Cavendish
Publishing

Statutes and Conventions on

INTERNATIONAL TRADE LAW

Fourth Edition

Indira Carr, MA, BPhil, LLM, PhD
Reader in International Commercial Law
University of Kent, Canterbury
and
Professor Richard Kidner, MA, BCL
Professor of Law, University of Wales, Aberystwyth

Cavendish
Publishing
Limited

London • Sydney • Portland, Oregon

Fourth edition first published in Great Britain 2003 by
Cavendish Publishing Limited, The Glass House,
Wharton Street, London WC1X 9PX, United Kingdom
Telephone: + 44 (0)20 7278 8000   Facsimile: + 44 (0)20 7278 8080
Email: info@cavendishpublishing.com
Website: www.cavendishpublishing.com

Published in the United States by Cavendish Publishing
c/o International Specialized Book Services,
5824 NE Hassalo Street, Portland,
Oregon 97213-3644, USA

Published in Australia by Cavendish Publishing (Australia) Pty Ltd
3/303 Barrenjoey Road, Newport, NSW 2106, Australia

© Carr, I and Kidner, R   2003
First edition   1993
Second edition   1995
Third edition   1999
Fourth edition   2003

British Library Cataloguing in Publication Data
Carr, Indira
Statutes and conventions on international trade law – 4th edn
1 Foreign trade regulation
I Title II Kidner, Richard, 1946–
III Statutes and conventions on international trade
341.7'54

Library of Congress Cataloguing in Publication Data
Data available

ISBN 1-85941-829-5

1 3 5 7 9 10 8 6 4 2

Printed and bound in Great Britain by MPG Books Ltd, Bodmin, Cornwall

ACKNOWLEDGMENTS

The publishers and editors thank the following organisations for their permission to reproduce the materials listed:

BIFA (BIFA Terms and Conditions 2000b).

Comité Maritime International (CMI Rules for Electronic Bills of Lading, 1990; CMI Rules for Sea Waybills, 1990, The York-Antwerp Rules 1994).

Institute of London Underwriters (Institute Cargo Clauses (A); Institute Cargo Clauses (B); Institute Strikes Clauses (C); Institute Strikes Clauses (Cargo); Institute War Clauses (Cargo); Marine Policy Form).

OTIF (Uniform Rules Concerning the Contract of International Carriage by Rail (CIM 1999)).

UNCITRAL (UNCITRAL Arbitration Rules, 1976; UNCITRAL Conciliation Rules, 1980; UNCITRAL Model Law on Electronic Commerce, 1996, as amended 1998; UNCITRAL Model Law on Electronic Signatures 2001; UNCITRAL Model Law on International Commercial Arbitration, 1985); UNCITRAL Model Law on International Commercial Conciliation 2003.

UNIDROIT (UNIDROIT Principles of International Commercial Contracts, 1994).

PREFACE

The study of International Trade Law requires access to a wide range of materials, many of which are not easily accessible, and the purpose of this book is to provide students with those documents which they are likely to be referred to in courses on this subject. We have provided extracts from statutes and conventions, all of which have been reproduced in their amended and updated form. In this edition, we have included the United Nations Conventions on the Liability of Operators of Transport Terminals in International Trade, 1991, the Model law on Electronic Signatures, 2001, and the Model Law on International Commercial Conciliation, 2003, all drafted by UNCITRAL. We have also included the Montreal Convention, 1999, CIM 1999 and the Cybercrime Convention, 2001.

A number of statutes have been amended, including the Bills of Exchange Act 1882, the Carriage by Air Act 1961 (incorporating the Montreal Convention), the Civil Jurisdiction and Judgments Act 1982 (to take account of the 'Brussels Regulation') and the Civil Procedure Rules (replacing RSC Order 111). New statutes and regulations include the Electronic Communications Act 2000, the Civil Jurisdiction and Judgments Order 2001 and the Financial Services and Markets Act 2000 (Law Applicable to Contracts of Insurance) Regulations 2001. Finally the two EC Directives on electronic commerce have been included in their final versions.

A new section has been added on Standard Trading Conditions.

The collection is necessarily highly selective as the potential range of material is very wide; nevertheless we believe we have selected all the documents which a student is likely to come across in any standard course on International Trade Law. We also believe that the materials in this collection will be of use to students following courses on commercial law and carriage of goods. We hope that this will provide a convenient and relatively inexpensive method of access to materials which might otherwise not be easily available.

The collection is divided into seven parts: Statutes, Statutory Instruments, European Union Materials, Conventions, Rules and Model Law, Standard Forms and Standard Trading Conditions. The material in the first four parts is arranged in chronological order (and alphabetically within years) and the material in the remaining parts is arranged alphabetically. The material is printed in its amended form but we have not indicated the source of these amendments and the text is printed as amended even if that amendment is not yet in force. Sections which have been omitted or repealed are noted.

The collection contains material available to us up to 1 April 2003.

Indira Carr
Richard Kidner

CONTENTS

CONVENTIONS

RULES AND MODEL LAWS

STANDARD FORMS

STANDARD TRADING CONDITIONS

SECTION I
STATUTES

CHAPTER 61
PART I
PRELIMINARY

PART III
CHEQUES ON A BANKER

PART I
PRELIMINARY

1.   [Omitted].

2.   Interpretation of terms
In this Act, unless the context otherwise requires—

'Acceptance' means an acceptance completed by delivery or notification.

'Action' includes counter claim and set off.

'Banker' includes a body of persons whether incorporated or not who carry on the business of banking.

'Bankrupt' includes any person whose estate is vested in a trustee or assignee under the law for the time being in force relating to bankruptcy.

'Bearer' means the person in possession of a bill or note which is payable to bearer.

'Bill' means bill of exchange, and 'note' means promissory note.

'Delivery' means transfer of possession, actual or constructive, from one person to another.

'Holder' means the payee or indorsee of a bill or note who is in possession of it, or the bearer thereof.

'Indorsement' means an indorsement completed by delivery.

'Issue' means the first delivery of a bill or note, complete in form to a person who takes it as a holder.

'Person' includes a body of persons whether incorporated or not.

'Postal operator' has the meaning given by section 125(1) of the Postal Services Act 2000.

'Value' means valuable consideration.

'Written' includes printed, and 'writing' includes print.

PART II
BILLS OF EXCHANGE

Form and interpretation

3.   Bill of exchange defined

(1)   A bill of exchange is an unconditional order in writing, addressed by one person to another, signed by the person giving it, requiring the person to whom it is addressed to pay on demand or at a fixed or determinable future time a sum certain in money to or to the order of a specified person, or to bearer.

(2)   An instrument which does not comply with these conditions, or which orders any act to be done in addition to the payment of money, is not a bill of exchange.

(3)   An order to pay out of a particular fund is not unconditional within the meaning of this section; but an unqualified order to pay, coupled with (a) an indication of a particular fund out of which the drawee is to re-imburse himself or a particular account to be debited with the amount, or (b) a statement of the transaction which gives rise to the bill is unconditional.

(4)   A bill is not invalid by reason—

(a)   that it is not dated;

(b)   that it does not specify the value given, or that any value has been given therefore;

(c)   that it does not specify the place where it is drawn or the place where it is payable.

4.   Inland and foreign bills

(1)   An inland bill is a bill which is or on the face of it purports to be—

(a)   both drawn and payable within the British Islands; or

(b)   drawn within the British Islands upon some person resident therein. Any other bill is a foreign bill.

For the purposes of the Act 'British Islands' mean any part of the United Kingdom of Great Britain and Ireland, the islands of Man, Guernsey, Jersey, Alderney, and Sark, and the islands adjacent to any of them being part of the dominions of Her Majesty.

(2)   Unless the contrary appear on the face of the bill the holder may treat it as an inland bill.

5.   Effect where different parties to bill are the same person

(1)   A bill may be drawn payable to, or to the order of, the drawer; or it may be drawn payable to, or to the order of, the drawee.

(2)   Where in a bill drawer and drawee are the same person, or where the drawee is a fictitious person or a person not having capacity to contract, the holder may treat the instrument, at his option, either as a bill of exchange or as a promissory note.

6.   Address to drawee

(1)   The drawee must be named or otherwise indicated in a bill with reasonable certainty.

(2)   A bill may be addressed to two or more drawees whether they are partners or not, but an order addressed to two drawees in the alternative or to two or more drawees in succession is not a bill of exchange.

7. **Certainty required as to payee**
  (1)　Where a bill is not payable to bearer, the payee must be named or otherwise indicated therein with reasonable certainty.
  (2)　A bill may be made payable to two or more payees jointly, or it may be made payable in the alternative to one of two, or one or some of several payees. A bill may also be made payable to the holder of an office for the time being.
  (3)　Where the payee is a fictitious or non-existing person the bill may be treated as payable to bearer.

8. **What bills are negotiable**
  (1)　When a bill contains words prohibiting transfer, or indicating an intention that it should not be transferable, it is valid as between the parties thereto, but is not negotiable.
  (2)　A negotiable bill may be payable either to order or to bearer.
  (3)　A bill is payable to bearer which is expressed to be so payable or on which the only or last indorsement is an indorsement in blank.
  (4)　A bill is payable to order which is expressed to be so payable, or which is expressed to be payable to a particular person, and does not contain words prohibiting transfer or indicating an intention that it should not be transferable.
  (5)　Where a bill, either originally or by indorsement, is expressed to be payable to the order of a specified person, and not to him or his order, it is nevertheless payable to him or his order at his option.

9. **Sum payable**
  (1)　The sum payable by a bill is a sum certain within the meaning of this Act, although it was required to be paid —
    (a)　with interest;
    (b)　by stated instalments;
    (c)　by stated instalments, with a provision that upon default in payment of any instalment the whole shall become due;
    (d)　according to an indicated rate of exchange or according to a rate of exchange to be ascertained as directed by the bill.
  (2)　Where the sum payable is expressed in words and also in figures, and there is a discrepancy between the two, the sum denoted by the words is the amount payable.
  (3)　Where a bill is expressed to be payable with interest, unless the instrument otherwise provides, interest runs from the date of the bill, and if the bill is undated from the issue thereof.

10. **Bill payable on demand**
  (1)　A bill is payable on demand —
    (a)　which is expressed to be payable on demand, or at sight, or on presentation; or
    (b)　in which no time for payment is expressed.
  (2)　Where a bill is accepted or indorsed when it is overdue, it shall, as regards the acceptor who so accepts, or any indorser who so indorses it, be deemed a bill payable on demand.

11. **Bill payable at a future time**
  A bill is payable at a determinable future time within the meaning of this Act which is expressed to be payable —
  (1)　At a fixed period after date or sight.
  (2)　On or at a fixed period after the occurrence of a specified event which is certain to happen, though the time of happening may be uncertain.

An instrument expressed to be payable on a contingency is not a bill, and the happening of the event does not cure the defect.

12.   Omission of date in bill payable after date

Where a bill expressed to be payable at a fixed period after date is issued undated, or where the acceptance of a bill payable at a fixed period after sight is undated, any holder may insert therein the true date of issue or acceptance, and the bill shall be payable accordingly.

Provided that — (1) where the holder in good faith and by mistake inserts a wrong date, and (2) in every case where a wrong date is inserted, if the bill subsequently comes into the hands of a holder in due course the bill shall not be avoided thereby, but shall operate and be payable as if the date so inserted had been the true date.

13.   Ante-dating and post-dating

(1)   Where a bill or an acceptance or any indorsement on a bill is dated, the date shall, unless the contrary be proved, be deemed to be the true date of the drawing, acceptance, or indorsement, as the case may be.

(2)   A bill is not invalid by reason only that it is ante-dated or post-dated, or that it bears date on a Sunday.

14.   Computation of time of payment

Where a bill is not payable on demand the day on which it falls due is determined as follows:

(1)   The bill is due and payable in all cases on the last day of the time of payment as fixed by the bill or, if that is a non-business day, on the succeeding business day.

(2)   Where a bill is payable at a fixed period after date, after sight, or after the happening of a specified event, the time of payment is determined by excluding the day from which the time is to begin to run and by including the day of payment.

(3)   Where a bill is payable at a fixed period after sight, the time begins to run from the date of the acceptance if the bill be accepted, and from the date of noting or protest if the bill be noted or protested for non-acceptance, or for non-delivery.

(4)   The term 'month' in a bill means a calendar month.

15.   Case of need

The drawer of a bill and any indorser may insert therein the name of a person to whom the holder may resort in case of need, that is to say, in case the bill is dishonoured by non-acceptance or non-payment. Such person is called the referee in case of need. It is in the option of the holder to resort to the referee in case of need or not as he may think fit.

16.   Optional stipulations by drawer or indorser

The drawer of a bill, and any indorser, may insert therein an express stipulation —

(1)   Negativing or limiting his own liability to the holder.

(2)   Waiving as regards himself some or all of the holder's duties.

17.   Definition and requisites of acceptance

(1)   The acceptance of a bill is the signification by the drawee of his assent to the order of the drawer.

(2)   An acceptance is invalid unless it complies with the following conditions, namely —

(a)   it must be written on the bill and be signed by the drawee. The mere signature of the drawee without additional words is sufficient;

(b) it must not express that the drawee will perform his promise by any other means than the payment of money.

18. Time for acceptance

A bill may be accepted—

(1) Before it has been signed by the drawer, or while otherwise incomplete.

(2) When it is overdue, or after it has been dishonoured by a previous refusal to accept, or by non-payment.

(3) When a bill payable after sight is dishonoured by non-acceptance, and the drawee subsequently accepts it, the holder, in the absence of any different agreement, is entitled to have the bill accepted as of the date of first presentment to the drawee for acceptance.

19. General and qualified acceptance

(1) An acceptance is either (a) general or (b) qualified.

(2) A general acceptance assents without qualification to the order of the drawer. A qualified acceptance in expressed terms varies the effect of the bill as drawn. In particular an acceptance is qualified which is—

(a) conditional, that is to say, which makes payment by the acceptor dependent on the fulfilment of a condition therein stated;

(b) partial, that is to say, an acceptance to pay part only of the amount for which the bill is drawn;

(c) local, that is to say, an acceptance to pay only at a particular specified place.

An acceptance to pay at a particular place is a general acceptance, unless it expressly states that the bill is to be paid there only and not elsewhere;

(d) qualified as to time;

(e) the acceptance of some one or more of the drawees, but not of all.

20. Inchoate instruments

(1) Where a simple signature on a blank paper is delivered by the signer in order that it may be converted into a bill, it operates as a *prima facie* authority to fill it up as a complete bill for any amount using the signature for that of the drawer, or the acceptor, or an indorser; and, in like manner, when a bill is wanting in any material particular, the person in possession of it has a *prima facie* authority to fill up the omission in any way he thinks fit.

(2) In order that any such instrument when completed may be enforceable against any person who became a party thereto prior to its completion, it must be filled up within a reasonable time, and strictly in accordance with the authority given. Reasonable time for this purpose is a question of fact. Provided that if any such instrument after completion is negotiated to a holder in due course it shall be valid and effectual for all purposes in his hands, and he may enforce it as if it had been filled up within a reasonable time and strictly in accordance with the authority given.

21. Delivery

(1) Every contract on a bill, whether it be the drawer's, the acceptor's, or an indorser's, is incomplete and revocable, until delivery of the instrument in order to give effect thereto.

Provided that where an acceptance is written on a bill, and the drawee gives notice to or according to the directions of the person entitled to the bill that he has accepted it, the acceptance then becomes complete and irrevocable.

(2) As between immediate parties, and as regards a remote party other than a holder in due course, the delivery—

(a) in order to be effectual must be made either by or under the authority of the party drawing, accepting, or indorsing, as the case may be;

(b) may be shown to have been conditional or for a special purpose only, and not for the purpose of transferring the property in the bill. But if the bill be in the hands of a holder in due course a valid delivery of the bill by all parties prior to him so as to make them liable to him is conclusively presumed.

(3) Where a bill is no longer in the possession of a party who has signed it as drawer, acceptor, or indorser, a valid and unconditional delivery by him is presumed until the contrary is proved.

Capacity and authority of parties

22. Capacity of parties

(1) Capacity to incur liability as a party to a bill is coextensive with capacity to contract.

Provided that nothing in this section shall enable a corporation to make itself liable as drawer, acceptor, or indorser of a bill unless it is competent to it so to do under the law for the time being in force relating to corporations.

(2) Where a bill is drawn or indorsed by an infant, minor, or corporation having no capacity or power to incur liability on a bill, the drawing or indorsement entitles the holder to receive payment of the bill, and to enforce it against any other party thereto.

23. Signature essential to liability

No person is liable as drawer, indorser, or acceptor of a bill who has not signed it as such: Provided that—

(1) Where a person signs a bill in a trade or assumed name, he is liable thereon as if he had signed it in his own name.

(2) The signature of the name of the firm is equivalent to the signature by the person so signing of the names of all persons liable as partners in that firm.

24. Forged or unauthorised signature

Subject to the provisions of this Act, where a signature on a bill is forged or placed thereon without the authority of the person whose signature it purports to be, the forged or unauthorised signature is wholly inoperative, and no right to retain the bill or to give a discharge therefore or to enforce payment thereof against any party thereto can be acquired through or under that signature, unless the party against whom it is sought to retain or enforce payment of the bill is precluded from setting up the forgery or want of authority.

Provided that nothing in this section shall affect the ratification of an unauthorised signature not amounting to a forgery.

25. Procuration signatures

A signature by procuration operates as notice that the agent has but a limited authority to sign, and the principal is only bound by such signature if the agent in so signing was acting within the actual limits of his authority.

26. Person signing as agent or in representative capacity

(1) Where a person signs a bill as drawer, indorser, or acceptor, and adds words to his signature, indicating that he signs for or on behalf of a principal, or in a representative character, he is not personally liable thereon; but the mere addition to his signature of words describing him as an agent, or as filling a representative character, does not exempt him from personal liability.

(2) In determining whether a signature on a bill is that of the principal or that of the agent by whose hand it is written, the construction most favourable to the validity of the instrument shall be adopted.

The consideration for a bill

27. Value and holder for value

    (1) Valuable consideration for a bill may be constituted by—

        (a) any consideration sufficient to support a simple contract;

        (b) an antecedent debt or liability. Such a debt or liability is deemed valuable consideration whether the bill is payable on demand or at a future time.

    (2) Where value has at any time been given for a bill the holder is deemed to be a holder for value as regards the acceptor and all parties to the bill who became parties prior to such time.

    (3) Where the holder of a bill has a lien on it arising either from contract or by implication of law, he is deemed to be a holder for value to the extent of the sum for which he has a lien.

28. Accommodation bill or party

    (1) An accommodation party to a bill is a person who has signed a bill as drawer, acceptor, or indorser, without receiving value therefore, and for the purpose of lending his name to some other person.

    (2) An accommodation party is liable on the bill to a holder for value; and it is immaterial whether, when such holder took the bill, he knew such party to be an accommodation party or not.

29. Holder in due course

    (1) A holder in due course is a holder who has taken a bill, complete and regular on the face of it, under the following conditions, namely—

        (a) that he became the holder of it before it was overdue, and without notice that it had been previously dishonoured, if such was the fact;

        (b) that he took the bill in good faith and for value, and that at the time the bill was negotiated to him he had no notice of any defect in the title of the person who negotiated it.

    (2) In particular the title of a person who negotiates a bill is defective within the meaning of this Act when he obtained the bill, or the acceptance thereof, by fraud, duress, or force and fear, or other unlawful means, or an illegal consideration, or when he negotiates it in breach of faith, or under such circumstances as amount to a fraud.

    (3) A holder (whether for value or not), who derives his title to a bill through a holder in due course, and who is not himself a party to any fraud or illegality affecting it, has all the rights of that holder in due course as regards the acceptor and all parties to the bill prior to that holder.

30. Presumption of value and good faith

    (1) Every party whose signature appears on a bill is *prima facie* deemed to have become a party thereto for value.

    (2) Every holder of a bill is *prima facie* deemed to be a holder in due course; but if in an action on a bill it is admitted or proved that the acceptance, issue, or subsequent negotiation of the bill is affected with fraud, duress, or force and fear, or illegality, the burden of proof is shifted, unless and until the holder proves that, subsequent to the alleged fraud or illegality, value has in good faith been given for the bill.

Negotiation of bills

31. Negotiation of bill

    (1) A bill is negotiated when it is transferred from one person to another in such a manner as to constitute the transferee the holder of the bill.

    (2) A bill payable to bearer is negotiated by delivery.

(3)   A bill payable to order is negotiated by the indorsement of the holder completed by delivery.

(4)   Where the holder of a bill payable to his order transfers it for value without indorsing it, the transfer gives the transferee such title as the transferor had in the bill, and the transferee in addition acquires the right to have the indorsement of the transferor.

(5)   Where any person is under obligation to indorse a bill in a representative capacity, he may indorse the bill in such terms as to negative personal liability.

32.   Requisites of a valid indorsement

An indorsement in order to operate as a negotiation must comply with the following conditions, namely—

(1)   It must be written on the bill itself and be signed by the indorser. The simple signature of the indorser on the bill without additional words is, sufficient.

     An indorsement written on an *allonge*, or on a 'copy' of a bill issued or negotiated in a country where 'copies' are recognised, is deemed to be written on the bill itself.

(2)   It must be an indorsement of the entire bill. A partial indorsement, that is to say, an indorsement which purports to transfer to the indorsee a part only of the amount payable, or which purports to transfer the bill to two or more indorsees severally, does not operate as a negotiation of the bill.

(3)   Where a bill is payable to the order of two or more payees or indorsees who are not partners all must indorse, unless the one indorsing has authority to indorse for the others.

(4)   Where, in a bill payable to order, the payee or indorsee is wrongly designated, or his name is mis-spelt, he may indorse the bill as therein described, adding, if he thinks fit, his proper signature.

(5)   Where there are two or more indorsements on a bill, each indorsement is deemed to have been made in the order in which it appears on the bill, until the contrary is proved.

(6)   An indorsement may be made in blank or special. It may also contain terms making it restrictive.

33.   Conditional indorsement

Where a bill purports to be indorsed conditionally the condition may be disregarded by the payer, and payment to the indorsee is valid whether the condition has been fulfilled or not.

34.   Indorsement in blank and special indorsement

(1)   An indorsement in blank specifies no indorsee, and a bill so indorsed becomes payable to bearer.

(2)   A special indorsement specifies the person to whom, or to whose order, the bill is to be payable.

(3)   The provisions of this Act relating to a payee apply with the necessary modifications to an indorsee under a special indorsement.

(4)   When a bill has been indorsed in blank, any holder may convert the blank indorsement into a special indorsement by writing above the indorser's signature a direction to pay the bill to or to the order of himself or some other person.

35.   Restrictive indorsement

(1)   An endorsement is restrictive which prohibits the further negotiation of the bill or which expresses that it is a mere authority to deal with the bill as thereby directed and not a transfer of the ownership thereof, as, for example, if a bill be indorsed 'Pay D. only,' or 'Pay D. for the account of X.,' or 'Pay D. or order for collection.'

(2)   A restrictive indorsement gives the indorsee the right to receive payment of the bill and to sue any party thereto that his indorser could have sued, but gives him no power to transfer his rights as indorsee unless it expressly authorise him to do so.

(3)   Where a restrictive indorsement authorises further transfer, all subsequent indorsees take the bill with the same rights and subject to the same liabilities as the first indorsee under the restrictive indorsement.

36.   Negotiation of overdue or dishonoured bill

(1)   Where a bill is negotiable in its origin it continues to be negotiable until it has been—

    (a)   restrictively indorsed; or

    (b)   discharged by payment or otherwise.

(2)   Where an overdue bill is negotiated, it can only be negotiated subject to any defect of title affecting it at its maturity, and thenceforward no person who takes it can acquire or give a better title than that which the person from whom he took it had.

(3)   A bill payable on demand is deemed to be overdue within the meaning and for the purposes of this section, when it appears on the face of it to have been in circulation for an unreasonable length of time. What is an unreasonable length of time for this purpose is a question of fact.

(4)   Except where an indorsement bears date after the maturity of the bill, every negotiation is *prima facie* deemed to have been effected before the bill was overdue.

(5)   Where a bill which is not overdue has been dishonoured any person who takes it with notice of the dishonour takes it subject to any defect of title attaching thereto at the time of dishonour, but nothing in this subsection shall affect the rights of a holder in due course.

37.   Negotiation of bill to party already liable thereon

Where a bill is negotiated back to the drawer, or to a prior indorser or to the acceptor, such party may, subject to the provisions of this Act, re-issue and further negotiate the bill, but he is not entitled to enforce payment of the bill against any intervening party to whom he was previously liable.

38.   Rights of the holder

The rights and powers of the holder of a bill are as follows—

(1)   He may sue on the bill in his own name.

(2)   Where he is a holder in due course, he holds the bill free from any defect of title of prior parties, as well as from mere personal defences available to prior parties among themselves, and may enforce payment against all parties liable on the bill.

(3)   Where his title is defective (a) if he negotiates the bill to a holder in due course, that holder obtains a good and complete title to the bill, and (b) if he obtains payment of the bill the person who pays him in due course gets a valid discharge for the bill.

General duties of the holder

39.   When presentment for acceptance is necessary

(1)   Where a bill is payable after sight, presentment for acceptance is necessary in order to fix the maturity of the instrument.

(2)   Where a bill expressly stipulates that it shall be presented for acceptance, or where a bill is drawn payable elsewhere than at the residence or place of business of the drawee, it must be presented for acceptance before it can be presented for payment.

(3)   In no other case is presentment for acceptance necessary in order to render liable any party to the bill.

(4)   Where the holder of a bill, drawn payable elsewhere than at the place of business or residence of the drawee, has not time, with the exercise of reasonable diligence, to present the bill for acceptance before presenting it for payment on the day that it falls due, the delay caused by presenting the bill for acceptance before presenting it for payment is excused, and does not discharge the drawer and indorsers.

40.   Time for presenting bill payable after sight

(1)   Subject to the provisions of this Act, when a bill payable after sight is negotiated, the holder must either present it for acceptance or negotiate it within a reasonable time.

(2)   If he do not do so, the drawer and all indorsers prior to that holder are discharged.

(3)   In determining what is a reasonable time within the meaning of this section, regard shall be had to the nature of the bill, the usage of trade with respect to similar bills, and the facts of the particular case.

41.   Rules as to presentment for acceptance, and excuses for non-presentment

(1)   A bill is duly presented for acceptance which is presented in accordance with the following rules—

(a)   the presentment must be made by or on behalf of the holder to the drawee or to some person authorised to accept or refuse acceptance on his behalf at a reasonable hour on a business day and before the bill is overdue;

(b)   where a bill is addressed to two or more drawees, who are not partners, presentment must be made to them all, unless one has authority to accept for all, then presentment may be made to him only;

(c)   where the drawee is dead presentment may be made to his personal representative;

(d)   where the drawee is bankrupt, presentment may be made to him or to his trustee;

(e)   where authorised by agreement or usage, a presentment through a postal operator is sufficient.

(2)   Presentment in accordance with these rules is excused, and a bill may be treated as dishonoured by non-acceptance—

(a)   where the drawee is dead or bankrupt, or is a fictitious person or a person not having capacity to contract by bill;

(b)   where, after the exercise of reasonable diligence, such presentment cannot be effected;

(c)   where, although the presentment has been irregular, acceptance has been refused on some other ground.

(3)   The fact that the holder has reason to believe that the bill, on presentment, will be dishonoured does not excuse presentment.

42.   Non-acceptance

When a bill is duly presented for acceptance and is not accepted within the customary time, the person presenting it must treat it as dishonoured by non-acceptance. If he do not, the holder shall lose his right of recourse against the drawer and indorsers.

43.   Dishonour by non-acceptance and its consequences

(1)   A bill is dishonoured by non-acceptance—

(a)   when it is duly presented for acceptance, and such an acceptance as is prescribed by this Act is refused or cannot be obtained; or

     (b) when presentment for acceptance is excused and the bill is not accepted.

(2)   Subject to the provisions of this Act when a bill is dishonoured by non-acceptance, an immediate right of recourse against the drawer and indorsers accrues to the holder, and no presentment for payment is necessary.

44.   Duties as to qualified acceptance

(1)   The holder of a bill may refuse to take a qualified acceptance, and if he does not obtain an unqualified acceptance may treat the bill as dishonoured by non-acceptance.

(2)   Where a qualified acceptance is taken, and the drawer or an indorser has not expressly or impliedly authorised the holder to take a qualified acceptance, or does not subsequently assent thereto, such drawer or indorser is discharged from his liability on the bill.

      The provisions of this sub-section do not apply to a partial acceptance, whereof due notice has been given. Where a foreign bill has been accepted as to part, it must be protested as to the balance.

(3)   When the drawer or indorser of a bill receives notice of a qualified acceptance, and does not within a reasonable time express his dissent to the holder he shall be deemed to have assented thereto.

45.   Rules as to presentment for payment

Subject to the provisions of this Act a bill must be duly presented for payment. If it be not so presented the drawer and indorsers shall be discharged. A bill is duly presented for payment which is presented in accordance with the following rules—

(1)   Where the bill is not payable on demand, presentment must be made on the day it falls due.

(2)   Where the bill is payable on demand, then, subject to the provisions of this Act, presentment must be made within a reasonable time after its issue in order to render the drawer liable, and within a reasonable time after its indorsement, in order to render the indorser liable. In determining what is a reasonable time, regard shall be had to the nature of the bill, the usage of trade with regard to similar bills, and the facts of the particular case.

(3)   Presentment must be made by the holder or by some person authorised to receive payment on his behalf at a reasonable hour on a business day, at the proper place as herein-after defined, either to the person designated by the bill as payer, or to some person authorised to pay or refuse payment on his behalf if with the exercise of reasonable diligence such person can there be found.

(4)   A bill is presented at the proper place—

    (a) where a place of payment is specified in the bill and the bill is there presented;

    (b) where no place of payment is specified, but the address of the drawee or acceptor is given in the bill, and the bill is there presented;

    (c) where no place of payment is specified and no address given, and the bill is presented at the drawee's or acceptor's place of business if known, and if not, at his ordinary residence if known;

    (d) in any other case if presented to the drawee or acceptor wherever he can be found, or if presented at his last known place of business or residence.

(5)   Where a bill is presented at the proper place, and after the exercise of reasonable diligence no person authorised to pay or refuse payment can be found there, no further presentment to the drawee or acceptor is required.

(6)   Where a bill is drawn upon, or accepted by two or more persons who are not partners, and no place of payment is specified, presentment must be made to them all.

    (7)   Where the drawee or acceptor of a bill is dead, and no place of payment is specified, presentment must be made to a personal representative, if such there be, and with the exercise of reasonable diligence can be found.

    (8)   Where authorised by agreement or usage a presentment through a postal operator is sufficient.

46.   Excuses for delay or non-presentment for payment

    (1)   Delay in making presentment for payment is excused when the delay is caused by circumstances beyond the control of the holder, and not imputable to his default, misconduct, or negligence. When the cause of delay ceases to operate presentment must be made with reasonable diligence.

    (2)   Presentment for payment is dispensed with—

        (a)   where, after the exercise of reasonable diligence presentment, as required by this Act, cannot be effected. The fact that the holder has reason to believe that the bill will, on presentment, be dishonoured, does not dispense with the necessity for presentment;

        (b)   where the drawee is a fictitious person;

        (c)   as regards the drawer where the drawee or acceptor is not bound as between himself and the drawer, to accept or pay the bill, and the drawer has no reason to believe that the bill would be paid if presented;

        (d)   as regards an indorser, where the bill was accepted or made for the accommodation of that indorser, and he has no reason to expect that the bill would be paid if presented;

        (e)   by waiver of presentment, express or implied.

47.   Dishonour by non-payment

    (1)   A bill is dishonoured by non-payment (a) when it is duly presented for payment and payment is refused or cannot be obtained, or (b) when presentment is excused and the bill is overdue and unpaid.

    (2)   Subject to the provisions of this Act, when a bill is dishonoured by non-payment, an immediate right of recourse against the drawer and indorsers accrues to the holder.

48.   Notice of dishonour and effect of non-notice

Subject to the provisions of this Act, when a bill has been dishonoured by non-acceptance or by non-payment, notice of dishonour must be given to the drawer and each indorser, and any drawer or indorser to whom such notice is not given is discharged. Provided that—

    (1)   Where a bill is dishonoured by non-acceptance, and notice of dishonour is not given, the rights of a holder in due course, subsequent to the omission, shall not be prejudiced by the omission.

    (2)   Where a bill is dishonoured by non-acceptance, and due notice of dishonour is given, it shall not be necessary to give notice of a subsequent dishonour by non-payment unless the bill shall in the meantime have been accepted.

49.   Rules as to notice of dishonour

Notice of dishonour in order to be valid and effectual must be given in accordance with the following rules—

    (1)   The notice must be given by or on behalf of the holder, or by or on behalf of an indorser who, at the time of giving it, is himself liable on the bill.

    (2)   Notice of dishonour may be given by an agent either in his own name, or in the name of any party entitled to give notice whether that party be his principal or not.

    (3)   Where the notice is given by or on behalf of the holder, it enures for the benefit of all subsequent holders and all prior indorsers who have a right of recourse against the party to whom it is given.

(4)   Where notice is given by or on behalf of an indorser entitled to give notice as herein-before provided, it enures for the benefit of the holder and all indorsers subsequent to the party to whom notice is given.

(5)   The notice may be given in writing or by personal communication, and may be given in any terms which sufficiently identify the bill, and intimate that the bill has been dishonoured by non-acceptance or non-payment.

(6)   The return of a dishonoured bill to the drawer or an indorser is, in point of form, deemed a sufficient notice of dishonour.

(7)   A written notice need not be signed, and an insufficient written notice may be supplemented and validated by verbal communication. A misdescription of the bill shall not vitiate the notice unless the party to whom the notice is given is in fact misled thereby.

(8)   Where notice of dishonour is required to be given to any person, it may be given either to the party himself, or to his agent in that behalf.

(9)   Where the drawer or indorser is dead, and the party giving notice knows it, the notice must be given to a personal representative if such there be, and with the exercise of reasonable diligence he can be found.

(10)   Where the drawer or indorser is bankrupt, notice may be given either to the party himself or to the trustee.

(11)   Where there are two or more drawers or indorsers who are not partners, notice must be given to each of them, unless one of them has authority to receive such notice for the others.

(12)   The notice may be given as soon as the bill is dishonoured and must be given within a reasonable time thereafter. In the absence of special circumstances notice is not deemed to have been given within a reasonable time, unless—

  (a)   where the person giving and the person to receive notice reside in the same place, the notice is given or sent off in time to reach the latter on the day after the dishonour of the bill;

  (b)   where the person giving and the person to receive notice reside in different places, the notice is sent off on the day after the dishonour of the bill, if there be a post at a convenient hour on that day, and if there be no such post on that day then by the next post thereafter.

(13)   Where a bill when dishonoured is in the hands of an agent, he may either himself give notice to the parties liable on the bill or he may give notice to his principal. If he give notice to his principal, he must do so within the same time as if he were the holder, and the principal upon receipt of such notice has himself the same time for giving notice as if the agent had been an independent holder.

(14)   Where a party to a bill receives due notice of dishonour, he has after the receipt of such notice the same period of time for giving notice to antecedent parties that the holder has after the dishonour.

(15)   Where a notice of dishonour is duly addressed and posted, the sender is deemed to have given due notice of dishonour, notwithstanding any miscarriage by the postal operator concerned.

50.   Excuses for non-notice and delay

(1)   Delay in giving notice of dishonour is excused where the delay is caused by circumstances beyond the control of the party giving notice, and not imputable to his default, misconduct, or negligence. When the cause of delay ceases to operate the notice must be given with reasonable diligence.

(2)   Notice of dishonour is dispensed with—

  (a)   when, after the exercise of reasonable diligence, notice as required by this Act cannot be given to or does not reach the drawer or indorser sought to be charged;

    (b) by waiver express or implied. Notice of dishonour may be waived before the time of giving notice has arrived, or after the omission to give due notice;

    (c) as regards the drawer in the following cases, namely, (1) where drawer and drawee are the same person, (2) where the drawee is a fictitious person or a person not having capacity to contract, (3) where the drawer is the person to whom the bill is presented for payment, (4) where the drawee or acceptor is as between himself and the drawer under no obligation to accept or pay the bill, (5) where the drawer has countermanded payment;

    (d) as regards the indorser in the following cases, namely, (1) where the drawee is a fictitious person or a person not having capacity to contract, and the indorser was aware of the fact at the time he indorsed the bill, (2) where the indorser is the person to whom the bill is presented for payment, (3) where the bill was accepted or made for his accommodation.

51.   Notice or protest of bill

    (1) Where an inland bill has been dishonoured it may, if the holder thinks fit, be noted for non-acceptance or non-payment, as the case may be; but it shall not be necessary to note or protest any such bill in order to preserve the recourse against the drawer or indorser.

    (2) Where a foreign bill, appearing on the face of it to be such, has been dishonoured by non-acceptance it must be duly protested for non-acceptance, and where such a bill, which has not been previously dishonoured by non-acceptance, is dishonoured by non-payment it must be duly protested for non-payment. If it be not so protested the drawer and indorsers are discharged. Where a bill does not appear on the face of it to be a foreign bill, protest thereof in case of dishonour is unnecessary.

    (3) A bill which has been protested for non-acceptance may be subsequently protested for non-payment.

    (4) Subject to the provisions of this Act, when a bill is noted or protested, it may be noted on the day of its dishonour and must be noted not later than the next succeeding business day. When a bill has been duly noted, the protest may be subsequently extended as of the date of the noting.

    (5) Where the acceptor of a bill becomes bankrupt or insolvent or suspends payment before it matures, the holder may cause the bill to be protested for better security against the drawer and indorsers.

    (6) A bill must be protested at the place where it is dishonoured: Provided that—

        (a) when a bill is presented through a postal operator, and returned by post dishonoured, it may be protested at the place to which it is returned and on the day of its return if received during business hours, and if not received during business hours, then not later than the next business day;

        (b) when a bill drawn payable at the place of business or residence of some person other than the drawee has been dishonoured by non-acceptance, it must be protested for non-payment at the place where it is expressed to be payable, and no further presentment for payment to, or demand on, the drawee is necessary.

    (7) A protest must contain a copy of the bill, and must be signed by the notary making it, and must specify—

        (a) the person at whose request the bill is protested;

        (b) the place and date of protest, the cause or reason for protesting the bill, the demand made, and the answer given, if any, or the fact that the drawee or acceptor could not be found.

(8)   Where a bill is lost or destroyed, or is wrongly detained from the person entitled to hold it, protest may be made on a copy or written particulars thereof.

(9)   Protest is dispensed with by any circumstance which would dispense with notice of dishonour. Delay in noting or protesting is excused when the delay is caused by circumstances beyond the control of the holder, and not imputable to his default, misconduct, or negligence. When the cause of delay ceases to operate the bill must be noted or protested with reasonable diligence.

52.   Duties of holder as regards drawee or acceptor

(1)   When a bill is accepted generally presentment for payment is not necessary in order to render the acceptor liable.

(2)   When by the terms of a qualified acceptance presentment for payment is required, the acceptor, in the absence of an express stipulation to that effect, is not discharged by the omission to present the bill for payment on the day that it matures.

(3)   In order to render the acceptor of a bill liable it is not necessary to protest it, or that notice dishonour should be given to him.

(4)   Where the holder of a bill presents it for payment, he shall exhibit the bill to the person from whom he demands payment, and when a bill is paid the holder shall forthwith deliver it up to the party paying it.

Liabilities of parties

53.   Funds in hands of drawee

(1)   A bill, of itself, does not operate as an assignment of funds in the hands of the drawee available for the payment thereof, and the drawee of a bill who does not accept as required by this Act is not liable on the instrument. This sub-section shall not extend to Scotland.

(2)   In Scotland, where the drawee of a bill has in his hands funds available for the payment thereof, the bill operates as an assignment of the sum for which it is drawn in favour of the holder, from the time when the bill is presented to the drawee.

54.   Liability of acceptor

The acceptor of a bill, by accepting it—

(1)   Engages that he will pay it according to the tenor of his acceptance.

(2)   Is precluded from denying to a holder in due course—

(a)   the existence of the drawer, the genuineness of his signature, and his capacity and authority to draw the bill;

(b)   in the case of a bill payable to drawer's order, the then capacity of the drawer to indorse, but not the genuineness or validity of his indorsement;

(c)   in the case of a bill payable to the order of a third person, the existence of the payee and his then capacity to indorse, but not the genuineness or validity of his indorsement.

55.   Liability of drawer or indorser

(1)   The drawer of a bill by drawing it—

(a)   engages that on due presentment it shall be accepted and paid according to its tenor, and that if it be dishonoured he will compensate the holder or any indorser who is compelled to pay it, provided that the requisite proceedings on dishonour be duly taken;

(b)   is precluded from denying to a holder in due course the existence of the payee and his then capacity to indorse.

(2)   The indorser of a bill by indorsing it—

    (a)   engages that on due presentment it shall be accepted and paid according to its tenor, and that if it be dishonoured he will compensate the holder or a subsequent indorser who is compelled to pay it, provided that the requisite proceedings on dishonour be duly taken.

    (b)   is precluded from denying to a holder in due course the genuineness and regularity in all respects of the drawer's signature and all previous endorsements;

    (c)   is precluded from denying to his immediate or a subsequent indorsee that the bill was at the time of his indorsement a valid and subsisting bill, and that he had then a good title thereto.

56.   Stranger signing bill liable as indorser

Where a person signs a bill otherwise than as drawer or acceptor, he thereby incurs the liabilities of an indorser to a holder in due course.

57.   Measure of damages against parties to dishonoured bill

Where a bill is dishonoured, the measure of damages, which shall be deemed to be liquidated damages, shall be as follows—

(1)   The holder may recover from any party liable on the bill, and the drawer who has been compelled to pay the bill may recover from the acceptor, and an indorser who has been compelled to pay the bill may recover from the acceptor or from the drawer, or from a prior indorser—

    (a)   the amount of the bill;

    (b)   interest thereon from the time of presentment for payment if the bill is payable on demand, and from the maturity of the bill in any other case;

    (c)   the expenses of noting, or, when protest is necessary, and the protest has been extended, the expenses of protest.

(2)   [Repealed].

(3)   Where by this Act interest may be recovered as damages, such interest may, if justice require it, be withheld wholly or in part, and where a bill is expressed to be payable with interest at a given rate, interest as damages may or may not be given at the same rate as interest proper.

58.   Transferor by delivery and transferee

(1)   Where the holder of a bill payable to bearer negotiates it by delivery without indorsing it he is called a 'transferor by delivery'.

(2)   A transferor by delivery is not liable on the instrument.

(3)   A transferor by delivery who negotiates a bill thereby warrants to his immediate transferee being a holder for value that the bill is what it purports to be, that he has a right to transfer it, and that at the time of transfer he is not aware of any fact which renders it valueless.

Discharge of bill

59.   Payment in due course

(1)   A bill is discharged by payment in due course by or on behalf of the drawee or acceptor. 'Payment in due course' means payment made at or after the maturity of the bill to the holder thereof in good faith and without notice that his title to the bill is defective.

(2)   Subject to the provisions herein-after contained, when a bill is paid by the drawer or an indorser it is not discharged; but—

    (a)   where a bill payable to, or to the order of, a third party is paid by the drawer, the drawer may enforce payment thereof against the acceptor, but may not re-issue the bill;

(b) where a bill is paid by an indorser, or where a bill payable to drawer's order is paid by the drawer, the party paying it is remitted to his former rights as regards the acceptor or antecedent parties, and he may, if he thinks fit, strike out his own subsequent indorsements, and again negotiate the bill.

(3) Where an accommodation bill is paid in due course by the party accommodated the bill is discharged.

60. Banker paying demand draft whereon indorsement is forged

When a bill payable to order on demand is drawn on a banker, and the banker on whom it is drawn pays the bill in good faith and in the ordinary course of business, it is not incumbent on the banker to show that the indorsement of the payee or any subsequent indorsement was made by or under the authority of the person whose indorsement it purports to be, and the banker is deemed to have paid the bill in due course, although such indorsement has been forged or made without authority.

61. Acceptor the holder at maturity

When the acceptor of a bill is or becomes the holder of it at or after its maturity, in his own right, the bill is discharged.

62. Express waiver

(1) When the holder of a bill at or after its maturity absolutely and unconditionally renounces his rights against the acceptor the bill is discharged. The renunciation must be in writing, unless the bill is delivered up to the acceptor.

(2) The liabilities of any party to a bill may in like manner be renounced by the holder before, at, or after its maturity: but nothing in this section shall affect the rights of a holder in due course without notice of the renunciation.

63. Cancellation

(1) Where a bill is intentionally cancelled by the holder or his agent, and the cancellation is apparent thereon, the bill is discharged.

(2) In like manner any party liable on a bill may be discharged by the intentional cancellation of his signature by the holder or his agent. In such case any indorser who would have had a right of recourse against the party whose signature is cancelled is also discharged.

(3) A cancellation made unintentionally, or under a mistake, or without the authority of the holder is inoperative; but where a bill or any signature thereon appears to have been cancelled the burden of proof lies on the party who alleges that the cancellation was made unintentionally, or under a mistake, or without authority.

64. Alteration of bill

(1) Where a bill or acceptance is materially altered without the assent of all parties liable on the bill, the bill is avoided except as against a party who has himself made, authorised, or assented to the alteration, and subsequent indorsers.

Provided that, where a bill has been materially altered, but the alteration is not apparent, and the bill is in the hands of a holder in due course, such holder may avail himself of the bill as if it had not been altered, and may enforce payment of it according to its original tenor.

(2) In particular the following alterations are material, namely, any alteration of the date, the sum payable, the time of payment, the place of payment, and, where a bill has been accepted generally, the addition of a place of payment without the acceptor's assent.

Acceptance and payment for honour

65.   Acceptance for honour supra protest

(1)   Where a bill of exchange has been protested for dishonour by non-acceptance, or protested for better security, and is not overdue, any person, not being a party already liable thereon, may, with the consent of the holder, intervene and accept the bill supra protest, for the honour of any party liable thereon, or for the honour of the person for whose account the bill is drawn.

(2)   A bill may be accepted for honour for part only of the sum for which it is drawn.

(3)   An acceptance for honour supra protest in order to be valid must—
(a)   be written on the bill, and indicate that it is an acceptance for honour;
(b)   be signed by the acceptor for honour.

(4)   Where an acceptance for honour does not expressly state for whose honour it is made, it is deemed to be an acceptance for the honour of the drawer.

(5)   Where a bill payable after sight is accepted for honour, its maturity is calculated from the date of the noting for non-acceptance, and not from the date of the acceptance for honour.

66.   Liability of acceptor for honour

(1)   The acceptor for honour of a bill by accepting it engages that he will, on due presentment, pay the bill according to the tenor of his acceptance, if it is not paid by the drawee, provided it has been duly presented for payment, and protested for non-payment, and that he receives notice of these facts.

(2)   The acceptor for honour is liable to the holder and to all parties to the bill subsequent to the party for whose honour he has accepted.

67.   Presentment to acceptor for honour

(1)   Where a dishonoured bill has been accepted for honour supra protest, or contains a reference in case of need, it must be protested for non-payment before it is presented for payment to the acceptor for honour, or referee in case of need.

(2)   Where the address of the acceptor for honour is in the same place where the bill is protested for non-payment, the bill must be presented to him not later than the day following its maturity; and where the address of the acceptor for honour is in some place other than the place where it was protested for non-payment, the bill must be forwarded not later than the day following its maturity for presentment to him.

(3)   Delay in presentment or non-presentment is excused by any circumstance which would excuse delay in presentment for payment or non-presentment for payment.

(4)   When a bill of exchange is dishonoured by the acceptor for honour it must be protested for non-payment by him.

68.   Payment for honour supra protest

(1)   Where a bill has been protested for non-payment, any person may intervene and pay it supra protest for the honour of any party liable thereon, or for the honour of the person for whose account the bill is drawn.

(2)   Where two or more persons offer to pay a bill for the honour of different parties, the person whose payment will discharge most parties to the bill shall have the preference.

(3)   Payment for honour supra protest, in order to operate as such and not as a mere voluntary payment, must be attested by a notarial act of honour which may be appended to the protest or form an extension of it.

(4)   The notarial act of honour must be founded on a declaration made by the payer for honour, or his agent in that behalf, declaring his intention to pay the bill for honour, and for whose honour he pays.

(5)   Where a bill has been paid for honour, all parties subsequent to the party for whose honour it is paid are discharged, but the payer for honour is subrogated for, and succeeds to both the rights and duties of, the holder as regards the party for whose honour he pays, and all parties liable to that party.

(6)   The payer for honour on paying to the holder the amount of the bill and the notarial expenses incidental to its dishonour is entitled to receive both the bill itself and the protest. If the holder do not on demand deliver them up he shall be liable to the payer for honour in damages.

(7)   Where the holder of a bill refuses to receive payment supra protest he shall lose his right of recourse against any party who would have been discharged by such payment.

Lost instruments

69.   Holder's right to duplicate of lost bill

Where a bill has been lost before it is overdue the person who was the holder of it may apply to the drawer to give him another bill of the same tenor, giving security to the drawer if required to indemnify him against all persons whatever in case the bill alleged to have been lost shall be found again. If the drawer on request as aforesaid refuses to give such duplicate bill he may be compelled to do so.

70.   Action on lost bill

In any action or proceeding upon a bill, the court or a judge may order that the loss of the instrument shall not be set up, provided an indemnity be given to the satisfaction of the court or judge against the claims of any other person upon the instrument in question.

Bill in a set

71.   Rules as to sets

(1)   Where a bill is drawn in a set, each part of the set being numbered, and containing a reference to the other parts the whole of the parts constitute one bill.

(2)   Where the holder of a set indorses two or more parts to different persons, he is liable on every such part, and every indorser subsequent to him is liable on the part he has himself indorsed as if the said parts were separate bills.

(3)   Where two or more parts of a set are negotiated to different holders in due course, the holder whose title first accrues is as between such holders deemed the true owner of the bill; but nothing in this sub-section shall affect the rights of a person who in due course accepts or pays the part first presented to him.

(4)   The acceptance may be written on any part, and it must be written on one part only. If the drawee accepts more than one part, and such accepted parts get into the hands of different holders in due course, he is liable on every such part as if it were a separate bill.

(5)   When the acceptor of a bill drawn in a set pays it without requiring the part bearing his acceptance to be delivered up to him, and that part at maturity is outstanding in the hands of a holder in due course, he is liable to the holder thereof.

(6)   Subject to the preceding rules, where any one part of a bill drawn in a set is discharged by payment or otherwise, the whole bill is discharged.

Conflict of laws

72. Rules where laws conflict

Where a bill drawn in one country is negotiated, accepted, or payable in another, the rights, duties, and liabilities of the parties thereto are determined as follows—

(1)   The validity of a bill as regards requisites in form is determined by the law of the place of issue, and the validity as regards requisites in form of the supervening contracts, such as acceptance, or indorsement, or acceptance supra protest, is determined by the law of the place where such contract was made.

Provided that—

(a)   where a bill is issued out of the United Kingdom it is not invalid by reason only that it is not stamped in accordance with the law of the place of issue;

(b)   where a bill, issued out of the United Kingdom, conforms, as regards requisites in form, to the law of the United Kingdom, it may, for the purpose of enforcing payment thereof, be treated as valid as between all persons who negotiate, hold, or become parties to it in the United Kingdom.

(2)   Subject to the provisions of this Act, the interpretation of the drawing, indorsement, acceptance, or acceptance supra protest of a bill, is determined by the law of the place where such contract is made. Provided that where an inland bill is indorsed in a foreign country the indorsement shall as regards the payer be interpreted according to the law of the United Kingdom.

(3)   The duties of the holder with respect to presentment for acceptance or payment and the necessity for or sufficiency of a protest or notice of dishonour, or otherwise, are determined by the law of the place where the act is done or the bill is dishonoured.

(4)   [Repealed].

(5)   Where a bill is drawn in one country and is payable in another, the due date thereof is determined according to the law of the place where it is payable.

PART III

CHEQUES ON A BANKER

73. Cheque defined

A cheque is a bill of exchange drawn on a banker payable on demand.

Except as otherwise provided in this Part, the provisions of this Act applicable to a bill of exchange payable on demand apply to a cheque.

74. Presentment of cheque for payment

Subject to the provisions of this Act—

(1)   Where a cheque is not presented for payment within a reasonable time of its issue, and the drawer or the person on whose account it is drawn had the right at the time of such presentment as between him and the banker to have the cheque paid and suffers actual damage through the delay, he is discharged to the extent of such damage, that is to say, to the extent to which such drawer or person is a creditor of such banker to a larger amount than he would have been had such cheque been paid.

(2)   In determining what is a reasonable time regard shall be had to the nature of the instrument, the usage of trade and of bankers, and the facts of the particular case.

(3)   The holder of such cheque as to which such drawer or person is discharged shall be a creditor, in lieu of such drawer or person, of such banker to the extent of such discharge, and entitled to recover the amount from him.

74A.   Presentment of cheque for payment: alternative place of presentment
Where the banker on whom a cheque is drawn—
(a)   has by notice published in the London, Edinburgh and Belfast Gazette specified an address at which cheques drawn on him may be presented; and
(b)   has not by notice so published cancelled the specification of that address,
the cheque is also presented at the proper place if it is presented there.

74B.   Presentment of cheque for payment: alternative place of presentment by banker
(1)   A banker may present a cheque for payment to the banker on whom it is drawn by notifying him of its essential features by electronic means or otherwise, instead of by presenting the cheque itself.
(2)   If a cheque is presented for payment under this section, presentment need not be made at the proper place or at a reasonable hour on a business day.
(3)   If, before the close of business on the next business day following presentment of a cheque under this section, the banker on whom the cheque is drawn requests the banker by whom the cheque was presented to present the cheque itself—
       (a)   the presentment under this section shall be disregarded; and
       (b)   this section shall not apply in relation to the subsequent presentment of the cheque.
(4)   A request under subsection (3) above for the presentment of a cheque shall not constitute dishonour of the cheque by non-payment.
(5)   Where presentment of a cheque is made under this section, the banker who presented the cheque and the banker on whom it is drawn shall be subject to the same duties in relation to the collection and payment of the cheque as if the cheque itself has been presented for payment.
(6)   For the purposes of this section, the essential features of a cheque are—
       (a)   the serial number of the cheque;
       (b)   the code which identifies the banker on whom the cheque is drawn;
       (c)   the account number of the drawer of the cheque; and
       (d)   the amount of the cheque is entered by the drawer of the cheque.

74C.   Cheques presented for payment: under s 74B: disapplication of s 52(4)
Section 52(4) above—
(a)   so far as relating to presenting a bill for payment, shall not apply to presenting a cheque for payment under s 74B above; and
(b)   so far as relating to a bill which is paid, shall not apply to a cheque which is paid following presentment under that section.

75.   Revocation of banker's authority
The duty and authority of a banker to pay a cheque drawn on him by his customer are determined by—
(1)   Countermand of payment.
(2)   Notice of the customer's death.

Crossed cheques

76.   General and special crossings defined
(1)   Where a cheque bears across its face an addition of—
       (a)   the words "and company" or any abbreviation thereof between two parallel transverse lines, either with or without the words "not negotiable"; or

(b)   two parallel transverse lines simply, either with or without the words "not negotiable",

that addition constitutes a crossing, and the cheque is crossed generally.

(2)   Where a cheque bears across its face an addition of the name of a banker, either with or without the words "not negotiable," that addition constitutes a crossing, and the cheque is crossed specially and to that banker.

77.   Crossing by drawer or after issue

(1)   A cheque may be crossed generally or specially by the drawer.

(2)   Where a cheque is uncrossed, the holder may cross it generally or specially.

(3)   Where a cheque is crossed generally the holder may cross it specially.

(4)   Where a cheque is crossed generally or specially, the holder may add the words "not negotiable".

(5)   Where a cheque is crossed specially, the banker to whom it is crossed may again cross it specially to another banker for collection.

(6)   Where an uncrossed cheque, or a cheque crossed generally, is sent to a banker for collection, he may cross it specially to himself.

78.   Crossing a material part of cheque

A crossing authorised by this Act is a material part of the cheque; it shall not be lawful for any person to obliterate or, except as authorised by this Act, to add to or alter the crossing.

79.   Duties of banker as to crossed cheques

(1)   Where a cheque is crossed specially to more than one banker except when crossed to an agent for collection being a banker, the banker on whom it is drawn shall refuse payment thereof.

(2)   Where the banker on whom a cheque is drawn which is so crossed nevertheless pays the same, or pays a cheque crossed generally otherwise than to a banker, or if crossed specially otherwise than to the banker to whom it is crossed, or his agent for collection being a banker, he is liable to the true owner of the cheque for any loss he may sustain owing to the cheque having been so paid.

Provided that where a cheque is presented for payment which does not at the time of presentment appear to be crossed, or to have had a crossing which has been obliterated, or to have been added to or altered otherwise than as authorised by this Act, the banker paying the cheque in good faith and without negligence shall not be responsible or incur any liability, nor shall the payment be questioned by reason of the cheque having been crossed, or of the crossing having been obliterated or having been added to or altered otherwise than as authorised by this Act, and of payment having been made otherwise than to a banker or to the banker to whom the cheque is or was crossed, or to his agent for collection being a banker, as the case may be.

80.   Protection to banker and drawer where cheque is crossed

Where the banker, on whom a crossed cheque (including a cheque which under section 81A below or otherwise is not transferable) is drawn, in good faith and without negligence pays it, if crossed generally, to a banker, and if crossed specially, to the banker to whom it is crossed, or his agent for collection being a banker, the banker paying the cheque, and, if the cheque has come into the hands of the payee, the drawer, shall respectively be entitled to the same rights and be placed in the same position as if payment of the cheque had been made to the true owner thereof.

81.   Effect of crossing on holder
Where a person takes a crossed cheque which bears on it the words "not negotiable," he shall not have and shall not be capable of giving a better title to the cheque than that which the person from whom he took it had.

81A.   Non-transferable cheques
(1)   Where a cheque is crossed and bears across its face the words "account payee" or "a/c payee", either with or without the word "only", the cheque shall not be transferable, but shall only be valid as between the parties thereto.

(2)   A banker is not to be treated for the purposes of section 80 above as having been negligent by reason only of his failure to concern himself with any purported indorsement of a cheque which under subsection (1) above or otherwise is not transferable.

82.   [Repealed].

PART IV
PROMISSORY NOTES

83.   Promissory note defined
(1)   A promissory note is an unconditional promise in writing made by one person to another signed by the maker, engaging to pay, on demand or at a fixed or determinable future time, a sum certain in money, to, or to the order of, a specified person or to bearer.

(2)   An instrument in the form of a note payable to maker's order is not a note within the meaning of this section unless and until it is indorsed by the maker.

(3)   A note is not invalid by reason only that it contains also a pledge of collateral security with authority to sell or dispose thereof.

(4)   A note which is, or on the face of it purports to be, both made and payable within the British Islands is an inland note. Any other note is a foreign note.

84.   Delivery necessary
A promissory note is inchoate and incomplete until delivery thereof to the payee or bearer.

85.   Joint and several notes
(1)   A promissory note may be made by two or more makers, and they may be liable thereon jointly, or jointly and severally according to its tenor.

(2)   Where a note runs "I promise to pay" and is signed by two or more persons it is deemed to be their joint and several note.

86.   Note payable on demand
(1)   Where a note payable on demand has been indorsed, it must be presented for payment within a reasonable time of the indorsement. If it be not so presented the indorser is discharged.

(2)   In determining what is reasonable time, regard shall be had to the nature of the instrument, the usage of trade, and the facts of the particular case.

(3)   Where a note payable on demand is negotiated, it is not deemed to be overdue, for the purpose of affecting the holder with defects of title of which he had no notice, by reason that it appears that a reasonable time for presenting it for payment has elapsed since its issue.

87. **Presentment of note for payment**
(1) Where a promissory note is in the body of it made payable at a particular place, it must be presented for payment at that place in order to render the maker liable. In any other case, presentment for payment is not necessary in order to render the maker liable.
(2) Presentment for payment is necessary in order to render the indorser of a note liable.
(3) Where a note is in the body of it made payable at a particular place, presentment at that place is necessary in order to render an indorser liable; but when a place of payment is indicated by way of memorandum only, presentment at that place is sufficient to render the indorser liable, but a presentment to the maker elsewhere, if sufficient in other respects, shall also suffice.

88. **Liability of maker**
The maker of a promissory note by making it—
(1) Engages that he will pay it according to its tenor.
(2) Is precluded from denying to a holder in due course the existence of the payee and his then capacity to indorse.

89. **Application of Part II to notes**
(1) Subject to the provisions in this part, and except as by this section provided, the provisions of this Act relating to bills of exchange apply, with the necessary modifications, to promissory notes.
(2) In applying those provisions the maker of a note shall be deemed to correspond with the acceptor of a bill, and the first indorser of a note shall be deemed to correspond with the drawer of an accepted bill payable to drawer's order.
(3) The following provisions as to bills do not apply to notes; namely, provisions relating to—
(a) presentment for acceptance;
(b) acceptance;
(c) acceptance supra protest;
(d) bills in a set.
(4) Where a foreign note is dishonoured protest thereof is unnecessary.

PART V

SUPPLEMENTARY

90. **Good faith**
A thing is deemed to be done in good faith, within the meaning of this Act, where it is in fact done honestly, whether it is done negligently or not.

91. **Signature**
(1) Where, by this Act, any instrument or writing is required to be signed by any person it is not necessary that he should sign it with his own hand, but it is sufficient if his signature is written thereon by some other person by or under his authority.
(2) In the case of a corporation, where, by this act, any instrument or writing is required to be signed, it is sufficient if the instrument or writing be sealed with the corporate seal. But nothing in this section shall be construed as requiring the bill or note of a corporation to be under seal.

92.   Computation of time
Where, by this Act, the time limited for doing any act or thing is less than three days, in reckoning time, non-business days are excluded.
    Non-business days' for the purposes of this Act mean—
(a)   Saturday, Sunday, Good Friday, Christmas Day;
(b)   a bank holiday under the Banking and Financial Dealings Act 1971;
(c)   a day appointed by Royal proclamation as a public fast or thanksgiving day;
(d)   a day declared by an order under section 2 of the Banking and Financial Dealings Act 1971 to be a non-business day.
Any other day is a business day.

93.   When noting equivalent to protest
For the purposes of this Act, where a bill or note is required to be protested within a specified time or before some further proceeding is taken, it is sufficient that the bill has been noted for protest before the expiration of the specified time or the taking of the proceeding; and the formal protest may be extended at any time thereafter as of the date of the noting.

94.   Protest when notary not accessible
Where a dishonoured bill or note is authorised or required to be protested, and the services of a notary cannot be obtained at the place where the bill is dishonoured, any householder or substantial resident of the place may, in the presence of two witnesses, give a certificate, signed by them, attesting the dishonour of the bill, and the certificate shall in respects operate as if it were a formal protest of the bill. The form given in Schedule 1 to this Act may be used with necessary modifications, and if used shall be sufficient.

95.–100.   [Omitted].

MARINE INSURANCE ACT 1906

CHAPTER 41
MARINE INSURANCE

SUPPLEMENTAL

86.   Ratification by assured.
87.   Implied obligations varied by agreement or usage.
88.   Reasonable time, &c a question of fact.
89.   Slip as evidence.
90.   Interpretation of terms.

SCHEDULE
SCHEDULE 1—FORM OF POLICY
MARINE INSURANCE

1.   Marine insurance defined
A contract of marine insurance is a contract whereby the insurer undertakes to indemnify the assured, in manner and to the extent thereby agreed, against marine losses, that is to say, the losses incident to marine adventure.

2.   Mixed sea and land risks
(1)   A contract of marine insurance may, by its express terms, or by usage of trade, be extended so as to protect the assured against losses on inland waters or on any land risk which may be incidental to any sea voyage.
(2)   Where a ship in course of building, or the launch of a ship, or any adventure analogous to a marine adventure, is covered by a policy in the form of a marine policy, the provisions of this Act, in so far as applicable, shall apply thereto; but, except as by this section provided, nothing in this Act shall alter or affect any rule of law applicable to any contract of insurance other than a contract of marine insurance as by this Act define.

3.   Marine adventure and maritime perils defined
(1)   Subject to the provisions of this Act, every lawful marine adventure may be the subject of a contract of marine insurance.
(2)   In particular there is a marine adventure where—
   (a)   any ship goods or other moveables are exposed to maritime perils. Such property is in this Act referred to as 'insurable property';
   (b)   the earning or acquisition of any freight, passage money, commission, profit, or other pecuniary benefit, or the security for any advances, loan, or disbursements, is endangered by the exposure of insurable property to maritime perils;
   (c)   any liability to a third party may be incurred by the owner of, or other person interested in or responsible for, insurable property, by reason of maritime perils.
'Maritime perils' means the perils consequent on, or incidental to, the navigation of the sea, that is to say, perils of the seas, fire, war, perils, pirates, rovers, thieves, captures, seizures, restraints, and detainment's of princes and peoples, jettisons, barratry, and any other perils, either of the like kind or which may be designated by the policy.

INSURABLE INTEREST

4.   Avoidance of wagering or gaming contracts
(1)   Every contract of marine insurance by way of gaming or wagering is void.
(2)   A contract of marine insurance is deemed to be a gaming or wagering contract—

(a) where the assured has not an insurable interest as defined by this Act, and the contract is entered into with no expectation of acquiring such an interest; or

(b) where the policy is made 'interest or no interest', or 'without further proof of interest than the policy itself', or 'without benefit of salvage to the insurer', or subject to any other like term.

Provided that, where there is no possibility of salvage, a policy may be effected without benefit of salvage to the insurer.

5. Insurable interest defined

(1) Subject to the provisions of this Act, every person has an insurable interest who is interested in a marine adventure.

(2) In particular a person is interested in a marine adventure where he stands in any legal or equitable relation to the adventure or to any insurable property at risk therein, in consequence of which he may benefit by the safety or due arrival of insurable property, or may be prejudiced by its loss, or by damage thereto, or by the detention thereof, or may incur liability in respect thereof.

6. When interest must attach

(1) The assured must be interested in the subject-matter insured at the time of the loss though he need not be interested when the insurance is effected: Provided that where the subject-matter is insured 'lost or not lost,' the assured may recover although he may not have acquired his interest until after the loss, unless at the time of effecting the contract of insurance the assured was aware of the loss, and the insurer was not.

(2) Where the assured has no interest at the time of the loss, he cannot acquire interest by any act or election after he is aware of the loss.

7. Defeasible or contingent interest

(1) A defeasible interest is insurable, as also is a contingent interest.

(2) In particular, where the buyer of goods has insured them, he has an insurable interest, notwithstanding that he might, at his election, have rejected the goods, or have treated them as at the seller's risk, by reason of the latter's delay in making delivery or otherwise.

8. Partial interest

A partial interest of any nature is insurable.

9. Re-insurance

(1) The insurer under a contract of marine insurance has an insurable interest in his risk, and may re-insure in respect of it.

(2) Unless the policy otherwise provides, the original assured has no right or interest in respect of such re-insurance.

10. Bottomry

The lender of money on bottomry or respondentia has an insurable interest in respect of the loan.

11. Master's and seamen's wages

The master or any member of the crew of a ship has an insurable interest in respect of his wages.

12. Advance freight

In the case of advance freight, the person advancing the freight has an insurable interest, in so far as such freight is not repayable in case of loss.

13. **Charges of insurance**
The assured has an insurable interest in the charges of any insurance which he may effect.

14. **Quantum of interest**
(1) Where the subject-matter insured is mortgaged, the mortgagor has an insurable interest in the full value thereof, and the mortgagee has an insurable interest in respect of any sum due or to become due under the mortgage.
(2) A mortgagee, consignee, or other person having an interest in the subject-matter insured may insure on behalf and for the benefit of other persons interested as well as for his own benefit.
(3) The owner of insurable property has an insurable interest in respect of the full value thereof, notwithstanding that some third person may have agreed, or be liable, to indemnify him in case of loss.

15. **Assignment of interest**
Where the assured assigns or otherwise parts with his interest in the subject-matter insured, he does not thereby transfer to the assignee his rights under the contract of insurance, unless there be an express or implied agreement with the assignee to that effect. But the provisions of this section do not affect a transmission of interest by operation of law.

INSURABLE VALUE

16. **Measure of insurable value**
Subject to any express provision or valuation in the policy, the insurable value of the subject-matter insured must be ascertained as follows—
(1) In insurance on ship, the insurable value is the value, at the commencement of the risk, of the ship, including her outfit, provisions and stores for the officers and crew, money advanced for seamen's wages, and other disbursements (if any) incurred to make the ship fit for the voyage or adventure contemplated by the policy, plus the charges of insurance upon the whole: The insurable value, in the case of a steamship, includes also the machinery, boilers, and coals and engine stores if owned by the assured, and, in the case of a ship engaged in a special trade, the ordinary fittings requisite for that trade.
(2) In insurance on freight, whether paid in advance or otherwise, the insurable value is the gross amount of the freight at the risk of the assured, plus the charges of insurance.
(3) In insurance on goods or merchandise, the insurable value is the prime cost of the property insured, plus the expenses of and incidental to shipping and the charges of insurance upon the whole.
(4) In insurance on any other subject-matter, the insurable value is the amount at the risk of the assured when the policy attaches, plus the charges of insurance.

DISCLOSURE AND REPRESENTATIONS

17. **Insurance is *uberrimae fidei***
A contract of marine insurance is a contract based upon the utmost good faith, and, if the utmost good faith be not observed by either party, the contract may be avoided by the other party.

18.   Disclosure by assured

(1)   Subject to the provisions of this section, the assured must disclose to the insurer, before the contract is concluded, every material circumstance which is known to the assured, and the assured is deemed to know every circumstance which, in the ordinary course of business, ought to be known by him. If the assured fails to make such disclosure, the insurer may avoid the contract.

(2)   Every circumstance is material which would influence the judgment of a prudent insurer in fixing the premium, or determining whether he will take the risk.

(3)   In the absence of inquiry the following circumstances need not be disclosed, namely—

(a)   any circumstance which diminishes the risk;

(b)   any circumstance which is known or presumed to be known to the insurer. The insurer is presumed to know matters of common notoriety or knowledge, and matters which an insurer in the ordinary course of his business, as such, ought to know;

(c)   any circumstances as to which information is waived by the insurer;

(d)   any circumstance which it is superfluous to disclose by reason of any express or implied warranty.

(4)   Whether any particular circumstance, which is not disclosed, be material or not is, in each case, a question of fact.

(5)   The term 'circumstance' includes any communication made to, or information received by, the assured.

19.   Disclosure by agent effecting insurance

Subject to the provisions of the preceding section as to circumstances which need not be disclosed, where an insurance is effected for the assured by an agent, the agent must disclose to the insurer—

(a)   every material circumstance which is known to himself, and an agent to insure is deemed to know every circumstance which in the ordinary course of business ought to be known by, or to have been communicated to, him; and

(b)   every material circumstance which the assured is bound to disclose, unless it come to his knowledge too late to communicate it to the agent.

20.   Representations pending negotiation of contract

(1)   Every material representation made by the assured or his agent to the insurer during the negotiations for the contract, and before the contract is concluded, must be true. If it be untrue the insurer may avoid the contract.

(2)   A representation is material which would influence the judgment of a prudent insurer in fixing the premium, or determining whether he will take the risk.

(3)   A representation may be either a representation as to a matter of fact, or as to a matter of expectation or belief.

(4)   A representation as to a matter of fact is true, if it be substantially correct, that is to say, if the difference between what is represented and what is actually correct would not be considered material by a prudent insurer.

(5)   A representation as to a matter of expectation or belief is true if it be made in good faith.

(6)   A representation may be withdrawn or corrected before the contract is concluded.

(7)   Whether a particular representation be material or not is, in each case, a question of fact.

21.   When contract is deemed to be concluded

A contract of marine insurance is deemed to be concluded when the proposal of the assured is accepted by the insurer, whether the policy be then issued or not; and, for the purpose of showing when the proposal was accepted, reference may be made to the slip or covering note or other customary memorandum of the contract.

THE POLICY

22.   Contract must be embodied in policy

Subject to the provisions of any statute, a contract of marine insurance is inadmissible in evidence unless it is embodied in a marine policy in accordance with this Act. The policy may be executed and issued either at the time when the contract is concluded, or afterwards.

23.   What policy must specify

A marine policy must specify—

(1)   The name of the assured, or of some person who effects the insurance on his behalf.

(2)–(5) [Repealed].

24.   Signature of insurer

(1)   A marine policy must be signed by or on behalf of the insurer, provided that in the case of a corporation the corporate seal may be sufficient, but nothing in this section shall be construed as requiring the subscription of a corporation to be under seal.

(2)   Where a policy is subscribed by or on behalf of two or more insurers, each subscription, unless the contrary be expressed, constitutes a distinct contract with the assured.

25.   Voyage and time policies

(1)   Where the contract is to insure the subject-matter 'at and from,' or from one place to another or other, the policy is called a 'voyage policy,' and where the contract is to insure the subject-matter for a definite period of time the policy is called a 'time policy.' A contract for both voyage and time may be included in the same policy.

(2)   [Repealed].

26.   Designation of subject-matter

(1)   The subject-matter insured must be designated in a marine policy with reasonable certainty.

(2)   The nature and extent of the interest of the assured in the subject-matter insured need not be specified in the policy.

(3)   Where the policy designates the subject-matter insured in general terms, its shall be construed to apply to the interest intended by the assured to be covered.

(4)   In the application of this section regard shall be had to any usage regulating the designation of the subject-matter insured.

27.   Valued policy

(1)   A policy may be either valued or unvalued.

(2)   A valued policy is a policy which specifies the agreed value of the subject-matter insured.

(3)   Subject to the provisions of this Act, and in the absence of fraud, the value fixed by the policy is, as between the insurer and assured, conclusive of the

insurable value of the subject intended to be insured, whether the loss be total or partial.

(4)   Unless the policy otherwise provides, the value fixed by the policy is not conclusive for the purpose of determining whether there has been a constructive total loss.

28.   Unvalued policy

An unvalued policy is a policy which does not specify the value of the subject-matter insured, but subject to the limit of the sum insured, leaves the insurable value to be subsequently ascertained, in the manner herein-before specified.

29.   Floating policy by ship or ships

(1)   A floating policy is a policy which describes the insurance in general terms, and leaves the name of the ship or ships and other particulars to be defined by subsequent declaration.

(2)   The subsequent declaration or declarations may be made by indorsement on the policy, or in other customary manner.

(3)   Unless the policy otherwise provides, the declarations must be made in the order of dispatch or shipment. They must, in the case of goods, comprise all consignments within the terms of the policy, and the value of the goods or other property must be honestly stated, but an omission or erroneous declaration may be rectified even after loss or arrival, provided the omission or declaration was made in good faith.

(4)   Unless the policy otherwise provides, where a declaration of value is not made until after notice of loss or arrival, the policy must be treated as an unvalued policy as regards the subject-matter of that declaration.

30.   Construction of terms in policy

(1)   A policy may be in the form in the First Schedule to this Act.

(2)   Subject to the provisions of this Act, and unless the context of the policy otherwise requires, the terms and expressions mentioned in the First Schedule to this Act shall be construed as having the scope and meaning in that schedule assigned to them.

31.   Premium to be arranged

(1)   Where an insurance is effected at a premium to be arranged, and no arrangement is made, a reasonable premium is payable.

(2)   Where an insurance is effected on the terms that an additional premium is to be arranged in a given event, and that event happens but no arrangement is made, then a reasonable additional premium is payable.

DOUBLE INSURANCE

32.   Double insurance

(1)   Where two or more policies are effected by or on behalf of the assured on the same adventure and interest or any part thereof, and the sums insured exceed the indemnity allowed by this Act, the assured is said to be over-insured by double insurance.

(2)   Where the assured is over-insured by double insurance—

(a)   the assured, unless the policy otherwise provides, may claim payment from the insurers in such order as he may think fit, provided that he is not entitled to receive any sum in excess of the indemnity allowed by this Act;

(b)   where the policy under which the assured claims is a valued policy, the assured must give credit as against the valuation for any sum received by him under any other policy without regard to the actual value of the subject-matter insured;

(c) where the policy under which the assured claims is an unvalued policy he must give credit, as against the full insurable value, for any sum received by him under any other policy;

(d) where the assured receives any sum in excess of the indemnity allowed by this Act, he is deemed to hold such sum in trust for the insurers, according to their right of contribution among themselves.

WARRANTIES, &C

33. Nature of warranty

(1) A warranty, in the following sections relating to warranties, means a promissory warranty, that is to say, a warranty by which the assured undertakes that some particular thing shall or shall not be done, or that some condition shall be fulfilled, or whereby he affirms or negatives the existence of a particular state of facts.

(2) A warranty may be express or implied.

(3) A warranty, as above defined, is a condition which must be exactly complied with, whether it be material to the risk or not. If it be not so complied with, then, subject to any express provision in the policy, the insurer is discharged from liability as from the date of the breach of warranty, but without prejudice to any liability incurred by him before that date.

34. When breach of warranty excused

(1) Non-compliance with a warranty is excused when by reason of a change of circumstances, the warranty ceases to be applicable to the circumstances of the contract, or when compliance with the warranty is rendered unlawful by any subsequent law.

(2) Where a warranty is broken, the assured cannot avail himself of the defence that the breach has been remedied, and the warranty complied with, before loss.

(3) A breach of warranty may be waived by the insurer.

35. Express warranties

(1) An express warranty may be in any form of words from which the intention to warrant is to be inferred.

(2) An express warranty must be included in, or written upon, the policy, or must be contained in some document incorporated by reference into the policy.

(3) An express warranty does not exclude an implied warranty, unless it be inconsistent therewith.

36. Warranty of neutrality

(1) Where insurable property, whether ship or goods, is expressly warranted neutral, there is an implied condition that the property shall have a neutral character at the commencement of the risk, and that, so far as the assured can control the matter, its neutral character shall be preserved during the risk.

(2) Where a ship is expressly warranted 'neutral' there is also an implied condition that, so far as the assured can control the matter she shall be properly documented, that is to say, that she shall carry the necessary papers to establish her neutrality, and that she shall not falsify or suppress her papers, or use simulated papers. If any loss occurs through breach of this condition, the insurer may avoid the contract.

37. No implied warranty of nationality
There is no implied warranty as to the nationality of a ship, or that her nationality shall not be changed during the risk.

38. Warranty of good safety
Where the subject-matter insured is warranted 'well' or 'in good safety' on a particular day, it is sufficient if it be safe at any time during that day.

39. Warranty of seaworthiness of ship
(1)   In a voyage policy there is an implied warranty that at the commencement of the voyage the ship shall be seaworthy for the purpose of the particular adventure insured.
(2)   Where the policy attaches while the ship is in port, there is also an implied warranty that she shall, at the commencement of the risk, be reasonably fit to encounter the ordinary perils of the port.
(3)   Where the policy relates to a voyage which is performed in different stages, during which the ship requires different kinds of or further preparation or equipment, there is an implied warranty that at the commencement of each stage the ship is seaworthy in respect of such preparation or equipment for the purposes of that stage.
(4)   A ship is deemed to be seaworthy when she is reasonably fit in all respects to encounter the ordinary perils of the seas of the adventure insured.
(5)   In a time policy there is no implied warranty that the ship shall be seaworthy at any stage of the adventure, but where, with the privity of the assured, the ship is sent to sea in an unseaworthy state, the insurer is not liable for any loss attributable to unseaworthiness.

40. No implied warranty that goods are seaworthy
(1)   In a policy on goods or other moveables there is no implied warranty that the goods or moveables are seaworthy.
(2)   In a voyage policy on goods or other moveables there is an implied warranty that at the commencement of the voyage the ship is not only seaworthy as a ship, but also that she is reasonably fit to carry the goods or other moveables to the destination contemplated by the policy.

41. Warranty of legality
There is an implied warranty that the adventure insured is a lawful one, and that, so far as the assured can control the matter, the adventure shall be carried out in a lawful manner.

THE VOYAGE

42. Implied condition as to commencement of risk
(1)   Where the subject-matter is insured by a voyage policy 'at and from' or 'from' a particular place, it is not necessary that the ship should be at that place when the contract is concluded, but there is an implied condition that the adventure shall be commenced within a reasonable time, and that if the adventure be not so commenced the insurer may avoid the contract.
(2)   The implied condition may be negatived by showing that the delay was caused by circumstances known to the insurer before the contract was concluded, or by showing that he waived the condition.

43. Alteration of port of departure
Where the place of departure is specified by the policy, and the ship instead of sailing from that place sails from any other place, the risk does not attach.

44. Sailing for different destination
Where the destination is specified in the policy, and the ship, instead of sailing for
that destination, sails for any other destination, the risk does not attach.

45. Change of voyage
(1)   Where, after the commencement of the risk, the destination of the ship is
       voluntarily changed from the destination contemplated by the policy, there is
       said to be a change of voyage.
(2)   Unless the policy otherwise provides, where there is a change of voyage, the
       insurer is discharged from liability as from the time of change, that is to say, as
       from the time when the determination to change it is manifested; and it is
       immaterial that the ship may not in fact have left the course of voyage
       contemplated by the policy when the loss occurs.

46. Deviation
(1)   Where a ship, without lawful excuse, deviates from the voyage contemplated
       by the policy, the insurer is discharged from liability as from the time of
       deviation, and it is immaterial that the ship may have regained her route
       before any loss occurs.
(2)   There is a deviation from the voyage contemplated by the policy—
       (a) where the course of the voyage is specifically designated by the policy,
            and that course is departed from; or
       (b) where the course of the voyage is not specifically designated by the
            policy, but the usual and customary course is departed from.
(3)   The intention to deviate is immaterial; there must be a deviation in fact to
       discharge the insurer from his liability under the contract.

47. Several ports of discharge
(1)   Where several ports of discharge are specified by the policy, the ship may
       proceed to all or any of them, but, in the absence of any usage or sufficient
       cause to the contrary, she must proceed to them, or such of them as she goes
       to, in the order designated by the policy. If she does not there is a deviation.
(2)   Where the policy is to 'ports of discharge,' within a given area, which are not
       named, the ship must, in the absence of any usage or sufficient cause to the
       contrary, proceed to them, or such of them as she goes to, in their
       geographical order. If she does not there is a deviation.

48. Delay in voyage
In the case of a voyage policy, the adventure insured must be prosecuted
throughout its course with reasonable dispatch, and, if without lawful excuse it is
not so prosecuted, the insurer is discharged from liability as from the time when
the delay became unreasonable.

49. Excuses for deviation or delay
(1)   Deviation or delay in prosecuting the voyage contemplated by the policy is
       excused—
       (a) where authorised by any special term in the policy; or
       (b) where caused by circumstances beyond the control of the master and his
            employer; or
       (c) where reasonably necessary in order to comply with an express or
            implied warranty; or
       (d) where reasonably necessary for the safety of the ship or subject-matter
            insured; or
       (e) for the purpose of saving human life, or aiding a ship in distress where
            human life may be in danger; or

(f)   where reasonably necessary for the purpose of obtaining medical or surgical aid for any person on board the ship; or

(g)   where caused by the barratrous conduct of the master or crew, if barratry be one of the perils insured against.

(2)   When the cause excusing the deviation or delay ceases to operate, the ship must resume her course, and prosecute her voyage, with reasonable dispatch.

ASSIGNMENT OF POLICY

50.   When and how policy is assignable

(1)   A marine policy is assignable unless it contains terms expressly prohibiting assignment. It may be assigned either before or after loss.

(2)   Where a marine policy has been assigned so as to pass the beneficial interest in such policy, the assignee of the policy is entitled to sue thereon in his own name; and the defendant is entitled to make any defence arising out of the contract which he would have been entitled to make if the action had been brought in the name of the person by or on behalf of whom the policy was effected.

51.   Assured who has no interest cannot assign

Where the assured has parted with or lost his interest in the subject-matter insured, and has not, before or at the time of so doing, expressly or impliedly agreed to assign the policy, any subsequent assignment of the policy is inoperative. Provided that nothing in this section affects the assignment of a policy after loss.

THE PREMIUM

52.   When premium payable

Unless otherwise agreed, the duty of the assured or his agent to pay the premium, and the duty of the insurer to issue the policy to the assured or his agent, are concurrent conditions, and the insurer is not bound to issue the policy until payment or tender of the premium.

53.   Policy effected through broker

(1)   Unless otherwise agreed, where a marine policy is effected on behalf of the assured by a broker, the broker is directly responsible to the insurer for the premium, and the insurer is directly responsible to the assured for the amount which may be payable in respect of losses, or in respect of returnable premium.

(2)   Unless otherwise agreed, the broker has, as against the assured, a lien upon the policy for the amount of the premium and his charges in respect of effecting the policy; and, where he has dealt with the person who employs him as a principal, he has also a lien on the policy in respect of any balance on any insurance account which may be due to him from such person, unless when the debt was incurred he had reason to believe that such person was only an agent.

54.   Effect of receipt on policy

Where a marine policy effected on behalf of the assured by a broker acknowledges the receipt of the premium, such acknowledgement is, in the absence of fraud, conclusive as between the insurer and the assured, but not as between the insurer and broker.

LOSS AND ABANDONMENT

55.   Included and excluded losses

(1)   Subject to the provisions of this Act, and unless the policy otherwise provides, the insurer is liable for any loss proximately caused by a peril insured against, but, subject as aforesaid, he is not liable for any loss which is not proximately caused by a peril insured against.

(2)   In particular—

(a)   the insurer is not liable for any loss attributable to the wilful misconduct of the assured, but, unless the policy otherwise provides, he is liable for any loss proximately caused by a peril insured against, even though the loss would not have happened but for the misconduct or negligence of the master or crew;

(b)   unless the policy otherwise provides, the insurer on ship or goods is not liable for any loss proximately caused by delay, although the delay be caused by a peril insured against;

(c)   unless the policy otherwise provides, the insurer is not liable for ordinary wear and tear, ordinary leakage and breakage, inherent vice or nature of the subject-matter insured, or for any loss proximately caused by rats or vermin, or for any injury to machinery not proximately caused by maritime perils.

56.   Partial and total loss

(1)   A loss may be either total or partial. Any loss other than a total loss, as hereinafter defined, is a partial loss.

(2)   A total loss may be either an actual total loss, or a constructive total loss.

(3)   Unless a different intention appears from the terms of the policy, an insurance against total loss includes a constructive, as well as an actual, total loss.

(4)   Where the assured brings an action for a total loss and the evidence proves only a partial loss, he may, unless the policy otherwise provides, recover for a partial loss.

(5)   Where goods reach their destination in specie, but by reason of obliteration of marks, or otherwise, they are incapable of identification, the loss, if any, is partial, and not total.

57.   Actual total loss

(1)   Where the subject-matter insured is destroyed, or so damaged as to cease to be a thing of the kind insured, or where the assured is irretrievably deprived thereof, there is an actual total loss.

(2)   In the case of an actual total loss no notice of abandonment need be given.

58.   Missing ship

Where the ship concerned in the adventure is missing, and after the lapse of a reasonable time no news of her has been received, an actual total loss may be presumed.

59.   Effect of transhipment, &c

Where, by a peril insured against, the voyage is interrupted at an intermediate port or place, under such circumstances as, apart from any special stipulation in the contract of affreightment, to justify the master in landing and reshipping the goods or other moveables, or in transhipping them, and sending them on to their destination, the liability of the insurer continues, notwithstanding the landing or transhipment.

60. Constructive total loss defined

(1)   Subject to any express provision in the policy, there is a constructive total loss where the subject-matter insured is reasonably abandoned on account of its actual total loss appearing to be unavoidable, or because it could not be preserved from actual total loss without an expenditure which would exceed its value when the expenditure had been incurred.

(2)   In particular, there is a constructive total loss—

    (i)   where the assured is deprived of the possession of his ship or goods by a peril insured against, and (a) it is unlikely that he can recover the ship or goods, as the case may be, or (b) the cost of recovering the ship or goods, as the case may be, would exceed their value when recovered; or

    (ii) in the case of damage to a ship, where she is so damaged by a peril insured against that the cost of repairing the damage would exceed the value of the ship when repaired. In estimating the cost of repairs, no deduction is to be made in respect of general average contributions to those repairs payable by other interests, but account is to be taken of the expense of future salvage operations and of any future general average contributions to which the ship would be liable if repaired; or

    (iii) in the case of damage to goods, where the cost of repairing the damage and forwarding the goods to their destination would exceed their value on arrival.

61. Effect of constructive total loss

Where there is a constructive total loss the assured may either treat the loss as a partial loss, or abandon the subject-matter insured to the insurer and treat the loss as if it were an actual total loss.

62. Notice of abandonment

(1)   Subject to the provisions of this section, where the assured elects to abandon the subject-matter insured to the insurer, he must give notice of abandonment. If he fails to do so the loss can only be treated as a partial loss.

(2)   Notice of abandonment may be given in writing, or by word of mouth, or partly in writing and partly by word of mouth, and may be given in any terms which indicate the intention of the assured to abandon his insured interest in the subject-matter insured unconditionally to the insurer.

(3)   Notice of abandonment must be given with reasonable diligence after the receipt of reliable information of the loss, but where the information is of a doubtful character the assured is entitled to a reasonable time to make inquiry.

(4)   Where notice of abandonment is properly given, the rights of the assured are not prejudiced by the fact that the insurer refuses to accept the abandonment.

(5)   The acceptance of an abandonment may be either express or implied from the conduct of the insurer. The mere silence of the insurer after notice is not acceptance.

(6)   Where notice of abandonment is accepted the abandonment is irrevocable. The acceptance of the notice conclusively admits liability for the loss and the sufficiency of the notice.

(7)   Notice of abandonment is unnecessary where, at the time when the assured receives information of the loss, there would be no possibility of benefit to the insurer if notice were given to him.

(8)   Notice of abandonment may be waived by the insurer.

(9)   Where an insurer has re-insured his risk, no notice of abandonment need by given by him.

63.   Effect of abandonment

(1)   Where there is a valid abandonment the insurer is entitled to take over the interest of the assured in whatever may remain of the subject-matter insured, and all proprietary rights incidental thereto.

(2)   Upon the abandonment of a ship, the insurer thereof is entitled to any freight in course of being earned, and which is earned by her subsequent to the casualty causing the loss, less the expenses of earning it incurred after the casualty; and, where the ship is carrying the owner's goods, the insurer is entitled to a reasonable remuneration for the carriage of them subsequent to the casualty causing the loss.

PARTIAL LOSSES (INCLUDING SALVAGE AND GENERAL AVERAGE AND PARTICULAR CHARGES)

64.   Particular average loss

(1)   A particular average loss is a partial loss of the subject-matter insured, caused by a peril insured against, and which is not a general average loss.

(2)   Expenses incurred by or on behalf of the assured for the safety or preservation of the subject-matter insured, other than general average and salvage charges, are called particular charges. Particular charges are not included in particular average.

65.   Salvage charges

(1)   Subject to any express provision in the policy, salvage charges incurred in preventing a loss by perils insured against may be recovered as a loss by those perils.

(2)   'Salvage charges' means the charges recoverable under maritime law by a salvor independently of contract. They do not include the expenses of services in the nature of salvage rendered by the assured or his agents, or any person employed for hire by them, for the purpose of averting a peril insured against. Such expenses, where properly incurred, may be recovered as particular charges or as a general average loss, according to the circumstances under which they were incurred.

66.   General average loss

(1)   A general average loss is a loss caused by or directly consequential on a general average act. It includes a general average expenditure as well as a general average sacrifice.

(2)   There is a general average act where any extraordinary sacrifice or expenditure is voluntarily and reasonably made or incurred in time of peril for the purpose of preserving the property imperilled in the common adventure.

(3)   Where there is a general average loss, the party on whom it falls is entitled, subject to the conditions imposed by maritime law, to a rateable contribution from the other parties interested, and such contribution is called a general average contribution.

(4)   Subject to any express provision in the policy, where the assured has incurred a general average expenditure, he may recover from the insurer in respect of the proportion of the loss which falls upon him; and, in the case of a general average sacrifice, he may recover from the insurer in respect of the whole loss without having enforced his right of contribution from the other parties liable to contribute.

(5)   Subject to any express provision in the policy, where the assured has paid, or is liable to pay, a general average contribution in respect of the subject insured, he may recover therefore from the insurer.

(6)   In the absence of express stipulation, the insurer is not liable for any general average loss or contribution where the loss was not incurred for the purpose of avoiding, or in connection with the avoidance of, a peril insured against.

(7)   Where ship, freight, and cargo, or any two of those interests, are owned by the same assured, the liability of the insurer in respect of general average losses or contributions is to be determined as if those subjects were owned by different persons.

MEASURE OF INDEMNITY

67.   Extent of liability of insurer for loss
(1)   The sum which the assured can recover in respect of a loss on a policy by which he is insured, in the case of an unvalued policy to the full extent of the insurable value, or, in the case of a valued policy to the full extent of the value fixed by the policy is called the measure of indemnity.

(2)   Where there is a loss recoverable under the policy, the insurer, or each insurer if there be more than one, is liable for such proportion of the measure of indemnity as the amount of his subscription bears to the value fixed by the policy in the case of a valued policy, or to the insurable value in the case of an unvalued policy.

68.   Total loss
Subject to the provisions of this Act and to any express provision in the policy, where there is a total loss of the subject-matter insured—
(1)   If the policy be a valued policy, the measure of indemnity is the sum fixed by the policy.

(2)   If the policy be an unvalued policy, the measure of indemnity is the insurable value of the subject-matter insured.

69.   Partial loss of ship
Where a ship is damaged, but is not totally lost, the measure of indemnity, subject to any express provision in the policy, is as follows—
(1)   Where the ship has been repaired, the assured is entitled to the reasonable cost of the repairs, less the customary deductions, but not exceeding the sum insured in respect of any one casualty.

(2)   Where the ship has been only partially repaired, the assured is entitled to the reasonable cost of such repairs, computed as above, and also to be indemnified for the reasonable depreciation, if any, arising from the unrepaired damage, provided that the aggregate amount shall not exceed the cost of repairing the whole damage, computed as above.

(3)   Where the ship has not been repaired, and has not been sold in her damaged state during the risk, the assured is entitled to be indemnified for the reasonable depreciation arising from the unrepaired damage, but not exceeding the reasonable cost of repairing such damage, computed as above.

70.   Partial loss of freight
Subject to any express provision in the policy, where there is a partial loss of freight, the measure of indemnity is such proportion of the sum fixed by the policy in the case of a valued policy, or of the insurable value in the case of an unvalued policy, as the proportion of freight lost by the assured bears to the whole freight at the risk of the assured under the policy.

71.   Partial loss of goods, merchandise, &c
Where there is a partial loss of goods, merchandise or other moveables, the measure of indemnity, subject to any express provision in the policy, is as follows—

(1)   Where part of the goods, merchandise or other moveables insured by a valued policy is totally lost, the measure of indemnity is such proportion of the sum fixed by the policy as the insurable value of the part lost bears to the insurable value of the whole, ascertained as in the case of an unvalued policy.

(2)   Where part of the goods, merchandise, or other moveables insured by an unvalued policy is totally lost, the measure of indemnity is the insurable value of the part lost, ascertained as in case of total loss.

(3)   Where the whole or any part of the goods or merchandise insured has been delivered damaged at its destination, the measure of indemnity is such proportion of the sum fixed by the policy in the case of a valued policy, or of the insurable value in the case of an unvalued policy, as the difference between the gross sound and damaged valued at the place of arrival bears to the gross sound value.

(4)   'Gross value' means the wholesale price, or, if there be no such price, the estimated value, with, in either case, freight, landing charges, and duty paid beforehand; provided that, in the case of goods or merchandise customarily sold in bond, the bonded price is deemed to be the gross value. 'Gross proceeds' means the actual price obtained at a sale where all charges on sale are paid by the sellers.

72.   Apportionment of valuation

(1)   Where different species of property are insured under a single valuation, the valuation must be apportioned over the different species in proportion to their respective insurable values, as in the case of an unvalued policy. The insured value of any part of a species is such proportion of the total insured value of the same as the insurable value of the part bears to the insurable value of the whole, ascertained in both cases as provided by this Act.

(2)   Where a valuation has to be apportioned, and particulars of the prime cost of each separate species, quality, or description of goods cannot be ascertained, the division of the valuation may be made over the net arrived sound values of the different species, qualities, or descriptions of goods.

73.   General average contributions and salvage charges

(1)   Subject to any express provision in the policy, where the assured has paid, or is liable for, any general average contribution, the measure of indemnity is the full amount of such contribution, if the subject-matter liable to contribution is insured for its full contributory value, or if only part of it be insured, the indemnity payable by the insurer must be reduced in proportion to the under insurance, and where there has been a particular average loss which constitutes a deduction from the contributory value, and for which the insurer is liable, that amount must be deducted from the insured value in order to ascertain what the insurer is liable to contribute.

(2)   Where the insurer is liable for salvage charges the extent of his liability must be determined on the like principle.

74.   Liabilities to third parties

Where the assured has effected an insurance in express terms against any liability to a third party, the measure of indemnity, subject to any express provision in the policy, is the amount paid or payable by him to such third party in respect of such liability.

75.   General provisions as to measure of indemnity

(1)   Where there has been a loss in respect of any subject-matter not expressly provided for in the foregoing provisions of this Act, the measure of indemnity shall be ascertained, as nearly as may be, in accordance with those provisions, in so far as applicable to the particular case.

(2) Nothing in the provisions of this Act relating to the measure of indemnity shall affect the rules relating to double insurance, or prohibit the insurer from disproving interest wholly or in part, or from showing that at the time of the loss the whole or any part of the subject-matter insured was not at risk under the policy.

76. Particular average warranties

(1) Where the subject-matter insured is warranted free from particular average, the assured cannot recover for a loss of part, other than a loss incurred by a general average sacrifice, unless the contract contained in the policy be apportionable; but, if the contract be apportionable, the assured may recover for a total loss of any apportionable part.

(2) Where the subject-matter insured is warranted free from particular average, either wholly or under a certain percentage, the insurer is nevertheless liable for salvage charges, and for particular charges and other expenses properly incurred pursuant to the provisions of the suing and labouring clause in order to avert a loss insured against.

(3) Unless the policy otherwise provides, where the subject-matter insured is warranted free from particular average under a specified percentage, a general average loss cannot be added to a particular average loss to make up the specified percentage.

(4) For the purpose of ascertaining whether the specified percentage has been reached, regard shall be had only to the actual loss suffered by the subject-matter insured. Particular charges and the expenses of and incidental to ascertaining and proving the loss must be excluded.

77. Successive losses

(1) Unless the policy otherwise provides, and subject to the provisions of this Act, the insurer is liable for successive losses, even though the total amount of such losses may exceed the sum insured.

(2) Where, under the same policy, a partial loss, which has not been repaired or otherwise made good, is followed by a total loss, the assured can only recover in respect of the total loss: Provided that nothing in this section shall affect the liability of the insurer under the suing and labouring clause.

78. Suing and labouring clause

(1) Where the policy contains a suing and labouring clause, the engagement thereby entered into is deemed to be supplementary to the contract of insurance, and the assured may recover from the insurer any expenses properly incurred pursuant to the clause, notwithstanding that the insurer may have paid for a total loss, or that the subject-matter may have been warranted free from particular average, either wholly or under a certain percentage.

(2) General average losses and contributions and salvage charges, as defined by this Act, are not recoverable under the suing and labouring clause.

(3) Expenses incurred for the purpose of averting or diminishing any loss not covered by the policy are not recoverable under the suing and labouring clause.

(4) It is the duty of the assured and his agents, in all cases, to take such measures as may be reasonable for the purpose of averting or minimising a loss.

RIGHTS OF INSURER ON PAYMENT

79.   Right of subrogation

(1)   Where the insurer pays for a total loss, either of the whole, or in the case of goods of any apportionable part, of the subject-matter insured, he thereupon becomes entitled to take over the interest of the assured in whatever may remain of the subject-matter so paid for, and he is thereby subrogated to all the rights and remedies of the assured in and in respect of that subject-matter as from the time of the casualty causing the loss.

(2)   Subject to the foregoing provisions, where the insurer pays for a partial loss, he acquires no title to the subject-matter insured, or such part of it as may remain, but he is thereupon subrogated to all rights and remedies of the assured in and in respect of the subject-matter insured as from the time of the casualty causing the loss, in so far as the assured has been indemnified, according to this Act, by such payment for the loss.

80.   Right of contribution

(1)   Where the assured is over-insured by double insurance, each insurer is bound, as between himself and the other insurers, to contribute rateably to the loss in proportion to the amount for which he is liable under his contract.

(2)   If any insurer pays more than his proportion of the loss, he is entitled to maintain an action for contribution against the other insurers, and is entitled to the like remedies as a surety who has paid more than his proportion of the debt.

81.   Effect of under insurance

Where the assured is insured for an amount less than the insurable value or, in the case of a valued policy, for an amount less than the policy valuation, he is deemed to be his own insurer in respect of the uninsured balance.

RETURN OF PREMIUM

82.   Enforcement of return

Where the premium or a proportionate part thereof is, by this Act, declared to be returnable—

(a)   if already paid, it may be recovered by the assured from the insurer; and

(b)   if unpaid, it may be retained by the assured or his agent.

83.   Return by agreement

Where the policy contains a stipulation for the return of the premium, or a proportionate part thereof, on the happening of a certain event, and that event happens, the premium, or, as the case may be, the proportionate part thereof, is thereupon returnable to the assured.

84.   Return for failure of consideration

(1)   Where the consideration for the payment of the premium totally fails, and there has been no fraud or illegality on the part of the assured or his agents, the premium is thereupon returnable to the assured.

(2)   Where the consideration for the payment of the premium is apportionable and there is a total failure of any apportionable part of the consideration, a proportionate part of the premium is, under the like conditions, thereupon returnable to the assured.

(3)   In particular—

(a)   where the policy is void, or is avoided by the insurer as from the commencement of the risk, the premium is returnable, provided that there has been no fraud or illegality on the part of the assured; but if the risk is not apportionable, and has once attached, the premium is not returnable;

(b) where the subject-matter insured, or part thereof, has never been imperilled, the premium, or, as the case may be, a proportionate part thereof, is returnable;

     Provided that where the subject-matter has been insured 'lost or not lost' and has arrived in safety at the time when the contract is concluded, the premium is returnable unless, at such time, the insurer knew of the safe arrival;

(c) where the assured has no insurable interest throughout the currency of the risk, the premium is returnable, provided that this rule does not apply to a policy effected by way of gaming or wagering;

(d) where the assured has a defeasible interest which is terminated during the currency of the risk, the premium is not returnable;

(e) where the assured has over-insured under an unvalued policy, a proportionate part of the several premiums is returnable;

(f) subject to the foregoing provisions, where the assured has over-insured by double insurance, a proportionate part of the several premiums is returnable;

Provided that, if the policies are effected at different times, and any earlier policy has at any time borne the entire risk, or if a claim has been paid on the policy in respect of the full sum insured thereby, no premium is returnable in respect of that policy, and when the double insurance is effected knowingly by the assured no premium is returnable.

MUTUAL INSURANCE

85. Modification of Act in case of mutual insurance

(1) Where two or more persons mutually agree to insure each other against marine losses there is said to be a mutual insurance.

(2) The provisions of this Act relating to the premium do not apply to mutual insurance, but a guarantee, or such other arrangement as may be agreed upon, may be substituted for the premium.

(3) The provisions of this Act, in so far as they may be modified by the agreement of the parties, may in the case of mutual insurance be modified by the terms of the policies issued by the association, or by the rules and regulations of the association.

(4) Subject to the exceptions mentioned in this section, the provisions of this Act apply to a mutual insurance.

SUPPLEMENTAL

86. Ratification by assured

Where a contract of marine insurance is in good faith effected by one person on behalf of another, the person on whose behalf it is effected may ratify the contract even after he is aware of a loss.

87. Implied obligations varied by agreement or usage

(1) Where any right, duty, or liability would arise under a contract of marine insurance by implication of law, it may be negatived or varied by express agreement, or by usage, if the usage be such as to bind both parties to the contract.

(2) The provisions of this section extend to any right, duty, or liability declared by this Act which may be lawfully modified by agreement.

88.   Reasonable time, &c a question of fact

Where by this Act any reference is made to reasonable time, reasonable premium, or reasonable diligence, the question what is reasonable is a question of fact.

89.   Slip as evidence

Where there is a duly stamped policy, reference may be made, as heretofore, to the slip or covering note, in any legal proceeding.

90.   Interpretation of terms

In this Act, unless the context or subject-matter otherwise requires—

'Action' includes counter-claim and set off.

'Freight' includes the profit derivable by a shipowner from the employment of his ship to carry his own goods or moveables, as well as freight payable by a third party, but does not include passage money.

'Moveables' means any moveable tangible property, other than the ship, and includes money, valuable securities, and other documents.

'Policy' means a marine policy.

91.–94.   [Omitted].

SCHEDULES
FIRST SCHEDULE
FORM OF POLICY

Be it known that   as well in

own name as for and in the name and names of all and every other person or persons to whom the same doth, may, or shall appertain, in part or in all doth make assurance and cause

and them, and every of them, to be insured lost or not lost, at and from

Upon any kind of goods and merchandises, and also upon the body, tackle, apparel, ordnance, munition, artillery, boat, and other furniture, of and in the good ship or vessel called the

whereof is master under God, for this present voyage,

or whosoever else shall go for master in the said ship, or by whatsoever other name or names the said ship, or the master thereof, is or shall be named or called; beginning the adventure upon the said goods and merchandised from the loading thereof aboard the said ship.

upon the said ship, &c

and so shall continue and endure, during her abode there, upon the said ship, &c. And further, until the said ship, with all her ordnance, tackle, apparel, &c., and goods and merchandises whatsoever shall be arrived at

upon the said ship, &c until she hath moored at anchor twenty-four hours in good safety; and upon the goods and merchandises, until the same be there discharged and safely landed. And it shall be lawful for the said ship, &c, in this voyage, to proceed and sail to and touch and stay at any ports or places whatsoever

without prejudice to this insurance. The said ship, &c, goods and merchandises, &c, for so much as concerns the assured by agreement between the assured and assurers in this policy, are and shall be valued at

Touching the adventures and perils which we the assurers are contented to bear and do take upon us in this voyage: they are of the seas, men of war, fire, enemies, pirates, rovers, thieves, jettisons, letters of mart and countermart, surprisals, takings at sea, arrests, restraints, and detainments of all kings, princes, and people, of what nation, condition, or quality soever, barratry of the master and mariners, and of all other perils, losses, and misfortunes, that have or shall come to the hurt, detriment, or damage of the said goods and merchandises, and ship, &c, or any part thereof. And in case of any loss or misfortune it shall be lawful to the assured, their factors, servants and assigns, to sue, labour, and travel for, in and about the defence, safeguards, and recovery of the said goods and merchandises, and ship, &c, or any part thereof, without prejudice to this insurance; to the charges whereof we, the assurers, will contribute each one according to the rate and quantity of his sum herein assured. And it is especially declared and agreed that no acts of the insurer or insured in recovering, saving, or preserving the property insured shall be considered as a waiver, or acceptance of abandonment. And it is agreed by us, the insurers, that this writing or policy of assurance shall be of as much force and effect as the surest writing or policy of assurance heretofore made in Lombard Street, or in the Royal Exchange, or elsewhere in London. And so we, the assurers, are contented, and do hereby promise and bind ourselves, each one for his own part, our heirs, executors, and goods to the assured, their executors, administrators, and assigns, for the true performance of the premises, confessing ourselves paid the consideration due unto us for this assurance by the assured, at and after the rate of

In Witness whereof we, the assurers, have subscribed our names and sums assured in London.

N.B. — Corn, fish, salt, fruit, flour, and seed are warranted free from average, unless general, or the ship be stranded-sugar, tobacco, hemp, flax, hides and skins are warranted free from average, under five pounds per cent., and all other goods, also the ship and freight, are warranted free from average, under three pounds per cent. unless general, or the ship be stranded.

RULES FOR CONSTRUCTION OF POLICY

The following are the rules referred to by this Act for the construction of a policy in the above or other like form, where the context does not otherwise require—

1. Where the subject-matter is insured 'lost or not lost', and the loss has occurred before the contract is concluded, the risk attaches unless, at such time the assured was aware of the loss, and the insurer was not.
2. Where the subject-matter is insured 'from' a particular place, the risk does not attach until the ship starts on the voyage insured.
3. —
    (a) Where a ship is insured 'at and from' a particular place, and she is at that place in good safety when the contract is concluded, the risk attaches immediately.
    (b) If she be not at that place when the contract is concluded, the risk attaches as soon as she arrives there in good safety, and, unless the policy otherwise provides, it is immaterial that she is covered by another policy for a specified time after arrival.
    (c) Where chartered freight is insured 'at and from' a particular place, and the ship is at that place in good safety when the contract is concluded the risk attaches immediately. If she be not there when the contract is concluded, the risk attaches as soon as she arrives there in good safety.
    (d) Where freight, other than chartered freight, is payable without special conditions and is insured 'at and from' a particular place, the risk attaches pro rata as the goods or merchandise are shipped; provided that if there be cargo in readiness which belongs to the shipowner, or which some other person has contracted with him to ship, the risk attaches as soon as the ship is ready to receive such cargo.

4.   Where goods or other moveables are insured 'from the loading thereof,' the risk does not attach until such goods or moveables are actually on board, and the insurer is not liable for them while in transit from the shore to the ship.

5.   Where the risk on goods or other moveables continues until they are 'safely landed,' they must be landed in the customary manner and within a reasonable time after arrival at the port of discharge, and if they are not so landed the risk ceases.

6.   In the absence of any further licence or usage, the liberty to touch and stay 'at any port or place whatsoever' does not authorise the ship to depart from the course of her voyage from the port of departure to the port of destination.

7.   The term 'perils of the seas' refers only to fortuitous accidents or casualties of the seas. It does not include the ordinary action of the winds and waves.

8.   The term 'pirates' includes passengers who mutiny and rioters who attack the ship from the shore.

9.   The term 'thieves' does not cover clandestine theft or a theft committed by any one of the ship's company, whether crew or passengers.

10.   The term 'arrests, &c, of kings, princes, and people' refers to a political or executive acts, and does not include a loss caused by riot or by ordinary judicial process.

11.   The term 'barratry' includes every wrongful act wilfully committed by the master or crew to the prejudice of the owner, or, as the case may be, the charterer.

12.   The term 'all other perils' includes only perils similar in kind to the perils specifically mentioned in the policy.

13.   The term 'average unless general' means a partial loss of subject-matter insured other than a general average loss, and does not include 'particular charges'.

14.   Where the ship has stranded, the insurer is liable for the excepted losses, although the loss is not attributable to the stranding, provided that when the stranding takes place the risk has attached and, if the policy be on goods, that the damaged goods are on board.

15.   The term 'ship' includes the hull, materials and outfit, stores and provisions for the officers and crew, and, in the case of vessels engaged in a special trade, the ordinary fittings requisite for the trade, and also, in the case of a steamship, the machinery, boilers, and coals and engine stores, if owned by the assured.

16.   The term 'freight' includes the profit derivable by a shipowner from the employment of his ship to carry his own goods or moveables, as well as freight payable by a third party, but does not include passage money.

17.   The term 'goods' means goods in the nature of merchandise, and does not include personal effects or provisions and stores for use on board.

In the absence of any usage to the contrary, deck cargo and living animals must be insured specifically, and not under the general denomination of goods.

[Note: by virtue of the Public Order Act 1986 the words 'rioters' in rule 8 and 'riot' in rule 10 shall be construed in accordance with section 1 of that Act.]

ADMINISTRATION OF JUSTICE ACT 1920

CHAPTER 81
PART II
RECIPROCAL ENFORCEMENT OF JUDGMENTS IN THE UNITED KINGDOM AND IN
OTHER PARTS OF HIS MAJESTY'S DOMINIONS

9. **Enforcement in the United Kingdom of judgements obtained in superior courts in other British dominions**

(1) Where a judgment has been obtained in a superior court in any part of His Majesty's dominions outside the United Kingdom to which this Part of this Act extends, the judgment creditor may apply to the High Court in England or Northern Ireland or to the Court of Session in Scotland, at any time within twelve months after the date of the judgment, or such longer period as may be allowed by the court, to have the judgment registered in the court, and on any such application the court may, if in all the circumstances of the case they think it just and convenient that the judgment should be enforced in the United Kingdom, and subject to the provisions of this section, order the judgment to be registered accordingly.

(2) No judgment shall be ordered to be registered under this section if—

(a) the original court acted without jurisdiction; or

(b) the judgment debtor, being a person who was neither carrying on business nor ordinarily resident within the jurisdiction of the original court, did not voluntarily appear or otherwise submit or agree to submit to the jurisdiction of that court; or

(c) the judgment debtor, being the defendant in the proceedings, was not duly served with the process of the original court and did not appear, notwithstanding that he was ordinarily resident or was carrying on business within the jurisdiction of that court or agreed to submit to the jurisdiction of that court; or

(d) the judgment was obtained by fraud; or

(e) the judgment debtor satisfies the registering court either that an appeal is pending, or that he is entitled and intends to appeal, against the judgment; or

(f) the judgment was in respect of a cause of action which for reasons of public policy or for some other similar reason could not have been entertained by the registering court.

(3) Where a judgment is registered under this section—

(a) the judgment shall, as from the date of registration, be of the same force and effect, and proceedings may be taken thereon, as if it had been a judgment originally obtained or entered up on the date of registration in the registering court;

(b) the registering court shall have the same control and jurisdiction over the judgment as it has over similar judgments given by itself, but in so far only as relates to execution under this section;

(c) the reasonable costs of and incidental to the registration of the judgment (including the costs of obtaining a certified copy thereof from the original court and of the application for registration) shall be recoverable in like manner as if they were sums payable under the judgment.

(4) and (5) [Omitted].

FOREIGN JUDGMENTS (RECIPROCAL ENFORCEMENT) ACT 1933

CHAPTER 13

PART I

Registration of foreign judgments

1. Power to extend Part I of Act to foreign countries giving reciprocaltreatment.
2. Application for, and effect of, registration of foreign judgment.
3. [Omitted].
4. Cases in which registered judgments must, or may, be set aside.
5. Powers of registering court on application to set aside registration.
6. Foreign judgments which can be registered not to be enforceableotherwise.
7. [Omitted].

PART II

Miscellaneous and general

8. General effect to certain foreign judgments
9.–14.[Omitted].

PART I

1. **Power to extend Part I of Act to foreign countries giving reciprocal treatment**
   (1) If, in the case of any foreign country, Her Majesty is satisfied that, in the event of the benefits conferred by this Part of this Act being extended to, or to any particular class of, judgments given in the courts of that country or in any particular class of those courts, substantial reciprocity of treatment will be assured as regards the enforcement in that country of similar judgments given in similar courts of the United Kingdom, She may order in Council direct—
      (a) that this Part of this Act shall extend to that country;
      (b) that such courts of that country as are specified in the Order shall be recognised courts of that country for the purposes of this Part of this Act; and
      (c) that judgments of any such recognised court, or such judgments of any class so specified, shall, if within subsection (2) of this section, be judgments to which this Part of this Act applies.
   (2) Subject to subsection (2A) of this section, a judgment of a recognised court is within this subsection if it satisfies the following conditions, namely—
      (a) it is either final and conclusive as between the judgment debtor and the judgment creditor or requires the former to make an interim payment to the latter; and
      (b) there is payable under it a sum of money, not being a sum payable in respect of taxes or other charges of a like nature or in respect of a fine or other penalty; and
      (c) it is given after the coming into force of the Order in Council which made that court a recognised court.
   (2A) The following judgments of a recognised court are not within subsection (2) of this section—
      (a) a judgment given by that court on appeal from a court which is not a recognised court;

(b) a judgment or other instrument which is regarded for the purposes of its enforcement as a judgment of that court but which was given or made in another country;

(c) a judgment given by that court in proceedings founded on a judgment of a court in another country and having as their object the enforcement of that judgment.

(3) For the purposes of this section, a judgment shall be deemed to be final and conclusive notwithstanding that an appeal may be pending against it, or that it may still be subject to appeal, in the courts of the country of the original court.

(4) and (5) [Omitted].

2. Application for, and effect of, registration of foreign judgement

(1) A person, being a judgment creditor under a judgment to which this Part of this Act applies, may apply to the High Court at any time within six years after the date of the judgment, or, where there have been proceedings by way of appeal against the judgment, after the date of the last judgment given in those proceedings, to have the judgment registered in the High Court, and on any such application the court shall, subject to proof of the prescribed matters and to the other provisions of this Act, order the judgment to be registered:

Provided that a judgment shall not be registered if at the date of the application—

(a) it has been wholly satisfied; or

(b) it could not be enforced by execution in the country of the original court.

(2) Subject to the provisions of this Act with respect to the setting aside of registration—

(a) a registered judgment shall, for the purposes of execution, be of the same force and effect; and

(b) proceedings may be taken on a registered judgment; and

(c) the sum for which a judgment is registered shall carry interest; and

(d) the registering court shall have the same control over the execution of a registered judgment;

as if the judgment had been a judgment originally given in the registering court and entered on the date of registration:

Provided that execution shall not issue on the judgment so long as, under this Part of this Act and the Rules of Court made thereunder, it is competent for any party to made an application to have the registration of the judgment set aside, or, where such an application is made, until after the application has been finally determined.

(3) [Repealed].

(4) If at the date of the application for registration the judgment of the original court has been partly satisfied, the judgment shall not be registered in respect of the whole sum payable under the judgment of the original court, but only in respect of the balance remaining payable at that date.

(5) If, on an application for the registration of a judgment, it appears to the registering court that the judgment is in respect of different matters and that some, but not all, of the provisions of the judgment are such that if those provisions had been contained in separate judgments those judgments could properly have been registered, the judgment may be registered in respect of the provisions aforesaid but not in respect of any other provisions contained therein.

(6) [Omitted].

3. [Omitted].

4.   Cases in which registered judgments must, or may, be set aside

(1)   On an application in that behalf duly made by any party against whom a registered judgment may be enforced, the registration of the judgment—

(a)   shall be set aside if the registering court is satisfied—

(i)   that the judgment is not a judgment to which this Part of the Act applied or was registered in contravention of the foregoing provisions of this Act; or

(ii)   that the courts of the country of the original court had no jurisdiction in the circumstances of the case; or

(iii)   that the judgment debtor, being the defendant in the proceedings in the original court, did not (notwithstanding that process may have been duly served on him in accordance with the law of the country of the original court) receive notice of those proceedings in sufficient time to enable him to defend the proceedings and did not appear; or

(iv)   that the judgment was obtained by fraud; or

(v)   that the enforcement of the judgment would be contrary to public policy in the country of the registering court; or

(vi)   that the rights under the judgment are not vested in the person by whom the application for registration was made;

(b)   may be set aside if the registering court is satisfied that the matter in dispute in the proceedings in the original court had previously to the date of the judgment in the original court been the subject of a final and conclusive judgment by a court having jurisdiction in the matter.

(2)   For the purposes of this section the courts of the country of the original court shall, subject to the provisions of subsection (3) of this section, be deemed to have had jurisdiction—

(a)   in the case of a judgment given in an action *in personam:*

(i)   if the judgment debtor, being a defendant in the original court, submitted to the jurisdiction of that court by voluntarily appearing in the proceedings; or

(ii)   if the judgment debtor was plaintiff in, or counter-claimed in, the proceedings in the original court; or

(iii)   if the judgment debtor, being a defendant in the original court, had before the commencement of the proceedings agreed, in respect of the subject matter of the proceedings, to submit to the jurisdiction of that court or of the courts of the country of that court; or

(iv)   if the judgment debtor, being a defendant in the original court, was at the time when the proceedings were instituted resident in, or being a body corporate had its principal place of business in, the country of that court; or

(v)   if the judgment debtor, being a defendant in the original court, had an office or place of business in the country of that court and the proceedings in that court were in respect of a transaction effected through or at that office or place;

(b)   in the case of a judgment given in an action of which the subject matter was immovable property or in an action *in rem* of which the subject matter was movable property, if the property in question was at the time of the proceedings in the original court situate in the country of that court;

(c)   in the case of a judgment given in an action other than any such action as is mentioned in paragraph (a) or paragraph (b) of this subsection, if the jurisdiction of the original court is recognised by the law of the registering court.

(3)   Notwithstanding anything in subsection (2) of this section, the courts of the country of the original court shall not be deemed to have had jurisdiction—

    (a)   if the subject matter of the proceedings was immovable property outside the country of the original court; or

    (b)   [repealed];

    (c)   if the judgment debtor, being a defendant in the original proceedings, was a person who under the rules of public international law was entitled to immunity from the jurisdiction of the courts of the country of the original court and did not submit to the jurisdiction of that court.

5.   Powers of registering court on application to set aside registration

(1)   If, on an application to set aside the registration of a judgment, the applicant satisfies the registering court either that an appeal is pending, or that he is entitled and intends to appeal, against the judgment, the court, if it thinks fit, may, on such terms as it may think just, either set aside the registration or adjourn the application to set aside the registration until after the expiration of such period as appears to the court to be reasonably sufficient to enable the applicant to take the necessary steps to have the appeal disposed of by the competent tribunal.

(2)   Where the registration of a judgment is set aside under the last foregoing subsection, or solely for the reason that the judgment was not at the date of the application for registration enforceable by execution in the country of the original court, the setting aside of the registration shall not prejudice a further application to register the judgment when the appeal has been disposed of or if and when the judgment becomes enforceable by execution in that country, as the case may be.

(3)   Where the registration of a judgment is set aside solely for the reason that the judgment, notwithstanding that it had at the date of application for registration been partly satisfied, was registered for the whole sum payable thereunder, the registering court shall, on the application of the judgment creditor, order judgment to be registered for the balance remaining payable at that date.

6.   Foreign judgments which can be registered not to be enforceable otherwise

No proceedings for the recovery of a sum payable under a foreign judgment, being a judgment to which the Part of this Act applies, other than proceedings by way of registration of the judgment, shall be entertained by any court in the United Kingdom.

7.   [Omitted].

PART II

Miscellaneous and general

8.   General effect of certain foreign judgments

(1)   Subject to the provisions of this section, a judgment to which Part I of this Act applies or would have applied if a sum of money had been payable thereunder, whether it can be registered or not, and whether, if it can be registered, it is registered or not, shall be recognised in any court in the United Kingdom as conclusive between the parties thereto in all proceedings founded on the same cause of action and may be relied on by way of defence or counter-claim in any such proceedings.

(2)   This section shall not apply in the case of any judgment—

    (a)   where the judgment has been registered and the registration thereof has been set aside on some ground other than:

(i)   that a sum of money was not payable under the judgment; or

(ii)   that the judgment had been wholly or partly satisfied; or

(iii)   that at the date of the application the judgment could not be enforced by execution in the country of the original court; or

(b) where the judgment has not been registered, it is shown (whether it could have been registered or not) that if it had been registered the registration thereof would have been set aside on an application for that purpose on some ground other than one of the grounds specified in paragraph (a) of this subsection.

(3)   Nothing in this section shall be taken to prevent any court in the United Kingdom recognising any judgment as conclusive of any matter of law or fact decided therein if that judgment would have been so recognised before the passing of this Act.

9.–14.   [Omitted].

LAW REFORM (FRUSTRATED CONTRACTS) ACT 1943

CHAPTER 40

1.   Adjustment of rights and liabilities of parties to frustrated contracts

(1)   Where a contract governed by English law has become impossible of performance or been otherwise frustrated, and the parties thereto have for that reason been discharged from the further performance of the contract, the following provisions of this section shall, subject to the provisions of section two of this Act, have effect in relation thereto.

(2)   All sums paid or payable to any party in pursuance of the contract before the time when the parties were so discharged (in this Act referred to as 'the time of discharge') shall, in the case of sums so paid, be recoverable from him as money received by him for the use of the party by whom the sums were paid, and, in the case of sums so payable, cease to be so payable:

Provided that, if the party to whom the sums were so paid or payable incurred expenses before the time of discharge in, or for the purpose of, the performance of the contract, the court may, if it considers it just to do so having regard to all the circumstances of the case, allow him to retain or, as the case may be, recover the whole or any part of the sums so paid or payable, not being an amount in excess of the expenses so incurred.

(3)   Where any party to the contract has, by reason of anything done by any other party thereto in, or for the purpose of, the performance of the contract, obtained a valuable benefit (other than a payment of money to which the last foregoing subsection applies) before the time of discharge, there shall be recoverable from him by the said other party such sum (if any), not exceeding the value of the said benefit to the party obtaining it, as the court considers just, having regard to all the circumstances of the case and, in particular—

(a) the amount of any expenses incurred before the time of discharge by the benefited party in, or for the purpose of, the performance of the contract, including any sums paid or payable by him to any other party in pursuance of the contract and retained or recoverable by that party under the last foregoing subsection; and

(b) the effect, in relation to the said benefit, of the circumstances giving rise to the frustration of the contract.

(4)   In estimating, for the purposes of the foregoing provisions of this section, the amount of any expenses incurred by any party to the contract, the court may,

without prejudice to the generality of the said provisions, include such sum as appears to be reasonable in respect of overhead expenses and in respect of any work or services performed personally by the said party.

(5) In considering whether any sum ought to be recovered or retained under the foregoing provisions of this section by any party to the contract, the court shall not take into account any sums which have, by reason of the circumstances giving rise to the frustration of the contract, become payable to that party under any contract of insurance unless there was an obligation to insure imposed by an express term of the frustrated contract or by or under any enactment.

(6) Where any person has assumed obligations under the contract in consideration of the conferring of a benefit by any other party to the contract upon any other person, whether a party to the contract or not, the court may, if in all the circumstances of the case it considers it just to do so, treat for the purposes of subsection (3) of this section any benefit so conferred as a benefit obtained by the person who has assumed the obligations as aforesaid.

2.   Provision as in application of this Act

(1) This Act shall apply to contracts, whether made before or after the commencement of this Act, as respects which the time of discharge is on or after the first day of July, nineteen hundred and forty-three, but not to contracts as respect which the time of discharge is before the said date.

(2) This Act shall apply to contracts to which the Crown is a party in like manner as to contracts between subject.

(3) Where any contract to which this Act applies contains any provisions which, upon the true construction of the contract, is intended to have effect in the event of circumstances arising which operate, or would but for the said provision operate, to frustrate the contract, or is intended to have effect whether such circumstances arise or not, the court shall give effect to the said provision and shall only give effect to the forgoing section of this Act to such extent, if any, as appears to the court to be consistent with the said provision.

(4) Where it appears to the court that a part of any contract to which this Act applies can properly be severed from the remainder of the contract, being a part wholly performed before the time of discharge, or so performed except for the payment in respect of that part of the contract of sums which are or can be ascertained under the contract, the court shall treat that part of the contract as if it were a separate contract and had not been frustrated and shall treat the foregoing section of this Act as only applicable to the remainder of that contract.

(5) This Act shall not apply—

(a) to any charterparty, except a time charterparty or a charterparty by way of demise, or to any contract (other than a charterparty) for the carriage of goods by sea; or

(b) to any contract of insurance, save as is provided by subsection (5) of the foregoing section; or

(c) to any contract to which section seven of the Sale of Goods Act 1979 (which avoids contracts for the sale of specific goods which perish before the risk has passed to the buyer) applies, or to any other contract for the sale, or for the sale and delivery, of specific goods, where the contract is frustrated by reason of the fact that the goods have perished.

3.   [Omitted].

ARBITRATION ACT 1950

CHAPTER 27
PART II
ENFORCEMENT OF CERTAIN FOREIGN AWARDS

PART II
ENFORCEMENT OF CERTAIN FOREIGN AWARDS

35.   Awards to which Part II applies
   (1)   This Part of this Act applies to any award made after the twenty-eighth day of
          July, nineteen hundred and twenty-four—
          (a)   in pursuance of an agreement for arbitration to which the protocol set
                out in the First Schedule to this Act applies; and
          (b)   between persons of whom one is subject to the jurisdiction of some one
                of such Powers as His Majesty, being satisfied that reciprocal provisions
                have been made, may by Order in Council declare to be parties to the
                convention set out in the Second Schedule to this Act, and of whom the
                other is subject to the jurisdiction of some other of the Powers aforesaid;
                and
          (c)   in one such territories as His Majesty, being satisfied that reciprocal
                provisions have been made; may by Order in Council declare to be
                territories to which the said convention applies;
          and an award to which this Part of this Act applies is in this Part of this Act
          referred to as 'a foreign award'.
   (2) and (3) [Omitted].

36.   Effect of foreign awards
   (1)   A foreign award shall, subject to the provisions of this Part of this Act, be
          enforceable in England either by action or in the same manner as the award
          of an arbitrator is enforceable by virtue of section sixty-six of the Arbitration
          Act 1996.
   (2)   Any foreign award which would be enforceable under this Part of this Act
          shall be treated as binding for all purposes on the persons as between whom
          it was made, and may accordingly be relied on by any of those persons by way
          of defence, set off or otherwise in any legal proceedings in England, and any
          references in this Part of this Act to enforcing a foreign award shall be
          construed as including references to relying on an award.

37.   Conditions for enforcement of foreign awards
   (1)   In order that a foreign award may be enforceable under this Part of this Act it
          must have—

(a) been made in pursuance of an agreement for arbitration which was valid under the law by which it was governed;

(b) been made by the tribunal provided for in the agreement or constituted in manner agreed upon by the parties;

(c) been made in conformity with the law governing the arbitration procedure;

(d) become final in the country in which it was made;

(e) been in respect of a matter which may lawfully be referred to arbitration under the law of England;

and the enforcement thereof must not be contrary to the public policy or the law of England.

(2) Subject to the provisions of this subsection, a foreign award shall not be enforceable under this Part of this Act if the court dealing with the case is satisfied that—

(a) the award has been annulled in the country in which it was made; or

(b) the party against whom it is sought to enforce the award was not given notice of the arbitration proceedings in sufficient time to enable him to present his case or was under some legal incapacity and was not properly represented; or

(c) the award does not deal with all the questions referred or contains decisions on matters beyond the scope of the agreement for arbitration.

Provided that, if the award does not deal with all the questions referred, the court may, if it thinks fit, either postpone the enforcement of the award or order its enforcement subject to the giving of such security by the person seeking to enforce it as the court may think fit.

(3) If a party seeking to resist the enforcement of a foreign award proves that there is any ground other than the non-existence of the conditions specified in paragraphs (a), (b) and (c) of subsection (1) of this section, or the existence of the conditions specified in paragraphs (b) and (c) of subsection (2) of this section, entitling him to contest the validity of the award, the court may, if it thinks fit, either refuse to enforce the award or adjourn the hearing until after the expiration of such period as appears to the court to be reasonably sufficient to enable that party to take the necessary steps to have the award annulled by the competent tribunal.

38. **[Omitted].**

39. **Meaning of 'final award'**
For the purposes of this Part of this Act, an award shall not be deemed final if any proceedings for the purpose of contesting the validity of the award are pending in the country in which it was made.

40.–42. **[Omitted].**

FIRST SCHEDULE
PROTOCOL ON ARBITRATION CLAUSES SIGNED ON BEHALF OF HIS MAJESTY AT A MEETING OF THE ASSEMBLY OF THE LEAGUE OF NATIONS HELD ON THE TWENTY-FOURTH DAY OF SEPTEMBER, NINETEEN HUNDRED AND TWENTY-THREE

The undersigned, being duly authorised, declare that they accept, on behalf of the countries which they represent, the following provisions:—

1. Each of the Contracting States recognises the validity of an agreement whether relating to existing or future differences between parties, subject respectively to the jurisdiction of different Contracting States by which the parties to a contract agree to submit to arbitration all or any differences that may arise in connection

with such contract relating to commercial matters or to any other matter capable of settlement by arbitration, whether or not the arbitration is to take place in a country to whose jurisdiction none of the parties is subject.

Each Contracting State reserves the right to limit the obligation mentioned above to contracts which are considered as commercial under its national law. Any Contracting State which avails itself of this right will notify the secretary-general of the League of Nations, in order that the other Contracting States may be so informed.

2.   The arbitral procedure, including the constitution of the arbitral tribunal, shall be governed by the will of the parties and by the law of the country in whose territory the arbitration takes place.

The Contracting States agree to facilitate all steps in the procedure which require to be taken in their own territories, in accordance with the provisions of their law governing arbitral procedure applicable to existing differences.

3.   Each Contracting State undertakes to ensure the execution by its authorities and in accordance with the provisions of its national laws of arbitral awards made in its own territory under the preceding Articles.

4.   The tribunals of the Contracting Parties, on being seized of a dispute regarding a contract made between persons to whom Article 1 applies and including an arbitration agreement whether referring to present or future differences which is valid in virtue of the said Article and capable of being carried into effect, shall refer the parties on the application of either of them to the decision of the arbitrators.

Such reference shall not prejudice the competence of the judicial tribunals in case the agreement or the arbitration cannot proceed or become inoperative.

Articles 5.–8. [Omitted].

SECOND SCHEDULE
CONVENTION ON THE EXECUTION OF FOREIGN ARBITRAL AWARDS SIGNED AT GENEVA ON BEHALF OF HIS MAJESTY OF THE TWENTY-SIXTH DAY OF SEPTEMBER, NINETEEN HUNDRED AND TWENTY-SEVEN

Article 1

In the territories of any High Contracting Party to which the present Convention applies, an arbitral award made in pursuance of an agreement, whether relating to existing or future differences (hereinafter called 'a submission to arbitration') covered by the Protocol on Arbitration Clauses, opened at Geneva on September 24, 1923, shall be recognised as binding and shall be enforced in accordance with the rules of the procedure of the territory where the award is relied upon, provided that the said award has been made in a territory of one of the High Contracting Parties to which the present Convention applies and between persons who are subject to the jurisdiction of one of the High Contracting Parties.

To obtain such recognition or enforcement, it shall, further, be necessary—

(a)   that the award has been made in pursuance of a submission to arbitration which is valid under the law applicable thereto;

(b)   that the subject-matter of the award is capable of settlement by arbitration under the law of the country in which the award is sought to be relied upon;

(c)   that the award has been made by the Arbitral Tribunal provided for in the submission to arbitration or constituted in the manner agreed upon by the parties and in conformity with the law governing the arbitration procedure;

(d)   that the award has become final in the country in which it has been made, in the sense that it will not be considered as such if it is open to opposition, *appel* or *pourvoi en cassation* (in the countries where such forms of procedure exist) or if it

is proved that any proceedings for the purpose of contesting the validity of the award are pending;
(e)   that the recognition or enforcement of the award is not contrary to the public policy or to the principles of the law of the country in which it is sought to be relied upon.

Article 2

Even if the conditions laid down in Article 1 hereof are fulfilled, recognition and enforcement of the award shall be refused if the Court is satisfied—
(a)   that the award has been annulled in the country in which it was made;
(b)   that the party against whom it is sought to use the award was not given notice of the arbitration proceedings in sufficient time to enable him to present his case; or that, being under a legal incapacity, he was not properly represented;
(c)   that the award does not deal with the differences contemplated by or falling within the terms of the submission to arbitration or that it contains decisions on matters beyond the scope of the submission to arbitration.
If the award has not covered all the questions submitted to the arbitral tribunal, the competent authority of the country where recognition or enforcement of the award is sought can, if it think fit, postpone such recognition or enforcement or grant it subject to such guarantee as that authority may decide.

Article 3

If the party against whom the award has been made proves that, under the law governing the arbitration procedure, there is a ground, other than the grounds referred to in Article 1 (a) and (c), and Article 2 (b) and (c), entitling him to contest the validity of the award in a Court of Law, the Court may, if it thinks fit, either refuse recognition or enforcement of the award or adjourn the consideration thereof, giving such party a reasonable time within which to have the award annulled by the competent tribunal.

Article 4

The party relying upon an award or claiming its enforcement must supply in particular—
(1)   The original award or a copy thereof duly authenticated, according to the requirements of the law of the country in which it was made.
(2)   Documentary or other evidence to prove that the award has become final, in the sense defined in Article 1 (d), in the country in which it was made.
(3)   When necessary, documentary or other evidence to prove that the conditions laid down in Article 1, paragraph 1 and paragraph 2 (a) and (c), have been fulfilled.
A translation of the award and of the other documents mentioned in this Article into the official language of the country where the award is sought to be relied upon may be demanded. Such translation must be certified correct by a diplomatic or consular agent of the country to which the party who seeks to rely upon the award belongs or by a sworn translator of the country where the award is sought to be relied upon.

Article 5

The provisions of the above Articles shall not deprive any interested party of the right of availing himself of an arbitral award in the manner and to the extent allowed by the law or the treaties of the country where such award is sought to be relied upon.

Articles 6.–11. [Omitted].

CHEQUES ACT 1957

CHAPTER 36

1. **Protection of bankers paying unindorsed or irregularly indorsed cheques, &c**
   (1) Where a banker in good faith and in the ordinary course of business pays a cheque drawn on him which is not indorsed or is irregularly indorsed, he does not, in doing so, incur any liability by reason only of the absence of, or irregularity in, indorsement, and he is deemed to have paid it in due course.
   (2) Where a banker in good faith and in the ordinary course of business pays any such instrument as the following, namely—
       (a) a document issued by a customer of his which, though not a bill of exchange, is intended to enable a person to obtain payment from him of the sum mentioned in the document;
       (b) a draft payable on demand drawn by him upon himself, whether payable at the head office or some other office of his bank;
       he does not, in doing so, incur any liability by reason only of the absence of, or irregularity in, indorsement, and the payment discharges the instrument.

2. **Rights of bankers collecting cheques not indorsed by holders**
   A banker who gives value for, or has a lien on, a cheque payable to order which the holder delivers to him for collection without indorsing it, has such (if any) rights as he would have had if, upon delivery the holder had indorsed it in blank.

3. **Unindorsed cheques as evidence of payment**
   (1) An unindorsed cheque which appears to have been paid by the banker on whom it is drawn is evidence of the receipt by the payee of the sum payable by the cheque.
   (2) For the purposes of subsection (1) above, a copy of a cheque to which that subsection applies is evidence of the cheque if—
       (a) the copy is made by the banker in whose possession the cheque is after presentment; and
       (b) it is certified by him to be a true copy of the original.

4. **Protection of bankers collecting payment of cheques, &c**
   (1) Where a banker, in good faith and without negligence—
       (a) receives payment for a customer of an instrument to which this section applies; or
       (b) having credited a customer's account with the amount of such an instrument, receives payment thereof for himself,
       and the customer has no title, or a defective title, to the instrument, the banker does not incur any liability to the true owner of the instrument by reason only of having received payment thereof.
   (2) This section applies to the following instruments, namely—
       (a) cheques (including cheques which under section 81A(1) of the Bills of Exchange Act 1882 or otherwise are not transferable);
       (b) any document issued by a customer of a banker which, though not a bill of exchange, is intended to enable a person to obtain payment from that banker of the sum mentioned in the document;
       (c) any document issued by a public officer which is intended to enable a person to obtain payment from the Paymaster General or the Queen's and Lord Treasurer's Remembrancer of the sum mentioned in the document but is not a bill of exchange;

      (d) any draft payable on demand drawn by a banker upon himself, whether payable at the head office or some other office of his bank.

  (3)   A banker is not to be treated for the purposes of this section as having been negligent by reason only of his failure to concern himself with absence of, or irregularity in, indorsement of an instrument.

5.   Application of certain provisions of Bills of Exchange Act, 1882, to instruments not being bills of exchange

The provisions of the Bills of Exchange Act 1882 relating to crossed cheques shall, so far as applicable, have effect in relation to instruments (other than cheques) to which the last foregoing section applies as they have effect in relation to cheques.

6.   Construction, saving and repeal

  (1)   This Act shall be construed as one with the Bills of Exchange Act 1882.

  (2)   The foregoing provisions of this Act do not make negotiable any instrument which, apart from them, is not negotiable.

CARRIAGE BY AIR ACT 1961

CHAPTER 27

1.   Convention to have force of law

  (1)   The applicable provisions of the Carriage by Air Conventions have the force of law in the United Kingdom in relation to any carriage by air to which they apply, irrespective of the nationality of the aircraft performing that carriage.

  (2)   Subsection (1) does not apply in relation to Community air carriers to the extent that the provisions of the Council Regulation have the force of law in the United Kingdom.

  (3)   Subsection (1) is subject to the other provisions of this Act.

  (4)   If more than one of the Carriage by Air Conventions applies to a carriage by air, the applicable provisions that have the force of law in the United Kingdom are those of whichever is the most recent applicable Convention in force.

  (5)   The Carriage by Air Conventions are—

      (a) the Convention known as 'the Warsaw Convention as amended at The Hague, 1955' ('the Convention');

      (b) that Convention as further amended by Protocol No. 4 of Montreal, 1975 ('the Convention as amended'); and

      (c) the Convention known as 'the Montreal Convention 1999' ('the Montreal Convention').

  (6)   'The applicable provisions' means—

      (a) the provisions of the Convention set out in Schedule 1;

      (b) the provisions of the Convention as amended set out in Schedule 1A; and

      (c) the provisions of the Montreal Convention set out in Schedule 1B,

    so far as they relate to the rights and liabilities of carriers, carriers' servants and agents, passengers, consignors, consignees and other persons.

  (7)   In this Act a reference to an Article of, or Protocol to, any of the Carriage by Air Conventions is a reference to that Article or Protocol as it appears in the Schedule in which it is set out.

  (8)   If there is any inconsistency between the text in English in Part I of Schedule 1 or 1A and the text in French in Part II of that Schedule, the French text shall prevail.

2. and 3.   [Omitted].

4.   Limitation of liability

(1)   It is hereby declared that the limitations on liability in the applicable provisions mentioned in subsection (1A) apply whatever the nature of the proceedings by which liability may be enforced.

(1A)   The provisions are—

(a)   Article 22 of the Convention;

(b)   Article 22 of the Convention as amended; and

(c)   Articles 21 and 22 of the Montreal Convention.

(1B)   The limitation for each passenger in—

(a)   paragraph (1) of Article 22 of the Convention or of the Convention as amended; and

(b)   Article 21 and paragraph (1) of Article 22 of the Montreal Convention, applies to the aggregate liability of the carrier in all proceedings which may be brought against him under the law of any part of the United Kingdom, together with any proceedings brought against him outside the United Kingdom.

(2)   A court before which proceedings are brought to enforce a liability which is limited by a provision mentioned in subsection 3A may at any stage of the proceedings make any such order as appears to the court to be just and equitable in view of that provision, and of any other proceedings which have been, or are likely to be, commenced in the United Kingdom or elsewhere to enforce the liability in whole or in part.

(3)   Without prejudice to the last foregoing subsection, a court before which proceedings are brought to enforce a liability which is limited by a provision mentioned in subsection 3A shall, where the liability is, or may be, partly enforceable in other proceedings in the United Kingdom or elsewhere, have jurisdiction to award an amount less than the court would have awarded if the limitation applied solely to the proceedings before the court, or to make any part of its award conditional on the result of any other proceedings.

(3A)   The provisions are—

(a)   Article 22 of the Convention;

(b)   Article 22 of the Convention as amended; and

(c)   Articles 21, 22 and 44 of the Montreal Convention.

(4) and (5) [Omitted].

4A.   Notice of partial loss

(1)   References to damage in the provisions mentioned in subsection (2) shall be construed as including loss of part of the baggage or cargo in question and the reference to the receipt of baggage or cargo shall, in relation to loss of part of it, be construed as receipt of the remainder of it.

(2)   The provisions are—

(a)   Article 26(2) of the Convention;

(b)   Article 26(2) of the Convention as amended; and

(c)   Article 31(2) of the Montreal Convention.

5.   Time for bringing proceedings

(1)   No action against a carrier's servant or agent which arises out of damage to which any of the Carriage by Air Conventions applies relates shall, if he was acting within the scope of his employment, be brought after more than two years, reckoned from the date of arrival at the destination or from the date on which the aircraft ought to have arrived, or from the date on which the carriage stopped.

(2)   The provisions mentioned in subsection (4) shall not be read as applying to any proceedings for contribution between persons liable for any damage to which any of the Carriage by Air Conventions relates, but no action shall be brought by a tortfeasor to obtain a contribution from a carrier in respect of a

tort to which the said Article 29 applies after the expiration of two years from the time when judgment is obtained against the person seeking to obtain the contribution.

(3) Subsections (1) and (2) and the provisions mentioned in subsection (4) shall have effect as if references in those provisions to an action included references to arbitral proceedings; and the provisions of section 14 of the Arbitration Act 1996 apply to determine when such proceedings are commenced.

(4) The provisions are—
  (a) Article 29 of the Convention;
  (b) Article 29 of the Convention as amended; and
  (c) Article 35 of the Montreal Convention.

(5) If the Montreal Convention applies, 'carrier' in this section includes an actual carrier as defined by Article 39 of that Convention.

6. Contributory negligence

(1) It is hereby declared that for the purposes of the provisions mentioned in subsection (2) the Law Reform (Contributory Negligence) Act 1945 (including that Act as applied to Scotland), and section two of the Law Reform (Miscellaneous Provisions) Act (Northern Ireland) 1948, are provisions of the law of the United Kingdom under which a court may exonerate the carrier wholly or partly from his liability.

(2) The provisions are—
  (a) Article 21 of the Convention;
  (b) Article 21 of the Convention as amended; and
  (c) Article 20 of the Montreal Convention.

7.–14. [Omitted].

SCHEDULE 1 [OMITTED]

SCHEDULE 1A
THE WARSAW CONVENTION WITH THE AMENDMENT MADE TO IT BY THE HAGUE PROTOCOL AND PROTOCOL NO. 4 SIGNED AT MONTREAL, 1975

PART I
THE ENGLISH TEXT

CONVENTION FOR THE UNIFICATION OF CERTAIN RULES RELATING TO INTERNATIONAL CARRIAGE BY AIR

CHAPTER I
SCOPE-DEFINITIONS

Article 1

(1) This Convention applies to all international carriage of persons, baggage or cargo performed by aircraft for reward. It applies equally to gratuitous carriage by aircraft performed by an air transport undertaking.

(2) For the purposes of this Convention, the expression international carriage means any carriage in which, according to the agreement between the parties, the place of departure and the place of destination, whether or not there be a break in the carriage or a trans-shipment, are situated either within the territories of two High Contracting Parties or within the territory of a single High Contracting Party if there

is an agreed stopping place within the territory of another State, even if that State is not a High Contracting Party. Carriage between two points within the territory of a single High Contracting Party without an agreed stopping place within the territory of another State is not international carriage for the purposes of this Convention.

(3)   Carriage to be performed by several successive air carriers is deemed, for the purposes of this Convention, to be one undivided carriage if it has been regarded by the parties as a single operation, whether it had been agreed upon under the form of a single contract or a series of contracts, and it does not lose its international character merely because one contract or a series of contracts is to be performed entirely within the territory of the same State.

Article 2

(1)   This Convention applies to carriage performed by the State or by legally constituted public bodies provided it falls within the conditions laid down in Article 1.

(2)   In the carriage of postal items the carrier shall be liable only to the relevant postal administration in accordance with the rules applicable to the relationship between the carriers and the postal administrations.

(3)   Except as provided in paragraph (2) of this Article, the provisions of this Convention shall not apply to the carriage of postal items.

CHAPTER II
DOCUMENTS OF CARRIAGE

SECTION 1—PASSENGER TICKET

Article 3

(1)   In respect of the carriage of passengers an individual or collective document of carriage shall be delivered containing—
    (a)   an indication of the places of departure and destination;
    (b)   if the places of departure and destination are within the territory of a single High Contracting Party, one or more agreed stopping places being within the territory of another State, an indication of at least one such stopping place;
    (c)   a notice to the effect that, if the passenger's journey involves an ultimate destination or stop in a country other than the country of departure, the Warsaw Convention may be applicable and that the Convention governs and in most cases limits the liability of carriers for death or personal injury and in respect of loss of or damage to baggage.

(2)   The passenger ticket shall constitute *prima facie* evidence of the conclusion and conditions of the contract of carriage. The absence, irregularity or loss of the passenger ticket does not affect the existence or the validity of the contract of carriage which shall, none the less, be subject to the rules of this Convention. Nevertheless, if, with the consent of the carrier, the passenger embarks without a passenger ticket having been delivered, or if the ticket does not include the notice required by paragraph (1)(c) of this Article, the carrier shall not be entitled to avail himself of the provisions of Article 22.

SECTION 2—BAGGAGE CHECK

Article 4

(1)   In respect of the carriage of checked baggage, a baggage check shall be delivered, which, unless combined with or incorporated in a document of carriage which complies with the provisions of Article 3, paragraph (1), shall contain—

(a) an indication of the places of departure and destination;

(b) if the places of departure and destination are within the territory of a single High Contracting Party, one or more agreed stopping places being within the territory of another State, an indication of at least one such stopping place;

(c) a notice to the effect that, if the carriage involves an ultimate destination or stop in a country other than the country of departure, the Warsaw Convention may be applicable and that the Convention governs and in most cases limits the liability of carriers in respect of loss or damage to baggage.

(2) The passenger ticket shall constitute *prima facie* evidence of the registration of the baggage and of the conditions of the contract of carriage. The absence, irregularity or loss of the baggage check does not affect the existence or the validity of the contract of carriage which shall, none the less, be subject to the rules of this Convention. Nevertheless, if the carrier takes charge of the baggage without a baggage check (unless combined with or incorporated in the passenger ticket which complies with the provisions of Article 3, paragraph (1)(c)) does not include the notice required by paragraph (1)(c) of this Article, he shall not be entitled to avail himself of the provisions of Article 22, paragraph (2).

SECTION 3—DOCUMENTATION RELATING TO CARGO

Article 5

(1) In respect of the carriage of cargo an air waybill shall be delivered.

(2) Any other means which would preserve a record of the carriage to be performed may, with the consent of the consignor, be substituted for the delivery of an air waybill. If such other means are used, the carrier shall, if so requested by the consignor, deliver to the consignor a receipt for the cargo permitting identification of the consignment and access to the information contained in the record preserved by such other means.

(3) The impossibility of using, at points of transit and destination, the other means which would preserve the record of the carriage referred to in paragraph (2) of this Article does not entitle the carrier to refuse to accept the cargo for carriage.

Article 6

(1) The air waybill shall be made out by the consignor in three original parts.

(2) The first part shall be marked 'for the carrier'; it shall be signed by the consignor. The second part shall be marked 'for the consignee'; it shall be signed by the consignor and by the carrier. The third part shall be signed by the carrier and handed by him to the consignor after the cargo has been accepted.

(3) The signature of the carrier and that of the consignor may be printed or stamped.

(4) If, at the request of the consignor, the carrier makes out the air waybill, he shall be deemed, subject to proof to the contrary, to have done so on behalf of the consignor.

Article 7

When there is more than one package—

(a) the carrier of cargo has the right to require the consignor to make out separate air waybills;

(b) the consignor has the right to require the carrier to deliver separate receipts when the other means referred to in paragraph (2) of Article 5 are used.

Article 8

The air waybill and the receipt for the cargo shall contain—
(a)   an indication of the places of departure and destination;
(b)   if the places of departure and destination are within the territory of a single High Contracting Party, one or more agreed stopping places being within the territory of another State, an indication of at least one such stopping place; and
(c)   an indication of the weight of the consignment.

Article 9

Non-compliance with the provisions of Articles 5 to 8 shall not affect the existence or the validity of the contract of carriage, which shall, none the less, be subject to the rules of this Convention including those relating to limitation of liability.

Article 10

(1)   The consignor is responsible for the correctness of the particulars and statements relating to the cargo inserted by him or on his behalf in the air waybill or furnished by him or on his behalf to the carrier for insertion in the receipt for the cargo or for insertion in the record preserved by the other means referred to in paragraph (2) of Article 5.
(2)   The consignor shall indemnify the carrier against all damage suffered by him, or by any other person to whom the carrier is liable, by reason of the irregularity, incorrectness or incompleteness of the particulars and statements furnished by the consignor or on his behalf.
(3)   Subject to the provisions of paragraphs (1) and (2) of this Article, the carrier shall indemnify the consignor against all damage suffered by him, or by any other person to whom the consignor is liable, by reason of the irregularity, incorrectness or incompleteness of the particulars and statements inserted by the carrier or on his behalf in the receipt for the cargo or in the record preserved by the other means referred to in paragraph (2) of Article 5.

Article 11

(1)   The air waybill or the receipt for the cargo is *prima facie* evidence of the conclusion of the contract, of the acceptance of the cargo and of the conditions of carriage mentioned therein.
(2)   Any statements in the air waybill or the receipt for the cargo relating to the weight, dimensions and packing of the cargo, as well as those relating to the number of packages, are *prima facie* evidence of the facts stated; those relating to the quantity, volume and condition of the cargo do not constitute evidence against the carrier except so far as they both have been, and are stated in the air waybill to have been, checked by him in the presence of the consignor, or relate to the apparent condition of the cargo.

Article 12

(1)   Subject to his liability to carry out all his obligations under the contract of carriage, the consignor has the right to dispose of the cargo by withdrawing it at the airport of departure or destination, or by stopping it in the course of the journey on any landing, or by calling for it to be delivered at the place of destination or in the course of the journey to a person other than the consignee originally designated, or by requiring it to be returned to the airport of departure. He must not exercise this right of disposition in such a way as to prejudice the carrier or other consignors and he must repay any expenses occasioned by the exercise of this right.

(2)   If it is impossible to carry out the orders of the consignor the carrier must so inform him forthwith.

(3)   If the carrier obeys the orders of the consignor for the disposition of the cargo without requiring the production of the part of the air waybill or the receipt for the cargo delivered to the latter, he will be liable, without prejudice to his right of recovery from the consignor, for any damage which may be caused thereby to any person who is lawfully in possession of that part of the air waybill or the receipt for the cargo.

(4)   The right conferred on the consignor ceases at the moment when that of the consignee begins in accordance with Article 13. Nevertheless, if the consignee declines to accept the cargo, or if he cannot be communicated with, the consignor resumes his right of disposition.

Article 13

(1)   Except when the consignor has exercised his right under Article 12, the consignee is entitled, on arrival of the cargo at the place of destination, to require the carrier to deliver the cargo to him, on payment of the charges due and on complying with the conditions of carriage.

(2)   Unless it is otherwise agreed, it is the duty of the carrier to give notice to the consignee as soon as the cargo arrives.

(3)   If the carrier admits the loss of the cargo, or if the cargo has not arrived at the expiration of seven days after the date on which it ought to have arrived, the consignee is entitled to enforce against the carrier the rights which flow from the contract of carriage.

Article 14

The consignor and the consignee can respectively enforce all the rights given them by Articles 12 and 13, each in his own name, whether he is acting in his own interest or in the interest of another, provided that he carries out the obligations imposed by the contract of carriage.

Article 15

(1)   Articles 12, 13, and 14 do not affect either the relations of the consignor and the consignee with each other or the mutual relations of third parties whose rights are derived either from the consignor or from the consignee.

(2)   The provisions of Articles 12, 13 and 14 can only be varied by express provision in the air waybill or the receipt for the cargo.

Article 16

(1)   The consignor must furnish such information and such documents as are necessary to meet the formalities of customs, octroi or police before the cargo can be delivered to the consignee. The consignor is liable to the carrier for any damage occasioned by the absence, insufficiency or irregularity of any such information or documents, unless the damage is due to the fault of the carrier, his servants or agents.

(2)   The carrier is under no obligation to enquire into the correctness or sufficiency of such information or documents.

CHAPTER III
LIABILITY OF THE CARRIER

Article 17

The carrier is liable for damage sustained in event of the death or personal wounding of a passenger or any other bodily injury suffered by a passenger, if the accident which caused the damage so sustained took place on board the aircraft or in the course of any of the operations of embarking or disembarking.

Article 18

(1)   The carrier is liable for damage sustained in the event of the destruction or loss of, or damage to, any registered baggage, if the occurrence which caused the damage so sustained took place during the carriage by air.

(2)   The carrier is liable for damage sustained in the event of the destruction or loss of, or damage to, cargo upon condition only that the occurrence which caused the damage so sustained took place during the carriage by air.

(3)   However, the carrier is not liable if he proves that the destruction, loss of, or damage to, the cargo resulted solely from one or more of the following—

    (a)   inherent defect, quality or vice of that cargo;

    (b)   defective packing of that cargo performed by a person other than the carrier or his servants or agents;

    (c)   an act of war or an armed conflict;

    (d)   an act of public authority carried out in connection with the entry, exit or transit of the cargo.

(4)   The carriage by air within the meaning of the preceding paragraphs of this Article comprises the period during which the cargo is in the charge of the carrier, whether in an airport or on board an aircraft, or, in the case of a landing outside an airport, in any place whatsoever.

(5)   The period of the carriage by air does not extend to any carriage by land, by sea or by river performed outside an airport. If, however, such carriage takes place in performance of a contract for carriage by air, for the purpose of loading, delivery or transhipment, any damage is presumed, subject to proof to the contrary, to have been the result of an event which took place during the carriage by air.

Article 19

The carrier is liable for damage occasioned by delay in the carriage by air of passengers, baggage or cargo.

Article 20

In the case of passengers and baggage, and in the case of damage occasioned by delay in the carriage of cargo, the carrier shall not be liable if he proves that he and his servants and agents have taken all necessary measures to avoid the damage or that it was impossible for them to take such measures.

Article 21

(1)   In the carriage of passengers and baggage, if the carrier proves that the damage was caused by or contributed to by the negligence of the person suffering the damage, the Court may, in accordance with the provisions of its own law, exonerate the carrier wholly or partly from his liability.

(2)   In the carriage of cargo, if the carrier proves that the damage was caused by or contributed to by the negligence or other wrongful act or omission of the person claiming compensation, or the person from whom he derives his rights, the carrier shall be wholly or partly exonerated from his liability to the claimant to the extent that such negligence or wrongful act or omission caused or contributed to the damage.

Article 22

(1)   In the carriage of persons the liability of the carrier for each passenger is limited to the sum of 16,600 Special Drawing Rights. Where, in accordance with the law of the court seised of the case, damages may be awarded in the form of periodical payments, the equivalent capital value of the said payments shall not exceed this limit. Nevertheless, by special contract, the carrier and the passenger may agree to a higher limit of liability.

(2)   —

     (a)   in the carriage of registered baggage, the liability of the carrier is limited to a sum of 17 special drawing rights per kilogramme, unless the consignor has made, at the time when the package was handed over to the carrier, a special declaration of interest in delivery at destination and has paid a supplementary sum if the case so requires. In that case the carrier will be liable to pay a sum not exceeding the declared sum, unless he proves that that sum is greater than the consignor's actual interest in delivery at destination;

     (b)   in the carriage of cargo, the liability of the carrier is limited to a sum of 17 Special Drawing Rights per kilogramme, unless the consignor has made, at the same time when the package was handed over to the carrier, a special declaration of interest in delivery at destination and has paid a supplementary sum if the case so requires. In that case the carrier will be liable to pay a sum not exceeding the declared sum, unless he proves that that sum is greater than the consignor's actual interest in delivery at destination;

     (c)   in the case of loss, damage or delay of part of registered baggage or cargo, or of any object contained therein, the weight to be taken into consideration in determining the amount to which the carrier's liability is limited shall be only the total weight of the package or packages concerned. Nevertheless, when the loss, damage or delay of a part of the registered baggage or cargo, or of an object contained therein, affects the value of other packages covered by the same baggage check or the same air waybill, the total weight of such package or packages shall also be taken into consideration in determining the limit of liability.

(3)   As regards objects of which the passenger takes charge himself the liability of the carrier is limited to 332 Special Drawing Rights per passenger.

(4)   The limits prescribed in this Article shall not prevent the court in an action relating to the carriage of cargo from awarding in accordance with its own law, in addition, the whole or part of the court costs and of the other expenses of the litigation incurred by the plaintiff. The foregoing provision shall not apply if the amount of the damages awarded, excluding court costs and other expenses of the litigation, does not exceed the sum which the carrier has offered in writing to the plaintiff within a period of six months from the date of the occurrence causing the damage, or before the commencement of the action, if that is later.

(5)   The sums mentioned in terms of special drawing right in this Article shall be deemed to refer to the special drawing right as defined by the International Monetary Fund. Conversion of the sums into national currencies shall, in case of judicial proceedings, be made according to the value of such currencies in terms of the special drawing right at the date of the judgment.

(6)   The value of a national currency, in terms of the Special Drawing Right, of a High
       Contracting Party which is a Member of the International Monetary Fund, shall be
       calculated in accordance with the method of valuation applied by the International
       Monetary Fund, in effect at the date of the judgment for its operations and
       transactions. The value of a national currency, in terms of the Special Drawing
       Right, of a High Contracting Party which is not a Member of the International
       Monetary Fund, shall be calculated in a manner determined by that High
       Contracting Party. Nevertheless, those States which are not Members of the
       International Monetary Fund and whose law does not permit the application of the
       provisions of paragraph (2)(b) of Article 22 may, at the time of ratification or
       accession or at any time thereafter, declare that the limit of liability of the carrier in
       judicial proceedings in their territories is fixed at a sum of two hundred and fifty
       monetary units per kilogramme. This monetary unit corresponds to sixty-five and a
       half milligrammes of gold of millesimal fineness nine hundred. This sum may be
       converted into the national currency concerned in round figures. The conversion
       of this sum into national currency shall be made according to the law of the State
       concerned.

Article 23

(1)   Any provision tending to relieve the carrier of liability or to fix a lower limit than
       that which is laid down in this Convention shall be null and void, but the nullity of
       any such provision does not involve the nullity of the whole contract, which shall
       remain subject to the provisions of this Convention.
(2)   Paragraph (1) of this Article shall not apply to provisions governing loss or damage
       resulting from the inherent defect, quality or vice of the cargo carried.

Article 24

(1)   In the carriage of passengers, baggage and cargo, any action for damages, however
       founded, can only be brought subject to the conditions and limits of liability set out
       in this Convention without prejudice to the question as to who are the persons
       who have the right to bring suit and what are their respective rights.
(2)   In the carriage of cargo, any action for damages, however founded, whether under
       this Convention or in contract or in tort or otherwise, can only be brought subject
       to the conditions and limits of liability set out in this Convention without prejudice
       to the question as to who are the persons who have the right to bring suit and what
       are their respective rights. Such limits of liability constitute maximum limits and
       may not be exceeded whatever the circumstances which give rise to the liability.

Article 25

In the carriage of passengers and baggage, the limits of liability specified in Article 22
shall not apply if it is proved that the damage resulted from an act or omission of the
carrier, his servants or agents, done with intent to cause damage or recklessly and with
knowledge that damage would probably result; provided that, in the case of such act or
omission of a servant or agent, it is also proved that he was acting within the scope of his
employment.

Article 25A

(1)   If an action is brought against a servant or agent of the carrier arising out of damage
       to which the Convention relates, such servant or agent, if he proves that he acted
       within the scope of his employment, shall be entitled to avail himself of the limits
       of liability which that carrier himself is entitled to invoke under Article 22.

(2) The aggregate of the amounts recoverable from the carrier, his servants and agents, in that case, shall not exceed the said limits.

(3) In the carriage of passengers and baggage, the provisions of paragraphs (1) and (2) of this Article shall not apply if it is proved that the damage resulted from an act or omission of the servant or agent done with intent to cause damage or recklessly and with knowledge that damage would probably result.

Article 26

(1) Receipt by the person entitled to delivery of baggage or cargo without complaint is *prima facie* evidence that the same have been delivered in good condition and in accordance with the document of carriage.

(2) In the case of damage, the person entitled to delivery must complain to the carrier forthwith after the discovery of the damage, and at the latest, within seven days from the date of receipt in the case of baggage and fourteen days from the date of receipt in the case of cargo. In the case of delay the complaint must be made at the latest within twenty-one days from the date on which the baggage or cargo has been placed at his disposal.

(3) Every complaint must be made in writing upon the document of carriage or by separate notice in writing despatched within the times aforesaid.

(4) Failing complaint within the times aforesaid, no action shall lie against the carrier, save in the case of fraud on his part.

Article 27

In the case of the death of the person liable, an action for damages lies in accordance with the terms of this Convention against those legally representing his estate.

Article 28

(1) An action for damages must be brought, at the option of the plaintiff, in the territory of one of the High Contracting Parties, either before the court having jurisdiction where the carrier is ordinarily resident, or has his principal place of business, or has an establishment by which the contract has been made or before the court having jurisdiction at the place of destination.

(2) Questions of procedure shall be governed by the law of the court seised of the case.

Article 29

(1) The right to damages shall be extinguished if an action is not brought within two years, reckoned from the date of arrival at the destination, or from the date on which the aircraft ought to have arrived, or from the date on which the carriage stopped.

(2) The method of calculating the period of limitation shall be determined by the law of the court seised of the case.

Article 30

(1) In the case of carriage to be performed by various successive carriers and falling within the definition set out in the third paragraph of Article 1, each carrier who accepts passengers, baggage or cargo is subjected to the rules set out in this Convention, and is deemed to be one of the contracting parties to the contract of carriage in so far as the contract deals with that part of the carriage which is performed under his supervision.

(2)   In the case of carriage of this nature, the passenger or his representative can take action only against the carrier who performed the carriage during which the accident or the delay occurred, save in the case where, by express agreement, the first carrier assumed liability for the whole journey.

(3)   As regards baggage or cargo, the passenger or consignor will have a right of action against the first carrier, and the passenger or consignee who is entitled to delivery will have a right of action against the last carrier, and further, each may take action against the carrier who performed the carriage during which the destruction, loss, damage or delay took place. These carriers will be jointly and severally liable to the passenger or to the consignor or consignee.

Article 30A

Nothing in this Convention shall prejudice the question whether a person liable for damage in accordance with its provisions has a right of recourse against any other person.

CHAPTER IV
PROVISIONS RELATING TO COMBINED CARRIAGE

Article 31

(1)   In the case of combined carriage performed partly by air and partly by any other mode of carriage, the provisions of this Convention apply only to the carriage by air, provided that the carriage by air falls within the terms of Article 1.

(2)   Nothing in this Convention shall prevent the parties in the case of combined carriage from inserting in the documents of air carriage conditions relating to other modes of carriage, provided that the provisions of this Convention are observed as regards the carriage by air.

CHAPTER V
GENERAL AND FINAL PROVISIONS

Article 32

Any clause contained in the contract and all special agreements entered into before the damage occurred by which the parties purport to infringe the rules laid down by this convention, whether by deciding the law to be applied, or by altering the rules as to jurisdiction, shall be null and void. Nevertheless for the carriage of cargo arbitration clauses are allowed, subject to this Convention, if the arbitration is to take place within one of the jurisdictions referred to in the first paragraph of Article 28.

Article 33

Except as provided in paragraph (3) of Article 5, nothing in this Convention shall prevent the carrier either from refusing to enter into any contract of carriage or from making regulations which do not conflict with the provisions of this Convention.

Article 34

The provisions of Articles 3 to 8 inclusive relating to documents of carriage shall not apply in the case of carriage performed in extra-ordinary circumstances outside the normal scope of an air carrier's business.

Article 35

The expression 'days' when used in this Convention means current days not working days.

Article 40A

(1) [Omitted].
(2) For the purposes of the Convention the word territory means not only the metropolitan territory of a State but also all other territories for the foreign relations of which that State is responsible.

Articles 36.–42. [Omitted].

SCHEDULE 1B

CONVENTION
FOR THE UNIFICATION OF CERTAIN RULES FOR
INTERNATIONAL CARRIAGE BY AIR

CHAPTER I

GENERAL PROVISIONS

Article 1   Scope of Application

1. This Convention applies to all international carriage of persons, baggage or cargo performed by aircraft for reward. It applies equally to gratuitous carriage by aircraft performed by an air transport undertaking.
2. For the purposes of this Convention, the expression *international carriage* means any carriage in which, according to the agreement between the parties, the place of departure and the place of destination, whether or not there be a break in the carriage or a transhipment, are situated either within the territories of two States Parties, or within the territory of a single State Party if there is an agreed stopping place within the territory of another State, even if that State is not a State Party. Carriage between two points within the territory of a single State Party without an agreed stopping place within the territory of another State is not international carriage for the purposes of this Convention.
3. Carriage to be performed by several successive carriers is deemed, for the purposes of this Convention, to be one undivided carriage if it has been regarded by the parties as a single operation, whether it had been agreed upon under the form of a single contract or of a series of contracts, and it does not lose its international character merely because one contract or a series of contracts is to be performed entirely within the territory of the same State.
4. This Convention applies also to carriage as set out in Chapter V, subject to the terms contained therein.

Article 2   Carriage Performed by State and Carriage of Postal Items

1. This Convention applies to carriage performed by the State or by legally constituted public bodies provided it falls within the conditions laid down in Article 1.
2. In the carriage of postal items, the carrier shall be liable only to the relevant postal administration in accordance with the rules applicable to the relationship between the carriers and the postal administrations.

3.   Except as provided in paragraph 2 of this Article, the provisions of this Convention shall not apply to the carriage of postal items.

CHAPTER II
DOCUMENTATION AND DUTIES OF THE PARTIES RELATING TO THE CARRIAGE OF PASSENGERS, BAGGAGE AND CARGO

Article 3   Passengers and Baggage

1.   In respect of carriage of passengers, an individual or collective document of carriage shall be delivered containing:
   (a)   an indication of the places of departure and destination;
   (b)   if the places of departure and destination are within the territory of a single State Party, one or more agreed stopping places being within the territory of another State, an indication of at least one such stopping place.
2.   Any other means which preserves the information indicated in paragraph 1 may be substituted for the delivery of the document referred to in that paragraph. If any such other means is used, the carrier shall offer to deliver to the passenger a written statement of the information so preserved.
3.   The carrier shall deliver to the passenger a baggage identification tag for each piece of checked baggage.
4.   The passenger shall be given written notice to the effect that where this Convention is applicable it governs and may limit the liability of carriers in respect of death or injury and for destruction or loss of, or damage to, baggage, and for delay.
5.   Non-compliance with the provisions of the foregoing paragraphs shall not affect the existence or the validity of the contract of carriage, which shall, nonetheless, be subject to the rules of this Convention including those relating to limitation of liability.

Article 4   Cargo

1.   In respect of the carriage of cargo, an air waybill shall be delivered.
2.   Any other means which preserves a record of the carriage to be performed may be substituted for the delivery of an air waybill. If such other means are used, the carrier shall, if so requested by the consignor, deliver to the consignor a cargo receipt permitting identification of the consignment and access to the information contained in the record preserved by such other means.

Article 5   Contents of Air Waybill or Cargo Receipt

The air waybill or the cargo receipt shall include:
(a)   an indication of the places of departure and destination;
(b)   if the places of departure and destination are within the territory of a single State Party, one or more agreed stopping places being within the territory of another State, an indication of at least one such stopping place; and
(c)   an indication of the weight of the consignment.

Article 6   Document Relating to the Nature of the Cargo

The consignor may be required, if necessary to meet the formalities of customs, police and similar public authorities, to deliver a document indicating the nature of the cargo. This provision creates for the carrier no duty, obligation or liability resulting therefrom.

Article 7   Description of Air Waybill

1.   The air waybill shall be made out by the consignor in three original parts.
2.   The first part shall be marked 'for the carrier; it shall be signed by the consignor. The second part shall be marked 'for the consignee'; it shall be signed by the consignor and by the carrier. The third part shall be signed by the carrier who shall hand it to the consignor after the cargo has been accepted.
3.   The signature of the carrier and that of the consignor may be printed or stamped.
4.   If, at the request of the consignor, the carrier makes out the air waybill, the carrier shall be deemed, subject to proof to the contrary, to have done so on behalf of the consignor.

Article 8   Documentation for Multiple Packages

When there is more than one package:
(a)   the carrier of cargo has the right to require the consignor to make out separate air waybills;
(b)   the consignor has the right to require the carrier to deliver separate cargo receipts when the other means referred to in paragraph 2 of Article 4 are used.

Article 9   Non-compliance with Documentary Requirements

Non-compliance with the provisions of Articles 4 to 8 shall not affect the existence or the validity of the contract of carriage, which shall, nonetheless, be subject to the rules of this Convention including those relating to limitation of liability.

Article 10   Responsibility for Particulars of Documentation

1.   The consignor is responsible for the correctness of the particulars and statements relating to the cargo inserted by it or on its behalf in the air waybill or furnished by it or on its behalf to the carrier for insertion in the cargo receipt or for insertion in the record preserved by the other means referred to in paragraph 2 of Article 4. The foregoing shall also apply where the person acting on behalf of the consignor is also the agent of the carrier.
2.   The consignor shall indemnify the carrier against all damage suffered by it, or by any other person to whom the carrier is liable, by reason of the irregularity, incorrectness or incompleteness of the particulars and statements furnished by the consignor or on its behalf.
3.   Subject to the provisions of paragraphs 1 and 2 of this Article, the carrier shall indemnify the consignor against all damage suffered by it, or by any other person to whom the consignor is liable, by reason of the irregularity, incorrectness or incompleteness of the particulars and statements inserted by the carrier or on its behalf in the cargo receipt or in the record preserved by the other means referred to in paragraph 2 of Article 4.

Article 11   Evidentiary Value of Documentation

1.   The air waybill or the cargo receipt is *prima facie* evidence of the conclusion of the contract, of the acceptance of the cargo and of the conditions of carriage mentioned therein.
2.   Any statements in the air waybill or the cargo receipt relating to the weight, dimensions and packing of the cargo, as well as those relating to the number of packages, are *prima facie* evidence of the facts stated; those relating to the quantity, volume and condition of the cargo do not constitute evidence against the carrier except so far as they both have been, and are stated in the air waybill or the cargo

receipt to have been, checked by it in the presence of the consignor, or relate to the apparent condition of the cargo.

Article 12   Right of Disposition of Cargo

1. Subject to its liability to carry out all its obligations under the contract of carriage, the consignor has the right to dispose of the cargo by withdrawing it at the airport of departure or destination, or by stopping it in the course of the journey on any landing, or by calling for it to be delivered at the place of destination or in the course of the journey to a person other than the consignee originally designated, or by requiring it to be returned to the airport of departure. The consignor must not exercise this right of disposition in such a way as to prejudice the carrier or other consignors and must reimburse any expenses occasioned by the exercise of this right.
2. If it is impossible to carry out the instructions of the consignor, the carrier must so inform the consignor forthwith.
3. If the carrier carries out the instructions of the consignor for the disposition of the cargo without requiring the production of the part of the air waybill or the cargo receipt delivered to the latter, the carrier will be liable, without prejudice to its right of recovery from the consignor, for any damage which may be caused thereby to any person who is lawfully in possession of that part of the air waybill or the cargo receipt.
4. The right conferred on the consignor ceases at the moment when that of the consignee begins in accordance with Article 13. Nevertheless, if the consignee declines to accept the cargo, or cannot be communicated with, the consignor resumes its right of disposition.

Article 13   Delivery of the Cargo

1. Except when the consignor has exercised its right under Article 12, the consignee is entitled, on arrival of the cargo at the place of destination, to require the carrier to deliver the cargo to it, on payment of the charges due and on complying with the conditions of carriage.
2. Unless it is otherwise agreed, it is the duty of the carrier to give notice to the consignee as soon as the cargo arrives.
3. If the carrier admits the loss of the cargo, or if the cargo has not arrived at the expiration of seven days after the date on which it ought to have arrived, the consignee is entitled to enforce against the carrier the rights which flow from the contract of carriage.

Article 14   Enforcement of the Rights of Consignor and Consignee

The consignor and the consignee can respectively enforce all the rights given to them by Articles 12 and 13, each in its own name, whether it is acting in its own interest or in the interest of another, provided that it carries out the obligations imposed by the contract of carriage.

Article 15   Relations of Consignor and Consignee or Mutual Relations of Third Parties

1. Articles 12, 13 and 14 do not affect either the relations of the consignor and the consignee with each other or the mutual relations of third parties whose rights are derived either from the consignor or from the consignee.
2. The provisions of Articles 12, 13 and 14 can only be varied by express provision in the air waybill or the cargo receipt.

Article 16   Formalities of Customs, Police or Other Public Authorities

1.   The consignor must furnish such information and such documents as are necessary to meet the formalities of customs, police and any other public authorities before the cargo can be delivered to the consignee. The consignor is liable to the carrier for any damage occasioned by the absence, insufficiency or irregularity of any such information or documents, unless the damage is due to the fault of the carrier, its servants or agents.

2.   The carrier is under no obligation to enquire into the correctness or sufficiency of such information or documents.

CHAPTER III
LIABILITY OF THE CARRIER AND EXTENT OF COMPENSATION FOR DAMAGE

Article 17   Death and Injury of Passengers—Damage to Baggage

1.   The carrier is liable for damage sustained in case of death or bodily injury of a passenger upon condition only that the accident which caused the death or injury took place on board the aircraft or in the course of any of the operations of embarking or disembarking.

2.   The carrier is liable for damage sustained in case of destruction or loss of, or of damage to, checked baggage upon condition only that the event which caused the destruction, loss or damage took place on board the aircraft or during any period within which the checked baggage was in the charge of the carrier. However, the carrier is not liable if and to the extent that the damage resulted from the inherent defect, quality or vice of the baggage. In the case of unchecked baggage, including personal items, the carrier is liable if the damage resulted from its fault or that of its servants or agents.

3.   If the carrier admits the loss of the checked baggage, or if the checked baggage has not arrived at the expiration of twenty-one days after the date on which it ought to have arrived, the passenger is entitled to enforce against the carrier the rights which flow from the contract of carriage.

4.   Unless otherwise specified, in this Convention the term 'baggage' means both checked baggage and unchecked baggage.

Article 18   Damage to Cargo

1.   The carrier is liable for damage sustained in the event of the destruction or loss of, or damage to, cargo upon condition only that the event which caused the damage so sustained took place during the carriage by air.

2.   However, the carrier is not liable if and to the extent it proves that the destruction, or loss of, or damage to, the cargo resulted from one or more of the following:
(a)   inherent defect, quality or vice of that cargo;
(b)   defective packing of that cargo performed by a person other than the carrier or its servants or agents;
(c)   an act of war or an armed conflict;
(d)   an act of public authority carried out in connection with the entry, exit or transit of the cargo.

3.   The carriage by air within the meaning of paragraph 1 of this Article comprises the period during which the cargo is in the charge of the carrier.

4.   The period of the carriage by air does not extend to any carriage by land, by sea or by inland waterway performed outside an airport. If, however, such carriage takes place in the performance of a contract for carriage by air, for the purpose of loading, delivery or transhipment, any damage is presumed, subject to proof to the contrary, to have been the result of an event which took place during the carriage

by air. If a carrier, without the consent of the consignor, substitutes carriage by another mode of transport for the whole or part of a carriage intended by the agreement between the parties to be carriage by air, such carriage by another mode of transport is deemed to be within the period of carriage by air.

Article 19   Delay

The carrier is liable for damage occasioned by delay in the carriage by air of passengers, baggage or cargo. Nevertheless, the carrier shall not be liable for damage occasioned by delay if it proves that it and its servants and agents took all measures that could reasonably be required to avoid the damage or that it was impossible for it or them to take such measures.

Article 20   Exoneration

If the carrier proves that the damage was caused or contributed to by the negligence or other wrongful act or omission of the person claiming compensation, or the person from whom he or she derives his or her rights, the carrier shall be wholly or partly exonerated from its liability to the claimant to the extent that such negligence or wrongful act or omission caused or contributed to the damage. When by reason of death or injury of a passenger compensation is claimed by a person other than the passenger, the carrier shall likewise be wholly or partly exonerated from its liability to the extent that it proves that the damage was caused or contributed to by the negligence or other wrongful act or omission of that passenger. This Article applies to all the liability provisions in this Convention, including paragraph 1 of Article 21.

Article 21   Compensation in Case of Death or Injury of Passengers

1. For damages arising under paragraph 1 of Article 17 not exceeding 100,000 Special Drawing Rights for each passenger, the carrier shall not be able to exclude or limit its liability.
2. The carrier shall not be liable for damages arising under paragraph 1 of Article 17 to the extent that they exceed for each passenger 100,000 Special Drawing Rights if the carrier proves that:
    (a) such damage was not due to the negligence or other wrongful act or omission of the carrier or its servants or agents; or
    (b) such damage was solely due to the negligence or other wrongful act or omission of a third party.

Article 22   Limits of Liability in Relation to Delay, Baggage and Cargo

1. In the case of damage caused by delay as specified in Article 19 in the carriage of persons, the liability of the carrier for each passenger is limited to 4,150 Special Drawing Rights.
2. In the carriage of baggage, the liability of the carrier in the case of destruction, loss, damage or delay is limited to 1,000 Special Drawing Rights for each passenger unless the passenger has made, at the time when the checked baggage was handed over to the carrier, a special declaration of interest in delivery at destination and has paid a supplementary sum if the case so requires. In that case the carrier will be liable to pay a sum not exceeding the declared sum, unless it proves that the sum is greater than the passenger's actual interest in delivery at destination.
3. In the carriage of cargo, the liability of the carrier in the case of destruction, loss, damage or delay is limited to a sum of 17 Special Drawing Rights per kilogramme, unless the consignor has made, at the time when the package was handed over to the carrier, a special declaration of interest in delivery at destination and has paid a supplementary sum if the case so requires. In that case the carrier will be liable to

pay a sum not exceeding the declared sum, unless it proves that the sum is greater than the consignor's actual interest in delivery at destination.

4.   In the case of destruction, loss, damage or delay of part of the cargo, or of any object contained therein, the weight to be taken into consideration in determining the amount to which the carrier's liability is limited shall be only the total weight of the package or packages concerned. Nevertheless, when the destruction, loss, damage or delay of a part of the cargo, or of an object contained therein, affects the value of other packages covered by the same air waybill, or the same receipt or, if they were not issued, by the same record preserved by the other means referred to in paragraph 2 of Article 4, the total weight of such package or packages shall also be taken into consideration in determining the limit of liability.

5.   The foregoing provisions of paragraphs 1 and 2 of this Article shall not apply if it is proved that the damage resulted from an act or omission of the carrier, its servants or agents, done with intent to cause damage or recklessly and with knowledge that damage would probably result; provided that, in the case of such act or omission of a servant or agent, it is also proved that such servant or agent was acting within the scope of its employment.

6.   The limits prescribed in Article 21 and in this Article shall not prevent the court from awarding, in accordance with its own law, in addition, the whole or part of the court costs and of the other expenses of the litigation incurred by the plaintiff, including interest. The foregoing provision shall not apply if the amount of the damages awarded, excluding court costs and other expenses of the litigation, does not exceed the sum which the carrier has offered in writing to the plaintiff within a period of six months from the date of the occurrence causing the damage, or before the commencement of the action, if that is later.

Articles 23 and 24 [Omitted].

Article 25   Stipulation on Limits

A carrier may stipulate that the contract of carriage shall be subject to higher limits of liability than those provided for in this Convention or to no limits of liability whatsoever.

Article 26   Invalidity of Contractual Provisions

Any provision tending to relieve the carrier of liability or to fix a lower limit than that which is laid down in this Convention shall be null and void, but the nullity of any such provision does not involve the nullity of the whole contract, which shall remain subject to the provisions of this Convention.

Article 27   Freedom to Contract

Nothing contained in this Convention shall prevent the carrier from refusing to enter into any contract of carriage, from waiving any defences available under the Convention, or from laying down conditions which do not conflict with the provisions of this Convention.

Article 28   Advance Payments

In the case of aircraft accidents resulting in death or injury of passengers, the carrier shall, if required by its national law, make advance payments without delay to a natural person or persons who are entitled to claim compensation in order to meet the immediate economic needs of such persons. Such advance payments shall not constitute a recognition of liability and may be offset against any amounts subsequently paid as damages by the carrier.

Article 29   Basis of Claims

In the carriage of passengers, baggage and cargo, any action for damages, however founded, whether under this Convention or in contract or in tort or otherwise, can only be brought subject to the conditions and such limits of liability as are set out in this Convention without prejudice to the question as to who are the persons who have the right to bring suit and what are their respective rights. In any such action, punitive, exemplary or any other non-compensatory damages shall not be recoverable.

Article 30   Servants, Agents—Aggregation of Claims

1. If an action is brought against a servant or agent of the carrier arising out of damage to which the Convention relates, such servant or agent, if they prove that they acted within the scope of their employment, shall be entitled to avail themselves of the conditions and limits of liability which the carrier itself is entitled to invoke under this Convention.
2. The aggregate of the amounts recoverable from the carrier, its servants and agents, in that case, shall not exceed the said limits.
3. Save in respect of the carriage of cargo, the provisions of paragraphs 1 and 2 of this Article shall not apply if it is proved that the damage resulted from an act or omission of the servant or agent done with intent to cause damage or recklessly and with knowledge that damage would probably result.

Article 31   Timely Notice of Complaints

1. Receipt by the person entitled to delivery of checked baggage or cargo without complaint is *prima facie* evidence that the same has been delivered in good condition and in accordance with the document of carriage or with the record preserved by the other means referred to in paragraph 2 of Article 3 and paragraph 2 of Article 4.
2. In the case of damage, the person entitled to delivery must complain to the carrier forthwith after the discovery of the damage, and, at the latest, within seven days from the date of receipt in the case of checked baggage and fourteen days from the date of receipt in the case of cargo. In the case of delay, the complaint must be made at the latest within twenty-one days from the date on which the baggage or cargo have been placed at his or her disposal.
3. Every complaint must be made in writing and given or dispatched within the times aforesaid.
4. If no complaint is made within the times aforesaid, no action shall lie against the carrier, save in the case of fraud on its part.

Article 32   Death of Person Liable

In the case of the death of the person liable, an action for damages lies in accordance with the terms of this Convention against those legally representing his or her estate.

Article 33   Jurisdiction

1. An action for damages must be brought, at the option of the plaintiff, in the territory of one of the States Parties, either before the court of the domicile of the carrier or of its principal place of business, or where it has a place of business through which the contract has been made or before the court at the place of destination.
2. In respect of damage resulting from the death or injury of a passenger, an action may be brought before one of the courts mentioned in paragraph 1 of this Article, or in the territory of a State Party in which at the time of the accident the passenger

has his or her principal and permanent residence and to or from which the carrier operates services for the carriage of passengers by air, either on its own aircraft, or on another carrier's aircraft pursuant to a commercial agreement, and in which that carrier conducts its business of carriage of passengers by air from premises leased or owned by the carrier itself or by another carrier with which it has a commercial agreement.

3. For the purposes of paragraph 2:

   (a) 'commercial agreement' means an agreement, other than an agency agreement, made between carriers and relating to the provision of their joint services for carriage of passengers by air;

   (b) 'principal and permanent residence' means the one fixed and permanent abode of the passenger at the time of the accident. The nationality of the passenger shall not be the determining factor in this regard.

4. Questions of procedure shall be governed by the law of the court seised of the case.

Article 34   Arbitration

1. Subject to the provisions of this Article, the parties to the contract of carriage for cargo may stipulate that any dispute relating to the liability of the carrier under this Convention shall be settled by arbitration. Such agreement shall be in writing.

2. The arbitration proceedings shall, at the option of the claimant, take place within one of the jurisdictions referred to in Article 33.

3. The arbitrator or arbitration tribunal shall apply the provisions of this Convention.

4. The provisions of paragraphs 2 and 3 of this Article shall be deemed to be part of every arbitration clause or agreement, and any term of such clause or agreement which is inconsistent therewith shall be null and void.

Article 35   Limitation of Actions

1. The right to damages shall be extinguished if an action is not brought within a period of two years, reckoned from the date of arrival at the destination, or from the date on which the aircraft ought to have arrived, or from the date on which the carriage stopped.

2. The method of calculating that period shall be determined by the law of the court seised of the case.

Article 36   Successive Carriage

1. In the case of carriage to be performed by various successive carriers and falling within the definition set out in paragraph 3 of Article 1, each carrier which accepts passengers, baggage or cargo is subject to the rules set out in this Convention and is deemed to be one of the parties to the contract of carriage in so far as the contract deals with that part of the carriage which is performed under its supervision.

2. In the case of carriage of this nature, the passenger or any person entitled to compensation in respect of him or her can take action only against the carrier which performed the carriage during which the accident or the delay occurred, save in the case where, by express agreement, the first carrier has assumed liability for the whole journey.

3. As regards baggage or cargo, the passenger or consignor will have a right of action against the first carrier, and the passenger or consignee who is entitled to delivery will have a right of action against the last carrier, and further, each may take action against the carrier which performed the carriage during which the destruction, loss, damage or delay took place. These carriers will be jointly and severally liable to the passenger or to the consignor or consignee.

Article 37   Right of Recourse against Third Parties

Nothing in this Convention shall prejudice the question whether a person liable for damage in accordance with its provisions has a right of recourse against any other person.

CHAPTER IV
COMBINED CARRIAGE

Article 38   Combined Carriage

1. In the case of combined carriage performed partly by air and partly by any other mode of carriage, the provisions of this Convention shall, subject to paragraph 4 of Article 18, apply only to the carriage by air, provided that the carriage by air falls within the terms of Article 1.
2. Nothing in this Convention shall prevent the parties in the case of combined carriage from inserting in the document of air carriage conditions relating to other modes of carriage, provided that the provisions of this Convention are observed as regards the carriage by air.

CHAPTER V
CARRIAGE BY AIR PERFORMED BY A PERSON OTHER THAN THE CONTRACTING CARRIER

Article 39   Contracting Carrier—Actual Carrier

The provisions of this Chapter apply when a person (hereinafter referred to as 'the contracting carrier') as a principal makes a contract governed by this Convention with a passenger or consignor or with a person acting on behalf of the passenger or consignor, and another person (hereinafter referred to as 'the actual carrier') performs, by virtue of authority from the contracting carrier, the whole or part of the carriage, but is not with respect to such part a successive carrier within the meaning of this Convention. Such authority shall be presumed in the absence of proof to the contrary.

Article 40   Respective Liability of Contracting and Actual Carriers

If an actual carrier performs the whole or part of carriage which, according to the contract referred to in Article 39, is governed by this Convention, both the contracting carrier and the actual carrier shall, except as otherwise provided in this Chapter, be subject to the rules of this Convention, the former for the whole of the carriage contemplated in the contract, the latter solely for the carriage which it performs.

Article 41   Mutual Liability

1. The acts and omissions of the actual carrier and of its servants and agents acting within the scope of their employment shall, in relation to the carriage performed by the actual carrier, be deemed to be also those of the contracting carrier.
2. The acts and omissions of the contracting carrier and of its servants and agents acting within the scope of their employment shall, in relation to the carriage performed by the actual carrier, be deemed to be also those of the actual carrier. Nevertheless, no such act or omission shall subject the actual carrier to liability exceeding the amounts referred to in Articles 21, 22, 23 and 24. Any special agreement under which the contracting carrier assumes obligations not imposed by this Convention or any waiver of rights or defences conferred by this

Convention or any special declaration of interest in delivery at destination contemplated in Article 22 shall not affect the actual carrier unless agreed to by it.

Article 42   Addressee of Complaints and Instructions

Any complaint to be made or instruction to be given under this Convention to the carrier shall have the same effect whether addressed to the contracting carrier or to the actual carrier. Nevertheless, instructions referred to in Article 12 shall only be effective if addressed to the contracting carrier.

Article 43   Servants and Agents

In relation to the carriage performed by the actual carrier, any servant or agent of that carrier or of the contracting carrier shall, if they prove that they acted within the scope of their employment, be entitled to avail themselves of the conditions and limits of liability which are applicable under this Convention to the carrier whose servant or agent they are, unless it is proved that they acted in a manner that prevents the limits of liability from being invoked in accordance with this Convention.

Article 44   Aggregation of Damages

In relation to the carriage performed by the actual carrier, the aggregate of the amounts recoverable from that carrier and the contracting carrier, and from their servants and agents acting within the scope of their employment, shall not exceed the highest amount which could be awarded against either the contracting carrier or the actual carrier under this Convention, but none of the persons mentioned shall be liable for a sum in excess of the limit applicable to that person.

Article 45   Addressee of Claims

In relation to the carriage performed by the actual carrier, an action for damages may be brought, at the option of the plaintiff, against that carrier or the contracting carrier, or against both together or separately. If the action is brought against only one of those carriers, that carrier shall have the right to require the other carrier to be joined in the proceedings, the procedure and effects being governed by the law of the court seised of the case.

Article 46   Additional Jurisdiction

Any action for damages contemplated in Article 45 must be brought, at the option of the plaintiff, in the territory of one of the States Parties, either before a court in which an action may be brought against the contracting carrier, as provided in Article 33, or before the court having jurisdiction at the place where the actual carrier has its domicile or its principal place of business.

Article 47   Invalidity of Contractual Provisions

Any contractual provision tending to relieve the contracting carrier or the actual carrier of liability under this Chapter or to fix a lower limit than that which is applicable according to this Chapter shall be null and void, but the nullity of any such provision does not involve the nullity of the whole contract, which shall remain subject to the provisions of this Chapter.

Article 48   Mutual Relations of Contracting and Actual Carriers

Except as provided in Article 45, nothing in this Chapter shall affect the rights and obligations of the carriers between themselves, including any right of recourse or indemnification.

CHAPTER VI
OTHER PROVISIONS

Article 49   Mandatory Application

Any clause contained in the contract of carriage and all special agreements entered into before the damage occurred by which the parties purport to infringe the rules laid down by this Convention, whether by deciding the law to be applied, or by altering the rules as to jurisdiction, shall be null and void.

Article 50   Insurance

States Parties shall require their carriers to maintain adequate insurance covering their liability under this Convention. A carrier may be required by the State Party into which it operates to furnish evidence that it maintains adequate insurance covering its liability under this Convention.

Article 51   Carriage Performed in Extraordinary Circumstances

The provisions of Articles 3 to 5, 7 and 8 relating to the documentation of carriage shall not apply in the case of carriage performed in extraordinary circumstances outside the normal scope of a carrier's business.

Article 52   Definition of Days

The expression 'days' when used in this Convention means calendar days, not working days.

CARRIAGE BY AIR (SUPPLEMENTARY PROVISIONS) ACT 1962

CHAPTER 43

1. **Supplementary Convention to have force of law**
   (1)   The provisions of the Convention, supplementary to the Warsaw Convention, for the unification of certain rules relating to International carriage by air performed by a person other than the contracting carrier, as set out in the Schedule to this Act, shall, so far as they relate to the rights and liabilities of carriers, carriers' servants and agents, passengers, consignors, consignees, and other persons, and subject to the provisions of this Act, have the force of law in the United Kingdom in relation to any carriage by air to which the Convention applies, irrespective of the nationality of the aircraft performing that carriage.
   (2)   If there is any inconsistency between the text in English in Part I of the Schedule to this Act and the text in French in Part II of that Schedule, the text in French shall prevail.

2.–7. [Omitted].

SCHEDULE

PART 1

THE ENGLISH TEXT

CONVENTION
SUPPLEMENTARY TO THE WARSAW CONVENTION, FOR THE UNIFICATION OF
CERTAIN RULES RELATING TO INTERNATIONAL CARRIAGE BY AIR PERFORMED BY
A PERSON OTHER THAN THE CONTRACTING CARRIER

Article I

In this Convention—
- (a)   [Omitted];
- (b)   'contracting carrier' means a person who as a principal makes an agreement for carriage governed by the Warsaw Convention with a passenger or consignor or with a person acting on behalf of the passenger or consignor;
- (c)   'actual carrier' means a person, other than the contracting carrier, who, by virtue of authority from the contracting carrier, performs the whole or part of the carriage contemplated in paragraph (b) but who is not with respect to such part a successive carrier within the meaning of the Warsaw Convention. Such authority is presumed in the absence of proof to the contrary.

Article II

If an actual carrier performs the whole or part of carriage which, according to the agreement referred to in Article I, paragraph (b), is governed by the Warsaw Convention, both the contracting carrier and the actual carrier shall, except as otherwise provided in this Convention, be subject to the rules of the Warsaw Convention, the former for the whole of the carriage contemplated in the agreement, the latter solely for the carriage which he performs.

Article III

1.   The acts and omissions of the actual carrier and of his servants and agents acting within the scope of their employment shall, in relation to the carriage performed by the actual carrier, be deemed to be also those of the contracting carrier.
2.   The acts and omissions of the contracting carrier and of his servants and agents acting within the scope of their employment shall, in relation to the carriage performed by the actual carrier, be deemed to be also those of the actual carrier. Nevertheless, no such act or omission shall subject the actual carrier to liability exceeding the limits specified in Article 22 or Article 22A of the Warsaw Convention. Any special agreement under which the contracting carrier assumes obligations not imposed by the Warsaw Convention or any waiver of rights conferred by that Convention or any special declaration of interest in delivery at destination contemplated in Article 22 of the said Convention, shall not affect the actual carrier unless agreed to by him.

Article IV

Any complaint to be made or order to be given under the Warsaw Convention to the carrier shall have the same effect whether addressed to the contracting carrier or to the actual carrier. Nevertheless, orders referred to in Article 12 of the Warsaw Convention shall only be effective if addressed to the contracting carrier.

Article V

In relation to the carriage performed by the actual carrier, any servant or agent of that carrier or of the contracting carrier shall, if he proves that he acted within the scope of his employment, be entitled to avail himself of the limits of liability which are applicable under this Convention to the carrier whose servant or agent he is unless it is proved that he acted in a manner which, under the Warsaw Convention, prevents the limits of liability from being invoked.

Article VI

In relation to the carriage performed by the actual carrier, the aggregate of the amounts recoverable from that carrier and the contracting carrier, and from their servants and agents acting within the scope of their employment, shall not exceed the highest amount which could be awarded against either the contracting carrier or the actual carrier under this Convention, but none of the persons mentioned shall be liable for a sum in excess of the limit applicable to him.

Article VII

In relation to the carriage performed by the actual carrier, an action for damages may be brought, at the option of the plaintiff, against that carrier or the contracting carrier, or against both together or separately. If the action is brought against only one of those carriers, that carrier shall have the right to require the other carrier to be joined in the proceedings, the procedure and effects being governed by the law of the court seised of the case.

Article VIII

Any action for damages contemplated in Article VII of this Convention must be brought, at the option of the plaintiff, either before a court in which an action may be brought against the contracting carrier, as provided in Article 28 of the Warsaw Convention, or before the court having jurisdiction at the place where the actual carrier is ordinarily resident or has his principal place of business.

Article IX

1. Any contractual provision tending to relieve the contracting carrier or the actual carrier of liability under this Convention or to fix a lower limit than that which is applicable according to this Convention shall be null and void, but the nullity of any such provision does not involve the nullity of the whole agreement, which shall remain subject to the provisions of this Convention.
2. In respect of the carriage performed by the actual carrier, the preceding paragraph shall not apply to contractual provisions governing loss or damage resulting from the inherent defect, quality or vice of the cargo carried.
3. Any clause contained in an agreement for carriage and all special agreements entered into before the damage occurred by which the parties purport to infringe the rules laid down by this Convention, whether by deciding the law to be applied, or by altering the rules as to jurisdiction, shall be null and void. Nevertheless, for

the carriage of cargo arbitration clauses are allowed, subject to this Convention, if the arbitration is to take place in one of the jurisdictions referred to in Article VIII.

Article X

Except as provided in Article VII, nothing in this Convention shall affect the rights and obligations of the two carriers between themselves.

Articles XI to XVIII [Omitted].

CARRIAGE OF GOODS BY ROAD ACT 1965

CHAPTER 37

1.   Convention to have force of law

Subject to the following provisions of this Act, the provisions of the Convention on the Contract for the International Carriage of Goods by Road (in this Act referred to as 'the Convention'), as set out in the Schedule to this Act, shall have the force of law in the United Kingdom so far as they relate to the rights and liabilities of persons concerned in the carriage of goods by road under a contract to which the Convention applies.

2.–13. [Omitted].

14.   Short title interpretation and commencement

(1)   [Omitted].

(2)   The persons who, for the purposes of this Act, are persons concerned in the carriage of goods by road under a contract to which the Convention applies are—

(a)   the sender;

(b)   the consignee;

(c)   any carrier who, in accordance with Article 34 in the Schedule to this Act or otherwise, is a party to the contract of carriage;

(d)   any person for whom such a carrier is responsible by virtue of Article 3 in the Schedule to this Act;

(e)   any person to whom the rights and liabilities of any of the persons referred to in paragraphs (a) to (d) of this subsection have passed (whether by assignment or assignation or by operation of law).

(3) and (4) [Omitted].

SCHEDULE
CONVENTION ON THE CONTRACT FOR THE INTERNATIONAL
CARRIAGE OF GOODS BY ROAD

CHAPTER I
SCOPE OF APPLICATION

Article 1

1.   This Convention shall apply to every contract for the carriage of goods by road in vehicles for reward, when the place of taking over of the goods and the place designated for delivery, as specified in the contract, are situated in two different

countries, of which at least one is a Contracting country, irrespective of the place of residence and the nationality of the parties.

2.   For the purposes of this Convention, 'vehicles' means motor vehicles, articulated vehicles, trailers and semi-trailers as defined in Article 4 of the Convention on Road Traffic dated 19th September 1949.

3.   This Convention shall apply also where carriage coming within its scope is carried out by States or by governmental institutions or organisations.

4.   This Convention shall not apply—
     (a)   to carriage performed under the terms of any international postal convention;
     (b)   to funeral consignments;
     (c)   to furniture removal.

5.   The Contracting Parties agree not to vary any of the provisions of this Convention by special agreements between two or more of them, except to make it inapplicable to their frontier traffic or to authorise the use in transport operations entirely confined to their territory of consignment notes representing a title to the goods.

Article 2

1.   Where the vehicle containing the goods is carried over part of the journey by sea, rail, inland waterways or air, and, except where the provisions of Article 14 are applicable, the goods are not unloaded from the vehicle, this Convention shall nevertheless apply to the whole of the carriage. Provided that to the extent that it is proved that any loss, damage or delay in delivery of the goods which occurs during the carriage by the other means of transport was not caused by an act or omission of the carrier by road, but by some event which could only have occurred in the course of and by reason of the carriage by that other means of transport, the liability of the carrier by road shall be determined not by this Convention but in the manner in which the liability of the carrier by the other means of transport would have been determined if a contract for the carriage of the goods alone had been made by the sender with the carrier by the other means of transport in accordance with the conditions prescribed by law for the carriage of goods by that means of transport. If, however, there are no such prescribed conditions, the liability of the carrier by road shall be determined by this Convention.

2.   If the carrier by road is also himself the carrier by the other means of transport, his liability shall also be determined in accordance with the provisions of paragraph 1 of this Article, but as if, in his capacities as carrier by road and as carrier by the other means of transport, he were two separate persons.

CHAPTER II
PERSONS FOR WHOM THE CARRIER IS RESPONSIBLE

Article 3

For the purposes of this Convention the carrier shall be responsible for the acts and omissions of his agents and servants and of any other persons of whose services he makes use for the performance of the carriage, when such agents, servants or other persons are acting within the scope of their employment, as if such acts or omissions were his own.

CHAPTER III
CONCLUSION AND PERFORMANCE OF THE CONTRACT OF CARRIAGE

Article 4

The contract of carriage shall be confirmed by the making out of a consignment note. The absence, irregularity or loss of the consignment note shall not affect the existence or the validity of the contract of carriage which shall remain subject to the provisions of this Convention.

Article 5

1. The consignment note shall be made out in three original copies signed by the sender and by the carrier. These signatures may be printed or replaced by the stamps of the sender and the carrier if the law of the country in which the consignment note has been made out so permits. The first copy shall be handed to the sender, the second shall accompany the goods and the third shall be retained by the carrier.
2. When the goods which are to be carried have to be loaded in different vehicles, or are of different kinds or are divided into different lots, the sender or the carrier shall have the right to require a separate consignment note to be made out for each vehicle used, or for each kind or lot of goods.

Article 6

1. The consignment note shall contain the following particulars—
   (a) the date of the consignment note and the place at which it is made out;
   (b) the name and address of the sender;
   (c) the name and address of the carrier;
   (d) the place and the date of taking over the goods and the place designated for delivery;
   (e) the name and address of the consignee;
   (f) the description in common use of the nature of the goods and the method of packing, and, in the case of dangerous goods, their generally recognised description;
   (g) the number of packages and their special marks and numbers;
   (h) the gross weight of the goods or their quantity otherwise expressed;
   (i) charges relating to the carriage (carriage charges, supplementary charges, customs duties and other charges incurred from the making of the contract to the time of delivery);
   (j) the requisite instructions for Customs and other formalities;
   (k) a statement that the carriage is subject, notwithstanding any clause to the contrary, to the provisions of this Convention.
2. Where applicable, the consignment note shall also contain the following particulars—
   (a) a statement that transhipment is not allowed;
   (b) the charges which the sender undertakes to pay;
   (c) the amount of 'cash on delivery' charges;
   (d) a declaration of the value of the goods and the amount representing special interest in delivery;
   (e) the sender's instructions to the carrier regarding insurance of the goods;
   (f) the agreed time-limit within which the carriage is to be carried out;
   (g) a list of the documents handed to the carrier.
3. The parties may enter in the consignment note any other particulars which they may deem useful.

Article 7

1. The sender shall be responsible for all expenses, loss and damage sustained by the carrier by reason of the inaccuracy or inadequacy of—
    (a) the particulars specified in Article 6, paragraph 1, (b), (d), (e), (f), (g), (h) and (j);
    (b) the particulars specified in Article 6, paragraph 2;
    (c) any other particulars or instructions given by him to enable the consignment note to be made out or for the purpose of their being entered therein.
2. If, at the request of the sender, the carrier enters in the consignment note the particulars referred to in paragraph 1 of this Article, he shall be deemed, unless the contrary is proved, to have done so on behalf of the sender.
3. If the consignment note does not contain the statement specified in Article 6, paragraph 1 (k), the carrier shall be liable for all expenses, loss and damage sustained through such omission by the person entitled to dispose of the goods.

Article 8

1. On taking over the goods, the carrier shall check—
    (a) the accuracy of the statements in the consignment note as to the number of packages and their marks and numbers, and
    (b) the apparent condition of the goods and their packaging.
2. Where the carrier has no reasonable means of checking the accuracy of the statements referred to in paragraph 1(a) of this Article, he shall enter his reservations in the consignment note together with the grounds on which they are based. He shall likewise specify the grounds for any reservations which he makes with regard to the apparent condition of the goods and their packaging. Such reservations shall not bind the sender unless he has expressly agreed to be bound by them in the consignment note.
3. The sender shall be entitled to require the carrier to check the gross weight of the goods or their quantity otherwise expressed. He may also require the contents of the packages to be checked. The carrier shall be entitled to claim the cost of such checking. The result of the checks shall be entered in the consignment note.

Article 9

1. The consignment note shall be *prima facie* evidence of the making of the contract of carriage, the conditions of the contract and the receipt of the goods by the carrier.
2. If the consignment note contains no specific reservations by the carrier, it shall be presumed, unless the contrary is proved, that the goods and their packaging appeared to be in good condition when the carrier took them over and that the number of packages, their marks and numbers corresponded with the statements in the consignment note.

Article 10

The sender shall be liable to the carrier for damage to persons, equipment or other goods, and for any expenses due to defective packing of the goods, unless the defect was apparent or known to the carrier at the time when he took over the goods and he made no reservations concerning it.

Article 11

1. For the purposes of the Customs or other formalities which have to be completed before delivery of the goods, the sender shall attach the necessary documents to

the consignment note or place them at the disposal of the carrier and shall furnish him with all the information which he requires.

2. The carrier shall not be under any duty to enquire into either the accuracy or the adequacy of such documents and information. The sender shall be liable to the carrier for any damage caused by the absence, inadequacy or irregularity of such documents and information, except in the case of some wrongful act or neglect on the part of the carrier.

3. The liability of the carrier for the consequences arising from the loss or incorrect use of the documents specified in and accompanying the consignment note or deposited with the carrier shall be that of an agent, provided that the compensation payable by the carrier shall not exceed that payable in the event of loss of the goods.

Article 12

1. The sender has the right to dispose of the goods, in particular by asking the carrier to stop the goods in transit, to change the place at which delivery is to take place or to deliver the goods to a consignee other than the consignee indicated in the consignment notice.

2. The right shall cease to exist when the second copy of the consignment note is handed to the consignee or when the consignee exercises his right under Article 13, paragraph 1; from that time onwards the carrier shall obey the orders of the consignee.

3. The consignee shall, however, have the right of disposal from the time when the consignment note is drawn up, if the sender makes an entry to that effect in the consignment note.

4. If in exercising his right of disposal the consignee has ordered the delivery of the goods to another person, that other person shall not be entitled to name other consignees.

5. The exercise of the right of disposal shall be subject to the following conditions—
   (a) that the sender or, in the case referred to in paragraph 3 of this Article, the consignee who wishes to exercise the right produces the first copy of the consignment note on which the new instructions to the carrier have been entered and indemnifies the carrier against all expenses, loss and damage involved in carrying out such instruction;
   (b) that the carrying out of such instructions is possible at the time when the instructions reach the person who is to carry them out and does not either interfere with the normal working of the carrier's undertaking or prejudice the senders or consignees of other consignments;
   (c) that the instructions do not result in a division of the consignment.

6. When, by reason of the provisions of paragraph 5(b) of this Article, the carrier cannot carry out the instructions which he receives, he shall immediately notify the person who give him such instructions.

7. A carrier who has not carried out the instructions given under the conditions provided for in this Article, or who has carried them out without requiring the first copy of the consignment note to be produced, shall be liable to the person entitled to make a claim for any loss or damage caused thereby.

Article 13

1. After arrival of the goods at the place designated for delivery, the consignee shall be entitled to require the carrier to deliver to him, against a receipt, the second copy of the consignment note and the goods. If the loss of the goods is established or if the goods have not arrived after the expiry of the period provided for in Article 19, the consignee shall be entitled to enforce in his own name against the carrier any rights arising from the contract of carriage.

2.   The consignee who avails himself of the rights granted to him under paragraph 1 of this Article shall pay the charges shown to be due on the consignment note, but in the event of dispute on this matter the carrier shall not be required to deliver the goods unless security has been furnished by the consignee.

Article 14

1.   If for any reason it is or becomes impossible to carry out the contract in accordance with the terms laid down in the consignment note before the goods reach the place designated for delivery, the carrier shall ask for instructions from the person entitled to dispose of the goods in accordance with the provisions of Article 12.

2.   Nevertheless, if circumstances are such as to allow the carriage to be carried out under conditions differing from those laid down in the consignment note and if the carrier has been unable to obtain instructions in reasonable time from the person entitled to dispose of the goods in accordance with the provisions of Article 12, he shall take such steps as seem to him to be in the best interests of the person entitled to dispose of the goods.

Article 15

1.   Where circumstances prevent delivery of the goods after their arrival at the place designated for delivery, the carrier shall ask the sender for his instructions. If the consignee refuses the goods the sender shall be entitled to dispose of them without being obliged to produce the first copy of the consignment note.

2.   Even if he has refused the goods, the consignee may nevertheless require delivery so long as the carrier has not received instruction to the contrary from the sender.

3.   When circumstances preventing delivery of the goods arise after the consignee, in exercise of his rights under Article 12, paragraph 3, has given an order for the goods to be delivered to another person, paragraphs 1 and 2 of this Article shall apply as if the consignee were the sender and that other person were the consignee.

Article 16

1.   The carrier shall be entitled to recover the cost of his request for instructions and any expenses entailed in carrying out such instructions, unless such expenses were caused by the wrongful act or neglect of the carrier.

2.   In the cases referred to in Article 14, paragraph 1, and in Article 15, the carrier may immediately unload the goods for account of the person entitled to dispose of them and thereupon the carriage shall be deemed to be at an end. The carrier shall then hold the goods on behalf of the person so entitled. He may however entrust them to a third party, and in that case he shall not be under any liability except for the exercise of reasonable care in the choice of such third party. The charges due under the consignment note and all other expenses shall remain chargeable against the goods.

3.   The carrier may sell the goods, without awaiting instructions from the person entitled to dispose of them, if the goods are perishable or their condition warrants such a course, or when the storage expenses would be out of proportion to the value of the goods. He may also proceed to the sale of the goods in other cases if after the expiry of a reasonable period he has not received from the person entitled to dispose of the goods instructions to the contrary which he may reasonably be required to carry out.

4.   If the goods have been sold pursuant to this Article, the proceeds of sale, after deduction of the expenses chargeable against the goods, shall be placed at the disposal of the person entitled to dispose of the goods. If these charges exceed the proceeds of sale, the carrier shall be entitled to the difference.

5. The procedure in the case of sale shall be determined by the law or custom of the place where the goods are situated.

CHAPTER IV
LIABILITY OF THE CARRIER

Article 17

1. The carrier shall be liable for the total or partial loss of the goods and for damage thereto occurring between the time when he takes over the goods and time of delivery, as well as for any delay in delivery.
2. The carrier shall however be relieved of liability if the loss, damage or delay was caused by the wrongful act or neglect of the claimant, by the instructions of the claimant given otherwise than as the result of a wrongful act or neglect on the part of the carrier, by inherent vice of the goods or through circumstances which the carrier could not avoid and the consequences of which he was unable to prevent.
3. The carrier shall not be relieved of liability by reason of the defective condition of the vehicle used by him in order to perform the carriage, or by reason of the wrongful act or neglect of the person from whom he may have hired the vehicle or of the agents or servants of the latter.
4. Subject to Article 18, paragraphs 2 to 5, the carrier shall be relieved of liability when the loss or damage arises from the special risks inherent in one or more of the following circumstances—
    (a) use of open unsheeted vehicles, when their use has been expressly agreed and specified in the consignment note;
    (b) the lack of, or defective condition of packing in the case of goods which, by their nature, are liable to wastage or to be damaged when not packed or when not properly packed;
    (c) handling, loading, stowage or unloading of the goods by sender, the consignee or persons acting on behalf of the sender or the consignee;
    (d) the nature of certain kinds of goods which particularly exposes them to total or partial loss or to damage, especially through breakage, rust, decay, desiccation, leakage, normal wastage, or the action of moth or vermin;
    (e) insufficiency or inadequacy of marks or numbers on the packages;
    (f) the carriage of livestock.
5. Where under this Article the carrier is not under any liability in respect of some of the factors causing the loss, damage or delay, he shall only be liable to the extent that those factors for which he is liable under this Article have contributed to the loss, damage or delay, he shall only be liable to the extent that those factors for which he is liable under this Article have contributed to the loss, damage or delay.

Article 18

1. The burden of proving that loss, damage or delay was due to one of the causes specified in Article 17, paragraph 2, shall rest upon the carrier.
2. When the carrier established that in the circumstances of the case, the loss or damage could be attributed to one or more of the special risks referred to in Article 17, paragraph 4, it shall be presumed that it was so caused. The claimant shall however be entitled to prove that the loss or damage was not, in fact, attributable either wholly or partly to one of these risks.
3. This presumption shall not apply in the circumstances set out in Article 17, paragraph 4 (a), if there has been an abnormal shortage, or a loss of any package.
4. If the carriage is performed in vehicles specially equipped to protect the goods from the effects of heat, cold, variations in temperature or the humidity of the air, the carrier shall not be entitled to claim the benefit of Article 17, paragraph 4(d),

unless he proves that all steps incumbent on him in the circumstances with respect to the choice, maintenance and use of such equipment were taken and that he complied with any special instructions issued to him.

5.   The carrier shall not be entitled to claim the benefit of Article 17, paragraph 4(f), unless he proves that all steps normally incumbent on him in the circumstances were taken and that he complied with any special instructions issued to him.

Article 19

Delay in delivery shall be said to occur when the goods have not been delivered within the agreed time-limit or when, failing an agreed time-limit, the actual duration of the carriage having regard to the circumstances of the case, and in particular, in the case of partial loads, the time required for making up a complete load in the normal way, exceeds the time it would be reasonable to allow a diligent carrier.

Article 20

1.   The fact that goods have not been delivered within thirty days following the expiry of the agreed time-limit, or, if there is no agreed time-limit, within sixty days from the time when the carrier took over the goods, shall be conclusive evidence of the loss of the goods, and the person entitled to make a claim may thereupon treat them as lost.

2.   The person so entitled may, on receipt of compensation for the missing goods, request in writing that he shall be notified immediately should the goods be recovered in the course of the year following the payment of compensation. He shall be given a written acknowledgement of such request.

3.   Within the thirty days following receipt of such notification, the person entitled as aforesaid may require the goods to be delivered to him against payment of the charges shown to be due on the consignment note and also against refund of the compensation he received less any charges included therein but without prejudice to any claims to compensation for delay in delivery under Article 23 and, where applicable, Article 26.

4.   In the absence of the request mentioned in paragraph 2 or of any instructions given within the period of thirty days specified in paragraph 3, or if the goods are not recovered until more than one year after the payment of compensation, the carrier shall be entitled to deal with them in accordance with the law of the place where the goods are situated.

Article 21

Should the goods have been delivered to the consignee without collection of the 'cash on delivery' charge which should have been collected by the carrier under the terms of the contract of carriage, the carrier shall be liable to the sender for compensation not exceeding the amount of such charge without prejudice to his right of action against the consignee.

Article 22

1.   When the sender hands goods of a dangerous nature to the carrier, he shall inform the carrier of the exact nature of the danger and indicate, if necessary, the precautions to be taken. If this information has not been entered in the consignment note, the burden of proving, by some other means, that the carrier knew the exact nature of the danger constituted by the carriage of the said goods shall rest upon the sender or the consignee.

2.   Goods of a dangerous nature which, in the circumstances referred to in paragraph 1 of this Article, the carrier did not know were dangerous, may, at any time or place,

be unloaded, destroyed or rendered harmless by the carrier without compensation; further, the sender shall be liable for all expenses, loss or damage arising out of their handing over for carriage or of their carriage.

Article 23

1. When, under the provisions of this Convention, a carrier is liable for compensation in respect of total or partial loss of goods, such compensation shall be calculated by reference to the value of the goods at the place and time at which they were accepted for carriage.
2. The value of the goods shall be fixed accordingly to the commodity exchange price or, if there is no such price, according to the current market price or, if there is no commodity exchange price or current market price, by reference to the normal value of goods of the same kind and quality.
3. Compensation shall not, however, exceed 8.33 units of account per kilogram of gross weight short.
4. In addition, the carriage charges, Customs duties and other charges incurred in respect of the carriage of the goods shall be refunded in full in case of total loss and in proportion to the loss sustained in case of partial loss, but no further damages shall be payable.
5. In the case of delay, if the claimant proves that damage has resulted therefrom the carrier shall pay compensation for such damage not exceeding the carriage charges.
6. Higher compensation may only be claimed where the value of the goods or a special interest in delivery has been declared in accordance with Articles 24 and 26.
7. The unit of account mentioned in this Convention is the Special Drawing Right as defined by the International Monetary Fund. The amount mentioned in paragraph 3 of this Article shall be converted into the national currency of the State of the Court seised of the case on the basis of the value of that currency on the date of the judgment or the date agreed upon by the Parties.

Article 24

The sender may, against payment of a surcharge to be agreed upon, declare in the consignment note a value for the goods exceeding the limit laid down in Article 23, paragraph 3, and in that case the amount of the declared value shall be substituted for that limit.

Article 25

1. In case of damage, the carrier shall be liable for the amount by which the goods have diminished in value, calculated by reference to the value of the goods fixed in accordance with Article 23, paragraphs 1, 2 and 4.
2. The compensation may not, however, exceed—
   (a) if the whole consignment has been damaged the amount payable in the case of total loss;
   (b) if part only of the consignment has been damaged, the amount payable in the case of loss of the part affected.

Article 26

1. The sender may, against payment of a surcharge to be agreed upon, fix the amount of a special interest in delivery in the case of loss or damage or of the agreed time-limit being exceeded, by entering such amount in the consignment note.
2. If a declaration of a special interest in delivery has been made, compensation for the additional loss or damage proved may be claimed, up to the total amount of the

interest declared, independently of the compensation provided for in Articles 23, 24 and 25.

Article 27

1.   The claimant shall be entitled to claim interest on compensation payable. Such interest, calculated at five per centum per annum, shall accrue from the date on which the claim was sent in writing to the carrier or, if no such claim has been made, from the date on which legal proceedings were instituted.
2.   When the amounts on which the calculation of the compensation is based are not expressed in the currency of the country in which payment is claimed, conversion shall be at the rate of exchange applicable on the day and at the place of payment of compensation.

Article 28

1.   In cases where, under the law applicable, loss, damage or delay arising out of carriage under this Convention gives rise to an extra-contractual claim, the carrier may avail himself of the provisions of this Convention which exclude his liability or which fix or limit the compensation due.
2.   In cases where the extra-contractual liability for loss, damage or delay of one of the persons for whom the carrier is responsible under the terms of Article 3 is in issue, such person may also avail himself of the provisions of this Convention which exclude the liability of the carrier or which fix or limit the compensation due.

Article 29

1.   The carrier shall not be entitled to avail himself of the provisions of this chapter which exclude or limit his liability or which shift the burden of proof if the damage was caused by his wilful misconduct or by such default on his part as, in accordance with the law of the court or tribunal seised of the case, is considered as equivalent to wilful misconduct.
2.   The same provision shall apply if the wilful misconduct or default is committed by the agents or servants of the carrier or by any other persons of whose services he makes use for the performance of the carriage, when such agents, servants or other persons are acting within the scope of their employment. Furthermore, in such a case such agents, servants or other persons shall not be entitled to avail themselves, with regard to their personal liability, of the provisions of this chapter referred to in paragraph 1.

CHAPTER V
CLAIMS AND ACTIONS

Article 30

1.   If the consignee takes delivery of the goods without duly checking their condition with the carrier or without sending him reservations giving a general indication of the loss or damage, not later than the time of delivery in the case of apparent loss or damage and within seven days of delivery, Sundays and public holidays excepted, in the case of loss or damage which is not apparent, the fact of his taking delivery shall be *prima facie* evidence that he has received the goods in the condition described in the consignment note. In the case of loss or damage which is not apparent the reservations referred to shall be made in writing.
2.   When the condition of the goods has been duly checked by the consignee and the carrier, evidence contradicting the result of this checking shall only be admissible

in the case of loss or damage which is not apparent and provided that the consignee has duly sent reservations in writing to the carrier within seven days, Sundays and public holidays excepted, from the date of checking.

3.   No compensation shall be payable for delay in delivery unless a reservation has been sent in writing to the carrier, within twenty-one days from the time that the goods were placed at the disposal of the consignee.

4.   In calculating the time-limits provided for in this Article the date of delivery, or the date of checking, or the date when the goods were placed at the disposal of the consignee, as the case may be, shall not be included.

5.   The carrier and the consignee shall give each other every reasonable facility for making the requisite investigations and checks.

Article 31

1.   In legal proceedings arising out of carriage under this Convention, the plaintiff may bring an action in any court or tribunal of a contracting country designated by agreement between the parties and, in addition, in the courts or tribunals of a country within whose territory—
    (a)   the defendant is ordinarily resident, or has his principal place of business, or the branch or agency through which the contract of carriage was made; or
    (b)   the place where the goods were taken over by the carrier or the place designated for delivery is situated, and in no other courts or tribunals.

2.   Where in respect of a claim referred to in paragraph 1 of this Article an action is pending before a court or tribunal competent under that paragraph, or where in respect of such a claim a judgment has been entered by such a court or tribunal no new action shall be started between the same parties on the same grounds unless the judgment of the court or tribunal before which the first action was brought is not enforceable in the country in which the fresh proceedings are brought.

3.   When a judgment entered by a court or tribunal of a contracting country in any such action as is referred to in paragraph 1 of this Article has become enforceable in that country, it shall also become enforceable in each of the other contracting States, as soon as the formalities required in the country concerned have been complied with. The formalities shall not permit the merits of the case to be re-opened.

4.   The provisions of paragraph 3 of this Article shall apply to judgments after trial, judgments by default and settlements confirmed by an order of the court, but shall not apply to interim judgments or to awards of damages, in addition to costs against a plaintiff who wholly or partly fails in his action.

5.   Security for costs shall not be required in proceedings arising out of carriage under the Convention from nationals of contracting countries resident or having their place of business in one of those countries.

Article 32

1.   The period of limitation for an action arising out of carriage under this Convention shall be one year. Nevertheless, in the case of wilful misconduct, or such default as in accordance with the law of the court or tribunal seised of the case, is considered as equivalent to wilful misconduct, the period of limitation shall be three years. The period of limitation shall begin to run—
    (a)   in the case of partial loss, damage or delay in delivery, from the date of delivery;
    (b)   in the case of total loss, from the thirtieth day after the expiry of the agreed time-limit or where there is no agreed time-limit from the sixtieth day from the date on which the goods were taken over by the carrier;
    (c)   in all other cases, on the expiry of a period of three months after the making of the contract of carriage.

The day on which the period of limitation begins to run shall not be included in the period.

2.   A written claim shall suspend the period of limitation until such date as the carrier rejects the claim by notification in writing and returns the documents attached thereto. If a part of the claim is admitted the period of limitation shall start to run again only in respect of that part of the claim still in dispute. The burden of proof of the receipt of the claim, or of the reply and of the return of the documents, shall rest with the party relying upon these facts. The running of the period of limitation shall not be suspended by further claims having the same object.

3.   Subject to the provisions of paragraph 2 above, the extension of the period of limitation shall be governed by the law of the court or tribunal seised of the case. That law shall also govern the fresh accrual of rights of action.

4.   A right of action which has become barred by lapse of time may not be exercised by way of counter-claim or set-off.

Article 33

The contract of carriage may contain a clause conferring competence on an arbitration tribunal if the clause conferring competence on the tribunal provides that the tribunal shall apply this Convention.

CHAPTER VI
PROVISIONS RELATING TO CARRIAGE PERFORMED BY SUCCESSIVE CARRIERS

Article 34

If carriage governed by a single contract is performed by successive road carriers, each of them shall be responsible for the performance of the whole operation, the second carrier and each succeeding carrier becoming a party to the contract of carriage, under the terms of the consignment note, by reason of his acceptance of the goods and the consignment note.

Article 35

1.   A carrier accepting the goods from a previous carrier shall give the latter a dated and signed receipt. He shall enter his name and address on the second copy of the consignment note. Where applicable, he shall enter on the second copy of the consignment note and on the receipt reservations of the kind provided for in Article 8, paragraph 2.

2.   The provisions of Article 9 shall apply to the relations between successive carriers.

Article 36

Except in the case of a counter-claim or a set-off raised in an action concerning a claim based on the same contract of carriage, legal proceedings in respect of liability for loss, damage or delay may only be brought against the first carrier, the last carrier or the carrier who was performing that portion of the carriage during which the event causing the loss, damage or delay occurred; an action may be brought at the same time against several of these carriers.

Article 37

A carrier who has paid compensation in compliance with the provisions of this Convention, shall be entitled to recover such compensation, together with interest thereon and all costs and expenses incurred by reason of the claim, from the other carriers who have taken part in the carriage, subject to the following provisions—

(a) the carrier responsible for the loss or damage shall be solely liable for the compensation whether paid by himself or by another carrier;

(b) when the loss or damage has been caused by the action of two or more carriers, each of them shall pay an amount proportionate to his share of liability; should it be impossible to apportion the liability, each carrier shall be liable in proportion to the share of the payment for the carriage which is due to him;

(c) if it cannot be ascertained to which carriers liability is attributable for the loss or damage, the amount of the compensation shall be apportioned between all the carriers as laid down in (b) above.

Article 38

If one of the carriers is insolvent, the share of the compensation due from him and unpaid by him shall be divided among the other carriers in proportion to the share of the payment for the carriage due to them.

Article 39

1. No carrier against whom a claim is made under Articles 37 and 38 shall be entitled to dispute the validity of the payment made by the carrier making the claim if the amount of the compensation was determined by judicial authority after the first mentioned carrier had been given due notice of the proceedings and afforded an opportunity of entering an appearance.

2. A carrier wishing to take proceedings to enforce his right of recovery may make his claim before the competent court or tribunal of the country in which one of the carriers concerned is ordinarily resident, or has his principal place of business or the branch or agency through which the contract of carriage was made. All the carriers concerned may be made defendants in the same action.

3. The provisions of Article 31, paragraphs 3 and 4, shall apply to judgments entered in the proceedings referred to in Articles 37 and 38.

4. The provisions of Article 32 shall apply to claims between carriers. The period of limitation shall, however, begin to run either on the date of the final judicial decision fixing the amount of compensation payable under the provisions of this Convention, or, if there is no such judicial decision, from the actual date of payment.

Article 40

Carriers shall be free to agree among themselves on provisions other than those laid down in Articles 37 and 38.

CHAPTER VII
NULLITY OF STIPULATIONS CONTRARY TO THE CONVENTION

Article 41

1. Subject to the provisions of Article 40, any stipulation which would directly or indirectly derogate from the provisions of this Convention shall be null and void. The nullity of such a stipulation shall not involve the nullity of the other provisions of the contract.

2. In particular, a benefit of insurance in favour of the carrier or any other similar clause, or any clause shifting the burden of proof shall be null and void.

PROTOCOL OF SIGNATURE

1.   This Convention shall not apply to traffic between the United Kingdom of Great Britain and Northern Ireland and the Republic of Ireland.

UNIFORM LAWS ON INTERNATIONAL SALES ACT 1967

CHAPTER 45

1.   **Application of Uniform Law on the International Sale of Goods**
   (1)   In this Act 'the Uniform Law on Sales' means the Uniform Law on the International Sale of Goods forming the Annex to the First Convention and set out, with the modification provided for by Article III of that Convention, in Schedule 1 to this Act; and 'the First Convention' means the Convention relating to a Uniform Law on the International Sale of Goods done at The Hague on 1st July 1964.
   (2)   The Uniform Law on Sales shall, subject to the following provisions of this section, have the force of the law in the United Kingdom.
   (3)   While an Order of Her Majesty in Council is in force declaring that a declaration by the United Kingdom under Article V of the First Convention (application only by choice of parties) has been made and not withdrawn the Uniform Law on Sales shall apply to a contract of sale only if it has been chosen by the parties to the contract as the law of the contract.
   (4)   In determining the extent of the application of the Uniform Law on Sales by virtue of Article 4 thereof (choice of parties) —
       (a) and (b) [Omitted];
       (c)   in relation to a contract made on or after 1 February 1978, no provision of that law shall be so regarded except sections 12 to 15B of the Sale of Goods Act 1979.
   (5) to (8) [Omitted].

2.   **Application of Uniform Law on the Formation of Contracts for the International Sale of Goods**
   (1)   In this Act 'the Uniform Law on Formation' means the Law forming Annex I to the Second Convention as set out, with the modifications provided for by paragraph 3 of Article I of that Convention, in Schedule 2 to this Act; and 'the Second Convention' means the Convention relating to a Uniform Law on the Formation of Contracts for the International Sale of Goods done at The Hague on 1st July 1964.
   (2)   Subject to subsection (3) of this section the Uniform Law on Formation shall have the force of law in the United Kingdom.
   (3)   The Uniform Law on Formation shall not apply to offers, replies and acceptances made before such date as Her Majesty may by Order in Council declare to be the date on which the Second Convention comes into force in respect of the United Kingdom.
   (4)   [Omitted].

3.–5. **[Omitted].**

SCHEDULES

SCHEDULE 1
THE UNIFORM LAW ON THE INTERNATIONAL SALE OF GOODS

CHAPTER I
SPHERE OF APPLICATION OF THE LAW

Article 1

1. The present Law shall apply to contracts of sale of goods entered into by parties whose places of business are in the territories of different Contracting States, in each of the following cases—
   (a) where the contract involves the sale of goods which are at the time of the conclusion of the contract in the course of carriage or will be carried from the territory of one State to the territory of another;
   (b) where the acts constituting the offer and the acceptance have been effected in the territories of different States;
   (c) where delivery of the goods is to be made in the territory of a State other than that within whose territory the acts constituting the offer and the acceptance have been effected.
2. Where a party to the contract does not have a place of business, reference shall be made to his habitual residence.
3. The application of the present Law shall not depend on the nationality of the parties.
4. In the case of contracts by correspondence, offer and acceptance shall be considered to have been effected in the territory of the same State only if the letters, telegrams or other documentary communications which contain them have been sent and received in the territory of that State.
5. For the purpose of determining whether the parties have their places of business or habitual residences in 'different States', any two or more States shall not be considered to be 'different State' if a valid declaration to that effect made under Article 11 of the Convention dated the 1st day of July 1964 relating to a Uniform Law on the International Sale of Goods is in force in respect of them.

Article 2

Rules of private international law shall be excluded for the purposes of the application of the present Law, subject to any provision to the contrary in the said Law.

Article 3

The parties to a contract of sale shall be free to exclude the application thereto of the present Law either entirely or partially. Such exclusion may be express or implied.

Article 4

The present Law shall also apply where it has been chosen as the law of the contract by the parties, whether or not their places of business or their habitual residences are in different States and whether or not such States are Parties to the Convention dated the 1st day of July 1964 relating to the Uniform Law on the International Sale of Goods, to the extent that it does not affect the application of any mandatory provisions of law which would have been applicable if the parties had not chosen the Uniform Law.

Article 5

1.   The present Law shall not apply to sales—
     (a)   of stocks, shares, investment securities, negotiable instruments or money;
     (b)   of any ship, vessel or aircraft, which is or will be subject to registration;
     (c)   of electricity;
     (d)   by authority of law or on execution or distress.
2.   The present Law shall not affect the application of any mandatory provision of national law for the protection of a party to a contract which contemplates the purchase of goods by that party by payment of the price by instalments.

Article 6

Contracts for the supply of goods to be manufactured or produced shall be considered to be sales within the meaning of the present Law, unless the party who orders the goods undertakes to supply an essential and substantial part of the materials necessary for such manufacture or production.

Article 7

The present Law shall apply to sales regardless of the commercial or civil character of the parties or of the contracts.

Article 8

The present Law shall govern only the obligations of the seller and the buyer arising from a contract of sale. In particular, the present Law shall not, except as otherwise expressly provided there, be concerned with the formation of the contract, nor with the effect which the contract may have on the property in the goods sold, nor with the validity of the contract or of any of its provisions or of any usage.

CHAPTER II
GENERAL PROVISIONS

Article 9

1.   The parties shall be bound by any usage which they have expressly or impliedly made applicable to their contract and by any practices which they have established between themselves.
2.   They shall also be bound by usages which reasonable persons in the same situation as the parties usually consider to be applicable to their contract. In the event of conflict with the present Law, the usages shall prevail unless otherwise agreed by the parties.
3.   Where expressions, provisions or forms of contract commonly used in commercial practice are employed, they shall be interpreted according to the meaning usually given to them in the trade concerned.

Article 10

For the purposes of the present Law, a breach of contract shall be regarded as fundamental wherever the party in breach knew, or ought to have known, at the time of the conclusion of the contract, that a reasonable person in the same situation as the other party would not have entered into the contract if he had foreseen the breach and its effects.

Article 11

Where under the present Law an act is required to be performed 'promptly', it shall be performed within as short a period as possible, in the circumstances, from the moment when the act could reasonably be performed.

Article 12

For the purposes of the present Law, the expression 'current price' means a price based upon an official market quotation, or, in the absence of such a quotation, upon those factors which, according to the usage of the market, serve to determine the price.

Article 13

For the purposes of the present Law, the expression 'a party knew or ought to have known', or any similar expression, refers to what should have been known to a reasonable person in the same situation.

Article 14

Communications provided for by the present Law shall be made by the means usual in the circumstances.

Article 15

A contract of sale need not be evidenced by writing and shall not be subject to any other requirements as to form. In particular, it may be proved by means of witnesses.

Article 16

Where under the provisions of the present Law one party to a contract of sale is entitled to require performance of any obligation by the other party, a court shall not be bound to enter or enforce a judgment providing for specific performance except in accordance with the provisions of Article VII of the Convention dated the 1st day of July 1964 relating to a Uniform Law on the International Sale of Goods.

Article 17

Questions concerning matters governed by the present Law which are not expressly settled therein shall be settled in conformity with the general principals on which the present Law is based.

CHAPTER III
OBLIGATIONS OF THE SELLER

Article 18

The seller shall effect delivery of the goods, hand over any documents relating thereto and transfer the property in the goods, as required by the contract and the present Law.

SECTION I—DELIVERY OF THE GOODS

Article 19

1.   Delivery consists in the handing over of goods which conform with the contract.

2.   Where the contract of sale involves carriage of the goods and no other place for delivery has been agreed upon, delivery shall be effected by handing over the goods to the carrier for transmission to the buyer.

3.   Where the goods handed over to the carrier are not clearly appropriated to performance of the contract by being marked with an address or by some other means, the seller shall, in addition to handing over the goods, sent to the buyer notice of the consignment and, if necessary, some document specifying the goods.

SUB-SECTION 1.   OBLIGATIONS OF THE SELLER AS REGARDS THE DATE AND PLACE OF DELIVERY

A—DATE OF DELIVERY

Article 20

Where the parties have agreed upon a date for delivery or where such date is fixed by usage, the seller shall, without the need for any other formality, be bound to deliver the goods at that date, provided that the date thus fixed is determined or determinable by the calendar or is fixed in relation to a definite event, the date of which can be ascertained by the parties.

Article 21

Where by agreement of the parties or by usage delivery shall be effected within a certain period (such as a particular month or season), the seller may fix the precise date of delivery, unless the circumstances indicate that the fixing of the date was reserved to the buyer.

Article 22

Where the date of delivery has not been determined in accordance with the provisions of Articles 20 or 21, the seller shall be bound to deliver the goods within a reasonable time after the conclusion of the contract, regard being had to the nature of the goods and to the circumstances.

B—PLACE OF DELIVERY

Article 23

1.   Where the contract of sale does not involve carriage of the goods, the seller shall deliver the goods at the place where he carried on business at the time of the conclusion of the contract, or, in the absence of a place of business, at his habitual residence.

2.   If the sale relates to specific goods and the parties knew that the goods were at a certain place at the time of the conclusion of the contract, the seller shall deliver the goods at that place. The same rule shall apply if the goods sold are unascertained goods to be taken from a specified stock or if they are to be manufactured or produced at a place known to the parties at the time of the conclusion of the contract.

C—REMEDIES FOR THE SELLER'S FAILURE TO PERFORM HIS OBLIGATIONS AS REGARDS THE DATE AND PLACE OF DELIVERY

Article 24

1.   Where the seller fails to perform his obligations as regards the date or the place of delivery, the buyer may, as provided in Articles 25 to 32—

     (a)   require performance of the contract by the seller;

     (b)   declare the contract avoided.

2.   The buyer may also claim damages as provided in Article 82 or in Articles 84 to 87.

3.   In no case shall the seller be entitled to apply to a court or arbitral tribunal to grant him a period of grace.

Article 25

The buyer shall not be entitled to require performance of the contract by the seller, if it is in conformity with usage and reasonably possible for the buyer to purchase goods to replace those to which the contract relates. In this case the contract shall be *ipso facto* avoided as from the time when such purchases should be effected.

(a)   Remedies as regards the date of delivery

Article 26

1.   Where the failure to deliver the goods at the date fixed amounts to a fundamental breach of the contract, the buyer may either require performance by the seller or declare the contract avoided. He shall inform the seller of his decision within a reasonable time; otherwise the contract shall be *ipso facto* avoided.

2.   If the seller requests the buyer to make known his decision under paragraph 1 of this Article and the buyer does not comply promptly, the contract shall be *ipso facto* avoided.

3.   If the seller has effected delivery before the buyer has made known his decision under paragraph 1 of this Article and the buyer does not exercise promptly his right to declare the contract avoided, the contract cannot be avoided.

4.   Where the buyer has chosen performance of the contract and does not obtain it within a reasonable time, he may declare the contract avoided.

Article 27

1.   Where failure to deliver the goods at the date fixed does not amount to a fundamental breach of the contract, the seller shall retain the right to effect delivery and the buyer shall retain the right to require performance of the contract by the seller.

2.   The buyer may however grant the seller an additional period of time of reasonable length. Failure to deliver the goods at the date fixed shall amount to a fundamental breach of the contract whenever a price for such goods is quoted on a market where the buyer can obtain them.

Article 28

Failure to deliver the goods at the date fixed shall amount to a fundamental breach of the contract whenever a price for such goods is quoted on a market where the buyer can obtain them.

Article 29

Where the seller tenders delivery of the goods before the date fixed, the buyer may accept or reject delivery; if he accepts, he may reserve the right to claim damages in accordance with Article 82.

(b) Remedies as regards the place of delivery

Article 30

1. Where failure to deliver the goods at the place fixed amounts to a fundamental breach of the contract, and failure to deliver the goods at the date fixed would also amount to a fundamental breach, the buyer may either require performance of the contract by the seller or declare the contract avoided. The buyer shall inform the seller of his decision within a reasonable time; otherwise the contract shall be *ipso facto* avoided.
2. If the seller requests the buyer to make known his decision under paragraph 1 of this Article and the buyer does not comply promptly, the contract shall be *ipso facto* avoided.
3. If the seller has transported the goods to the place fixed before the buyer has made known his decision under paragraph 1 of this Article and the buyer does not exercise promptly his right to declare the contract avoided, the contract cannot be avoided.

Article 31

1. In cases not provided for in Article 30, the seller shall retain the right to effect delivery at the place fixed and the buyer shall retain the right to require performance of the contract by the seller.
2. The buyer may however grant the seller an additional period of time of reasonable length. Failure to deliver within this period at the place fixed shall amount to a fundamental breach of the contract.

Article 32

1. If delivery is to be effected by handing over the goods to a carrier and the goods have been handed over at a place other than that fixed, the buyer may declare the contract avoided, whenever the failure to deliver the goods at the place fixed amounts to a fundamental breach of the contract. He shall lose this right if he has not promptly declared the contract avoided.
2. The buyer shall have the same right, in the circumstances and on the conditions provided in paragraph 1 of this Article, if the goods have been despatched to some place other than that fixed.
3. If despatch from a place or to a place other than that fixed does not amount to a fundamental breach of the contract, the buyer may only claim damages in accordance with Article 82.

SUB-SECTION 2. OBLIGATIONS OF THE SELLER AS REGARDS THE CONFORMITY OF THE GOODS

A—LACK OF CONFORMITY

Article 33

1. The seller shall not have fulfilled his obligation to deliver the goods, where he has handed over—
   - (a) part only of the goods sold or a larger or a smaller quantity of the goods than he contracted to sell;
   - (b) goods which are not those to which the contract relates or goods of a different kind;

(c)   goods which lack the qualities of a sample or model which the seller has handed over or sent to the buyer, unless the seller has submitted it without any express or implied undertaking that the goods would conform therewith;

(d)   goods which do not possess the qualities necessary for their ordinary or commercial use;

(e)   goods which do not possess the qualities for some particular purpose expressly or impliedly contemplated by the contract;

(f)   in general, goods which do not possess the qualities and characteristics expressly or impliedly contemplated by the contract.

2.   No difference in quantity, lack of part of the goods or absence of any quality or characteristic shall be taken into consideration where it is not material.

Article 34

In the cases to which Article 33 relates, the rights conferred on the buyer by the present Law exclude all other remedies based on lack of conformity of the goods.

Article 35

1.   Whether the goods are in conformity with the contract shall be determined by their condition at the time when risk passes. However, if risk does not pass because of a declaration of avoidance of the contract or of a demand for other goods in replacement, the conformity of the goods with the contract shall be determined by their condition at the time when risk would have passed had they been in conformity with the contract.

2.   The seller shall be liable for the consequences of any lack of conformity occurring after the time fixed in paragraph 1 of this Article if it was due to an act of the seller or of a person for whose conduct he is responsible.

Article 36

The seller shall not be liable for the consequences of any lack of conformity of the kind referred to in sub-paragraphs (d), (e) or (f) of paragraph 1 of Article 33, if at the time of the conclusion of the contract the buyer knew, or could not have been unaware of, such lack of conformity.

Article 37

If the seller has handed over goods before the date fixed for delivery he may, up to that date, deliver other goods which are in conformity with the contract or remedy any defects in the goods handed over, provided that the exercise of this right does not cause the buyer either unreasonable inconvenience or unreasonable expense.

B—ASCERTAINMENT AND NOTIFICATION OF LACK OF CONFORMITY

Article 38

1.   The buyer shall examine the goods, or cause them to be examined, promptly.

2.   In case of carriage of the goods the buyer shall examine them at the place of destination.

3.   If the goods are redespatched by the buyer without transhipment and the seller knew or ought to have known, at the time when the contract was concluded, of the possibility of such redespatch, examination of the goods may be deferred until they arrive at the new destination.

4.   The methods of examination shall be governed by the agreement of the parties or, in the absence of such agreement, by the law or usage of the place where the examination is to be effected.

Article 39

1.   The buyer shall lose the right to rely on a lack of conformity of the goods if he has not given the seller notice thereof promptly after he has discovered the lack of conformity or ought to have discovered it. If a defect which could not have been revealed by the examination of the goods provided for in Article 38 is found later, the buyer may nonetheless rely on that defect, provided that he gives the seller notice thereof promptly after its discovery. In any event, the buyer shall lose the right to rely on a lack of conformity of the goods if he has not given notice thereof to the seller within a period of two years from the date on which the goods were handed over, unless the lack of conformity constituted a breach of a guarantee covering a longer period.
2.   In giving notice to the seller of any lack of conformity, the buyer shall specify its nature and invite the seller to examine the goods or to cause them to be examined by his agent.
3.   Where any notice referred to in paragraph 1 of this Article has been sent by letter, telegram or other appropriate means, the fact that such notice is delayed or fails to arrive at its destination shall not deprive the buyer of the right to rely thereon.

Article 40

The seller shall not be entitled to rely on the provisions of Articles 38 and 39 if the lack of conformity relates to facts of which he knew, or of which he could not have been unaware, and which he did not disclose.

C—REMEDIES FOR LACK OF CONFORMITY

Article 41

1.   Where the buyer has given due notice to the seller of the failure of the goods to confirm with the contract, the buyer may, as provided in Articles 42 to 46—
      (a)   require performance of the contract by the seller;
      (b)   declare the contract avoided;
      (c)   reduce the price.
2.   The buyer may also claim damages as provided in Article 82 or in Articles 84 to 87.

Article 42

1.   The buyer may require the seller to perform the contract—
      (a)   if the sale relates to goods to be produced or manufactured by the seller, by remedying defects in the goods, provided the seller is in a position to remedy the defects;
      (b)   if the sales relates to specific goods, by delivering the goods to which the contract refers or the missing part thereof;
      (c)   if the sale relates to unascertained goods, by delivering other goods which are in conformity with the contract or by delivering the missing part or quantity, except where the purchase of goods in replacement is in conformity with usage and reasonably possible.
2.   If the buyer does not obtain performance of the contract by the seller within a reasonable time, he shall retain the rights provided in Articles 43 to 46.

Article 43

The buyer may declare the contract avoided if the failure of the goods to conform to the contract and also the failure to deliver on the date fixed amount to fundamental breaches of the contract. The buyer shall lose his right to declare the contract avoided if he does not exercise it promptly after giving the seller notice of the lack of conformity or, in the case to which paragraph 2 of Article 42 applies, after the expiration of the period referred to in that paragraph.

Article 44

1. In cases not provided for in Article 43, the seller shall retain, after the date fixed for the delivery of the goods, the right to deliver any missing part or quantity of the goods or to deliver other goods which are in conformity with the contract or to remedy any defect in the goods handed over, provided that the exercise of this right does not cause the buyer either unreasonable inconvenience or unreasonable expense.
2. The buyer may however fix an additional period of time of reasonable length for the further delivery or for the remedying of the defect. If at the expiration of the additional period the seller has not delivered to goods or remedied the defect, the buyer may choose between requiring the performance of the contract or reducing the price in accordance with Article 46 or, provided that he does so promptly, declare the contract avoided.

Article 45

1. Where the seller has handed over part only of the goods or an insufficient quantity or where part only of the goods handed over is in conformity with the contract, the provisions of Articles 43 and 44 shall apply in respect of the part or quantity which is missing or which does not conform with the contract.
2. The buyer may declare the contract avoided in its entirety only if the failure to effect delivery completely and in conformity with the contract amounts to a fundamental breach of the contract.

Article 46

Where the buyer has neither obtained performance of the contract by the seller nor declared the contract avoided, the buyer may reduce the price in the same proportion as the value of the goods at the time of the conclusion of the contract has been diminished because of their lack of conformity with the contract.

Article 47

Where the seller has proffered to the buyer a quantity of unascertained goods greater than that provided for in the contract, the buyer may reject or accept the excess quantity. If the buyer rejects the excess quantity, the seller shall be liable only for damages in accordance with Article 82. If the buyer accepts the whole or part of the excess quantity, he shall pay for it at the contract rate.

Article 48

The buyer may exercise the rights provided in Articles 43 to 46, even before the time fixed for delivery, if it is clear that goods which would be handed over would not be in conformity with the contract.

Article 49

1.   The buyer shall lose his right to reply on lack of conformity with the contract at the expiration of a period of one year after he has given notice as provided in Article 39, unless he has been prevented from exercising his right because of fraud on the part of the seller.

2.   After the expiration of this period, the buyer shall not be entitled to rely on the lack of conformity, even by way of defence to an action. Nevertheless, if the buyer has not paid for the goods and provided that he has given due notice of the lack of conformity promptly, as provided in Article 39, he may advance as a defence to a claim for payment of the price a claim for a reduction in the price or for damages.

SECTION II—HANDING OVER DOCUMENTS

Article 50

Where the seller is bound to hand over to the buyer any documents relating to the goods, he shall do so at the time and place fixed by the contract or by usage.

Article 51

If the seller fails to hand over the documents as provided in Article 50 at the time and place fixed or if he hands over documents which are not in conformity with those which he was bound to hand over, the buyer shall have the same rights as those provided under Articles 24 to 32 or under Articles 41 to 49, as the case may be.

SECTION III—TRANSFER OF PROPERTY

Article 52

1.   Where the goods are subject to a right or claim of a third person, the buyer, unless he agreed to take the goods subject to such right or claim, shall notify the seller of such right or claim, unless the seller already knows thereof, and request that the goods should be freed therefrom within reasonable time or that other goods free from all rights and claims of third persons to be delivered to him by the seller.

2.   If the seller complies with a request made under paragraph 1 of this Article and the buyer nevertheless suffers a loss, the buyer may claim damages in accordance with Article 82.

3.   If the seller fails to comply with a request made under paragraph 1 of the Article and a fundamental breach of the contract results thereby, the buyer may declare the contract avoided and claim damages in accordance with Articles 84 to 87. If the buyer does not declare the contract avoided or if there is no fundamental breach of the contract, the buyer shall have the right to claim damages in accordance with Article 82.

4.   The buyer shall lose his right to declare the contract avoided if he fails to act in accordance with paragraph 1 of this Article within a reasonable time from the moment when he became aware or ought to have become aware of the right or claim of the third person in respect of the goods.

Article 53

The rights conferred on the buyer by Article 52 exclude all other remedies based on the fact that the seller has failed to perform his obligation to transfer the property in the goods or that the goods are subject to a right or claim of a third person.

SECTION IV—OTHER OBLIGATIONS OF THE SELLER

Article 54

1. If the seller is bound to despatch the goods to the buyer, he shall make, in the usual way and on the usual terms, such contracts as are necessary for the carriage of the goods to the place fixed.
2. If the seller is not bound by the contract to effect insurance in respect of the carriage of the goods, he shall provide the buyer, at his request, with all information necessary to enable him to effect such insurance.

Article 55

1. If the seller fails to perform any obligation other than those referred to in Articles 20 to 53, the buyer may—
   (a) where such failure amounts to a fundamental breach of the contract, declare the contract avoided, provided that he does so promptly, and claim damages in accordance with Articles 84 to 87, or
   (b) in any other case, claim damages in accordance with Article 82.
2. The buyer may also require performance by the seller of his obligation unless the contract is avoided.

CHAPTER IV
OBLIGATIONS OF THE BUYER

Article 56

The buyer shall pay the price for the goods and take delivery of them, as required by the contract and the present law.

SECTION I—PAYMENT OF THE PRICE

A—FIXING THE PRICE

Article 57

Where a contract has been concluded but does not state a price or make provision for the determination of the price, the buyer shall be bound to pay the price generally charged by the seller at the time of the conclusion of the contract.

Article 58

Where the price is fixed according to the weight of the goods, it shall, in case of doubt, be determined by the net weight.

B—PLACE AND DATE OF PAYMENT

Article 59

1. The buyer shall pay the price to the seller at the seller's place of business or, if he does not have a place of business, at his habitual residence, or where the payment is to be made against the handing over of the goods or of documents, at the place where such handing over takes place.

2.   Where in consequence of a change in the place of business or habitual residence of the seller subsequent to the conclusion of the contract, the expenses incidental to payment are increased, such increase shall be borne by the seller.

Article 60

Where the parties have agreed upon a date for the payment of the price or where such a date is fixed by usage, the buyer shall, without the need for any other formality, pay the price at that date.

C—REMEDIES FOR NON-PAYMENT

Article 61

1.   If the buyer fails to pay the price in accordance with the contract and with the present law, the seller may require the buyer to perform his obligation.
2.   The seller shall not be entitled to require payment of the price by the buyer if it is in conformity with usage and reasonably possible for the seller to resell the goods. In that case the contract shall be *ipso facto* avoided as from the time when such resale should be effected.

Article 62

1.   Where failure to pay the price at the date fixed amounts to a fundamental breach of the contract, the seller may either require the buyer to pay the price or declare the contract avoided. He shall inform the buyer of his decision within a reasonable time; otherwise the contract shall be *ipso facto* avoided.
2.   Where the failure to pay the price at the date fixed does not amount to a fundamental breach of the contract, the seller may grant to the buyer an additional period of time of reasonable length. If the buyer has not paid the price at the expiration of the additional period, the seller may either require the payment of the price by the buyer or provided that he does so promptly, declare the contract avoided.

Article 63

1.   Where the contract is avoided because of failure to pay the price, the seller shall have the right to claim damages in accordance with Articles 84 to 87.
2.   Where the contract is not avoided, the seller shall have the right to claim damages in accordance with Articles 82 and 83.

Article 64

In no case shall the buyer be entitled to apply to a court or arbitral tribunal to grant him a period of grace for the payment of the price.

SECTION II—TAKING DELIVERY

Article 65

Taking delivery consists in the buyer's doing all such acts as are necessary in order to enable the seller to hand over the goods and actually taking them over.

Article 66

1. Where the buyer's failure to take delivery of the goods in accordance with the contract amounts to a fundamental breach of the contract or gives the seller good grounds for fearing that the buyer will not pay the price, the seller may declare the contract avoided.
2. Where the failure to take delivery of the goods does not amount to a fundamental breach of contract, the seller may grant to the buyer an additional period, the seller may declare the contract avoided, provided that he does so promptly.

Article 67

1. If the contract reserves to the buyer the right subsequently to determine the form, measurement or other features of the goods (sale by specification) and he fails to make such specification either on the date expressly or impliedly agreed upon or within a reasonable time after receipt of a request from the seller, the seller may declare the contract avoided, provided that he does so promptly, or to make the specification himself in accordance with the requirements of the buyer in so far as these are known to him.
2. If the seller makes the specification himself, he shall inform the buyer of the details thereof and shall fix a reasonable period of time within which the buyer may submit a different specification. If the buyer fails to do so the specification made by the seller shall be binding.

Article 68

1. Where the contract is avoided because of the failure of the buyer to accept delivery of the goods or to make a specification, the seller shall have the right to claim damages in accordance with Articles 84 to 87.
2. Where the contract is not avoided, the seller shall have the right to claim damages in accordance with Article 82.

SECTION III—OTHER OBLIGATIONS OF THE BUYER

Article 69

The buyer shall take the steps provided for in the contract, by usage or by laws and regulations in force, for the purpose of making provision for or guaranteeing payment of the price, such as the acceptance of a bill of exchange, the opening of a documentary credit or the giving of a banker's guarantee.

Article 70

1. If the buyer fails to perform any obligation other than those referred to in Sections I and II of this Chapter, the seller may—
   (a) where such failure amounts to a fundamental breach of the contract, declare the contract avoided, provided that he does so promptly, and claim damages in accordance with Articles 84 to 87; or
   (b) in any other case, claim damages in accordance with Article 82.
2. The seller may also require performance by the buyer of his obligation, unless the contract is avoided.

CHAPTER V
PROVISIONS COMMON TO THE OBLIGATIONS OF THE SELLER
AND OF THE BUYER

SECTION I—CONCURRENCE BETWEEN DELIVERY
OF THE GOODS AND PAYMENT OF THE PRICE

Article 71

Except as otherwise provided in Article 72, delivery of the goods and payment of the price shall be concurrent conditions. Nevertheless, the buyer shall not be obliged to pay the price until he has had an opportunity to examine the goods.

Article 72

1.   Where the contract involves carriage of the goods and where delivery is by virtue of paragraph 2 of Article 19, effected by handing over the goods to the carrier, the seller may either postpone despatch of the goods until he receives payment or proceed to despatch them on terms that reserve to himself the right of disposal of the goods during transit. In the latter case, he may require that the goods shall not be handed over to the buyer at the place of destination except against payment of the price and the buyer shall not be bound to pay the price until he has had an opportunity to examine the goods.
2.   Nevertheless, when the contract requires payment against documents, the buyer shall not be entitled to refuse payment of the price on the ground that he has not had the opportunity to examine the goods.

Article 73

1.   Each party may suspend the performance of his obligations whenever, after the conclusion of the contract, the economic situation of the other party appears to have become so difficult that there is good reason to fear that he will not perform a material part of his obligations.
2.   If the seller has already despatched the goods before the economic situation of the buyer described in paragraph 1 of this Article becomes evident, he may prevent the handing over of the goods to the buyer even if the latter holds a document which entitles him to obtain them.
3.   Nevertheless, the seller shall not be entitled to prevent the handing over of the goods if they are claimed by a third person who is a lawful holder of a document which entitles him to obtain the goods unless the document contains a reservation concerning the effects of its transfer or unless the seller can prove that the holder of the document when he acquired it, knowingly acted to the detriment of the seller.

SECTION II—EXEMPTIONS

Article 74

1.   Where one of the parties has not performed one of his obligations, he shall not be liable for such non-performance if he can prove that it was due to circumstances which according to the intention of the parties at the time of the conclusion of the contract, he was not bound to take into account or to avoid or to overcome; in the absence of any expression of the intention of the parties, regard shall be had to what reasonable persons in the same situation would have intended.

2. Where the circumstances which gave rise to the non-performance of the obligation constituted only a temporary impediment to performance, the party in default shall nevertheless be permanently relieved of his obligation if, by reason of the delay, performance would be so radically changed as to amount to the performance of an obligation quite different from that contemplated by the contract.

3. The relief provided by this Article for one of the parties shall not include the avoidance of the contract under some other provision of the present Law or deprive the other party of any right which he has under the present Law to reduce the price, unless the circumstances which entitled the first party to relief were caused by the act of the other party or of some person for whose conduct he was responsible.

SECTION III—SUPPLEMENTARY RULES CONCERNING THE AVOIDANCE OF THE CONTRACT

A—SUPPLEMENTARY GROUNDS FOR AVOIDANCE

Article 75

1. Where, in the case of contracts for delivery of goods by instalments, by reason of any failure by one party of his obligations under the contract in respect of any instalment, the other party has good reason to fear failure of performance in respect of future instalments, he may declare the contract avoided for the future, provided that he does so promptly.

2. The buyer may also, provided that he does so promptly, declare the contract avoided in respect of future deliveries or in respect of deliveries already made or both, if by reason of their interdependence such deliveries would be worthless to him.

Article 76

Where prior to the date fixed for performance of the contract it is clear that one of the parties will commit a fundamental breach of the contract, the other party shall have the right to declare the contract avoided.

Article 77

Where the contract has been avoided under Article 75 or Article 76, the party declaring the contract avoided may claim damages in accordance with Articles 84 to 87.

B—EFFECTS OF AVOIDANCE

Article 78

1. Avoidance of the contract releases both parties from their obligations thereunder, subject to any damages which may be due.

2. If one party has performed the contract either wholly or in part, he may claim the return of whatever he has supplied or paid under the contract. If both parties are required to make restitution, they shall do so concurrently.

Article 79

1. The buyer shall lose his right to declare the contract avoided where it is impossible for him to return the goods in the condition in which he received them.

2. Nevertheless, the buyer may declare the contract avoided—

(a)   if the goods or part of the goods have perished or deteriorated as a result of the defect which justifies the avoidance;

(b)   if the goods or part of the goods have perished or deteriorated as a result of the examination prescribed in Article 38;

(c)   if part of the goods have been consumed or transformed by the buyer in the course of normal use before the lack of conformity with the contract was discovered;

(d)   if the impossibility of returning the goods or of returning them in the condition in which they were received is not due to the act of the buyer, or of some other person for whose conduct he is responsible;

(e)   if the deterioration of transformation of the goods is unimportant.

Article 80

The buyer who has lost the right to declare the contract avoided by virtue of Article 79 shall retain all the other rights conferred on him by the present Law.

Article 81

1.   Where the seller is under an obligation to refund the price, he shall also be liable for the interest thereon at the rate fixed by Article 83, as from the date of payment.

2.   The buyer shall be liable to account to the seller for all benefits which he has derived from the goods or part of them, as the case may be—

(a)   where he is under an obligation to return the goods or part of them;

(b)   where it is impossible for him to return the goods or part of them, but the contract is nevertheless avoided.

SECTION IV—SUPPLEMENTARY RULES CONCERNING DAMAGES

A—DAMAGES WHERE THE CONTRACT IS NOT AVOIDED

Article 82

Where the contract is not avoided, damages for a breach of contract by one party shall consist of a sum equal to the loss of profit, suffered by the other party. Such damages shall not exceed the loss which the party in breach ought to have foreseen at the time of the conclusion of the contract, in the light of the facts and matters which then were known or ought to have been known to him, as a possible consequence of the breach of the contract.

Article 83

Where the breach of contract consists of delay in the payment of the price, the seller shall in any event be entitled to interest on such sum as in arrear at a rate equal to the official discount rate in the country where he has his place of business, or if he has no place of business, his habitual residence, plus 1%.

B—DAMAGES WHERE THE CONTRACT IS AVOIDED

Article 84

1.   In the case of avoidance of the contract, where there is a current price for the goods, damages shall be equal to the difference between the price fixed by the contract and the current price on the date on which the contract is avoided.

2.   In calculating the amount of damages under paragraph 1 of this Article, the current price to be taken into account shall be that prevailing in the market in which the transaction took place, if there is no such current price or if its application is inappropriate, the price in a market which serves as a reasonable substitute, making due allowance for differences in the cost of transporting goods.

Article 85

If the buyer has bought goods in replacement or the seller has resold goods in a reasonable manner, he may recover the difference between the contract price and the price paid for the goods bought in replacement or that obtained by the resale.

Article 86

The damages referred to in Articles 84 and 85 may be increased by the amount of any reasonable expenses incurred as a result of the breach or up to the amount of any loss, including loss of profit, which should have been foreseen by the party in breach, at the time of the conclusion of the contract, in the light of the facts and matters which were known or ought to have been known to him, as a possible consequence of the breach of the contract.

Article 87

If there is no current price for the goods, damages shall be calculated on the same basis as that provided in Article 82.

C—GENERAL PROVISIONS CONCERNING DAMAGES

Article 88

The party who relies on a breach of the contract shall adopt all reasonable measures to mitigate the loss resulting from the breach. If he fails to adopt such measures, the party in breach may claim reduction in the damages.

Article 89

In case of fraud, damages shall be determined by the rules applicable in respect of contracts of sale not governed by the present law.

SECTION V—EXPENSES

Article 90

The expenses of delivery shall be borne by the seller; all expenses after delivery shall be borne by the buyer.

SECTION VI—PRESERVATION OF THE GOODS

Article 91

Where the buyer is in delay in taking delivery of the goods or in paying the price, the seller shall take reasonable steps to preserve the goods; he shall have the right to retain them until he has been reimbursed his reasonable expenses by the buyer.

Article 92

1. Where the goods have been received by the buyer, he shall take reasonable steps to preserve them if he intends to reject them: he shall have the right to retain them until he has been reimbursed his reasonable expenses by the seller.
2. Where the goods despatched to the buyer have been put at his disposal at their place of destination and he exercises the right to reject them he shall be bound to take possession of them on behalf of the seller, provided that this may be done without payment of the price and without reasonable inconvenience or unreasonable expense. This provision shall not apply where the seller or a person authorised to take charge of the goods on his behalf is present at such destination.

Article 93

The party who is under an obligation to take steps to preserve the goods may deposit them in the warehouse of a third person at the expense of the other party provided that the expense incurred is not unreasonable.

Article 94

1. The party who, in the cases to which Articles 91 and 92 apply, is under an obligation to take steps to preserve the goods may sell them by any appropriate means, provided that there has been unreasonable delay by the other party in accepting them or taking them back or in paying the costs of preservation and provided that due notice has been given to the other party of the intention to sell.
2. The party selling the goods shall have the right to retain out of the proceeds of sale an amount equal to the reasonable costs of preserving the goods and of selling them and shall transmit the balance to the other party.

Article 95

Where, in the cases to which Articles 91 and 92 apply, the goods are subject to loss or rapid deterioration or their preservation would involve unreasonable expense, the party under the duty to preserve them is bound to sell them in accordance with Article 94.

CHAPTER VI
PASSING OF THE RISK

Article 96

Where the risk has passed to the buyer, he shall pay the price notwithstanding the loss or deterioration of the goods, unless this is due to the act of the seller or of some other person for whose conduct the seller is responsible.

Article 97

1. The risk shall pass to the buyer when delivery of the goods is effected in accordance with the provision of the contract and the present Law.
2. In the case of the handing over of goods which are not in conformity with the contract, the risk shall pass to the buyer from the moment when the handing over has, apart from the lack of conformity, been effected in accordance with the provisions of the contract and of the present Law, where the buyer has neither declared the contract avoided nor required goods in replacement.

Article 98

1. Where the handing over of the goods is delayed owing to the breach of an obligation of the buyer, the risk shall pass to the buyer as from the last date when, apart from such breach, the handing over could have been made in accordance with the contract.
2. Where the contract relates to a sale of unascertained goods, delay on the part of the buyer shall cause the risk to pass only when the seller has set aside goods manifestly appropriated to the contract and has notified the buyer that this has been done.
3. Where unascertained goods are of such a kind that the seller cannot set aside a part of them until the buyer takes delivery, it shall be sufficient for the seller to do all acts necessary to enable the buyer to take delivery.

Article 99

1. Where the sale is of goods in transit by sea, the risk shall be borne by the buyer as from the time at which the goods were handed over to the carrier.
2. here the seller, at the time of the conclusion of the contract, knew or ought to have known that the goods had been lost or had deteriorated, the risk shall remain with him until the time of the conclusion of the contract.

Article 100

If, in the case to which paragraph 3 of Article 19 applies, the seller, at the time of sending the notice or other document referred to in that paragraph knew or ought to have known that the goods had been lost or had deteriorated after they were handed over to the carrier, the risk shall remain with the seller until the time of sending such notice or document.

Article 101

The passing of the risk shall not necessarily be determined by the provisions of the contract concerning expenses.

SCHEDULE 2

THE UNIFORM LAW ON THE FORMATION OF CONTRACTS FOR THE INTERNATIONAL SALES OF GOODS

Article 1

The present law shall apply to the formation of contracts of sale of goods which, if they were concluded, would be governed by the Uniform Law on the International Sale of Goods.

Article 2

1. The provision of the following Articles shall apply except to the extent that it appears from the preliminary negotiations, the offer, the reply, the practices which the parties have established between themselves or usage, that other rules apply.
2. However, a term of the offer stipulating that silence shall amount to acceptance is invalid.

Article 3

An offer or an acceptance need not be evidenced by writing and shall not be subject to any other requirement as to form. In particular, they may be proved by means of witnesses.

Article 4

1. The communication which one person addresses to one or more specific persons with the object of concluding a contract of sale shall not constitute an offer unless it is sufficiently definite to permit the conclusion of the contract by acceptance and indicates the intention of the offeror to be bound.
2. This communication may be interpreted by reference to and supplemented by the preliminary negotiations, any practices which the parties have established between themselves, usage and the provisions of the Uniform Law on the International Sale of Goods.

Article 5

1. The offer shall not bind the offeror until it has been communicated to the offeree; it shall lapse if its withdrawal is communicated to the offeree before or at the same time as the offer.
2. After an offer has been communicated to the offeree it can be revoked unless the revocation is not made in good faith or in conformity with fair dealing or unless the offer states a fixed time for acceptance or otherwise indicates that it is firm or irrevocable.
3. An indication that the offer is firm or irrevocable may be express or implied from the circumstances, the preliminary negotiations, any practices which the parties have established between themselves or usage.
4. A revocation of an offer shall only have effect if it has been communicated to the offeree before he has despatched his acceptance or has done any act treated as acceptance under paragraph 2 of Article 6.

Article 6

1. Acceptance of an offer consists of a declaration communicated by any means whatsoever to the offeror.
2. Acceptance may also consist of the despatch of the goods or of the price or of any other act which my be considered to be equivalent to the declaration referred to in paragraph 1 of this Article either by virtue of the offer or as a result of practices which the parties have established between themselves or usage.

Article 7

1. An acceptance containing additions, limitations or other modifications shall be a rejection of the offer and shall constitute a counter-offer.
2. However, a reply to an offer which purports to be an acceptance but which contains additional or different terms which do not materially alter the terms of the offer shall constitute an acceptance unless the offeror promptly objects to the discrepancy; if he does not so object the terms of the contract shall be the terms of the offer with the modifications contained in the acceptance.

Article 8

1. A declaration of acceptance of an offer shall have effect only if it is communicated to the offeror within the time he has fixed or, if no such time is fixed, within a

reasonable time, due account being taken of the circumstances of the transaction, including the rapidity of the means of communication employed by the offeror, and usage. In the case of an oral offer, the acceptance shall be immediate, if the circumstances do not show that the offeree shall have time for reflection.

2.   If a time for acceptance is fixed by an offeror in a letter or in a telegram, it shall be presumed to begin to run from the day the letter was dated or the hour of the day the telegram was handed in for despatch.

3.   If an acceptance consists of an act referred to in paragraph 2 of Article 6, the act shall have effect only if it is done within the period laid down in paragraph 1 of the present Article.

Article 9

1.   If the acceptance is late, the offeror may nevertheless consider it to have arrived in due time on condition that he promptly so informs the acceptor orally or by despatch of a notice.

2.   If however the acceptance is communicated late, it shall be considered to have been communicated in due time, if the letter or document which contains the acceptance shows that it has been sent in such circumstances that if its transmission had been normal it would have been communicated in due time; this provision shall not however apply if the offeror has promptly informed the acceptor orally or by despatch of a notice that he considers his offer as having lapsed.

Article 10

An acceptance cannot be revoked except by a revocation which is communicated to the offeror before or at the same time as the acceptance.

Article 11

The formation of the contract is not affected by the death of the parties or by his becoming incapable of contracting before acceptance unless the contrary results from the intention of the parties, usage or the nature of the transaction.

Article 12

1.   For the purpose of the present law, the expression 'to be communicated' means to be delivered at the address of the person to whom the communication is directed.

2.   Communications provided for by the present Law shall be made by the means usual in the circumstances.

Article 13

1.   'Usage' means any practice or method of dealing which reasonable persons in the same situation as the parties usually consider to be applicable to the formation of their contract.

2.   Where expressions, provisions or forms of contract commonly used in commercial practice are employed, they shall be interpreted according to the meaning usually given to them in the trade concerned.

CARRIAGE OF GOODS BY SEA ACT 1971

CHAPTER 19

1.   Application of Hague Rules as amended

(1)   In this Act, 'the Rules' means the International Convention for the unification of certain rules of law relating to bills of lading signed at Brussels on 25th August 1924, as amended by the Protocol signed at Brussels on 23rd February 1968 and by the Protocol signed at Brussels on 21st December 1979.

(2)   The provisions of the Rules as set out in the Schedule to this Act shall have the force of law.

(3)   Without prejudice to subsection (2) above, the said provisions shall have effect (and have the force of law) in relation to and in connection with the carriage of goods by sea in ships where the port of shipment is a port in the United Kingdom, whether or not the carriage is between ports in two different states within the meaning of Article X of the Rules.

(4)   Subject to subsection (6) below, nothing in this section shall be taken as applying anything in the Rules to any contract for the carriage of goods by sea, unless the contract expressly or by implication provides for the issue of a bill of lading or any similar document of title.

(5)   [Repealed].

(6)   Without prejudice to Article X(c) of the Rules, the Rules shall have the force of law in relation to—

(a)   any bill of lading if the contract contained in or evidenced by it expressly provides that the Rules shall govern the contract; and

(b)   any receipt which is a non-negotiable document marked as such if the contract contained in or evidenced by it is a contract for the carriage of goods by sea which expressly provides that the Rules are to govern the contract as if the receipt were a bill of lading,

but subject, where paragraph (b) applies, to any necessary modifications and in particular with the omission in Article III of the Rules of the second sentence of paragraph 4 and of paragraph 7.

(7)   If and so far as the contract contained in or evidenced by a bill of lading or receipt within paragraph (a) or (b) of subsection (6) above applies to deck cargo or live animals, the Rules as given the force of law by that subsection shall have effect as it Article 1(c) did not exclude deck cargo and live animals.

In this subsection 'deck cargo' means cargo which by the contract of carriage is stated as being carried on deck and is so carried.

1A.   Conversion of special drawing rights into sterling

(1)   For the purposes of Article IV of the Rules the value on a particular day of one special drawing right shall be treated as equal to such a sum in sterling as the International Monetary Fund have fixed as being the equivalent of one special drawing right—

(a)   for that day; or

(b)   if no sum has been so fixed for that day, for the last day before that day for which a sum has been so fixed.

(2)   A certificate given by or on behalf of the Treasury stating—

(a)   that a particular sum in sterling has been fixed as aforesaid for a particular day; or

(b)   that no sum has been so fixed for a particular day and that a particular sum in sterling has been so fixed for a day which is the last day for which a sum has been so fixed before the particular day, shall be conclusive evidence of those matters for the purpose of subsection (1) above; and a document purporting to be such a certificate shall in any proceedings be received in evidence and, unless the contrary is proved, be deemed to be such a certificate.

(3)   The Treasury may charge a reasonable fee for any certificate given in pursuance of subsection (2) above, and any fee received by the Treasury by virtue of this subsection shall be paid into the Consolidated Fund.

2.   **[Omitted].**

3.   **Absolute warranty of seaworthiness not to be implied in contracts to which Rules apply**
There shall not be implied in any contract for the carriage of goods by sea to which Rules apply by virtue of this Act any absolute undertaking by the carrier of the goods to provide a seaworthy ship.

4.–5. **[Omitted].**

6.   **Supplemental**
(1)–(3) [Omitted].
(4)   It is hereby declared that for the purposes of Article VIII of the Rules section 186 of the Merchant Shipping Act 1995 (which entirely exempts shipowners and others in certain circumstances for loss of, or damage to, goods) is a provision relating to limitation of liability.

SCHEDULE
THE HAGUE RULES AS AMENDED BY THE BRUSSELS PROTOCOL 1968

Article I

In these Rules the following words are employed with the meaning set out below—

(a)   'Carrier' includes the owner or the charterer who enters into a contract of carriage with a shipper.

(b)   'Contract of carriage' applies only to contracts of carriage covered by a bill of lading or any similar document of title, in so far as such document relates to the carriage of goods by sea, including any bill of lading or any similar document as aforesaid issued under or pursuant to a charter party from the moment at which such bill of lading or similar document of title regulates the relations between a carrier and a holder of the same.

(c)   'Goods' includes goods, wares, merchandise and articles of every kind whatsoever except live animals and cargo which by the contract of carriage is stated as being carried on deck and is so carried.

(d)   'Ship' means any vessel used for the carriage of goods by sea.

(e)   'Carriage of goods' covers the period from the time when the goods are loaded on to the time they are discharged from the ship.

Article II

Subject to the provisions of Article VI, under every contract of carriage of goods by sea the carrier, in relation to the loading, handling, stowage, carriage, custody, care and discharge of such goods, shall be subject to the responsibilities and liabilities, and entitled to the rights and immunities hereinafter set forth.

Article III

1. The carrier shall be bound before and at the beginning of the voyage to exercise due diligence to—
    (a)   make the ship seaworthy;
    (b)   properly man, equip and supply the ship;
    (c)   make the holds, refrigerating and cool chambers, and all other parts of the ship in which goods are carried, fit and safe for their reception, carriage and preservation.

2. Subject to the provisions of Article IV, the carrier shall properly and carefully load, handle, stow, carry, keep, care for, and discharge the goods carried.

3. After receiving the goods into his charge the carrier or the master or agent of the carrier shall, on demand of the shipper, issue to the shipper a bill of lading showing among other things—
    (a)   the leading marks necessary for identification of the goods as the same are furnished in writing by the shipper before the loading of such goods starts, provided such marks are stamped or otherwise shown clearly upon the goods if uncovered, or on the cases or coverings in which such goods are contained, in such a manner as should ordinarily remain legible until the end of the voyage;
    (b)   either the number of packages or pieces, or the quantity, or weight, as the case may be, as furnished in writing by the shipper;
    (c)   the apparent order and conditions of the goods.
    Provided that no carrier, master or agent of the carrier shall be bound to state or show in the bill of lading any marks, number, quantity, or weight which he has reasonable ground for suspecting not accurately to represent the goods actually received or which he has had no reasonable means of checking.

4. Such a bill of lading shall be *prima facie* evidence of the receipt by the carrier of the goods as therein described in accordance with paragraph 3(a), (b) and (c). However, proof to the contrary shall not be admissible when the bill of lading has been transferred to a third party acting in good faith.

5. The shipper shall be deemed to have guaranteed to the carrier the accuracy at the time of shipment of the marks, number, quantity and weight, as furnished by him, and the shipper shall indemnify the carrier against all loss, damages and expenses arising or resulting from inaccuracies in such particulars. The right of the carrier to such indemnity shall in no way limit his responsibility and liability under the contract of carriage to any person other than the shipper.

6. Unless notice of loss or damage and the general nature of such loss or damage be given in writing to the carrier or his agent at the port of discharge before or at the time of the removal of the goods into the custody of the person entitled to delivery thereof under the contract of carriage, or, if the loss or damage be not apparent, within three days, such removal shall be *prima facie* evidence of the delivery by the carrier of the goods as described in the bill of lading.
    The notice in writing need not be given if the state of the goods has, at the time of their receipt been the subject of joint survey or inspection.
    Subject to paragraph 6*bis* the carrier and the ship shall in any event be discharged from all liability whatsoever in respect of the goods, unless suit is brought within one year of their delivery or of the date when they should have been delivered. This period may, however, be extended if the parties so agree after the cause of action has arisen.
    In the case of any actual or apprehended loss or damage the carrier and the receiver shall give all reasonable facilities to each other for inspecting and tallying the goods.

6 *bis*. An action for indemnity against a third person may be brought even after the expiration of the year provided for in the preceding paragraph if brought within the time allowed by the law of the Court seized of the case. However, the time allowed

shall be not less than three months, commencing from the day when the person bringing such action for indemnity has settled the claim or has been served with process in the action against himself.

7. After the goods are loaded the bill of lading to be issued by the carrier, master, or agent of the carrier to the shipper shall, if the shipper so demands, be a 'shipped' bill of lading, provided that if the shipper shall have previously taken up any document of title to such goods, he shall surrender the same as against the issue of the 'shipped' bill of lading, but at the option of the carrier such document of title may be noted at the port of shipment by the carrier, master, or agent with the name or names of the ship or ships upon which the goods have been shipped and the date or dates of shipment, and when so noted, if it shows the particulars mentioned in paragraph 3 of Article III, shall for the purpose of this Article be deemed to constitute a 'shipped' bill of lading.

8. Any clause, covenant, or agreement in a contract of carriage relieving the carrier or the ship from liability for loss or damage to, or in connection with goods, arising from negligence, fault, or failure in the duties and obligations provided in this Article or lessening such liability otherwise than as provided in these Rules shall be null and void and of no effect. A benefit of insurance in favour of the carrier or similar clause shall be deemed to be clause relieving the carrier from liability.

Article IV

1. Neither the carrier nor the ship shall be liable for loss or damage arising or resulting from unseaworthiness unless caused by want of due diligence on the part of the carrier to make the ship seaworthy, and to secure that the ship is properly manned, equipped and supplied, and to make the holds, refrigerating and cool chambers and all other parts of the ship in which goods are carried fit and safe for their reception, carriage and preservation in accordance with the provisions of paragraph 1 of Article III. Whenever loss or damage has resulted from unseaworthiness the burden of proving the exercise of due diligence shall be on the carrier or other person claiming exemption under this article.

2. Neither the carrier nor the ship shall be liable for loss or damage arising or resulting from—

    (a) act, neglect, or default of the master, mariner, pilot, or the servants of the carrier in the navigation or in the management of the ship;

    (b) fire, unless caused by the actual fault or privity of the carrier;

    (c) perils, dangers and accidents of the sea or other navigable waters;

    (d) act of God;

    (e) act of war;

    (f) act of public enemies;

    (g) arrest or restraint of princes, rulers or people, or seizure under legal process;

    (h) quarantine restrictions;

    (i) act or omission of the shipper or owner of the goods, his agent or representative;

    (j) strikes or lockouts or stoppage or restraint of labour from whatever cause, whether partial or general;

    (k) riots and civil commotions;

    (l) saving or attempting to save life or property at sea;

    (m) wastage in bulk or weight or any other loss or damage arising from inherent defect, quality or vice of the goods;

    (n) insufficiency of packing;

    (o) insufficiency or inadequacy of marks;

    (p) latent defects not discoverable by due diligence;

    (q) any other cause arising without the actual fault or privity of the carrier, or without the fault or neglect of the agents or servants of the carrier, but the burden of proof shall be on the person claiming the benefit of this exception to show that neither the actual fault or privity of the carrier nor the fault or neglect of the agents or servants of the carrier contributed to the loss or damage.

3.   The shipper shall not be responsible for loss or damage sustained by the carrier or the ship arising or resulting from any cause without the act, fault or neglect of the shipper, his agents or his servants.

4.   ~~Any~~ deviation in saving or attempting to save life or property at sea or ~~any reasonable deviation~~ shall not be deemed to be an infringement or breach of these Rules or of the contract of carriage, and the carrier shall not be liable for any loss or damage resulting therefrom.

5.   —

(a)   Unless the nature and value of such goods have been declared by the shipper before shipment and inserted in the bill of lading, neither the carrier nor the ship shall in any event be or become liable for any loss or damage to or in connection with the goods in an amount exceeding 666.67 units of account per package or unit or 2 units of account per kilogram of gross weight of the goods lost or damaged, whichever is the higher.

(b)   The total amount recoverable shall be calculated by reference to the value of such goods at the place and time at which the goods are discharged from the ship in accordance with the contract or should have been so discharged.

      The value of the goods shall be fixed according to the commodity exchange price, or, if there be no such price, according to the current market price, or if there be no commodity exchange price or current market price, by reference to the normal value of goods of the same kind and quality.

(c)   Where a container, pallet or similar article of transport is used to consolidate goods, the number of packages or units enumerated in the bill of lading as packed in such article of transport shall be deemed the number of packages or units for the purpose of this paragraph as far as these packages or units are concerned. Except as aforesaid such article of transport shall be considered the package or unit.

(d)   The unit of account mentioned in this Article is the special drawing right as defined by the International Monetary Fund. The amounts mentioned in sub-paragraph (a) of this paragraph shall be converted into national currency on the basis of the value of that currency on a date to be determined by the law of the Court seized of the case.

(e)   Neither the carrier nor the ship shall be entitled to the benefit of the limitation of liability provided for in this paragraph if it is proved that the damage resulted from an act or omission of the carrier done with intent to cause damage, or recklessly and with knowledge that damage would probably result.

(f)   The declaration mentioned in sub-paragraph (a) of this paragraph if embodied in the bill of lading shall be *prima facie* evidence, but shall not be binding or conclusive on the carrier.

(g)   By agreement between the carrier, master or agent of the carrier and the shipper other maximum amounts than those mentioned in sub-paragraph (a) of this paragraph may be fixed, provided that no maximum amount so fixed shall be less than the appropriate maximum mentioned in that sub-paragraph.

(h)   Neither the carrier nor the ship shall be responsible in any event for loss or damage to, or in connection with goods, if the nature or value thereof has been knowingly mis-stated by the shipper in the bill of lading.

6.   Goods of an inflammable, explosive or dangerous nature to the shipment whereof the carrier, master or agent of the carrier has not consented with knowledge of their nature and character, may at any time before discharge be landed at any place, or destroyed or rendered innocuous by the carrier without compensation and the shipper of such goods shall be liable for all damages and expenses directly or

indirectly arising out of or resulting from such shipment. If any such goods shipped with such knowledge and consent shall become a danger to the ship or cargo, they may in like manner be landed at any place, or destroyed or rendered innocuous by the carrier without liability on the part of the carrier except to general average, if any.

Article IV bis

1. The defences and limits of liability provided for in these Rules shall apply in any action against the carrier in respect of loss or damage to goods covered by a contract of carriage whether the action be founded in contract or in tort.
2. If such an action is bought against a servant or agent of the carrier (such servant or agent not being an independent contractor), such servant or agent shall be entitled to avail himself of the defences and limits of liability which the carrier is entitled to invoke under these Rules.
3. The aggregate of the amounts recoverable from the carrier, and such servants and agents, shall in no case exceed the limit provided for in these Rules.
4. Nevertheless, a servant or agent of the carrier shall not be entitled to avail himself of the provisions of this Article, if it is proved that the damage resulted from an act or omission of the servant or agent done with intent to cause damage or recklessly and with knowledge that damage would probably result.

Article V

A carrier shall be at liberty to surrender in whole or in part all or any of his rights and immunities or to increase any of his responsibilities and obligations under these Rules, provided such surrender or increase shall be embodied in the bill of lading issued to the shipper. The provisions of these Rules shall not be applicable to charter parties, but if bills of lading are issued in the case of a ship under a charter party they shall comply with the terms of these Rules. Nothing in these Rules shall be held to prevent the insertion in a bill of lading of any lawful provision regarding general average.

Article VI

Notwithstanding the provisions of the preceding Articles, a carrier, master or agent of the carrier and a shipper shall in regard to any particular goods be at liberty to enter into any agreement in any terms as to the responsibility and liability of the carrier for such goods, and as to the rights and immunities of the carrier in respect of such goods, or his obligation as to seaworthiness, so far as this stipulation is not contrary to public policy, or the care or diligence of his servant or agents in regard to the loading, handling, stowage, carriage, custody, care and discharge of the goods carried by sea, provided that in this case no bill of lading has been or shall be issued and that the terms agreed shall be embodied in a receipt which shall be a non-negotiable document and shall be marked as such.

Any agreement so entered into shall have legal effect.

Provided that this Article shall not apply to ordinary commercial shipments made in the ordinary course of trade, but only to other shipments where the character or condition of the property to be carried or the circumstances, terms and conditions under which the carriage is to be performed are such as reasonably to justify a special agreement.

Article VII

Nothing herein contained shall prevent a carrier or a shipper from entering into any agreement, stipulation, condition, reservation or exemption as to the responsibility and liability of the carrier or the ship for the loss or damage to, or in connection with, the custody and care and handling of goods prior to the loading on, and subsequent to the discharge from, the ship on which the goods are carried by sea.

Article VIII

The provisions of these Rules shall not affect the rights and obligations or the carrier under any statute for the time being in force relating to the limitation of the liability of owners of sea-going vessels.

Article IX

These rules shall not affect the provisions of any international Convention or national law governing liability for nuclear damage.

Article X

The provisions of these Rules shall apply to every bill of lading relating to the carriage of goods between ports in two different States if—
(a)   the bill of lading is issued in a contracting State; or
(b)   the carriage is from a port in a contracting State; or
(c)   the contract contained in or evidenced by the bill of lading provides that these
        Rules or legislation of any State giving effect to them are to govern the contract,
whatever may be the nationality of the ship, the carrier, the shipper, the consignee, or any other interested person.

Articles XI–XVI [Omitted].

UNFAIR CONTRACT TERMS ACT 1977

CHAPTER 50

1.   [Omitted].

2.   Negligence liability
   (1)   A person cannot by reference to any contract term or to a notice given to
           persons generally or to particular persons exclude or restrict his liability for
           death or personal injury resulting from negligence.
   (2)   In the case of other loss or damage, a person cannot so exclude or restrict his
           liability for negligence except in so far as the term or notice satisfies the
           requirement of reasonableness.
   (3)   Where a contract term or notice purports to exclude or restrict liability for
           negligence a person's agreement to or awareness of it is not of itself to be
           taken as indicating his voluntary acceptance of any risk.

3.–25.   [Omitted].

MISCELLANEOUS

26.   International supply contracts
   (1)   The limits imposed by this Act on the extent to which a person may exclude
           or restrict liability by reference to a contract term do not apply to liability
           arising under such a contract as is described in subsection (3) below.
   (2)   The terms of such a contract are not subject to any requirement of
           reasonableness under Section 3 or 4; and nothing in Part II of this Act shall
           require the incorporation of the terms of such a contract to be fair and
           reasonable for them to have effect.

(3)　Subject to subsection (4), that description of contract is one whose characteristics are the following—

　(a)　either it is a contract of sale or goods or it is one under or in pursuance of which the possession or ownership of goods passes; and

　(b)　it is made by parties whose places of business (or, if they have none, habitual residences) are in the territories of different States (the Channel Islands and the Isle of Man being treated for this purpose as different States from the United Kingdom).

(4)　A contract falls within subsection (3) above only if either—

　(a)　the goods in question are, at the time of the conclusion of the contract, in the course of carriage, or will be carried, from the territory of one State to the territory of another; or

　(b)　the acts constituting the offer and acceptance have been done in territories of different states; or

　(c)　the contract provides for the goods to be delivered to the territory of a State other than that within those territory those acts were done.

27.　Choice of law clauses

(1)　Where the law applicable to a contract is the law of any part of the United Kingdom only by choice of the parties (and apart from that choice would be the law of some country outside the United Kingdom) sections 2 to 7 and 16 to 21 of this Act operate as part of the law applicable to the contract.

(2)　This Act has effect notwithstanding any contract term which applies or purports to apply the law of some country outside the United Kingdom, where (either or both)—

　(a)　the term appears to the court, or arbitrator or arbiter to have been imposed wholly or mainly for the purpose of enabling the party imposing it to evade the operation of this Act; or

　(b)　in the making of the contract one of the parties dealt as consumer, and he was than habitually resident in the United Kingdom, and the essential steps necessary for the making of the contract were taken there, whether by him or by others on his behalf.

(3)　In the application of subsection (2) above to Scotland, for paragraph (b) there shall be substituted—

　'(b)　the contract is a consumer contract as defined in Part II of this Act, and the consumer at the date when the contract was made was habitually resident in the United Kingdom, and the essential steps necessary for the making of the contract were taken there, whether by him or by others on his behalf.'

28.–32. [Omitted].

SCHEDULE 1
SCOPE OF SECTIONS 2 TO 4 AND 7

1.　Sections 2 to 4 of this Act do not extend to—

　(a)　any contract of marine salvage or towage;

　(b)　any charterparty of a ship or hovercraft; and

　(c)　any contract for the carriage of goods by ship or hovercraft;

but, subject to this, sections 2 to 4 and 7 do not extend to any such contract except in favour of a person dealing as consumer.

2.–5. [Omitted].

STATE IMMUNITY ACT 1978

CHAPTER 33

PART I
PROCEEDINGS IN UNITED KINGDOM BY OR AGAINST OTHER STATES

Immunity from jurisdiction

PART I
PROCEEDINGS IN UNITED KINGDOM BY OR AGAINST OTHER STATES

Immunity from jurisdiction

1.   General immunity from jurisdiction
  (1)   A State is immune from the jurisdiction of the courts of the United Kingdom except as provided in the following provisions of this part of the Act.
  (2)   A court shall give effect to the immunity conferred by this section even though the State does not appear in the proceedings in question.

Exceptions from immunity

2.   Submission to jurisdiction
  (1)   A state is not immune as respects proceedings in respect of which it has submitted to the jurisdiction of the courts of the United Kingdom.
  (2)   A state may submit after the dispute giving rise to the proceedings has arisen or by a prior written agreement: but a provision in any agreement that it is to be governed by the law of the United Kingdom is not be regarded as a submission.
  (3)   A state is deemed to have submitted—
    (a)   if it has instituted the proceedings; or
    (b)   subject to subsections (4) and (5) below, if it has intervened or taken any step in the proceedings.
  (4)   Subsection (3)(b) above does not apply to intervention or any step taken for the purpose only of—
    (a)   claiming immunity; or
    (b)   asserting an interest in property in circumstances such that the State would have been entitled to immunity if the proceedings had been brought against it.

(5) Subsection (3)(b) above does not apply to any step taken by the State in ignorance of facts entitling it to immunity if those facts could not reasonably have been ascertained and immunity is claimed as soon as reasonably practicable.

(6) A submission in respect of any proceedings extends to any appeal but not to any counter-claim unless it arises out of the same legal relationship or facts as the claim.

(7) The head of a State's diplomatic mission in the United Kingdom, or the person for the time being performing his functions, shall be deemed to have authority to submit on behalf of the State in respect of any proceedings; and any person who has entered into a contract on behalf of and with the authority of a State shall be deemed to have authority to submit on its behalf in respect of proceedings arising out of the contract.

3. **Commercial transactions and contracts to be performed in the United Kingdom**

(1) A state is not immune as respects proceedings relating to —
   (a) a commercial transaction entered into by the State; or
   (b) an obligation of the State which by virtue of a contract (whether a commercial transaction or not) falls to be performed wholly or partly in the United Kingdom.

(2) This section does not apply if the parties to the dispute are States or have otherwise agreed in writing; and subsection (1)(b) above does not apply if the contract (not being a commercial transaction) was made in the territory of the State concerned and the obligation in question is governed by its administrative law.

(3) In this section 'commercial transaction' means —
   (a) any contract for the supply of goods or services;
   (b) any loan or other transaction for the provision of finance and any guarantee or indemnity in respect of any such transaction or of any other financial obligation; and
   (c) any other transaction or activity (whether of a commercial industrial, financial, professional or other similar character) into which a state enters or in which it engages otherwise than in the exercise of sovereign authority,

but neither paragraph of subsection (1) above applies to a contract of employment between a State and an individual.

4.–8. **[Omitted].**

9. **Arbitrations**

(1) Where a State has agreed in writing to submit a dispute which has arisen, or may arise, to arbitration, the State is not immune as respects proceedings in the courts of the United Kingdom which relate to the arbitration.

(2) This section has effect subject to any contrary provision in the arbitration agreement and does not apply to any arbitration agreement between states.

10. **Ships used for commercial purposes**

(1) This section applies to —
   (a) Admiralty proceedings; and
   (b) proceedings on any claim which could be made the subject of Admiralty proceedings.

(2) A State is not immune as respects —
   (a) an action *in rem* against a ship belonging to that State; or
   (b) an action *in personam* for enforcing a claim in connection with such a ship,

if, at the time when the cause of action arose, the ship was in use or intended for use for commercial purposes.

(3)　Where an action *in rem* is brought against a ship belonging to a State for enforcing a claim in connection with another ship belonging to that State, subsection (2) (a) above does not apply as respects the first-mentioned ship unless at the time when the cause of action relating to the other ship arose, both ships were in use or intended for use for commercial purposes.

(4)　A State is not immune as respects—

　(a)　an action *in rem* against a cargo belonging to that State if both the cargo and the ship carrying it were, at the time when the cause of action arose, in use or intended for use for commercial purposes; or

　(b)　an action *in personam* for enforcing a claim in connection with such a cargo if the ship carrying it was then in use or intended for use as aforesaid.

(5)　In the foregoing provisions references to a ship or cargo belonging to a State include references to a ship or cargo in its possession or control or in which it claims an interest; and, subject to subsection (4) above, subsection (2) above applies to property other than a ship as it applies to a ship.

(6)　Sections 3 to 5 above do not apply to proceedings of the kind described in subsection (1) above if the State in question is a party to the Brussels Convention and the claim relates to the operation of a ship owned or operated by that State, the carriage of cargo or passengers on any such ship or the carriage of cargo owned by that State on any other ship.

11.–13.　[Omitted].

Supplementary provisions

14.　States entitled to immunities and privileges

(1)　The immunities and privileges conferred by this Part of this Act apply to any foreign or commonwealth State other than the United Kingdom; and references to a State include references to—

　(a)　the sovereign or other head of that State in his public capacity;

　(b)　the government of that State; and

　(c)　any department of that government,

but not to any entity (hereafter referred to as a 'separate entity') which is distinct from the executive organs of the government of the State and capable of suing or being sued.

(2)　A separate entity is immune from the jurisdiction of the courts of the United Kingdom if, and only if—

　(a)　the proceedings relate to anything done by it in the exercise of sovereign authority; and

　(b)　the circumstances are such that a State (or, in the case of proceedings to which Section 10 above applies, a State which is not a party to the Brussels Convention) would have been so immune.

(3)　If a separate entity (not being a State's central bank or other monetary authority) submits to the jurisdiction in respect of proceedings in the case of which it is entitled to immunity by virtue of subsection (2) above, subsections (1) to (4) of section 13 above shall apply to it in respect of those proceedings as if references to a State were references to that entity.

(4)　Property of a State's central bank or other monetary authority shall not be regarded for the purposes of subsection (4) of section 13 above as in use or intended for use for commercial purposes; and where any such bank or authority is a separate entity subsections (1) to (3) of that section shall apply to it as if references to a State were references to the bank or authority.

(5) Section 12 above applies to proceedings against the constituent territories of a federal State; and her Majesty may by Order in Council provide for the other provisions of this Part of this Act to apply to any such constituent territory specified in the Order as they apply to a State.

(6) Where the provisions of this Part of this Act do not apply to a constituent territory by virtue of any such Order subsections (2) and (3) above shall apply to it as if it were a separate entity.

15.–16. [Omitted].

17. Interpretation of Part I

(1) In this Part of the Act 'the Brussels Convention' means the International Convention for the Unification of Certain Rules Concerning the Immunity of State-owned Ships signed in Brussels on 10th April 1926.

'commercial purposes' means purposes of such transactions or activities as are mentioned in section 3(3) above;

'ship' includes hovercraft.

(2) In sections 2(2) and 13(3) above references to an agreement include references to a treaty, convention or other international agreement.

(3) For the purposes of sections 3 to 8 above the territory of the United Kingdom shall be deemed to include any dependent territory in respect of which the United Kingdom is a party to the European Convention on State Immunity.

(4) In sections 3(1), 4(1), 5 and 16(2) above references to the United Kingdom include references to its territorial waters and any area designated under section 1(7) of the Continental Shelf Act 1964.

(5) In relation to Scotland in this Part of this Act 'action *in rem*' means such an action only in relation to Admiralty proceedings.

18.–23. [Omitted].

SALE OF GOODS ACT 1979

CHAPTER 54
PART II
FORMATION OF THE CONTRACT

Contract of sale

2. Contract of sale.
3. Capacity to buy and sell.

Formalities of contract

4. How contract of sale is made.

Subject matter of contract

5. Existing or future goods.
6. Goods which have perished.
7. Goods perishing before sale but after agreement to sell.

PART II
FORMATION OF THE CONTRACT

Contract of sale

2.   Contract of sale
(1)   A contract of sale of goods is a contract by which the seller transfers or agrees to transfer the property in goods to the buyer for a money consideration, called the price.
(2)   There may be a contract of sale between one part owner and another.
(3)   A contract of sale may be absolute or conditional.
(4)   Where under a contract of sale the property in the goods is transferred from the seller to the buyer the contract is called a sale.
(5)   Where under a contract of sale the transfer of the property in the goods is to take place at a future time or subject to some condition later to be fulfilled the contract is called an agreement to sell.
(6)   An agreement to sell becomes a sale when the time elapses or the conditions are fulfilled subject to which the property in the goods is to be transferred.

3.   Capacity to buy and sell
(1)   Capacity to buy and sell is regulated by the general law concerning capacity to contract and to transfer and acquire property.
(2)   Where necessaries are sold and delivered to a minor or a person who by reason of mental incapacity or drunkenness is incompetent to contract, he must pay a reasonable price for them.
(3)   In subsection (2) above 'necessaries' means goods suitable to the condition in life of the minor or other person concerned and to his actual requirements at the time of the sale and delivery.

Formalities of contract

4.   How contract of sale is made
(1)   Subject to this and any other Act, a contract of sale may be made in writing (either with or without seal), or by world of mouth, or partly in writing and partly by word of mouth, or may be implied from the conduct of the parties.
(2)   Nothing in this section affects the law relating to corporations.

Subject matter of contract

5.   Existing or future goods
(1)   The goods which form the subject of a contract of sale may be either existing goods, owned or possessed by the seller, or goods to be manufactured or acquired by him after the making of the contract of sale, in this Act called future goods.
(2)   There may be a contract for the sale of goods the acquisition of which by the seller depends on a contingency which may or may not happen.
(3)   Where by a contract of sale the seller purports to effect a present sale of future goods, the contract operates as an agreement to sell the goods.

6.   Goods which have perished
Where there is a contract for the sale of specific goods, and the goods without the knowledge of the seller have perished at the time when the contract is made, the contract is void.

7.   Goods perishing before sale but after agreement to sell
Where there is an agreement to sell specific goods and subsequently the goods, without any fault on the part of the seller or buyer perish before the risk passes to the buyer, the agreement is avoided.
The price

8.   Ascertainment of price
(1)   The price in a contract of sale may be fixed by the contract, or may be left to be fixed in a manner agreed by the contract, or may be determined by the course of dealing between the parties.
(2)   Where the price is not determined as mentioned in subsection (1) above the buyer must pay a reasonable price.
(3)   What is a reasonable price is a question of fact dependent on the circumstances of each particular case.

9.   Agreement to sell at valuation
(1)   Where there is an agreement to sell goods on the terms that the price is to be fixed by the valuation of a third party, and he cannot or does not make the valuation, the agreement is avoided; but if the goods or any part of them have been delivered to and appropriated by the buyer he must pay a reasonable price for them.
(2)   Where the third party is prevented from making the valuation by the fault of the seller or buyer, the party not at fault may maintain an action for damages against the party at fault.

Implied terms, etc

10.   Stipulations about time
(1)   Unless a different intention appears from the terms of the contract, stipulations as to time of payment are not of the essence of a contract of sale.
(2)   Whether any other stipulation as to time is or is not of the essence of the contract depends on the terms of the contract.
(3)   In a contract of sale 'month' *prima facie* means calendar month.

11.   When condition to be treated as warranty
(1)   This section does not apply to Scotland.
(2)   Where a contract of sale is subject to a condition to be fulfilled by the seller the buyer may waive the condition, or may elect to treat the breach of the condition as a breach of warranty and not as a ground for treating the contract as repudiated.
(3)   Whether a stipulation in a contract of sale is a condition, the breach of which may give rise to a right to treat the contract as repudiated, or a warranty, the breach of which may give rise to a claim for damages but not a right to reject the goods and treat the contract as repudiated, depends in each case on the construction of the contract; and a stipulation may be a condition, although called a warranty in the contract.
(4)   Subject to section 35A below, where a contract of sale is not severable and the buyer has accepted the goods or part of them, the breach of a condition to be fulfilled by the seller can only be treated as a breach of warranty, and not as a ground for rejecting the goods and treating the contract as repudiated, unless there is an express or implied term of the contract to that effect.
(5)   [Repealed].
(6)   Nothing in this section affects a condition or warranty whose fulfilment is excused by law by reason of impossibility or otherwise.
(7)   [Omitted].

12. **Implied terms about title, etc**

(1)   In a contract of sale, other than one to which subsection (3) below applies, there is an implied term on the part of the seller that in the case of a sale he has the right to sell the goods, and in the case of an agreement to sell he will have such a right at the time when the property is to pass.

(2)   In a contract of sale, other than one to which subsection (3) below applies, there is also an implied term that—

(a)   the goods are free, and will remain free until the time when the property is to pass, from any charge or encumbrance not disclosed or known to the buyer before the contract is made; and

(b)   the buyer will enjoy quiet possession of the goods except so far as it may be disturbed by the owner or other person entitled to the benefit of any charge or encumbrance so disclosed or known.

(3)   This subsection applies to a contract of sale in the case of which there appears from the contract or is to be inferred from its circumstances an intention that the seller should transfer only such title as he or a third person may have.

(4)   In a contract to which subsection (3) above applies there is an implied term that all charges or encumbrances known to the seller and not known to the buyer have been disclosed to the buyer before the contract is made.

(5)   In a contract to which subsection (3) above applies there is also an implied term that none of the following will disturb the buyer's quiet possession of the goods, namely—

(a)   the seller;

(b)   in a case where the parties to the contract intend that the seller should transfer only such title as a third person may have, that person;

(c)   anyone claiming through or under the seller or that third person otherwise than under a charge or encumbrance disclosed or known to the buyer before the contract is made.

(5A)   As regards England and Wales and Northern Ireland, the term implied by subsection (1) above is a condition and the terms implied by subsections (2), (4) and (5) above are warranties.

(6)   [Omitted].

13. **Sale by description**

(1)   Where there is a contract for the sale of goods by description, there is an implied term that the goods will correspond with the description.

(1A)   As regards England and Wales and Northern Ireland, the term implied by subsection (1) above is a condition.

(2)   If the sale is by sample as well as by description it is not sufficient that the bulk of the goods corresponds with the sample if the goods do not also correspond with the description.

(3)   A sale of goods is not prevented from being a sale by description by reason only that, being exposed for sale or hire, they are selected by the buyer.

(4)   [Omitted].

14. **Implied terms about quality or fitness**

(1)   Except as provided by this section and section 15 below and subject to any other enactment, there is no implied term about the quality or fitness for any particular purpose of goods supplied under a contract of sale.

(2)   Where the seller sells goods in the course of a business, there is an implied term that the goods supplied under the contract are of satisfactory quality.

(2A)   For the purposes of this Act, goods are of satisfactory quality if they meet the standard that a reasonable person would regard as satisfactory, taking account of any description of the goods, the price (if relevant) and all the other relevant circumstances.

(2B)   For the purposes of this Act, the quality of the goods includes their state and condition and the following (among others) are in appropriate cases aspects of the quality of goods—
   (a)   fitness for all the purposes for which goods of the kind in question are commonly supplied,
   (b)   appearance and finish,
   (c)   freedom from minor defects,
   (d)   safety, and
   (e)   durability.

(2C)   The term implied by subsection (2) above does not extend to any matter making the quality of goods unsatisfactory—
   (a)   which is specifically drawn to the buyer's attention before the contract is made;
   (b)   where the buyer examines the goods before the contract is made, which that examination ought to reveal; or
   (c)   in the case of a contract for sale by sample, which would have been apparent on a reasonable examination of the sample.

(3)   Where the seller sells goods in the course of a business and the buyer, expressly or by implication, makes known—
   (a)   to the seller; or
   (b)   where the purchase price or part of it is payable by instalments and the goods were previously sold by a credit-broker to the seller, to that credit-broker,
   any particular purpose for which the goods are being bought, there is an implied term that the goods supplied under the contract are reasonable fit for that purpose, whether or not that is a purpose for which such goods are commonly supplied, except where the circumstances show that the buyer does not rely, or that it is unreasonable for him to rely, on the skill or judgment of the seller or credit-broker.

(4)   An implied term or warranty about quality or fitness for a particular purpose may be annexed to a contract of sale by usage.

(5)   The preceding provisions of this section apply to a sale by a person who in the course of a business is acting as agent for another as they apply to a sale by a principal in the course of a business, except where that other is not selling in the course of a business and either the buyer knows that fact or reasonable steps are taken to bring it to the notice of the buyer before the contract is made.

(6)   As regards England and Wales and Northern Ireland, the terms implied by subsections (2) and (3) above are conditions.

(7) and (8) [Omitted].

2D to 2F [Omitted].

Sale by sample

15.   Sale by sample
(1)   A contract of sale is a contract for sale by sample where there is an express or implied term to that effect in the contract.
(2)   In the case of a contract for sale by sample there is an implied term—
   (a)   that the bulk will correspond with the sample in quality;
   (b)   [Repealed];
   (c)   that the goods will be free from any defect, making their quality unsatisfactory, which would not be apparent on reasonable examination of the sample.
(3)   As regards England and Wales and Northern Ireland, the term implied by subsection (2) above is a condition.
(4)   [Omitted].

Miscellaneous

15A. Modification of remedies for breach of condition in non-consumer cases
    (1)   Where in the case of a contract of sale—
        (a) the buyer would, apart from this subsection, have the right to reject goods by reason of a breach on the part of the seller of a term implied by section 13, 14 or 15 above, but
        (b) the breach is so slight that it would be unreasonable for him to reject them,
    then, if the buyer does not deal as consumer, the breach is not to be treated as a breach of condition but may be treated as a breach of warranty.
    (2)   This section applies unless a contrary intention appears in, or is to be implied from, the contract.
    (3)   It is for the seller to show that a breach fell within subsection (1)(b) above.
    (4)   This section does not apply to Scotland.

PART III
EFFECTS OF THE CONTRACT

Transfer of property as between seller and buyer

16. Goods must be ascertained
Subject to section 20A below, where there is a contract for the sale of unascertained goods no property in the goods is transferred to the buyer unless and until the goods are ascertained.

17. Property passes when intended to pass
    (1)   Where there is a contract for the sale of specific or ascertained goods the property in them is transferred to the buyer at such time as the parties to the contract intend it to be transferred.
    (2)   For the purpose of ascertaining the intention of the parties regard shall be had to the terms of the contract, the conduct of the parties and the circumstances of the case.

18. Rules for ascertaining intention
Unless a different intention appears, the following are rules for ascertaining the intention of the parties as to the time at which the property in the goods is to pass to the buyer.
    Rule 1—Where there is an unconditional contract for the sale of specific goods in a deliverable state the property in the goods passes to the buyer when the contract is made, and it is immaterial whether the time of payment or the time of delivery, or both, be postponed.
    Rule 2—Where there is a contract for the sale of specific goods and the seller is bound to do something to the goods for the purpose of putting them into a deliverable state, the property does not pass until the thing is done and the buyer has notice that it has been done.
    Rule 3—Where there is a contract for the sale of specific goods in a deliverable state but the seller is bound to weigh, measure, test or do some other act or thing with reference to the goods for the purpose of ascertaining the price, the property does not pass until the act or thing is done and the buyer has notice that it has been done.
    Rule 4—When goods are delivered to the buyer on approval or on sale or return or other similar terms the property in the goods passes to the buyer—
        (a) when he signifies his approval or acceptance to the seller or does any other act adopting the transaction;

(b) if he does not signify his approval or acceptance to the seller but retains the goods without giving notice of rejection, then, if a time has been fixed for the return of the goods on the expiration of that time, and if no time has been fixed, on the expiration of a reasonable time.

Rule 5—

(1) Where there is a contract for the sale of unascertained or future goods by description, and goods of that description and in a deliverable state are unconditionally appropriated to the contract, either by the seller with the assent of the buyer or by the buyer with the assent of the seller, the property in the goods then passes to the buyer; and the assent may be express or implied, and may be given either before or after the appropriation is made.

(2) Where, in pursuance of the contract, the seller delivers the goods to the buyer or to a carrier or other bailee or custodier (whether named by the buyer or not) for the purpose of transmission to the buyer, and does not reserve the right of disposal, he is to be taken to have unconditionally appropriated the goods to the contract.

(3) Where there is a contract for the sale of a specified quantity of unascertained goods in a deliverable state forming part of a bulk which is identified either in the contract or by subsequent agreement between the parties and the bulk is reduced to (or to less than) that quantity, then, if the buyer under that contract is the only buyer to whom goods are then due out of the bulk—

(a) the remaining goods are to be taken as appropriated to that contract at the time when the bulk is so reduced; and

(b) the property in those goods then passes to that buyer.

(4) Paragraph (3) above applies also (with the necessary modifications) where a bulk is reduced to (or to less than) the aggregate of the quantities due to a single buyer under separate contracts relating to that bulk and he is the only buyer to whom goods are then due out of that bulk.

19. Reservation of right of disposal

(1) Where there is a contract for the sale of specific goods or where goods are subsequently appropriated to the contract, the seller may, by the terms of the contract or appropriation, reserve the right of disposal of the goods until certain conditions are fulfilled; and in such a case, notwithstanding the delivery of the goods to the buyer, or to the carrier or other bailee or custodier for the purpose of transmission to the buyer, the property in the goods does not pass to the buyer until the conditions imposed by the seller are fulfilled.

(2) Where goods are shipped and by the bill of lading the goods are deliverable to the order of the seller or his agent, the seller is *prima facie* to be taken to reserve the right of disposal.

(3) Where the seller of goods draws on the buyer for the price and transmits the bill of exchange and bill of lading to the buyer together to secure acceptance or payment of the bill of exchange, the buyer is bound to return the bill of lading if he does not honour the bill of exchange, and if he wrongfully retains the bill of lading the property in the goods does not pass to him.

20. Risk *prima facie* passes with property

(1) Unless otherwise agreed, the goods remain at the seller's risk until the property in them is transferred to the buyer, but when the property in them is transferred to the buyer the goods are at the buyer's risk whether delivery has been made or not.

(2) But where delivery has been delayed through the fault of either buyer or seller the goods are at the risk of the party at fault as regards any loss which might not have occurred but for such fault.

(3)   Nothing in this section affects the duties or liabilities of either seller or buyer as a bailee or custodier of the goods of the other party.

(4)   [Omitted].

20A. Undivided shares in goods forming part of a bulk

(1)   This section applies to a contract for the sale of a specified quantity of unascertained goods if the following conditions are met—

    (a)   the goods or some of them form part of a bulk which is identified either in the contract or by subsequent agreement between the parties; and

    (b)   the buyer has paid the price for some or all of the goods which are the subject of the contract and which form part of the bulk.

(2)   Where this section applies, then (unless the parties agree otherwise), as soon as the conditions specified in paragraphs (a) and (b) of subsection (1) above are met or at such later time as the parties may agree—

    (a)   property in an undivided share in the bulk is transferred to the buyer; and

    (b)   the buyer becomes an owner in common of the bulk.

(3)   Subject to subsection (4) below, for the purposes of this section, the undivided share of a buyer in a bulk at any time shall be such share as the quantity of goods paid for and due to the buyer out of the bulk bears to the quantity of goods in the bulk at that time.

(4)   Where the aggregate of the undivided shares of buyers in a bulk determined under subsection (3) above would at any time exceed the whole of the bulk at that time, the undivided share in the bulk of each buyer shall be reduced proportionately so that the aggregate of the undivided shares is equal to the whole bulk.

(5)   Where a buyer has paid the price for only some of the goods due to him out of a bulk, any delivery to the buyer out of the bulk shall, for the purposes of this section, be ascribed in the first place to the goods in respect of which payment has been made.

(6)   For the purposes of this section payment of part of the price for any goods shall be treated as payment for a corresponding part of the goods.

20B. Deemed consent by co-owner to dealings in bulk goods

(1)   A person who has become an owner in common of a bulk by virtue of section 20A above shall be deemed to have consented to—

    (a)   any delivery of goods out of the bulk to any other owner in common of the bulk, being goods which are due to him under his contract;

    (b)   any dealing with or removal, delivery or disposal of goods in the bulk by any other person who is an owner in common of the bulk in so far as the goods fall within that co-owner's undivided share in the bulk at the time of the dealing, removal, delivery or disposal.

(2)   No cause of action shall accrue to anyone against a person by reason of that person having acted in accordance with paragraph (a) or (b) of subsection (1) above in reliance on any consent deemed to have been given under that subsection.

(3)   Nothing in this section or section 20A above shall—

    (a)   impose an obligation on a buyer of goods out of a bulk to compensate any other buyer of goods out of that bulk for any shortfall in the goods received by that other buyer;

    (b)   affect any contractual arrangement between buyers of goods out of a bulk for adjustments between themselves; or

    (c)   affect the rights of any buyer under his contract.

Transfer of title

21. Sale by person not the owner

(1)   Subject to this Act, where goods are sold by a person who is not their owner and who does not sell them under the authority or with the consent of the owner, the buyer acquires no better title to the goods than the seller had, unless the owner of the goods is by his conduct precluded from denying the seller's authority to sell.

(2)   Nothing in this Act affects—

(a)   the provisions of the Factors Acts or any enactment enabling the apparent owner of goods to dispose of them as if he were their true owner;

(b)   the validity of any contract of sale under any special common law or statutory power of sale or under the order of a court of competent jurisdiction.

22.   [Repealed].

23.   Sale under voidable title

When the seller of goods has a voidable title to them, but his title has not been avoided at the time of the sale, the buyer acquires a good title to the goods, provided he buys them in good faith and without notice of the seller's defect of title.

24.   Seller in possession after sale

Where a person having sold goods continues or is in possession of the goods, or of the documents of title to the goods, the delivery or transfer by that person, or by a mercantile agent acting for him, of the goods or documents of title under any sale, pledge, or other disposition thereof, to any person receiving the same in good faith and without notice of the previous sale, has the same effect as if the person making the delivery or transfer were expressly authorised by the owner of the goods to make the same.

25. Buyer in possession after sale

(1)   Where a person having bought or agreed to buy goods obtains, with the consent of the seller, possession of the goods or the documents of title to the goods or documents of title, under any sale, pledge, or other disposition thereof, to any person receiving the same in good faith and without notice of any lien or other right of the original seller in respect of the goods, has the same effect as if the person making the delivery or transfer were a mercantile agent in possession of the goods or documents of title with the consent of the owner.

(2)   For the purposes of subsection (1) above—

(a)   the buyer under a conditional sale agreement is to be taken not to be a person who has bought or agreed to buy goods; and

(b)   'conditional sale agreement' means an agreement for the sale of goods which is a consumer credit agreement within the meaning of the Consumer Credit Act 1974 under which the purchase price or part of it is payable by instalments, and the property in the goods is to remain in the seller (notwithstanding that the buyer is to be in possession of the goods) until such conditions as to the payment of instalments or otherwise as may be specified in the agreement are fulfilled.

(3) and (4) [Omitted].

26. **Supplementary to sections 24 and 25**

In sections 24 and 25 above 'mercantile agent' means a mercantile agent having in the customary course of his business as such agent authority either—

(a)   to sell goods; or
(b)   to consign goods for the purpose of sale; or
(c)   to buy goods; or
(d)   to raise money on the security of goods.

PART IV
PERFORMANCE OF THE CONTRACT

27.   **Duties of seller and buyer**

It is the duty of the seller to deliver the goods, and of the buyer to accept and pay for them, in accordance with the terms of the contract of sale.

28.   **Payment and delivery are concurrent conditions**

Unless otherwise agreed, delivery of the goods and payment of the price are concurrent conditions, that is to say, the seller must be ready and willing to give possession of the goods to the buyer in exchange for the price and the buyer must be ready and willing to pay the price in exchange for possession of the goods.

29.   **Rules about delivery**

(1)   Whether it is for the buyer to take possession of the goods or for the seller to send them to the buyer is a question depending in each case on the contract, express or implied, between the parties.

(2)   Apart from any such contract, express or implied, the place of delivery is the seller's place of business if he has one, and if not, his residence; except that, if the contract is for the sale of specific goods, which to the knowledge of the parties when the contract is made are in some other place, then that place is the place of delivery.

(3)   Where under the contract of sale the seller is bound to send the goods to the buyer, but no time for sending them is fixed, the seller is bound to send them within a reasonable time.

(4)   Where the goods at the time of sale are in the possession of a third person, there is no delivery by seller to buyer unless and until the third person acknowledges to the buyer that he holds the goods on his behalf; but nothing in this section affects the operation of the issue or transfer of any document of title to goods.

(5)   Demand or tender of delivery may be treated as ineffectual unless made at a reasonable hour; and what is a reasonable hour is a question of fact.

(6)   Unless otherwise agreed, the expenses of and incidental to putting the goods into a deliverable state must be borne by the seller.

30.   **Delivery of wrong quantity**

(1)   Where the seller delivers to the buyer a quantity of goods less than he contracted to sell, the buyer may reject them, but if the buyer accepts the goods so delivered he must pay for them at the contract rate.

(2)   Where the seller delivers to the buyer a quantity of goods larger than he contracted to sell, the buyer may accept the goods included in the contract and reject the rest, or he may reject the whole.

(2A)   A buyer who does not deal as consumer may not—

(a)   where the seller delivers a quantity of goods less than he contracted to sell, reject the goods under subsection (1) above; or

(b)   where the seller delivers a quantity of goods larger than he contracted to sell, reject the whole under subsection (2) above, if the shortfall or, as the case may be, excess is so slight that it would be unreasonable for him to do so.

(2B) It is for the seller to show that a shortfall or excess fell within subsection (2A) above.

(2C) Subsections (2A) and (2B) above do not apply to Scotland.

(3) Where the seller delivers to the buyer a quantity of goods larger than he contracted to sell and the buyer accepts the whole of the goods so delivered he must pay for them at the contract rate.

(4) [Repealed].

(5) This section is subject to any usage of trade, special agreement, or of course of dealing between the parties.

31. Instalment deliveries

(1) Unless otherwise agreed, the buyer of goods is not bound to accept delivery of them by instalments.

(2) Where there is a contract for the sale of goods to be delivered by stated instalments, which are to be separately paid for, and the seller makes defective deliveries in respect of one or more instalments or the buyer neglects or refuses to take delivery of or pay for one or more instalments, it is a question in each case depending on the terms of the contract and the circumstances of the case whether the breach of contract is a repudiation of the whole contract or whether it is a severable breach giving rise to a claim for compensation but not to a right to treat the whole contract as repudiated.

32. Delivery to carrier

(1) Where, in pursuance of a contract of sale, the seller is authorised or required to send the goods to the buyer, delivery of the goods to a carrier (whether named by the buyer or not) for the purpose of transmission to the buyer is *prima facie* deemed to be a delivery of the goods to the buyer.

(2) Unless otherwise authorised by the buyer, the seller must make such contract with the carrier on behalf of the buyer as may be reasonable having regard to the nature of the goods and the other circumstances of the case; and if the seller omits to do so, and the goods are lost or damaged in course of transit, the buyer may decline to treat the delivery to the carrier as a delivery to himself or may hold the seller responsible in damages.

(3) Unless otherwise agreed, where goods are sent by the seller to the buyer by a route involving sea transit, under circumstances in which it is usual to insure, the seller must give such notice to the buyer as may enable him to insure them during their sea transit; and if the seller fails to do so, the goods are at his risk during such sea transit.

(4) [Omitted].

33. Risk where goods are delivered at distant place

Where the seller of goods agrees to deliver them at his own risk at a place other than that where they are when sold, the buyer must nevertheless (unless otherwise agreed) take any risk of deterioration in the goods necessarily incident to the course of transit.

34. Buyer's right of examining the goods

Unless otherwise agreed, when the seller tenders delivery of goods to the buyer, he is bound on request to afford the buyer a reasonable opportunity of examining the goods for the purpose of ascertaining whether they are in conformity with the contract and, in the case of a contract for sale by sample, of comparing the bulk with the sample.

35. Acceptance
   (1) The buyer is deemed to have accepted the goods subject to subsection (2)
        below—
        (a) when he intimates to the seller that he has accepted them; or
        (b) when the goods have been delivered to him and he does any act in
             relation to them which is inconsistent with the ownership of the seller.
   (2) Where goods are delivered to the buyer, and he has not previously examined
        them, he is not deemed to have accepted them under subsection (1) above
        until he has had a reasonable opportunity of examining them for the
        purpose—
        (a) of ascertaining whether they are in conformity with the contract; and
        (b) in the case of a contract for sale by sample, of comparing the bulk with
             the sample.
   (3) Where the buyer deals as consumer or (in Scotland) the contract of sale is a
        consumer contract, the buyer cannot lose his right to rely on subsection (2)
        above by agreement, waiver or otherwise.
   (4) The buyer is also deemed to have accepted the goods when after the lapse of
        a reasonable time he retains the goods without intimating to the seller that he
        has rejected them.
   (5) The questions that are material in determining for the purposes of subsection
        (4) above whether a reasonable time has elapsed include whether the buyer
        has had a reasonable opportunity of examining the goods for the purpose
        mentioned in subsection (2) above.
   (6) The buyer is not by virtue of this section deemed to have accepted the goods
        merely because—
        (a) he asks for, or agrees to, their repair by or under an arrangement with the
             seller; or
        (b) the goods are delivered to another under a sub-sale or other disposition.
   (7) Where the contract is for the sale of goods making one or more commercial
        units, a buyer accepting any goods included in a unit is deemed to have
        accepted all the goods making the unit; and in this subsection 'commercial
        unit' means a unit division of which would materially impair the value of the
        goods or the character of the unit.
   (8) [Omitted].

35A. Right of partial rejection
   (1) If the buyer—
        (a) has the right to reject the goods by reason of a breach on the part of the
             seller that affects some or all of them; but
        (b) accepts some of the goods, including, where there are any goods
             unaffected by the breach, all such goods,
        he does not by accepting them lose his right to reject the rest.
   (2) In the case of a buyer having the right to reject an instalment of goods,
        subsection (1) above applies as if references to the goods were references to
        the goods comprised in the instalment.
   (3) For the purposes of subsection (1) above, goods are affected by a breach if by
        reason of the breach they are not in conformity with the contract.
   (4) This section applies unless a contrary intention appears in, or is to be implied
        from, the contract.

36. Buyer not bound to return rejected goods
   Unless otherwise agreed, where goods are delivered to the buyer, and he refuses
   to accept them, having the right to do so, he is not bound to return them to the
   seller, but it is sufficient if he intimates to the seller that he refuses to accept them.

37.   Buyer's liability for not taking delivery of goods

(1)   When the seller is ready and willing to deliver the goods, and requests the buyer to take delivery, and the buyer does not within a reasonable time after such request take delivery of the goods, he is liable to the seller for any loss occasioned by his neglect or refusal to take delivery, and also for a reasonable charge for the care and custody of the goods.

(2)   Nothing in this section affects the rights of the seller where the neglect or refusal of the buyer to take delivery amounts to a repudiation of the contract.

PART V
RIGHTS OF UNPAID SELLER AGAINST THE GOODS

Preliminary

38.   Unpaid seller defined

(1)   The seller of goods is an unpaid seller within the meaning of this Act—

(a)   when the whole of the price has not been paid or tendered;

(b)   when a bill of exchange or other negotiable instrument has been received as conditional payment, and the condition on which it was received has not been fulfilled by reason of the dishonour of the instrument or otherwise.

(2)   In this Part of this Act 'seller' includes any person who is in the position of a seller, as, for instance, an agent of the seller to whom the bill of lading has been indorsed, or a consignor or agent who has himself paid (or is directly responsible for) the price.

39.   Unpaid seller's rights

(1)   Subject to this and any other Act, notwithstanding that the property in the goods may have passed to the buyer, the unpaid seller of goods, as such, has by implication of law—

(a)   a lien on the goods or right to retain them for the price while he is in possession of them;

(b)   in case of the insolvency of the buyer, a right of stopping the goods in transit after he has parted with the possession of them;

(c)   a right of re-sale as limited by this Act.

(2)   Where the property in goods has not passed to the buyer, the unpaid seller has (in addition to his other remedies) a right of withholding delivery similar to and co-extensive with his rights of lien or retention and stoppage in transit where the property has passed to the buyer.

40.   [Repealed].

Unpaid seller's lien

41.   Seller's lien

(1)   Subject to this Act, the unpaid seller of goods who is in possession of them is entitled to retain possession of them until payment or tender of the price in the following cases—

(a)   where the goods have been sold without any stipulation as to credit;

(b)   where the goods have been sold on credit but the term of credit has expired;

(c)   where the buyer becomes insolvent.

(2)   The seller may exercise his lien or right of retention notwithstanding that he is in possession of the goods as agent or bailee or custodier for the buyer.

42.   Part delivery

Where an unpaid seller has made part delivery of the goods, he may exercise his lien or right of retention on the remainder, unless such part delivery has been made under such circumstances as to show an agreement to waive the lien or right of retention.

43.   Termination of lien

(1)   The unpaid seller of goods loses his lien or right of retention in respect of them—

(a)   when he delivers the goods to a carrier or other bailee or custodier for the purpose of transmission to the buyer without reserving the right of disposal of the goods;

(b)   when the buyer or his agent lawfully obtains possession of the goods;

(c)   by waiver of the lien or right of retention.

(2)   An unpaid seller of goods who has a lien or right of retention in respect of them does not lose his lien or right of retention by reason only that he has obtained judgment or decree for the price of the goods.

Stoppage in transit

44.   Right of stoppage in transit

Subject to this Act, when the buyer of goods becomes insolvent the unpaid seller who has parted with the possession of the goods has the right of stopping them in transit, that is to say, he may resume possession of the goods as long as they are in course of transit, and may retain them until payment or tender the price.

45.   Duration of transit

(1)   Goods are deemed to be in course of transit from the time when they are delivered to a carrier or other bailee or custodier for the purpose of transmission to the buyer, until the buyer or his agent in that behalf takes delivery of them from the carrier or other bailee or custodier.

(2)   If the buyer or his agent in that behalf obtains delivery of the goods before their arrival at the appointed destination, the transit is at an end.

(3)   If, after the arrival of the goods at the appointed destination, the carrier or other bailee or custodier acknowledges to the buyer or his agent that he holds the goods on his behalf and continues in possession of them as bailee or custodier for the buyer or his agent, the transit is at an end, and it is immaterial that a further destination for the goods may have been indicated by the buyer.

(4)   If the goods are rejected by the buyer, and the carrier or other bailee or custodier continues in possession of them, the transit is not deemed to be at an end, even if the seller has refused to receive them back.

(5)   When goods are delivered to a ship chartered by the buyer it is a question depending on the circumstances of the particular case whether they are in the possession of the master as a carrier or as agent to the buyer.

(6)   Where the carrier or other bailee or custodier wrongfully refuses to deliver the goods to the buyer or his agent in that behalf, the transit is deemed to be at an end.

(7)   Where part delivery of the goods has been made to the buyer or his agent in that behalf, the remainder of the goods may be stopped in transit, unless such part delivery has been made under such circumstances as to show an agreement to give up possession of the whole of the goods.

46.   How stoppage in transit is effected

(1)   The unpaid seller may exercise his right of stoppage in transit either by taking actual possession of the goods or by giving notice of his claim to the carrier or other bailee or custodier in whose possession the goods are.

(2)   The notice may be given either to the person in actual possession of the goods or to his principal.

(3)   If given to the principal, the notice is ineffective unless given at such time and under such circumstances that the principal, by the exercise of reasonable diligence, may communicate it to his servant or agent in time to prevent a delivery to the buyer.

(4)   When notice of stoppage in transit is given by the seller to the carrier or other bailee or custodier in possession of the goods, he must re-deliver the goods to, or according to the directions of, the seller; and the expenses of the re-delivery must be borne by the seller.

Re-sale, etc, by buyer

47.   Effect of sub-sale, etc, by buyer

(1)   Subject to this Act, the unpaid seller's right of lien or retention or stoppage in transit is not affected by any sale or other disposition of the goods which the buyer may have made, unless the seller has assented to it.

(2)   Where a document of title to goods has been lawfully transferred to any person as buyer or owner of the goods, and that person transfers the document to a person who takes it in good faith and for valuable consideration, then—

(a)   if the last-mentioned transfer was by way of sale the unpaid seller's right of lien or retention or stoppage in transit is defeated; and

(b)   if the last-mentioned transfer was made by way of pledge or other disposition for value, the unpaid seller's right of lien or retention or stoppage in transit can only be exercised subject to the rights of the transferee.

Rescission and re-sale by seller

48.   Rescission and re-sale by seller

(1)   Subject to this section, a contract of sale is not rescinded by the mere exercise by an unpaid seller of his right of lien or retention or stoppage in transit.

(2)   Where an unpaid seller who has exercised his right of lien or retention or stoppage in transit re-sells the goods, the buyer acquires a good title to them as against the original buyer.

(3)   Where the goods are of a perishable nature, or where the unpaid seller gives notice to the buyer of his intention to re-sell, and the buyer does not within a reasonable time pay or tender the price, the unpaid seller may re-sell the goods and recover from the original buyer damages for any loss occasioned by his breach of contract.

(4)   Where the seller expressly reserves the right of re-sale in case the buyer should make default, and on the buyer making default re-sells the goods, the original contract of sale is rescinded but without prejudice to any claim the seller may have for damages.

PART VA

48A.–48F. [Omitted].

PART VI
ACTIONS FOR BREACH OF THE CONTRACT

Seller's remedies

49.   Action for price

(1)   Where, under a contract of sale, the property in the goods has passed to the buyer and he wrongfully neglects or refuses to pay for the goods according to the terms of the contract, the seller may maintain an action against him for the price of the goods.

(2)   Where, under a contract of sale, the price is payable on a day certain irrespective of delivery and the buyer wrongfully neglects or refuses to pay such price, the seller may maintain an action for the price, although the property in the goods has not passed and the goods have not been appropriated to the contract.

(3)   Nothing in this section prejudices the right of the seller in Scotland to recover interest on the price from the date of tender of the goods, or from the date on which the price was payable, as the case may be.

50.   Damages for non-acceptance

(1)   Where the buyer wrongfully neglects or refuses to accept and pay for the goods, the seller may maintain an action against him for damages for non-acceptance.

(2)   The measure of damages is the estimated loss directly and naturally resulting, in the ordinary course of events, from the buyer's breach of contract.

(3)   Where there is an available market for the goods in question the measure of damages is *prima facie* to be ascertained by the difference between the contract price and the market or current price at the time or times when the goods ought to have been accepted or (if no time was fixed for acceptance) at the time of the refusal to accept.

Buyer's remedies

51.   Damages for non-delivery

(1)   Where the seller wrongfully neglects or refuses to deliver the goods to the buyer, the buyer may maintain an action against the seller for damages for non-delivery.

(2)   The measure of damages is the estimated loss directly and naturally resulting, in the ordinary course of events, from the seller's breach of contract.

(3)   Where there is an available market for the goods in question the measure of damages is *prima facie* to be ascertained by the difference between the contract price and the market or current price of the goods at the time or times when they ought to have been delivered or (if no time was fixed) at the time of the refusal to deliver.

52.   Specific performance

(1)   In any action for breach of contract to deliver specific or ascertained goods the court may, if it thinks fit, on the plaintiff's application, by its judgement or decree direct that the contract shall be performed specifically, without giving the defendant the option of retaining the goods on payment of damages.

(2)   The plaintiff's application may be made at any time before judgement or decree.

(3)   The judgement or decree may be unconditional, or on such terms and conditions as to damages, payment of the price and otherwise as seem just to the court.

(4) The provisions of this section shall be deemed to be supplementary to, and not in derogation of, the right of specific implement in Scotland.

53. Remedy for breach of warranty

(1) Where there is a breach of warranty by the seller, or where the buyer elects (or is compelled) to treat any breach of a condition on the part of the seller as a breach of warranty, the buyer is not by reason only of such breach of warranty entitled to reject the goods; but he may:

(a) set up against the seller the breach of warranty in diminution or extinction of the price, or

(b) maintain an action against the seller for damages for the breach of warranty.

(2) The measure of damages for breach of warranty is the estimated loss directly and naturally resulting, in the ordinary course of events, from the breach of warranty.

(3) In the case of breach of warranty of quality such loss is *prima facie* the difference between the value of the goods at the time of delivery to the buyer and the value they would have had if they had fulfilled the warranty.

(4) The fact that the buyer has set up the breach of warranty in diminution or extinction of the price does not prevent him from maintaining an action for the same breach of warranty if he has suffered further damage.

(5) This section does not apply to Scotland.

Interest, etc

54. Interest, etc

Nothing in this Act affects the right of the buyer or the seller to recover interest or special damages in any case where by law interest or special damages may be recoverable, or to recover money paid where the consideration for the payment of it has failed.

PART VII
SUPPLEMENTARY

55. Exclusion of implied terms

(1) Where a right, duty or liability would arise under a contract of sale of goods by implication of law, it may (subject to the Unfair Contract Terms Act 1977) be negatived or varied by express agreement, or by the course of dealing between the parties, or by such usage as binds both parties to the contract.

(2) An express condition or warranty does not negative a condition or warranty implied by this Act unless inconsistent with it.

(3) [Omitted].

56. [Omitted].

57. Auction sales

(1) Where goods are put up for sale by auction in lots, each lot is *prima facie* deemed to be the subject of a separate contract of sale.

(2) A sale by auction is complete when the auctioneer announces its completion by the fall of the hammer, or in other customary manner; and until the announcement is made any bidder may retract his bid.

(3) A sale by auction may be notified to be subject to a reserve or upset price, and a right to bid may also be reserved expressly by or on behalf of the seller.

(4) Where a sale by auction is not notified to be subject to a right to bid by or on behalf of the seller, it is not lawful for the seller to bid himself or to employ

any person to bid at the sale, or for the auctioneer knowingly to take any bid from the seller or any such person.

(5)   A sale contravening subsection (4) above may be treated as fraudulent by the buyer.

(6)   Where, in respect of a sale by auction, a right to bid is expressly reserved (but not otherwise) the seller or any one person on his behalf may bid at the auction.

58.   [Omitted].

59.   Reasonable time a question of fact

Where a reference is made in this Act to a reasonable time the question what is a reasonable time is a question of fact.

60.   Rights, etc, enforceable by action

Where a right, duty or liability is declared by this Act, it may (unless otherwise provided by this Act) be enforced by action.

61.   Interpretation

(1)   In this Act, unless the context or subject matter otherwise requires—

'action' includes counterclaim and set-off, and in Scotland condescendence and claim and compensation;

'bulk' means a mass or collection of goods of the same kind which—

(a)   is contained in a defined space or area; and

(b)   is such that any goods in the bulk are interchangeable with any other goods therein of the same number or quantity;

'business' includes a profession and the activities of any Government department (including a Northern Ireland department) or local or public authority;

'buyer' means a person who buys or agrees to buy goods;

'consumer contract' has the same meaning as in section 25(1) of the Unfair Contract Terms Act 1977; and for the purposes of this Act the onus of proving that a contract is not to be regarded as a consumer contract shall lie on the seller;

'contract of sale' includes an agreement to sell as well as a sale;

'credit-broker' means a person acting in the course of a business of credit brokerage carried on by him, that is a business of effecting introduction of individuals desiring to obtain credit—

(a)   to persons carrying on any business so far as it relates to the provision of credit; or

(b)   to other persons engaged in credit brokerage;

'defendant' includes in Scotland defender, respondent, and claimant in a multiplepoinding;

'delivery' means voluntary transfer of possession from one person to another, except that in relation to sections 20A and 20B above it includes such appropriation of goods to the contract as results in property in the goods being transferred to the buyer;

'document of title to goods' has the same meaning as it has in the Factors Acts;

'Factors Acts' means the Factors Act 1889, the Factors (Scotland) Act 1890, and any enactment amending or substituted for the same;

'fault' means wrongful act or default;

'future goods' means goods to be manufactured or acquired by the seller after the making of the contract of sale;

'goods' includes all personal chattels other than things in action and money, and in Scotland all corporeal moveables except money; and in particular 'goods' includes emblements, industrial growing crops, and things attached to or forming part of the land which are agreed to be severed before sale or under the contract of sale and includes an undivided share in goods;

'plaintiff' includes pursuer, complainer, claimant in a multiple poinding and defendant or defender counter-claiming;

'producer' means the manufacturer of goods, the importer of goods into the European Economic Area or any person purporting to be a producer by placing his name, trade mark or other distinctive sign on the goods;

'property' means the general property in goods, and not merely a special property;

'repair' means, in cases where there is a lack of conformity in goods for the purposes of section 48F of this Act, to bring the goods into conformity with the contract;

'sale' includes a bargain and sale as well as a sale and delivery;

'seller' means a person who sells or agrees to sell goods;

'specific goods' means goods identified and agreed on at the time a contract of sale is made and includes an undivided share, specified as a fraction or percentage, of goods identified and agreed on as aforesaid;

'warranty' (as regards England and Wales and Northern Ireland) means an agreement with reference to goods which are the subject of a contract of sale, but collateral to the main purpose of such contract, the breach of which gives rise to a claim for damages, but not to a right to reject the goods and treat the contract as repudiated.

(2) [Repealed].

(3) A thing is deemed to be done in good faith within the meaning of this Act when it is in fact done honestly, whether it is done negligently or not.

(4) A person is deemed to be insolvent within the meaning of this Act if he has either ceased to pay his debts in the ordinary course of business or he cannot pay his debts as they become due.

(5) Goods are in a deliverable state within the meaning of this Act when they are in such a state that the buyer would under the contract be bound to take delivery of them.

(5A) References in this Act to dealing as consumer are to be construed in accordance with Part I of the Unfair Contract Terms Act 1977; and, for the purposes of this Act, it is for a seller claiming that the buyer does not deal as consumer to show that he does not.

(6) [Omitted].

62.–64. and Schedules 1–4 [Omitted].

LIMITATION ACT 1980

CHAPTER 58

PART I

ORDINARY TIME LIMITS FOR DIFFERENT CLASSES OF ACTION

Time limits under Part I subject to extension or exclusion under Part II

Actions founded on tort

2. Time limit for actions founded on tort.
3. Time limit in case of successive conversions and extinction of title of owner of converted goods.

Actions founded on simple contract

5.   Time limit for actions founded on simple contract.
6.   Special time limit for actions in respects of certain loans.
7.   Time limit for actions to enforce certain awards.

General rule for actions on a specialty

8.   Time limit for actions on a specialty.

Actions for sums recoverable by statute

9.   Time limit for actions for sums recoverable by statute.
10.   Special time limit for claiming contribution.

Actions in respect of latent damage not involving personal injuries

14A.   Special time limit for negligence actions where facts relevant to cause of action are not known at date of accrual.
14B.   Overriding time limit for negligence actions not involving personal injuries.

PART I
ORDINARY TIME LIMITS FOR DIFFERENT CLASSES OF ACTION

1.   **[Omitted].**

Actions founded on tort

2.   **Time limit for actions founded on tort**
An action founded on tort shall not be brought after the expiration of six years from the date on which the cause of action accrued.

3.   **Time limit in case of successive conversions and extinction of title of owner of converted goods**
(1)   Where any cause of action in respect of the conversion of a chattel has accrued to any person and, before he recovers possession of the chattel, a further conversion take place, no action shall be brought in respect of the further conversion after the expiration of six years from the accrual of the cause of action in respect of the original conversion.
(2)   Where any such cause of action has accrued to any person and the period prescribed for bringing that action has expired and he has not during that period recovered possession of the chattel, the title of that person to the chattel shall be extinguished.

4. and 4A. [Omitted].

Actions founded on simple contract

5.   **Time limit for actions founded on simple contract**
An action founded on simple contract shall not be brought after the expiration of six years from the date on which the cause of action accrued.

6.   **Special time limit for actions in respect of certain loans**
(1)   Subject to subsection (3) below, section 5 of this Act shall not bar the right of action on a contract of loan to which this section applies.

(2)   This section applies to any contract of loan which—
  (a) does not provide for repayment of the debt on or before a fixed or determinable date; and
  (b) does not effectively (whether or not it purports to do so) make the obligation to repay the debt conditional on a demand for repayment made by or on behalf of the creditor or on any other matter;
  except where in connection with taking the loan the debtor enters into any collateral obligation to pay the amount of the debt or any part of it (as, for example, by delivering a promissory note as security for the debt) on terms which would exclude the application of this section to the contract of loan if they applied directly to repayment of the debt.

(3)   Where a demand in writing for repayment of the debt under a contract of loan to which this section applies is made by or on behalf of the creditor (or, where there are joint creditors, by or on behalf of any one of them) section 5 of this Act shall thereupon apply as if the cause of action to recover the debt had accrued on the date on which the demand was made.

(4)   In this section 'promissory note' has the same meaning as in the Bills of Exchange Act 1882.

7.   Time limit for actions to enforce certain awards

An action to enforce an award, where the submission is not by an instrument under seal, shall not be brought after the expiration of six years from the date on which the cause of action accrued.

General rule for actions on a specialty

8.   Time limit for actions on a specialty

(1)   An action upon a specialty shall not be brought after the expiration of twelve years from the date on which the cause of action accrued.

(2)   Subsection (1) above shall not affect any action for which a shorter period of limitation is prescribed by any other provision of this Act.

Actions for sums recoverable by statute

9.   Time limit for actions for sums recoverable by statute

(1)   An action to recover any sum recoverable by virtue of any enactment shall not be brought after the expiration of six years from the date on which the cause of action accrued.

(2)   Subsection (1) above shall not affect any action to which section 10 of this Act applies.

10.   Special time limit for claiming contribution

(1)   Where under section 1 of the Civil Liability (Contribution) Act 1978 any person becomes entitled to a right to recover contribution in respect of any other person, no action to recover contribution by virtue of that right shall be brought after the expiration of two years from the date on which that right accrued.

(2)   For the purposes of this section the date on which a right to recover contribution in respect of any damage accrues to any person (referred to below in this section as 'the relevant date') shall be ascertained as provided in subsection (3) and (4) below.

(3)   If the person in question is held liable in respect of that damage—
  (a) by a judgment given in any civil proceedings; or
  (b) by an award made on any arbitration;
  the relevant date shall be the date on which the judgement is given, or the date of the award (as the case may be).

For the purposes of this subsection no account shall be taken of any judgement or award given or made on appeal in so far as it varies the amount of damages awarded against the person in question.

(4)   If, in any case not within subsection (3) above, the person in question makes or agrees to make any payment to one or more persons in compensation for that damage (whether he admits any liability in respect of the damage or not), the relevant date shall be the earliest date on which the amount to be paid by him is agreed between him (or his representative) and the person (or each of the persons, as the case may be) to whom the payment is to be made.

(5)   An action to recover contribution shall be one to which sections 28, 32, and 35 of this Act apply, but otherwise Parts II and III of this Act (except sections 34, 27 and 38) shall not apply for the purposes of this section.

11.–14.   [Omitted].

Actions in respect of latent damage not involving personal injuries

14A.   Special time limit for negligence actions where facts relevant to cause of action are not known at date of accrual

(1)   This section applies to any action for damages for negligence, other than one to which section 11 of this Act applies, where the starting date for reckoning the period of limitation under subsection (4)(b) below falls after the date on which the cause of action accrued.

(2)   Section 2 of this Act shall not apply to an action to which this section applies.

(3)   An action to which this section applies shall not be brought after the expiration of the period applicable in accordance with subsection (4) below.

(4)   That period is either—
        (a)   six years from the date on which the cause of action accrued; or
        (b)   three years from the starting date as defined by subsection (5) below, if that period expires later than the period mentioned in paragraph (a) above.

(5)   For the purposes of this section, the starting date for reckoning the period of limitation under subsection (4)(b) above is the earliest date on which the plaintiff or any person in whom the cause of action was vested before him first had both the knowledge required for bringing an action for damages in respect of the relevant damage and a right to bring such an action.

(6)   In subsection (5) above "the knowledge required for bringing an action for damages in respect of the relevant damage" means knowledge both—
        (a)   of the material facts about the damage in respect of which damages are claimed; and
        (b)   of the other facts relevant to the current action mentioned in subsection (8) below.

(7)   For the purposes of subsection (6)(a) above, the material facts about the damage are such facts about the damage as would lead a reasonable person who had suffered such damage to consider it sufficiently serious to justify his instituting proceedings for damages against a defendant who did not dispute liability and was able to satisfy a judgement.

(8)   The other facts referred to in subsection (6)(b) above are—
        (a)   that the damage was attributable in whole or in part to the act or omission which is alleged to constitute negligence; and
        (b)   the identity of the defendant; and
        (c)   if it is alleged that the act or omission was that of a person other than the defendant, the identity of that person and the additional facts supporting the bringing of an action against the defendant.

(9)   Knowledge that any acts or omissions did or did not, as a matter of law, involve negligence is irrelevant for the purposes of subsection (5) above.

(10)   For the purposes of this section a person's knowledge includes knowledge which he might reasonably have been expected to acquire—

(a)   from facts observable or ascertainable by him; or

(b)   from facts ascertainable by him with the help of appropriate expert advice which it is reasonable for him to seek,

but a person shall not be taken by virtue of this subsection to have knowledge of a fact ascertainable only with the help of expert advice so long as he has taken all reasonable steps to obtain (and, where appropriate, to act on) that advice.

14B.   Overriding time limit for negligence actions not involving personal injuries

(1)   An action for damages for negligence, other than one to which section 11 of this Act applies, shall not be brought after the expiration of fifteen years from the date (or, if more than one, from the last of the dates) on which there occurred any act or omission—

(a)   which is alleged to constitute negligence; and

(b)   to which the damage in respect of which damages are claimed is alleged to be attributable (in whole or in part).

(2)   This section bars the right of action in a case to which subsection (1) above applies notwithstanding that:

(a)   the cause of action has not yet accrued; or

(b)   where section 14A of this Act applies to the action, the date which is for the purposes of that section the starting date for reckoning the period mentioned in subsection (4)(b) of that section has not yet occurred,

before the end of the period of limitation prescribed by this section.

[Note: Section 11 applies for actions in relation to personal injuries or death.]

15.–41. [Omitted].

CIVIL JURISDICTION AND JUDGMENTS ACT 1982

CHAPTER 27

PART I

IMPLEMENTATION OF THE CONVENTIONS

Main implementing provisions

PART IV

MISCELLANEOUS PROVISIONS

Provisions relating to jurisdiction

26.   Security in Admiralty proceedings in England and Wales or Northern Ireland in case of stay, etc.

Provisions relating to recognition and enforcement of judgments

31.   Overseas judgments given against States, etc.
32.   Overseas judgments given in proceedings brought in breach of agreements for settlement of disputes.
33.   Certain steps not to amount to submission to jurisdiction of overseas court.

PART V
SUPPLEMENTARY AND GENERAL PROVISIONS

Domicile

46.   Domicile and seat of the Crown.
49.   Saving for powers to stay, sist, strike out or dismiss proceedings.

PART I
IMPLEMENTATION OF THE CONVENTIONS

Main implementing provisions

1.   Interpretation of references to the Conventions and Contracting States
    (1)   In this Act—
            'the 1968 Convention' means the Convention on jurisdiction and the enforcement of judgments in civil and commercial matters (including the Protocol annexed to that Convention), signed at Brussels on 27th September 1968;
            'the 1971 Protocol' means the Protocol on the interpretation of the 1968 Convention by the European Court, signed at Luxembourg on 3rd June 1971;
            'the Accession convention' means the Convention on the accession to the 1968 convention and the 1971 Protocol of Denmark, the Republic of Ireland and the United Kingdom, signed at Luxembourg on 9th October 1978;
            'the 1982 Accession Convention' means the Convention on the accession of the Hellenic republic to the 1968 Convention and the 1971 Protocol, with the adjustments made to them by the Accession Convention, signed at Luxembourg on 25th October 1982;
            'the 1989 Accession Convention' means the Convention on the accession of the Kingdom of Spain and the Portuguese Republic to the 1968 convention and the 1971 Protocol, with the adjustments made to them by the Accession convention and the 1982 Accession Convention, signed at Donostia-San Sebastian on 26th May 1989;
            'the 1996 Accession Convention' means the Convention on the accession of the Republic of Austria, the Republic of Finland and the Kingdom of Sweden to the 1968 Convention and the 1971 Protocol, with the adjustments made to them by the Accession Convention, the 1982 Accession Convention and the 1989 Accession Convention, signed at Brussels on 29th November 1996;
            'the Brussels Conventions' means the 1968 Convention, the 1971 Protocol, the Accession Convention, the 1982 Accession Convention, the 1989 Accession Convention and the 1996 Accession Convention;

'the Lugano Convention' means the Convention on jurisdiction and the enforcement of judgments in civil and commercial matters (including the Protocols annexed to that Convention) opened for signature at Lugano on 16th September 1988 and signed by the United Kingdom on 18th September 1989;

'the Regulation' means Council Regulation (EC) No. 44/2001 of 22nd December 2000 on jurisdiction and the recognition and enforcement of judgments in civil and commercial matters.

(2) [Omitted].

(3) In this Act—

'Contracting State', without more, in any provision means—

(a) in the application of the provision in relation to the Brussels Conventions, a Brussels Contracting State; and

(b) in the application of the provision in relation to the Lugano Convention, a Lugano Contracting State.

'Brussels Contracting State' means Denmark (which is not bound by the Regulation, but was one of the parties acceding to the 1968 Convention under the Accession Convention);

'Lugano Contracting State' means—

(a) one of the original parties to the Lugano Convention, that is to say—

Austria, Belgium, Denmark, Finland, France, the Federal Republic of Germany, the Hellenic Republic, Iceland, the Republic of Ireland, Italy, Luxembourg, the Netherlands, Norway, Portugal, Spain, Sweden, Switzerland and the United Kingdom; or

(b) a party who has subsequently acceded to that Convention, that is to say, Poland.

being a State in relation to which that convention has taken effect in accordance with paragraph 3 or 4 of Article 61.

'Regulation State' in any provision, in the application of that provision in relation to the Regulation, has the same meaning as 'Member State' in the Regulation, that is all Members States except Denmark.

(4) Any question arising as to whether it is the Regulation, any of the Brussels Conventions, or the Lugano Convention which applies in the circumstances of a particular case shall be determined as follows—

(a) in accordance with Article 54B of the Lugano Convention (which determines the relationship between the Brussels Conventions and the Lugano Convention); and

(b) in accordance with Article 68 of the Regulation (which determines the relationship between the Brussels Conventions and the Regulation).

2. The Conventions to have the force of law

(1) The Brussels Conventions shall have the force of law in the United Kingdom, and judicial notice shall be taken of them.

(2) [Omitted].

3. Interpretation of the Conventions

(1) Any question as to the meaning or effect of any provision of the Brussels Conventions shall, if not referred to the European Court in accordance with the 1971 Protocol, be determined in accordance with the principles laid down by any relevant decision of the European Court.

(2) Judicial notice shall be taken of any decision of, or expression of opinion by, the European Court on any such question.

(3) Without prejudice to the generality of subsection (1), the following reports (which are reproduced in the Official Journal of the Communities), namely—

(a) the reports by Mr P Jenard on the 1968 Convention and the 1971 Protocol;

    (b)   the report by Professor Peter Schlosser on the Accession Convention;

    (c)   the report by Professor Demetrios I Evvigenis and Professor K D Kerameus on the 1982 Accession Convention; and

    (d)   the report by Mr Martinho de Almeida Cruz, Mr Manuel Desantes Real and Mr P Jenard on the 1989 Accession Convention,

may be considered in ascertaining the meaning or effect of any provision of the Brussels Conventions and shall be given such weight as is appropriate in the circumstances.

3A. The Lugano Convention to have the force of law

(1)   The Lugano Convention shall have the force of law in the United Kingdom, and judicial notice shall be taken of it.

(2)   [Omitted].

3B. Interpretation of the Lugano Convention

(1)   In determining any question as to the meaning or effect of a provision of the Lugano Convention, a court in the United Kingdom shall, in accordance with Protocol No 2 to that Convention, take account of any principles laid down in any relevant decision delivered by a court of any other Lugano Contracting State concerning provisions of the Convention.

(2)   Without prejudice to any practice of the courts as to the matters which may be considered apart from this section, the report on the Lugano Convention by Mr P Jenard and Mr G Moller (which is reproduced in the official Journal of the communities of 28th July 1990) may be considered in ascertaining the meaning or effect of any provision of the Convention and shall be given such weight as is appropriate in the circumstances.

4.–23. [Omitted].

PART IV
MISCELLANEOUS PROVISIONS

Provisions relating to jurisdiction

24. Interim relief and protective measures in cases of doubtful jurisdiction

(1)   Any power of a court in England and Wales or Northern Ireland to grant interim relief pending trial or pending the determination of an appeal shall extend to a case where—

    (a)   the issue to be tried, or which is the subject of the appeal, relates to the jurisdiction of the court to entertain the proceedings; or

    (b)   the proceedings involve the reference of any matter to the European Court under the 1971 Protocol; or

    (c)   the proceedings involve a reference of any matter relating to the Regulation to the European Court under Article 68 of the Treaty establishing the European Community.

(2)   Any power of a court in Scotland to grant protective measures pending the decision of any hearing shall apply to a case where—

    (a)   the subject of the proceedings includes a question as to the jurisdiction of the court to entertain them; or

    (b)   the proceedings involve the reference of a matter to the European Court under the 1971 Protocol; or

    (c)   the proceedings involve a reference of any matter relating to the Regulation to the European Court under Article 68 of the Treaty establishing the European Community.

(3)   Subsections (1) and (2) shall not be construed as restricting any power to grant relief of protective measures which a court may have apart from this section.

25.   Interim relief in England and Wales and Northern Ireland in the absence of substantive proceedings

(1)   The High Court in England and Wales or Northern Ireland shall have power to grant interim relief where—

    (a)   proceedings have been or are to be commenced in a Brussels or Lugano Contracting State or a Regulation State other than the United Kingdom or in a part of the United Kingdom other than that in which the High Court in question exercises jurisdiction; and

    (b)   they are or will be proceedings whose subject-matter is within the scope of the Regulation as determined by Article 1 of the Regulation (whether or not the Regulation has effect in relation to the proceedings).

(2)   On an application for any interim relief under subsection (1) the court may refuse to grant that relief if, in the opinion of the court, the fact that the court has no jurisdiction apart from this section in relation to the subject-matter of the proceedings in question makes it inexpedient for the court to grant it.

(3) and (4) [Omitted]; (5) [Repealed] and (6) [Omitted].

(7)   In this section 'interim relief', in relation to the High Court in England and Wales or Northern Ireland, means interim relief of any kind which that court has power to grant in proceedings relating to matters within its jurisdiction, other than—

    (a)   a warrant for the arrest of property; or

    (b)   provision for obtaining evidence.

26.   Security in Admiralty proceedings in England and Wales or Northern Ireland in case of stay, etc

(1)   Where in England and Wales or Northern Ireland a court stays or dismisses Admiralty proceedings on the ground that the dispute in question should be submitted to the determination of the courts of another part of the United Kingdom or of an overseas country, the court may, if in those proceedings property has been arrested or bail or other security has been given to prevent or obtain release from arrest—

    (a)   order that the property arrested be retained as security for the satisfaction of any award or judgment which—

        (i)   is given in respect of the dispute in the legal proceedings in favour of which those proceedings are stayed or dismissed; and

        (ii)   is enforceable in England and Wales or, as the case may be, in Northern Ireland; or

    (b)   order that the stay or dismissal of those proceedings be conditional on the provision of equivalent security for the satisfaction of any such award or judgment.

(2)   Where a court makes an order under subsection (1), it may attach such conditions to the order as it thinks fit, in particular conditions with respect to the institution or prosecution of the relevant legal proceedings.

(3)   Subject to any provision made by rules of court and to any necessary modifications, the same law and practice shall apply in relation to property retained in pursuance of an order made by a court under subsection (1) as would apply if it were held for the purposes of proceedings in that court.

Provisions relating to recognition and enforcement of judgments

31.   Overseas judgments given against States, etc

    (1)   A judgment given by a court of an overseas country against a State to which that court belongs shall be recognised and enforced in the United Kingdom if, and only if—

        (a) it would be so recognised and enforced if it had not been given against a State; and

        (b) that court would have had jurisdiction in the matter if it had applied rules corresponding to those applicable to such matters in the United Kingdom in accordance with sections 2 to 11 of the State Immunity Act 1978.

    (2)   References in subsection (1) to a judgment given against a State include references to judgments of any of the following descriptions given in relation to a State—

        (a) judgments against the government, or a department of the government, of the State but not (except as mentioned in paragraph (c)) judgments against an entity which is distinct from the executive organs of Government;

        (b) judgments against the sovereign or head of State in his public capacity;

        (c) judgments against any such separate entity as is mentioned in paragraph (a) given in proceedings relating to anything done by it in the exercise of the sovereign authority of the State.

    (3)   Nothing in subsection (1) shall affect the recognition or enforcement in the United Kingdom of a judgment to which Part I of the Foreign Judgements (Reciprocal Enforcement) Act 1933 applies by virtue of section 4 of the Carriage of Goods by Road Act 1965, section 17(4) of the Nuclear Installations Act 1965, section 166(4) of the Merchant Shipping Act 1995, section 6 of the International Transport Conventions Act 1983 or section 5 of the Carriage of Passengers by Road Act 1974.

    (4)   Sections 12, 13 and 14(3) and (4) of the State Immunity Act 1978 (service of process and procedural privileges) shall apply to proceedings for the recognition or enforcement in the United Kingdom of a judgment given by a court of an overseas country (whether or not that judgment is within subsection (1) of this section) as they apply to other proceedings.

    (5)   In this section 'state', in the case of a federal State, includes any of its constituent territories.

32.   Overseas judgments given in proceedings brought in breach of agreement for settlement of disputes

    (1)   Subject to the following provisions of this section, a judgment given by a court of an overseas country in any proceedings shall not be recognised or enforced in the United Kingdom if—

        (a) the bringing of those proceedings in that court was contrary to an agreement under which the dispute in question was to be settled otherwise than by proceedings in the courts of that country; and

        (b) those proceedings were not brought in that court by, or with the agreement of, the person against whom the judgment was given; and

        (c) that person did not counterclaim in the proceedings or otherwise submit to the jurisdiction of that court.

    (2)   Subsection (1) does not apply where the agreement referred to in paragraph (a) of that subsection was illegal, void or unenforceable or was incapable of being performed for reasons not attributable to the fault of the party bringing the proceedings in which the judgment was given.

    (3)   In determining whether a judgment given by a court of an overseas country should be recognised or enforced in the United Kingdom, a court in the

United Kingdom shall not be bound by any decision of the overseas court relating to any of the matters mentioned in subsection (1) or (2).

(4)   Nothing in subsection (1) shall affect the recognition or enforcement in the United Kingdom of—

   (a)   a judgment which is required to be recognised or enforced there under the 1968 Convention or the Lugano Convention or the Regulation.

   (b)   a judgment to which Part I of the Foreign Judgements (Reciprocal Enforcement) Act 1933 applies by virtue of section 4 of the Carriage of Goods by Road Act 1965, section 17(4) of the Nuclear Installations Act 1965, section 6 of the International Transport Conventions Act 1983, section 5 of the Carriage of Passengers by Road Act 1974 or section 177(4) of the Merchant Shipping Act 1995).

33.   Certain steps not to amount to submission to jurisdiction of overseas court

(1)   For the purposes of determining whether a judgment given by a court of an overseas country should be recognised or enforced in England and Wales or Northern Ireland, the person against whom the judgment was given shall not be regarded as having submitted to the jurisdiction of the court by reason only of the fact that he appeared (conditionally or otherwise) in the proceedings for all or any one or more of the following purposes, namely—

   (a)   to contest the jurisdiction of the court;

   (b)   to ask the court to dismiss or start the proceedings on the ground that the dispute in question should be submitted to arbitration or to the determination of the courts of another country;

   (c)   to protect, or obtain the release of, property seized or threatened with seizure in the proceedings.

(2)   Nothing in this section shall affect the recognition or enforcement in England and Wales or Northern Ireland of a judgment which is required to be recognised or enforced there under the 1968 Convention or the Lugano Convention or the Regulation.

34.   Certain judgments a bar to further proceedings on the same cause of action

No proceedings may be brought by a person in England and Wales or Northern Ireland on a cause of action in respect of which a judgment has been given in his favour in proceedings between the same parties, or their privies, in a court in another part of the United Kingdom or in a court of an overseas country, unless that judgment is not enforceable or entitled to recognition in England and Wales or, as the case may be, in Northern Ireland.

35.–45.   [Omitted].

46.   Domicile and seat of the Crown

(1)   For the purposes of this Act the seat of the Crown (as determined by this section) shall be treated as its domicile.

(2)   The following provisions of this section determine where the Crown has its seat—

   (a)   for the purposes of the 1968 Convention and the Lugano Convention, (in each of which Article 53 equates the domicile of a legal person with its seat); and

   (b)   for the purposes of this Act.

(3)   Subject to the provisions of any Order in Council for the time being in force under subsection (4)—

   (a)   the Crown in right of Her Majesty's government in the United Kingdom has its seat in every part of, and every place in, the United Kingdom; and

   (aa) the Crown in the right of the Scottish Administration has its seat in, and in every place in, Scotland;

        (b) the Crown in right of Her Majesty's government in Northern Ireland has its seat in, and in every place in, Northern Ireland.

(4)   Her Majesty may by Order in Council provide that, in the case of proceedings of any specified description against the Crown in right of Her Majesty's government in the United Kingdom, the Crown shall be treated for the purposes of the 1968 Convention, the Lugano Convention and this Act as having its seat in, and in every place in, a specified part of the United Kingdom and not in any other part of the United Kingdom.

(5)   An Order in council under subsection (4) may frame a description of proceedings in any way, and in particular may do so by reference to the government department or officer of the Crown against which or against whom they fall to be instituted.

(6)   [Omitted].

(7)   Nothing in this section applies to the Crown otherwise than in right of Her Majesty's government in the United Kingdom or Her Majesty's government in Northern Ireland.

47.–48.   [Omitted].

49.   Saving for powers to stay, sist, strike out or dismiss proceedings
Nothing in this Act shall prevent any court in the United Kingdom from staying, sisting, striking out or dismissing any proceedings before it, on the ground of forum non conveniens or otherwise, where to do so is not inconsistent with the 1968 Convention.

50.–55.   [Omitted].

INTERNATIONAL TRANSPORT CONVENTIONS ACT 1983

CHAPTER 14

THE RAILWAY CONVENTION

1.   Convention to have the force of law

(1)   The Convention concerning International Carriage by Rail signed on behalf of the United Kingdom on 9th May 1980 shall have the force of law in the United Kingdom.

(2)   In this Act 'the Convention' means the Convention referred to in subsection (1) above including, except where the context otherwise requires—

     (a) the protocol on the privileges and immunities of the intergovernmental organisation set up by the Convention; and

     (b) the uniform rules in Appendix A and Appendix B to the Convention together with the Annexes to Appendix B.

(3)   The provisions having the force of law by virtue of this section are—

     (a) the provisions of the Convention as presented to Parliament in April 1982 and set out in Command Paper 8535 as amended by:

        (i) Part I of the Protocol of Decisions adopted by the Revision Committee constituted by the Convention in the course of its first session held at Berne from 14th to 21st December 1989, presented to Parliament in 1991 and set out in Command paper 1690; and

       (ii) Part I of the Protocol of Decisions adopted by that Committee in the course of its second session held at Berne from 28th to 31st May 1990 as so presented and set out in Command paper 1689; and

        (iii)   the Protocol amending the Convention adopted by the 2nd General Assembly of the Intergovernmental Organisation for International Carriage by Rail (OTIF) constituted by the Convention held at Berne from 17th to 20th December 1990 as presented to Parliament in 1993 and set out in Command Paper 2232;

and

     (b)   as respects Annexes I, II and III to Appendix B to the Convention, the provisions referred to in that Command Paper;

and judicial notice shall be taken of those provisions as if they were contained in this Act.

    (4)   [Omitted].

2.   **[Omitted].**

3.   **Fatal accidents**

    (1)   Where by virtue of the Convention any person has a right of action in respect of the death of a passenger by reason of his being a person whom the passenger was under a legal duty to maintain—

     (a)   subject to subsection (2) below, no action in respect of the passenger's death shall be brought for the benefit of that person under the Fatal Accidents Act 1976; but

     (b)   nothing in section 2(3) of that Act (not more than one action in respect of the same subject-matter of complaint) shall prevent an action being brought under that Act for the benefit of any other person.

    (2)   Nothing in subsection (1)(a) above affects the right of any person to claim for damages for bereavement under section 1A of the said Act of 1976.

    (3)   Section 4 of the said Act of 1976 (exclusion of certain benefits in assessment of damages) shall apply in relation to an action brought by any person under the Convention as it applied in relation to an action under that Act.

    (4)   Where separate proceedings are brought under the Convention and under the said Act of 1976 in respect of the death of a passenger, a court, in awarding damages under that Act, shall take into account any damages awarded in the proceedings brought under the Convention and shall have jurisdiction to make any part of its award conditional on the result of those proceedings.

    (5) and (6) [Omitted].

4.–11. and Schedules [Omitted].

FOREIGN LIMITATION PERIODS ACT 1984

CHAPTER 16

1.   **Application of foreign limitation law**

    (1)   Subject to the following provisions of this Act, where in any action or proceedings in a court in England and Wales the law of any other country falls (in accordance with rules of private international law applicable by any such court) to be taken into account in the determination of any matter—

     (a)   the law of that country relating to limitation shall apply in respect of that matter for the purposes of the action or proceedings; and

(b) except where that matter falls within subsection (2) below, the law of England and Wales relating to limitation shall not so apply.

(2)   A matter falls within this subsection if it is a matter in the determination of which both the law of England and Wales and the law of some other country fall to be taken into account.

(3)   The law of England and Wales shall determine for the purposes of any law applicable by virtue of subsection (1)(a) above whether, and the time at which, proceedings have been commenced in respect of any matter; and, accordingly, section 35 of the Limitation Act 1980 (new claims in pending proceedings) shall apply in relation to time limits applicable by virtue of subsection (1)(a) above as it applies in relation to time limits under that Act.

(4)   A court in England and Wales, in exercising in pursuance of subsection (1)(a) above any discretion conferred by the law of any other country, shall so far as practicable exercise that discretion in the manner in which it is exercised in comparable cases by the courts of that other country.

(5)   In this section 'law', in relation to any country, shall not include rules of private international law applicable by the courts of that country or, in the case of England and Wales, this Act.

2.   Exceptions to section 1

(1)   In any case in which the application of section 1 above would to any extent conflict (whether under subsection (2) below or otherwise) with public policy, that section shall not apply to the extent that its application would so conflict.

(2)   The application of section 1 above in relation to any action or proceedings shall conflict with public policy to the extent that its application would cause undue hardship to a person who is, or might be made, a party to the action or proceedings.

(3)   Where, under a law applicable by virtue of section 1(1)(a) above for the purposes of any action or proceedings, a limitation period is or may be extended or interrupted in respect of the absence of a party to the action or proceedings from any specified jurisdiction or country, so much of that law as provides for the extension or interruption shall be disregarded for those purposes.

(4)   [Omitted].

3.   Foreign judgments on limitation points

Where a court in any country outside England and Wales has determined any matter wholly or partly by reference to the law of that or any other country (including England and Wales) relating to limitation, then, for the purposes of the law relating to the effect to be given in England and Wales to that determination, that court shall, to the extent that it has so determined the matter, be deemed to have determined it on its merits.

4.   Meaning of law relating to limitation

(1)   Subject to subsection (3) below, references in this Act to the law of any country (including England and Wales) relating to limitation shall, in relation to any matter, be construed as references to so much of the relevant law of that country as (in any manner) makes provision with respect to a limitation period applicable to the bringing of proceedings in respect of that matter in the courts of that country and shall include —

(a)   references to so much of that law as relates to, and to the effect of, the application, extension, reduction or interruption of that period; and

(b)   a reference, where under that law there is no limitation period which is so applicable, to the rule that such proceedings may be brought within an indefinite period.

(2)   In subsection (1) above 'relevant law', in relation to any country, means the procedural and substantive law applicable, apart from any rules of private international law, by the courts of that country.

(3)   References in this Act to the law of England and Wales relating to limitation shall not include the rules by virtue of which a court may, in the exercise of any discretion, refuse equitable relief on the grounds of acquiescence or otherwise; but, in applying those rules to a case in relation to which the law of any country outside England and Wales is applicable by virtue of section 1(1)(a) above (not being a law that provides for a limitation period that has expired), a court in England and Wales shall have regard, in particular, to the provisions of the law that is so applicable.

5.   [Repealed]; 6. and 7. [Omitted].

LATENT DAMAGE ACT 1986

CHAPTER 37

3.   Accrual of cause of action to successive owners in respect of latent damage to property.

3.   Accrual of cause of action to successive owners in respect of latent damage to property

(1)   Subject to the following provisions of this section, where—

    (a) a cause of action ('the original cause of action') has accrued to any person in respect of any negligence to which damage to any property in which he has an interest is attributable (in whole or in part); and

    (b) another person acquires an interest in that property after the date on which the original cause of action accrued but before the material facts about the damage have become known to any person who, at the time when he first has knowledge of those facts, has any interest in the property,

a fresh cause of action in respect of that negligence shall accrue to that other person on the date on which he acquires his interest in the property.

(2)   A cause of action accruing to any person by virtue of subsection (1) above—

    (a) shall be treated as if based on breach of a duty of care at common law owed to the person to whom it accrues; and

    (b) shall be treated for the purposes of section 14A of the 1980 Act (special time limit for negligence actions where facts relevant to cause of action are not known at date of accrual) as having accrued on the date on which the original cause of action accrued.

(3)   [Omitted].

(4)   Subsection (1) above shall not apply in any case where the person acquiring an interest in the damaged property is either—

    (a) a person in whom the original cause of action vests by operation of law; or

    (b) a person in whom the interest in that property vests by virtue of any order made by a court under section 538 of the Companies Act 1985 (vesting of company property in liquidator).

(5)   For the purposes of subsection (1)(b) above, the material facts about the damage are such facts about the damage as would lead a reasonable person who has an interest in the damaged property at the time when those facts become known to him to consider it sufficiently serious to justify his instituting proceedings for damages against a defendant who did not dispute liability and was able to satisfy a judgment.

(6)   For the purposes of this section a person's knowledge includes knowledge which he might reasonably have been expected to acquire—

(a) from facts observable or ascertainable by him; or

(b) from facts ascertainable by him with the help of appropriate expert advice which it is reasonable for him to seek;

but a person shall not be taken by virtue of this subsection to have knowledge of a fact ascertainable by him only with the help of expert advice so long as he has taken all reasonable steps to obtain (and, where appropriate to act on) that advice.

(7) [Omitted].

COMPUTER MISUSE ACT 1990

CHAPTER 18

Computer misuse offences

Computer misuse offences

1.   Unauthorised access to computer material

(1)   A person is guilty of an offence if—

(a) he causes a computer to perform any function with intent to secure access to any program or data held in any computer;

(b) the access he intends to secure is unauthorised; and

(c) he knows at the time when he causes the computer to perform the function that that is the case.

(2)   The intent a person has to have to commit an offence under this section need not be directed at—

(a) any particular program or data;

(b) a program or data of any particular kind; or

(c) a program or data held in any particular computer.

(3)   A person guilty of an offence under this section shall be liable on summary conviction to imprisonment for a term not exceeding six months or to a fine not exceeding level 5 on the standard scale or to both.

2.   Unauthorised access with intent to commit or facilitate commission of further offences

(1)   A person is guilty of an offence under this section if he commits an offence under section 1 above ('the unauthorised access offence') with intent—

      (a) to commit an offence to which this section applies; or

      (b) to facilitate the commission of such an offence (whether by himself or by any other person),

and the offence he intends to commit or facilitate is referred to below in this section as the further offence.

(2)   This section applies to offences—

      (a) for which the sentence is fixed by law; or

      (b) for which a person who has attained the age of twenty-one years (eighteen in relation to England and Wales) and has no previous convictions may be sentenced to imprisonment for a term of five years (or, in England and Wales, might be so sentenced but for the restrictions imposed by section 33 of the Magistrates' Courts Act 1980).

(3)   It is immaterial for the purposes of this section whether the further offence is to be committed on the same occasion as the unauthorised access offence or on any future occasion.

(4)   A person may be guilty of an offence under this section even though the facts are such that the commission of the further offence is impossible.

(5)   A person guilty of an offence under this section shall be liable—

      (a) on summary conviction, to imprisonment for a term not exceeding six months or to a fine not exceeding the statutory maximum or to both; and

      (b) on conviction on indictment, to imprisonment for a term not exceeding five years or to a fine or to both.

3.   Unauthorised modification of computer material

(1)   A person is guilty of an offence if—

      (a) he does any act which causes an unauthorised modification of the contents of any computer; and

      (b) at the time when he does the act he has the requisite intent and the requisite knowledge.

(2)   For the purposes of subsection (1)(b) above the requisite intent is an intent to cause a modification of the contents of any computer and by so doing—

      (a) to impair the operation of any computer;

      (b) to prevent or hinder access to any program or data held in any computer; or

      (c) to impair the operation of any such program or the reliability of any such data.

(3)   The intent need not be directed at—

      (a) any particular computer;

      (b) any particular program or data or a program or data of any particular kind; or

      (c) any particular modification or a modification of any particular kind.

(4)   For the purposes of subsection (1)(b) above the requisite knowledge is knowledge that any modification he intends to cause is unauthorised.

(5)   It is immaterial for the purposes of this section whether an unauthorised modification or any intended effect of it of a kind mentioned in subsection (2) above is, or is intended to be, permanent or merely temporary.

(6)   For the purposes of the Criminal Damage Act 1971 a modification of the contents of a computer shall not be regarded as damaging any computer or computer storage medium unless its effect on that computer or computer storage medium impairs its physical condition.

(7)   A person guilty of an offence under this section shall be liable—

      (a) on summary conviction, to imprisonment for a term not exceeding six months or to a fine not exceeding the statutory maximum or to both; and

      (b) on conviction on indictment, to imprisonment for a term not exceeding five years or to a fine or to both.

Jurisdiction

4.   Territorial scope of offences under this Act

(1)   Except as provided below in this section, it is immaterial for the purposes of any offence under section 1 or 3 above —

(a)   whether any act or other event proof of which is required for conviction of the offence occurred in the home country concerned; or

(b)   whether the accused was in the home country concerned at the time of any such act or event.

(2)   Subject to subsection (3) below, in the case of such an offence at least one significant link with domestic jurisdiction must exist in the circumstances of the case for the offence to be committed.

(3)   There is no need for any such link to exist for the commission of an offence under section 1 above to be established in proof of an allegation to that effect in proceedings for an offence under section 2 above.

(4)   Subject to section 8 below, where —

(a)   any such link does in fact exist in the case of an offence under section 1 above; and

(b)   commission of that offence is alleged in proceedings for an offence under section 2 above;

section 2 above shall apply as if anything the accused intended to do or facilitate in any place outside the home country concerned which would be an offence to which section 2 applies if it took place in the home country concerned were the offence in question.

(5)   This section is without prejudice to any jurisdiction exercisable by a court in Scotland apart from this section.

(6)   References in this Act to the home country concerned are references —

(a)   in the application of this Act to England and Wales, to England and Wales;

(b)   in the application of this Act to Scotland, to Scotland; and

(c)   in the application of this Act to Northern Ireland, to Northern Ireland.

5.   Significant links with domestic jurisdiction

(1)   The following provisions of this section apply for the interpretation of section 4 above.

(2)   In relation to an offence under section 1, either of the following is a significant link with domestic jurisdiction —

(a)   that the accused was in the home country concerned at the time when he did the act which caused the computer to perform the function; or

(b)   that any computer containing any program or data to which the accused secured or intended to secure unauthorised access by doing that act was in the home country concerned at that time.

(3)   In relation to an offence under section 3, either of the following is a significant link with domestic jurisdiction —

(a)   that the accused was in the home country concerned at the time when he did the act which caused the unauthorised modification; or

(b)   that the unauthorised modification took place in the home country concerned.

6.   Territorial scope of inchoate offences related to offences under this Act

(1)   On a charge of conspiracy to commit an offence under this Act the following questions are immaterial to the accused's guilt —

(a)   the question where any person became a party to the conspiracy; and

(b)   the question whether any act, omission or other event occurred in the home country concerned.

(2)   On a charge of attempting to commit an offence under section 3 above the following questions are immaterial to the accused's guilt —

(a) the question where the attempt was made; and

(b) the question whether it had an effect in the home country concerned.

(3) On a charge of incitement to commit an offence under this Act the question where the incitement took place is immaterial to the accused's guilt.

(4) This section does not extend to Scotland.

7. [Omitted].

8. Relevance of external law

(1) A person is guilty of an offence triable by virtue of section 4(4) above only if what he intended to do or facilitate would involve the commission of an offence under the law in force where the whole or any part of it was intended to take place.

(2) A person is guilty of an offence triable by virtue of section 1(lA) of the Criminal Law Act 1977 only if the pursuit of the agreed course of conduct would at some stage involve—

(a) an act or omission by one or more of the parties; or

(b) the happening of some other event;

constituting an offence under the law in force where the act, omission or other event was intended to take place.

(3) A person is guilty of an offence triable by virtue of section 1(lA) of the Criminal Attempts Act 1981 or by virtue of section 7(4) above only if what he had in view would involve the commission of an offence under the law in force where the whole or any part of it was intended to take place.

(4) Conduct punishable under the law in force in any place is an offence under that law for the purposes of this section, however it is described in that law.

(5) Subject to subsection (7) below, a condition specified in any of subsections (1) to (3) above shall be taken to be satisfied unless not later than rules of court may provide the defence serve on the prosecution a notice—

(a) stating that, on the facts as alleged with respect to the relevant conduct, the condition is not in their opinion satisfied;

(b) showing their grounds for that opinion; and

(c) requiring the prosecution to show that it is satisfied.

(6) In subsection (5) above 'the relevant conduct' means—

(a) where the condition in subsection (1) above is in question, what the accused intended to do or facilitate;

(b) where the condition in subsection (2) above is in question, the agreed course of conduct; and

(c) where the condition in subsection (3) above is in question, what the accused had in view.

(7) The court, if it thinks fit, may permit the defence to require the prosecution to show that the condition is satisfied without the prior service of a notice under subsection (5) above.

(8) If by virtue of subsection (7) above a court of solemn jurisdiction in Scotland permits the defence to require the prosecution to show that the condition is satisfied, it shall be competent for the prosecution for that purpose to examine any witness or to put in evidence any production not included in the lists lodged by it.

(9) In the Crown Court the question whether the condition is satisfied shall be decided by the judge alone.

(10) In the High Court of Justiciary and in the sheriff court the question whether the condition is satisfied shall be decided by the judge or, as the case may be, the sheriff alone.

9.— (1) In any proceedings brought in England and Wales in respect of British any offence to which this section applies it is immaterial to guilt whether or not the accused was a British citizen at the time of any act, omission or other event proof of which is required for conviction of the offence.

(2)   This section applies to the following offences—
   (a) any offence under this Act;
   (b) conspiracy to commit an offence under this Act;
   (c) any attempt to commit an offence under section 3 above; and
   (d) incitement to commit an offence under this Act.

10.–16.   [Omitted].

17.   Interpretation
   (1)   The following provisions of this section apply for the interpretation of this Act.
   (2)   A person secures access to any program or data held in a computer if by causing a computer to perform any function he—
      (a) alters or erases the program or data;
      (b) copies or moves it to any storage medium other than that in which it is held or to a different location in the storage medium in which it is held;
      (c) uses it; or
      (d) has it output from the computer in which it is held (whether by having it displayed or in any other manner);
      and references to access to a program or data (and to an intent to secure such access) shall be read accordingly.
   (3)   For the purposes of subsection (2)(c) above a person uses a program if the function he causes the computer to perform—
      (a) causes the program to be executed; or
      (b) is itself a function of the program.
   (4)   For the purposes of subsection (2)(d) above—
      (a) a program is output if the instructions of which it consists are output; and
      (b) the form in which any such instructions or any other data is output (and in particular whether or not it represents a form in which, in the case of instructions, they are capable of being executed or, in the case of data, it is capable of being processed by a computer) is immaterial.
   (5)   Access of any kind by any person to any program or data held in a computer is unauthorised if—
      (a) he is not himself entitled to control access of the kind in question to the program or data; and
      (b) he does not have consent to access by him of the kind in question to the program or data from any person who is so entitled,
      but this subsection is subject to section 10.
   (6)   References to any program or data held in a computer include references to any program or data held in any removable storage medium which is for the time being in the computer; and a computer is to be regarded as containing any program or data held in any such medium.
   (7)   A modification of the contents of any computer takes place if, by the operation of any function of the computer concerned or any other computer—
      (a) any program or data held in the computer concerned is altered or erased; or
      (b) any program or data is added to its contents;
      and any act which contributes towards causing such a modification shall be regarded as causing it.
   (8)   Such a modification is unauthorised if—
      (a) the person whose act causes it is not himself entitled to determine whether the modification should be made; and

       (b) he does not have consent to the modification from any person who is so entitled.

(9)   References to the home country concerned shall be read in accordance with section 4(6) above.

(10)   References to a program include references to part of a program.

18.   **[Omitted].**

CONTRACTS (APPLICABLE LAW) ACT 1990

CHAPTER 36

1.   **Meaning of 'the Conventions'**
In this Act—

    (a) 'the Rome Convention' means the Convention on the law applicable to contractual obligations opened for signature in Rome on 19th June 1980 and signed by the United Kingdom on 7th December 1981;

    (b) 'the Luxembourg Convention' means the Convention on the accession of the Hellenic Republic to the Rome Convention signed by the United Kingdom in Luxembourg on 10th April 1984;

    (c) 'the Brussels Protocol' means the first Protocol on the interpretation of the Rome Convention by the European Court signed by the United Kingdom in Brussels on 19th December 1988;

    (d) 'the Funchal Convention' means the Convention on the accession of the Kingdom of Spain and the Portuguese Republic to the Rome Convention and the Brussels Protocol, with adjustments made to the Rome Convention by the Luxembourg Convention, signed by the United Kingdom in Funchal on 18th May 1992;

    (e) 'the 1996 Accession Convention' means the Convention on the accession of the Republic of Austria, the Republic of Finland and the Kingdom of Sweden to the Rome Convention and the Brussels Protocol, with the adjustments made to the Rome Convention by the Luxembourg Convention and the Funchal Convention, signed by the United Kingdom in Brussels on 29th November 1996;

and these Conventions and this Protocol are together referred to as 'the Conventions'.

2.   **Conventions to have force of law**

(1)   Subject to subsections (2) and (3) below, the Conventions shall have the force of law in the United Kingdom.

(1A) The internal law for the purposes of Article 1(3) of the Rome Convention is the provisions of the regulations for the time being in force under section 424(3) of the Financial Services and Markets Act 2000.

(2)   Articles 7(1) and 10(1)(e) of the Rome Convention shall not have the force of law in the United Kingdom.

(3)   Notwithstanding Article 19(2) of the Rome Convention, the Conventions shall apply in the case of conflicts between the laws of different parts of the United Kingdom.

(4)   [Omitted].

3.   **Interpretation of Conventions**

(1)   Any question as to the meaning or effect of any provision of the Conventions shall, if not referred to the European Court in accordance with the Brussels

Protocol, be determined in accordance with the principles laid down by, and any relevant decision of, the European Court.

(2)   Judicial notice shall be taken of any decision of, or expression of opinion by, the European Court on any such question.

(3)   Without prejudice to any practice of the courts as to the matters which may be considered apart from this subsection—

(a)   the report on the Rome Convention by Professor Mario Giuliano and Professor Paul Lagarde which is reproduced in the Official Journal of the Communities of 31st October 1980 may be considered in ascertaining the meaning or effect of any provision of that Convention; and

(b)   any report on the Brussels Protocol which is reproduced in the Official Journal of the Communities may be considered in ascertaining the meaning of effect of any provision of that Protocol.

4.–9. [Omitted].

SCHEDULE 1
THE ROME CONVENTION

TITLE 1
SCOPE OF THE CONVENTION

Article 1
Scope of the Convention

1.   The rules of this Convention shall apply to contractual obligations in any situation involving a choice between the laws of different countries.

2.   They shall not apply to—

(a)   questions involving the status or legal capacity of natural persons, without prejudice to Article 11;

(b)   contractual obligations relating to:
— wills and succession;
— rights in property arising out of a matrimonial relationship;
— rights and duties arising out of a family relationship, parentage, marriage or affinity, including maintenance obligations in respect of children who are not legitimate;

(c)   obligations arising under bills of exchange, cheques and promissory notes and other negotiable instruments to the extent that the obligations under such other negotiable instruments arise out of their negotiable character;

(d)   arbitration agreements and agreements on the choice of court;

(e)   questions governed by the law of companies and other bodies corporate or unincorporate such as the creation, by registration or otherwise, legal capacity, internal organisation or winding up of companies and other bodies corporate or unincorporate and the personal liability of officers and members as such for the obligations of the company or body;

(f)   the question whether an agent is able to bind a principal, or an organ to bind a company or body corporate or unincorporate, to a third party;

(g)   the constitution of trusts and the relationship between settlors, trustees and beneficiaries;

(h)   evidence and procedure, without prejudice to Article 14.

3.   The rules of this Convention do not apply to contracts of insurance which cover risks situated in the territories of the Member States of the European Economic Community. In order to determine whether a risk is situated in these territories the court shall apply its internal law.

4.   The preceding paragraph does not apply to contracts of re-insurance.

Article 2
Application of law of non-contracting States

Any law specified by this Convention shall be applied whether or not it is the law of a Contracting State.

TITLE II
UNIFORM RULES

Article 3
Freedom of choice

1. A contract shall be governed by the law chosen by the parties. The choice must be express or demonstrated with reasonable certainty by the terms of the contract or the circumstances of the case. By their choice the parties can select the law applicable to the whole or a part only of the contract.
2. The parties may at any time agree to subject the contract to a law other than that which previously governed it, whether as a result of an earlier choice under this Article or of other provisions of this Convention. Any variation by the parties of the law to be applied made after the conclusion of the contract shall not prejudice its formal validity under Article 9 or adversely affect the rights of third parties.
3. The fact that the parties have chosen a foreign law, whether or not accompanied by the choice of a foreign tribunal, shall not, where all the other elements relevant to the situation at the time of the choice are connected with one country only, prejudice the application of rules of the law of that country which cannot be derogated from by contract, hereinafter called "mandatory rules".
4. The existence and validity of the consent of the parties as to the choice of the applicable law shall be determined in accordance with the provisions of Articles 8, 9 and 11.

Article 4
Applicable law in the absence of choice

1. To the extent that the law applicable to the contract has not been chosen in accordance with Article 3, the contract shall be governed by the law of the country with which it is most closely connected. Nevertheless, a severable part of the contract which has a closer connection with another country may by way of exception be governed by the law of that other country.
2. Subject to the provisions of paragraph 5 of this Article, it shall be presumed that the contract is most closely connected with the country where the party who is to effect the performance which is characteristic of the contract has, at the time of conclusion of the contract, his habitual residence, or, in the case of a body corporate or unincorporate, its central administration. However, if the contract is entered into in the course of that party's trade or profession, that country shall be the country in which the principal place of business is situated or, where under the terms of the contract the performance is to be effected through a place of business other than the principal place of business, the country in which that other place of business is situated.
3. Notwithstanding the provisions of paragraph 2 of this Article, to the extent that the subject matter of the contract is a right in immovable property or a right to use immovable property it shall be presumed that the contract is most closely connected with the country where the immovable property is situated.
4. A contract for the carriage of goods shall not be subject to the presumption in paragraph 2. In such a contract if the country in which, at the time the contract is concluded, the carrier has his principal place of business is also the country in

which the place of loading or the place of discharge or the principal place of business of the consignor is situated, it shall be presumed that the contract is most closely connected with that country. In applying this paragraph single voyage charter-parties and other contracts the main purpose of which is the carriage of goods shall be treated as contracts for the carriage of goods.

5.   Paragraph 2 shall not apply if the characteristic performance cannot be determined, and the presumptions in paragraphs 2, 3 and 4 shall be disregarded if it appears from the circumstances as a whole that the contract is more closely connected with another country.

Article 5
Certain consumer contracts

1.   This Article applies to a contract the object of which is the supply of goods or services to a person ('the consumer') for a purpose which can be regarded as being outside his trade or profession, or a contract for the provision of credit for that object.

2.   Notwithstanding the provisions of Article 3, a choice of law made by the parties shall not have the result of depriving the consumer of the protection afforded to him by the mandatory rules of the law of the country in which he has his habitual residence:
   —   if in that country the conclusion of the contract was preceded by a specific invitation addressed to him or by advertising, and he had taken in that country all the steps necessary on his part for the conclusion of the contract, or
   —   if the other party or his agent received the consumer's order in that country, or
   —   if the contract is for the sale of goods and the consumer travelled from that country to another country and there gave his order, provided that the consumer's journey was arranged by the seller for the purpose of inducing the consumer to buy.

3.   Notwithstanding the provisions of Article 4, a contract to which this Article applies will, in the absence of choice in accordance with Article 3, be governed by the law of the country in which the consumer has his habitual residence if it is entered into in the circumstances described in paragraph 2 of this Article.

4.   This Article shall not apply to—
   (a)   a contract of carriage;
   (b)   a contract for the supply of services where the services are to be supplied to the consumer exclusively in a country other than that in which he has his habitual residence.

5.   Notwithstanding the provisions of paragraph 4, this Article shall apply to a contract which, for an inclusive price, provides for a combination of travel and accommodation.

Article 6
Individual employment contracts

1.   Notwithstanding the provisions of Article 3, in a contract of employment a choice of law made by the parties shall not have the result of depriving the employee of the protection afforded to him by the mandatory rules of the law which would be applicable under paragraph 2 in the absence of choice.

2.   Notwithstanding the provisions of Article 4, a contract of employment shall, in the absence of choice in accordance with Article 3, be governed—
   (a)   by the law of the country in which the employee habitually carries out his work in performance of the contract, even if he is temporarily employed in another country; or

(b)   if the employee does not habitually carry out his work in any one country, by
       the law of the country in which the place of business through which he was
       engaged is situated,
unless it appears from the circumstances as a whole that the contract is more
closely connected with another country, in which case the contract shall be
governed by the law of that country.

Article 7
Mandatory rules

1.   When applying under this Convention the law of a country, effect may be given to
      the mandatory rules of the law of another country with which the situation has a
      close connection, if and in so far as, under the law of the latter country, those rules
      must be applied whatever the law applicable to the contract. In considering
      whether to give effect to these mandatory rules, regard shall be had to their nature
      and purpose and to the consequences of their application or non-application.
2.   Nothing in this Convention shall restrict the application of the rules of the law of
      the forum in a situation where they are mandatory irrespective of the law otherwise
      applicable to the contract.

Article 8
Material validity

1.   The existence and validity of a contract, or of any term of a contract, shall be
      determined by the law which would govern it under this Convention if the contract
      or term were valid.
2.   Nevertheless a party may rely upon the law of the country in which he has his
      habitual residence to establish that he did not consent if it appears from the
      circumstances that it would not be reasonable to determine the effect of his
      conduct in accordance with the law specified in the preceding paragraph.

Article 9
Formal validity

1.   A contract concluded between persons who are in the same country is formally
      valid if it satisfies the formal requirements of the law which governs it under this
      Convention or of the law of the country where it is concluded.
2.   A contract concluded between persons who are in different countries is formally
      valid if it satisfies the formal requirements of the law which governs it under this
      Convention or of the law of one of those countries.
3.   Where a contract is concluded by an agent, the country in which the agent acts is
      the relevant country for the purposes of paragraphs 1 and 2.
4.   An act intended to have legal effect relating to an existing or contemplated contract
      is formally valid if it satisfies the formal requirements of the law which under this
      Convention governs or would govern the contract or of the law of the country
      where the act was done.
5.   The provisions of the preceding paragraphs shall not apply to a contract to which
      Article 5 applies, concluded in the circumstances described in paragraph 2 of
      Article 5. The formal validity of such a contract is governed by the law of the
      country in which the consumer has his habitual residence.
6.   Notwithstanding paragraphs 1 to 4 of this Article, a contract the subject matter of
      which is a right in immovable property or a right to use immovable property shall
      be subject to the mandatory requirements of form of the law of the country where
      the property is situated if by that law those requirements are imposed irrespective
      of the country where the contract is concluded and irrespective of the law
      governing the contract.

Article 10
Scope of the applicable law

1.   The law applicable to a contract by virtue of Articles 3 to 6 and 12 of this
      Convention shall govern in particular—
      (a)   interpretation;
      (b)   performance;
      (c)   within the limits of the powers conferred on the court by its procedural law,
            the consequences of breach, including the assessment of damages in so far
            as it is governed by rules of law;
      (d)   the various ways of extinguishing obligations and prescription and limitation
            of actions;
      (e)   the consequences of nullity of the contract.
2.   In relation to the manner of performance and the steps to be taken in the event of
      defective performance regard shall be had to the law of the country in which
      performance takes place.

Article 11
Incapacity

In a contract concluded between persons who are in the same country, a natural person
who would have capacity under the law of that country may invoke his incapacity
resulting from another law only if the other party to the contract was aware of this
incapacity at the time of the conclusion of the contract or was not aware thereof as a
result of negligence.

Article 12
Voluntary assignment

1.   The mutual obligations of assignor and assignee under a voluntary assignment of a
      right against another person ('the debtor') shall be governed by the law which
      under this Convention applies to the contract between the assignor and assignee.
2.   The law governing the right to which the assignment relates shall determine its
      assignability, the relationship between the assignee and the debtor, the conditions
      under which the assignment can be invoked against the debtor and any question
      whether the debtor's obligations have been discharged.

Article 13
Subrogation

1.   Where a person ('the creditor') has a contractual claim upon another ('the debtor'),
      and a third person has a duty to satisfy the creditor, or has in fact satisfied the
      creditor in discharge of that duty, the law which governs the third person's duty to
      satisfy the creditor shall determine whether the third person is entitled to exercise
      against the debtor the rights which the creditor had against the debtor under the
      law governing their relationship and, if so, whether he may do so in full or only to a
      limited extent.
2.   The same rule applies where several persons are subject to the same contractual
      claim and one of them has satisfied the creditor.

Article 14
Burden of proof, etc

1.   The law governing the contract under this Convention applies to the extent that it
      contains, in the law of contract, rules which raise presumptions of law or determine
      the burden of proof.

2. A contract or an act intended to have legal effect may be proved by any mode of proof recognised by the law of the forum or by any of the laws referred to in Article 9 under which that contract or act is formally valid, provided that such mode of proof can be administered by the forum.

Article 15
Exclusion of renvoi

The application of the law of any country specified by this Convention means the application of the rules of law in force in that country other than its rules of private international law.

Article 16
'Ordre public'

The application of a rule of the law of any country specified by this Convention may be refused only if such application is manifestly incompatible with the public policy ('ordre public') of the forum.

Article 17
No retrospective effect

This Convention shall apply in a Contracting State to contracts made after the date on which this Convention has entered into force with respect to that State.

Article 18
Uniform interpretation

In the interpretation and application of the preceding uniform rules, regard shall be had to their international character and to the desirability of achieving uniformity in their interpretation and application.

Article 19
States with more than one legal system

1. Where a State comprises several territorial units each of which has its own rules of law in respect of contractual obligations, each territorial unit shall be considered as a country for the purposes of identifying the law applicable under this Convention.
2. A State within which different territorial units have their own rules of law in respect of contractual obligations shall not be bound to apply this Convention to conflicts solely between the laws of such units.

Article 20
Precedence of Community law

This Convention shall not affect the application of provisions which, in relation to particular matters, lay down choice of law rules relating to contractual obligations and which are or will be contained in acts of the institutions of the European Communities or in national laws harmonised in implementation of such acts.

Article 21

Relationship with other conventions

This Convention shall not prejudice the application of international conventions to which a Contracting State is, or becomes, a party.

Articles 22–26 [Omitted].

Article 27 [Revoked].

Articles 28–33 [Omitted].

SCHEDULE 3
THE BRUSSELS PROTOCOL

Article 1

The Court of Justice of the European Communities shall have jurisdiction to give rulings on the interpretation of—
(a)   the Convention on the law applicable to contractual obligations, opened for signature in Rome on 19 June 1980, hereinafter referred to as 'the Rome Convention';
(b)   the Convention on accession to the Rome Convention by the States which have become Members of the European Communities since the date on which it was opened for signature;
(c)   this Protocol.

Articles 2–11 [Omitted].

CARRIAGE OF GOODS BY SEA ACT 1992

CHAPTER 50

1.   Shipping documents, etc, to which Act applies
(1)   This Act applies to the following documents, that is to say—
    (a)   any bill of lading;
    (b)   any sea waybill; and
    (c)   any ship's delivery order.
(2)   References in this Act to a bill of lading—
    (a)   do not include references to a document which is incapable of transfer either by endorsement or, as a bearer bill, by delivery without endorsement; but
    (b)   subject to that, do include references to a received for shipment bill of lading.
(3)   References in this Act to a sea waybill are references to any document which is not a bill of lading but—
    (a)   is such a receipt for goods as contains or evidences a contract for the carriage of goods by sea; and
    (b)   identifies the person to whom delivery of the goods is to be made by the carrier in accordance with that contract.
(4)   References in this Act to a ship's delivery order are references to any document which is neither a bill of lading nor a sea waybill but contains an undertaking which—
    (a)   is given under or for the purposes of a contract for the carriage by sea of the goods to which the document relates, or of goods which include those goods; and
    (b)   is an undertaking by the carrier to a person identified in the document to deliver the goods to which the document relates to that person.

(5)   The Secretary of State may by regulations make provision for the application of this Act to cases where a telecommunication system or any other information technology is used for effecting transactions corresponding to—
  (a)   the issue of a document to which this Act applies;
  (b)   the endorsement, delivery or other transfer of such a document; or
  (c)   the doing of anything else in relation to such a document.

(6)   [Omitted].

2.   Rights under shipping documents
(1)   Subject to the following provisions of this section, a person who becomes—
  (a)   the lawful holder of a bill of lading;
  (b)   the person who (without being an original party to the contract of carriage) is the person to whom delivery of the goods to which a sea waybill relates is to be made by the carrier in accordance with that contract; or
  (c)   the person to whom delivery of the goods to which a ship's delivery order relates is to be made in accordance with the undertaking contained in the order,
shall (by virtue of becoming the holder of the bill or, as the case may be, the person to whom delivery is to be made) have transferred to and vested in him all rights of suit under the contract of carriage as if he had been a party to that contract.

(2)   Where, when a person becomes the lawful holder of a bill of lading, possession of the bill no longer gives a right (as against the carrier) to possession of the goods to which the bill relates, that person shall not have any rights transferred to him by virtue of subsection (1) above unless he becomes the holder of the bill—
  (a)   by virtue of a transaction effected in pursuance of any contractual of other arrangements made before the time when such a right to possession ceased to attach to possession of the bill; or
  (b)   as a result of the rejection to that person by another person of goods or documents delivered to the other person in pursuance of any such arrangements.

(3)   The rights vested in any person by virtue of the operation of subsection (1) above in relation to a ship's delivery order–
  (a)   shall be so vested subject to the terms of the order; and
  (b)   where the goods to which the order relates form a part only of the goods to which the contract of carriage relates, shall be confined to rights in respect of the goods to which the order relates.

(4)   Where, in the case of any document to which this Act applies—
  (a)   a person with any interest or right in or in relation to goods to which the document relates sustains loss or damage in consequence of a breach of the contract of carriage; but
  (b)   subsection (1) above operates in relation to that document so that rights of suit in respect of that breach are vested in another person,
the other person shall be entitled to exercise those rights for the benefit of the person who sustained the loss or damage to the same extent as they could have been exercised if they had been vested in the person for whose benefit they are exercised.

(5)   Where rights are transferred by virtue of the operation of subsection (1) above in relation to any document, the transfer for which that subsection provides shall extinguish any entitlement to those rights which derives—
  (a)   where that document is a bill of lading, from a person's having been an original party to the contract of carriage; or
  (b)   in the case of any document to which this Act applies, from the previous operation of that subsection in relation to that document;

but the operation of that subsection shall be without prejudice to any rights which derive from a person's having been an original party to the contract contained in, or evidenced by, a sea waybill and, in relation to a ship's delivery order, shall be without prejudice to any rights deriving otherwise than from the previous operation of that subsection in relation to that order.

3.   Liabilities under shipping documents

(1)   Where subsection (1) of section 2 of this Act operates in relation to any document to which this Act applies and the person in whom rights are vested by virtue of that subsection —

(a)   takes or demands delivery from the carrier of any of the goods to which the document relates;

(b)   makes a claim under the contract of carriage against the carrier in respect of any of those goods; or

(c)   is a person who, at a time before those rights were vested in him, took or demanded delivery from the carrier of any of those goods,

that person shall (by virtue of taking or demanding delivery or making the claim or, in a case falling within paragraph (c) above, of having the rights vested in him) become subject to the same liabilities under that contract as if he had been a party to that contract.

(2)   Where the goods to which a ship's delivery order relates form a part only of the goods to which the contract of carriage relates, the liabilities to which any person is subject by virtue of the operation of this section in relation to that order shall exclude liabilities in respect of any goods to which the order does not relate.

(3)   This section, so far as it imposes liabilities under any contract on any person, shall be without prejudice to the liabilities under the contract of any person as an original party to the contract.

4.   Representations in bills of lading

A bill of lading which —

(a)   represents goods to have been shipped on board a vessel or to have been received for shipment on board a vessel; and

(b)   has been signed by the master of the vessel or by a person who was not the master but has the express, implied or apparent authority of the carrier to sign bills of lading,

shall, in favour of a person who has become the lawful holder of the bill, be conclusive evidence against the carrier of the shipment of the goods or, as the case may be, of their receipt for shipment.

5.   Interpretation, etc

(1)   In this Act —

'bill of lading', 'sea waybill' and 'ship's delivery order' shall be construed in accordance with section 1 above;

'the contract of carriage' —

(a)   in relation to a bill of lading or sea waybill, means the contract contained in or evidenced by that bill or waybill; and

(b)   in relation to a ship's delivery order, means the contract under or for the purposes of which the undertaking contained in the order is given;

'holder', in relation to a bill of lading, shall be construed in accordance with subsection (2) below;

'information technology' includes any computer or other technology by means of which information or other matter may be recorded or communicated without being reduced to documentary form; and 'telecommunication system' has the same meaning as in the Telecommunications Act 1984.

(2)   References in this Act to the holder of a bill of lading are references to any of the following persons, that is to say—

(a)   a person with possession of the bill who, by virtue of being the person identified in the bill, is the consignee of the goods to which the bill relates;

(b)   a person with possession of the bill as a result of the completion, by delivery of the bill, of any endorsement of the bill or, in the case of a bearer bill, of any other transfer of the bill;

(c)   a person with possession of the bill as a result of any transaction by virtue of which he would have become a holder falling within paragraph (a) or (b) above had not the transaction been effected at a time when possession of the bill no longer gave a right (as against the carrier) to possession of the goods to which the bill relates;

and a person shall be regarded for the purposes of this Act as having become the lawful holder of a bill of lading wherever he has become the holder of the bill in good faith.

(3)   References in this Act to a person's being identified in a document include references to his being identified by a description which allows for the identity of the person in question to be varied, in accordance with the terms of the document, after its issue; and the reference in section 1(3)(b) of this Act to a document's identifying a person shall be construed accordingly.

(4)   Without prejudice to sections 2(2) and 4 above, nothing in this Act shall preclude its operation in relation to a case where the goods to which a document relates—

(a)   cease to exist after the issue of the document; or

(b)   cannot be identified (whether because they are mixed with other goods or for any other reason);

and references in this Act to the goods to which a document relates shall be construed accordingly.

(5)   The preceding provisions of this Act shall have effect without prejudice to the application, in relation to any case, of the rules (the Hague-Visby Rules) which for the time being have the force of law by virtue of section 1 of the Carriage of Goods by Sea Act 1971.

6.   [Omitted].

MERCHANT SHIPPING ACT 1995

CHAPTER 21

1.–184.   [Omitted].

PART VII

Limitation of liability of shipowners, etc and salvors for maritime claims

185.   Limitation of liability for maritime claims

(1)   The provisions of the Convention on Limitation of Liability for Maritime Claims 1976 as set out in Part I of Schedule 7 (in this section and Part II of that Schedule referred to as 'the Convention') shall have the force of law in the United Kingdom.

(2)   The provisions of Part II of that Schedule shall have effect in connection with the Convention, and subsection (1) above shall have effect subject to the provisions of that Part.

(2A)–(2E) [Omitted].

(3)   The provisions having the force of law under this section shall apply in relation to Her Majesty's ships as they apply in relation to other ships.

(4)   The provisions having the force of law under this section shall not apply to any liability in respect of loss of life or personal injury caused to, or loss of or damage to any property of, a person who is on board the ship in question or employed in connection with that ship or with the salvage operations in question if—

(a) he is so on board or employed under a contract of service governed by the law of any part of the United Kingdom; and

(b) the liability arises from an occurrence which took place after the commencement of this Act.

In this subsection, 'ship' and 'salvage operations' have the same meaning as in the Convention.

(5)   [Omitted].

186. Exclusion of liability

(1)   Subject to subsection (3) below, the owner of a United Kingdom ship shall not be liable for any loss or damage in the following cases, namely—

(a) where any property on board the ship is lost or damaged by reason of fire on board the ship; or

(b) where any gold, silver, watches, jewels or precious stones on board the ship are lost or damaged by reason of theft, robbery or other dishonest conduct and their nature and value were not at the time of shipment declared by their owner or shipper to the owner or master of the ship in the bill of lading or otherwise in writing.

(2)   Subject to subsection (3) below, where the loss or damage arises from anything done or omitted by any person in his capacity of master or member of the crew or (otherwise than in that capacity) in the course of his employment as a servant of the owner of the ship, subsection (1) above shall also exclude the liability of—

(a) the master, member of the crew or servant; and

(b) in a case where the master or member of the crew is the servant of a person whose liability would not be excluded by that subsection apart from this paragraph, the person whose servant he is.

(3)   This section does not exclude the liability of any person for any loss or damage resulting from any such personal act or omission of his as is mentioned in Article 4 of the Convention set out in Part I of Schedule 7.

(4)   This section shall apply in relation to Her Majesty's ships as it applies in relation to other ships.

(5)   In this section 'owner', in relation to a ship, includes any part owner and any charterer, manager or operator of the ship.

Multiple fault; apportionment, liability and contribution

187. Damage or loss: apportionment of liability

(1)   Where, by the fault of two or more ships, damage or loss is caused to one or more of those ships, to their cargoes or freight, or to any property on board, the liability to make good the damage or loss shall be in proportion to the degree in which each ship was in fault.

(2)   If, in any such case, having regard to all the circumstances, it is not possible to establish different degrees of fault, the liability shall be apportioned equally.

(3) This section applies to persons other than the owners of a ship who are responsible for the fault of the ships, as well as to the owners of a ship and where, by virtue of any charter or demise, or for any other reason, the owners are not responsible for the navigation and management of the ship, this section applies to the charterers or other persons for the time being so responsible instead of the owners.

(4) Nothing in this section shall operate so as to render any ship liable for any loss or damage to which the fault of the ship has not contributed.

(5) Nothing in this section shall affect the liability of any person under a contract of carriage or any contract, or shall be construed as imposing any liability upon any person from which he is exempted by any contract or by any provision of law, or as affecting the right of any person to limit hi. liability in the manner provided by law.

(6) In this section 'freight' includes passage money and hire.

(7) In this section references to damage or loss caused by the fault of a ship include references to any salvage or other expenses, consequent upon that fault, recoverable at law by way of damages.

188. Loss of life or personal injuries: joint and several liability

(1) Where loss of life or personal injuries are suffered by any person on board a ship owing to the fault of that ship and of any other ship or ships, the liability of the owners of the ships shall be joint and several.

(2) Subsection (3) of section 187 applies also to this section.

(3) Nothing in this section shall be construed as depriving any person of any right of defence on which, apart from this section, he might have relied in an action brought against him by the person injured, or any person or persons entitled to sue in respect of such loss of life, or shall affect the right of any person to limit his liability in the manner provided by law.

(4) Subsection (7) of section 187 applies also for the interpretation of this section.

189. Loss of life or personal injuries: right of contribution

(1) Where loss of life or personal injuries are suffered by any person on board a ship owing to the fault of that ship and any other ship or ships, and a proportion of the damages is recovered against the owners of one of the ships which exceeds the proportion in which the ship was in fault, they may recover by way of contribution the amount of the excess from the owners of the other ship or ships to the extent to which those ships were respectively in fault.

(2) Subsection (3) of section 187 applies also to this section.

(3) Nothing in this section authorises the recovery of any amount which could not, by reason of any statutory or contractual limitation of, or exemption from, liability, or which could not for any other reason, have been recovered in the first instance as damages by the persons entitled to sue therefor.

(4) In addition to any other remedy provided by law, the persons entitled to any contribution recoverable under this section shall, for the purposes of recovering it, have the same rights and powers as the persons entitled to sue for damages in the first instance.

190. Time limit for proceedings against owners or ship

(1) This section applies to any proceedings to enforce any claim or lien against a ship or her owners—
   (a) in respect of damage or loss caused by the fault of that ship to another ship, its cargo or freight or any property on board it; or
   (b) for damages for loss of life or personal injury caused by the fault of that ship to any person on board another ship.

(2) The extent of the fault is immaterial for the purposes of this section.

(3)   Subject to subsections (5) and (6) below, no proceedings to which this section applies shall be brought after the period of two years from the date when—
       (a)   the damage or loss was caused; or
       (b)   the loss of life or injury was suffered.

(4)   Subject to subsections (5) and (6) below, no proceedings under any of sections 187 to 189 to enforce any contribution in respect of any overpaid proportion of any damages for loss of life or personal injury shall be brought after the period of one year from the date of payment.

(5)   Any court having jurisdiction in such proceedings may, in accordance with rules of court, extend the period allowed for bringing proceedings to such extent and on such conditions as it thinks fit.

(6)   Any such court, if satisfied that there has not been during any period allowed for bringing proceedings any reasonable opportunity of arresting the defendant ship within—
       (a)   the jurisdiction of the court; or
       (b)   the territorial sea of the country to which the plaintiff's ship belongs or in which the plaintiff resides or has his principal place of business,
       shall extend the period allowed for bringing proceedings to an extent sufficient to give a reasonable opportunity of so arresting the ship.

SCHEDULE 7
CONVENTION ON LIMITATION OF LIABILITY FOR MARITIME CLAIMS 1976

PART I
TEXT OF CONVENTION

CHAPTER I
THE RIGHT OF LIMITATION

Article 1
Persons entitled to limit liability

1.   Shipowners and salvors, as hereinafter defined, may limit their liability in accordance with the rules of this Convention for claims set out in Article 2.
2.   The term 'shipowner' shall mean the owner, charterer, manager or operator of a seagoing ship.
3.   Salvor shall mean any person rendering services in direct connection with salvage operations. Salvage operations shall also include operations referred to in Article 2, paragraph 1(d), (e) and (f).
4.   If any claims set out in Article 2 are made against any person for whose act, neglect or default the shipowner or salvor is responsible, such person shall be entitled to avail himself of the limitation of liability provided for in this Convention.
5.   In this Convention the liability of a shipowner shall include liability in an action brought against the vessel herself.
6.   An insurer of liability for claims subject to limitation in accordance with the rules of this Convention shall be entitled to the benefits of this Convention to the same extent as the assured himself.
7.   The act of invoking limitation of liability shall not constitute an admission of liability.

Article 2
Claims subject to limitation

1.   Subject to Articles 3 and 4 the following claims, whatever the basis of liability may be, shall be subject to limitation of liability—

(a) claims in respect of loss of life or personal injury or loss of or damage to property (including damage to harbour works, basins and waterways and aids to navigation) occurring on board or in direct connection with the operation of the ship or with salvage operations and consequential loss resulting therefrom;

(b) claims in respect of loss resulting from delay in the carriage by sea of cargo, passengers or their luggage;

(c) claims in respect of other loss resulting from infringement of rights other than contractual rights, occurring in direct connection with the operation of the ship or salvage operations;

(d) claims in respect of the raising, removal, destruction or the rendering harmless of a ship which is sunk, wrecked, stranded or abandoned, including anything that is or has been on board such ship;

(e) claims in respect of the removal, destruction or the rendering harmless of the cargo of the ship;

(f) claims of a person other than the person liable in respect of measures taken in order to avert or minimise loss for which the person liable may limit his liability in accordance with this Convention, and further loss caused by such measures.

2. Claims set out in paragraph 1 shall be subject to limitation of liability even if brought by way of recourse or for indemnity under a contract or otherwise. However, claims set out under paragraph (d), (e) and (f) shall not be subject to limitation of liability to the extent that they relate to remuneration under a contract with the person liable.

Article 3
Claims excepted from limitation

The rules of this Convention shall not apply to—

(a) claims for salvage, including, if applicable, any claim for special compensation under Article 14 of the International Convention on Salvage 1989, as amended, or contribution in general average;

(b) claims for oil pollution damage within the meaning of the international Convention on Civil Liability for Oil Pollution Damage dated 29th November 1969 or of any amendment or Protocol thereto which is in force;

(c) claims subject to any international convention or national legislation governing or prohibiting limitation of liability for nuclear damage;

(d) claims against the shipowner of a nuclear ship for nuclear damage;

(e) claims by servant of the shipowner or salvor whose duties are connected with the ship or the salvage operations, including claims of their heirs, dependants or other persons entitled to make such claims, if under the law governing the contract of service between the shipowner or salvor and such servant the shipowner or salvor is not entitled to limit his liability in respect of such claims, or if he is by such law only permitted to limit his liability to an amount greater than that provided for in Article 6.

Article 4
Conduct barring limitation

A person liable shall not be entitled to limit his liability if it is proved that the loss resulted from his personal act or omission, committed with the intent to cause such loss, or recklessly and with knowledge that such loss would probably result.

Article 5
Counterclaims

Where a person entitled to limitation of liability under the rules of this Convention has a claim against the claimant arising out of the same occurrence, their respective claims shall be set off against each other and the provisions of this Convention shall only apply to the balance, if any.

CHAPTER II
LIMITS OF LIABILITY

Article 6
The general limits

1. The limits of liability for claims other than those mentioned in Article 7, arising on any distinct occasion, shall be calculated as follows—
    (a) in respect of claims for loss of life or personal injury:
        (i)   2 million Units of Account for a ship with a tonnage not exceeding 2,000 tons;
        (ii) for a ship with a tonnage in excess thereof, the following amount in addition to that mentioned in (i)—
            for each ton from 2,001 to 30,000 tons, 800 Units of Account;
            for each ton from 30,001 to 70,000 tons, 600 Units of Account; and
            for each ton in excess of 70,000 tons, 400 Units of Account;
    (b) in respect of any other claims:
        (i)   1 million Units of Account for a ship with a tonnage not exceeding 2,000 tons;
        (ii) for a ship with a tonnage in excess thereof the following amount in addition to that mentioned in (i)—
            for each ton from 2,001 to 30,000 tons, 400 Units of Account;
            for each ton from 30,0001 to 70,000 tons, 300 Units of Account; and
            for each ton in excess of 70,000 tons, 200 Units of Account.
2. Where the amount calculated in accordance with paragraph 1(a) is insufficient to pay the claims mentioned therein in full, the amount calculated in accordance with paragraph 1(b) shall be available for payment of the unpaid balance of claims under paragraph 1(a) and such unpaid balance shall rank rateably with claims mentioned under paragraph 1(b).
3. The limits of liability for any salvor not operating from any ship or for any salvor operating solely on the ship to, or in respect of which he is rendering salvage services, shall be calculated according to a tonnage of 1,500 tons.

Article 7
The limit for passenger claims

1. In respect of claims arising on any distinct occasion for loss of life or personal injury to passengers of a ship, the limit of liability of the shipowner thereof shall be an amount of 175,000 Units of Account multiplied by the number of passengers which the ship is authorised to carry according to the ship's certificate.
2. For the purpose of this Article 'claims for loss of life or personal injury to passengers of a ship' shall mean any such claims brought by or on behalf of any person carried in that ship—
    (a) under a contract of passenger carriage; or
    (b) who, with the consent of the carrier, is accompanying a vehicle or live animals which are covered by a contract for the carriage of goods.

Article 8
Unit of Account

1. The Unit of Account referred to in Articles 6 and 7 is the Special Drawing Right as defined by the International Monetary Fund. The amounts mentioned in Articles 6 and 7 shall be converted into the national currency of the State in which limitation is sought, according to the value of that currency at the date the limitation fund shall have been constituted, payment is made, or security is given which under the law of that State is equivalent to such payment.

Article 9
Aggregation of claims

1. The limits of liability determined in accordance with Article 6 shall apply to the aggregate of all claims which arise on any distinct occasion—
   (a) against the person or persons mentioned in paragraph 2 of Article 1 and any person for whose act, neglect or default he or they areresponsible; or
   (b) against the shipowner of a ship rendering salvage services from that ship and the salvor or salvors operating from such ship and any person for whose act, neglect or default he or they are responsible; or
   (c) against the salvor or salvors who are not operating from a ship or who are operating solely on the ship to, or in respect of which, the salvage services are rendered and any person for whose act, neglect or default he or they are responsible.
2. The limits of liability determined in accordance with Article 7 shall apply to the aggregate of all claims subject thereto which may arise on any distinct occasion against the person or persons mentioned in paragraph 2 of Article 1 in respect of the ship referred to in Article 7 and any person for whose act, neglect or default he or they are responsible.

Article 10
Limitation of liability without constitution of a limitation fund

1. Limitation of liability may be invoked notwithstanding that a limitation fund as mentioned in Article 11 has not been constituted.
2. If limitation of liability is invoked without the constitution of a limitation fund, the provisions of Article 12 shall apply correspondingly.
3. Questions of procedure arising under the rules of this Article shall be decided in accordance with the national law of the State Party in which action is brought.

CHAPTER III
THE LIMITATION FUND

Article 11
Constitution of the fund

1. Any person alleged to be liable may constitute a fund with the Court or other competent authority in any State Party in which legal proceedings are instituted in respect of claims subject to limitation. The fund shall be constituted in the sum of such of the amounts set out in Articles 6 and 7 as are applicable to claims for which that person may be liable, together with interest thereon from the date of the occurrence giving rise to the liability until the date of the constitution of the fund. Any fund thus constituted shall be available only for the payment of claims in respect of which limitation of liability can be invoked.

2.   A fund may be constituted, either by depositing the sum, or by producing a guarantee acceptable under the legislation of the State Party where the fund is constituted and considered to be adequate by the court or other competent authority.

3.   A fund constituted by one of the persons mentioned in paragraph 1(a), (b) or (c) or paragraph 2 of Article 9 or his insurer shall be deemed constituted by all persons mentioned in paragraph 1(a), (b) or (c) or paragraph 2, respectively.

Article 12
Distribution of the fund

1.   Subject to the provisions of paragraphs 1 and 2 of Article 6 and of Article 7, the fund shall be distributed among the claimants in proportion to their established claims against the fund.

2.   If, before the fund is distributed, the person liable, or his insurer, has settled a claim against the fund such person shall up to the amount he has paid, acquire by subrogation the rights which the person so compensated would have enjoyed under this Convention.

3.   The right of subrogation provided for in paragraph 2 may also be exercised by persons other than those therein mentioned in respect of any amount of compensation which they may have paid, but only to the extent that such subrogation is permitted under the applicable national law.

4.   Where the person liable or any other person establishes that he may be compelled to pay, at a later day, in whole or in part any such amount of compensation with regard to which such person would have enjoyed a right of subrogation pursuant to paragraphs 2 and 3 had the compensation been paid before the fund was distributed, the Court or other competent authority of the State where the fund has been constituted may order that a sufficient sum shall be provisionally set aside to enable such person at such later date to enforce his claim against the fund.

Article 13
Bar to other actions

1.   Where a limitation fund has been constituted in accordance with Article 11, any person having made a claim against the fund shall be barred from exercising any right in respect of such a claim against any other assets of a person by or on behalf of whom the fund has been constituted.

2.   After a limitation fund has been constituted in accordance with Article 11, any ship or other property, belonging to a person on behalf of whom the fund has been constituted, which has been arrested or attached within the jurisdiction of a State Party for a claim which may be raised against the fund, or any security given, may be released by order of the Court or other competent authority of such State. However, such release shall always be ordered if the limitation fund has been constituted—
   (a)   at the port where the occurrence took place, or, if it took place out of port, at the first port of call thereafter; or
   (b)   at the port of disembarkation in respect of claims for loss of life or personal injury; or
   (c)   at the port of discharge in respect of damage to cargo; or
   (d)   in the State where the arrest is made.

3.   The rules of paragraphs 1 and 2 shall apply only if the claimant may bring a claim against the limitation fund before the Court administering that fund and the fund is actually available and freely transferable in respect of that claim.

Article 14
Governing Law

Subject to the provisions of this Chapter the rules relating to the constitution and distribution of a limitation fund, and all rules of procedure in connection therewith, shall be governed by the law of the State Party in which the fund is constituted.

CHAPTER IV
SCOPE OF APPLICATION

Article 15

(1) This Convention shall apply whenever any person referred to in Article 1 seeks to limit his liability before the Court of a State Party or seeks to procure the release of a ship or other property or the discharge of any security given within the jurisdiction of any such State.

(2) A State Party may regulate by specific provisions of national law the system of limitation of liability to be applied to vessels which are—
   (a) according to the law of that State, ships intended for navigation on inland waterways;
   (b) ships of less than 300 tons.
   A State Party which makes use of the option provided for in this paragraph shall inform the depositary of the limits of liability adopted in its national legislation or of the fact that there are none.

(3) *bis* Notwithstanding the limit of liability prescribed in paragraph 1 of Article 7, a State Party may regulate by specific provisions of national law the system of liability to be applied to claims for loss of life or personal injury to passengers of a ship, provided that the limit of liability is not lower than that prescribed in paragraph 1 of Article 7. A State Party which makes use of the option provided for in this paragraph shall inform the Secretary-General of the limits of liability adopted or of the fact that there are none.

Article 18
Reservations

1. Any State may, at the time of signature, ratification, acceptance, approval or accession, or at any time thereafter, reserve the right—
   (a) to exclude the application of article 2, paragraphs 1(d) and (e);
   (b) to exclude claims for damage within the meaning of the International Convention on Liability and Compensation for Damage in Connection with the Carriage of Hazardous and Noxious Substances by Sea, 1996 or of any amendment or Protocol thereto.
   No other reservations shall be admissible to the substantive provisions of this Convention.

PART II

PROVISIONS HAVING EFFECT IN CONNECTION WITH CONVENTION

Interpretation

1. In this part of this Schedule any reference to a numbered Article is a reference to the Article of the Convention which is so numbered.

Right to limit liability

2.   Subject to paragraph 6 below, the right to limit liability under the convention shall apply in relation to any ship whether seagoing or not, and the definition of 'shipowner' in paragraph 2 of Article 1 shall be construed accordingly.

Claims subject to limitation

2A.   Paragraph 1(a) of article 2 shall have effect as if the reference to "loss of life or personal injury" did not include a reference to loss of life or personal injury to passengers of seagoing ships.

3.   (1)   Paragraph 1(d) of Article 2 shall not apply unless provision has been made by an order of the Secretary of State for the setting up and management of a fund to be used for the making to harbour or conservancy authorities of payments needed to compensate them for the reduction, in consequence of the said paragraph 1(d), of amounts recoverable by them in claims of the kind there mentioned, and to be maintained by contributions from such authorities raised and collected by them in respect of vessels in like manner as other sums so raised by them.

        (2)   Any order under sub-paragraph (1) above may contain such incidental and supplemental provisions as appear to the Secretary of State to be necessary or expedient

Claims excluded from limitation

4.   (1)   Claims for damage within the meaning of the International Convention on Liability and Compensation for Damage in Connection with the Carriage of Hazardous and Noxious Substances by Sea 1996, or any amendment of or Protocol to that Convention, which arise from occurrences which take place after the coming into force of the first Order in Council made by Her Majesty under section 182B of this Act shall be excluded from the Convention.

        (2)   The claims excluded from the Convention by paragraph (b) of Article 3 are claims in respect of any liability incurred under section 153 of this Act.

        (3)   The claims excluded from the Convention by paragraph (c) of Article 3 are claims made by virtue of any of sections 7 to 11 of the Nuclear Installations Act 1965.

The general limits

5.   (1)   In the application of Article 6 to a ship with a tonnage less than 300 tons that Article shall have effect as if—
                (a) paragraph (a)(i) referred to 1,000,000 Units of Account; and
                (b) paragraph (b)(i) referred to 500,000 Units of Account.

        (2)   For the purposes of Article 6 and this paragraph a ship's tonnage shall be its gross tonnage calculated in such manner as may be prescribed by an order made by the Secretary of State.

        (3)   Any order under this paragraph shall, so far as appears to the Secretary of State to be practicable, give effect to the regulations in Annex 1 of the International Convention on Tonnage Measurement of Ships 1969.

Limit for passenger claims

6.   (1)   Article 7 shall not apply in respect of any seagoing ship; and shall have effect in respect of any ship which is not seagoing as if, in paragraph 1 of that article—
                (a) after 'thereof' there were inserted 'in respect of each passenger,';

(b) the words from 'multiplied' onwards were omitted.

(2) In paragraph 2 of Article 7 the reference to claims brought on behalf of a person includes a reference to any claim in respect of the death of a person under the Fatal Accidents Act 1976, the Fatal Accidents (Northern Ireland) Order 1977 or the Damages (Scotland) Act 1976.

Units of Account

7. (1) For the purpose of converting the amounts mentioned in Articles 6 and 7 from special drawing rights into sterling one special drawing right shall be treated as equal to such a sum in sterling as the International Monetary Fund have fixed as being the equivalent of one special drawing right for—
(a) the relevant date under paragraph 1 of Article 8; or
(b) if no sum has been so fixed for that date, the last proceeding date for which a sum has been so fixed.

(2) A certificate given by or on behalf of the Treasury stating—
(a) that a particular sum in sterling has been fixed as mentioned in the preceding sub-paragraph for a particular date; or
(b) that no sum has been so fixed for that date and that a particular sum in sterling has been so fixed for a date which is the last preceding date for which a sum has been so fixed,

shall be conclusive evidence of those matters for the purposes of those Articles; and a document purporting to be such a certificate shall, in any proceedings, be received in evidence and unless the contrary is proved be deemed to be such a certificate.

Constitution of fund

8. (1) The Secretary of State may from time to time with the concurrence of the Treasury, by order prescribe the rate of interest to be applied for the purposes of paragraph 1 of Article 11.

(2) Any statutory instrument containing an order under sub-paragraph (1) above, shall be laid before Parliament after being made.

(3) Where a fund is constituted with the court in accordance with Article 11 for the payment of claims arising out of any occurrence, the court may stay any proceedings relating to any claim arising out of that occurrence which are pending against the person by whom the fund has been constituted.

Distribution of fund

9. No lien or other right in respect of any ship or property shall affect the proportions in which under Article 12 the fund is distributed among several claimants.

Bar to other actions

10. Where the release of a ship or other property is ordered under paragraph 2 of Article 13 the person on whose application it is ordered to be release shall be deemed to have submitted to (or, in Scotland, prorogated) the jurisdiction of the court to adjudicate on the claim for which the ship or property was arrested or attached.

Meaning of 'court'

11. References in the Convention and the preceding provisions of this Part of this Schedule to the court are references to the High Court or, in relation to Scotland, the Court of Session.

Meaning of 'ship'

12. References in the Convention and in the preceding provisions of this Part of this Schedule to a ship include references to any structure (whether completed or in course of completion) launched and intended for use in navigation as a ship or part of a ship.

Meaning of 'State Party'

13. An Order in Council made for the purposes of this paragraph and declaring that any State specified in the Order is a party to the Convention as amended by the 1996 Protocol shall, subject to the provisions of any subsequent Order made for those purposes be conclusive evidence that the State is a party to the Convention as amended by the 1996 Protocol.

PRIVATE INTERNATIONAL LAW (MISCELLANEOUS PROVISIONS) ACT 1995

CHAPTER 42

PART III
CHOICE OF LAW IN TORT AND DELICT

9. **Purpose of Part III**
   (1) The rules in this Part apply for choosing the law (in this Part referred to as 'the applicable law') to be used for determining issues relating to tort or (for the purposes of the law of Scotland) delict.
   (2) The characterisation for the purposes of private international law of issues arising in a claim as issues relating to tort or delict is a matter for the courts of the forum.
   (3) The rules in this Part do not apply in relation to issues arising in any claim excluded from the operation of this Part by section 13 below.
   (4) The applicable law shall be used for determining the issues arising in a claim, including in particular the question whether an actionable tort or delict has occurred.
   (5) The applicable law to be used for determining the issues arising in a claim shall exclude any choice of law rules forming part of the law of the country or countries concerned.
   (6) For the avoidance of doubt (and without prejudice to the operation of section 14 below) this Part applies in relation to events occurring in the forum as it applies in relation to events occurring in any other country.
   (7) In this Part as it extends to any country within the United Kingdom, 'the forum' means England and Wales, Scotland or Northern Ireland, as the case may be.
   (8) In this Part 'delict' includes quasi-delict.

10. **Abolition of certain common law rules**
    The rules of the common law, in so far as they—
    (a) require actionability under both the law of the forum and the law of another country for the purpose of determining whether a tort or delict is actionable; or
    (b) allow (as an exception from the rules falling within paragraph (a) above) for the law of a single country to be applied for the purpose of determining the issues, or any of the issues, arising in the case in question,

are hereby abolished so far as they apply to any claim in tort or delict which is not excluded from the operation of this Part by section 13 below.

11. Choice of applicable law: the general rule

(1) The general rule is that the applicable law is the law of the country in which the events constituting the tort or delict in question occur.

(2) Where elements of those events occur in different countries, the applicable law under the general rule is to be taken as being—

    (a) for a cause of action in respect of personal injury caused to an individual or death resulting from personal injury, the law of the country where the individual was when he sustained the injury;

    (b) for a cause of action in respect of damage to property, the law of the country where the property was when it was damaged; and

    (c) in any other case, the law of the country in which the most significant element or elements of those events occurred.

(3) In this section 'personal injury' includes disease or any impairment of physical or mental condition.

12. Choice of applicable law: displacement of general rule

(1) If it appears, in all the circumstances, from a comparison of—

    (a) the significance of the factors which connect a tort or delict with the country whose law would be the applicable law under the general rule; and

    (b) the significance of any factors connecting the tort or delict with another country,

that it is substantially more appropriate for the applicable law for determining the issues arising in the case, or any of those issues, to be the law of the other country, the general rule is displaced and the applicable law for determining those issues or that issue (as the case may be) is the law of that other country.

(2) The factors that may be taken into account as connecting a tort or delict with a country for the purposes of this section include, in particular, factors relating to the parties, to any of the events which constitute the tort or delict in question or to any of the circumstances or consequences of those events.

13. Exclusion of defamation claims from Part III

(1) Nothing in this Part applies to affect the determination of issues arising in any defamation claim.

(2) For the purposes of this section 'defamation claim' means—

    (a) any claim under the law of any part of the United Kingdom for libel or slander or for slander of title, slander of goods or other malicious falsehood and any claim under the law of Scotland for verbal injury; and

    (b) any claim under the law of any other country corresponding to or otherwise in the nature of a claim mentioned in paragraph (a) above.

14. Transitional provision and savings

(1) Nothing in this Part applies to acts or omissions giving rise to a claim which occur before the commencement of this Part.

(2) Nothing in this Part affects any rules of law (including rules of private international law) except those abolished by section 10 above.

(3) Without prejudice to the generality of subsection (2) above, nothing in this Part—

    (a) authorises the application of the law of a country outside the forum as the applicable law for determining issues arising in any claim in so far as to do so:

        (i) would conflict with principles of public policy; or

(ii)   would give effect to such a penal, revenue or other public law as
        would not otherwise be enforceable under the law of the forum; or
(b) affects any rules of evidence, pleading or practice or authorises
     questions of procedure in any proceedings to be determined otherwise
     than in accordance with the law of the forum.
(4)   This Part has effect without prejudice to the operation of any rule of law
       which either has effect notwithstanding the rules of private international law
       applicable in the particular circumstances or modifies the rules of private
       international law that would otherwise be so applicable.

15.   Crown application
(1)   This Part applies in relation to claims by or against the Crown as it applies in
       relation to claims to which the Crown is not a party.
(2)   In subsection (1) above a reference to the Crown does not include a
       reference to Her Majesty in Her private capacity or to Her Majesty in right of
       Her Duchy of Lancaster or to the Duke of Cornwall.
(3)   Without prejudice to the generality of section 14(2) above, nothing in this
       section affects any rule of law as to whether proceedings of any description
       may be brought against the Crown.

ARBITRATION ACT 1996

CHAPTER 23

PART I
ARBITRATION PURSUANT TO AN ARBITRATION AGREEMENT

Introductory

The arbitration agreement

Stay of legal proceedings

Commencement of arbitral proceedings

The arbitral tribunal

Jurisdiction of the arbitral tribunal

The arbitral proceeding

Powers of court in relation to arbitral proceedings

The award

PART II
OTHER PROVISIONS RELATING TO ARBITRATION

Domestic arbitration agreements

Appointment of judges as arbitrators

PART I
ARBITRATION PURSUANT TO AN ARBITRATION AGREEMENT

Introductory

1.   **General principles**
     The provisions of this Part are founded on the following principles, and shall be construed accordingly—
     (a)   the object of arbitration is to obtain the fair resolution of disputes by an impartial tribunal without unnecessary delay or expense;
     (b)   the parties should be free to agree how their disputes are resolved, subject only to such safeguards as are necessary in the public interest;
     (c)   in matters governed by this Part the court should not intervene except as provided by this Part.

2.   **Scope of application of provisions**
     (1)   The provisions of this Part apply where the seat of the arbitration is in England and Wales or Northern Ireland.

(2)   The following sections apply even if the seat of the arbitration is outside England and Wales or Northern Ireland or no seat has been designated or determined—

       (a)   sections 9 to 11 (stay of legal proceedings, &c); and

       (b)   section 66 (enforcement of arbitral awards).

(3)   The powers conferred by the following sections apply even if the seat of the arbitration is outside England and Wales or Northern Ireland or no seat has been designated or determined—

       (a)   section 43 (securing the attendance of witnesses); and

       (b)   section 44 (court powers exercisable in support of arbitral proceedings),

       but the court may refuse to exercise any such power if, in the opinion of the court, the fact that the seat of the arbitration is outside England and Wales or Northern Ireland, or that when designated or determined the seat is likely to be outside England and Wales or Northern Ireland, makes it inappropriate to do so.

(4)   The court may exercise a power conferred by any provision of this Part not mentioned in subsection (2) or (3) for the purpose of supporting the arbitral process where—

       (a)   no seat of the arbitration has been designated or determined; and

       (b)   by reason of a connection with England and Wales or Northern Ireland the court is satisfied that it is appropriate to do so.

(5)   Section 7 (separability of arbitration agreement) and section 8 (death of a party) apply where the law applicable to the arbitration agreement is the law of England and Wales or Northern Ireland even if the seat of the arbitration is outside England and Wales or Northern Ireland or has not been designated or determined.

3.   The seat of the arbitration

In this Part 'the seat of the arbitration' means the juridical seat of the arbitration designated—

(a)   by the parties to the arbitration agreement; or

(b)   by any arbitral or other institution or person vested by the parties with powers in that regard; or

(c)   by the arbitral tribunal if so authorised by the parties,

or determined, in the absence of any such designation, having regard to the parties' agreement and all the relevant circumstances.

4.   Mandatory and non-mandatory provisions

(1)   The mandatory provisions of this Part are listed in Schedule 1 and have effect notwithstanding any agreement to the contrary.

(2)   The other provisions of this Part (the 'non-mandatory provisions') allow the parties to make their own arrangements by agreement but provide rules which apply in the absence of such agreement.

(3)   The parties may make such arrangements by agreeing to the application of institutional rules or providing any other means by which a matter may be decided.

(4)   It is immaterial whether or not the law applicable to the parties' agreement is the law of England and Wales or, as the case may be, Northern Ireland.

(5)   The choice of a law other than the law of England and Wales or Northern Ireland as the applicable law in respect of a matter provided for by a non-mandatory provision of this Part is equivalent to an agreement making provision about that matter.

     For this purpose an applicable law determined in accordance with the parties' agreement, or which is objectively determined in the absence of any express or implied choice, shall be treated as chosen by the parties.

5.   Agreements to be in writing

(1)   The provisions of this Part apply only where the arbitration agreement is in writing, and any other agreement between the parties as to any matter is effective for the purposes of this Part only if in writing.

The expressions 'agreement', 'agree' and 'agreed' shall be construed accordingly.

(2)   There is an agreement in writing—

(a)   if the agreement is made in writing (whether or not it is signed by the parties);

(b)   if the agreement is made by exchange of communications in writing; or

(c)   if the agreement is evidenced in writing.

(3)   Where parties agree otherwise than in writing by reference to terms which are in writing, they make an agreement in writing.

(4)   An agreement is evidenced in writing if an agreement made otherwise than in writing is recorded by one of the parties, or by a third party, with the authority of the parties to the agreement.

(5)   An exchange of written submissions in arbitral or legal proceedings in which the existence of an agreement otherwise than in writing is alleged by one party against another party and not denied by the other party in his response constitutes as between those parties an agreement in writing to the effect alleged.

(6)   References in this Part to anything being written or in writing include its being recorded by any means.

The arbitration agreement

6.   Definition of arbitration agreement

(1)   In this Part an 'arbitration agreement' means an agreement to submit to arbitration present or future disputes (whether they are contractual or not).

(2)   The reference in an agreement to a written form of arbitration clause or to a document containing an arbitration clause constitutes an arbitration agreement if the reference is such as to make that clause part of the agreement.

7.   Separability of arbitration agreement

Unless otherwise agreed by the parties, an arbitration agreement which forms or was intended to form part of another agreement (whether or not in writing) shall not be regarded as invalid, non-existent or ineffective because that other agreement is invalid, or did not come into existence or has become ineffective, and it shall for that purpose be treated as a distinct agreement.

8.   Whether agreement discharged by death of a party

(1)   Unless otherwise agreed by the parties, an arbitration agreement is not discharged by the death of a party and may be enforced by or against the personal representatives of that party.

(2)   Subsection (1) does not affect the operation of any enactment or rule of law by virtue of which a substantive right or obligation is extinguished by death.

Stay of legal proceedings

9.   Stay of legal proceedings

(1)   A party to an arbitration agreement against whom legal proceedings are brought (whether by way of claim or counterclaim) in respect of a matter which under the agreement is to be referred to arbitration may (upon notice to the other parties to the proceedings) apply to the court in which the

proceedings have been brought to stay the proceedings so far as they concern that matter.

(2)   An application may be made notwithstanding that the matter is to be referred to arbitration only after the exhaustion of other dispute resolution procedures.

(3)   An application may not be made by a person before taking the appropriate procedural step (if any) to acknowledge the legal proceedings against him or after he has taken any step in those proceedings to answer the substantive claim.

(4)   On an application under this section the court shall grant a stay unless satisfied that the arbitration agreement is null and void, inoperative, or incapable of being performed.

(5)   If the court refuses to stay the legal proceedings, any provision that an award is a condition precedent to the bringing of legal proceedings in respect of any matter is of no effect in relation to those proceedings.

10.   Reference of interpleader issue to arbitration

(1)   Where in legal proceedings relief by way of interpleader is granted and any issue between the claimants is one in respect of which there is an arbitration agreement between them, the court granting the relief shall direct that the issue be determined in accordance with the agreement unless the circumstances are such that proceedings brought by a claimant in respect of the matter would not be stayed.

(2)   Where subsection (1) applies but the court does not direct that the issue be determined in accordance with the arbitration agreement, any provision that an award is a condition precedent to the bringing of legal proceedings in respect of any matter shall not affect the determination of that issue by the court.

11.   Retention of security where Admiralty proceedings stayed

(1)   Where Admiralty proceedings are stayed on the ground that the dispute in question should be submitted to arbitration, the court granting the stay may, if in those proceedings property has been arrested or bail or other security has been given to prevent or obtain release from arrest—

(a)   order that the property arrested be retained as security for the satisfaction of any award given in the arbitration in respect of that dispute; or

(b)   order that the stay of those proceedings be conditional on the provision of equivalent security for the satisfaction of any such award.

(2)   Subject to any provision made by rules of court and to any necessary modifications, the same law and practice shall apply in relation to property retained in pursuance of an order as would apply if it were held for the purposes of proceedings in the court making the order.

Commencement of arbitral proceedings

12.   Power of court to extend time for beginning arbitral proceedings, &c

(1)   Where an arbitration agreement to refer future disputes to arbitration provides that a claim shall be barred, or the claimant's right extinguished, unless the claimant takes within a time fixed by the agreement some step—

(a)   to begin arbitral proceedings; or

(b)   to begin other dispute resolution procedures which must be exhausted before arbitral proceedings can be begun,

the court may by order extend the time for taking that step.

(2)	Any party to the arbitration agreement may apply for such an order (upon notice to the other parties), but only after a claim has arisen and after exhausting any available arbitral process for obtaining an extension of time.

(3)	The court shall make an order only if satisfied—
   (a) that the circumstances are such as were outside the reasonable contemplation of the parties when they agreed the provision in question, and that it would be just to extend the time; or
   (b) that the conduct of one party makes it unjust to hold the other party to the strict terms of the provision in question.

(4)	The court may extend the time for such period and on such terms as it thinks fit, and may do so whether or not the time previously fixed (by agreement or by a previous order) has expired.

(5)	An order under this section does not affect the operation of the Limitation Acts (see section 13).

(6)	The leave of the court is required for any appeal from a decision of the court under this section.

## 13.	Application of Limitation Acts

(1)	The Limitation Acts apply to arbitral proceedings as they apply to legal proceedings.

(2)	The court may order that in computing the time prescribed by the Limitation Acts for the commencement of proceedings (including arbitral proceedings) in respect of a dispute which was the subject matter—
   (a) of an award which the court orders to be set aside or declares to be of no effect; or
   (b) of the affected part of an award which the court orders to be set aside in part, or declares to be in part of no effect,
   the period between the commencement of the arbitration and the date of the order referred to in paragraph (a) or (b) shall be excluded.

(3)	In determining for the purposes of the Limitation Acts when a cause of action accrued, any provision that an award is a condition precedent to the bringing of legal proceedings in respect of a matter to which an arbitration agreement applies shall be disregarded.

(4)	In this Part 'the Limitation Acts' means—
   (a) in England and Wales, the Limitation Act 1980, the Foreign Limitation Periods Act 1984 and any other enactment (whenever passed) relating to the limitation of actions;
   (b) in Northern Ireland, the Limitation (Northern Ireland) Order 1985 and any other enactment (whenever passed) relating to the limitation of actions.

## 14.	Commencement of arbitral proceedings

(1)	The parties are free to agree when arbitral proceedings are to be regarded as commenced for the purposes of this Part and for the purposes of the Limitation Acts.

(2)	If there is no such agreement the following provisions apply.

(3)	Where the arbitrator is named or designated in the arbitration agreement, arbitral proceedings are commenced in respect of a matter when one party serves on the other party or parties a notice in writing requiring him or them to submit that matter to the person so named or designated.

(4)	Where the arbitrator or arbitrators are to be appointed by the parties, arbitral proceedings are commenced in respect of a matter when one party serves on the other party or parties notice in writing requiring him or them to appoint an arbitrator or to agree to the appointment of an arbitrator in respect of that matter.

(5)   Where the arbitrator or arbitrators are to be appointed by a person other than a party to the proceedings, arbitral proceedings are commenced in respect of a matter when one party gives notice in writing to that person requesting him to make the appointment in respect of that matter.

The arbitral tribunal

15. The arbitral tribunal

(1)   The parties are free to agree on the number of arbitrators to form the tribunal and whether there is to be a chairman or umpire.

(2)   Unless otherwise agreed by the parties, an agreement that the number of arbitrators shall be two or any other even number shall be understood as requiring the appointment of an additional arbitrator as chairman of the tribunal.

(3)   If there is no agreement as to the number of arbitrators, the tribunal shall consist of a sole arbitrator.

16. Procedure for appointment of arbitrators

(1)   The parties are free to agree on the procedure for appointing the arbitrator or arbitrators, including the procedure for appointing any chairman or umpire.

(2)   If or to the extent that there is no such agreement, the following provisions apply.

(3)   If the tribunal is to consist of a sole arbitrator, the parties shall jointly appoint the arbitrator not later than 28 days after service of a request in writing by either party to do so.

(4)   If the tribunal is to consist of two arbitrators, each party shall appoint one arbitrator not later than 14 days after service of a request in writing by either party to do so.

(5)   If the tribunal is to consist of three arbitrators—
   (a)   each party shall appoint one arbitrator not later than 14 days after service of a request in writing by either party to do so; and
   (b)   the two so appointed shall forthwith appoint a third arbitrator as the chairman of the tribunal.

(6)   If the tribunal is to consist of two arbitrators and an umpire—
   (a)   each party shall appoint one arbitrator not later than 14 days after service of a request in writing by either party to do so; and
   (b)   the two so appointed may appoint an umpire at any time after they themselves are appointed and shall do so before any substantive hearing or forthwith if they cannot agree on a matter relating to the arbitration.

(7)   In any other case (in particular, if there are more than two parties) section 18 applies as in the case of a failure of the agreed appointment procedure.

17. Power in case of default to appoint sole arbitrator

(1)   Unless the parties otherwise agree, where each of two parties to an arbitration agreement is to appoint an arbitrator and one party ('the party in default') refuses to do so, or fails to do so within the time specified, the other party, having duly appointed his arbitrator, may give notice in writing to the party in default that he proposes to appoint his arbitrator to act as sole arbitrator.

(2)   If the party in default does not within 7 clear days of that notice being given—
   (a)   make the required appointment; and
   (b)   notify the other party that he has done so,
   the other party may appoint his arbitrator as sole arbitrator whose award shall be binding on both parties as if he had been so appointed by agreement.

(3)   Where a sole arbitrator has been appointed under subsection (2), the party in default may (upon notice to the appointing party) apply to the court which may set aside the appointment.

(4)   The leave of the court is required for any appeal from a decision of the court under this section.

18. Failure of appointment procedure

(1)   The parties are free to agree what is to happen in the event of a failure of the procedure for the appointment of the arbitral tribunal.

There is no failure if an appointment is duly made under section 17 (power in case of default to appoint sole arbitrator), unless that appointment is set aside.

(2)   If or to the extent that there is no such agreement any party to the arbitration agreement may (upon notice to the other parties) apply to the court to exercise its powers under this section.

(3)   Those powers are—
    (a)   to give directions as to the making of any necessary appointments;
    (b)   to direct that the tribunal shall be constituted by such appointments (or any one or more of them) as have been made;
    (c)   to revoke any appointments already made;
    (d)   to make any necessary appointments itself.

(4)   An appointment made by the court under this section has effect as if made with the agreement of the parties.

(5)   The leave of the court is required for any appeal from a decision of the court under this section.

19. Court to have regard to agreed qualifications

In deciding whether to exercise, and in considering how to exercise, any of its powers under section 16 (procedure for appointment of arbitrators) or section 18 (failure of appointment procedure), the court shall have due regard to any agreement of the parties as to the qualifications required of the arbitrators.

20. Chairman

(1)   Where the parties have agreed that there is to be a chairman, they are free to agree what the functions of the chairman are to be in relation to the making of decisions, orders and awards.

(2)   If or to the extent that there is no such agreement, the following provisions apply.

(3)   Decisions, orders and awards shall be made by all or a majority of the arbitrators (including the chairman).

(4)   The view of the chairman shall prevail in relation to a decision, order or award in respect of which there is neither unanimity nor a majority under subsection (3).

21. Umpire

(1)   Where the parties have agreed that there is to be an umpire, they are free to agree what the functions of the umpire are to be, and in particular—
    (a)   whether he is to attend the proceedings; and
    (b)   when he is to replace the other arbitrators as the tribunal with power to make decisions, orders and awards.

(2)   If or to the extent that there is no such agreement, the following provisions apply.

(3)   The umpire shall attend the proceedings and be supplied with the same documents and other materials as are supplied to the other arbitrators.

(4)   Decisions, orders and awards shall be made by the other arbitrators unless and until they cannot agree on a matter relating to the arbitration.

In that event they shall forthwith give notice in writing to the parties and the umpire, whereupon the umpire shall replace them as the tribunal with power to make decisions, orders and awards as if he were sole arbitrator.

(5)   If the arbitrators cannot agree but fail to give notice of that fact, or if any of them fails to join in the giving of notice, any party to the arbitral proceedings may (upon notice to the other parties and to the tribunal) apply to the court which may order that the umpire shall replace the other arbitrators as the tribunal with power to make decisions, orders and awards as if he were sole arbitrator.

(6)   The leave of the court is required for any appeal from a decision of the court under this section.

22.   Decision-making where no chairman or umpire

(1)   Where the parties agree that there shall be two or more arbitrators with no chairman or umpire, the parties are free to agree how the tribunal is to make decisions, orders and awards.

(2)   If there is no such agreement, decisions, orders and awards shall be made by all or a majority of the arbitrators.

23.   Revocation of arbitrator's authority

(1)   The parties are free to agree in what circumstances the authority of an arbitrator may be revoked.

(2)   If or to the extent that there is no such agreement the following provisions apply.

(3)   The authority of an arbitrator may not be revoked except—
   (a)   by the parties acting jointly; or
   (b)   by an arbitral or other institution or person vested by the parties with powers in that regard.

(4)   Revocation of the authority of an arbitrator by the parties acting jointly must be agreed in writing unless the parties also agree (whether or not in writing) to terminate the arbitration agreement.

(5)   Nothing in this section affects the power of the court—
   (a)   to revoke an appointment under section 18 (powers exercisable in case of failure of appointment procedure); or
   (b)   to remove an arbitrator on the grounds specified in section 24.

24.   Power of court to remove arbitrator

(1)   A party to arbitral proceedings may (upon notice to the other parties, to the arbitrator concerned and to any other arbitrator) apply to the court to remove an arbitrator on any of the following grounds—
   (a)   that circumstances exist that give rise to justifiable doubts as to his impartiality;
   (b)   that he does not possess the qualifications required by the arbitration agreement;
   (c)   that he is physically or mentally incapable of conducting the proceedings or there are justifiable doubts as to his capacity to do so;
   (d)   that he has refused or failed:
      (i)   properly to conduct the proceedings; or
      (ii)   to use all reasonable despatch in conducting the proceedings or making an award,
      and that substantial injustice has been or will be caused to the applicant.

(2)   If there is an arbitral or other institution or person vested by the parties with power to remove an arbitrator, the court shall not exercise its power of removal unless satisfied that the applicant has first exhausted any available recourse to that institution or person.

(3)   The arbitral tribunal may continue the arbitral proceedings and make an award while an application to the court under this section is pending.

(4)   Where the court removes an arbitrator, it may make such order as it thinks fit with respect to his entitlement (if any) to fees or expenses, or the repayment of any fees or expenses already paid.

(5)   The arbitrator concerned is entitled to appear and be heard by the court before it makes any order under this section.

(6)   The leave of the court is required for any appeal from a decision of the court under this section.

25.   Resignation of arbitrator

(1)   The parties are free to agree with an arbitrator as to the consequences of his resignation as regards—
    (a)   his entitlement (if any) to fees or expenses; and
    (b)   any liability thereby incurred by him.

(2)   If or to the extent that there is no such agreement the following provisions apply.

(3)   An arbitrator who resigns his appointment may (upon notice to the parties) apply to the court—
    (a)   to grant him relief from any liability thereby incurred by him; and
    (b)   to make such order as it thinks fit with respect to his entitlement (if any) to fees or expenses or the repayment of any fees or expenses already paid.

(4)   If the court is satisfied that in all the circumstances it was reasonable for the arbitrator to resign, it may grant such relief as is mentioned in subsection (3)(a) on such terms as it thinks fit.

(5)   The leave of the court is required for any appeal from a decision of the court under this section.

26.   Death of arbitrator or person appointing him

(1)   The authority of an arbitrator is personal and ceases on his death.

(2)   Unless otherwise agreed by the parties, the death of the person by whom an arbitrator was appointed does not revoke the arbitrator's authority.

27.   Filling of vacancy, &c

(1)   Where an arbitrator ceases to hold office, the parties are free to agree—
    (a)   whether and if so how the vacancy is to be filled;
    (b)   whether and if so to what extent the previous proceedings should stand; and
    (c)   what effect (if any) his ceasing to hold office has on any appointment made by him (alone or jointly).

(2)   If or to the extent that there is no such agreement, the following provisions apply.

(3)   The provisions of sections 16 (procedure for appointment of arbitrators) and 18 (failure of appointment procedure) apply in relation to the filling of the vacancy as in relation to an original appointment.

(4)   The tribunal (when reconstituted) shall determine whether and if so to what extent the previous proceedings should stand.
    This does not affect any right of a party to challenge those proceedings on any ground which had arisen before the arbitrator ceased to hold office.

(5)   His ceasing to hold office does not affect any appointment by him (alone or jointly) of another arbitrator, in particular any appointment of a chairman or umpire.

28.   Joint and several liability of parties to arbitrators for fees and expenses

(1)   The parties are jointly and severally liable to pay to the arbitrators such reasonable fees and expenses (if any) as are appropriate in the circumstances.

(2)   Any party may apply to the court (upon notice to the other parties and to the arbitrators) which may order that the amount of the arbitrators' fees and expenses shall be considered and adjusted by such means and upon such terms as it may direct.

(3)   If the application is made after any amount has been paid to the arbitrators by way of fees or expenses, the court may order the repayment of such amount (if any) as is shown to be excessive, but shall not do so unless it is shown that it is reasonable in the circumstances to order repayment.

(4)   The above provisions have effect subject to any order of the court under section 24(4) or 25(3)(b) (order as to entitlement to fees or expenses in case of removal or resignation of arbitrator).

(5)   Nothing in this section affects any liability of a party to any other party to pay all or any of the costs of the arbitration (see sections 59 to 65) or any contractual right of an arbitrator to payment of his fees and expenses.

(6)   In this section references to arbitrators include an arbitrator who has ceased to act and an umpire who has not replaced the other arbitrators.

29.   Immunity of arbitrator

(1)   An arbitrator is not liable for anything done or omitted in the discharge or purported discharge of his functions as arbitrator unless the act or omission is shown to have been in bad faith.

(2)   Subsection (1) applies to an employee or agent of an arbitrator as it applies to the arbitrator himself.

(3)   This section does not affect any liability incurred by an arbitrator by reason of his resigning (but see section 25).

Jurisdiction of the arbitral tribunal

30.   Competence of tribunal to rule on its own jurisdiction

(1)   Unless otherwise agreed by the parties, the arbitral tribunal may rule on its own substantive jurisdiction, that is, as to—

(a)   whether there is a valid arbitration agreement;

(b)   whether the tribunal is properly constituted; and

(c)   what matters have been submitted to arbitration in accordance with the arbitration agreement.

(2)   Any such ruling may be challenged by any available arbitral process of appeal or review or in accordance with the provisions of this Part.

31.   Objection to substantive jurisdiction of tribunal

(1)   An objection that the arbitral tribunal lacks substantive jurisdiction at the outset of the proceedings must be raised by a party not later than the time he takes the first step in the proceedings to contest the merits of any matter in relation to which he challenges the tribunal's jurisdiction.

    A party is not precluded from raising such an objection by the fact that he has appointed or participated in the appointment of an arbitrator.

(2)   Any objection during the course of the arbitral proceedings that the arbitral tribunal is exceeding its substantive jurisdiction must be made as soon as possible after the matter alleged to be beyond its jurisdiction is raised.

(3)   The arbitral tribunal may admit an objection later than the time specified in subsection (1) or (2) if it considers the delay justified.

(4)   Where an objection is duly taken to the tribunal's substantive jurisdiction and the tribunal has power to rule on its own jurisdiction, it may—

(a)   rule on the matter in an award as to jurisdiction; or

(b) deal with the objection in its award on the merits.

If the parties agree which of these courses the tribunal should take, the tribunal shall proceed accordingly.

(5) The tribunal may in any case, and shall if the parties so agree, stay proceedings whilst an application is made to the court under section 32 (determination of preliminary point of jurisdiction).

32. Determination of preliminary point of jurisdiction

(1) The court may, on the application of a party to arbitral proceedings (upon notice to the other parties), determine any question as to the substantive jurisdiction of the tribunal.

A party may lose the right to object (see section 73).

(2) An application under this section shall not be considered unless—

(a) it is made with the agreement in writing of all the other parties to the proceedings; or

(b) it is made with the permission of the tribunal and the court is satisfied:

(i) that the determination of the question is likely to produce substantial savings in costs;

(ii) that the application was made without delay; and

(iii) that there is good reason why the matter should be decided by the court.

(3) An application under this section, unless made with the agreement of all the other parties to the proceedings, shall state the grounds on which it is said that the matter should be decided by the court.

(4) Unless otherwise agreed by the parties, the arbitral tribunal may continue the arbitral proceedings and make an award while an application to the court under this section is pending.

(5) Unless the court gives leave, no appeal lies from a decision of the court whether the conditions specified in subsection (2) are met.

(6) The decision of the court on the question of jurisdiction shall be treated as a judgment of the court for the purposes of an appeal.

But no appeal lies without the leave of the court which shall not be given unless the court considers that the question involves a point of law which is one of general importance or is one which for some other special reason should be considered by the Court of Appeal.

The arbitral proceedings

33. General duty of the tribunal

(1) The tribunal shall—

(a) act fairly and impartially as between the parties, giving each party a reasonable opportunity of putting his case and dealing with that of his opponent; and

(b) adopt procedures suitable to the circumstances of the particular case, avoiding unnecessary delay or expense, so as to provide a fair means for the resolution of the matters falling to be determined.

(2) The tribunal shall comply with that general duty in conducting the arbitral proceedings, in its decisions on matters of procedure and evidence and in the exercise of all other powers conferred on it.

34. Procedural and evidential matters

(1) It shall be for the tribunal to decide all procedural and evidential matters, subject to the right of the parties to agree any matter.

(2) Procedural and evidential matters include—

(a) when and where any part of the proceedings is to be held;

    (b) the language or languages to be used in the proceedings and whether translations of any relevant documents are to be supplied;

    (c) whether any and if so what form of written statements of claim and defence are to be used, when these should be supplied and the extent to which such statements can be later amended;

    (d) whether any and if so which documents or classes of documents should be disclosed between and produced by the parties and at what stage;

    (e) whether any and if so what questions should be put to and answered by the respective parties and when and in what form this should be done;

    (f) whether to apply strict rules of evidence (or any other rules) as to the admissibility, relevance or weight of any material (oral, written or other) sought to be tendered on any matters of fact or opinion, and the time, manner and form in which such material should be exchanged and presented;

    (g) whether and to what extent the tribunal should itself take the initiative in ascertaining the facts and the law;

    (h) whether and to what extent there should be oral or written evidence or submissions.

(3)   The tribunal may fix the time within which any directions given by it are to be complied with, and may if it thinks fit extend the time so fixed (whether or not it has expired).

35.　Consolidation of proceedings and concurrent hearings

(1)   The parties are free to agree—

    (a) that the arbitral proceedings shall be consolidated with other hearings, arbitral proceedings; or

    (b) that concurrent hearings shall be held,

    on such terms as may be agreed.

(2)   Unless the parties agree to confer such power on the tribunal, the tribunal has no power to order consolidation of proceedings or concurrent hearings.

36.　Legal or other representation

Unless otherwise agreed by the parties, a party to arbitral proceedings may be represented in the proceedings by a lawyer or other person chosen by him.

37.　Power to appoint experts, legal advisers or assessors

(1)   Unless otherwise agreed by the parties—

    (a) the tribunal may:

        (i)   appoint experts or legal advisers to report to it and the parties; or

        (ii) appoint assessors to assist it on technical matters,

      and may allow any such expert, legal adviser or assessor to attend the proceedings; and

    (b) the parties shall be given a reasonable opportunity to comment on any information, opinion or advice offered by any such person.

(2)   The fees and expenses of an expert, legal adviser or assessor appointed by the tribunal for which the arbitrators are liable are expenses of the arbitrators for the purposes of this Part.

38.　General powers exercisable by the tribunal

(1)   The parties are free to agree on the powers exercisable by the arbitral tribunal for the purposes of and in relation to the proceedings.

(2)   Unless otherwise agreed by the parties the tribunal has the following powers.

(3)   The tribunal may order a claimant to provide security for the costs of the arbitration.

      This power shall not be exercised on the ground that the claimant is—

    (a) an individual ordinarily resident outside the United Kingdom; or

(b) a corporation or association incorporated or formed under the law of a country outside the United Kingdom, or whose central management and control is exercised outside the United Kingdom.

(4) The tribunal may give directions in relation to any property which is the subject of the proceedings or as to which any question arises in the proceedings, and which is owned by or is in the possession of a party to the proceedings—

(a) for the inspection, photographing, preservation, custody or detention of the property by the tribunal, an expert or a party; or

(b) ordering that samples be taken from, or any observation be made of or experiment conducted upon, the property.

(5) The tribunal may direct that a party or witness shall be examined on oath or affirmation, and may for that purpose administer any necessary oath or take any necessary affirmation.

(6) The tribunal may give directions to a party for the preservation for the purposes of the proceedings of any evidence in his custody or control.

39. Power to make provisional awards

(1) The parties are free to agree that the tribunal shall have power to order on a provisional basis any relief which it would have power to grant in a final award.

(2) This includes, for instance, making—

(a) a provisional order for the payment of money or the disposition of property as between the parties; or

(b) an order to make an interim payment on account of the costs of the arbitration.

(3) Any such order shall be subject to the tribunal's final adjudication; and the tribunal's final award, on the merits or as to costs, shall take account of any such order.

(4) Unless the parties agree to confer such power on the tribunal, the 'tribunal has no such power.

This does not affect its powers under section 47 (awards on different issues, &c).

40. General duty of parties

(1) The parties shall do all things necessary for the proper and expeditious conduct of the arbitral proceedings.

(2) This includes—

(a) complying without delay with any determination of the tribunal as to procedural or evidential matters, or with any order or directions of the tribunal; and

(b) where appropriate, taking without delay any necessary steps to obtain a decision of the court on a preliminary question of jurisdiction or law (see sections 32 and 45).

41. Powers of tribunal in case of party's default

(1) The parties are free to agree on the powers of the tribunal in case of a party's failure to do something necessary for the proper and expeditious conduct of the arbitration.

(2) Unless otherwise agreed by the parties, the following provisions apply.

(3) If the tribunal is satisfied that there has been inordinate and inexcusable delay on the part of the claimant in pursuing his claim and that the delay—

(a) gives rise, or is likely to give rise, to a substantial risk that it is not possible to have a fair resolution of the issues in that claim; or

(b) has caused, or is likely to cause, serious prejudice to the respondent, the tribunal may make an award dismissing the claim.

(4)   If without showing sufficient cause a party—
    (a) fails to attend or be represented at an oral hearing of which due notice was given; or
    (b) where matters are to be dealt with in writing, fails after due notice to submit written evidence or make written submission,
the tribunal may continue the proceedings in the absence of that party or as the case may be, without any written evidence or submissions on his behalf, and may make an award on the basis of the evidence before it.

(5)   If without showing sufficient cause a party fails to comply with an order or directions of the tribunal, the tribunal may make a peremptory order to the same effect, prescribing such time for compliance with it as the tribunal considers appropriate.

(6)   If a claimant fails to comply with a peremptory order of the tribunal to provide security for costs, the tribunal may make an award dismissing his claim.

(7)   If a party fails to comply with any other kind of peremptory order then, without prejudice to section 42 (enforcement by court of tribunal peremptory orders), the tribunal may do any of the following—
    (a) direct that the party in default shall not be entitled to rely upon any allegation or material which was the subject matter of the order;
    (b) draw such adverse inferences from the act of non-compliance as the circumstances justify;
    (c) proceed to an award on the basis of such materials as have been properly provided to it;
    (d) make such order as it thinks fit as to the payment of costs of the arbitration incurred in consequence of the non-compliance.

Powers of court in relation to arbitral proceedings

42.   Enforcement of peremptory orders of tribunal

(1)   Unless otherwise agreed by the parties the court may make an order requiring a party to comply with a peremptory order made by the tribunal.

(2)   An application for an order under this section may be made—
    (a) by the tribunal (upon notice to the parties);
    (b) by a party to the arbitral proceedings with the permission of the tribunal (and upon notice to the other parties); or
    (c) where the parties have agreed that the powers of the court under this section shall be available.

(3)   The court shall not act unless it is satisfied that the applicant has exhausted any available arbitral process in respect of failure to comply with the tribunal's order.

(4)   No order shall be made under this section unless the court is satisfied that the person to whom the tribunal's order was directed has failed to comply with it within the time prescribed in the order or, if no time was prescribed, within a reasonable time.

(5)   The leave of the court is required for any appeal from a decision of the court under this section.

43.   Securing the attendance of witnesses

(1)   A party to arbitral proceedings may use the same court procedures as are available in relation to legal proceedings to secure the attendance before the tribunal of a witness in order to give oral testimony or to produce documents or other material evidence.

(2)   This may only be done with the permission of the tribunal or the agreement of the other parties.

(3)   The court procedures may only be used if—

(a)   the witness is in the United Kingdom; and

(b)   the arbitral proceedings are being conducted in England and Wales or, as the case may be, Northern Ireland.

(4)   A person shall not be compelled by virtue of this section to produce any document or other material evidence which he could not be compelled to produce in legal proceedings.

44.   Court powers exercisable in support of arbitral proceedings

(1)   Unless otherwise agreed by the parties, the court has for the purposes of and in relation to arbitral proceedings the same power of making orders about the matters listed below as it has for the purposes of and in relation to legal proceedings.

(2)   Those matters are—

(a)   the taking of the evidence of witnesses;

(b)   the preservation of evidence;

(c)   making orders relating to property which is the subject of the proceedings or as to which any question arises in the proceedings:

    (i)   for the inspection, photographing, preservation, custody or detention of the property; or

    (ii)   ordering that samples be taken from, or any observation be made of or experiment conducted upon, the property;

and for that purpose authorising any person to enter any premises in the possession or control of a party to the arbitration;

(d)   the sale of any goods the subject of the proceedings;

(e)   the granting of an interim injunction or the appointment of a receiver.

(3)   If the case is one of urgency, the court may, on the application of a party or proposed party to the arbitral proceedings, make such orders as it thinks necessary for the purpose of preserving evidence or assets.

(4)   If the case is not one of urgency, the court shall act only on the application of a party to the arbitral proceedings (upon notice to the other parties and to the tribunal) made with the permission of the tribunal or the agreement in writing of the other parties.

(5)   In any case the court shall act only if or to the extent that the arbitral tribunal, and any arbitral or other institution or person vested by the parties with power in that regard, has no power or is unable for the time being to act effectively.

(6)   If the court so orders, an order made by it under this section shall cease to have effect in whole or in part on the order of the tribunal or of any such arbitral or other institution or person having power to act in relation to the subject-matter of the order.

(7)   The leave of the court is required for any appeal from a decision of the court under this section.

45.   Determination of preliminary point of law

(1)   Unless otherwise agreed by the parties, the court may on the application of a party to arbitral proceedings (upon notice to the other parties) determine any question of law arising in the course of the proceedings which the court is satisfied substantially affects the rights of one or more of the parties.

An agreement to dispense with reasons for the tribunal's award shall be considered an agreement to exclude the court's jurisdiction under this section.

(2)   An application under this section shall not be considered unless—

(a)   it is made with the agreement of all the other parties to the proceedings; or

(b)   it is made with the permission of the tribunal and the court is satisfied:

         (i)   that the determination of the question is likely to produce substantial savings in costs; and

         (ii)   that the application was made without delay.

(3)   The application shall identify the question of law to be determined and, unless made with the agreement of all the other parties to the proceedings, shall state the grounds on which it is said that the question should be decided by the court.

(4)   Unless otherwise agreed by the parties, the arbitral tribunal may continue the arbitral proceedings and make an award while an application to the court under this section is pending.

(5)   Unless the court gives leave, no appeal lies from a decision of the court whether the conditions specified in subsection (2) are met.

(6)   The decision of the court on the question of law shall be treated as a judgment of the court for the purposes of an appeal.

But no appeal lies without the leave of the court which shall not be given unless the court considers that the question is one of general importance, or is one which for some other special reason should be considered by the Court of Appeal.

The award

46. Rules applicable to substance of dispute

(1)   The arbitral tribunal shall decide the dispute—

    (a) in accordance with the law chosen by the parties as applicable to the substance of the dispute; or

    (b) if the parties so agree, in accordance with such other considerations as are agreed by them or determined by the tribunal.

(2)   For this purpose the choice of the laws of a country shall be understood to refer to the substantive laws of that country and not its conflict of laws rules.

(3)   If or to the extent that there is no such choice or agreement, the tribunal shall apply the law determined by the conflict of laws rules which it considers applicable.

47. Awards on different issues, &c

(1)   Unless otherwise agreed by the parties, the tribunal may make more than one award at different times on different aspects of the matters to be determined.

(2)   The tribunal may, in particular, make an award relating—

    (a) to an issue affecting the whole claim; or

    (b) to a part only of the claims or cross-claims submitted to it for decision.

(3)   If the tribunal does so, it shall specify in its award the issue, or the claim or part of a claim, which is the subject matter of the award.

48. Remedies

(1)   The parties are free to agree on the powers exercisable by the arbitral tribunal as regards remedies.

(2)   Unless otherwise agreed by the parties, the tribunal has the following powers.

(3)   The tribunal may make a declaration as to any matter to be determined in the proceedings.

(4)   The tribunal may order the payment of a sum of money, in any currency.

(5)   The tribunal has the same powers as the court—

    (a) to order a party to do or refrain from doing anything;

    (b) to order specific performance of a contract (other than a contract relating to land);

    (c) to order the rectification, setting aside or cancellation of a deed or other document.

49. Interest

(1) The parties are free to agree on the powers of the tribunal as regards the award of interest.

(2) Unless otherwise agreed by the parties the following provisions apply.

(3) The tribunal may award simple or compound interest from such dates, at such rates and with such rests as it considers meets the justice of the case—

    (a) on the whole or part of any amount awarded by the tribunal, in respect of any period up to the date of the award;

    (b) on the whole or part of any amount claimed in the arbitration and outstanding at the commencement of the arbitral proceedings but paid before the award was made, in respect of any period up to the date of payment.

(4) The tribunal may award simple or compound interest from the date of the award (or any later date) until payment, at such rates and with such rests as it considers meets the justice of the case, on the outstanding amount of any award (including any award of interest under subsection (3) and any award as to costs).

(5) References in this section to an amount awarded by the tribunal include an amount payable in consequence of a declaratory award by the tribunal.

(6) The above provisions do not affect any other power of the tribunal to award interest.

50. Extension of time for making award

(1) Where the time for making an award is limited by or in pursuance of the arbitration agreement, then, unless otherwise agreed by the parties, the court may in accordance with the following provisions by order extend that time.

(2) An application for an order under this section may be made—

    (a) by the tribunal (upon notice to the parties); or

    (b) by any party to the proceedings (upon notice to the tribunal and the other parties),

but only after exhausting any available arbitral process for obtaining an extension of time.

(3) The court shall only make an order if satisfied that a substantial injustice would otherwise be done.

(4) The court may extend the time for such period and on such term as it thinks fit, and may do so whether or not the time previously fixed (by or under the agreement or by a previous order) has expired.

(5) The leave of the court is required for any appeal from a decision of the court under this section.

51. Settlement

(1) If during arbitral proceedings the parties settle the dispute, the following provisions apply unless otherwise agreed by the parties.

(2) The tribunal shall terminate the substantive proceedings and, if so requested by the parties and not objected to by the tribunal, shall record the settlement in the form of an agreed award.

(3) An agreed award shall state that it is an award of the tribunal and shall have the same status and effect as any other award on the merits of the case.

(4) The following provisions of this Part relating to awards (sections 52 to 58) apply to an agreed award.

(5) Unless the parties have also settled the matter of the payment of the costs of the arbitration, the provisions of this Part relating to costs (sections 59 to 65) continue to apply.

52. Form of award

(1) The parties are free to agree on the form of an award.

(2)   If or to the extent that there is no such agreement, the following provisions apply.

(3)   The award shall be in writing signed by all the arbitrators or all those assenting to the award.

(4)   The award shall contain the reasons for the award unless it is an agreed award or the parties have agreed to dispense with reasons.

(5)   The award shall state the seat of the arbitration and the date when the award is made.

53.   Place where award treated as made

Unless otherwise agreed by the parties, where the seat of the arbitration is in England and Wales or Northern Ireland, any award in the proceedings shall be treated as made there, regardless of where it was signed, despatched or delivered to any of the parties.

54.   Date of award

(1)   Unless otherwise agreed by the parties, the tribunal may decide what is to be taken to be the date on which the award was made.

(2)   In the absence of any such decision, the date of the award shall be taken to be the date on which it is signed by the arbitrator or, where more than one arbitrator signs the award, by the last of them.

55.   Notification of award

(1)   The parties are free to agree on the requirements as to notification of the award to the parties.

(2)   If there is no such agreement, the award shall be notified to the parties by service on them of copies of the award, which shall be done without delay after the award is made.

(3)   Nothing in this section affects section 56 (power to withhold award in case of non-payment).

56.   Power to withhold award in case of non-payment

(1)   The tribunal may refuse to deliver an award to the parties except upon full payment of the fees and expenses of the arbitrators.

(2)   If the tribunal refuses on that ground to deliver an award, a party to the arbitral proceedings may (upon notice to the other parties and the tribunal) apply to the court, which may order that—

(a)   the tribunal shall deliver the award on the payment into court by the applicant of the fees and expenses demanded, or such lesser amount as the court may specify;

(b)   the amount of the fees and expenses properly payable shall be determined by such means and upon such terms as the court may direct; and

(c)   out of the money paid into court there shall be paid out such fees and expenses as may be found to be properly payable and the balance of the money (if any) shall be paid out to the applicant.

(3)   For this purpose the amount of fees and expenses properly payable is the amount the applicant is liable to pay under section 28 or any agreement relating to the payment of the arbitrators.

(4)   No application to the court may be made where there is any available arbitral process for appeal or review of the amount of the fees or expenses demanded.

(5)   References in this section to arbitrators include an arbitrator who has ceased to act and an umpire who has not replaced the other arbitrators.

(6)   The above provisions of this section also apply in relation to any arbitral or other institution or person vested by the parties with powers in relation to the delivery of the tribunal's award.

     As they so apply, the references to the fees and expenses of the arbitrators shall be construed as including the fees and expenses of that institution or person.

(7)   The leave of the court is required for any appeal from a decision of the court under this section.

(8)   Nothing in this section shall be construed as excluding an application under section 28 where payment has been made to the arbitrators in order to obtain the award.

57.   Correction of award or additional award

(1)   The parties are free to agree on the powers of the tribunal to correct an award or make an additional award.

(2)   If or to the extent there is no such agreement, the following provisions apply.

(3)   The tribunal may on its own initiative or on the application of a party—

    (a)   correct an award so as to remove any clerical mistake or error arising from an accidental slip or omission or clarify or remove any ambiguity in the award; or

    (b)   make an additional award in respect of any claim (including a claim for interest or costs) which was presented to the tribunal but was not dealt with in the award.

These powers shall not be exercised without first affording the other parties a reasonable opportunity to make representations to the tribunal.

(4)   Any application for the exercise of those powers must be made within 28 days of the date of the award or such longer period as the parties may agree.

(5)   Any correction of an award shall be made within 28 days of the date the application was received by the tribunal or, where the correction is made by the tribunal on its own initiative, within 28 days of the date of the award or, in either case, such longer period as the parties may agree.

(6)   Any additional award shall be made within 56 days of the date of the original award or such longer period as the parties may agree.

(7)   Any correction of an award shall form part of the award.

58.   Effect of award

(1)   Unless otherwise agreed by the parties, an award made by the tribunal pursuant to an arbitration agreement is final and binding both on the parties and on any persons claiming through or under them.

(2)   This does not affect the right of a person to challenge the award by any available arbitral process of appeal or review or in accordance with the provisions of this Part.

Costs of the arbitration

59.   Costs of the arbitration

(1)   References in this Part to the costs of the arbitration are to—

    (a)   the arbitrators' fees and expenses;

    (b)   the fees and expenses of any arbitral institution concerned; and

    (c)   the legal or other costs of the parties.

(2)   Any such reference includes the costs of or incidental to any proceedings to determine the amount of the recoverable costs of the arbitration (see section 63).

60.   Agreement to pay costs in any event

An agreement which has the effect that a party is to pay the whole or part of the costs of the arbitration in any event is only valid if made after the dispute in question has arisen.

61.   Award of costs

(1)   The tribunal may make an award allocating the costs of the arbitration as between the parties, subject to any agreement of the parties.

(2)   Unless the parties otherwise agree, the tribunal shall award costs on the general principle that costs should follow the event except where it appears to the tribunal that in the circumstances this is not appropriate in relation to the whole or part of the costs.

62.   Effect of agreement or award about costs

Unless the parties otherwise agree, any obligation under an effect of agreement between them as to how the costs of the arbitration are to be borne, or under an award allocating the costs of the arbitration, extends only to such costs as are recoverable.

63.   The recoverable costs of the arbitration

(1)   The parties are free to agree what costs of the arbitration are recoverable.

(2)   If or to the extent there is no such agreement, the following provisions apply.

(3)   The tribunal may determine by award the recoverable costs of the arbitration on such basis as it thinks fit.

If it does so, it shall specify—

(a)   the basis on which it has acted; and

(b)   the items of recoverable costs and the amount referable to each.

(4)   If the tribunal does not determine the recoverable costs of the arbitration, any party to the arbitral proceedings may apply to the court (upon notice to the other parties) which may—

(a)   determine the recoverable costs of the arbitration on such basis as it thinks fit; or

(b)   order that they shall be determined by such means and upon such terms as it may specify.

(5)   Unless the tribunal or the court determines otherwise—

(a)   the recoverable costs of the arbitration shall be determined on the basis that there shall be allowed a reasonable amount in respect of all costs reasonably incurred; and

(b)   any doubt as to whether costs were reasonably incurred or were reasonable in amount shall be resolved in favour of the paying party.

(6)   The above provisions have effect subject to section 64 (recoverable fees and expenses of arbitrators).

(7)   Nothing in this section affects any right of the arbitrators, any expert, legal adviser or assessor appointed by the tribunal, or any arbitral institution, to payment of their fees and expenses.

64.   Recoverable fees and expenses of arbitrators

(1)   Unless otherwise agreed by the parties, the recoverable costs of the arbitration shall include in respect of the fees and expenses of the arbitrators only such reasonable fees and expenses as are appropriate in the circumstances.

(2)   If there is any question as to what reasonable fees and expenses are appropriate in the circumstances, and the matter is not already before the court on an application under section 63(4), the court may on the application of any party (upon notice to the other parties)—

(a)   determine the matter; or

(b) order that it be determined by such means and upon such terms as the court may specify.

(3) Subsection (1) has effect subject to any order of the court under section 24(4) or 25(3)(b) (order as to entitlement to fees or expenses in case of removal or resignation of arbitrator).

(4) Nothing in this section affects any right of the arbitrator to payment of his fees and expenses.

65. Power to limit recoverable costs

(1) Unless otherwise agreed by the parties, the tribunal may direct that the recoverable costs of the arbitration, or of any part of the arbitral proceedings, shall be limited to a specified amount.

(2) Any direction may be made or varied at any stage, but this must be done sufficiently in advance of the incurring of costs to which it relates, or the taking of any steps in the proceedings which may be affected by it, for the limit to be taken into account.

Powers of the court in relation to award

66. Enforcement of the award

(1) An award made by the tribunal pursuant to an arbitration agreement may, by leave of the court, be enforced in the same manner as a judgment or order of the court to the same effect.

(2) Where leave is so given, judgment may be entered in terms of the award.

(3) Leave to enforce an award shall not be given where, or to the extent that, the person against whom it is sought to be enforced shows that the tribunal lacked substantive jurisdiction to make the award. The right to raise such an objection may have been lost (see section 73).

(4) Nothing in this section affects the recognition or enforcement of an award under any other enactment or rule of law, in particular under Part II of the Arbitration Act 1950 (enforcement of awards under Geneva Convention) or the provisions of Part III of this Act relating to the recognition and enforcement of awards under the New York Convention or by an action on the award.

67. Challenging the award: substantive jurisdiction

(1) A party to arbitral proceedings may (upon notice to the other parties and to the tribunal) apply to the court—

(a) challenging any award of the arbitral tribunal as to its substantive jurisdiction; or

(b) for an order declaring an award made by the tribunal on the merits to be of no effect, in whole or in part, because the tribunal did not have substantive jurisdiction.

A party may lose the right to object (see section 73) and the right to apply is subject to the restrictions in section 70(2) and (3).

(2) The arbitral tribunal may continue the arbitral proceedings and make a further award while an application to the court under this section is pending in relation to an award as to jurisdiction.

(3) On an application under this section challenging an award of the arbitral tribunal as to its substantive jurisdiction, the court may by order—

(a) confirm the award;

(b) vary the award; or

(c) set aside the award in whole or in part.

(4) The leave of the court is required for any appeal from a decision of the court under this section.

68.   Challenging the award: serious irregularity

(1)   A party to arbitral proceedings may (upon notice to the other parties and to the tribunal) apply to the court challenging an award in the proceedings on the ground of serious irregularity affecting the tribunal, the proceedings or the award.

        A party may lose the right to object (see section 73) and the right to apply is subject to the restrictions in section 70(2) and (3).

(2)   Serious irregularity means an irregularity of one or more of the following kinds which the court considers has caused or will cause substantial injustice to the applicant—

    (a)   failure by the tribunal to comply with section 33 (general duty of tribunal);

    (b)   the tribunal exceeding its powers (otherwise than by exceeding its substantive jurisdiction: see section 67);

    (c)   failure by the tribunal to conduct the proceedings in accordance with the procedure agreed by the parties;

    (d)   failure by the tribunal to deal with all the issues that were put to it;

    (e)   any arbitral or other institution or person vested by the parties with powers in relation to the proceedings or the award exceeding its powers;

    (f)   uncertainty or ambiguity as to the effect of the award;

    (g)   the award being obtained by fraud or the award or the way in which it was procured being contrary to public policy;

    (h)   failure to comply with the requirements as to the form of the award; or

    (i)   any irregularity in the conduct of the proceedings or in the award which is admitted by the tribunal or by any arbitral or other institution or person vested by the parties with powers in relation to the proceedings or the award.

(3)   If there is shown to be serious irregularity affecting the tribunal, the proceedings or the award, the court may—

    (a)   remit the award to the tribunal, in whole or in part, for reconsideration;

    (b)   set the award aside in whole or in part; or

    (c)   declare the award to be of no effect, in whole or in part.

        The court shall not exercise its power to set aside or to declare an award to be of no effect, in whole or in part, unless it is satisfied that it would be inappropriate to remit the matters in question to the tribunal for reconsideration.

(4)   The leave of the court is required for any appeal from a decision of the court under this section.

69.   Appeal on point of law

(1)   Unless otherwise agreed by the parties, a party to arbitral proceedings may (upon notice to the other parties and to the tribunal) appeal to the court on a question of law arising out of an award made in the proceedings.

        An agreement to dispense with reasons for the tribunal's award shall be considered an agreement to exclude the court's jurisdiction under this section.

(2)   An appeal shall not be brought under this section except—

    (a)   with the agreement of all the other parties to the proceedings; or

    (b)   with the leave of the court.

        The right to appeal is also subject to the restrictions in section 70(2).

(3)   Leave to appeal shall be given only if the court is satisfied—

    (a)   that the determination of the question will substantially affect the rights of one or more of the parties;

    (b)   that the question is one which the tribunal was asked to determine;

    (c)   that, on the basis of the findings of fact in the award:

        (i)   the decision of the tribunal on the question is obviously wrong; or

        (ii)   the question is one of general public importance and the decision of the tribunal is at least open to serious doubt; and

    (d) that, despite the agreement of the parties to resolve the matter by arbitration, it is just and proper in all the circumstances for the court to determine the question.

(4)   An application for leave to appeal under this section shall identify the question of law to be determined and state the grounds on which it is alleged that leave to appeal should be granted.

(5)   The court shall determine an application for leave to appeal under this section without a hearing unless it appears to the court that a hearing is required.

(6)   The leave of the court is required for any appeal from a decision of the court under this section to grant or refuse leave to appeal.

(7)   On an appeal under this section the court may by order—
    (a) confirm the award;
    (b) vary the award;
    (c) remit the award to the tribunal, in whole or in part, for reconsideration in the light of the court's determination; or
    (d) set aside the award in whole or in part.
The court shall not exercise its power to set aside an award, in whole or in part, unless it is satisfied that it would be inappropriate to remit the matters in question to the tribunal for reconsideration.

(8)   The decision of the court on an appeal under this section shall be treated as a judgment of the court for the purposes of a further appeal.

    But no such appeal lies without the leave of the court which shall not be given unless the court considers that the question is one of general importance or is one which for some other special reason should be considered by the Court of Appeal.

70.   Challenge or appeal: supplementary provisions

(1)   The following provisions apply to an application or appeal under section 67, 68 or 69.

(2)   An application or appeal may not be brought if the applicant or provisions appellant has not first exhausted—
    (a) any available arbitral process of appeal or review; and
    (b) any available recourse under section 57 (correction of award or additional award).

(3)   Any application or appeal must be brought within 28 days of the date of the award or, if there has been any arbitral process of appeal or review, of the date when the applicant or appellant was notified of the result of that process.

(4)   If on an application or appeal it appears to the court that the award—
    (a) does not contain the tribunal's reasons; or
    (b) does not set out the tribunal's reasons in sufficient detail to enable the court properly to consider the application or appeal,
the court may order the tribunal to state the reasons for its award in sufficient detail for that purpose.

(5)   Where the court makes an order under subsection (4), it may make such further order as it thinks fit with respect to any additional costs of the arbitration resulting from its order.

(6)   The court may order the applicant or appellant to provide security for the costs of the application or appeal, and may direct that the application or appeal be dismissed if the order is not complied with.

    The power to order security for costs shall not be exercised on the ground that the applicant or appellant is—
    (a) an individual ordinarily resident outside the United Kingdom; or

       (b) a corporation or association incorporated or formed under the law of a country outside the United Kingdom, or whose central management and control is exercised outside the United Kingdom.

    (7)   The court may order that any money payable under the award shall be brought into court or otherwise secured pending the determination of the application or appeal, and may direct that the application or appeal be dismissed if the order is not complied with.

    (8)   The court may grant leave to appeal subject to conditions to the same or similar effect as an order under subsection (6) or (7).

           This does not affect the general discretion of the court to grant leave subject to conditions.

71. Challenge or appeal: effect of order of court

    (1)   The following provisions have effect where the court makes an order under section 67, 68 or 69 with respect to an award.

    (2)   Where the award is varied, the variation has effect as part of the tribunal's award.

    (3)   Where the award is remitted to the tribunal, in whole or in part, for reconsideration, the tribunal shall make a fresh award in respect of the matters remitted within three months of the date of the order for remission or such longer or shorter period as the court may direct.

    (4)   Where the award is set aside or declared to be of no effect, in whole or in part, the court may also order that any provision that an award is a condition precedent to the bringing of legal proceedings in respect of a matter to which the arbitration agreement applies, is of no effect as regards the subject matter of the award or, as the case may be, the relevant part of the award.

Miscellaneous

72. Saving for rights of person who takes no part in proceedings

    (1)   A person alleged to be a party to arbitral proceedings but who takes no part in the proceedings may question —

       (a) whether there is a valid arbitration agreement;

       (b) whether the tribunal is properly constituted; or

       (c) what matters have been submitted to arbitration in accordance with the arbitration agreement,

      by proceedings in the court for a declaration or injunction or other appropriate relief.

    (2)   He also has the same right as a party to the arbitral proceedings to challenge an award —

       (a) by an application under section 67 on the ground of lack of substantive jurisdiction in relation to him; or

       (b) by an application under section 68 on the ground of serious irregularity (within the meaning of that section) affecting him,

      and section 70(2) (duty to exhaust arbitral procedures) does not apply in his case.

73. Loss of right to object

    (1)   If a party to arbitral proceedings takes part, or continues to take part, in the proceedings without making, either forthwith or within such time as is allowed by the arbitration agreement or the tribunal or by any provision of this Part, any objection —

       (a) that the tribunal lacks substantive jurisdiction;

       (b) that the proceedings have been improperly conducted;

       (c) that there has been a failure to comply with the arbitration agreement or with any provision of this Part; or

(d) that there has been any other irregularity affecting the tribunal or the proceedings,

he may not raise that objection later, before the tribunal or the court, unless he shows that, at the time he took part or continued to take part in the proceedings, he did not know and could not with reasonable diligence have discovered the grounds for the objection.

(2) Where the arbitral tribunal rules that it has substantive jurisdiction and a party to arbitral proceedings who could have questioned that ruling—

(a) by any available arbitral process of appeal or review; or

(b) by challenging the award,

does not do so, or does not do so within the time allowed by the arbitration agreement or any provision of this Part, he may not object later to the tribunal's substantive jurisdiction on any ground which was the subject of that ruling.

74. Immunity of arbitral institutions, &c

(1) An arbitral or other institution or person designated or requested by the parties to appoint or nominate an arbitrator is not liable for anything done or omitted in the discharge or purported discharge of that function unless the act or omission is shown to have been in bad faith.

(2) An arbitral or other institution or person by whom an arbitrator is appointed or nominated is not liable, by reason of having appointed or nominated him, for anything done or omitted by the arbitrator (or his employees or agents) in the discharge or purported discharge of his functions as arbitrator.

(3) The above provisions apply to an employee or agent of an arbitral or other institution or person as they apply to the institution or person himself.

75. Charge to secure payment of solicitors' costs

The powers of the court to make declarations and orders under section 73 of the Solicitors Act 1974 or Article 71H of the Solicitors (Northern Ireland) Order 1976 (power to charge property recovered in the proceedings with the payment of solicitors' costs) may be exercised in relation to arbitral proceedings as if those proceedings were proceedings in the court.

Supplementary

76. Service of notices, &c

(1) The parties are free to agree on the manner of service of any notice or other document required or authorised to be given or served in pursuance of the arbitration agreement or for the purposes of the arbitral proceedings.

(2) If or to the extent that there is no such agreement the following provisions apply.

(3) A notice or other document may be served on a person by any effective means.

(4) If a notice or other document is addressed, pre-paid and delivered by post—

(a) to the addressee's last known principal residence or, if he is or has been carrying on a trade, profession or business, his last known principal business address; or

(b) where the addressee is a body corporate, to the body's registered or principal office,

it shall be treated as effectively served.

(5) This section does not apply to the service of documents for the purposes of legal proceedings, for which provision is made by rules of court.

(6) References in this Part to a notice or other document include any form of communication in writing and references to giving or serving a notice or other document shall be construed accordingly.

77. Powers of court in relation to service of documents

(1)   This section applies where service of a document on a person in the manner agreed by the parties, or in accordance with provisions of section 76 having effect in default of agreement, is not reasonably practicable.

(2)   Unless otherwise agreed by the parties, the court may make such order as it thinks fit—
    (a) for service in such manner as the court may direct; or
    (b) dispensing with service of the document.

(3)   Any party to the arbitration agreement may apply for an order, but only after exhausting any available arbitral process for resolving the matter.

(4)   The leave of the court is required for any appeal from a decision of the court under this section.

78. Reckoning periods of time

(1)   The parties are free to agree on the method of reckoning periods of time for the purposes of any provision agreed by them or any provision of this Part having effect in default of such agreement.

(2)   If or to the extent there is no such agreement, periods of time shall be reckoned in accordance with the following provisions.

(3)   Where the act is required to be done within a specified period after or from a specified date, the period begins immediately after that date.

(4)   Where the act is required to be done a specified number of clear days after a specified date, at least that number of days must intervene between the day on which the act is done and that date.

(5)   Where the period is a period of seven days or less which would include a Saturday, Sunday or a public holiday in the place where anything which has to be done within the period falls to be done, that day shall be excluded.

    In relation to England and Wales or Northern Ireland, a 'public holiday' means Christmas Day, Good Friday or a day which under the Banking and Financial Dealings Act 1971 is a bank holiday.

79. Power of court to extend time limits relating to arbitral proceedings

(1)   Unless the parties otherwise agree, the court may by order extend any time limit agreed by them in relation to any matter relating to the arbitral proceedings or specified in any provision of this Part having effect in default of such agreement.

    This section does not apply to a time limit to which section 12 applies (power of court to extend time for beginning arbitral proceedings, &c).

(2)   An application for an order may be made—
    (a) by any party to the arbitral proceedings (upon notice to the other parties and to the tribunal); or
    (b) by the arbitral tribunal (upon notice to the parties).

(3)   The court shall not exercise its power to extend a time limit unless it is satisfied—
    (a) that any available recourse to the tribunal, or to any arbitral or other institution or person vested by the parties with power in that regard, has first been exhausted; and
    (b) that a substantial injustice would otherwise be done.

(4)   The court's power under this section may be exercised whether or not the time has already expired.

(5)   An order under this section may be made on such terms as the court thinks fit.

(6)   The leave of the court is required for any appeal from a decision of the court under this section.

80. Notice and other requirements in connection with legal proceedings

(1) References in this Part to an application, appeal or other step in relation to legal proceedings being taken 'upon notice' to the other parties to the arbitral proceedings, or to the tribunal, are to such notice of the originating process as is required by rules of court and do not impose any separate requirement.

(2) Rules of court shall be made—

(a) requiring such notice to be given as indicated by any provision of this Part; and

(b) as to the manner, form and content of any such notice.

(3) Subject to any provision made by rules of court, a requirement to give notice to the tribunal of legal proceedings shall be construed—

(a) if there is more than one arbitrator, as a requirement to give notice to each of them; and

(b) if the tribunal is not fully constituted, as a requirement to give notice to any arbitrator who has been appointed.

(4) References in this Part to making an application or appeal to the court within a specified period are to the issue within that period of the appropriate originating process in accordance with rules of court.

(5) Where any provision of this Part requires an application or appeal to be made to the court within a specified time, the rules of court relating to the reckoning of periods, the extending or abridging of periods, and the consequences of not taking a step within the period prescribed by the rules, apply in relation to that requirement.

(6) Provision may be made by rules of court amending the provisions of this Part—

(a) with respect to the time within which any application or appeal to the court must be made;

(b) so as to keep any provision made by this Part in relation to arbitral proceedings in step with the corresponding provision of rules of court applying in relation to proceedings in the court; or

(c) so as to keep any provision made by this Part in relation to legal proceedings in step with the corresponding provision of rules of court applying generally in relation to proceedings in the court.

(7) Nothing in this section affects the generality of the power to make rules of court.

81. Saving for certain matters governed by common law

(1) Nothing in this Part shall be construed as excluding the operation of any rule of law consistent with the provisions of this Part, in particular, any rule of law as to—

(a) matters which are not capable of settlement by arbitration;

(b) the effect of an oral arbitration agreement; or

(c) the refusal of recognition or enforcement of an arbitral award on grounds of public policy.

(2) Nothing in this Act shall be construed as reviving any jurisdiction of the court to set aside or remit an award on the ground of errors of fact or law on the face of the award.

82. Minor definitions

(1) In this Part—

'arbitrator', unless the context otherwise requires, includes an umpire;

'available arbitral process', in relation to any matter, includes any process of appeal to or review by an arbitral or other institution or person vested by the parties with powers in relation to that matter;

'claimant', unless the context otherwise requires, includes a counterclaimant, and related expressions shall be construed accordingly;

'dispute' includes any difference;

'enactment' includes an enactment contained in Northern Ireland legislation;

'legal proceedings' means civil proceedings in the High Court or a county court;

'peremptory order' means an order made under section 41(5) or made in exercise of any corresponding power conferred by the parties;

'premises' includes land, buildings, moveable structures, vehicles, vessels, aircraft and hovercraft;

'question of law' means—

    (a)   for a court in England and Wales, a question of the law of England and Wales, and

    (b)   for a court in Northern Ireland, a question of the law of Northern Ireland;

'substantive jurisdiction', in relation to an arbitral tribunal, refers to the matters specified in section 30(1)(a) to (c), and references to the tribunal exceeding its substantive jurisdiction shall be construed accordingly.

(2)   References in this Part to a party to an arbitration agreement include any person claiming under or through a party to the agreement.

83.   Index of defined expressions: Part I

In this Part the expressions listed explained by the provisions indicated—

agreement, agree and agreed	section 5(1)
agreement in writing	section 5(2) to (5)
arbitration agreement	sections 6 and 5(1)
arbitrator	section 82(1)
available arbitral process	section 82(1)
claimant	section 82(1)
commencement (in relation to arbitral proceedings)	section 14
costs of the arbitration	section 59
the court	section 105
dispute	section 82(1)
enactment	section 82(1)
legal proceedings	section 82(1)
Limitation Acts	section 13(4)
notice (or other document),	section 76(6)
party—	
—in relation to an arbitration agreement	section 82(2)
—where section 106(2) or (3) applies	section 106(4)
peremptory order	section 82(1) (and see section 41(5))
premises	section 82(1)
question of law	section 82(1)
recoverable costs	sections 63 and 64
seat of the arbitration	section 3
serve and service (of notice or other document)	section 76(6)
substantive jurisdiction (in relation to an arbitral tribunal)	section 82(1) (and see section 30(1)(a) to (c))
upon notice (to the parties or the tribunal)	section 80
written and in writing	section 5(6)

84. **[Omitted].**

PART II
OTHER PROVISIONS RELATING TO ARBITRATION

Domestic arbitration agreements

85. **Modification of Part I in relation to domestic arbitration agreement**

(1)   In the case of a domestic arbitration agreement the provisions of Part I are modified in accordance with the following sections.

(2)   For this purpose a 'domestic arbitration agreement' means an arbitration agreement to which none of the parties is—

(a)   an individual who is a national of, or habitually resident in, a state other than the United Kingdom; or

(b)   a body corporate which is incorporated in, or whose central control and management is exercised in, a state other than the United Kingdom, and under which the seat of the arbitration (if the seat has been designated or determined) is in the United Kingdom.

(3)   In subsection (2) 'arbitration agreement' and 'seat of the arbitration' have the same meaning as in Part I (see sections 3, 5(1) and 6).

86. **Staying of legal proceedings**

(1)   In section 9 (stay of legal proceedings), subsection (4) (stay unless the arbitration agreement is null and void, inoperative, or incapable of being performed) does not apply to a domestic arbitration agreement.

(2)   On an application under that section in relation to a domestic arbitration agreement the court shall grant a stay unless satisfied—

(a)   that the arbitration agreement is null and void, inoperative, or incapable of being performed; or

(b)   that there are other sufficient grounds for not requiring the parties to abide by the arbitration agreement.

(3)   The court may treat as a sufficient ground under subsection (2)(b) the fact that the applicant is or was at any material time not ready and willing to do all things necessary for the proper conduct of the arbitration or of any other dispute resolution procedures required to be exhausted before resorting to arbitration.

(4)   For the purposes of this section the question whether an arbitration agreement is a domestic arbitration agreement shall be determined by reference to the facts at the time the legal proceedings are commenced.

87. **Effectiveness of agreement to exclude court's jurisdiction**

(1)   In the case of a domestic arbitration agreement any agreement to exclude the jurisdiction of the court under—

(a)   section 45 (determination of preliminary point of law); or

(b)   section 69 (challenging the award: appeal on point of law),

is not effective unless entered into after the commencement of the arbitral proceedings in which the question arises or the award is made.

(2)   For this purpose the commencement of the arbitral proceedings has the same meaning as in Part I (see section 14).

(3)   For the purposes of this section the question whether an arbitration agreement is a domestic arbitration agreement shall be determined by reference to the facts at the time the agreement is entered into.

88.–92. [Omitted].

Appointment of judges as arbitrators

93. Appointment of judges as arbitrators

   (1)   A judge of the Commercial Court or an official referee may, if in all the circumstances he thinks fit, accept appointment as a sole arbitrator or as umpire by or by virtue of an arbitration agreement.

   (2)   A judge of the Commercial Court shall not do so unless the Lord Chief Justice has informed him that, having regard to the state of business in the High Court and the Crown Court, he can be made available.

   (3)   An official referee shall not do so unless the Lord Chief Justice has informed him that, having regard to the state of official referees' business, he can be made available.

   (4)   The fees payable for the services of a judge of the Commercial Court or official referee as arbitrator or umpire shall be taken in the High Court.

   (5)   In this section—

         'arbitration agreement' has the same meaning as in Part I; and

         'official referee' means a person nominated under section 68(1)(a) of the Supreme Court Act 1981 to deal with official referees' business.

   (6)   The provisions of Part I of this Act apply to arbitration before a person appointed under this section with the modifications specified in Schedule 2.

Statutory arbitrations

94. Application of Part I to statutory arbitrations

   (1)   The provisions of Part I apply to every arbitration under an enactment (a 'statutory arbitration'), whether the enactment was passed or made before or after the commencement of this Act, subject to the adaptations and exclusions specified in sections 95 to 98.

   (2)   The provisions of Part I do not apply to a statutory arbitration if or to the extent that their application—

       (a)   is inconsistent with the provisions of the enactment concerned, with any rules or procedure authorised or recognised by it; or

       (b)   is excluded by any other enactment.

   (3)   In this section and the following provisions of this Part 'enactment'—

       (a)   in England and Wales, includes an enactment contained in subordinate legislation within the meaning of the Interpretation Act 1978;

       (b)   in Northern Ireland, means a statutory provision within the meaning of section 1(f) of the Interpretation Act (Northern Ireland) 1954.

95. General adaptation of provisions in relation to statutory arbitrations

   (1)   The provisions of Part I apply to a statutory arbitration—

       (a)   as if the arbitration were pursuant to an arbitration agreement and as if the enactment were that agreement; and

       (b)   as if the persons by and against whom a claim subject to arbitration in pursuance of the enactment may be or has been made were parties to that agreement.

   (2)   Every statutory arbitration shall be taken to have its seat in England and Wales or, as the case may be, in Northern Ireland.

96. Specific adaptations of provisions in relation to statutory arbitrations

   (1)   The following provisions of Part I apply to a statutory arbitration with the following adaptations.

   (2)   In section 30(1) (competence of tribunal to rule on its own relation to jurisdiction), the reference in paragraph (a) to whether there is a valid statutory arbitration agreement shall be construed as a reference to whether the arbitrations enactment applies to the dispute or difference in question.

(3) Section 35 (consolidation of proceedings and concurrent hearings) applies only so as to authorise the consolidation of proceedings, or concurrent hearings in proceedings, under the same enactment.

(4) Section 46 (rules applicable to substance of dispute) applies with the omission of subsection (l)(b) (determination in accordance with considerations agreed by parties).

97. Provisions excluded from applying to statutory arbitrations

The following provisions of Part I do not apply in relation to a statutory arbitration—

(a) section 8 (whether agreement discharged by death of a party);

(b) section 12 (power of court to extend agreed time limits);

(c) sections 9(5), 10(2) and 71(4) (restrictions on effect of provision that award condition precedent to right to bring legal proceedings).

98. [Omitted].

PART III
RECOGNITION AND ENFORCEMENT OF CERTAIN FOREIGN AWARDS

Enforcement of Geneva Convention awards

99. Continuation of Part II of the Arbitration Act 1950

Part II of the Arbitration Act 1950 (enforcement of certain foreign awards) continues to apply in relation to foreign awards within the meaning of that Part which are not also New York Convention awards.

Recognition and enforcement of New York Convention awards

100. New York Convention awards

(1) In this Part a 'New York Convention award' means an award made, in pursuance of an arbitration agreement, in the territory of a state (other than the United Kingdom) which is a party to the New York Convention.

(2) For the purposes of subsection (1) and of the provisions of this Part relating to such awards—

(a) 'arbitration agreement' means an arbitration agreement in writing; and

(b) an award shall be treated as made at the seat of the arbitration, regardless of where it was signed, despatched or delivered to any of the parties.

In this subsection 'agreement in writing' and 'seat of the arbitration' have the same meaning as in Part I.

(3) If Her Majesty by Order in Council declares that a state specified in the Order is a party to the New York Convention, or is a party in respect of any territory so specified, the Order shall, while in force, be conclusive evidence of that fact.

(4) In this section 'the New York Convention' means the Convention on the Recognition and Enforcement of Foreign Arbitral Awards adopted by the United Nations Conference on International Commercial Arbitration on 10th June 1958.

101. Recognition and enforcement of awards

(1) A New York Convention award shall be recognised as binding on the persons as between whom it was made, and may accordingly be relied on by those persons by way of defence, set-off or otherwise in any legal proceedings in England and Wales or Northern Ireland.

(2)   A New York Convention award may, by leave of the court, be enforced in the same manner as a judgment or order of the court to the same effect.

As to the meaning of 'the court' see section 105.

(3)   Where leave is so given, judgment may be entered in terms of the award.

102.   Evidence to be produced by party seeking recognition or enforcement

(1)   A party seeking the recognition or enforcement of a New York Convention award must produce—

(a)   the duly authenticated original award or a duly certified copy of it; and

(b)   the original arbitration agreement or a duly certified copy of it.

(2)   If the award or agreement is in a foreign language, the party must also produce a translation of it certified by an official or sworn translator or by a diplomatic or consular agent.

103.   Refusal of recognition or enforcement

(1)   Recognition or enforcement of a New York Convention award shall not be refused except in the following cases.

(2)   Recognition or enforcement of the award may be refused if the person against whom it is invoked proves—

(a)   that a party to the arbitration agreement was (under the law applicable to him) under some incapacity;

(b)   that the arbitration agreement was not valid under the law to which the parties subjected it or, failing any indication thereon, under the law of the country where the award was made;

(c)   that he was not given proper notice of the appointment of the arbitrator or of the arbitration proceedings or was otherwise unable to present his case;

(d)   that the award deals with a difference not contemplated by or not falling within the terms of the submission to arbitration or contains decisions on matters beyond the scope of the submission to arbitration (but see subsection (4));

(e)   that the composition of the arbitral tribunal or the arbitral procedure was not in accordance with the agreement of the parties or, failing such agreement, with the law of the country in which the arbitration took place;

(f)   that the award has not yet become binding on the parties, or has been set aside or suspended by a competent authority of the country in which, or under the law of which, it was made.

(3)   Recognition or enforcement of the award may also be refused if the award is in respect of a matter which is not capable of settlement by arbitration, or if it would be contrary to public policy to recognise or enforce the award.

(4)   An award which contains decisions on matters not submitted to arbitration may be recognised or enforced to the extent that it contains decisions on matters submitted to arbitration which can be separated from those on matters not so submitted.

(5)   Where an application for the setting aside or suspension of the award has been made to such a competent authority as is mentioned in subsection (2)(f), the court before which the award is sought to be relied upon may, if it considers it proper, adjourn the decision on the recognition or enforcement of the award.

It may also on the application of the party claiming recognition or enforcement of the award order the other party to give suitable security.

104.   Saving for other bases of recognition or enforcement

Nothing in the preceding provisions of this Part affects any right to rely upon or enforce a New York Convention award at common law or under section 66.

105. [Omitted].

106. **Crown application**
    (1)   Part I of this Act applies to any arbitration agreement to which Her Majesty, either in right of the Crown or of the Duchy of Lancaster or otherwise, or the Duke of Cornwall, is a party.
    (2)   Where Her Majesty is party to an arbitration agreement otherwise than in right of the Crown, Her Majesty shall be represented for the purposes of any arbitral proceedings—
        (a)   where the agreement was entered into by Her Majesty in right of the Duchy of Lancaster, by the Chancellor of the Duchy or such person as he may appoint; and
        (b)   in any other case, by such person as Her Majesty may appoint in writing under the Royal Sign Manual.
    (3)   Where the Duke of Cornwall is party to an arbitration agreement, he shall be represented for the purposes of any arbitral proceedings by such person as he may appoint.
    (4)   References in Part I to a party or the parties to the arbitration agreement or to arbitral proceedings shall be construed, where subsection (2) or (3) applies, as references to the person representing Her Majesty or the Duke of Cornwall.

107.–110. [Omitted].

SCHEDULE 1

MANDATORY PROVISIONS OF PART I

sections 9 to 11 (stay of legal proceedings);
section 12 (power of court to extend agreed time limits);
section 13 (application of Limitation Acts);
section 24 (power of court to remove arbitrator);
section 26(1) (effect of death of arbitrator);
section 28 (liability of parties for fees and expenses of arbitrators);
section 29 (immunity of arbitrator);
section 31 (objection to substantive jurisdiction of tribunal);
section 32 (determination of preliminary point of jurisdiction);
section 33 (general duty of tribunal);
section 37(2) (items to be treated as expenses of arbitrators);
section 40 (general duty of parties);
section 43 (securing the attendance of witnesses);
section 56 (power to withhold award in case of non-payment);
section 60 (effectiveness of agreement for payment of costs in any event);
section 66 (enforcement of award);
sections 67 and 68 (challenging the award: substantive jurisdiction and serious irregularity), and sections 70 and 71 (supplementary provisions; effect of order of court) so far as relating to those sections;
section 72 (saving for rights of person who takes no part in proceedings);
section 73 (loss of right to object);
section 74 (immunity of arbitral institutions, &c);
section 75 (charge to secure payment of solicitors' costs).
section 93(6).

SCHEDULE 2

MODIFICATIONS OF PART I IN RELATION TO JUDGE-ARBITRATORS

Introductory

1.   In this Schedule 'judge-arbitrator' means a judge of the Commercial Court or official referee appointed as arbitrator or umpire under section 93.

General

2.   (1)   Subject to the following provisions of this Schedule, references in Part I to the court shall be construed in relation to a judge-arbitrator, or in relation to the appointment of a judge-arbitrator, as references to the Court of Appeal.

        (2)   The references in sections 32(6), 45(6) and 69(8) to the Court of Appeal shall in such a case be construed as references to the House of Lords.

Arbitrator's fees

3.   (1)   The power of the court in section 28(2) to order consideration and adjustment of the liability of a party for the fees of an arbitrator may be exercised by a judge-arbitrator.

        (2)   Any such exercise of the power is subject to the powers of the Court of Appeal under sections 24(4) and 25(3)(b) (directions as to entitlement to fees or expenses in case of removal or resignation).

Exercise of court powers in support of arbitration

4.   (1)   Where the arbitral tribunal consists of or includes a judge-arbitrator the powers of the court under sections 42 to 44 (enforcement of peremptory orders, summoning witnesses, and other court powers) are exercisable by the High Court and also by the judge-arbitrator himself.

        (2)   Anything done by a judge-arbitrator in the exercise of those powers shall be regarded as done by him in his capacity as judge of the High Court and have effect as if done by that court.

                Nothing in this sub-paragraph prejudices any power vested in him as arbitrator or umpire.

Extension of time for making award

5.   (1)   The power conferred by section 50 (extension of time for making award) is exercisable by the judge-arbitrator himself.

        (2)   Any appeal from a decision of a judge-arbitrator under that section lies to the Court of Appeal with the leave of that court.

Withholding award in case of non-payment

6.   (1)   The provisions of paragraph 7 apply in place of the provisions of section 56 (power to withhold award in the case of non-payment) in relation to the withholding of an award for non-payment of the fees and expenses of a judge-arbitrator.

        (2)   This does not affect the application of section 56 in relation to the delivery of such an award by an arbitral or other institution or person vested by the parties with powers in relation to the delivery of the award.

7.　(1)　A judge-arbitrator may refuse to deliver an award except upon payment of the fees and expenses mentioned in section 56(1).

　　(2)　The judge-arbitrator may, on an application by a party to the arbitral proceedings, order that if he pays into the High Court the fees and expenses demanded, or such lesser amount as the judge-arbitrator may specify—

　　　(a)　the award shall be delivered;

　　　(b)　the amount of the fees and expenses. properly payable shall be determined by such means and upon such terms as he may direct; and

　　　(c)　out of the money paid into court there shall be paid out such fees and expenses as may be found to be properly payable and the balance of the money (if any) shall be paid out to the applicant.

　　(3)　For this purpose the amount of fees and expenses properly payable is the amount the applicant is liable to pay under section 28 or any agreement relating to the payment of the arbitrator.

　　(4)　No application to the judge-arbitrator under this paragraph may be made where there is any available arbitral process for appeal or review of the amount of the fees or expenses demanded.

　　(5)　Any appeal from a decision of a judge-arbitrator under this paragraph lies to the Court of Appeal with the leave of that court.

　　(6)　Where a party to arbitral proceedings appeals under sub-paragraph (5), an arbitrator is entitled to appear and be heard.

Correction of award or additional award

8.　Subsections (4) to (6) of section 57 (correction of award or additional award: time limit for application or exercise of power) do not apply to a judge-arbitrator.

Costs

9.　Where the arbitral tribunal consists of or includes a judge-arbitrator the powers of the court under section 63(4) (determination of recoverable costs) shall be exercised by the High Court.

10.　(1)　The power of the court under section 64 to determine an arbitrator's reasonable fees and expenses may be exercised by a judge-arbitrator.

　　(2)　Any such exercise of the power is subject to the powers of the Court of Appeal under sections 24(4) and 25(3)(b) (directions as to entitlement to fees or expenses in case of removal or resignation).

Enforcement of award

11.　The leave of the court required by section 66 (enforcement of award) may in the case of an award of a judge-arbitrator be given by the judge-arbitrator himself.

Solicitors' costs

12.　The powers of the court to make declarations and orders under the provisions applied by section 75 (power to charge property recovered in arbitral proceedings with the payment of solicitors' costs) may be exercised by the judge-arbitrator.

Powers of court in relation to service of documents

13.　(1)　The power of the court under section 77(2) (powers of court in relation to service of documents) is exercisable by the judge-arbitrator.

　　(2)　Any appeal from a decision of a judge-arbitrator under that section lies to the Court of Appeal with the leave of that court.

Powers of court to extend time limits relating to arbitral proceedings

14.   (1)   The power conferred by section 79 (power of court to extend time limits relating to arbitral proceedings) is exercisable by the judge-arbitrator himself.

      (2)   Any appeal from a decision of a judge-arbitrator under that section lies to the Court of Appeal with the leave of that court.

CONTRACTS (RIGHTS OF THIRD PARTIES) ACT 1999

CHAPTER 31

1.   **Right of third party to enforce contractual term**
     (1)   Subject to the provisions of this Act, a person who is not a party to a contract (a 'third party') may in his own right enforce a term of the contract if—
           (a)   the contract expressly provides that he may; or
           (b)   subject to subsection (2), the term purports to confer a benefit on him.
     (2)   Subsection (1)(b) does not apply if on a proper construction of the contract it appears that the parties did not intend the term to be enforceable by the third party.
     (3)   The third party must be expressly identified in the contract by name, as a member of a class or as answering a particular description but need not be in existence when the contract is entered into.
     (4)   This section does not confer a right on a third party to enforce a term of a contract otherwise than subject to and in accordance with any other relevant terms of the contract.
     (5)   For the purpose of exercising his right to enforce a term of the contract, there shall be available to the third party any remedy that would have been available to him in an action for breach of contract if he had been a party to the contract (and the rules relating to damages, injunctions, specific performance and other relief shall apply accordingly).
     (6)   Where a term of a contract excludes or limits liability in relation to any matter references in this Act to the third party enforcing the term shall be construed as references to his availing himself of the exclusion or limitation.
     (7)   In this Act, in relation to a term of a contract which is enforceable by a third party—
           'the promisor' means the party to the contract against whom the term is enforceable by the third party; and
           'the promisee' means the party to the contract by whom the term is enforceable against the promisor.

2.   **Variation and cancellation of contract**
     (1)   Subject to the provisions of this section, where a third party has a right under section 1 to enforce a term of the contract, the parties to the contract may not without his consent cancel the contract, or vary it in such a way as to extinguish, or alter his entitlement under, that right, if—

      (a) the third party has communicated his assent to the term to the promisor;

      (b) the promisor is aware that the third party has relied on the term; or

      (c) the promisor can reasonably be expected to have foreseen that the third party would rely on the term and the third party has in fact relied on it.

(2)   The assent referred to in subsection (1)(a)—

      (a) may be by words or conduct; and

      (b) if sent to the promisor by post or other means, shall not be regarded as communicated to the promisor until received by him.

(3)   Subsection (1) is subject to any express term of the contract under which—

      (a) the contract may be cancelled or varied without the consent of the third party; or

      (b) the consent of the third party is required in circumstances specified in the contract instead of those set out in subsection (1)(a) to (c).

(4)   Where the consent of a third party is required under subsection (1) or (3), the court may, on the application of the parties to the contract, dispense with his consent if satisfied—

      (a) that his consent cannot be obtained because his whereabouts cannot reasonably be ascertained; or

      (b) that he is mentally incapable of giving his consent.

(5)   The court may, on the application of the parties to a contract, dispense with any consent that may be required under subsection (1)(c) if satisfied that it cannot reasonably be ascertained whether or not the third party has in fact relied on the term.

(6)   If the court dispenses with a third party's consent, it may impose such conditions as it thinks fit, including a condition requiring the payment of compensation to the third party.

(7)   The jurisdiction conferred by subsections (4) to (6) is exercisable by both the High Court and a county court.

3.   Defences, etc, available to promisor

(1)   Subsections (2) to (5) apply where, in reliance on section 1, proceedings for the enforcement of a term of a contract are brought by a third party.

(2)   The promisor shall have available to him by way of defence or set-off any matter that—

      (a) arises from or in connection with the contract and is relevant to the term; and

      (b) would have been available to him by way of defence or set-off if the proceedings had been brought by the promisee.

(3)   The promisor shall also have available to him by way of defence or set-off any matter if—

      (a) an express term of the contract provides for it to be available to him in proceedings brought by the third party; and

      (b) it would have been available to him by way of defence or set-off if the proceedings had been brought by the promisee.

(4)   The promisor shall also have available to him—

      (a) by way of defence or set-off any matter; and

      (b) by way of counterclaim any matter not arising from the contract,

      that would have been available to him by way of defence or set-off or, as the case may be, by way of counterclaim against the third party if the third party had been a party to the contract.

(5)   Subsections (2) and (4) are subject to any express term of the contract as to the matters that are not to be available to the promisor by way of defence, set-off or counterclaim.

(6)   Where in any proceedings brought against him a third party seeks in reliance on section 1 to enforce a term of a contract (including, in particular, a term purporting to exclude or limit liability), he may not do so if he could not have

done so (whether by reason of any particular circumstances relating to him or otherwise) had he been a party to the contract.

4. Enforcement of contract by promisee
Section 1 does not affect any right of the promisee to enforce any term of the contract.

5. Protection of promisor from double liability
Where under section 1 a term of a contract is enforceable by a third party, and the promisee has recovered from the promisor a sum in respect of—
(a)   the third party's loss in respect of the term; or
(b)   the expense to the promisee of making good to the third party the default of the promisor,
then, in any proceedings brought in reliance on that section by the third party, the court shall reduce any award to the third party to such extent as it thinks appropriate to take account of the sum recovered by the promisee.

6. Exceptions
(1)   Section 1 confers no rights on a third party in the case of a contract on a bill of exchange, promissory note or other negotiable instrument.
(2) to (4) [Omitted].
(5)   Section 1 confers no rights on a third party in the case of—
(a)   a contract for the carriage of goods by sea; or
(b)   a contract for the carriage of goods by rail or road, or for the carriage of cargo by air, which is subject to the rules of the appropriate international transport convention,
except that a third party may in reliance on that section avail himself of an exclusion or limitation of liability in such a contract.
(6)   In subsection (5) 'contract for the carriage of goods by sea' means a contract of carriage—
(a)   contained in or evidenced by a bill of lading, sea waybill or a corresponding electronic transaction; or
(b)   under or for the purposes of which there is given an undertaking which is contained in a ship's delivery order or a corresponding electronic transaction.
(7)   For the purposes of subsection (6)—
(a)   'bill of lading', 'sea waybill' and 'ship's delivery order' have the same meaning as in the Carriage of Goods by Sea Act 1992; and
(b)   a corresponding electronic transaction is a transaction within section 1(5) of that Act which corresponds to the issue, indorsement, delivery or transfer of a bill of lading, sea waybill or ship's delivery order.
(8)   In subsection (5) 'the appropriate international transport convention' means—
(a)   in relation to a contract for the carriage of goods by rail, the Convention which has the force of law in the United Kingdom under section 1 of the International Transport Conventions Act 1983;
(b)   in relation to a contract for the carriage of goods by road, the Convention which has the force of law in the United Kingdom under section 1 of the Carriage of Goods by Road Act 1965; and
(c)   in relation to a contract for the carriage of cargo by air:
(i)   the Convention which has the force of law in the United Kingdom under section 1 of the Carriage by Air Act 1961; or
(ii)   the Convention which has the force of law under section 1 of the Carriage by Air (Supplementary Provisions) Act 1962; or

(iii)   either of the amended Conventions set out in Part B of Schedule 2 or 3 to the Carriage by Air Acts (Application of Provisions) Order 1967.

7.   **Supplementary provisions relating to third party**

(1)   Section 1 does not affect any right or remedy of a third party that exists or is available apart from this Act.

(2)   Section 2(2) of the Unfair Contract Terms Act 1977 (restriction on exclusion etc. of liability for negligence) shall not apply where the negligence consists of the breach of an obligation arising from a term of a contract and the person seeking to enforce it is a third party acting in reliance on section 1.

(3)   In sections 5 and 8 of the Limitation Act 1980 the references to an action founded on a simple contract and an action upon a specialty shall respectively include references to an action brought in reliance on section 1 relating to a simple contract and an action brought in reliance on that section relating to a specialty.

(4)   A third party shall not, by virtue of section 1(5) or 3(4) or (6), be treated as a party to the contract for the purposes of any other Act (or any instrument made under any other Act).

8.   **Arbitration provisions**

(1)   Where—

(a)   a right under section 1 to enforce a term ('the substantive term') is subject to a term providing for the submission of disputes to arbitration ('the arbitration agreement'), and

(b)   the arbitration agreement is an agreement in writing for the purposes of Part I of the Arbitration Act 1996,

the third party shall be treated for the purposes of that Act as a party to the arbitration agreement as regards disputes between himself and the promisor relating to the enforcement of the substantive term by the third party.

(2)   Where—

(a)   a third party has a right under section 1 to enforce a term providing for one or more descriptions of dispute between the third party and the promisor to be submitted to arbitration ('the arbitration agreement'),

(b)   the arbitration agreement is an agreement in writing for the purposes of Part I of the Arbitration Act 1996, and

(c)   the third party does not fall to be treated under subsection (1) as a party to the arbitration agreement,

the third party shall, if he exercises the right, be treated for the purposes of that Act as a party to the arbitration agreement in relation to the matter with respect to which the right is exercised, and be treated as having been so immediately before the exercise of the right.

9. and 10.   [Omitted].

ELECTRONIC COMMUNICATIONS ACT 2000

CHAPTER 7

7.   **Electronic signatures and related certificates**

(1)   In any legal proceedings—

(a)   an electronic signature incorporated into or logically associated with a particular electronic communication or particular electronic data, and

(b)   the certification by any person of such a signature,

shall each be admissible in evidence in relation to any question as to the authenticity of the communication or data or as to the integrity of the communication or data.

(2)   For the purposes of this section an electronic signature is so much of anything in electronic form as—

   (a)   is incorporated into or otherwise logically associated with any electronic communication or electronic data; and

   (b)   purports to be so incorporated or associated for the purpose of being used in establishing the authenticity of the communication or data, the integrity of the communication or data, or both.

(3)   For the purposes of this section an electronic signature incorporated into or associated with a particular electronic communication or particular electronic data is certified by any person if that person (whether before or after the making of the communication) has made a statement confirming that—

   (a)   the signature,

   (b)   a means of producing, communicating or verifying the signature, or

   (c)   a procedure applied to the signature,

   is (either alone or in combination with other factors) a valid means of establishing the authenticity of the communication or data, the integrity of the communication or data, or both.

SECTION II
STATUTORY INSTRUMENTS

CIVIL PROCEDURE RULES AND PRACTICE
SI 1998 NO 3132

PART 6
SERVICE OF DOCUMENTS

I GENERAL RULES ABOUT SERVICE

6.1 The rules in this Part apply to the service of documents, except where—
  (a) any other enactment, a rule in another Part, or a practice direction makes a different provision; or
  (b) the court orders otherwise.

Methods of service—general

6.2 (1) A document may be served by any of the following methods—
  (a) personal service, in accordance with rule 6.4;
  (b) first class post;
  (c) leaving the document at a place specified in rule 6.5;
  (d) through a document exchange in accordance with the relevant practice direction; or
  (e) by fax or other means of electronic communication in accordance with the relevant practice direction.
  (Rule 6.8 provides for the court to permit service by an alternative method.)
  (2) A company may be served by any method permitted under this Part as an alternative to the methods of service set out in—
  (a) section 725 of the Companies Act 1985 (service by leaving a document at or posting it to an authorised place);
  (b) section 695 of that Act (service on overseas companies); and
  (c) section 694A of that Act (service of documents on companies incorporated outside the UK and Gibraltar and having a branch in Great Britain).
6.3 (1) The court will serve a document which it has issued or prepared except where—
  (a) a rule provides that a party must serve the document in question;
  (b) the party on whose behalf the document is to be served notifies the court that he wishes to serve it himself;
  (c) a practice direction provides otherwise;
  (d) the court orders otherwise; or
  (e) the court has failed to serve and has sent a notice of non-service to the party on whose behalf the document is to be served in accordance with rule 6.11.
  (2) Where the court is to serve a document, it is for the court to decide which of the methods of service specified in rule 6.2 is to be used.
  (3) Where a party prepares a document which is to be served by the court, that party must file a copy for the court, and for each party to be served.
6.4 (1) A document to be served may be served personally, except as provided in paragraph (2).
  (2) Where a solicitor—
  (a) is authorised to accept service on behalf of a party; and
  (b) has notified the party serving the document in writing that he is so authorised,

a document must be served on the solicitor, unless personal service is required by an enactment, rule, practice direction or court order.

(3) A document is served personally on an individual by leaving it with that individual.

(4) A document is served personally on a company or other corporation by leaving it with a person holding a senior position within the company or corporation.

(The service practice direction sets out the meaning of 'senior position'.)

(5) A document is served personally on a partnership where partners are being sued in the name of their firm by leaving it with—

(a) a partner; or

(b) a person who, at the time of service, has the control or management of the partnership business at its principal place of business.

Address for service

6.5 (1) Except as provided by Section III of this Part (service out of the jurisdiction) a document must be served within the jurisdiction.

('Jurisdiction' is defined in Rule 2.3.)

(2) A party must give an address for service within the jurisdiction.

(3) Where a party—

(a) does not give the business address of his solicitor as his address for service; and

(b) resides or carries on business within the jurisdiction,

he must give his residence or place of business as his address for service.

(4) Any document to be served—

(a) by first class post;

(b) by leaving it at the place of service;

(c) through a document exchange;

(d) by fax or by other means of electronic communication,

must be sent or transmitted to, or left at, the address for service given by the party to be served.

(5) Where—

(a) a solicitor is acting for the party to be served; and

(b) the document to be served is not the claim form;

the party's address for service is the business address of his solicitor (Rule 6.13 specifies when the business address of a defendant's solicitor may be the defendant's address for service in relation to the claim form).

(6) Where—

(a) no solicitor is acting for the party to be served; and

(b) the party has not given an address for service,

the document must be sent or transmitted to, or left at, the place shown in the following table.

(Rule 6.2(2) sets out the statutory methods of service on a company.)

Nature of party to be served	Place of service
Individual	• Usual or last known residence.
Proprietor of a business	• Usual or last known residence; or
	• Place of business or last known place of business.
Individual who is suing or being sued in the name of a firm	• Usual or last known residence; or
	• Principal or last known place of business of the firm.

Nature of party to be served	Place of service
Corporation incorporated in England and Wales other than a company	• Principal office of the corporation; or • Any place within the jurisdiction where the corporation carries on its activities and which has a real connection with the claim
Company registered in England and Wales	• Principal office of the company; or • Any place of business of the company within the jurisdiction which has a real connection with the claim.
Any other company or corporation	• Any place within the jurisdiction where the corporation carries on its activities; or • Any place of business of the company within the jurisdiction.

    (7)   This rule does not apply where an order made by the court under rule 6.8 (service by an alternative method) specifies where the document in question maybe served.

6.6 to 6.14 [Omitted].

II SPECIAL PROVISIONS ABOUT SERVICE OF THE CLAIM FORM

Service of the claim form by contractually agreed method

6.15   (1)   Where—
       (a) a contract contains a term providing that, in the event of a claim being issued in relation to the contract, the claim form may be served by a method specified in the contract; and
       (b) a claim form containing only a claim in respect of that contract is issued,
      the claim form shall, subject to paragraph (2), be deemed to be served on the defendant if it is served by a method specified in the contract.
         Where the claim form is served out of the jurisdiction in accordance with the contract, it shall not be deemed to be served on the defendant unless
       (a) permission to serve it out of the jurisdiction has been granted under rule 6.20; or
       (b) it may be served without permission under rule 6.19.

Service of claim form on agent of principal who is overseas

6.16   (1)   Where—
       (a) the defendant is overseas; and
       (b) the conditions specified in paragraph (2) are satisfied,
      the court may, on an application only, permit a claim form relating to a contract to be served on a defendant's agent.
    (2)   The court may not make an order under this rule unless it is satisfied that—
       (a) the contract to which the claim relates was entered into within the jurisdiction with or through the defendant's agent; and
       (b) at the time of the application either the agent's authority has not been terminated or he is still in business relations with his principal.
    (3)   An application under this rule—
       (a) must be supported by evidence; and
       (b) may be made without notice.

(4)   An order under this rule must state a period within which the defendant must respond to the particulars of claim.
       (Rule 9.2 sets out how a defendant may respond to particulars of claim.)
(5)   The power conferred by this rule is additional to the power conferred by rule 6.8 (service by an alternative method).
(6)   Where the court makes an order under this rule, the claimant must send to the defendant copies of—
       (a) the order; and
       (b) the claim form.

III   SPECIAL PROVISIONS ABOUT SERVICE OUT OF THE JURISDICTION

Scope of this section
6.17   This Section contains rules about—
        (a)   service out of the jurisdiction;
        (b)   how to obtain the permission of the court to serve out of the jurisdiction; and
        (c)   the procedure for serving out of the jurisdiction.
        (Rule 2.3 defines 'jurisdiction'.)

Definitions
6.18   For the purposes of this Part—
        (a)   'the 1982 Act' means the Civil Jurisdiction and Judgments Act 1982;
        (b)   'the Hague Convention' means the Convention on the service abroad of judicial and extra-judicial documents in civil or commercial matters signed at the Hague on November 15, 1965;
        (c)   'Contracting State' has the meaning given by section 1(3) of the 1982 Act;
        (d)   'Convention territory' means the territory or territories of any Contracting State to which the Brussels or Lugano Conventions (as defined in section 1(1) of the 1982 Act) apply;
        (e)   'Civil Procedure Convention' means the Brussels and Lugano Conventions and any other Convention entered into by the United Kingdom regarding service outside the jurisdiction;
        (ea)   'the Service regulation' means Council Regulation (EC) No 1348/2000 of 29 May 2000 on the service in the Member States of judicial and extrajudicial documents in civil or commercial matters;
        (f)   'United Kingdom Overseas Territory' means those territories as set out in the relevant practice direction;
        (g)   'domicile' is to be determined—
               (i)   in relation to a Convention territory, in accordance with sections 41 to 46 of the 1982 Act;
               (ii)   in relation to a Regulation State, in accordance with the Judgments Regulation and paragraphs 9 to 12 of Schedule I to the Civil Jurisdiction and Judgments Order 2001;
        (h)   'claim form' includes petition and application notice;
        (i)   'claim' includes petition and application;
        (j)   'the Judgments Regulation' means Council Regulation (EC) No. 44/2001 of 22nd December 2000 on jurisdiction and the recognition and enforcement of judgments in civil and commercial matters; and
        (k)   'Regulation State' has the same meaning as 'Member State' in the Judgments Regulation, that is all Member States except Denmark.
        (Rule 6.30 provides that where an application notice is to be served out of the jurisdiction under this Part, Rules 6.21(4), 6.22 and 6.23 do not apply.)

Service out of the jurisdiction where the permission of the court is not required
6.19   (1)   A claim form may be served on a defendant out of the jurisdiction where each
claim included in the claim form made against the defendant to be served is a
claim which the court has power to determine under the 1982 Act and—
(a)   no proceedings between the parties concerning the same claim are
pending in the courts of any other part of the United Kingdom or any
other Convention territory; and
(b)   (i)   the defendant is domiciled in the United Kingdom or in any
Convention territory;
(ii)   Article 16 of Schedule 1 or 3C to the 1982 Act, or paragraph 11 of
Schedule 4 to that Act, refers to the proceedings; or
(iii)   the defendant is a party to an agreement conferring jurisdiction to
which Article 17 of Schedule 1 or 3C to the 1982 Act, or paragraph
12 of Schedule 4 to that Act, refers.
(1A)   A claim form may be served on a defendant out of the jurisdiction where each
claim included in the claim form made against the defendant to be served is a
claim which the court has power to determine under the Judgments
Regulation and—
(a)   no proceedings between the parties concerning the same claim are
pending in the courts of any other part of the United Kingdom or any
other Regulation State; and
(b)   (i)   the defendant is domiciled in the United Kingdom or in any
Regulation State;
(ii)   Article 22 of the Judgments Regulation refers to the proceedings; or
(iii)   the defendant is a party to an agreement conferring jurisdiction to
which Article 23 of the Judgments Regulation refers.
(2)   A claim form may be served on a defendant out of the jurisdiction where each
claim included in the claim form made against the defendant to be served is a
claim which, under any other enactment, the court has power to determine,
although—
(a)   the person against whom the claim is made is not within the jurisdiction;
or
(b)   the facts giving rise to the claim did not occur within the jurisdiction.
(3)   Where a claim form is to be served out of the jurisdiction under this rule, it
must contain a statement of the grounds on which the claimant is entitled to
serve it out of the jurisdiction.

Service out of the jurisdiction where the permission of the court is required
6.20   In any proceedings to which Rule 6.19 does not apply, a claim form may be
served out of the jurisdiction with the permission of the court if—

General grounds
(1)   a claim is made for a remedy against a person domiciled within the
jurisdiction.
(2)   a claim is made for an injunction ordering the defendant to do or refrain from
doing an act within the jurisdiction.
(3)   a claim is made against someone on whom the claim form has been or will be
served and—
(a)   there is between the claimant and that person a real issue which it is
reasonable for the court to try; and
(b)   the claimant wishes to serve the claim form on another person who is a
necessary or proper party to that claim.
(3A)   a claim is a Part 20 claim and the person to be served is a necessary or proper
party to the claim against the Part 20 claimant.

Claims for interim remedies
(4)   a claim is made for an interim remedy under section 25(1) of the 1982 Act.

Claims in relation to contracts
  (5)   a claim is made in respect of a contract where the contract—
         (a) was made within the jurisdiction;
         (b) was made by or through an agent trading or residing within the
              jurisdiction;
         (c) is governed by English law; or
         (d) contains a term to the effect that the court shall have jurisdiction to
              determine any claim in respect of the contract.
  (6)   a claim is made in respect of a breach of contract committed within the
         jurisdiction.
  (7)   a claim is made for a declaration that no contract exists where, if the contract
         was found to exist, it would comply with the conditions set out in paragraph
         (5).

Claims in tort
  (8)   a claim is made in tort where—
         (a) damage was sustained within the jurisdiction; or
         (b) the damage sustained resulted from an act committed within the
              jurisdiction.

Enforcement
  (9)   a claim is made to enforce any judgment or arbitral award.

Claims about property within the jurisdiction
  (10)   the whole subject matter of a claim relates to property located within the
         jurisdiction.

Claims about trusts etc.
  (11)   a claim is made for any remedy which might be obtained in proceedings to
         execute the trusts of a written instrument where—
         (a) the trusts ought to be executed according to English law; and
         (b) the person on whom the claim form is to be served is a trustee of the
              trusts.
  (12)   a claim is made for any remedy which might be obtained in proceedings for
         the administration of the estate of a person who died domiciled within the
         jurisdiction.
  (13)   a claim is made in probate proceedings which includes a claim for the
         rectification of a will.
  (14)   a claim is made for a remedy against the defendant as constructive trustee
         where the defendant's alleged liability arises out of acts committed within the
         jurisdiction.
  (15)   a claim is made for restitution where the defendant's alleged liability arises
         out of acts committed within the jurisdiction.

Claims by the Inland Revenue
  (16)   a claim is made by the Commissioners of the Inland Revenue relating to
         duties or taxes against a defendant not domiciled in Scotland or Northern
         Ireland.

Claim for costs order in favour of or against third parties
  (17)   a claim is made by a party to proceedings for an order that the court exercise
         its power under section 51 of the Supreme Court Act 1981 to make a costs
         order in favour of or against a person who is not a party to those proceedings.
              (Rule 48.2 sets out the procedure where the court is considering whether to
         exercise its discretion to make a costs order in favour of or against a non-
         party.)

Admiralty claims
  (17A) a claim is—
         (a) in the nature of salvage and any part of the services took place within the
              jurisdiction; or

      (b) to enforce a claim under section 153, 154 or 175 of the Merchant Shipping Act 1995.

Claims under various enactments

    (18) a claim is made under an enactment specified in the relevant practice direction.

Application for permission to serve claim form out of jurisdiction

6.21   (1)   An application for permission under Rule 6.20 must be supported by written evidence stating—

      (a) the grounds on which the application is made and the paragraph or paragraphs of Rule 6.20 relied on;

      (b) that the claimant believes that his claim has a reasonable prospect of success; and

      (c) the defendant's address or, if not known, in what place or country the defendant is, or is likely, to be found.

     (2)   Where the application is made in respect of a claim referred to in Rule 6.20(3), the written evidence must also state the grounds on which the witness believes that there is between the claimant and the person on whom the claim form has been, or will be served, a real issue which it is reasonable for the court to try.

  (2A) The court will not give permission unless satisfied that England and Wales is the proper place in which to bring the claim.

     (3)   Where—

      (a) the application is for permission to serve a claim form in Scotland or Northern Ireland; and

      (b) it appears to the court that the claimant may also be entitled to a remedy there, the court, in deciding whether to give permission, shall—

         (i)   compare the cost and convenience of proceeding there or in the jurisdiction; and

        (ii)   (where relevant) have regard to the powers and jurisdiction of the Sheriff court in Scotland or the county courts or courts of summary jurisdiction in Northern Ireland.

     (4)   An order giving permission to serve a claim form out of the jurisdiction must specify the periods within which the defendant may—

      (a) file an acknowledgment of service;

      (b) file or serve an admission; and

      (c) file a defence.

(Part 11 sets out the procedure by which a defendant may dispute the court's jurisdiction.)

    (The second practice direction to this Part sets out how the periods referred to in paragraphs (a), (b) and (c) are calculated.)

THE COMMERCIAL AGENTS (COUNCIL DIRECTIVE) REGULATIONS 1993

SI 1993 NO 3053

ARRANGEMENT OF REGULATIONS

PART I

GENERAL

1.   Citation, commencement and applicable law.

2.   Interpretation, application and extent.

PART II
RIGHTS AND OBLIGATIONS

3. Duties of a commercial agent to his principal.
4. Duties of a principal to his commercial agent.
5. Prohibition on derogation from regulations 3 and 4 and consequence of breach.

PART III
REMUNERATION

6. Form and amount of remuneration in absence of agreement.
7. Entitlement to commission on transactions concluded during agency contract.
8. Entitlement to commission on transactions concluded after agency contract has terminated.
9. Apportionment of commission between new and previous commercial agents.
10. When commission due and date for payment.
11. Extinction of right to commission.
12. Periodic supply of information as to commission due and right of inspection of principal's books.

PART IV
CONCLUSION AND TERMINATION OF THE AGENCY CONTRACT

13. Right to signed written statement of terms of agency contract.
14. Conversion of agency contract after expiry of fixed period.
15. Minimum periods of notice for termination of agency contract.
16. Savings with regard to immediate termination.
17. Entitlement of commercial agent to indemnity or compensation on termination of agency contract.
18. Grounds for excluding payment of indemnity or compensation under regulation 17.
19. Prohibition on derogation from regulations 17 and 18.
20. Restraint of trade clauses.

PART V
MISCELLANEOUS AND SUPPLEMENTAL

21. Disclosure of information.
22. Service of notice, etc.
23. Transitional provisions.

PART I
GENERAL

Citation, commencement and applicable law

1. (1) These Regulations may be cited as the Commercial Agents (Council Directive) Regulations 1993 and shall come into force on 1st January 1994.
    (2) These Regulations govern the relations between commercial agents and their principals and, subject to paragraph (3), apply in relation to the activities of commercial agents in Great Britain.
    (3) A court or tribunal shall—
        (a) apply the law of the other Member State concerned in place of regulations 3 to 22 where the parties have agreed that the agency contract is to be governed by the law of that Member State;

(b) (whether or not it is required to do so) apply these regulations where the law of another member State corresponding to these regulations enables the parties to agree that the agency contract is to be governed by the law of a different member State and the parties have agreed that it is to be governed by the law of England and Wales or Scotland.

Interpretation, application and extent

2.   (1)   In these Regulations—
'commercial agent' means a self-employed intermediary who has continuing authority to negotiate the sale or purchase of goods on behalf of another person (the 'principal'), or to negotiate and conclude the sale or purchase of goods on behalf of and in the name of that principal; but shall be understood as not including in particular:
   (i)   a person who, in his capacity as an officer of a company or association, is empowered to enter into commitments binding on that company or association;
   (ii)   a partner who is lawfully authorised to enter into commitments binding on his partners;
   (iii) a person who acts as an insolvency practitioner (as that expression is defined in section 388 of the Insolvency Act 1986) or the equivalent in any other jurisdiction;
'commission' means any part of the remuneration of a commercial agent which varies with the number or value of business transactions;
'EEA Agreement' means the Agreement on the European Economic Area signed at Oporto on 2nd May 1992 as adjusted by the Protocol signed at Brussels on 17th March 1993;
'Member State' includes a State which is a contracting party to the EEA Agreement;
'restraint of trade clause' means an agreement restricting the business activities of a commercial agent following termination of the agency contract.
   (2)   These Regulations do not apply to—
      (a) commercial agents whose activities are unpaid;
      (b) commercial agents when they operate on commodity exchanges or in the commodity market;
      (c) the Crown Agents for Overseas Governments and Administrations, as set up under the Crown Agents Act 1979 or its subsidiaries.
   (3)   The provisions of the Schedule to these Regulations have effect for the purpose of determining the persons whose activities as commercial agents are to be considered secondary.
   (4)   These Regulations shall not apply to the persons referred to in paragraph (3) above.
   (5)   These Regulations do not extend to Northern Ireland.

PART II
RIGHTS AND OBLIGATIONS

Duties of a commercial agent to his principal

3.   (1)   In performing his activities a commercial agent must look after the interests of his principal and act dutifully and in good faith.
   (2)   In particular, a commercial agent must—
      (a) make proper efforts to negotiate and, where appropriate, conclude the transactions he is instructed to take care of;

(b) communicate to his principal all the necessary information available to him;

(c) comply with reasonable instructions given by his principal.

Duties of a principal to his commercial agent

4. (1) In his relations with his commercial agent a principal must act dutifully and in good faith.

   (2) In particular, a principal must—

   (a) provide his commercial agent with the necessary documentation relating to the goods concerned;

   (b) obtain for his commercial agent the information necessary for the performance of the agency contract, and in particular notify his commercial agent within a reasonable period once he anticipates that the volume of commercial transactions will be significantly lower than that which the commercial agent could normally have expected.

   (3) A principal shall, in addition, inform his commercial agent within a reasonable period of his acceptance or refusal of, and of any non-execution by him of, a commercial transaction which the commercial agent has procured for him.

Prohibition on derogation from regulations 3 and 4 and consequence of breach

5. (1) The parties may not derogate from regulations 3 and 4 above.

   (2) The law applicable to the contract shall govern the consequence of breach of the rights and obligations under regulations 3 and 4 above.

PART III
REMUNERATION

Form and amount of remuneration in absence of agreement

6. (1) In the absence of any agreement as to remuneration between the parties, a commercial agent shall be entitled to the remuneration that commercial agents appointed for the goods forming the subject of his agency contract are customarily allowed in the place where he carries on his activities and, if there is no such customary practice, a commercial agent shall be entitled to reasonable remuneration taking into account all the aspects of the transaction.

   (2) This regulation is without prejudice to the application of any enactment or rule of law concerning the level of remuneration.

   (3) Where a commercial agent is not remunerated (wholly or in part) by commission, regulations 7 to 12 below shall not apply.

Entitlement to commission on transactions concluded during agency contract

7. (1) A commercial agent shall be entitled to commission on commercial transactions concluded during the period covered by the agency contract—

   (a) where the transaction has been concluded as a result of his action; or

   (b) where the transaction is concluded with a third party whom he has previously acquired as a customer for transactions of the same kind.

   (2) A commercial agent shall also be entitled to commission on transactions concluded during the period covered by the agency contract where he has an exclusive right to a specific geographical area or to a specific group of

customers and where the transaction has been entered into with a customer belonging to that area or group.

Entitlement to commission on transactions concluded after agency contract has terminated

8. Subject to regulation 9 below, a commercial agent shall be entitled to commission on commercial transactions concluded after the agency contract has terminated if—

    (a) the transaction is mainly attributable to his efforts during the period covered by the agency contract and if the transaction was entered into within a reasonable period after that contract terminated; or

    (b) in accordance with the conditions mentioned in regulation 7 above, the order of the third party reached the principal or the commercial agent before the agency contract terminated.

Apportionment of commission between new and previous commercial agents

9. (1) A commercial agent shall not be entitled to the commission referred to in regulation 7 above if that commission is payable, by virtue of regulation 8 above, to the previous commercial agent, unless it is equitable because of the circumstances for the commission to be shared between the commercial agents.

    (2) The principal shall be liable for any sum due under paragraph (1) above to the person entitled to it in accordance with that paragraph, and any sum which the other commercial agent receives to which he is not entitled shall be refunded to the principal.

When commission due and date for payment

10. (1) Commission shall become due as soon as, and to the extent that one of the following circumstances occurs—

    (a) the principal has executed the transaction; or

    (b) the principal should, according to his agreement with the third party, have executed the transaction; or

    (c) the third party has executed the transaction.

    (2) Commission shall become due at the latest when the third party has executed his part of the transaction or should have done so if the principal had executed his part of the transaction, as he should have.

    (3) The commission shall be paid not later than on the last day of the month following the quarter in which it became due, and, for the purposes of these Regulations, unless otherwise agreed between the parties, the first quarter period shall run from the date the agency contract takes effect, and subsequent periods shall run from that date in the third month thereafter or the beginning of the fourth month, whichever is the sooner.

    (4) Any agreement to derogate from paragraphs (2) and (3) above to the detriment of the commercial agent shall be void.

Extinction of right to commission

11. (1) The right to commission can be extinguished only if and to the extent that—

    (a) it is established that the contract between the third party and the principal will not be executed; and

    (b) that fact is due to a reason for which the principal is not to blame.

    (2) Any commission which the commercial agent has already received shall be refunded if the right to it is extinguished.

(3)   Any agreement to derogate from paragraph (1) above to the detriment of the commercial agent shall be void.

Periodic supply of information as to commission due and
right of inspection of principal's books

12.   (1)   The principal shall supply his commercial agent with a statement of the commission due, not later than the last day of the month following the quarter in which the commission has become due, and such statement shall set out the main components used in calculating the amount of the commission.

(2)   A commercial agent shall be entitled to demand that he be provided with all the information (and in particular an extract from the books) which is available to his principal and which he needs in order to check the amount of the commission due to him.

(3)   Any agreement to derogate from paragraphs (1) and (2) above shall be void.

(4)   Nothing in this regulation shall remove or restrict the effect of, or prevent reliance upon, any enactment or rule of law which recognises the right of an agent to inspect the books of a principal.

PART IV
CONCLUSION AND TERMINATION OF THE AGENCY CONTRACT

Right to signed written statement of terms of agency contract

13.   (1)   The commercial agent and principal shall each be entitled to receive from the other, on request, a signed written document setting out the terms of the agency contract including any terms subsequently agreed.

(2)   Any purported waiver of the right referred to in paragraph (1) above shall be void.

Conversion of agency contract after expiry of fixed period

14.   An agency contract for a fixed period which continues to be performed by both parties after that period has expired shall be deemed to be converted into an agency contract for an indefinite period.

Minimum periods of notice for termination of agency contract

15.   (1)   Where an agency contract is concluded for an indefinite period either party may terminate it by notice.

(2)   The period of notice shall be—
(a)   1 month for the first year of the contract;
(b)   2 months for the second year commenced;
(c)   3 months for the third year commenced and for the subsequent years,
and the parties may not agree on any shorter periods of notice.

(3)   If the parties agree on longer periods than those laid down in paragraph (2) above, the period of notice to be observed by the principal must not be shorter than that to be observed by the commercial agent.

(4)   Unless otherwise agreed by the parties, the end of the period of notice must coincide with the end of a calendar month.

(5)   The provisions of this regulation shall also apply to an agency contract for a fixed period where it is converted under regulation 14 above into an agency contract for an indefinite period subject to the proviso that the earlier fixed period must be taken into account in the calculation of the period of notice.

Savings with regard to immediate termination

16.   These Regulations shall not affect the application of any enactment or rule of law which provides for the immediate termination of the agency contract—

    (a)   because of the failure of one party to carry out all or part of his obligations under that contract; or

    (b)   where exceptional circumstances arise.

Entitlement of commercial agent to indemnity or
compensation on termination by contract

17.   (1)   This regulation has effect for the purpose of ensuring that the commercial agent is, after termination of the agency contract, indemnified in accordance with paragraphs (3) to (5) below or compensated for damage in accordance with paragraphs (6) and (7) below.

    (2)   Except where the agency contract otherwise provides, the commercial agent shall be entitled to be compensated rather than indemnified.

    (3)   Subject to paragraph (9) and to regulation 18 below, the commercial agent shall be entitled to an indemnity if and to the extent that—

        (a)   he has brought the principal new customers or has significantly increased the volume of business with existing customers and the principal continues to derive substantial benefits from the business with such customers; and

        (b)   the payment of this indemnity is equitable having regard to all the circumstances and, in particular, the commission lost by the commercial agent on the business transacted with such customers.

    (4)   The amount of the indemnity shall not exceed a figure equivalent to an indemnity for one year calculated from the commercial agent's average annual remuneration over the preceding five years and if the contract goes back less than five years the indemnity shall be calculated on the average for the period in question.

    (5)   The grant of an indemnity as mentioned above shall not prevent the commercial agent from seeking damages.

    (6)   Subject to paragraph (9) and to regulation 18 below, the commercial agent shall be entitled to compensation for the damage he suffers as a result of the termination of his relations with his principal.

    (7)   For the purpose of these Regulations such damage shall be deemed to occur particularly when the termination takes place in either or both of the following circumstances, namely circumstances which—

        (a)   deprive the commercial agent of the commission which proper performance of the agency contract would have procured for him whilst providing his principal with substantial benefits linked to the activities of the commercial agent; or

        (b)   have not enabled the commercial agent to amortize the costs and expenses that he had incurred in the performance of the agency contract on the advice of his principal.

    (8)   Entitlement to the indemnity or compensation for damage as provided for under paragraphs (2) to (7) above shall also arise where the agency contract is terminated as a result of the death of the commercial agent.

    (9)   The commercial agent shall lose his entitlement to the indemnity or compensation for damage in the instances provided for in paragraphs (2) to (8) above if within one year following termination of his agency contract he has not notified his principal that he intends pursuing his entitlement.

Grounds for excluding payment of indemnity or
compensation under regulation 17

18.   The compensation referred to in regulation 17 above shall not be payable to the commercial agent where—

(a)   the principal has terminated the agency contract because of default attributable to the commercial agent which would justify immediate termination of the agency contract pursuant to regulation 16 above; or

(b)   the commercial agent has himself terminated the agency contract, unless such termination is justified:

(i)   by circumstances attributable to the principal; or

(ii)   on grounds of the age, infirmity or illness of the commercial agent in consequence of which he cannot reasonably be required to continue his activities; or

(c)   the commercial agent, with the agreement of his principal, assigns his rights and duties under the agency contract to another person.

Prohibition on derogation from regulations 17 and 18

19.   The parties may not derogate from regulations 17 and 18 to the detriment of the commercial agent before the agency contract expires.

Restraint of trade clauses

20.   (1)   A restraint of trade clause shall be valid only if and to the extent that—

(a)   it is concluded in writing; and

(b)   it relates to the geographical area or the group of customers and the geographical area entrusted to the commercial agent and to the kind of goods covered by his agency under the contract.

(2)   A restraint of trade clause shall be valid for not more than two years after termination of the agency contract.

(3)   Nothing in this regulation shall affect any enactment or rule of law which imposes other restrictions on the validity or enforceability of restraint of trade clauses or which enables a court to reduce the obligations on the parties resulting from such clauses.

PART V
MISCELLANEOUS AND SUPPLEMENTAL

Disclosure of information

21.   Nothing in these Regulations shall require information to be given where such disclosure would be contrary to public policy.

Service of notice, etc

22.   (1)   Any notice, statement or other document to be given or supplied to a commercial agent or to be given or supplied to the principal under these Regulations may be so given or supplied—

(a)   by delivering it to him;

(b)   by leaving it at his proper address addressed to him by name;

(c)   by sending it by post to him addressed either to his registered address or to the address of his registered or principal office,

or by any other means provided for in the agency contract.

(2)   Any such notice, statement or document may—

    (a)   in the case of a body corporate, be given or served on the secretary or clerk of that body;

    (b)   in the case of a partnership, be given to or served on any partner or on any person having the control or management of the partnership business.

Transitional provisions

23.   (1)   Notwithstanding any provision in an agency contract made before 1st January 1994, these Regulations shall apply to that contract after that date and, accordingly any provision which is inconsistent with these Regulations shall have effect subject to them.

    (2)   Nothing in these Regulations shall affect the rights and liabilities of a commercial agent or a principal which have accrued before 1st January 1994.

THE SCHEDULE

Regulation 2(3)

1.   The activities of a person as a commercial agent are to be considered secondary where it may reasonably be taken that the primary purpose of the arrangement with his principal is other than as set out in paragraph 2 below.

2.   An arrangement falls within this paragraph if—

    (a)   the business of the principal is the sale, or as the case may be purchase, of goods of a particular kind; and

    (b)   the goods concerned are such that:

       (i)   transactions are normally individually negotiated and concluded on a commercial basis; and

      (ii)   procuring a transaction on one occasion is likely to lead to further transactions in those goods with that customer on future occasions, or to transactions in those goods with other customers in the same geographical area or among the same group of customers, and

that accordingly it is in the commercial interests of the principal in developing the market in those goods to appoint a representative to such customers with a view to the representative devoting effort, skill and expenditure from his own resources to that end.

3.   The following are indications that an arrangement falls within paragraph 2 above, and the absence of any of them is an indication to the contrary—

    (a)   the principal is the manufacturer, importer or distributor of the goods;

    (b)   the goods are specifically identified with the principal in the market in question rather than, or to a greater extent than, with any other person;

    (c)   the agent devotes substantially the whole of his time to representative activities (whether for one principal or for a number of principals whose interests are not conflicting);

    (d)   the goods are not normally available in the market in question other than by means of the agent;

    (e)   the arrangement is described as one of commercial agency.

4.   The following are indications that an arrangement does not fall within paragraph 2 above—

    (a)   promotional material is supplied direct to potential customers;

    (b)   persons are granted agencies without reference to existing agents in a particular area or in relation to a particular group;

    (c)   customers normally select the goods for themselves and merely place their orders through the agent.

5.   The activities of the following categories of persons are presumed, unless the contrary is established, not to fall within paragraph 2 above—
      Mail order catalogue agents for consumer goods.
      Consumer credit agents.

THE CIVIL JURISDICTION AND JUDGMENTS ACT 1982 (INTERIM RELIEF) ORDER 1997

SI 1997 NO 302

2.   The High Court in England and Wales or Northern Ireland shall have power to grant interim relief under section 25(1) of the Civil Jurisdiction and Judgments Act 1982 in relation to proceedings of the following descriptions, namely—
      (a)   proceedings commenced or to be commenced otherwise than in a Brussels or Lugano Contracting State or Regulation State;
      (b)   proceedings whose subject-matter is not within the scope of the Regulation as determined by Article 1 thereof.

THE CIVIL JURISDICTION AND JUDGMENTS ORDER 2001

SI 2001 NO 3929

1.   **[Omitted].**

2.   **Interpretation**
      (1)   In this Order—
            'the Act' means the Civil Jurisdiction and Judgments Act 1982;
            'the Regulation' means Council Regulation (EC) No 44/2001 of 22nd December 2000 on jurisdiction and the recognition and enforcement of judgments in civil and commercial matters;
            'Regulation State' in any provision, in the application of that provision in relation to the Regulation, has the same meaning as 'Member State' in the Regulation, that is all Member States except Denmark.
      (2)   In Schedule 2 to this Order, a section, Part, Schedule or paragraph referred to by number alone is a reference to the section, Part, Schedule or paragraph so numbered in the Act.

3. to 6. **[Omitted].**

SCHEDULE 1

Article 3

THE REGULATION

1.   **Interpretation**
      (1)   In this Schedule—
            'court', without more, includes a tribunal;
            'judgment' has the meaning given by Article 32 of the Regulation;
            'magistrates' court', in relation to Northern Ireland, means a court of summary jurisdiction;

'maintenance order' means a maintenance judgment within the meaning of the Regulation;

'part of the United Kingdom' means England and Wales, Scotland or Northern Ireland;

'payer', in relation to a maintenance order, means the person liable to make the payments for which the order provides;

'prescribed' means prescribed by rules of court.

(2)   In this Schedule, any reference to a numbered Article or Annex is a reference to the Article or Annex so numbered in the Regulation, and any reference to a sub-division of a numbered Article shall be construed accordingly.

(3)   References in paragraphs 2 to 8 to a judgment registered under the Regulation include, to the extent of its registration, references to a judgment so registered to a limited extent only.

(4)   Anything authorised or required by the Regulation or paragraphs 2 to 8 to be done by, to or before a particular magistrates' court may be done by, to or before any magistrates' court acting for the same petty sessions area (or, in Northern Ireland, petty sessions district) as that court.

2.   Enforcement of judgments other than maintenance orders (section 4)

(1)   Where a judgment is registered under the Regulation, the reasonable costs or expenses of and incidental to its registration shall be recoverable as if they were sums recoverable under the judgment.

(2)   A judgment registered under the Regulation shall, for the purposes of its enforcement, be of the same force and effect, the registering court shall have in relation to its enforcement the same powers, and proceedings for or with respect to its enforcement may be taken, as if the judgment had been originally given by the registering court and had (where relevant) been entered.

(3)   Sub-paragraph (2) is subject to Article 47 (restriction on enforcement where appeal pending or time for appeal unexpired), to paragraph 5 and to any provision made by rules of court as to the manner in which and conditions subject to which a judgment registered under the Regulation may be enforced.

3. and 4. [Omitted].

5.   Interest on registered judgments (section 7)

(1)   Subject to sub-paragraph (3), where in connection with an application for registration of a judgment under the Regulation the applicant shows—

(a)   that the judgment provides for the payment of a sum of money; and

(b)   that in accordance with the law of the Regulation State in which the judgment was given interest on that sum is recoverable under the judgment from a particular date or time,

the rate of interest and the date or time from which it is so recoverable shall be registered with the judgment and, subject to rules of court, the debt resulting, apart from paragraph 2(1), from the registration of the judgment shall carry interest in accordance with the registered particulars.

(2)   Costs or expenses recoverable by virtue of paragraph 2(1) shall carry interest as if they were the subject of an order for the payment of costs or expenses made by the registering court on the date of registration.

(3)   Interest on arrears of sums payable under a maintenance order registered under the Regulation in a magistrates' court in England and Wales or Northern Ireland shall not be recoverable in that court, but without prejudice to the operation in relation to any such order of section 2A of the Maintenance Orders Act 1958 or section 11A of the Maintenance and

Affiliation Orders Act (Northern Ireland) 1966 (which enable interest to be recovered if the order is re-registered for enforcement in the High Court).

(4) Except as mentioned in sub-paragraph (3), debts under judgments registered under the Regulation shall carry interest only as provided by this paragraph.

6. and 7.   [Omitted].

8.   Proof and admissibility of certain judgments and related documents (section 11)

(1) For the purposes of the Regulation—

(a) a document, duly authenticated, which purports to be a copy of a judgment given by a court of a Regulation State other than the United Kingdom shall without further proof be deemed to be a true copy, unless the contrary is shown; and

(b) a certificate obtained in accordance with Article 54 and Annex V shall be evidence, and in Scotland sufficient evidence, that the judgment is enforceable in the Regulation State of origin.

(2) A document purporting to be a copy of a judgment given by any such court as is mentioned in sub-paragraph (1)(a) is duly authenticated for the purposes of this paragraph if it purports—

(a) to bear the seal of that court; or

(b) to be certified by any person in his capacity as a judge or officer of that court to be a true copy of a judgment given by that court.

(3) Nothing in this paragraph shall prejudice the admission in evidence of any document which is admissible apart from this paragraph.

9.   Domicile of individuals (section 41)

(1) Subject to Article 59 (which contains provisions for determining whether a party is domiciled in a Regulation State), the following provisions of this paragraph determine, for the purposes of the Regulation, whether an individual is domiciled in the United Kingdom or in a particular part of, or place in, the United Kingdom or in a state other than a Regulation State.

(2) An individual is domiciled in the United Kingdom if and only if—

(a) he is resident in the United Kingdom; and

(b) the nature and circumstances of his residence indicate that he has a substantial connection with the United Kingdom.

(3) Subject to sub-paragraph (5), an individual is domiciled in a particular part of the United Kingdom if and only if—

(a) he is resident in that part; and

(b) the nature and circumstances of his residence indicate that he has a substantial connection with that part.

(4) An individual is domiciled in a particular place in the United Kingdom if and only if he—

(a) is domiciled in the part of the United Kingdom in which that place is situated; and

(b) is resident in that place.

(5) An individual who is domiciled in the United Kingdom but in whose case the requirements of sub-paragraph (3)(b) are not satisfied in relation to any particular part of the United Kingdom shall be treated as domiciled in the part of the United Kingdom in which he is resident.

(6) In the case of an individual who—

(a) is resident in the United Kingdom, or in a particular part of the United Kingdom; and

(b) has been so resident for the last three months or more,

the requirements of sub-paragraph (2)(b) or, as the case may be, sub-paragraph (3)(b) shall be presumed to be fulfilled unless the contrary is proved.

(7)   An individual is domiciled in a state other than a Regulation State if and only if—
    (a) he is resident in that state; and
    (b) the nature and circumstances of his residence indicate that he has a substantial connection with that state.

10. Seat of company, or other legal person or association for purposes of Article 22(2) (section 43)

(1)   The following provisions of this paragraph determine where a company, legal person or association has its seat for the purposes of Article 22(2) (which confers exclusive jurisdiction over proceedings relating to the formation or dissolution of such bodies, or to the decisions of their organs).

(2)   A company, legal person or association has its seat in the United Kingdom if and only if—
    (a) it was incorporated or formed under the law of a part of the United Kingdom; or
    (b) its central management and control is exercised in the United Kingdom.

(3)   Subject to sub-paragraph (4), a company, legal person or association has its seat in a Regulation State other than the United Kingdom if and only if—
    (a) it was incorporated or formed under the law of that state; or
    (b) its central management and control is exercised in that state.

(4)   A company, legal person or association shall not be regarded as having its seat in a Regulation State other than the United Kingdom if—
    (a) it has its seat in the United Kingdom by virtue of sub-paragraph (2)(a); or
    (b) it is shown that the courts of that other state would not regard it for the purposes of Article 22(2) as having its seat there.

11. Persons deemed to be domiciled in the United Kingdom for certain purposes (section 44)

(1)   This paragraph applies to—
    (a) proceedings within Section 3 of Chapter II of the Regulation (insurance contracts),
    (b) proceedings within Section 4 of Chapter II of the Regulation (consumer contracts), and
    (c) proceedings within Section 5 of Chapter II of the Regulation (employment contracts).

(2)   A person who, for the purposes of proceedings to which this paragraph applies arising out of the operations of a branch, agency or other establishment in the United Kingdom, is deemed for the purposes of the Regulation to be domiciled in the United Kingdom by virtue of—
    (a) Article 9(2) (insurers); or
    (b) Article 15(2) (suppliers of goods, services or credit to consumers); or
    (c) Article 18(2) (employers),
shall, for the purposes of those proceedings, be treated as so domiciled and as domiciled in the part of the United Kingdom in which the branch, agency or establishment in question is situated.

12. Domicile of trusts (section 45)

(1)   The following provisions of this paragraph determine for the purposes of the Regulation where a trust is domiciled.

(2)   A trust is domiciled in the United Kingdom if and only if it is by virtue of sub-paragraph (3) domiciled in a part of the United Kingdom.

(3)   A trust is domiciled in a part of the United Kingdom if and only if the system of law of that part is the system of law with which the trust has its closest and most real connection.

THE FINANCIAL SERVICES AND MARKETS ACT 2000
(LAW APPLICABLE TO CONTRACTS OF INSURANCE) REGULATIONS 2001

SI 2001 NO 2635

PART I

GENERAL

1.   [Omitted].

2.   Interpretation
(1)   In these Regulations—
'the Act' means the Financial Services and Markets Act 2000;
'the 1990 Act' means the Contracts (Applicable Law) Act 1990;
'applicable law', in relation to a contract of insurance, means the law that is applicable to that contract;
'contract of general insurance' and 'contract of long-term insurance' have the meanings given by the Regulated Activities Order;
'EEA State of the commitment' means, in relation to a contract of long-term insurance entered into on a date—
(a)   if the policyholder is an individual, the EEA State in which he resides on that date; or
(b)   otherwise, the EEA State in which the establishment of the policyholder to which the contract relates is situated on that date;
'establishment', in relation to a person ('A'), means—
(a)   A's head office;
(b)   any of A's agencies;
(c)   any of A's branches; or
(d)   any permanent presence of A in an EEA State, which need not take the form of a branch or agency and which may consist of an office managed by A's staff or by a person who is independent of A but has permanent authority to act for A as if he were an agency;
'large risk' has the meaning given by Article 5(d) of the first non-life insurance directive and includes risks specified by paragraph (iii) of that definition insured by professional associations, joint ventures or temporary groups;
'mandatory rules' means the rules from which the law allows no derogation by way of contract;
'the Regulated Activities Order' means the Financial Services and Markets Act 2000 (Regulated Activities) Order 2001.
(2)   References to the EEA State where the risk covered by a contract of insurance is situated are to—
(a)   if the contract relates to buildings or to buildings and their contents (in so far as the contents are covered by the same contract of insurance), the EEA State in which the property is situated;
(b)   if the contract relates to vehicles of any type, the EEA State of registration;
(c)   if the contract covers travel or holidays risks and has a duration of four months or less, the EEA State in which the policyholder entered into the contract;
(d)   in any other case—
(i)   if the policyholder is an individual, the EEA State in which he resides on the date the contract is entered into;
(ii)   otherwise, the EEA State in which the establishment of the policyholder to which the contract relates is situated on that date.

(3)   References to the country in which a person resides are to—
      (a) if he is an individual, the country in which he has his habitual residence;
      (b) in any other case, the country in which he has his central administration.
(4)   Where an EEA State (including the United Kingdom) includes several territorial units, each of which has its own laws concerning contractual obligations, each unit is to be considered as a separate state for the purposes of identifying the applicable law under these Regulations.

3.   **Scope of these Regulations**
(1)   These Regulations do not apply to contracts of reinsurance.
(2)   [Omitted].

PART II
CONTRACTS OF GENERAL INSURANCE

4.   **Applicable law**
(1)   This Part applies to a contract of general insurance which covers risks situated in an EEA State.
(2)   If the policyholder resides in the EEA State in which the risk is situated, the applicable law is the law of that EEA State unless, if such a choice is permitted under the law of that EEA State, the parties to the contract choose the law of another country.
(3)   If the policyholder does not reside in the EEA State in which the risk is situated, the parties to the contract may choose as the applicable law either—
      (a) the law of the EEA State in which the risk is situated; or
      (b) the law of the country in which the policyholder resides.
(4)   If the policyholder carries on a business (including a trade or profession) and the contract covers two or more risks relating to that business which are situated in different EEA States, the freedom of the parties to choose the applicable law conferred by this regulation extends to the law of any of those EEA States and of the country in which the policyholder resides.
(5)   If any of the EEA States referred to in paragraph (3) or (4) grant greater freedom of choice of the applicable law, the parties to the contract may take advantage of that freedom.
(6)   Notwithstanding paragraphs (2) to (4), if the risks covered by the contract are limited to events occurring in one EEA State other than the EEA State in which the risk is situated, the parties may choose the law of the former EEA State as the applicable law.
(7)   Notwithstanding paragraphs (2) to (4), if the risk covered by the contract is a large risk the parties may choose any law as the applicable law.
(8)   Where the foregoing provisions of this regulation allow the parties to the contract to choose the applicable law and if no choice has been made, or no choice has been made which satisfies the requirement set out in regulation 6(1), the applicable law is the law of the country, from amongst those considered in the relevant paragraph ('the relevant countries'), which is most closely connected with the contract; however, where a severable part of the contract has a closer connection with another relevant country, the law applicable to that part is, by way of exception, the law of that relevant country.
(9)   For the purposes of paragraph (8), the contract is rebuttably presumed to be most closely connected with the EEA State in which the risk is situated.

5.   **Mandatory rules**
(1)   Nothing in regulation 4 restricts the application of the mandatory rules of any part of the United Kingdom, irrespective of the applicable law of the contract.

(2)   If the parties to the contract choose the applicable law under regulation 4 and if all the other elements relevant to the situation at the time when the parties make their choice are connected with one EEA State only, the application of the mandatory rules of that EEA State is not prejudiced.

6.   Choice of law

(1)   Any choice made by the parties under regulation 4 must be expressed or demonstrated with reasonable certainty by the terms of the contract or the circumstances of the case.

(2)   Where the parties to the contract may choose the applicable law under regulation 4, and where the risk to which the contract relates is covered by Community co-insurance (within the meaning of Council Directive 78/473/EEC on the coordination of laws, regulations and administrative provisions relating to Community co-insurance), co-insurers other than the leading insurer (within the meaning of that Directive) are not to be treated as parties to the contract.

7.   The 1990 Act

(1)   Subject to the preceding provisions of this Part, the 1990 Act is to be treated as applying to the contract for the purposes of determining the applicable law.

(2)   In determining whether the mandatory rules of another EEA State should be applied in accordance with regulation 5(2) where the parties have chosen the law of a part of the United Kingdom as the applicable law, the 1990 Act is to be treated as applying to the contract.

(3)   In determining what freedom of choice the parties have under the law of a part of the United Kingdom, the 1990 Act is to be treated as applying to the contract.

PART III
CONTRACTS OF LONG-TERM INSURANCE

8.   Applicable law

(1)   This Part applies to a contract of long-term insurance if—

    (a)   where the policyholder is an individual, he resides in an EEA State;

    (b)   otherwise, the establishment of the policyholder to which the contract relates is situated in an EEA State.

(2)   The applicable law is the law of the EEA State of the commitment unless, if such a choice is permitted under the law of that EEA State, the parties choose the law of another country.

(3)   If the policyholder is an individual and resides in one EEA State but is a national or citizen of another, the parties to the contract may choose the law of the EEA State of which he is a national or citizen as the applicable law.

9.   Mandatory rules

Nothing in regulation 8 affects the application of the mandatory rules of any part of the United Kingdom, irrespective of the applicable law of the contract.

10.   The 1990 Act

(1)   Subject to the preceding provisions of this Part, the 1990 Act is to be treated as applying to the contract for the purposes of determining the applicable law.

(2)   In determining what freedom of choice the parties have under the law of a part of the United Kingdom, the 1990 Act is to be treated as applying to the contract.

SECTION III
EUROPEAN UNION MATERIALS

COUNCIL REGULATION NO 44/2001 ON JURISDICTION AND THE RECOGNITION AND ENFORCEMENT IN CIVIL AND COMMERCIAL MATTERS

OJ 2001 L12/1 (16/1/2001)

CHAPTER I
SCOPE

Article 1

(1) This Regulation shall apply in civil and commercial matters whatever the nature of the court or tribunal. It shall not extend, in particular, to revenue, customs or administrative matters.

(2) The Regulation shall not apply to—
   (a) the status or legal capacity of natural persons, rights in property arising out of a matrimonial relationship, wills and succession;
   (b) bankruptcy, proceedings related to the winding up of insolvent companies or other legal persons, judicial arrangements, compositions and analogous proceedings;
   (c) social security;
   (d) arbitration.

(3) In this Regulation the term 'Member State' shall mean Member State with the exception of Denmark.

CHAPTER II
JURISDICTION

SECTION 1
GENERAL PROVISIONS

Article 2

(1) Subject to the provisions of this Regulation, persons domiciled in a Member State shall, whatever their nationality, be sued in the courts of that Member State.

(2) Persons who are not nationals of the Member State in which they are domiciled shall be governed by the rules of jurisdiction applicable to nationals of that State.

Article 3

(1) Persons domiciled in a Member State may be sued in the courts of another Member State only by virtue of the rules set out in Sections 2 to 7 of this Chapter.

(2) In particular the rules of national jurisdiction set out in Annex 1 shall not be applicable as against them.

Article 4

(1) If the defendant is not domiciled in a Member State, the jurisdiction of the courts of each Member State shall, subject to the provisions of Articles 22 and 23, be determined by the law of that Member State.

(2) As against such a defendant, any person domiciled in a Member State may, whatever his nationality, avail himself in that State of the rules of jurisdiction there in force, and in particular those specified in Annex 1, in the same way as the nationals of that State.

SECTION 2
SPECIAL JURISDICTION

Article 5

A person domiciled in a Member State may, in another Member State, be sued—

(1)   (a)   in matters relating to a contract, in the courts for the place of performance of the obligation in question;

        (b)   for the purpose of this provision and unless otherwise agreed, the place of performance of the obligation in question shall be:

            —   in the case of the sale of goods, the place in a Member State where, under the contract, the goods were delivered or should have been delivered;

            —   in the case of the provision of services, the place in a Member State where, under the contract, the services were provided or should have been provided;

        (c)   if subparagraph (b) does not apply then subparagraph (a) applies.

(2)   In matters relating to maintenance, in the courts for the place where the maintenance creditor is domiciled or habitually resident or, if the matter is ancillary to proceedings concerning the status of a person, in the court which, according to its own law, has jurisdiction to entertain those proceedings, unless that jurisdiction is based solely on the nationality of one of the parties.

(3)   In matters relating to tort, delict or quasi-delict, in the courts for the place where the harmful event occurred.

(4)   As regards a civil claim for damages or restitution which is based on an act giving rise to criminal proceedings, in the court seised of those proceedings, to the extent that that court has jurisdiction under its own law to entertain civil proceedings.

(5)   As regards a dispute arising out of the operations of a branch, agency or other establishment, in the courts for the place in which the branch, agency or other establishment is situated.

(6)   As settlor, trustee or beneficiary of a trust created by the operation of a statute, or by a written instrument, or created orally and evidenced in writing, in the courts of the Contracting State in which the trust is domiciled.

(7)   As regards a dispute concerning the payment of remuneration claimed in respect of the salvage of cargo or freight, in the court under the authority of which the cargo and freight in question—

    (a)   has been arrested to secure such payment; or

    (b)   could have been so arrested, but bail or other security has been given,

provided that this provision shall apply only if it is claimed that the defendant has an interest in the cargo or freight or had such an interest at the time of salvage.

Article 6

A person domiciled in a Member State may also be sued—

(1)   Where he is one of a number of defendants, in the courts for the place where any one of them is domiciled, provided the claims are so closely connected that it is expedient to hear and determine them together to avoid the risk of irreconcilable judgments resulting from separate proceedings.

(2)   As a third party in an action on a warranty or guarantee or in any other third party proceedings, in the court seised of the original proceedings, unless these were instituted solely with the objective of removing him from the jurisdiction of the court which would be competent in his case.

(3)   On a counter-claim arising from the same contract or facts on which the original claim was based, in the court in which the original claim is pending.

(4)   In matters relating to a contract, if the action may be combined with an action against the same defendant in matters relating to rights *in rem* in immovable property, in the court of the Member State in which the property is situated.

Article 7

Where by virtue of this Regulation a court of a Member State has jurisdiction in actions relating to liability from the use or operation of a ship, that court, or any other court substituted for this purpose by the internal law of that Member State, shall also have jurisdiction over claims for limitation of such liability.

SECTION 3
JURISDICTION IN MATTERS RELATING TO INSURANCE

Article 8

In matters relating to insurance, jurisdiction shall be determined by this section, without prejudice to the provisions of Articles 4 and 5(5).

Article 9

(1)   An insurer domiciled in a Member State may be sued—
       (a)   in the courts of the Member State where he is domiciled; or
       (b)   in another Member State, in the case of actions brought by the policyholder, the insured or a beneficiary, in the courts for the place where the plaintiff is domiciled;
       (c)   if he is a co-insurer, in the courts of a Member State in which proceedings are brought against the leading insurer.
(2)   An insurer who is not domiciled in a Member State but has a branch, agency or other establishment in one of the Member States shall, in disputes arising out of the operations of the branch, agency or establishment, be deemed to be domiciled in that Member State.

Article 10

In respect of liability insurance or insurance of immovable property, the insurer may in addition be sued in the courts for the place where the harmful event occurred. The same applies if moveable and immovable property are covered by the same insurance policy and both are adversely affected by the same contingency.

Article 11

(1)   In respect of liability insurance, the insurer may also, if the law of the court permits it, be joined in proceedings which the injured party had brought against the insured.
(2)   The provisions of Articles 8, 9 and 10 shall apply to actions brought by the insured party directly against the insurer, where such direct actions are permitted.
(3)   If the law governing such direct actions provides that the policy-holder or the insured may be joined as a party to the action, the same court shall have jurisdiction over them.

Article 12

(1)   Without prejudice to the provisions of Article 11(3), an insurer may bring proceedings only in the courts of the Member State in which the defendant is

domiciled, irrespective of whether he is the policy-holder, the insured or a beneficiary.

(2)   The provisions of this section should not affect the right to bring a counterclaim in the court in which, in accordance with this Section, the original claim is pending.

Article 13

The provisions of this Section may be departed from only by an agreement—
(1)   which is entered into after the dispute has arisen; or
(2)   which allows the policy-holder, the insured or a beneficiary to bring proceedings in courts other than those indicated in this Section; or
(3)   which is concluded between a policy-holder and an insurer, both of whom are domiciled in the same Member State, and which has the effect of conferring jurisdiction on the courts of that State even if the harmful event were to occur abroad, provided that such an agreement is not contrary to the law of that State; or
(4)   which is concluded with a policy-holder who is not domiciled in a Member State, except in so far as the insurance is compulsory or relates to immovable property in a Member State; or
(5)   which relates to a contract of insurance in so far as it covers one or more of the risks set out in Article 14.

Article 14

The following are the risks referred to in Article 13(5)—
(1)   Any loss or damage to—
    (a)   sea-going ships, installations situated offshore or on the high seas, or aircraft, arising from perils which relate to their use for commercial purposes;
    (b)   goods in transit other than passengers' baggage where the transit consists of or includes carriage by such ships or aircraft.
(2)   Any liability, other than for bodily injury to passengers or loss of or damage to their baggage—
    (a)   arising out of the use or operation of ships, installations or aircraft as referred to in point 1(a) above in so far as the law of the Member State in which such aircraft are registered does not prohibit agreements on jurisdiction regarding insurance of such risks;
    (b)   for loss or damage caused by goods in transit as described in point 1(b) above.
(3)   Any financial loss connected with the use or operation of ships, installations or aircraft as referred to in 1(a) above, in particular loss of freight or charter-hire.
(4)   Any risk or interest connected with any of those referred to in points 1 to 3 above.
(5)   notwithstanding points 1 to 4, all 'large risks' as defined in Council Directive 73/239/EEC(7), as amended by Council Directives 88/357/EEC(8) and 90/618/EEC(9), as they may be amended.

SECTION 4
JURISDICTION OVER CONSUMER CONTRACTS

Article 15

(1)   In matters relating to a contract concluded by a person, the consumer, for a purpose which can be regarded as being outside his trade or profession, jurisdiction shall be determined by this Section, without prejudice to the provisions of Article 4 and Article 5(5), if it is—
    (a)   A contract for the sale of goods on instalment credit terms; or

(b)   it is a contract for a loan repayable by instalments, or for any other form of
       credit, made to finance the sale of goods; or
(c)   in all other cases, the contract has been concluded with a person who
       pursues commercial or professional activities in the Member State of the
       consumer's domicile or, by any means, directs such activities to that Member
       State or to several States including that Member State, and the contract falls
       within the scope of such activities.
(2) Where a consumer enters into a contract with a party who is not domiciled in the
     Member State but has a branch, agency or other establishment in one of the
     Member States, that party shall, in disputes arising out of the operations of the
     branch, agency or establishment, be deemed to be domiciled in that State.
(3) This Section shall not apply to a contract of transport other than a contract which,
     for an inclusive price, provides for a combination of travel and accommodation.

Article 16

(1) A consumer may bring proceedings against the other party to a contract either in
     the courts of the Member State in which that party is domiciled or in the courts of
     the Member State in which he is himself domiciled.
(2) Proceedings may be brought against a consumer by the other party to the contract
     only in the courts of the Member State in which the consumer is domiciled.
(3) This Article shall not affect the right to bring a counter-claim in the court in which,
     in accordance with this section, the original claim is pending.

Article 17

The provisions of this section may be departed from only by an agreement—
(1)   which is entered into after the dispute has arisen; or
(2)   which allows the consumer to bring proceedings in courts other than those
       indicated in this Section; or
(3)   which is entered into by the consumer and the other party to the contract, both of
       whom are at the time of conclusion of the contract domiciled or habitually resident
       in the same Member State, and which confers jurisdiction on the courts of that
       Member State, provided that such an agreement is not contrary to the law of that
       Member State.

SECTION 5
JURISDICTION OVER INDIVIDUAL CONTRACTS OF EMPLOYMENT

Article 18

(1) In matters relating to individual contracts of employment, jurisdiction shall be
     determined by this Section, without prejudice to Article 4 and point 5 of Article 5.
(2) Where an employee enters into an individual contract of employment with an
     employer who is not domiciled in a Member State but has a branch, agency or
     other establishment in one of the Member States, the employer shall, in disputes
     arising out of the operations of the branch, agency or establishment, be deemed to
     be domiciled in that Member State.

Article 19

An employer domiciled in a Member State may be sued:
(1)   in the courts of the Member State where he is domiciled; or
(2)   in another Member State:

(a)   in the courts for the place where the employee habitually carries out his work or in the courts for the last place where he did so, or

(b)   if the employee does not or did not habitually carry out his work in any one country, in the courts for the place where the business which engaged the employee is or was situated.

Article 20

(1)   An employer may bring proceedings only in the courts of the Member State in which the employee is domiciled.

(2)   The provisions of this Section shall not affect the right to bring a counter-claim in the court in which, in accordance with this Section, the original claim is pending.

Article 21

The provisions of this Section may be departed from only by an agreement on jurisdiction:

(1)   which is entered into after the dispute has arisen; or

(2)   which allows the employee to bring proceedings in courts other than those indicated in this Section.

SECTION 6
EXCLUSIVE JURISDICTION

Article 22

The following courts shall have exclusive jurisdiction, regardless of domicile—

(1)   In proceedings which have as their object rights *in rem* in immovable property or tenancies of immovable property, the courts of the Member State in which the property is situated.

However, in proceedings which have as their object tenancies of immovable property concluded for temporary private use for a maximum period of six consecutive months, the courts of the Member State in which the defendant is domiciled shall also have jurisdiction, provided that the landlord and the tenant are natural persons and are domiciled in the same Member State.

(2)   In proceedings which have as their object the validity of the constitution, the nullity or the dissolution of companies or other legal persons or associations of natural or legal persons, or the decisions of their organs, the courts of the Member State in which the company, legal person or association has its seat. In order to determine that seat, the court shall apply its rules of private international law.

(3)   In proceedings which have as their object the validity of entries in public registers, the courts of the Member State in which the register is kept.

(4)   In proceedings concerned with the registration or validity of patents, trademarks, designs, or other similar rights required to be deposited or registered, the courts of the Member State in which the deposit or registration has been applied for, has taken place or is under the terms of an international convention deemed to have taken place.

Without prejudice to the jurisdiction of the European Patent Office under the Convention on the Grant of European Patents, signed at Munich on 5 October 1973, the courts of each Member State shall have exclusive jurisdiction, regardless of domicile, in proceedings concerned with the registration or validity of any European patent granted for that State.

(5)   In proceedings concerned with the enforcement of judgments, the courts of the Member State in which the judgment has been or is to be enforced.

SECTION 7
PROROGATION OF JURISDICTION

Article 23

(1)   If the parties, one or more of whom is domiciled in a Member State, have agreed that a court or the courts of a Member State are to have jurisdiction to settle any disputes which have arisen or which may arise in connection with a particular legal relationship, that court or those courts shall have jurisdiction. Such jurisdiction shall be exclusive unless the parties have agreed otherwise.

       Such an agreement conferring jurisdiction shall be either:

    (a)   in writing or evidenced in writing; or

    (b)   in a form which accords with practices which the parties have established between themselves; or

    (c)   in international trade or commerce, in a form which accords with a usage of which the parties are or ought to have been aware and which in such trade or commerce is widely known to, and regularly observed by, parties to contracts of the type involved in the particular trade or commerce concerned.

(2)   Any communication by electronic means which provides a durable record of the agreement shall be equivalent to 'writing'.

(3)   Where such an agreement is concluded by parties, none of whom is domiciled in a Member State, the courts of other Member States shall have no jurisdiction over their disputes unless the court or courts chosen have declined jurisdiction.

(4)   The court or courts of a Member State on which a trust instrument has conferred jurisdiction shall have exclusive jurisdiction in any proceedings brought against a settlor, trustee or beneficiary, if relations between these persons or their rights or obligations under the trust are involved.

(5)   Agreements or provisions of a trust instrument conferring jurisdiction shall have no legal force if they are contrary to Articles 13, 17 or 21, or if the courts whose jurisdiction they purport to exclude have exclusive jurisdiction by virtue of Article 22.

Article 24

Apart from jurisdiction derived from other provisions of this Regulation, a court of a Member State before whom a defendant enters an appearance shall have jurisdiction. This rule shall not apply where appearance was entered solely to contest the jurisdiction, or where another court has exclusive jurisdiction by virtue of Article 22.

SECTION 8
EXAMINATION AS TO JURISDICTION AND ADMISSIBILITY

Article 25

Where a court of a Member State is seised of a claim which is principally concerned with a matter over which the courts of another Member State have exclusive jurisdiction by virtue of Article 22, it shall declare of its own motion that it has no jurisdiction.

Article 26

(1)   Where a defendant domiciled in one Member State is sued in a court of another Member State and does not enter an appearance, the court shall declare of its own motion that it has no jurisdiction unless its jurisdiction is derived from the provisions of this Regulation.

(2)   The court shall stay the proceedings so long as it is not shown that the defendant has been able to receive the document instituting the proceedings or an equivalent document in sufficient time to enable him to arrange for his defence, or that all necessary steps have been taken to this end.

(3)   Article 19 of Council Regulation (EC) No 1348/2000 of 29 May 2000 on the service in the Member States of judicial and extrajudicial documents in civil or commercial matters shall apply instead of the provisions of paragraph 2 if the document instituting the proceedings or an equivalent document had to be transmitted from one Member State to another pursuant to this Regulation.

(4)   Where the provisions of Regulation (EC) No 1348/2000 are not applicable, Article 15 of the Hague Convention of 15 November 1965 on the Service Abroad of Judicial and Extrajudicial Documents in Civil or Commercial Matters shall apply if the document instituting the proceedings or an equivalent document had to be transmitted pursuant to that Convention.

SECTION 9
LIS PENDENS-RELATED ACTIONS

Article 27

(1)   Where proceedings involving the same cause of action and between the same parties are brought in the courts of different Member States, any court other than the court first seised shall of its own motion stay its proceedings until such time as the jurisdiction of the court first seised is established.

(2)   Where the jurisdiction of the court first seised is established, any court other than the court first seised shall decline jurisdiction in favour of that court.

Article 28

(1)   Where related actions are brought in the courts of different Member States, any court other than the court first seised may, while the actions are pending at first instance, stay its proceedings.

(2)   Where these actions are pending at first instance, any court other than the court first seised may also, on the application of one of the parties, decline jurisdiction if the court first seised has jurisdiction over the actions in question and its law permits the consolidation thereof.

(3)   For the purposes of this Article, actions are deemed to be related where they are so closely connected that it is expedient to hear and determine them together to avoid the risk of irreconcilable judgments resulting from separate proceedings.

Article 29

Where actions come within the exclusive jurisdiction of several courts, any court other than the court first seised shall decline jurisdiction in favour of that court.

Article 30

For the purposes of this Section, a court shall be deemed to be seised:

(1)   at the time when the document instituting the proceedings or an equivalent document is lodged with the court, provided that the plaintiff has not subsequently failed to take the steps he was required to take to have service effected on the defendant, or

(2)   if the document has to be served before being lodged with the court, at the time when it is received by the authority responsible for service, provided that the

plaintiff has not subsequently failed to take the steps he was required to take to have the document lodged with the court.

SECTION 10
PROVISIONAL, INCLUDING PROTECTIVE, MEASURES

Article 31

Application may be made to the courts of a Member State for such provisional, including protective, measures as may be available under the law of that State, even if, under this Regulation, the courts of another Member State have jurisdiction as to the substance of the matter.

CHAPTER III
RECOGNITION AND ENFORCEMENT

Article 32

For the purposes of this Regulation, 'judgment' means any judgment given by a court or tribunal of a Member State, whatever the judgment may be called, including a decree, order, decision or writ of execution, as well as the determination of costs or expenses by an officer of the court.

SECTION 1
RECOGNITION

Article 33

(1)   A judgment given in a Member State shall be recognised in the other Member States without any special procedure being required.
(2)   Any interested party who raises the recognition of a judgment as the principal issue in a dispute may, in accordance with the procedures provided for in Sections 2 and 3 of this Chapter, apply for a decision that the judgment be recognised.
        If the outcome of proceedings in a court of a Member State depends on the determination of an incidental question of recognition that court shall have jurisdiction over that question.

Article 34

A judgment shall not be recognised—
(1)   If such recognition is manifestly contrary to public policy in the Member State in which recognition is sought.
(2)   Where it was given in default of appearance, if the defendant was not duly served with the document which instituted the proceedings or with an equivalent document in sufficient time to enable him to arrange for his defence unless the defendant failed to commence proceedings to challenge the judgment when it was possible for him to do so.
(3)   If it is irreconcilable with a judgment given in a dispute between the same parties in the Member State in which recognition is sought.
(4)   If it is irreconcilable with an earlier judgment given in another Member State or in a third State involving the same cause of action and between the same parties, provided that the earlier judgment fulfils the conditions necessary for its recognition in the Member State addressed.

Article 35

(1) Moreover, a judgment shall not be recognised if it conflicts with the provisions of Sections 3, 4 or 5 of Chapter II, or in a case provided for in Article 72.

(2) In its examination of the grounds of jurisdiction referred to in the foregoing paragraph, the court or authority applied to shall be bound by the findings of fact on which the court of the Member State of origin based its jurisdiction.

(3) Subject to paragraph 1, the jurisdiction of the court of the Member State of origin may not be reviewed. The test of public policy referred to in Article 34 may not be applied to the rules relating to jurisdiction.

Article 36

Under no circumstances may a foreign judgment be reviewed as to its substance.

Article 37

(1) A court of a Member State in which recognition is sought of a judgment given in another Member State may stay the proceedings if an ordinary appeal against the judgment has been lodged.

(2) A court of a Member State in which recognition is sought of a judgment given in Ireland or the United Kingdom may stay the proceedings if enforcement is suspended in the State of origin, by reason of an appeal.

SECTION 2
ENFORCEMENT

Article 38

(1) A judgment given in a Member State and enforceable in that State shall be enforced in another Member State when, on the application of any interested party, it has been declared enforceable there.

(2) However, in the United Kingdom, such a judgment shall be enforced in England and Wales, in Scotland, or in Northern Ireland when, on the application of any interested party, it has been registered for enforcement in that part of the United Kingdom.

Articles 35–58 [Omitted].

CHAPTER V
GENERAL PROVISIONS

Article 59

(1) In order to determine whether a party is domiciled in the Member State whose courts are seised of a matter, the Court shall apply its internal law.

(2) If a party is not domiciled in the Member State whose courts are seised of the matter, then, in order to determine whether the party is domiciled in another Member State, the court shall apply the law of that Member State.

Article 60

(1) For the purposes of this Regulation, a company or other legal person or association of natural or legal persons is domiciled at the place where it has its:
   (a) statutory seat, or

     (b)   central administration, or
     (c)   principal place of business.

(2)   For the purposes of the United Kingdom and Ireland 'statutory seat' means the registered office or, where there is no such office anywhere, the place of incorporation or, where there is no such place anywhere, the place under the law of which the formation took place.

(3)   In order to determine whether a trust is domiciled in the Member State whose courts are seised of the matter, the court shall apply its rules of private international law.

Article 61

Without prejudice to any more favourable provisions of national laws, persons domiciled in a Member State who are being prosecuted in the criminal courts of another Member State of which they are not nationals for an offence which was not intentionally committed may be defended by persons qualified to do so, even if they do not appear in person. However, the court seised of the matter may order appearance in person; in the case of failure to appear, a judgment given in the civil action without the person concerned having had the opportunity to arrange for his defence need not be recognised or enforced in the other Member States.

Articles 62–66 [Omitted].

CHAPTER VII
RELATIONS WITH OTHER INSTRUMENTS

Article 67

This Regulation shall not prejudice the application of provisions governing jurisdiction and the recognition and enforcement of judgments in specific matters which are contained in Community instruments or in national legislation harmonised pursuant to such instruments.

Article 68

(1)   This Regulation shall, as between the Member States, supersede the Brussels Convention, except as regards the territories of the Member States which fall within the territorial scope of that Convention and which are excluded from this Regulation pursuant to Article 299 of the Treaty.

(2)   In so far as this Regulation replaces the provisions of the Brussels Convention between Member States, any reference to the Convention shall be understood as a reference to this Regulation.

Articles 69–76 [Omitted].

DIRECTIVE 1999/93/EC OF THE EUROPEAN PARLIAMENT AND OF THE COUNCIL

OF 13 DECEMBER 1999
ON A COMMUNITY FRAMEWORK FOR ELECTRONIC SIGNATURES
OJ 2000/L13/12 (19/1/2000)

Article 1

Scope

The purpose of this Directive is to facilitate the use of electronic signatures and to contribute to their legal recognition. It establishes a legal framework for electronic signatures and certain certification-services in order to ensure the proper functioning of the internal market.

It does not cover aspects related to the conclusion and validity of contracts or other legal obligations where there are requirements as regards form prescribed by national or Community law nor does it affect rules and limits, contained in national or Community law, governing the use of documents.

Article 2

Definitions

For the purpose of this Directive:
1.   'electronic signature' means data in electronic form which are attached to or logically associated with other electronic data and which serve as a method of authentication;
2.   'advanced electronic signature' means an electronic signature which meets the following requirements:
       (a)   it is uniquely linked to the signatory;
       (b)   it is capable of identifying the signatory;
       (c)   it is created using means that the signatory can maintain under his sole control; and
       (d)   it is linked to the data to which it relates in such a manner that any subsequent change of the data is detectable;
3.   'signatory' means a person who holds a signature-creation device and acts either on his own behalf or on behalf of the natural or legal person or entity he represents;
4.   'signature-creation data' means unique data, such as codes or private cryptographic keys, which are used by the signatory to create an electronic signature;
5.   'signature-creation device' means configured software or hardware used to implement the signature-creation data;
6.   'secure-signature-creation device' means a signature-creation device which meets the requirements laid down in Annex III;
7.   'signature-verification-data' means data, such as codes or public cryptographic keys, which are used for the purpose of verifying an electronic signature;
8.   'signature-verification device' means configured software or hardware used to implement the signature-verification-data;
9.   'certificate' means an electronic attestation which links signature-verification data to a person and confirms the identity of that person;
10.   'qualified certificate' means a certificate which meets the requirements laid down in Annex I and is provided by a certification-service-provider who fulfils the requirements laid down in Annex II;
11.   'certification-service-provider' means an entity or a legal or natural person who issues certificates or provides other services related to electronic signatures;

12.   'electronic-signature product' means hardware or software, or relevant components thereof, which are intended to be used by a certification-service-provider for the provision of electronic-signature services or are intended to be used for the creation or verification of electronic signatures;

13.   'voluntary accreditation' means any permission, setting out rights and obligations specific to the provision of certification services, to be granted upon request by the certification-service-provider concerned, by the public or private body charged with the elaboration of, and supervision of compliance with, such rights and obligations, where the certification-service-provider is not entitled to exercise the rights stemming from the permission until it has received the decision by the body.

Article 3

Market access

1.   Member States shall not make the provision of certification services subject to prior authorisation.

2.   Without prejudice to the provisions of paragraph 1, Member States may introduce or maintain voluntary accreditation schemes aiming at enhanced levels of certification-service provision. All conditions related to such schemes must be objective, transparent, proportionate and non-discriminatory. Member States may not limit the number of accredited certification-service-providers for reasons which fall within the scope of this Directive.

3.   Each Member State shall ensure the establishment of an appropriate system that allows for supervision of certification-service-providers which are established on its territory and issue qualified certificates to the public.

4.   The conformity of secure signature-creation-devices with the requirements laid down in Annex III shall be determined by appropriate public or private bodies designated by Member States. The Commission shall, pursuant to the procedure laid down in Article 9, establish criteria for Member States to determine whether a body should be designated.

   A determination of conformity with the requirements laid down in Annex III made by the bodies referred to in the first subparagraph shall be recognised by all Member States.

5.   The Commission may, in accordance with the procedure laid down in Article 9, establish and publish reference numbers of generally recognised standards for electronic-signature products in the *Official Journal of the European Communities*. Member States shall presume that there is compliance with the requirements laid down in Annex II, point (f), and Annex III when an electronic signature product meets those standards.

6.   Member States and the Commission shall work together to promote the development and use of signature-verification devices in the light of the recommendations for secure signature-verification laid down in Annex IV and in the interests of the consumer.

7.   Member States may make the use of electronic signatures in the public sector subject to possible additional requirements. Such requirements shall be objective, transparent, proportionate and non-discriminatory and shall relate only to the specific characteristics of the application concerned. Such requirements may not constitute an obstacle to cross-border services for citizens.

Article 4

Internal market principles

1.   Each Member State shall apply the national provisions which it adopts pursuant to this Directive to certification-service-providers established on its territory and to the services which they provide. Member States may not restrict the provision of

certification-services originating in another Member State in the fields covered by
this Directive.
2.   Member States shall ensure that electronic-signature products which comply with
this Directive are permitted to circulate freely in the internal market.

Article 5

Legal effects of electronic signatures
1.   Member States shall ensure that advanced electronic signatures which are based
on a qualified certificate and which are created by a secure-signature-creation
device:
(a)   satisfy the legal requirements of a signature in relation to data in electronic
form in the same manner as a hand-written signature satisfies those
requirements in relation to paper-based data; and
(b)   are admissible as evidence in legal proceedings.
2.   Member States shall ensure that an electronic signature is not denied legal
effectiveness and admissibility as evidence in legal proceedings solely on the
grounds that it is:
—   in electronic form, or
—   not based upon a qualified certificate, or
—   not based upon a qualified certificate issued by an accredited certification-
service-provider, or
—   not created by a secure signature-creation device.

Article 6

Liability
1.   As a minimum, Member States shall ensure that by issuing a certificate as a
qualified certificate to the public or by guaranteeing such a certificate to the public
a certification-service-provider is liable for damage caused to any entity or legal or
natural person who reasonably relies on that certificate;
(a)   as regards the accuracy at the time of issuance of all information contained in
the qualified certificate and as regards the fact that the certificate contains all
the details prescribed for a qualified certificate;
(b)   for assurance that at the time of the issuance of the certificate, the signatory
identified in the qualified certificate held the signature-creation data
corresponding to the signature-verification data given or identified in the
certificate;
(c)   for assurance that the signature-creation data and the signature-verification
data can be used in a complementary manner in cases where the
certification-service-provider generates them both;
unless the certification-service-provider proves that he has not acted negligently.
2.   As a minimum Member States shall ensure that a certification-service-provider who
has issued a certificate as a qualified certificate to the public is liable for damage
caused to any entity or legal or natural person who reasonably relies on the
certificate for failure to register revocation of the certificate unless the
certification-service-provider proves that he has not acted negligently.
3.   Member States shall ensure that a certification-service-provider may indicate in a
qualified certificate limitations on the use of that certificate, provided that the
limitations are recognisable to third parties. The certification-service-provider shall
not be liable for damage arising from use of a qualified certificate which exceeds
the limitations placed on it.
4.   Member States shall ensure that a certification-service-provider may indicate in the
qualified certificate a limit on the value of transactions for which the certificate can
be used, provided that the limit is recognisable to third parties.

The certification-service-provider shall not be liable for damage resulting from this maximum limit being exceeded.

5. The provisions of paragraphs 1 to 4 shall be without prejudice to Council Directive 93/13/EEC of 5 April 1993 on unfair terms in consumer contracts.

Article 7

International aspects

1. Member States shall ensure that certificates which are issued as qualified certificates to the public by a certification-service-provider established in a third country are recognised as legally equivalent to certificates issued by a certification-service-provider established within the Community if:

   (a) the certification-service-provider fulfils the requirements laid down in this Directive and has been accredited under a voluntary accreditation scheme established in a Member State; or

   (b) a certification-service-provider established within the Community which fulfils the requirements laid down in this Directive guarantees the certificate; or

   (c) the certificate or the certification-service-provider is recognised under a bilateral or multilateral agreement between the Community and third countries or international organisations.

2. In order to facilitate cross-border certification services with third countries and legal recognition of advanced electronic signatures originating in third countries, the Commission shall make proposals, where appropriate, to achieve the effective implementation of standards and international agreements applicable to certification services. In particular, and where necessary, it shall submit proposals to the Council for appropriate mandates for the negotiation of bilateral and multilateral agreements with third countries and international organisations. The Council shall decide by qualified majority.

3. Whenever the Commission is informed of any difficulties encountered by Community undertakings with respect to market access in third countries, it may, if necessary, submit proposals to the Council for an appropriate mandate for the negotiation of comparable rights for Community undertakings in these third countries. The Council shall decide by qualified majority.

   Measures taken pursuant to this paragraph shall be without prejudice to the obligations of the Community and of the Member States under relevant international agreements.

Article 8

Data protection

1. Member States shall ensure that certification-service-providers and national bodies responsible for accreditation or supervision comply with the requirements laid down in Directive 95/46/EC of the European Parliament and of the Council of 24 October 1995 on the protection of individuals with regard to the processing of personal data and on the free movement of such data.

2. Member States shall ensure that a certification-service-provider which issues certificates to the public may collect personal data only directly from the data subject, or after the explicit consent of the data subject, and only insofar as it is necessary for the purposes of issuing and maintaining the certificate. The data may not be collected or processed for any other purposes without the explicit consent of the data subject.

3. Without prejudice to the legal effect given to pseudonyms under national law, Member States shall not prevent certification service providers from indicating in the certificate a pseudonym instead of the signatory's name.

Articles 9—15 [Omitted].

ANNEX I
REQUIREMENTS FOR QUALIFIED CERTIFICATES

Qualified certificates must contain:

(a)   an indication that the certificate is issued as a qualified certificate;
(b)   the identification of the certification-service-provider and the State in which it is established;
(c)   the name of the signatory or a pseudonym, which shall be identified as such;
(d)   provision for a specific attribute of the signatory to be included if relevant, depending on the purpose for which the certificate is intended;
(e)   signature-verification data which correspond to signature-creation data under the control of the signatory;
(f)   an indication of the beginning and end of the period of validity of the certificate;
(g)   the identity code of the certificate;
(h)   the advanced electronic signature of the certification-service-provider issuing it;
(i)   limitations on the scope of use of the certificate, if applicable; and
(j)   limits on the value of transactions for which the certificate can be used, if applicable.

ANNEX II
REQUIREMENTS FOR CERTIFICATION-SERVICE-PROVIDERS ISSUING QUALIFIED CERTIFICATES

Certification-service-providers must:

(a)   demonstrate the reliability necessary for providing certification services;
(b)   ensure the operation of a prompt and secure directory and a secure and immediate revocation service;
(c)   ensure that the date and time when a certificate is issued or revoked can be determined precisely;
(d)   verify, by appropriate means in accordance with national law, the identity and, if applicable, any specific attributes of the person to which a qualified certificate is issued;
(e)   employ personnel who possess the expert knowledge, experience, and qualifications necessary for the services provided, in particular competence at managerial level, expertise in electronic signature technology and familiarity with proper security procedures; they must also apply administrative and management procedures which are adequate and correspond to recognised standards;
(f)   use trustworthy systems and products which are protected against modification and ensure the technical and cryptographic security of the process supported by them;
(g)   take measures against forgery of certificates, and, in cases where the certification-service-provider generates signature-creation data, guarantee confidentiality during the process of generating such data;
(h)   maintain sufficient financial resources to operate in conformity with the requirements laid down in the Directive, in particular to bear the risk of liability for damages, for example, by obtaining appropriate insurance;
(i)   record all relevant information concerning a qualified certificate for an appropriate period of time, in particular for the purpose of providing evidence of certification for the purposes of legal proceedings. Such recording may be done electronically;
(j)   not store or copy signature-creation data of the person to whom the certification-service-provider provided key management services;
(k)   before entering into a contractual relationship with a person seeking a certificate to support his electronic signature inform that person by a durable means of communication of the precise terms and conditions regarding the use of the

certificate, including any limitations on its use, the existence of a voluntary accreditation scheme and procedures for complaints and dispute settlement. Such information, which may be transmitted electronically, must be in writing and in readily understandable language. Relevant parts of this information must also be made available on request to third-parties relying on the certificate;

(l) use trustworthy systems to store certificates in a verifiable form so that:
— only authorised persons can make entries and changes,
— information can be checked for authenticity,
— certificates are publicly available for retrieval in only those cases for which the certificate-holder's consent has been obtained, and
— any technical changes compromising these security requirements are apparent to the operator.

ANNEX III
REQUIREMENTS FOR SECURE SIGNATURE-CREATION DEVICES

1. Secure signature-creation devices must, by appropriate technical and procedural means, ensure at the least that:
   (a) the signature-creation-data used for signature generation can practically occur only once, and that their secrecy is reasonably assured;
   (b) the signature-creation-data used for signature generation cannot, with reasonable assurance, be derived and the signature is protected against forgery using currently available technology;
   (c) the signature-creation-data used for signature generation can be reliably protected by the legitimate signatory against the use of others.
2. Secure signature-creation devices must not alter the data to be signed or prevent such data from being presented to the signatory prior to the signature process.

ANNEX IV
RECOMMENDATIONS FOR SECURE SIGNATURE VERIFICATION

During the signature-verification process it should be ensured with reasonable certainty that:
(a) the data used for verifying the signature correspond to the data displayed to the verifier;
(b) the signature is reliably verified and the result of that verification is correctly displayed;
(c) the verifier can, as necessary, reliably establish the contents of the signed data:
(d) the authenticity and validity of the certificate required at the time of signature verification are reliably verified;
(e) the result of verification and the signatory's identity are correctly displayed;
(f) the use of a pseudonym is clearly indicated; and
(g) any security-relevant changes can be detected.

DIRECTIVE 2000/31/EC OF THE EUROPEAN PARLIAMENT AND OF THE COUNCIL

OF 8 JUNE 2000
ON CERTAIN LEGAL ASPECTS OF INFORMATION SOCIETY SERVICES,
IN PARTICULAR ELECTRONIC COMMERCE, IN THE INTERNAL MARKET
(DIRECTIVE ON ELECTRONIC COMMERCE)
OJ 2000/L178/1 (17/7/2000)

CHAPTER I
GENERAL PROVISIONS

Article 1

Objective and scope
1.   This Directive seeks to contribute to the proper functioning of the internal market
       by ensuring the free movement of information society services between the
       Member States.
2.   This Directive approximates, to the extent necessary for the achievement of the
       objective set out in paragraph 1, certain national provisions on information society
       services relating to the internal market, the establishment of service providers,
       commercial communications, electronic contracts, the liability of intermediaries,
       codes of conduct, out-of-court dispute settlements, court actions and cooperation
       between Member States.
3.   This Directive complements Community law applicable to information society
       services without prejudice to the level of protection for, in particular, public health
       and consumer interests, as established by Community acts and national legislation
       implementing them in so far as this does not restrict the freedom to provide
       information society services.
4.   This Directive does not establish additional rules on private international law nor
       does it deal with the jurisdiction of Courts.
5.   This Directive shall not apply to:
       (a)   the field of taxation;
       (b)   questions relating to information society services covered by Directives 95/46/
              EC and 97/66/EC;
       (c)   questions relating to agreements or practices governed by cartel law;
       (d)   the following activities of information society services:
              —   the activities of notaries or equivalent professions to the extent that they
                    involve a direct and specific connection with the exercise of public
                    authority,
              —   the representation of a client and defence of his interests before the
                    courts,
              —   gambling activities which involve wagering a stake with monetary value
                    in games of chance, including lotteries and betting transactions.
6.   This Directive does not affect measures taken at Community or national level, in
       the respect of Community law, in order to promote cultural and linguistic diversity
       and to ensure the defence of pluralism.

Article 2

Definitions
For the purpose of this Directive, the following terms shall bear the following meanings:
(a)   'information society services': services within the meaning of Article 1(2) of
       Directive 98/34/EC as amended by Directive 98/48/EC;

(b)   'service provider': any natural or legal person providing an information society service;

(c)   'established service provider': a service provider who effectively pursues an economic activity using a fixed establishment for an indefinite period. The presence and use of the technical means and technologies required to provide the service do not, in themselves, constitute an establishment of the provider;

(d)   'recipient of the service': any natural or legal person who, for professional ends or otherwise, uses an information society service, in particular for the purposes of seeking information or making it accessible;

(e)   'consumer': any natural person who is acting for purposes which are outside his or her trade, business or profession;

(f)   'commercial communication': any form of communication designed to promote, directly or indirectly, the goods, services or image of a company, organisation or person pursuing a commercial, industrial or craft activity or exercising a regulated profession. The following do not in themselves constitute commercial communications:
    —   information allowing direct access to the activity of the company, organisation or person, in particular a domain name or an electronic-mail address,
    —   communications relating to the goods, services or image of the company, organisation or person compiled in an independent manner, particularly when this is without financial consideration;

(g)   'regulated profession': any profession within the meaning of either Article 1(d) of Council Directive 89/48/EEC of 21 December 1988 on a general system for the recognition of higher-education diplomas awarded on completion of professional education and training of at least three-years' duration or of Article 1(f) of Council Directive 92/51/EEC of 18 June 1992 on a second general system for the recognition of professional education and training to supplement Directive 89/48/EEC;

(h)   'coordinated field': requirements laid down in Member States' legal systems applicable to information society service providers or information society services, regardless of whether they are of a general nature or specifically designed for them.
    (i)   The coordinated field concerns requirements with which the service provider has to comply in respect of:
        —   the taking up of the activity of an information society service, such as requirements concerning qualifications, authorisation or notification,
        —   the pursuit of the activity of an information society service, such as requirements concerning the behaviour of the service provider, requirements regarding the quality or content of the service including those applicable to advertising and contracts, or requirements concerning the liability of the service provider;
    (ii)   The coordinated field does not cover requirements such as:
        —   requirements applicable to goods as such,
        —   requirements applicable to the delivery of goods,
        —   requirements applicable to services not provided by electronic means.

Article 3

Internal market

1.   Each Member State shall ensure that the information society services provided by a service provider established on its territory comply with the national provisions applicable in the Member State in question which fall within the coordinated field.

2.   Member States may not, for reasons falling within the coordinated field, restrict the freedom to provide information society services from another Member State.

3.   Paragraphs 1 and 2 shall not apply to the fields referred to in the Annex.

4.   Member States may take measures to derogate from paragraph 2 in respect of a given information society service if the following conditions are fulfilled:
      (a)   the measures shall be:
            (i)   necessary for one of the following reasons:
                  —   public policy, in particular the prevention, investigation, detection and prosecution of criminal offences, including the protection of minors and the fight against any incitement to hatred on grounds of race, sex, religion or nationality, and violations of human dignity concerning individual persons,
                  —   the protection of public health,
                  —   public security, including the safeguarding of national security and defence,
                  —   the protection of consumers, including investors;
            (ii) taken against a given information society service which prejudices the objectives referred to in point (i) or which presents a serious and grave risk of prejudice to those objectives;
            (iii) proportionate to those objectives;
      (b)   before taking the measures in question and without prejudice to court proceedings, including preliminary proceedings and acts carried out in the framework of a criminal investigation, the Member State has:
            —   asked the Member State referred to in paragraph 1 to take measures and the latter did not take such measures, or they were inadequate,
            —   notified the Commission and the Member State referred to in paragraph 1 of its intention to take such measures.
5.   Member States may, in the case of urgency, derogate from the conditions stipulated in paragraph 4(b). Where this is the case, the measures shall be notified in the shortest possible time to the Commission and to the Member State referred to in paragraph 1, indicating the reasons for which the Member State considers that there is urgency.
6.   Without prejudice to the Member State's possibility of proceeding with the measures in question, the Commission shall examine the compatibility of the notified measures with Community law in the shortest possible time; where it comes to the conclusion that the measure is incompatible with Community law, the Commission shall ask the Member State in question to refrain from taking any proposed measures or urgently to put an end to the measures in question.

CHAPTER II
PRINCIPLES

SECTION 1: ESTABLISHMENT AND INFORMATION REQUIREMENTS

Article 4

Principle excluding prior authorisation
1.   Member States shall ensure that the taking up and pursuit of the activity of an information society service provider may not be made subject to prior authorisation or any other requirement having equivalent effect.
2.   Paragraph 1 shall be without prejudice to authorisation schemes which are not specifically and exclusively targeted at information society services, or which are covered by Directive 97/13/EC of the European Parliament and of the Council of 10 April 1997 on a common framework for general authorisations and individual licences in the field of telecommunications services.

Article 5

General information to be provided
1.   In addition to other information requirements established by Community law, Member States shall ensure that the service provider shall render easily, directly and permanently accessible to the recipients of the service and competent authorities, at least the following information:
(a)   the name of the service provider;
(b)   the geographic address at which the service provider is established;
(c)   the details of the service provider, including his electronic mail address, which allow him to be contacted rapidly and communicated with in a direct and effective manner;
(d)   where the service provider is registered in a trade or similar public register, the trade register in which the service provider is entered and his registration number, or equivalent means of identification in that register;
(e)   where the activity is subject to an authorisation scheme, the particulars of the relevant supervisory authority;
(f)   as concerns the regulated professions:
       —   any professional body or similar institution with which the service provider is registered,
       —   the professional title and the Member State where it has been granted,
       —   a reference to the applicable professional rules in the Member State of establishment and the means to access them;
(g)   where the service provider undertakes an activity that is subject to VAT, the identification number referred to in Article 22(1) of the sixth Council Directive 77/388/EEC of 17 May 1977 on the harmonisation of the laws of the Member States relating to turnover taxes—Common system of value added tax: uniform basis of assessment.
2.   In addition to other information requirements established by Community law, Member States shall at least ensure that, where information society services refer to prices, these are to be indicated clearly and unambiguously and, in particular, must indicate whether they are inclusive of tax and delivery costs.

SECTION 2: COMMERCIAL COMMUNICATIONS

Article 6

Information to be provided
In addition to other information requirements established by Community law, Member States shall ensure that commercial communications which are part of, or constitute, an information society service comply at least with the following conditions:
(a)   the commercial communication shall be clearly identifiable as such;
(b)   the natural or legal person on whose behalf the commercial communication is made shall be clearly identifiable;
(c)   promotional offers, such as discounts, premiums and gifts, where permitted in the Member State where the service provider is established, shall be clearly identifiable as such, and the conditions which are to be met to qualify for them shall be easily accessible and be presented clearly and unambiguously;
(d)   promotional competitions or games, where permitted in the Member State where the service provider is established, shall be clearly identifiable as such, and the conditions for participation shall be easily accessible and be presented clearly and unambiguously.

Article 7

Unsolicited commercial communication
1.   In addition to other requirements established by Community law, Member States which permit unsolicited commercial communication by electronic mail shall ensure that such commercial communication by a service provider established in their territory shall be identifiable clearly and unambiguously as such as soon as it is received by the recipient.
2.   Without prejudice to Directive 9 7/7/EC and Directive 97/66/EC, Member States shall take measures to ensure that service providers undertaking unsolicited commercial communications by electronic mail consult regularly and respect the opt-out registers in which natural persons not wishing to receive such commercial communications can register themselves.

Article 8

Regulated professions
1.   Member States shall ensure that the use of commercial communications which are part of, or constitute, an information society service provided by a member of a regulated profession is permitted subject to compliance with the professional rules regarding, in particular, the independence, dignity and honour of the profession, professional secrecy and fairness towards clients and other members of the profession.
2.   Without prejudice to the autonomy of professional bodies and associations, Member States and the Commission shall encourage professional associations and bodies to establish codes of conduct at Community level in order to determine the types of information that can be given for the purposes of commercial communication in conformity with the rules referred to in paragraph 1.
3.   When drawing up proposals for Community initiatives which may become necessary to ensure the proper functioning of the Internal Market with regard to the information referred to in paragraph 2, the Commission shall take due account of codes of conduct applicable at Community level and shall act in close cooperation with the relevant professional associations and bodies.
4.   This Directive shall apply in addition to Community Directives concerning access to, and the exercise of, activities of the regulated professions.

SECTION 3: CONTRACTS CONCLUDED BY ELECTRONIC MEANS

Article 9

Treatment of contracts
1.   Member States shall ensure that their legal system allows contracts to be concluded by electronic means. Member States shall in particular ensure that the legal requirements applicable to the contractual process neither create obstacles for the use of electronic contracts nor result in such contracts being deprived of legal effectiveness and validity on account of their having been made by electronic means.
2.   Member States may lay down that paragraph 1 shall not apply to all or certain contracts falling into one of the following categories:
(a)   contracts that create or transfer rights in real estate, except for rental rights;
(b)   contracts requiring by law the involvement of courts, public authorities or professions exercising public authority;
(c)   contracts of suretyship granted and on collateral securities furnished by persons acting for purposes outside their trade, business or profession;
(d)   contracts governed by family law or by the law of succession.

3. Member States shall indicate to the Commission the categories referred to in paragraph 2 to which they do not apply paragraph 1. Member States shall submit to the Commission every five years a report on the application of paragraph 2 explaining the reasons why they consider it necessary to maintain the category referred to in paragraph 2(b) to which they do not apply paragraph 1.

Article 10

Information to be provided

1. In addition to other information requirements established by Community law, Member States shall ensure, except when otherwise agreed by parties who are not consumers, that at least the following information is given by the service provider clearly, comprehensibly and unambiguously and prior to the order being placed by the recipient of the service:
   (a) the different technical steps to follow to conclude the contract;
   (b) whether or not the concluded contract will be filed by the service provider and whether it will be accessible;
   (c) the technical means for identifying and correcting input errors prior to the placing of the order;
   (d) the languages offered for the conclusion of the contract.
2. Member States shall ensure that, except when otherwise agreed by parties who are not consumers, the service provider indicates any relevant codes of conduct to which he subscribes and information on how those codes can be consulted electronically.
3. Contract terms and general conditions provided to the recipient must be made available in a way that allows him to store and reproduce them.
4. Paragraphs 1 and 2 shall not apply to contracts concluded exclusively by exchange of electronic mail or by equivalent individual communications.

Article 11

Placing of the order

1. Member States shall ensure, except when otherwise agreed by parties who are not consumers, that in cases where the recipient of the service places his order through technological means, the following principles apply:
   — the service provider has to acknowledge the receipt of the recipient's order without undue delay and by electronic means,
   — the order and the acknowledgement of receipt are deemed to be received when the parties to whom they are addressed are able to access them.
2. Member States shall ensure that, except when otherwise agreed by parties who are not consumers, the service provider makes available to the recipient of the service appropriate, effective and accessible technical means allowing him to identify and correct input errors, prior to the placing of the order.
3. Paragraph 1, first indent, and paragraph 2 shall not apply to contracts concluded exclusively by exchange of electronic mail or by equivalent individual communications.

SECTION 4: LIABILITY OF INTERMEDIARY SERVICE PROVIDERS

Article 12

'Mere conduit'

1. Where an information society service is provided that consists of the transmission in a communication network of information provided by a recipient of the service, or the provision of access to a communication network, Member States shall

ensure that the service provider is not liable for the information transmitted, on condition that the provider:

    (a)   does not initiate the transmission;

    (b)   does not select the receiver of the transmission; and

    (c)   does not select or modify the information contained in the transmission.

2.   The acts of transmission and of provision of access referred to in paragraph 1 include the automatic, intermediate and transient storage of the information transmitted in so far as this takes place for the sole purpose of carrying out the transmission in the communication network, and provided that the information is not stored for any period longer than is reasonably necessary for the transmission.

3.   This Article shall not affect the possibility for a court or administrative authority, in accordance with Member States' legal systems, of requiring the service provider to terminate or prevent an infringement.

Article 13

'Caching'

1.   Where an information society service is provided that consists of the transmission in a communication network of information provided by a recipient of the service, Member States shall ensure that the service provider is not liable for the automatic, intermediate and temporary storage of that information, performed for the sole purpose of making more efficient the information's onward transmission to other recipients of the service upon their request, on condition that:

    (a)   the provider does not modify the information;

    (b)   the provider complies with conditions on access to the information;

    (c)   the provider complies with rules regarding the updating of the information, specified in a manner widely recognised and used by industry;

    (d)   the provider does not interfere with the lawful use of technology, widely recognised and used by industry, to obtain data on the use of the information; and

    (e)   the provider acts expeditiously to remove or to disable access to the information it has stored upon obtaining actual knowledge of the fact that the information at the initial source of the transmission has been removed from the network, or access to it has been disabled, or that a court or an administrative authority has ordered such removal or disablement.

2.   This Article shall not affect the possibility for a court or administrative authority, in accordance with Member States' legal systems, of requiring the service provider to terminate or prevent an infringement.

Article 14

Hosting

1.   Where an information society service is provided that consists of the storage of information provided by a recipient of the service, Member States shall ensure that the service provider is not liable for the information stored at the request of a recipient of the service, on condition that:

    (a)   the provider does not have actual knowledge of illegal activity or information and, as regards claims for damages, is not aware of facts or circumstances from which the illegal activity or information is apparent; or

    (b)   the provider, upon obtaining such knowledge or awareness, acts expeditiously to remove or to disable access to the information.

2.   Paragraph 1 shall not apply when the recipient of the service is acting under the authority or the control of the provider.

3.   This Article shall not affect the possibility for a court or administrative authority, in accordance with Member States' legal systems, of requiring the service provider to terminate or prevent an infringement, nor does it affect the possibility for Member

States of establishing procedures governing the removal or disabling of access to information.

Article 15

No general obligation to monitor
1.   Member States shall not impose a general obligation on providers, when providing the services covered by Articles 12, 13 and 14, to monitor the information which they transmit or store, nor a general obligation actively to seek facts or circumstances indicating illegal activity.
2.   Member States may establish obligations for information society service providers promptly to inform the competent public authorities of alleged illegal activities undertaken or information provided by recipients of their service or obligations to communicate to the competent authorities, at their request, information enabling the identification of recipients of their service with whom they have storage agreements.

CHAPTER III
IMPLEMENTATION

Article 16

Codes of conduct
1.   Member States and the Commission shall encourage:
   (a)   the drawing up of codes of conduct at Community level, by trade, professional and consumer associations or organisations, designed to contribute to the proper implementation of Articles 5 to 15;
   (b)   the voluntary transmission of draft codes of conduct at national or Community level to the Commission;
   (c)   the accessibility of these codes of conduct in the Community languages by electronic means;
   (d)   the communication to the Member States and the Commission, by trade, professional and consumer associations or organisations, of their assessment of the application of their codes of conduct and their impact upon practices, habits or customs relating to electronic commerce;
   (e)   the drawing up of codes of conduct regarding the protection of minors and human dignity.
2.   Member States and the Commission shall encourage the involvement of associations or organisations representing consumers in the drafting and implementation of codes of conduct affecting their interests and drawn up in accordance with paragraph 1(a). Where appropriate, to take account of their specific needs, associations representing the visually impaired and disabled should be consulted.

Article 17

Out-of-court dispute settlement
1.   Member States shall ensure that, in the event of disagreement between an information society service provider and the recipient of the service, their legislation does not hamper the use of out-of-court schemes, available under national law, for dispute settlement, including appropriate electronic means.
2.   Member States shall encourage bodies responsible for the out-of-court settlement of, in particular, consumer disputes to operate in a way which provides adequate procedural guarantees for the parties concerned.

3.   Member States shall encourage bodies responsible for out-of-court dispute settlement to inform the Commission of the significant decisions they take regarding information society services and to transmit any other information on the practices, usages or customs relating to electronic commerce.

Article 18

Court actions
1.   Member States shall ensure that court actions available under national law concerning information society services' activities allow for the rapid adoption of measures, including interim measures, designed to terminate any alleged infringement and to prevent any further impairment of the interests involved.
2.   The Annex to Directive 98/27/EC shall be supplemented as follows:
        '11.   Directive 2000/31/EC of the European Parliament and of the Council of 8 June 2000 on certain legal aspects on information society services, in particular electronic commerce, in the internal market (Directive on electronic commerce) (OJ L 178, 17.7.2000, p. 1).'

Article 19

Cooperation
1.   Member States shall have adequate means of supervision and investigation necessary to implement this Directive effectively and shall ensure that service providers supply them with the requisite information.
2.   Member States shall cooperate with other Member States; they shall, to that end, appoint one or several contact points, whose details they shall communicate to the other Member States and to the Commission.
3.   Member States shall, as quickly as possible, and in conformity with national law, provide the assistance and information requested by other Member States or by the Commission, including by appropriate electronic means.
4.   Member States shall establish contact points which shall be accessible at least by electronic means and from which recipients and service providers may:
        (a)   obtain general information on contractual rights and obligations as well as on the complaint and redress mechanisms available in the event of disputes, including practical aspects involved in the use of such mechanisms;
        (b)   obtain the details of authorities, associations or organisations from which they may obtain further information or practical assistance.
5.   Member States shall encourage the communication to the Commission of any significant administrative or judicial decisions taken in their territory regarding disputes relating to information society services and practices, usages and customs relating to electronic commerce. The Commission shall communicate these decisions to the other Member States.

Article 20

Sanctions
Member States shall determine the sanctions applicable to infringements of national provisions adopted pursuant to this Directive and shall take all measures necessary to ensure that they are enforced. The sanctions they provide for shall be effective, proportionate and dissuasive.

ANNEX
DEROGATIONS FROM ARTICLE 3

As provided for in Article 3(3), Article 3(1) and (2) do not apply to:

- copyright, neighbouring rights, rights referred to in Directive 87/54/EEC and Directive 96/9/EC as well as industrial property rights,
- the emission of electronic money by institutions in respect of which Member States have applied one of the derogations provided for in Article 8(1) of Directive 2000/46/EC,
- Article 44(2) of Directive 85/611/EEC,
- Article 30 and Title IV of Directive 92/49/EEC, Title IV of Directive 92/96/EEC, Articles 7 and 8 of Directive 88/357/EEC and Article 4 of Directive 90/619/EEC,
- the freedom of the parties to choose the law applicable to their contract,
- contractual obligations concerning consumer contacts,
- formal validity of contracts creating or transferring rights in real estate where such contracts are subject to mandatory formal requirements of the law of the Member State where the real estate is situated,
- the permissibility of unsolicited commercial communications by electronic mail.

SECTION IV
CONVENTIONS

GENEVA PROTOCOL ON ARBITRATION CLAUSES 1923

See the First Schedule to the Arbitration Act 1950 for text of the Convention.

INTERNATIONAL CONVENTION FOR THE UNIFICATION OF CERTAIN RULES RELATING TO BILLS OF LADING, BRUSSELS, 1924 (THE HAGUE RULES)

Article 1

In this convention the following words are employed with the meanings set out below—
(a)   'carrier' includes the owner of the vessel or the charterer who enters into a contract of carriage with a shipper;
(b)   'contract of carriage' applies only to contracts of carriage covered by a bill of lading or any similar document of title, in so far as such document relates to the carriage of goods by sea; it also applies to any bill of lading or any similar document as aforesaid issued under or pursuant to a charter party from the moment at which such instrument regulates the relations between a carrier and a holder of the same;
(c)   'goods' includes goods, wares, merchandise, and articles of every kind whatsoever except live animals and cargo which by the contract of carriage is stated as being carried on deck and is so carried;
(d)   'ship' means any vessel used for the carriage of goods by sea;
(e)   'carriage of goods' covers the period from the time when the goods are loaded on to the time they are discharged from the ship.

Article 2

Subject to the provisions of Article 6, under every contract of carriage of goods by sea the carrier, in relation to the loading, handling, stowage, carriage, custody, care, and discharge of such goods shall be subject to the responsibilities and liabilities, and entitled to the rights and immunities hereinafter set forth.

Article 3

1.   The carrier shall be bound before and at the beginning of the voyage to exercise due diligence to—
(a)   make the ship seaworthy;
(b)   properly man, equip, and supply the ship;
(c)   make the holds, refrigerating and cool chambers, and all other parts of the ship in which goods are carried, fit and safe for their reception, carriage, and preservation.
2.   Subject to the provisions of Article 4, the carrier shall properly and carefully load, handle, stow, carry, keep, care for, and discharge the goods carried.
3.   After receiving the goods into his charge, the carrier or the master or agent of the carrier shall, on demand of the shipper, issue to the shipper a bill of lading showing among other things—
(a)   the leading marks necessary for identification of the goods as the same are furnished in writing by the shipper before the loading of such goods starts, provided such marks are stamped or otherwise shown clearly upon the goods if uncovered, or on the cases or coverings in which such goods are contained, in such a manner as should ordinarily remain legible until the end of the voyage;

    (b)   either the number of packages or pieces, or the quantity; or weight, as the case may be, as furnished in writing by the shipper;

    (c)   the apparent order and condition of the goods.

Provided that no carrier, master, or agent of the carrier shall be bound to state or show in the bill of lading any marks, number, quantity, or weight which he has reasonable grounds for suspecting not accurately to represent the goods actually received or which he has had no reasonable means of checking.

4.   Such a bill of lading shall be *prima facie* evidence of the receipt by the carrier of the goods as therein described in accordance with paragraph 3(a), (b) and (c).

5.   The shipper shall be deemed to have guaranteed to the carrier the accuracy at the time of shipment of the marks, number, quantity, and weight, as furnished by him, and the shipper shall indemnify the carrier against all loss, damages, and expenses arising or resulting from inaccuracies in such particulars. The right of the carrier to such indemnity shall in no way limit his responsibility and liability under the contract of carriage to any person other than the shipper.

6.   Unless notice of loss or damage and the general nature of such loss or damage be given in writing to the carrier or his agent at the port of discharge before or at the time of the removal of the goods into the custody of the person entitled to delivery thereof under the contract of carriage, such removal shall be *prima facie* evidence of the delivery by the carrier of the goods as described in the bill of lading.

If the loss or damage is not apparent, the notice must be given within three days of the delivery.

The notice in writing need not be given if the state of the goods has at the time of their receipt been the subject of joint survey or inspection.

In any event the carrier and the ship shall be discharged from all liability in respect of loss or damage unless suit is brought within one year after delivery of the goods or the date when the goods should have been delivered.

In the case of any actual or apprehended loss or damage the carrier and the receiver shall give all reasonable facilities to each other for inspecting and tallying the goods.

7.   After the goods are loaded, the bill of lading to be issued by the carrier, master, or agent of the carrier to the shipper shall, if the shipper so demands, be a 'shipped' bill of lading, provided that if the shipper shall have previously taken up any document of title to such goods, he shall surrender the same as against the issue of the 'shipped' bill of lading. At the option of the carrier such document of title may be noted at the port of shipment by the carrier, master, or agent with the name or names of the ship or ships upon which he goods have been shipped and the date or dates of shipment, and when so noted, if it shows the particulars mentioned in paragraph 3 or Article 3, it shall for the purpose of this Article be deemed to constitute a 'shipped' bill of lading.

8.   Any clause, covenant, or agreement in a contract of carriage relieving the carrier or the ship from liability for loss or damage to or in connection with goods arising from negligence, fault, or failure in the duties and obligations provided in this Article, or lessening such liability otherwise than as provided in this convention, shall be null and void and of no effect. A benefit of insurance in favour of the carrier or similar clause shall be deemed to be a clause relieving the carrier from liability.

Article 4

1.   Neither the carrier nor the ship shall be liable for loss or damage arising or resulting from unseaworthiness unless caused by want of due diligence on the part of the carrier to make the ship seaworthy and to secure that the ship is properly manned, equipped, and supplied and to make the holds, refrigerating and cool chambers, and all other parts of the ship in which goods are carried fit and safe for their reception, carriage, and preservation in accordance with the provisions of

paragraph 1 of Article 3. Whenever loss or damage has resulted from unseaworthiness, the burden of proving the exercise of due diligence shall be on the carrier or other person claiming exemption under this Article.

2. Neither the carrier nor the ship shall be responsible for loss or damage arising or resulting from—

    (a) act, neglect, or default of the master, mariner, pilot, or the servants of the carrier in the navigation or in the management of the ship;

    (b) fire, unless caused by the actual fault or privity of the carrier;

    (c) perils, dangers, and accidents of the sea or other navigable waters;

    (d) act of God;

    (e) act of war;

    (f) act of public enemies;

    (g) arrest or restraint of princes, rulers, or people or seizure under legal process;

    (h) quarantine restrictions;

    (i) Act or omission of the shipper or owner of the goods, his agent, or representative;

    (j) strikes or lock-outs or stoppage or restraint of labour from whatever cause, whether partial or general;

    (k) riots and civil commotions;

    (l) saving or attempting to save life or property at sea;

    (m) wastage in bulk or weight or any other loss or damage arising from inherent defect, quality, or vice of the goods;

    (n) insufficiency of packing;

    (o) insufficiency or inadequacy of marks;

    (p) latent defects not discoverable by due diligence;

    (q) any other cause arising without the actual fault or privity of the carrier, or without the fault or neglect of the agents or servants of the carrier, but the burden of proof shall be on the person claiming the benefit of this exception to show that neither the actual fault or privity of the carrier nor the fault or neglect of the agents or servants of the carrier contributed to the loss or damage.

3. The shipper shall not be responsible for loss or damage sustained by the carrier or the ship arising or resulting from any cause without the act, fault, or neglect of the shipper, his agents, or his servants.

4. Any deviation in saving or attempting to save a life or property at sea or any reasonable deviation shall not be deemed to be an infringement or breach of this convention or of the contract of carriage, and the carrier shall not be liable for any loss or damage resulting therefrom.

5. Neither the carrier nor the ship shall in any event be or become liable for any loss or damage to or in connection with goods in an amount exceeding 100 pounds sterling per package or unit or the equivalent of that sum in other currency unless the nature and value of such goods have been declared by the shipper before shipment and inserted in the bill of lading.

    This declaration if embodied in the bill of lading shall be *prima facie* evidence but shall not be binding or conclusive on the carrier.

    By agreement between the carrier, master, or agent of the carrier and the shipper another maximum amount than that mentioned in this paragraph may be fixed, provided that such maximum shall not be less than the figure above named.

    Neither the carrier nor the ship shall be responsible in any event for loss or damage to, or in connection with, goods if the nature or value thereof has been knowingly mis-stated by the shipper in the bill of lading.

6. Goods of an inflammable, explosive, or dangerous nature to the shipment whereof the carrier, master, or agent of the carrier has not consented with knowledge of their nature and character may at any time before discharge be landed at any place or destroyed or rendered innocuous by the carrier without compensation, and the shipper of such goods shall be liable for all damages and expenses directly or

indirectly arising out of or resulting from such shipment. If any such goods shipped with such knowledge and consent shall become a danger to the ship or cargo, they may in like manner be landed at any place or destroyed or rendered innocuous by the carrier without liability on the part of the carrier except to general average, if any.

Article 5

A carrier shall be at liberty to surrender in whole or in part all or any of his rights and immunities, or to increase any of his responsibilities and liabilities under this convention provided such surrender or increase shall be embodied in the bill of lading issued to the shipper.

The provisions of this convention shall not be applicable to charter-parties, but if bills of lading are issued in the case of a ship under a charter-party they shall comply with the terms of this convention. Nothing in these rules shall be held to prevent the insertion in a bill of lading of any lawful provision regarding general average.

Article 6

Notwithstanding the provisions of the preceding Articles, a carrier, master, or agent of the carrier and a shipper shall in regard to any particular goods be at liberty to enter into any agreement in any terms as to the responsibility and liability of the carrier for such goods, and as to the rights and immunities of the carrier in respect of such goods, or concerning his obligation as to seaworthiness so far as this stipulation is not contrary to public policy, or concerning the care or diligence of his servants or agents in regard to the loading, handling, stowage, carriage, custody, care, and discharge of the goods carried by sea, provided that in this case no bill of lading has been or shall be issued and that the terms agreed shall be embodied in a receipt which shall be a non-negotiable document and shall be marked as such.

Any agreement so entered into shall have full legal effect—

Provided that this Article shall not apply to ordinary commercial shipments made in the ordinary course of trade, but only to other shipments where the character or condition of the property to be carried or the circumstances, terms, and conditions under which the carriage is to be performed are such as reasonably to justify a special agreement.

Article 7

Nothing herein contained shall prevent a carrier or a shipper from entering into any agreement stipulation, condition, reservation, or exemption as to the responsibility and liability of the carrier or the ship for the loss or damage to, or in connection with, the custody and care and handling of goods prior to the loading on, and subsequent to the discharge from, the ship on which the goods are carried by sea.

Article 8

The provisions of this convention shall not affect the rights and obligations of the carrier under any statute for the time being in force relating to the limitation of the liability of owners of seagoing vessels.

Article 9

The monetary units mentioned in this convention are to be taken to be gold value. Those contracting states in which the pound sterling is not a monetary unit reserve to themselves the right of translating the sums indicated in this convention in terms of pound sterling into terms of their own monetary system in round figures. The national laws may reserve to the debtor the right of discharging his debt in national currency according to the rate of exchange prevailing on the day of their arrival of the ship at the port of discharge of the goods concerned.

Article 10

The provisions of this convention shall apply to all bills of lading issued in any of the Contracting States.

Articles 11–16 [Omitted].

GENEVA CONVENTION ON THE EXECUTION OF FOREIGN ARBITRAL AWARDS 1927

See the Second Schedule to the Arbitration Act 1950 for text of the Convention.

CONVENTION FOR THE UNIFICATION OF CERTAIN RULES RELATING TO INTERNATIONAL CARRIAGE BY AIR, WARSAW, 1929 (WARSAW CONVENTION)

CHAPTER I
SCOPE—DEFINITIONS

Article 1

1. This Convention applies to all international carriage of persons, luggage or goods performed by aircraft for reward. It applies equally to gratuitous carriage by aircraft performed by an air transport undertaking.

2. For the purpose of this Convention the expression 'international carriage' means any carriage in which, according to the contract made by the parties, the place of departure and the place of destination, whether or not there be a break in the carriage or a transhipment, are situated either within the territories of two High Contracting Parties, or within the territory of a single High Contracting party, if there is an agreed stopping place within a territory subject to the sovereignty, suzerainty, mandate or authority of another Power, even though that Power is not a party to this convention. A carriage without such an agreed stopping place between territories subject to the sovereignty, suzerainty, mandate or authority of the same High Contracting Party is not deemed to be international for the purposes of this Convention.

3. A carriage to be performed by several successive air carriers is deemed, for the purposes of this convention, to be one undivided carriage, if it has been regarded by the parties as a single operation, whether it had been agreed upon under the form of a single contract or of a series of contracts, and it does not lose its international character merely because one contract or a series of contracts is to be performed entirely within a territory subject to the sovereignty, suzerainty, mandate or authority of the same High Contracting Party.

Article 2

1. This Convention applies to carriage performed by the State or by legally constituted public bodies provided it falls within the conditions laid down in Article 1.

2.   This Convention does not apply to carriage performed under the terms of any international postal Convention.

CHAPTER II
DOCUMENTS OF CARRIAGE

SECTION 1— PASSENGER TICKET

Article 3 [Omitted].

SECTION 2—LUGGAGE TICKET

Article 4 [Omitted].

SECTION 3—AIR CONSIGNMENT NOTE

Article 5

1.   Every carrier of goods has the right to require the consignor to make out and over to him a document called an 'air consignment note'; every consignor has the right to require the carrier to accept this document.
2.   The absence, irregularity or loss of this document does not affect the existence or the validity of the contract of carriage which shall, subject to the provisions of Article 9, be none the less governed by the rules of this Convention.

Article 6

1.   The air consignment note shall be made out by the consignor in three original parts and be handed over with the goods.
2.   The first part shall be marked 'for the carrier,' and shall be signed by the consignor. The second part shall be marked 'for the consignee', it shall be signed by the consignor and by the carrier and shall accompany the goods. The third part shall be signed by the carrier and handed by him to the consignor after the goods have been accepted.
3.   The carrier shall sign on acceptance of the goods.
4.   The signature of the carrier may be stamped; that of the consignor may be printed or stamped.
5.   If, at the request of the consignor, the carrier makes out the air consignment note, he shall be deemed, subject to proof to the contrary, to have done so on behalf of the consignor.

Article 7

The carrier of goods has the right to require the consignor to make out separate consignment notes when there is more than one package.

Article 8

The air consignment note shall contain the following particulars—
(a)   the place and date of its execution;
(b)   the place of departure and of destination;
(c)   the agreed stopping places, provided that the carrier may reserve the right to alter the stopping places in case of necessity, and that if he exercises that right the alteration shall not have the affect of depriving the carriage of its international character;

(d) the name and address of the consignor;
(e) the name and address of the first carrier;
(f) the name and address of the consignee, if the case so requires;
(g) the nature of the goods;
(h) the number of the packages, the method of packing and the particular marks or numbers upon them;
(i) the weight, the quantity and the volume or dimensions of the goods;
(j) the apparent condition of the goods and of the packing;
(k) the freight, if it has been agreed upon, the date and place of payment, and the person who is to pay it;
(l) if the goods are sent for payment on delivery, the price of the goods, and, if the case so requires, the amount of the expenses incurred;
(m) the amount of the value declared in accordance with Article 22(2);
(n) the number of parts of the air consignment note;
(o) the document handed to the carrier to accompany the air consignment note;
(p) the time fixed for the completion of the carriage and a brief note of the route to be followed, if these matters have been agreed upon;
(q) a statement that the carriage is subject to the rules relating to liability established by this Convention.

Article 9

If the carrier accepts goods without an air consignment note having been made out, or if the air consignment note does not contain all the particulars set out in Article 8 (a) to (i) inclusive and (q), the carrier shall not be entitled to avail himself of the provisions of this Convention which exclude or limit his liability.

Article 10

1. The consignor is responsible for the correctness of the particulars and statements relating to the goods which he inserts in the air consignment note.
2. The consignor will be liable for all damage suffered by the carrier or any other person by reason of the irregularity, incorrectness or incompleteness of the said particulars and statements.

Article 11

1. The air consignment note is *prima facie* evidence of the conclusion of the contract, of the receipt of the goods and of the conditions of carriage.
2. The statements in the air consignment note relating to the weight, dimensions and packing of the goods, as well as those relating to the number of packages, are *prima facie* evidence of the facts stated; those relating to the quantity, volume and condition of the goods do not constitute evidence against the carrier except so far as they both have been, and are stated in the air consignment note to have been, checked by him in the presence of the consignor, or relate to the apparent condition of the goods.

Article 12

1. Subject to his liability to carry out all his obligations under the contract of carriage, the consignor has the right to dispose of the goods by withdrawing them at the aerodrome of departure or destination, or by stopping them in the course of the journey on any landing, or by calling for them to be delivered at the place of destination or in the course of the journey to a person other than the consignee named in the air consignment note, or by requiring them to be returned to the aerodrome of departure. He must not exercise this right of disposition in such a

way as to prejudice the carrier or other consignors and he must repay any expenses occasioned by the exercise of this right.

2.   If it is impossible to carry out the orders of the consignor the carrier must so inform him forthwith.

3.   If the carrier obeys the orders of the consignor for the disposition of the goods without requiring the production of the part of the air consignment note delivered to the latter, he will be liable, without prejudice to his right of recovery from the consignor, for any damage which may be caused thereby to any person who is lawfully in possession of that part of the air consignment note.

4.   The right conferred on the consignor ceases at the moment when that of the consignee begins in accordance with Article 13. Nevertheless, if the consignee declines to accept the consignment note or the goods, or if he cannot be communicated with, the consignor resumes his right of disposition.

Article 13

1.   Except in the circumstances set out in the preceding Article, the consignee is entitled, on arrival of the goods at the place of destination, to require the carrier to hand over to him the air consignment note and to deliver the goods to him, on payment of the charges due and on complying with the conditions of carriage set out in the air consignment note.

2.   Unless it is otherwise agreed, it is the duty of the carrier to give notice to the consignee as soon as the goods arrive.

3.   If the carrier admits the loss of the goods have not arrived at the expiration of seven days after date on which they ought to have arrived, the consignee is entitled to put into force against the carrier the rights which flow from the contract of carriage.

Article 14

The consignor and the consignee can respectively enforce all the rights given them by Articles 12 and 13, each in his own name, whether he is acting in his own interest or in the interest of another, provided that he carries out the obligations imposed by the contract.

Article 15

1.   Articles 12, 13 and 14 do not affect either the relations of the consignor or the consignee with each other or the mutual relations of third parties whose rights are derived either from the consignor or from the consignee.

2.   The provisions of Articles 12, 13 and 14 can only be varied by express provision in the air consignment note.

Article 16

1.   The consignor must furnish such information and attach to the air consignment note such documents as are necessary to meet the formalities of customs, octroi or police before the goods can be delivered to the consignee. The consignor is liable to the carrier for any damage occasioned by the absence, insufficiency or irregularity of any such information or documents, unless the damage is due to the fault of the carrier or his agents.

2.   The carrier is under no obligation to enquire into the correctness or sufficiency of such information or documents.

CHAPTER III
LIABILITY OF THE CARRIER

Article 17

The carrier is liable for damage sustained in the event of the death or wounding of a passenger or any other bodily injury suffered by a passenger, if the accident which caused the damage so sustained took place on board the aircraft or in the course of any of the operations of embarking or disembarking.

Article 18

1. The carrier is liable for damage sustained in the event of the destruction or loss of, or of damage to, any registered luggage or any goods, if the occurrence which caused the damage so sustained took place during the carriage by air.
2. The carriage by air within the meaning for the preceding paragraph comprises the period during which the luggage or goods are in charge of the carrier, whether in an aerodrome or on board an aircraft, or, in the case of a landing outside an aerodrome, in any place whatsoever.
3. The period of the carriage by air does not extend to any carriage by land, by sea or by river performed outside an aerodrome. If, however, such a carriage takes place in the performance of a contract for carriage by air, for the purpose of loading, delivery or trans-shipment, any damage is presumed, subject to proof to the contrary, to have been the result of an event which took place during the carriage by air.

Article 19

The carrier is liable for damage occasioned by delay in the carriage by air of passengers, luggage or goods.

Article 20

1. The carrier is not liable if he proves that he and his agents have taken all necessary measures to avoid the damage or that it was impossible for him or them to take such measures.
2. In the carriage of goods and luggage the carrier is not liable if he proves that the damage was occasioned by negligent pilotage or negligence in the handling of the aircraft or in navigation and that, in all other respects, he and his agents have taken all necessary measures to avoid the damage.

Article 21

If the carrier proves that the damage was caused by or contributed to by the negligence of the injured person the court may, in accordance with the provisions of its own law, exonerate the carrier wholly or partly from his liability.

Article 22

1. In the carriage of passengers the liability of the carrier for each passenger is limited to the sum of 125,000 francs. Where, in accordance with the law of the Court seised of the case, damages may be awarded in the form of periodical payments, the equivalent capital value of the said payment shall not exceed 125,000 francs. Nevertheless, by special contract, the carrier and the passenger may agree to a higher limit of liability.

2.   In the carriage of registered luggage and of goods, the liability of the carrier is limited to a sum of 250 francs per kilogram, unless the consignor has made, at the time when the package was handed over to the carrier, a special declaration of the value at delivery and has paid a supplementary sum if the case so requires. In that case the carrier will be liable to pay a sum not exceeding the declared sum, unless he proves that the sum is greater than the actual value to the consignor at delivery.

3.   As regards objects of which the passenger takes charge himself the liability of the carrier is limited to 5000 francs per passenger.

4.   The sums mentioned above shall be deemed to refer to the French franc consisting of 65 1/2 milligrams gold of millesimal fineness 900. These sums may be converted into any national currency in round figures.

Article 23

Any provision tending to relieve the carrier of liability or to fix a lower limit than that which is laid down in this convention shall be null and void, but the nullity of any such provision does not involve the nullity of the whole contract, which shall remain subject to the provisions of this Convention.

Article 24

1.   In the cases covered by Articles 18 and 19 any action for damages, however founded, can only be brought subject to the conditions and limits set out in this Convention.

2.   In the cases covered by Article 17 the provisions of the preceding paragraph also apply, without prejudice to the questions as to who are the persons who have the right to bring suit and what are their respective rights.

Article 25

1.   The carrier shall not be entitled to avail himself of the provisions of this Convention which exclude or limit his liability, if the damage is caused by his wilful misconduct or by such default on his part as, in accordance with the law of the Court seised of the case, is considered to be equivalent to wilful misconduct.

2.   Similarly the carrier shall not be entitled to avail himself of the said provisions, if the damage is caused as aforesaid by any agent of the carrier acting within the scope of his employment.

Article 26

1.   Receipt by the person entitled to delivery of luggage or goods without complaint is *prima facie* evidence that the same have been delivered in good condition and in accordance with the document of carriage.

2.   In the case of damage, the person entitled to delivery must complain to the carrier forthwith after the discovery of the damage, and, at the latest, within three days from the date of receipt in the case of luggage and seven days from the date of receipt in the case of goods. In the case of delay the complaint must be made at the latest within fourteen days from the date on which the luggage or goods have been placed at his disposal.

3.   Every complaint must be made in writing upon the document of carriage or by separate notice in writing despatched within the times aforesaid.

4.   Failing complaint within the times aforesaid, no action shall lie against the carrier, save in the case of fraud on his part.

Article 27

In the case of the death of the person liable, an action for damages lies in accordance with the terms of this Convention against those legally representing his estate.

Article 28

1.   An action for damages must be brought, at the option of the plaintiff, in the territory of one of the High Contracting Parties, either before the Court having jurisdiction where the carrier is ordinarily resident, or has his principal place of business, or has an establishment by which the contract has been made or before the Court having jurisdiction at the place of destination.
2.   Questions of procedure shall be governed by the law of the Court seised of the case.

Article 29

1.   The right to damages shall be extinguished if an action is not brought within two years, reckoned from the date of arrival at the destination, or from the date on which the aircraft ought to have arrived, or from the date on which the carriage stopped.
2.   The method of calculating the period of limitation shall be determined by the law of the Court seised of the case.

Article 30

1.   In the case of carriage to be performed by various successive carriers and falling within the definition set out in the third paragraph of Article I, each carrier who accepts passengers, luggage or goods is subjected to the rules set out in this Convention, and is deemed to be one of the contracting parties to the contract of carriage in so far as the contract deals with that part of the carriage which is performed under his supervision.
2.   In the case of carriage of this nature, the passenger or his representative can take action only against the carrier who performed the carriage during which the accident or the delay occurred, save in the case where, by express agreement, the first carrier has assumed liability for the whole journey.
3.   As regards luggage or goods, the passenger or consignor will have a right of action against the first carrier, and the passenger or consignee who is entitled to delivery will have a right of action against the last carrier, and further, each may take action against the carrier who performed the carriage during which the destruction, loss, damage or delay took place. These carriers will be jointly and severally liable to the passenger or to the consignor or consignee.

CHAPTER IV
PROVISIONS TO COMBINED CARRIAGE

Article 31

1.   In the case of combined carriage performed partly by air and partly by any other mode of carriage, the provisions of the Convention apply only to the carriage by air, provided that the carriage by air falls within the terms of Article 1.
2.   Nothing in this Convention shall prevent the parties in the case of combined carriage from inserting in the document of air carriage conditions relating to other modes of carriage, provided that the provisions of this Convention are observed as regards the carriage by air.

CHAPTER V
GENERAL AND FINAL PROVISIONS

Article 32

Any clause contained in the contract and all special agreements entered into before the damage occurred by which the parties purport to infringe the rules laid down by this Convention, whether by deciding the law to be applied, or by altering the rules as to jurisdiction, shall be null and void. Nevertheless for the carriage of goods arbitration clauses are allowed, subject to this Convention, if the arbitration is to take place within one of the jurisdictions referred to in the first paragraph of Article 28.

Article 33

Nothing contained in this Convention shall prevent the carrier either from refusing to enter into any contract of carriage, or from making regulations which do not conflict with the provisions of this Convention.

Article 34

This Convention does not apply to international carriage by air performed by way of experimental trial by air navigation undertakings with the view to the establishment of a regular line of air navigation, nor does it apply to carriage performed in extraordinary circumstances outside the normal scope of an air carrier's business.

Article 35

The expression 'days' when used in this Convention means current days not working days.

Articles 36–41 [Omitted].

CONVENTION PROVIDING A UNIFORM LAW FOR BILLS OF EXCHANGE AND PROMISSORY NOTES, GENEVA, 1930

Articles I–XI [Omitted].

ANNEX I
UNIFORM LAW ON BILLS OF EXCHANGE AND PROMISSORY NOTES

TITLE I
BILLS OF EXCHANGE

CHAPTER I
ISSUE AND FORM OF A BILL OF EXCHANGE

Article 1

A bill of exchange contains—
1.   the term 'bill of exchange' inserted in the body of the instrument and expressed in the language employed in drawing up the instrument;
2.   an unconditional order to pay a determinate sum of money;

3.   the name of the person who is to pay (drawee);
4.   a statement of the time of payment;
5.   a statement of the place where payment is to be made;
6.   the name of the person to whom or to whose order payment is to be made;
7.   a statement of the date and of the place where the bill is issued;
8.   the signature of the person who issues the bill (drawer).

Article 2

An instrument in which any of the requirements mentioned in the preceding Article is
wanting is invalid as a bill of exchange, except in the cases specified in the following
paragraphs —
    A bill of exchange in which the time of payment is not specified is deemed to be
payable at sight.
    In default of special mention, the place specified beside the name of the drawee is
deemed to be the place of payment, and at the same time the place of the domicile of the
drawee.
    A bill of exchange which does not mention the place of its issue is deemed to have
been drawn in the place mentioned beside the name of the drawer.

Article 3

A bill of exchange may be drawn payable to drawer's order.
    It may be drawn on the drawer himself.
    It may be drawn for account of a third person.

Article 4

A bill of exchange may be payable at the domicile of a third person either in the locality
where the drawee has his domicile or in another locality.

Article 5

When a bill of exchange is payable at sight, or at a fixed period after sight, the drawer may
stipulate that the sum payable shall bear interest. In the case of any other bill of exchange,
this stipulation is deemed not to be written (non écrite).
    The rate of interest must be specified in the bill; in default of such specification, the
stipulation shall be deemed not to be written (non écrite).
    Interest runs from the date of the bill of exchange, unless some other date is specified.

Article 6

When the sum payable by a bill of exchange is expressed in words and also in figures, and
there is a discrepancy between the two, the sum denoted by the words is the amount
payable. Where the sum payable by a bill of exchange is expressed more than once in
words or more than once in figures, and there is a discrepancy, the smaller sum is the sum
payable.

Article 7

If a bill of exchange bears signatures of persons incapable of binding themselves by a bill
of exchange, or forged signatures, or signatures of fictitious persons, or signatures which
for any other reason cannot bind the persons who signed the bill of exchange or on
whose behalf it was signed, the obligations of the other persons who signed it are none
the less valid.

Article 8

Whosoever puts his signature on a bill of exchange as representing a person for whom he had no power to act is bound himself as a party to the bill and, if he pays, has the same rights as the person for whom he purported to act. The same rule applies to a representative who has exceeded his powers.

Article 9

The drawer guarantees both acceptance and payment.

He may release himself from guaranteeing acceptance; every stipulation by which he releases himself from the guarantee of payment is deemed not to be written (non écrite).

Article 10

If a bill of exchange, which was incomplete when issued, has been completed otherwise than in accordance with the agreements entered into, the non-observance of such agreements may not be set up against the holder unless he has acquired the bill of exchange in bad faith or, in acquiring it, has been guilty of gross negligence.

CHAPTER II
ENDORSEMENT

Article 11

Every bill of exchange, even if not expressly drawn to order, may be transferred by means of endorsement.

When the drawer has inserted in a bill of exchange the words 'not to order' or an equivalent expression, the instrument can only be transferred according to the form, and with the effects of an ordinary assignment.

The bill may be endorsed even in favour of the drawee, whether he has accepted or not, or of the drawer, or of any other party to the bill. These persons may re-endorse the bill.

Article 12

An endorsement must be unconditional. Any condition to which it is made subject is deemed not to be written (non écrite).

A partial endorsement is null and void.

An endorsement 'to bearer' is equivalent to an endorsement in blank.

Article 13

An endorsement must be written on the bill of exchange or on a slip affixed thereto (allonge). It must be signed by the endorser.

The endorsement may leave the beneficiary unspecified or may consist simply of the signature of the endorser (endorsement in blank). In the latter case, the endorsement, to be valid, must be written on the back of the bill of exchange or on the slip attached thereto (allonge).

Article 14

An endorsement transfers all the rights arising out of a bill of exchange.

If the endorsement is in blank, the holder may—

1.   fill up the blank either with his own name or with the name of some other person;

2.   re-endorse the bill in blank, or to some other person;
3.   transfer the bill to a third person without filling up the blank, and without
        endorsing it.

Article 15

In the absence of any contrary stipulation, the endorser guarantees acceptance and
payment. He may prohibit any further endorsement; in this case, he gives no guarantee to
the persons to whom the bill is subsequently endorsed.

Article 16

The possessor of a bill of exchange is deemed to be the lawful holder if he establishes his
title to the bill through an uninterrupted series of endorsements, even if the last
endorsement is in blank. In this connection, cancelled endorsements are deemed not to
be written (*non écrits*). When an endorsement in blank is followed by another
endorsement, the person who signed this last endorsement is deemed to have acquired
the bill by the endorsement in blank.

Where a person has been dispossessed of a bill of exchange, in any manner
whatsoever, the holder who establishes his right thereto in the manner mentioned in the
preceding paragraph is not bound to give up the bill unless he has acquired it in bad faith,
or unless in acquiring it he has been guilty of gross negligence.

Article 17

Persons sued on a bill of exchange cannot set up against the holder defences founded on
their personal relations with the drawer or with previous holders, unless the holder, in
acquiring the bill, has knowingly acted to the detriment of the debtor.

Article 18

When an endorsement contains the statements 'value in collection' ('*valeur en
recouvrement*'), 'for collection' ('*pour encaissement*'), 'by procuration' ('*par procuration*')
or any other phrase implying a simple mandate, the holder may exercise all rights arising
out of the bill of exchange, but he can only endorse it in his capacity as agent.

In this case, the parties liable can only set up against the holder defences which could
be set up against the endorser.

The mandate contained in an endorsement by procuration does not terminate by
reason of the death of the party giving the mandate or by reason of his becoming legally
incapable.

Article 19

When an endorsement contains the statements 'value in security' ('*valeur en garantie*'),
'value in pledge' ('*valeur en gage*'), or any other statement implying a pledge, the holder
may exercise all the rights arising out of the bill of exchange, but an endorsement by him
has the effects only of an endorsement by an agent.

The parties liable cannot set up against the holder defences founded on their personal
relations with the endorser, unless the holder, in receiving the bill, has knowingly acted
to the detriment of the debtor.

Article 20

An endorsement after maturity has the same effects as an endorsement before maturity.
Nevertheless, an endorsement after protest for non-payment, or after the expiration of

the limit of time fixed for drawing up the protest, operates only as an ordinary assignment.

Failing proof to the contrary, an endorsement without date is deemed to have been placed on the bill before the expiration of the limit of time fixed for drawing up the protest.

CHAPTER III
ACCEPTANCE

Article 21

Until maturity, a bill of exchange may be presented to the drawee for acceptance at his domicile, either by the holder or by a person who is merely in possession of the bill.

Article 22

In any bill of exchange, the drawer may stipulate that it shall be presented for acceptance with or without fixing a limit of time for presentment.

Except in the case of a bill payable at the address of a third party or in a locality other than that of the domicile of the drawee, or, except in the case of a bill drawn payable at a fixed period after sight, the drawer may prohibit presentment for acceptance.

He may also stipulate that presentment for acceptance shall not take place before a named date.

Unless the drawer has prohibited acceptance, every endorser may stipulate that the bill shall be presented for acceptance, with or without fixing a limit of time for presentment.

Article 23

Bills of exchange payable at a fixed period after sight must be presented for acceptance within one year of their date. The drawer may abridge or extend this period. These periods may be abridged by the endorsers.

Article 24

The drawee may demand that a bill shall be presented to him a second time on the day after the first presentment. Parties interested are not allowed to set up that this demand has not been complied with unless this request is mentioned in the protest.

The holder is not obliged to surrender to the drawee a bill presented for acceptance.

Article 25

An acceptance is written on the bill of exchange. It is expressed by the word 'accepted' or any other equivalent term. It is signed by the drawee. The simple signature of the drawee on the face of the bill constitutes an acceptance.

When the bill is payable at a certain time after sight, or when it must be presented for acceptance within a certain limit of time in accordance with a special stipulation, the acceptance must be dated as of the day when the acceptance is given, unless the holder requires it shall be dated as of the day of presentment. If it is undated, the holder, in order to preserve his right of recourse against the endorsers and the drawer, must authenticate the omission by a protest drawn up within the proper time.

Article 26

An acceptance is unconditional, but the drawee may restrict it to part of the sum payable.

Every other modification introduced by an acceptance into the tenor of the bill of exchange operates as a refusal to accept. Nevertheless, the acceptor is bound according to the terms of his acceptance.

Article 27

When the drawer of a bill has indicated a place of payment other than the domicile of the drawee without specifying a third party at whose address payment must be made, the drawee may name such third party at the time of acceptance. In default of this indication, the acceptor is deemed to have undertaken to pay the bill himself at the place of payment.

If a bill is payable at the domicile of the drawee, the latter may in his acceptance indicate an address in the same place where payment is to be made.

Article 28

By accepting, the drawee undertakes to pay the bill of exchange at its maturity.

In default of payment, the holder, even if he is the drawer, has a direct action on the bill of exchange against the acceptor for all that can be demanded in accordance with Articles 48 and 49.

Article 29

Where the drawee who has put his acceptance on a bill has cancelled it before restoring the bill, acceptance is deemed to be refused. Failing proof to the contrary, the cancellation is deemed to have taken place before the bill was restored.

Nevertheless, if the drawee has notified his acceptance in writing to the holder or to any party who has signed the bill, he is liable to such parties according to the terms of his acceptance.

CHAPTER IV
'AVALS'

Article 30

Payment of a bill of exchange may be guaranteed by an 'aval' as to the whole or part of its amount.

This guarantee may be given by a third person or even by a person who has signed as a party to the bill.

Article 31

The 'aval' is given either on the bill itself or on an 'allonge'.

It is expressed by the words 'good as aval' ('bon pour aval') or by any other equivalent formula. It is signed by the giver of the 'aval'.

It is deemed to be constituted by the mere signature of the giver of the 'aval' placed on the face of the bill, except in the case of the signature of the drawee or of the drawer.

An 'aval' must specify for whose account it is given. In default of this it is deemed to be given for the drawer.

Article 32

The giver of an 'aval' is bound in the same manner as the person for whom he has become guarantor.

His undertaking is valid even when the liability which he has guaranteed is inoperative for any reason other than defect of form.

He has, when he pays a bill of exchange, the rights arising out of the bill of exchange against the person guaranteed and against those who are liable to the latter on the bill of exchange.

CHAPTER V
MATURITY

Article 33

A bill of exchange may be drawn payable—
   at sight;
   at a fixed period after sight;
   at a fixed period after date;
   at a fixed date.
   Bills of exchange at other maturities or payable by instalments are null and void.

Article 34

A bill of exchange at sight is payable on presentment. It must be presented for payment within a year of its date. The drawer may abridge or extend this period. These periods may be abridged by the endorsers.

The drawer may prescribe that a bill of exchange payable at sight must not be presented for payment before a named date. In this case, the period for presentation begins from the said date.

Article 35

The maturity of a bill of exchange payable at a fixed period after sight is determined either by the date of the acceptance or by the date of the protest.

In the absence of the protest, an undated acceptance is deemed, so far as regards the acceptor, to have been given on the last day of the limit of time for presentment for acceptance.

Article 36

Where a bill of exchange is drawn at one or more months after date or after sight, the bill matures on the corresponding date of the month when payment must be made. If there be no corresponding date, the bill matures on the last day of this month.

When a bill of exchange is drawn at one or more months and a-half after date or sight, entire months must first be calculated.

If the maturity is fixed at the commencement, in the middle (mid-January or mid-February, etc) or at the end of the month, the first, fifteenth or last day of the month is to be understood.

The expressions 'eight days' or 'fifteen days' indicate not one or two weeks, but a period of eight or fifteen actual days.

The expression 'half-month' means a period of fifteen days.

Article 37

When a bill of exchange is payable on a fixed day in a place where the calendar is different from the calendar in the place of issue, the day of maturity is deemed to be fixed according to the calendar of the place of payment.

When a bill of exchange drawn between two places having different calendars is payable at a fixed period after date, the day of issue is referred to the corresponding day of the calendar in the place of payment, and the maturity is fixed accordingly.

The time for presenting bills of exchange is calculated in accordance with the rules of the preceding paragraph.

These rules do not apply if a stipulation in the bill or even the simple terms of the instrument indicate an intention to adopt some different rule.

CHAPTER VI
PAYMENT

Article 38

The holder of a bill of exchange payable on a fixed day or at a fixed period after date or after sight must present the bill for payment either on the day on which it is payable or on one of the two business days which follow.

The presentment of a bill of exchange at a clearing-house is equivalent to a presentment for payment.

Article 39

The drawee who pays a bill of exchange may require that it shall be given up to him receipted by the holder.

The holder may not refuse partial payment.

In case of partial payment the drawee may require that mention of this payment shall be made on the bill, and that a receipt therefor shall be given to him.

Article 40

The holder of a bill of exchange cannot be compelled to receive a payment thereof before maturity.

The drawee who pays before maturity does so at his own risk and peril. He who pays at maturity is validly discharged, unless he has been guilty of fraud or gross negligence. He is bound to verify the regularity of the series of endorsements, but not the signature of the endorsers.

Article 41

When a bill of exchange is drawn payable in a currency which is not that of the place of payment, the sum payable may be paid in the currency of the country, according to its value on the date of maturity. If the debtor is in default, the holder may at his option demand that the amount of the bill be paid in the currency of the country according to the rate on the day of maturity or the day of payment.

The usages of the place of payment determine the value of foreign currency. Nevertheless, the drawer may stipulate that the sum payable shall be calculated according to a rate expressed in the bill.

The foregoing rules shall not apply to the case in which the drawer has stipulated that payment must be made in a certain specified currency (stipulation for effective payment in foreign currency).

If the amount of the bill of exchange is specified in a currency having the same denomination, but a different value in the country of issue and the country of payment, reference is deemed to be made to the currency of the place of payment.

Article 42

When a bill of exchange is not presented for payment within the limit of time fixed by Article 38, every debtor is authorised to deposit the amount with the competent authority at the charge, risk and peril of the holder.

CHAPTER VII
RECOURSE FOR NON-ACCEPTANCE OR NON-PAYMENT

Article 43

The holder may exercise his right of recourse against the endorsers, the drawer and the other parties liable—
  At maturity:
      If payment has not been made;
  Even before maturity:
      1.   if there has been total or partial refusal to accept;
      2.   in the event of the bankruptcy (*faillite*) of the drawee, whether he has accepted or not, or in the event of a stoppage of payment on his part, even when not declared by a judgment, or where execution has been levied against his goods without result;
      3.   in the event of the bankruptcy (*faillite*) of the drawer of a non-acceptable bill.

Article 44

Default of acceptance or on payment must be evidenced by an authentic act (protest for non-acceptance or non-payment).

   Protest for non-acceptance must be made within the limit of time fixed for presentment for acceptance. If in the case contemplated by Article 24, paragraph I, the first presentment takes place on the last day of that time, the protest may nevertheless be drawn up on the next day.

   Protest for non-payment of a bill of exchange payable on a fixed day or at a fixed period after date or sight must be made on one of the two business days following the day on which the bill is payable. In the case of a bill payable at sight, the protest must be drawn up under the conditions specified in the foregoing paragraph for the drawing up of a protest for non-acceptance.

   Protest for non-acceptance dispenses with presentment for payment and protest for non-payment.

   If there is a stoppage of payment on the part of the drawee, whether he has accepted or not, or if execution has been levied against his goods without result, the holder cannot exercise his right of recourse until after presentment of the bill to the drawee for payment and after the protest has been drawn up.

   If the drawee, whether he accepted or not, is declared bankrupt (*faillite déclarée*), or in the event of the declared bankruptcy of the drawer of a non-acceptable bill, the production of the judgment declaring the bankruptcy suffices to enable the holder to exercise his right of recourse.

Article 45

The holder must give notice of non-acceptance or non-payment to his endorser and to the drawer within the four business days which follow the day for protest or, in case of a stipulation '*retour sans frais*', the day for presentment. Every endorser must, within the two business days following the day on which he receives notice, notify his endorser of the notice he has received, mentioning the names and addresses of those who have given the previous notices, and so on through the series until the drawer is reached. The periods mentioned above run from the receipt of the preceding notice.

When, in conformity with the preceding paragraph, notice is given to a person who has signed a bill of exchange, the same notice must be given within the same limit of time to his *avaliseur*.

Where an endorser either has not specified his address or has specified it in an illegible manner, it is sufficient that notice should be given to the preceding endorser.

A person who must give notice may give it in any form whatever, even by simply returning the bill of exchange.

He must prove that he has given notice within the time allowed. this time-limit shall be regarded as having been observed if a letter giving the notice has been posted within the prescribed time.

A person who does not give notice within the limit of time mentioned above does not forfeit his rights. He is responsible for the injury, if any, caused by his negligence, but the damages shall not exceed the amount of the bill of exchange.

Article 46

The drawer, an endorser, or a person guaranteeing payment by *aval* (*avaliseur*) may, by the stipulation '*retour sans frais*', '*sans protet*', or any other equivalent expression written on the instrument and signed, release the holder from having a protest of non-acceptance or non-payment drawn up in order to exercise his right of recourse.

This stipulation does not release the holder from presenting the bill within the prescribed time, or from the notices he has to give. The burden of proving the non-observance of the limits of time lies on the person who seeks to set it up against the holder.

If the stipulation is written by the drawer, it is operative in respect of all persons who have signed the bill; if it is written by an endorser or an *avaliseur*, it is operative only in respect of such endorser or *avaliseur*. If, in spite of the stipulation written by the drawer, the holder has the protest drawn up, he must bear the expenses thereof. When the stipulation emanates from an endorser or *avaliseur*, the costs of the protest, if one is drawn up, may be recovered from all the persons who have signed the bill.

Article 47

All drawers, acceptors, endorsers or guarantors by *aval* of a bill of exchange are jointly and severally liable to the holder.

The holder has the right of proceeding against all these persons individually or collectively without being required to observe the order in which they have become bound.

The same right is possessed by any person signing the bill who has taken it up and paid it.

Proceedings against one of the parties liable do not prevent proceedings against the others, even though they may be subsequent to the party first proceeded against.

Article 48

The holder may recover from the person against whom he exercises his right of recourse—
1.   the amount of the unaccepted or unpaid bill of exchange with interest, if interest has been stipulated for;
2.   interest at the rate of 6 per cent from the date of maturity;
3.   the expenses of protest and of the notices given as well as other expenses.

If the right of recourse is exercised before maturity, the amount of the bill shall be subject to a discount. This discount shall be calculated according to the official rate of discount (bank-rate) ruling on the date when recourse is exercised at the place of domicile of the holder.

Article 49

A party who takes up and pays a bill of exchange can recover from the parties liable to him—
1.   the entire sum which he has paid;
2.   interest on the said sum calculated at the rate of 6 per cent, starting from the day when he made payment;
3.   any expenses which he has incurred.

Article 50

Every party liable against whom a right of recourse is or may be exercised can require against payment that the bill shall be given up to him with the protest and a receipted account.
   Every endorser who has taken up and paid a bill of exchange may cancel his own endorsement and those of subsequent endorsers.

Article 51

In the case of the exercise of the right of recourse after a partial acceptance, the party who pays the sum in respect of which the bill has not been accepted can require that this payment shall be specified on the bill and that he shall be given a receipt therefor. The holder must also give him a certified copy of the bill, together with the protest, in order to enable subsequent recourse to be exercised.

Article 52

Every person having the right of recourse may, in the absence of agreement to the contrary, reimburse himself by means of a fresh bill (redraft) to be drawn at sight on one of the parties liable to him and payable at the domicile of that party.
   The redraft includes, in addition to the sums mentioned in Articles 48 and 49, brokerage and the cost of stamping the redraft.
   If the redraft is drawn by the holder, the sum payable is fixed according to the rate for a sight bill drawn at the place where the original bill was payable upon the party liable at the place of his domicile. If the redraft is drawn by an endorser, the sum payable is fixed according to the rate for a sight bill drawn at the place where the drawer of the redraft is domiciled upon the place of domicile of the party liable.

Article 53

After the expiration of the limits of time fixed—
   for the presentment of a bill of exchange drawn at sight or at a fixed period after sight;
   for drawing up the protest for non-acceptance or non-payment;
   for presentment for payment in the case of a stipulation *retour sans frais,*
the holder loses his rights of recourse against the endorsers, against the drawer and against the other parties liable, with the exception of the acceptor.
   In default of presentment for acceptance within the limit of time stipulated by the drawer, the holder loses his right of recourse for non-payment, as well as for non-acceptance, unless it appears from the terms of the stipulation that the drawer only meant to release himself from the guarantee of acceptance.
   If the stipulation for a limit of time for presentment is contained in an endorsement, the endorser alone can avail himself of it.

Article 54

Should the presentment of the bill of exchange or the drawing up of the protest within the prescribed limits of time be prevented by an insurmountable obstacle (legal prohibition (prescription légale) by any State or other case of vis major), these limits of time shall be extended. The holder is bound to give notice without delay of the case of vis major to his endorser and to specify this notice, which he must date and sign, on the bill or on an *allonge*; in other respects the provisions of Article 45 shall apply.

When vis major has terminated, the holder must without delay present the bill of exchange for acceptance or payment and, if need be, draw up the protest.

If vis major continues to operate beyond thirty days after maturity, recourse may be exercised, and neither presentment nor the drawing up of a protest shall be necessary.

In the case of bills of exchange drawn at sight or at a fixed period after sight, the time-limit of thirty days shall run from the date on which the holder, even before the expiration of the time for presentment, has given notice of vis major to his endorser. In the case of bill of exchange drawn at a certain time after sight, the above time-limit of thirty days shall be added to the period after sight specified in the bill of exchange.

Facts which are purely personal to the holder or to the person whom he has entrusted with the presentment of the bill or drawing up of the bill or drawing up of the protest are not deemed to constitute cases of vis major.

CHAPTER VIII
INTERVENTION FOR HONOUR

1. GENERAL PROVISIONS

Article 55

The drawer, an endorser, or a person giving an *aval* may specify a person who is to accept or pay in case of need.

A bill of exchange may, subject as hereinafter mentioned, be accepted or paid by a person who intervenes for the honour of any debtor against whom a right of recourse exists.

The person intervening may be a third party, even the drawee, or, save the acceptor, a party already liable on the bill of exchange.

The person intervening is bound to give, within two business days, notice of his intervention to the party for whose honour he has intervened. In default, he is responsible for the injury, if any, due to his negligence, but the damages shall not exceed the amount of the bill of exchange.

2. ACCEPTANCE BY INTERVENTION (FOR HONOUR)

Article 56

There may be acceptance by intervention in all cases where the holder has a right of recourse before maturity on a bill which is capable of acceptance.

When the bill of exchange indicates a person who is designated to accept or pay it in case of need at the place of payment, the holder may not exercise his rights of recourse before maturity against the person naming such referee in case of need and against subsequent signatories, unless he has presented the bill of exchange to the referee in case of need and until, if acceptance is refused by the latter, this refusal has been authenticated by a protest.

In other cases of intervention the holder may refuse an acceptance by intervention. Nevertheless, if he allows it, he loses his right of recourse before maturity against the person on whose behalf such acceptance was given and against subsequent signatories.

Article 57

Acceptance by intervention is specified on the bill of exchange. It is signed by the person intervening. It mentions the person for whose honour it has been given and, in default of such mention, the acceptance is deemed to have been given for the honour of the drawer.

Article 58

The acceptor by intervention is liable to the holder and to the endorsers, subsequent to the party for whose honour he intervened, in the same manner as such party.

Notwithstanding an acceptance by intervention, the party for whose honour it has been given and the parties liable to him may require the holder, in exchange for payment of the sum mentioned in Article 48, to deliver the bill, the protest, and a receipted account, if any.

3.   PAYMENT BY INTERVENTION

Article 59

Payment by intervention may take place in all cases where, either at maturity or before maturity, the holder has a right of recourse on the bill.

Payment must include the whole amount payable by the party for whose honour it is made.

It must be made at the latest on the day following the last day allowed for drawing up the protest for non-payment.

Article 60

If a bill of exchange has been accepted by persons intervening who are domiciled in the place of payment, or if persons domiciled therein have been named as referees in case of need, the holder must present the bill to all these persons and, if necessary, have a protest for non-payment drawn up at latest on the day following the last day allowed for drawing up the protest.

In default of protest within this limit of time, the party who has named the referee in case of need, or for whose account the bill has been accepted, and the subsequent endorsers are discharged.

Article 61

The holder who refuses payment by intervention loses his right of recourse against any persons who would have been discharged thereby.

Article 62

Payment by intervention must be authenticated by a receipt given on the bill of exchange mentioning the person for whose honour payment has been made. In default of such mention, payment is deemed to have been made for the honour of the drawer.

The bill of exchange and the protest, if any, must be given up to the person paying by intervention.

Article 63

The person paying by intervention acquires the rights arising out of the bill of exchange against the party for whose honour he has paid and against persons who are liable to the latter on the bill of exchange. Nevertheless, he cannot re-endorse the bill of exchange.

Endorsers subsequent to the party for whose honour payment has been made are discharged.

In case of competition for payment by intervention, the payment which effects the greater number of releases has the preference. Any person who, with a knowledge of the facts, intervenes in a manner contrary to this rule, loses his right of recourse against those who would have been discharged.

CHAPTER IX
PARTS OF A SET, AND COPIES

1. PARTS OF A SET

Article 64

A bill of exchange can be drawn in a set of two or more identical parts.

These parts must be numbered in the body of the instrument itself; in default, each part is considered as a separate bill of exchange.

Every holder of a bill which does not specify that it has been drawn as a sole bill may, at his own expense, require the delivery of two or more parts. For this purpose he must apply to his immediate endorser, who is bound to assist him in proceeding against his own endorser, and so on in the series until the drawer is reached. The endorsers are bound to reproduce their endorsements on the new parts of the set.

Article 65

Payment made on one part of a set operates as a discharge, even though there is no stipulation that this payment annuls the effect on the other parts. Nevertheless, the drawee is liable on each accepted part which he has not recovered.

An endorser who has transferred parts of a set to different persons, as well as subsequent endorsers, are liable on all the parts bearing their signature which have not been restored.

Article 66

A party who has sent one part for acceptance must indicate on the other parts the name of the person in whose hands this part is to be found. That person is bound to give it up to the lawful holder of another part.

If he refuses, the holder cannot exercise his right of recourse until he has had a protest drawn us specifying—
1.   that the part sent for acceptance has not been given up to him on his demand;
2.   that acceptance or payment could not be obtained on another of the parts.

2. COPIES

Article 67

Every holder of a bill of exchange has the right to make copies of it. A copy must reproduce the original exactly, with the endorsements and all other statements to be found therein. It must specify where the copy ends. It may be endorsed and guaranteed by *aval* in the same manner and with the same effects as the original.

Article 68

A copy must specify the person in possession of the original instrument. The latter is bound to hand over the said instrument to the lawful holder of the copy.

If he refuses, the holder may not exercise his right of recourse against the persons who have endorsed the copy or guaranteed it by *aval* until he has had a protest drawn up specifying that the original has not been given up to him on his demand.

Where the original instrument, after the last endorsement before the making of the copy contains a clause 'commencing from here an endorsement is only valid if made on the copy' or some equivalent formula, a subsequent endorsement on the original is null and void.

CHAPTER X
ALTERATIONS

Article 69

In case of alteration of the text of a bill of exchange, parties who have signed subsequent to the alteration are bound according to the terms of the altered text; parties who have signed before the alteration are bound according to the terms of the original text.

CHAPTER XI
LIMITATION OF ACTIONS

Article 70

All actions arising out of a bill of exchange against the acceptor are barred after three years, reckoned from the date of maturity.

Actions by the holder against the endorsers and against the drawer are barred after one year from the date of a protest drawn up within proper time, or from the date of maturity where there is a stipulation *retour sans frais*.

Actions by endorsers against each other and against the drawer are barred after six months, reckoned from the day when the endorser took up and paid the bill or from the day when he himself was sued.

Article 71

Interruption of the period of limitation is only effective against the person in respect of whom the period has been interrupted.

CHAPTER XII
GENERAL PROVISIONS

Article 72

Payment of a bill of exchange which falls due on a legal holiday (jour férié légal) cannot be demanded until the next business day. So, too, all other proceedings relating to a bill of exchange, in particular presentment for acceptance and protest, can only be taken on a business day.

Where any of these proceedings must be taken within a certain limit of time the last day of which is a legal holiday (jour férié légal), the limit of time is extended until the first business day which follows the expiration of that time. Intermediate holidays (jours fériés) are included in computing limits of time.

Article 73

Legal or contractual limits of time do not include the day on which the period commences.

Article 74

No days of grace, whether legal or judicial, are permitted.

TITLE II
PROMISSORY NOTES

Article 75

A promissory note contains—
1. the term 'promissory note' inserted in the body of the instrument and expressed in the language employed in drawing up the instrument;
2. an unconditional promise to pay a determinate sum of money;
3. a statement of the time of payment;
4. a statement of the place where payment is to be made;
5. the name of the person to whom or to whose order payment is to be made;
6. a statement of the date and of the place where the promissory note is issued;
7. the signature of the person who issues the instrument (maker).

Article 76

An instrument in which any of the requirements mentioned in the preceding Article are wanting is invalid as a promissory note except in the cases specified in the following paragraphs.

A promissory note in which the time of payment is not specified is deemed to be payable at sight.

In default of special mention, the place where the instrument is made is deemed to be the place of payment and at the same time the place of the domicile of the maker.

A promissory note which does not mention the place of its issue is deemed to have been made in the place mentioned beside the name of the maker.

Article 77

The following provisions relating to bills of exchange apply to promissory notes so far as they are not inconsistent with the nature of these instruments, viz—

endorsement (Article 11 to 20);
time of payment (Articles 33 to 37);
payment (Articles 38 to 42);
recourse in case of non-payment (Articles 43 to 50, 52 to 54);
payment by intervention (Articles 55, 59 to 63);
copies (Articles 67 and 68);
alterations (Article 69);
limitation of actions (Articles 70 and 71);
holidays, computation of limits of time and prohibition of days of grace (Articles 72, 73 and 74).

The following provisions are also applicable to a promissory note: The provisions concerning a bill of exchange payable at the address of a third party or in a locality other than that of the domicile of the drawee (Articles 4 and 27): stipulation for interest (Article 5); discrepancies as regards the sum payable (Article 6); the consequences of signature under the conditions mentioned in Article 7, the consequences of signature by a person who acts without authority or who exceeds his authority (Article 8); and provisions concerning a bill of exchange in blank (Article 10).

The following provisions are also applicable to a promissory note: Provisions relating to guarantee by *aval* (Articles 30–32); in the case provided for in Article 31, last paragraph, if the *aval* does not specify on whose behalf it has been given, it is deemed to have been given on behalf of the maker of the promissory note.

Article 78

The maker of a promissory note is bound in the same manner as an acceptor of a bill of exchange.

Promissory notes payable at a certain time after sight must be presented for the visa of the maker within the limits of time fixed by Article 23. The limit of time runs from the date of which marks the commencement of the period of time after sight.

ANNEX II

Articles 1–23 [Omitted].

CONVENTION ON THE LAW APPLICABLE TO INTERNATIONAL SALES OF GOODS, THE HAGUE, 1955

Article 1

This Convention shall apply to international sales of goods.

It shall not apply to sales of securities, to sales of ships and of registered boats or aircraft, or to sales upon judicial order or by way of execution. It shall apply to sales based on documents.

For the purposes of this Convention, contracts to deliver goods to be manufactured or produced shall be placed on the same footing as sales, provided the party who assumes delivery is to furnish the necessary raw materials for their manufacture or production.

The mere declaration of the parties, relative to the application of a law or the competence of a judge or arbitrator, shall not be sufficient to confer upon a sale the international character provided for in the first paragraph of this Article.

Article 2

A sale shall be governed by the domestic law of the country designated by the Contracting Parties.

Such designation must be contained in an express clause, or unambiguously result from the provisions of the contract.

Conditions affecting the consent of the parties to the law declared applicable shall be determined by such law.

Article 3

In default of a law declared applicable by the parties under the conditions provided in the preceding Article, a sale shall be governed by the domestic law of the country in which the vendor has his habitual residence at the time when he receives the order. If the order is received by an establishment of the vendor, the sale shall be governed by the domestic law of the country in which the establishment is situated.

Nevertheless, a sale shall be governed by the domestic law of the country in which the purchaser has his habitual residence, or in which he has the establishment that has given the order, if the order has been received in such country, whether by the vendor or by his representative, agent or commercial traveller.

In case of a sale at an exchange or at a public auction, the sale shall be governed by the domestic law of the country in which the exchange is situated or the auction takes place.

Article 4

In the absence of an express clause to the contrary, the domestic law of the country in which inspection of goods delivered pursuant to a sale is to take place shall apply in respect of the form in which and the periods within which the inspection must take place, the notifications concerning the inspection and the measures to be taken in case of refusal of the goods.

Article 5

This Convention shall not apply to—
1. the capacity of the parties;
2. the form of the contract;
3. the transfer of ownership, provided that the various obligations of the parties, and especially those relating to risks, shall be subject to the law applicable to the sale pursuant to this Convention;
4. the effects of the sale as regards all persons other than the parties.

Article 6

In each of the Contracting States, the application of the law determined by this convention may be excluded on a ground of public policy.

Article 7

The Contracting States have agreed to incorporate the provisions of Articles 1-6 of this Convention in the national law of their respective countries.

Articles 8–12 [Omitted].

HAGUE PROTOCOL TO AMEND THE CONVENTION FOR THE UNIFICATION OF CERTAIN RULES RELATING TO INTERNATIONAL CARRIAGE BY AIR SIGNED AT WARSAW ON 12 OCTOBER 1929 (THE HAGUE PROTOCOL) 1955

CHAPTER 1
AMENDMENTS TO THE CONVENTION

Article 1

In Article 1 of the Convention—
(a) paragraph (2) shall be deleted and replaced by the following:
   '(2)   For the purposes of this convention, the expression international carriage means any carriage in which, according to the agreement between the parties, the place of departure and the place of destination, whether or not there be a break in the carriage or a transhipment, are situated either within the territories of two High Contracting Parties or within the territory of a single High Contracting Party if there is an agreed stopping place within the territory of another State, even if that State is not a High Contracting Party. Carriage between two points within the territory of a single High Contracting Party without an agreed stopping place within the territory of another State is not international carriage for the purposes of this Convention.'
(b) paragraph (3) shall be deleted and replaced by the following:

'(3)   Carriage to be performed by several successive air carriers is deemed, for the purposes of this Convention, to be one undivided carriage if it has been regarded by the parties as a single operation, whether it has been agreed upon under the form of a single contract or of a series of contracts, and it does not lose its international character merely because one contract or a series of contracts is to be performed entirely within the territory of the same State.'

Article 2

In Article 2 of the Convention—
    paragraph (2) shall be deleted and replaced by the following:
    '(2)   This Convention shall not apply to carriage of mail and postal packages.'

Article 3

In Article 3 of the Convention—
(a)   paragraph (1) shall be deleted and replaced by the following:
    '(1)   In respect of the carriage of passengers a ticket shall be delivered containing—
      (a)   an indication of the places of departure and destination;
      (b)   if the places of departure and destination are within the territory of a single High Contracting Party, one or more agreed stopping places being within the territory of another State, an indication of at least one such stopping place;
      (c)   a notice to the effect that, if the passenger's journey involves an ultimate destination or stop in a country other than the country of departure, the Warsaw Convention may be applicable and that the Convention governs and in most cases limits the liability of carriers for death or personal injury and in respect of loss of or damage to baggage.'
(b)   paragraph (2) shall be deleted and replaced by the following:
    '(2)   The passenger ticket shall constitute *prima facie* evidence of the conclusion and conditions of the contract of carriage. The absence, irregularity or loss of the passenger ticket does not affect the existence or the validity of the contract of carriage which shall, none the less, be subject to the rules of this Convention. Nevertheless, if, with the consent of the carrier, the passenger embarks without a passenger ticket having been delivered, or if the ticket does not include the notice required by paragraph (1) (c) of this Article, the carrier shall not be entitled to avail himself of the provisions of Article 22.'

Article 4

In Article 4 of the Convention—
(a)   paragraphs (1), (2) and (3) shall be deleted and replaced by the following:
    '(1)   In respect of the carriage of registered baggage, a baggage check shall be delivered, which, unless combined with or incorporated in a passenger ticket which complies with the provisions of Article 3, paragraph (1), shall contain:
      (a)   an indication of the places of departure and destination;
      (b)   if the places of departure and destination are within the territory of a single High Contracting Party, one or more agreed stopping places being within the territory of another State, an indication of at least one such stopping place;
      (c)   a notice to the effect that, if the carriage involves an ultimate destination or stop in a country other than the country of departure, the Warsaw Convention may be applicable and that the Convention governs and in most cases limits the liability of carriers in respect of loss or damage to baggage.'

(b) paragraph (4) shall be deleted and replaced by the following:
'(2) The baggage check shall constitute *prima facie* evidence of the registration of
the baggage and of the conditions of the contract of carriage. The absence,
irregularity or loss of the baggage check does not affect the existence or the
validity of the contract of carriage which shall, none the less, be subject to the
rules of this Convention. Nevertheless, if the carrier takes charge of the
baggage without a baggage check having been delivered or if the baggage
check (unless combined with or incorporated in the passenger ticket which
complies with the provisions of Article 3, paragraph (1)(c)) does not include
the notice required by paragraph (1)(c) of this Article, he shall not be entitled
to avail himself of the provisions of Article 22, paragraph (2).'

Article 5

In Article 6 of the Convention—
paragraph (3) shall be deleted and replaced by the following:
'(3) The carrier shall sign prior to the loading of the cargo on board the aircraft.'

Article 6

Article 8 of the Convention shall be deleted and replaced by the following—
'The air waybill shall contain:
(a) an indication of the places of departure and destination;
(b) if the places of departure and destination are within the territory of a
single High Contracting Party, one or more agreed stopping places being
within the territory of another State, an indication of at least one such
stopping place;
(c) a notice to the consignor to the effect that, if the carriage involves an
ultimate destination or stop in a country other than the country of
departure, the Warsaw Convention may be applicable and that the
Convention governs and in most cases limits the liability of carriers in
respect of loss of or damage to cargo.'

Article 7

Article 9 of the Convention shall be deleted and replaced by the following—
'If, with the consent of the carrier, cargo is loaded on board the aircraft without an
air waybill having been made out, or if the air waybill does not include the notice
required by Article 8, paragraph (c), the carrier shall not be entitled to avail himself
of the provisions of Article 22, paragraph (2).'

Article 8

In Article 10 of the Convention—
paragraph (2) shall be deleted and replaced by the following:
'(2) The consignor shall indemnify the carrier against all damage suffered by him,
or by any other person to whom the carrier is liable, by reason of the
irregularities, incorrectness or incompleteness of the particulars and
statements furnished by the consignor.'

Article 9

To Article 15 of the Convention—
the following paragraph shall be added:
'(3) Nothing in this Convention prevents the issue of a negotiable air waybill.'

Article 10

Paragraph (2) of Article 20 of the Convention shall be deleted.

Article 11

Article 22 of the Convention shall be deleted and replaced by the following—

'(1) In the carriage of persons the liability of the carrier for each passenger is limited to the sum of two hundred and fifty thousand francs. Where, in accordance with the law of the court seised of the case, damages may be awarded in the form of periodical payments, the equivalent capital value of the said payments shall not exceed two hundred and fifty thousand francs. Nevertheless, by special contract, the carrier and the passenger may agree to a higher limit of liability.

(2) (a) In the carriage of registered baggage and of cargo, the liability of the carrier is limited to a sum of two hundred and fifty francs per kilogramme, unless the passenger or consignor has made, at the time when the package was handed over to the carrier, a special declaration of interest in delivery at destination and has paid a supplementary sum if the case so requires. In that case the carrier will be liable to pay a sum not exceeding the declared sum, unless he proves that that sum is greater than the passenger's or consignor's actual interest in delivery at destination.

(b) In the case of loss, damage or delay of part of registered baggage or cargo, or of any object contained therein, the weight to be taken into consideration in determining the amount to which the carrier's liability is limited shall be only the total weight of the package or packages concerned. Nevertheless, when the loss, damage or delay of a part of the registered baggage or cargo, or of an object contained therein, affects the value of other packages covered by the same baggage check or the same air waybill, the total weight of such package or packages shall also be taken into consideration in determining the limit of liability.

(3) As regards objects of which the passenger takes charge himself the liability of the carrier is limited to five thousand francs per passenger.

(4) The limits prescribed in this article shall not prevent the court from awarding, in accordance with its own law, in addition, the whole or part of the court costs and of the other expenses of the litigation incurred by the plaintiff. The foregoing provision shall not apply if the amount of the damages awarded, excluding court costs and other expenses of the litigation, does not exceed the sum which the carrier has offered in writing to the plaintiff within a period of six months from the date of the occurrence causing the damage, or before the commencement of the action, if that is later.

(5) The sums mentioned in francs in this Article shall be deemed to refer to a currency unit consisting of sixty-five and a half milligrammes of gold of millesimal fineness nine hundred. These sums may be converted into national currencies in round figures. Conversion of the sums into national currencies other than gold shall, in case of judicial proceedings, be made according to the gold value of such currencies at the date of the judgment.'

Article 12

In Article 23 of the Convention, the existing provision shall be renumbered as paragraph (1) and another paragraph shall be added as follows—

'(2) Paragraph (1) of this Article shall not apply to provisions governing loss or damage resulting from the inherent defect, quality or vice of the cargo carried.'

Article 13

In Article 25 of the Convention—
  paragraphs (1) and (2) shall be deleted and replaced by the following—
  'The limits of liability specified in Article 22 shall not apply if it is proved that the
  damage resulted from an act or omission of the carrier, his servants or agents, done
  with intent to cause damage or recklessly and with knowledge that damage would
  probably result; provided that, in the case of such act or omission of a servant or
  agent, it is also proved that he was acting within the scope of his employment.'

Article 14

After Article 25 of the Convention the following article shall be inserted—
  'Article 25A
  (1) If an action is brought against a servant or agent of the carrier arising out of
       damage to which this Convention relates, such servant or agent, if he proves that
       he acted within the scope of his employment, shall be entitled to avail himself of
       the limits of liability which that carrier himself is entitled to invoke under Article
       22.
  (2) The aggregate of the amounts recoverable from the carrier, his servants and
       agents, in that case, shall not exceed the said limits.
  (3) The provisions of paragraphs (l) and (2) of this article shall not apply if it is proved
       that the damage resulted from an act or omission of the servant or agent done
       with intent to cause damage or recklessly and with knowledge that damage would
       probably result.'

Article 15

In Article 26 of the Convention—
  paragraph (2) shall be deleted and replaced by the following:
  '(2) In the case of damage, the person entitled to delivery must complain to the
       carrier forthwith after the discovery of the damage, and, at the latest, within seven
       days from the date of receipt in the case of baggage and fourteen days from the
       date of receipt in the case of cargo. In the case of delay the complaint must be
       made at the latest within twenty-one days from the date on which the baggage or
       cargo have been placed at his disposal.'

Article 16

Article 34 of the Convention shall be deleted and replaced by the following—
  'The provisions of Articles 3 to 9 inclusive relating to documents of carriage shall not
  apply in the case of carriage performed in extraordinary circumstances outside the
  normal scope of an air carrier's business.'

Article 17

After Article 40 of the Convention the following Article shall be inserted—
  'Article 40A
  (1) In Article 37, paragraph (2) and Article 40, paragraph (1), the expression High
       Contracting Party shall mean State. In all other cases, the expression High
       Contracting Party shall mean a State whose ratification of or adherence to the
       Convention has become effective and whose denunciation thereof has not
       become effective.
  (2) For the purposes of the Convention the word territory means not only the
       metropolitan territory of a State but also all other territories for the foreign
       relations of which that State is responsible.'

CHAPTER II
SCOPE OF APPLICATION OF THE CONVENTION AS AMENDED

Article 18

The Convention as amended by this Protocol shall apply to international carriage as defined in Article 1 of the Convention, provided that the places of departure and destination referred to in that Article are situated either in the territories of two parties to this Protocol or within the territory of a single party to this Protocol with an agreed stopping place within the territory of another State.

CHAPTER III
FINAL CLAUSE

Articles 19–27 [Omitted].

CONVENTION ON THE CONTRACT FOR THE INTERNATIONAL CARRIAGE OF GOODS BY ROAD, GENEVA, 1956

See the Schedule to the Carriage of Goods by Road Act 1965 for text of the Convention.

CONVENTION ON THE RECOGNITION AND ENFORCEMENT OF FOREIGN ARBITRAL AWARDS, NEW YORK, 1958

Article I

1. This Convention shall apply to the recognition and enforcement of arbitral awards made in the territory of a State other than the State where the recognition and enforcement of such awards are sought, and arising out of differences between persons, whether physical or legal. It shall also apply to arbitral awards not considered as domestic awards in the State where their recognition and enforcement are sought.
2. The term 'arbitral awards' shall include not only awards made by arbitrators appointed for each case but also those made by permanent arbitral bodies to which the parties have submitted.
3. When signing, ratifying or acceding to this convention, or notifying extension under Article X hereof, any State may on the basis of reciprocity declare that it will apply the Convention to the recognition and enforcement of awards made only in the territory of another Contracting State. It may also declare that it will apply the Convention only to differences arising out of legal relationships, whether contractual or not, which are considered as commercial under the national law of the State making such declaration.

Article II

1. Each Contracting State shall recognize an agreement in writing under which the parties undertake to submit to arbitration all or any differences which have arisen or which may arise between them in respect of a defined legal relationship, whether contractual or not, concerning a subject matter capable of settlement by arbitration.

2.   The term 'agreement in writing' shall include an arbitral clause in a contract or an arbitration agreement, signed by the parties or contained in an exchange of letters or telegrams.

3.   The court of a Contracting State, when seised of an action in a matter in respect of which the parties have made an agreement within the meaning of this Article, at the request of one of the parties, refer the parties to arbitration, unless it finds that the said agreement is null and void, inoperative or incapable of being performed.

Article III

Each Contracting State shall recognize arbitral awards as binding and enforce them in accordance with the rules of procedure of the territory where the award is relied upon, under the conditions laid down in the following Articles. There shall not be imposed substantially more onerous conditions or higher fees or charges on the recognition or enforcement of arbitral awards to which this Convention applies than are imposed on the recognition or enforcement of domestic arbitral awards.

Article IV

1.   To obtain the recognition and enforcement mentioned in the preceding Article, the party applying for recognition and enforcement shall, at the time of the application, supply—

     (a)   the duly authenticated original award or a duly certified copy thereof;

     (b)   the original agreement referred to in Article II or a duly certified copy thereof.

2.   If the said award or agreement is not made in an official language of the country in which the award is relied upon, the party applying for recognition and enforcement of the award shall produce a translation of these documents into such language. The translation shall be certified by an official or sworn translator or by a diplomatic or consular agent.

Article V

1.   Recognition and enforcement of the award may be refused, at the request of the party against whom it is invoked, only if that party furnishes to the competent authority where the recognition and enforcement is sought, proof that—

     (a)   the parties to the agreement referred to in Article II were, under the law applicable to them, under some incapacity, or the said agreement is not valid under the law to which the parties have subjected it or, failing any indication thereon, under the law of the country where the award was made; or

     (b)   the party against whom the award is invoked was not given proper notice of the appointment of the arbitrator or of the arbitration proceedings or was otherwise unable to present his case; or

     (c)   the award deals with a difference not contemplated by or not falling within the terms of the submission to arbitration, or it contains decisions on matters beyond the scope of the submission to arbitration, provided that, if the decisions on matters submitted to arbitration can be separated from those not so submitted, that part of the award which contains decisions on matters submitted to arbitration may be recognized and enforced; or

     (d)   the composition of the arbitral authority or the arbitral procedure was not in accordance with the agreement of the parties, or, failing such agreement, was not in accordance with the law of the country where the arbitration took place; or

     (e)   the award has not yet become binding on the parties, or has been set aside or suspended by a competent authority of the country in which, or under the law of which, that award was made.

2.   Recognition and enforcement of an arbitral award may also be refused if the competent authority in the country where recognition and enforcement is sought finds that—
     (a)   the subject matter of the difference is not capable of settlement by arbitration under the law of that country; or
     (b)   the recognition or enforcement of the award would be contrary to the public policy of that country.

Articles VI–XVI [Omitted].

CONVENTION SUPPLEMENTARY TO THE WARSAW CONVENTION FOR THE UNIFICATION OF CERTAIN RULES RELATING TO INTERNATIONAL CARRIAGE BY AIR PERFORMED BY A PERSON OTHER THAN THE CONTRACTING CARRIER (GUADALAJARA) 1961

See the Schedule to the Carriage by Air (Supplementary Provisions) Act 1962.

EUROPEAN CONVENTION ON INTERNATIONAL COMMERCIAL ARBITRATION, GENEVA, 1961

Article I
Scope of the Convention

1.   This Convention shall apply—
     (a)   to arbitration agreements concluded for the purpose of settling disputes arising from international trade between physical or legal persons having, when concluding the agreement, their habitual place of residence or their seat in different contracting states;
     (b)   to arbitral procedures and awards based on agreements referred to in paragraph 1(a) above.
2.   For the purpose of this Convention—
     (a)   the term 'arbitration agreement' shall mean either an arbitral clause in a contract or an arbitration agreement, the contract or arbitration agreement being signed by the parties, or contained in an exchange of letters, telegrams, or in a communication by teleprinter and, in relations between States whose laws do not require that an arbitration agreement be made in writing, any arbitration agreement concluded in the form authorized by these laws;
     (b)   the term 'arbitration' shall mean not only settlement by arbitrators appointed for each case (ad hoc arbitration) but also by permanent arbitral institutions;
     (c)   the term 'seat' shall mean the place of the situation of the establishment that has made the arbitration agreement.

Article II
Right of legal persons of public law to resort to arbitration

1.   In the cases referred to in Article I, paragraph 1, of this Convention, legal persons considered by the law which is applicable to them as 'legal persons of public law' have the right to conclude valid arbitration agreements.
2.   On signing, ratifying or acceding to this convention any State shall be entitled to declare that it limits the above faculty to such conditions as may be stated in its declaration.

Article III
Right of foreign nationals to be designated as arbitrators

In arbitration covered by this Convention, foreign nationals may be designated as arbitrators.

Article IV
Organization of the arbitration

1.   The parties to an arbitration agreement shall be free to submit their disputes —
      (a)   to a permanent arbitral institution; in this case, the arbitration proceedings shall be held in conformity with the rules of the said institution;
      (b)   to an *ad hoc* arbitral procedure; in this case, they shall be free *inter alia:*
             (i)   to appoint arbitrators or to establish means for their appointment in the event of an actual dispute;
             (ii)   to determine the place of arbitration; and
             (iii) to lay down the procedure to be followed by the arbitrators.
2.   Where the parties have agreed to submit any disputes to an ad hoc arbitration, and where within thirty days of the notification of the request for arbitration to the respondent one of the parties fails to appoint his arbitrator, the latter shall, unless otherwise provided, be appointed at the request of the other party by the President of the competent Chamber of Commerce of the country of the defaulting party's habitual place of residence or seat at the time of the introduction of the request for arbitration. This paragraph shall also apply to the replacement of the arbitrator(s) appointed by one of the parties or by the President of the Chamber of Commerce above referred to.
3.   Where the parties have agreed to submit any disputes to an ad hoc arbitration by one or more arbitrators and the arbitration agreement contains no indication regarding the organization of the arbitration, as mentioned in paragraph 1 of this Article, the necessary steps shall be taken by the arbitrator(s) already appointed, unless the parties are able to agree thereon and without prejudice to the case referred to in paragraph 2 above. Where the parties cannot agree on the appointment of the sole arbitrator or where the arbitrators appointed cannot agree on the measures to be taken, the claimant shall apply for the necessary action, where the place of arbitration has been agreed upon by the parties, at his option to the President of the Chamber of Commerce of the place of arbitration agreed upon or to the President of the competent Chamber of Commerce of the respondent's habitual place of residence or seat at the time of the introduction of the request for arbitration. Where such a place has not been agreed upon, the claimant shall be entitled at his option to apply for the necessary action either to the President of the competent Chamber of Commerce of the country of the respondent's habitual place of residence or seat at the time of the introduction of the request for arbitration, or to the Special Committee whose composition and procedure are specified in the Annex to this Convention. Where the claimant fails to exercise the rights given to him under this paragraph the respondent or the arbitrator(s) shall be entitled to do so.
4.   When seised of a request the President or the Special Committee shall be entitled as need be —
      (a)   to appoint the sole arbitrator, presiding arbitrator, umpire, or referee;
      (b)   to replace the arbitrator(s) appointed under any procedure other than that referred to in paragraph 2 above;
      (c)   to determine the place of arbitration, provided that the arbitrator(s) may fix another place of arbitration;
      (d)   to establish directly or by reference to the rules and statutes of a permanent arbitral institution the rules of procedure to be followed by the arbitrator(s),

provided that the arbitrators have not established these rules themselves in the absence of any agreement thereon between the parties.

5. Where the parties have agreed to submit their disputes to a permanent arbitral institution without determining the institution in question and cannot agree thereon, the claimant may request the determination of such institution in conformity with the procedure referred to in paragraph 3 above.

6. Where the arbitration agreement does not specify the mode of arbitration (arbitration by a permanent arbitral institution or an ad hoc arbitration) to which the parties have agreed to submit their dispute, and where the parties cannot agree thereon, the claimant shall be entitled to have recourse in this case to the procedure referred to in paragraph 3 above to determine the question. The President of the competent Chamber of Commerce or the Special Committee, shall be entitled either to refer the parties to a permanent arbitral institution or to request the parties to appoint their arbitrators within such time-limits as the President of the competent Chamber of Commerce or the Special Committee may have fixed and to agree within such time-limits on the necessary measures for the functioning of the arbitration. In the latter case, the provisions of paragraphs 2, 3 and 4 of this Article shall apply.

7. Where within a period of sixty days from the moment when he was requested to fulfil one of the functions set out in paragraphs 2, 3, 4, 5 and 6 of this Article, the President of the Chamber of Commerce designated by virtue of these paragraphs has not fulfilled one of these functions, the party requesting shall be entitled to ask the Special Committee to do so.

Article V
Plea as to arbitral jurisdiction

1. The party which intends to raise a plea as to the arbitrator's jurisdiction based on the fact that the arbitration agreement was either non-existent or null and void or had lapsed shall do so during the arbitration proceedings, not later than the delivery of its statement of claim or defence relating to the substance of the dispute; those based on the fact that an arbitrator has exceeded his terms of reference shall be raised during the arbitration proceedings as soon as the question on which the arbitrator is alleged to have no jurisdiction is raised during the arbitral procedure. Where the delay in raising the plea is due to a cause which the arbitrator deems justified, the arbitrator shall declare the plea admissible.

2. Pleas to the jurisdiction referred to in paragraph 1 above that have not been raised during the time-limits there referred to, may not be entered either during a subsequent stage of the arbitral proceedings where they are pleas left to the sole discretion of the parties under the law applicable by the arbitrator, or during subsequent court proceedings concerning the substance or the enforcement of the award where such pleas are left to the discretion of the parties under the rule of conflict of the court seised of the substance of the dispute or the enforcement of the award. The arbitrator's decision on the delay in raising the plea, will, however, be subject to judicial control.

3. Subject to any subsequent judicial control provided for under the *lex fori*, the arbitrator whose jurisdiction is called in question shall be entitled to proceed with the arbitration, to rule on his own jurisdiction and to decide upon the existence or the validity of the arbitration agreement or of the contract of which the agreement forms part.

Article VI
Jurisdiction of courts of law

1. A plea as to the jurisdiction of the court made before the court seised by either party to the arbitration agreement, on the basis of the fact that an arbitration

agreement exists shall, under penalty of estoppel, be presented by the respondent before or at the same time as the presentation of his substantial defence, depending upon whether the law of the court seised regards this plea as one of procedure or of substance.

2.   In taking a decision concerning the existing or the validity of an arbitration agreement, courts of Contracting States shall examine the validity of such agreement with reference to the capacity of the parties, under the law applicable to them, and with reference to other questions—

(a)   under the law to which the parties have subjected their arbitration agreement;

(b)   failing any indication thereon, under the law of the country in which the award is to be made;

(c)   failing any indication as to the law to which the parties have subjected the agreement, and where at the time when the question is raised in court the country in which the award is to be made cannot be determined, under the competent law by virtue of the rules of conflict of the court seised of the dispute.

The court may also refuse recognition of the arbitration agreement if under the law of their country the dispute is not capable of settlement by arbitration.

3.   Where either party to an arbitration agreement has initiated arbitration proceedings before any resort is had to a court, courts of Contracting States subsequently asked to deal with the same subject-matter between the same parties or with the question whether the arbitration agreement was non-existent or null and void or had lapsed, shall stay their ruling on the arbitrator's jurisdiction until the arbitral award is made, unless they have good and substantial reasons to the contrary.

4.   A request for interim measures or measures of conservation addressed to a judicial authority shall not be deemed incompatible with the arbitration agreement, or regarded as a submission of the substance of the case to the court.

Article VII
Applicable law

1.   The parties shall be free to determine, by agreement, the law to be applied by the arbitrators to the substance of the dispute. Failing any indication by the parties as to the applicable law, the arbitrators shall apply the proper law under the rule of conflict that the arbitrators deem applicable. In both cases the arbitrators shall take account of the terms of the contract and trade usages.

2.   The arbitrators shall act as *amiables compositeurs* if the parties so decide and if they may do so under the law applicable to the arbitration.

Article VIII
Reasons for the award

The parties shall be presumed to have agreed that reasons shall be given for the award unless they—

(a)   either expressly declare that reasons shall not be given; or

(b)   have assented to an arbitral procedure under which it is not customary to give reasons for awards, provided that in this case neither party requests before the end of the hearing, or if there has not been a hearing then before the making of the award, that reasons be given.

Article IX
Setting aside of the arbitral award

1.   The setting aside in a Contracting State of an arbitral award covered by this convention shall only constitute a ground for the refusal or recognition or enforcement in another Contracting State where such setting aside took place in a State in which, or under the law of which, the award has been made and for one of the following reasons—
      (a)   the parties to the arbitration agreement were under the law applicable to them, under some incapacity or the said agreement is not valid under the law to which the parties have subjected it or, failing any indication thereon, under the law of the country where the award was made; or
      (b)   the party requesting the setting aside of the award was not given proper notice of appointment of the arbitrator or of the arbitration proceedings or was otherwise unable to present his case; or
      (c)   the award deals with a difference not contemplated by or not falling within the terms of the submission to arbitration, or it contains decision on matters beyond the scope of the submission to arbitration, provided that, if the decisions on matters submitted to arbitration can be separated from those not so submitted, that part of the award which contains decisions on matters submitted to arbitration need not be set aside;
      (d)   the composition of the arbitral authority or the arbitral procedure was not in accordance with the agreement of the parties, or failing such agreement, with the provisions of Article IV of this Convention.
2.   In relations between Contracting States that are also parties to the New York convention on the Recognition and Enforcement of Foreign Arbitral Awards of 10th June 1958, paragraph 1 of this Article limits the application of Article V (1)(e) of the New York Convention solely to the cases of setting aside set out under paragraph 1 above.

Article X [Omitted].

AGREEMENT RELATING TO APPLICATION OF THE EUROPEAN CONVENTION ON INTERNATIONAL COMMERCIAL ARBITRATION, PARIS, 1962

Article 1

In relations between physical or legal persons whose habitual residence or seat is in States Parties to the present Agreement, paragraphs 2 to 7 of Article IV of the European convention on International Commercial Arbitration, opened for signature at Geneva on 21st April 1961, are replaced by the following provision:
      'If the arbitral Agreement contains no indication regarding the measures referred to in paragraph 1 of Article IV of the European Convention on International Commercial Arbitration as a whole, or some of these measures, any difficulties arising with regard to the constitution or functioning of the arbitral tribunal shall be submitted to the decision of the competent authority at the request of the party instituting proceedings.'

Articles 2–6 [Omitted].

CONVENTION RELATING TO A UNIFORM LAW ON THE INTERNATIONAL SALE OF GOODS, THE HAGUE, 1964

See Schedule 1 to the Uniform Law on International Sales Act 1967 for the text of the Convention.

CONVENTION RELATING TO A UNIFORM LAW ON THE FORMATION OF CONTRACTS FOR THE INTERNATIONAL SALE OF GOODS, 1964

See Schedule 2 to the Uniform Laws on International Sales Act 1967 for text of the Convention.

CONVENTION ON THE SERVICE ABROAD OF JUDICIAL AND EXTRAJUDICIAL DOCUMENTS IN CIVIL OR COMMERCIAL MATTERS, THE HAGUE, 1965

Article 1

The present convention shall apply in all cases, in civil or commercial matters, where there is occasion to transmit a judicial or extrajudicial document for service abroad.

This Convention shall not apply where the address of the person to be served with the document is not known.

CHAPTER I
JUDICIAL DOCUMENTS

Article 2

Each Contracting State shall designate a Central Authority which will undertake to receive requests for service coming from other Contracting States and to proceed in conformity with the provisions of Articles 3 to 6.

Each State shall organise the Central Authority in conformity with its own law.

Article 3

The authority or judicial officer competent under the law of the State in which the documents originate shall forward to the Central Authority of the State addressed a request conforming to the model annexed to the present convention, without any requirement of legalisation or other equivalent formality.

The document to be served or a copy thereof shall be annexed to the request. The request and the document shall both be furnished in duplicate.

Article 4

If the Central Authority considers that the request does not comply with the provisions of the present Convention it shall promptly inform the applicant and specify its objections to the request.

Article 5

The Central Authority of the State addressed shall itself serve the document or shall arrange to have it served by an appropriate agency, either—
(a)   by a method prescribed by its internal law for the service of documents in domestic actions upon persons who are within its territory; or
(b)   by a particular method requested by the applicant, unless such a method is incompatible with the law of the State addressed.
Subject to sub-paragraph (b) of the first paragraph of this Article, the document may always be served by delivery to an addressee who accepts it voluntarily.

If the document is to be served under the first paragraph above, the Central authority may require the document to be written in, or translated into, the official language or one of the official languages of the State addressed.

The part of the request, in the form attached to the present Convention, which contains a summary of the document to be served, shall be served with the document.

Article 6

The Central Authority of the State addressed or any authority which it may have designated for that purpose, shall complete a certificate in the form of the model annexed to the present Convention.

The certificate shall state that the document has been served and shall include the method, the place and the date of service and the person to whom the document was delivered. If the document has not been served, the certificate shall set out the reasons which have prevented service.

The applicant may require that a certificate not completed by a Central Authority or by a judicial authority shall be countersigned by one of these authorities.

The certificate shall be forwarded directly to the applicant.

Article 7

The standard terms in the model annexed to the present convention shall in all cases be written either in French or in English. They may also be written in the official language, or in one of the official languages, of the State in which the documents originate.

The corresponding blanks shall be completed either in the language of the State addressed or in French or in English.

Article 8

Each Contracting State shall be free to effect service of judicial documents upon persons abroad, without application of any compulsion, directly through its diplomatic or consular agents.

Any State may declare that it is opposed to such service within its territory, unless the document is to be served upon a national of the State in which the documents originate.

Article 9

Each Contracting State shall be free, in addition, to use consular channels to forward documents, for the purpose of service, to those authorities of another Contracting State which are designated by the latter for this purpose.

Each Contracting State may, if exceptional circumstances so require, use diplomatic channels for the same purpose.

Article 10

Provided the State of destination does not object, the present Convention shall not interfere with —

(a)   the freedom to send judicial documents, by postal channels, directly to persons abroad;
(b)   the freedom of judicial officers, officials or other competent persons of the State of origin to effect service of judicial documents directly through the judicial officers, officials or other competent persons of the State of destination;
(c)   the freedom of any person interested in a judicial proceeding to effect service of judicial documents directly through the judicial officers, officials or other competent persons of the State of destination.

Article 11

The present Convention shall not prevent two or more Contracting States from agreeing to permit, for the purpose of service of judicial documents, channels of transmission other than those provided for in the preceding Articles and, in particular, direct communication between their respective authorities.

Article 12

The service of judicial documents coming from a Contracting State shall not give rise to any payment or reimbursement of taxes or costs for the services rendered by the State addressed.

The applicant shall pay or reimburse the costs occasioned by —

(a)   the employment of a judicial officer or of a person competent under the law of the State of destination;
(b)   the use of a particular method of service.

Article 13

Where a request for service complies with the terms of the present convention, the State addressed may refuse to comply therewith only if it deems that compliance would infringe its sovereignty or security.

It may not refuse to comply solely on the ground that, under its internal law, it claims exclusive jurisdiction over the subject-matter of the action or that its internal law would not permit the action upon which the application is based.

The Central Authority shall, in case of refusal, promptly inform the applicant and state the reasons for the refusal.

Article 14

Difficulties which may arise in connection with the transmission of judicial documents for service shall be settled through diplomatic channels.

Article 15

Where a writ of summons or an equivalent document had to be transmitted abroad for the purpose of service, under the provisions of the present Convention, and the defendant has not appeared, judgment shall not be given until it is established that —

(a)   the document was served by a method prescribed by the internal law of the State addressed for the service of documents in domestic actions upon persons who are within its territory; or
(b)   the document was actually delivered to the defendant or to his residence by another method provided for by this Convention,

and that in either of these cases the service or the delivery was effected in sufficient time to enable the defendant to defend.

Each Contracting State shall be free to declare that the judge, notwithstanding the provisions of the first paragraph of this Article, may give judgment even if no certificate of service or delivery has been received, if all the following conditions are fulfilled —

(a)   the document was transmitted by one of the methods provided for in this convention;

(b)   a period of time of not less than six months, considered adequate by the judge in the particular case, has elapsed since the date of the transmission of the document;

(c)   no certificate of any kind has been received, even though every reasonable effort has been made to obtain it through the competent authorities of the State addressed.

Notwithstanding the provisions of the preceding paragraphs the judge may order, in case of urgency, any provisional or protective measures.

Article 16

When a writ of summons or an equivalent document had to be transmitted abroad for the purpose of service, under the provisions of the present Convention, and a judgment has been entered against a defendant who has not appeared, the judge shall have the power to relieve the defendant from the effects of the expiration of the time for appeal from the judgment if the following conditions are fulfilled —

(a)   the defendant, without any fault on his part, did not have knowledge of the document in sufficient time to defend, or knowledge of the judgment in sufficient time to appeal; and

(b)   the defendant has disclosed a *prima facie* defence to the action on the merits.

An application for relief may be filled only within a reasonable time after the defendant has knowledge of the judgment.

Each Contracting State may declare that the application will not be entertained if it is filed after the expiration of a time to be stated in the declaration, but which shall in no case be less than one year following the date of the judgment.

CHAPTER II
EXTRAJUDICIAL DOCUMENTS

Article 17

Extrajudicial documents emanating from authorities and judicial officers of a Contracting State may be transmitted for the purpose of service in another Contracting State by the methods and under the provisions of the present Convention.

CHAPTER III
GENERAL CLAUSES

Article 18

Each Contracting State may designate other authorities in addition to the Central Authority and shall determine the extent of their competence. The applicant shall, however, in all cases, have the right to address a request directly to the Central Authority. Federal States shall be free to designate more than one Central Authority.

Article 19

To the extent that the internal law of a Contracting State permits methods of transmission, other than those provided for in the preceding Articles, of documents coming from abroad, for service within its territory, the present Convention shall not affect such provisions.

Article 20

The present Convention shall not prevent an agreement between any two or more Contracting States to dispense with—
(a)   the necessity for duplicate copies of transmitted documents as required by the second paragraph of Article 3;
(b)   the language requirements of the third paragraph of Article 5 and Article 7;
(c)   the provisions of the fourth paragraph of Article 5;
(d)   the provisions of the second paragraph of Article 12.

ANNEX TO THE CONVENTION

Forms

*Request for Service Abroad of Judicial
or Extrajudicial Documents*

Convention on the service abroad of judicial and extrajudicial documents in civil or commercial matters, signed at The Hague, _____ 1965

The undersigned applicant has the honour to transmit—in duplicate—the documents listed below and, in conformity with Article 5 of the above-mentioned Convention, requests prompt service of one copy thereof on the addressee, i.e.

(identity and address) _____

_____

    (a) in accordance with the provisions of sub-paragraph a of the first paragraph of Article 5 of the convention*

    (b) in accordance with the following particular method (sub-paragraph b of the first paragraph of Article 5):* _____

_____

    (c) by delivery to the addressee, if he accepts it voluntarily (second paragraph of Article 5).*

The authority is requested to return or to have returned to the applicant a copy of the documents—and of the annexes*—with a certificate as provided on the reverse side.

List of documents

_____   Done at _____ , the _____

_____   Signature and/or stamp

_____

* Delete if inappropriate.

Reverse of the request

CERTIFICATE

The undersigned authority has the honour to certify, in conformity with Article 6 of the Convention,

1) that the document has been served*

  — the (date) _____

  — at (place, street, number) _____

  _____

  — in one of the following methods authorised by Article 5—

  (a) in accordance with the provisions of sub-paragraph a of the first para of Article 5 of the Convention*.

  (b) in accordance with the following particular method.* _____

  _____

  (c) by delivery to the addressee, who accepted it voluntarily.*

  The documents referred to in the request have been delivered to:

  — (identity and description of person) _____

  _____

  — relationship to the addressee (family, business or other): _____

  _____

2) that the document has not been served, by reason of the following facts.*

  _____

  _____

In conformity with the second paragraph of Article 12 of the Convention, the applicant is requested to pay or reimburse the expenses detailed in the attached statement.*

Annexes

Documents returned: _____

_____

_____

In appropriate cases, documents

establishing the service: _____

Done at _____, the _____

Signature and/or stamp.

* Delete if inappropriate.

SUMMARY OF THE DOCUMENT TO BE SERVED

Convention on the service abroad of judicial and extrajudicial documents in civil or commercial matters, signed at The Hague, the _____ 196

(Article 5, fourth paragraph)

Name and address of the requesting authority; _____

_____

Particulars of the parties:* _____

_____

JUDICIAL DOCUMENT**

Nature and purpose of the document: _____

_____

Nature and purpose of the proceedings and, where appropriate, the amount in dispute:

_____

_____

Date and place for entering appearance:** _____

_____

Court which has given judgment:** _____

_____

Date of judgment:** _____

Time limits stated in the document:** _____

_____

EXTRAJUDICIAL DOCUMENT**

Nature and purpose of the document: _____

_____

Time limits stated in the document:** _____

_____

* If appropriate, identity and address of the person interested in the transmission of the document.
** Delete if inappropriate.

BRUSSELS PROTOCOL AMENDING THE HAGUE RULES RELATING
TO BILLS OF LADING 1968
(HAGUE-VISBY RULES)

See the Schedule to the Carriage of Goods by Sea Act 1972 for text of the Convention.

GUATEMALA PROTOCOL 1971
PROTOCOL TO AMEND THE CONVENTION FOR THE UNIFICATION OF CERTAIN RULES
RELATING TO INTERNATIONAL CARRIAGE BY AIR SIGNED AT WARSAW ON 12TH
OCTOBER 1929 AS AMENDED BY THE PROTOCOL DONE AT THE HAGUE ON 28TH
SEPTEMBER 1955, GUATEMALA CITY, 8TH MARCH 1971

CHAPTER I
AMENDMENT TO THE CONVENTION

Article I

The Convention which the provisions of the present Chapter modify is the Warsaw Convention as amended at The Hague in 1955.

Article II

Article 3 of the Convention shall be deleted and replaced by the following—
'Article 3

1. In respect of the carriage of passengers an individual or collective document of carriage shall be delivered containing:
   (a) an indication of the places of departure and destination;
   (b) if the places of departure and destination are within the territory of a single High Contracting Party, one or more agreed stopping places being within the territory of another State, an indication of at least one such stopping place.
2. Any other means which would preserve a record of the information indicated in (a) and (b) of the foregoing paragraph may be substituted for the delivery of the document referred to in that paragraph.
3. Non-compliance with the provisions of the foregoing paragraphs shall not affect the existence or the validity of the contract of carriage, which shall, none the less be subject to the rules of this Convention including those relating to limitation of liability.'

Article III

Article 4 of the Convention shall be deleted and replaced by the following—
'Article 4

1. In respect of the carriage of checked baggage, a baggage check shall be delivered, which, unless combined with or incorporated in a document of carriage which complies with the provisions of Article 3, paragraph 1, shall contain:
   (a) an indication of the places of departure and destination;
   (b) if the places of departure and destination are within the territory of a single High Contracting Party, one or more agreed stopping places being within the territory of another State, an indication of at least one such stopping place.

2. Any other means which would preserve a record of the information indicated in (a) and (b) of the foregoing paragraph may be substituted for the delivery of the baggage check referred to in that paragraph.

3. Non-compliance with the provisions of the foregoing paragraphs shall not affect the existence or the validity of the contract of carriage, which shall, none the less, be subject to the rules of this Convention including those relating to limitation of liability.'

Article IV

Article 17 of the Convention shall be deleted and replaced by the following—
'Article 17

1. The carrier is liable for damage sustained in case of death or personal injury of a passenger upon condition only that the event which caused the death or injury took place on board the aircraft or in the course of any of the operations of embarking or disembarking. However, the carrier is not liable if the death or injury resulted solely from the state of health of the passenger.

2. The carrier is liable for damage sustained in case of destruction or loss of, or of damage to, baggage upon condition only that the event which caused the destruction, loss or damage took place on board the aircraft or in the course of any of the operations of embarking or disembarking or during any period within which the baggage was in charge of the carrier. However, the carrier is not liable if the damage resulted solely from the inherent defect, quality or vice of the baggage.

3. Unless otherwise specified in this Convention, the term "baggage" means both checked baggage and objects carried by the passenger.'

Article V

In Article 18 of the Convention, paragraphs 1 and 2 shall be deleted and replaced by the following—
'1. The carrier is liable for damage sustained in the event of the destruction or loss of, or of damage to, any cargo, if the occurrence which caused the damage so sustained took place during the carriage by air.

2. The carriage by air within the meaning of the preceding paragraph comprises the period during which the cargo is in charge of the carrier, whether in an airport or on board an aircraft, or, in the case of a landing outside an airport, in any place whatsoever.'

Article VI

Article 20 of the Convention shall be deleted and replaced by the following—
'Article 20

1. In the carriage of passengers and baggage the carrier shall not be liable for damage occasioned by delay if he proves that he and his servants and agents have taken all necessary measures to avoid the damage or that it was impossible for them to take such measures.

2. In the carriage of cargo the carrier shall not be liable for damage resulting from destruction, loss, damage or delay if he proves that he and his servants and agents have taken all necessary measures to avoid the damage or that it was impossible for them to take such measures.'

Article VII

Article 21 of the Convention shall be deleted and replaced by the following—
  'Article 21
      If the carrier proves that the damage was caused or contributed to by the
      negligence or other wrongful act or omission of the person claiming
      compensation, the carrier shall be wholly or partly exonerated from his liability
      to such person to the extent that such negligence or wrongful act or omission
      caused or contributed to the damage. When by reason of the death or injury of a
      passenger compensation is claimed by a person other than the passenger, the
      carrier shall likewise be wholly or partly exonerated from his liability to the
      extent that he proves that the damage was caused or contributed to by the
      negligence or other wrongful act or omission of that passenger.'

Article VIII

Article 22 of the Convention shall be deleted and replaced by the following—
  'Article 22
  1.   (a) In the carriage of persons the liability of the carrier is limited to the sum
             of one million five hundred thousand francs for the aggregate of the
             claims, however founded in respect of damage suffered as a result of the
             death or personal injury of each passenger. Where, in accordance with
             the law of the court seized of the case, damages may be awarded in the
             form of periodic payments, the equivalent capital value of the said
             payments shall not exceed one million five hundred thousand francs.
         (b) In the case of delay in the carriage of persons the liability of the carrier
             for each passenger is limited to sixty-two thousand five hundred francs.
         (c) In the carriage of baggage the liability of the carrier in the case of
             destruction, loss, damage or delay is limited to fifteen thousand francs
             for each passenger.
  2.   (a) In the carriage of cargo, the liability of the carrier is limited to a sum of
             two hundred and fifty francs per kilogramme, unless the consignor has
             made, at the time when the package was handed over to the carrier, a
             special declaration of interest in delivery at destination and has paid a
             supplementary sum if the case so requires. In that case the carrier will be
             liable to pay a sum not exceeding the declared sum, unless he proves
             that that sum is greater than the consignor's actual interest in delivery at
             destination.
         (b) In the case of loss, damage or delay of part of the cargo, or of any object
             contained therein, the weight to be taken into consideration in
             determining the amount to which the carrier's liability is limited shall be
             only the total weight of the package or packages concerned.
             Nevertheless, when the loss, damage or delay of a part of the cargo, or of
             any object contained therein, affects the value of other packages covered
             by the same air waybill, the total weight of such package or packages
             shall be taken into consideration in determining the limit of liability.
  3.   (a) The courts of the High Contracting Parties which are not authorised
             under their law to award the costs of the action, including lawyers' fees,
             shall, in actions to which this Convention applies, have the power to
             award, in their discretion, to the claimant the whole or part of the costs
             of the action, including lawyers' fees which the court considers
             reasonable.
         (b) The costs of the action including lawyers' fees shall be awarded in
             accordance with subparagraph (a) only if the claimant gives a written
             notice to the carrier of the amount claimed including the particulars of
             the calculation of that amount and the carrier does not make, within a

period of six months after his receipt of such notice, a written offer of settlement in an amount at least equal to the compensation awarded within the applicable limit. This period will be extended until the time of commencement of the action if that is later.

(c) The costs of the action including lawyers' fees shall not be taken into account in applying the limits under this Article.

4. The sums mentioned in francs in this Article and Article 42 shall be deemed to refer to a currency unit consisting of sixty-five and a half milligrammes of gold of millesimal fineness nine hundred. These sums may be converted into national currencies in round figures. Conversion of the sums into national currencies other than gold shall, in case of judicial proceedings, be made according to the gold value of such currencies at the date of the judgment.'

Article IX

Article 24 of the Convention shall be deleted and replaced by the following—

'Article 24

1. In the carriage of cargo, any action for damages, however founded, can only be brought subject to the conditions and limits set out in this Convention.

2. In the carriage of passengers and baggage any action for damages, however founded, whether under this Convention or in contract or in tort or otherwise, can only be brought subject to the conditions and limits of liability set out in this Convention, without prejudice to the question as to who are the persons who have the right to bring suit and what are their respective rights. Such limits of liability constitute maximum limits and may not be exceeded whatever the circumstances which gave rise to the liability.'

Article X

Article 25 of the Convention shall be deleted and replaced by the following—

'Article 25

The limit of liability specified in paragraph 2 of Article 27 shall not apply if it is proved that the damage resulted from an act or omission of the carrier, his servants or agents, done with intent to cause damage or recklessly and with knowledge that damage would probably result; provided that, in the case of such act or omission of a servant or agent, it is also proved that he was acting within the scope of his employment.'

Article XI

In Article 25A of the Convention, paragraphs 1 and 3 shall be deleted and replaced by the following—

'1. If an action is brought against a servant or agent of the carrier arising out of damage to which the Convention relates, such servant or agent if he proves that he acted within the scope of his employment, shall be entitled to avail himself of the limits of liability which that carrier himself is entitled to invoke under this Convention.

3. The provisions of paragraphs 1 and 2 of this Article shall not apply to the carriage of cargo if it is proved that the damage resulted from an act or omission of the servant or agent done with intent to cause damage or recklessly and with knowledge that damage would probably result.'

Article XII

In Article 28 of the Convention, the present paragraph 2 shall be renumbered as paragraph 3 and a new paragraph 2 shall be inserted as follows—

'2.   In respect of damage resulting from the death, injury or delay of a passenger or the destruction, loss, damage or delay of baggage, the action may be brought before one of the Courts mentioned in paragraph 1 of this Article, or in the territory of one of the High Contracting Parties, before the Court within the jurisdiction of which the carrier has an establishment if the passenger has his domicile or permanent residence in the territory of the same High Contracting Party.'

Article XIII

After Article 30 of the Convention, the following Article shall be inserted —
'Article 30A
Nothing in this Convention shall prejudice the question whether a person liable for damage in accordance with its provisions has a right of recourse against any other person.'

Article XIV

After Article 35 of the Convention, the following Article shall be inserted —
'Article 35A
No provision contained in this Convention shall prevent a State from establishing and operating within its territory a system to supplement the compensation payable to claimants under the Convention in respect of death, or personal injury, of passengers. Such a system shall fulfil the following conditions:

(a)   it shall not in any circumstances impose upon the carrier, his servants or agents, any liability in addition to that provided under this Convention;

(b)   it shall not impose upon the carrier any financial or administrative burden other than collecting in that State contributions from passengers if required so to do;

(c)   it shall not give rise to any discrimination between carriers with regard to the passengers concerned and the benefits available to the said passengers under the system shall be extended to them regardless of the carrier whose services they have used;

(d)   if a passenger has contributed to the system, any person suffering damage as a consequence of death or personal injury of such passenger shall be entitled to the benefit of the system.'

Article XV

After Article 41 of the Convention the following Article shall be inserted —
'Article 42

1.   Without prejudice to the provisions of Article 41, Conferences of the Parties to the Protocol done at Guatemala City on the eighth March 1971, shall be convened during the fifth and tenth years respectively after the date of entry into force of the said Protocol for the purpose of reviewing the limit established in Article 22, paragraph 1(a) of the Convention as intended by that Protocol.

2.   At each of the Conferences mentioned in paragraph 1 of this Article the limit of liability in Article 22, paragraph 1(a) in force at the respective dates of these Conferences shall not be increased by an amount exceeding one hundred and eighty-seven thousand five hundred francs.

3.   Subject to paragraph 2 of this Article, unless before the thirty-first December of the fifth and tenth years after the date of entry into force of the Protocol referred to in paragraph 1 of this Article the aforesaid Conferences decide otherwise by a two-thirds majority vote of the parties present and voting the limit of liability in Article 22, paragraph 1(a) in force at the respective date of

these Conferences shall on those dates be increased by one hundred and eighty-seven thousand five hundred francs.

4.   The applicable limit shall be that which, in accordance with the preceding paragraphs, is in effect on the date of the event which caused the death or personal injury of the passenger.'

CHAPTER II
SCOPE OF APPLICATION OF THE CONVENTION AS AMENDED

Article XVI

The Warsaw Convention as amended at The Hague in 1955 and by this Protocol shall apply to international carriage as defined in Article 1 of the Convention provided that the places of departure and destination referred to in that Article are situated either in the territories of two Parties to this Protocol or within the territory of a single Party to this Protocol with an agreed stopping place in the territory of another State.

CHAPTER III
FINAL CLAUSES

Articles XVII–XXVI [Omitted].

UNITED NATIONS CONVENTION ON THE LIMITATION PERIOD IN THE INTERNATIONAL SALE OF GOODS, NEW YORK, 1974

PART I
SUBSTANTIVE PROVISIONS

Sphere of application

Article 1

1.   This Convention shall determine when claims of a buyer and a seller against each other arising from a contract of international sale of goods or relating to its breach, termination or invalidity can no longer be exercised by reason on the expiration of a period of time. Such period of time is hereinafter referred to as 'the limitation period'.

2.   This Convention shall not affect a particular time-limit within which one party is required, as a condition for the acquisition or exercise of his claim to give notice to the other party or perform any act other than the institution of legal proceedings.

3.   In this Convention—

    (a)   'buyer', 'seller' and 'party' mean persons who buy or sell, or agree to buy or sell, goods, and the successors to and assigns of their rights or obligations under the contract of sale;

    (b)   'creditor' means a party who asserts a claim, whether or not such a claim is for a sum of money;

    (c)   'debtor' means a party against whom a creditor asserts a claim;

    (d)   'breach of contract' means the failure of a party to perform the contract or any performance not in conformity with the contract;

    (e)   'legal proceedings' includes judicial, arbitral and administrative proceedings;

    (f)   'person' includes corporation, company, partnership, association or entity, whether private or public, which can sue or be sued;

(g)   'writing' includes telegram and telex;
(h)   'year' means a year according to the Gregorian calendar.

Article 2

For the purposes of this Convention—
(a)   a contract of sale of goods shall be considered international if, at the time of the conclusion of the contract, the buyer and the seller have their places of business in different States;
(b)   the fact that the parties have their places of business in different States shall be disregarded whenever this fact does not appear either from the contract or from any dealings between, or from information disclosed by, the parties at any time before or at the conclusion of the contract;
(c)   where a party to a contract of sale of goods has places of business in more than one State, the place of business shall be that which has the closest relationship to the contract and its performance, having regard to the circumstances known to or contemplated by the parties at the time of the conclusion of the contract;
(d)   his habitual residence;
(e)   neither the nationality of the parties nor the civil or commercial character of the parties or of the contract shall be taken into consideration.

Article 3

1.   This Convention shall apply only if, at the time of the conclusion of the contract, the places of business of the parties to a contract of international sale of goods are in Contracting States.
2.   Unless this Convention provides otherwise, it shall apply irrespective of the law which would otherwise by applicable by virtue of the rules of private international law.
3.   This Convention shall not apply when the parties have expressly excluded its application.

Article 4

This Convention shall not apply to sales—
(a)   of goods bought for personal, family or household use;
(b)   by auction;
(c)   on execution or otherwise by authority of law;
(d)   of stocks, shares, investment securities, negotiable instruments or money;
(e)   of ships, vessels or aircraft;
(f)   of electricity.

Article 5

This Convention shall not apply to claims based upon—
(a)   death of, or personal injury to, any person;
(b)   nuclear damage caused by the goods sold;
(c)   a lien, mortgage or other security interest in property;
(d)   a judgment or award made in legal proceedings;
(e)   a document on which direct enforcement or execution can be obtained in accordance with the law of the place where such enforcement or execution is sought;
(f)   a bill of exchange, cheque or promissory note.

Article 6

1.   This Convention shall not apply to contracts in which the preponderant part of the obligations of the seller consists in the supply of labour or other services.
2.   Contracts for the supply of goods to be manufactured or produced shall be considered to be sales, unless the party who orders the goods undertakes to supply a substantial part of the materials necessary for such manufacture or production.

Article 7

In the interpretation and application of the provisions of this convention, regard shall be had to its international character and to the need to promote uniformity.

The duration and commencement of the limitation period

Article 8

The limitation period shall be four years.

Article 9

1.   Subject to the provisions of Articles 10, 11 and 12 the limitation period shall commence on the date on which the claim accrues.
2.   The commencement of the limitation period shall not be postponed by—
     (a)   a requirement that the party be given a notice as described in paragraph 2 of Article 1; or
     (b)   a provision in an arbitration agreement that no right shall arise until an arbitration award has been made.

Article 10

1.   A claim arising from a breach of contract shall accrue on the date on which such breach occurs.
2.   A claim arising from a defect or other lack of conformity shall accrue on the date on which the goods are actually handed over to, or their tender is refused by, the buyer.
3.   A claim based on fraud committed before or at the time of the conclusion of the contract or during its performance shall accrue on the date on which the fraud was or reasonably could have been discovered.

Article 11

If the seller has given an express undertaking relating to the goods which is stated to have effect for a certain period of time, whether expressed in terms of a specific period of time or otherwise, the limitation period in respect of any claim arising from the undertaking shall commence on the date on which the buyer notifies the seller of the fact on which the claim is based, but not later than on the date of the expiration of the period of the undertaking.

Article 12

1.   If, in circumstances provided for by the law applicable to the contract, one party is entitled to declare the contract terminated before the time for performance is due, and exercises this right, the limitation period in respect of a claim based on any such circumstances shall commence on the date on which the declaration is made

to the other party. If the contract is not declared to be terminated before performance becomes due, the limitation period shall commence on the date on which performance is due.

2. The limitation period in respect of a claim arising out of a breach by one party of a contract for the delivery of or payment for goods by instalments shall, in relation to each separate instalment, commence on the date on which the particular breach occurs. If, under the law applicable to the contract, one party is entitled to declare the contract terminated by reason of such breach, and exercises this right, the limitation period in respect of all relevant instalments shall commence on the date on which the declaration is made to the other party.

Cessation and extension of the limitation period

Article 13

The limitation period shall cease to run when the creditor performs any act which, under the law of the court where the proceedings are instituted, is recognised as commencing judicial proceedings against the debtor or as asserting his claim in such proceedings already instituted against the debtor, for the purpose of obtaining satisfaction or recognition of his claim.

Article 14

1. Where the parties have agreed to submit to arbitration, the limitation period shall cease to run when either party commences arbitral proceedings in the manner provided for in the arbitration agreement or by the law applicable to such proceedings.

2. In the absence of any such provision, arbitral proceedings shall be deemed to commence on the date on which a request that the claim in dispute be referred to arbitration is delivered at the habitual residence or place of business of the other party or, if he has no such residence or place of business, then at his last known residence or place of business.

Article 15

If any legal proceedings other than those mentioned in Articles 13 and 14, including legal proceedings commenced upon the occurrence of —
(a) the death or incapacity of the debtor;
(b) the bankruptcy or any state of insolvency affecting the whole of the property of the debtor; or
(c) the dissolution or liquidation of a corporation, company, partnership, association or entity when it is the debtor.

The limitation period shall cease to run when the creditor asserts his claim in such proceedings for the purpose of obtaining satisfaction or recognition of the claim, subject to the law governing the proceedings.

Article 16

For the purposes of Articles 13, 14 and 15, any act performed by way of counterclaim shall be deemed to have been performed on the same date as the act performed in relation to the claim against which the counterclaim is raised, provided that both the claim and the counterclaim relate to the same contract or to several contracts concluded in the course of the same transaction.

Article 17

1.   Where a claim has been asserted in legal proceedings within the limitation period in accordance with Articles 13, 14, 15 or 16, but such legal proceedings have ended without a decision binding on the merits of the claim, the limitation period shall be deemed to have continued to run.
2.   If, at the time such legal proceedings ended, the limitation period has expired or has less than one year to run, the creditor shall be entitled to a period of one year from the date on which the legal proceedings ended.

Article 18

1.   Where legal proceedings have been commenced against one debtor, the limitation period prescribed in this Convention shall cease to run against any other party jointly and severally liable with the debtor, provided that the creditor informs such party in writing within that period that the proceedings have been commenced.
2.   Where legal proceedings have been commenced by a subpurchaser against the buyer, the limitation period prescribed in this Convention shall cease to run in relation to the buyer's claim over against the seller, if the buyer informs the seller in writing within that period that the proceedings have been commenced.
3.   Where the legal proceedings referred to in paragraphs 1 and 2 of this Article have ended, the limitation period in respect of the claim of the creditor or the buyer against the party jointly and severally liable or against the seller shall be deemed not to have ceased running by virtue of paragraphs 1 and 2 of this Article, but the creditor or the buyer shall be entitled to an additional year from the date on which the legal proceedings ended, if at that time the limitation period had expired or had less than one year to run.

Article 19

Where the creditor performs, in the State in which the debtor has his place of business and before the expiration of the limitation period, any act, other than the acts described in Articles 13, 14, 15 and 16, which under the law of that State has the effect of recommencing a limitation period, a new limitation period of four years shall commence on the date prescribed by that law.

Article 20

1.   Where the debtor, before the expiration of the limitation period, acknowledges in writing his obligation to the creditor, a new limitation period of four years shall commence to run from the date of such acknowledgement.
2.   Payment of interest or partial performance of an obligation by the debtor shall have the same effect as an acknowledgement under paragraph 1 of this Article if it can reasonably be inferred from such payment or performance that the debtor acknowledges that obligation.

Article 21

Where, as a result of a circumstance which is beyond the control of the creditor and which he could neither avoid nor overcome, the creditor has been prevented from causing the limitation period to cease to run, the limitation period shall be extended so as not to expire before the expiration of one year from the date on which the relevant circumstance ceased to exist.

Modification of the limitation period by the parties

Article 22

1. The limitation period cannot be modified or affected by any declaration or agreement between the parties, except in the cases provided for in paragraph 2 of this Article.
2. The debtor may at any time during the running of the limitation period extend the period by a declaration in writing to the creditor. This declaration may be renewed.
3. The provisions of this Article shall not affect the validity of a clause in the contract of sale which stipulates that arbitral proceedings shall be commenced within a shorter period of limitation than that prescribed by this Convention, provided that such clause is valid under the law applicable to the contract of sale.

General limit of the limitation period

Article 23

Notwithstanding the provisions of this Convention, a limitation period shall in any event expire not later than 10 years from the date on which it commenced to run under Articles 9, 10, 11 and 12 of this Convention.

Consequences of expiration of the limitation period

Article 24

Expiration of the limitation period shall be taken into consideration in any legal proceedings only if invoked by a party to such proceedings.

Article 25

1. Subject to the provisions of paragraph 2 of this Article and of Article 24, no claim shall be recognised or enforced in any legal proceedings commenced after the expiration of the limitation period.
2. Notwithstanding the expiration of the limitation period, one party may rely on his claim as a defence or for the purpose of set-off against a claim asserted by the other party, provided that in the latter case this may only be done—
    (a) if both claims relate to the same contract or to several contracts concluded in the course of the same transaction; or
    (b) if the claims could have been set-off at any time before the expiration of the limitation period.

Article 26

Where the debtor performs his obligation after the expiration of the limitation period, he shall not on that ground be entitled in any way to claim restitution even if he did not know at the time when he performed his obligation that the limitation period had expired.

Article 27

The expiration of the limitation period with respect to a principal debt shall have the same effect with respect to an obligation to pay interest on that debt.

Calculation of the period

Article 28

1.   The limitation period shall be calculated in such a way that it shall expire at the end
      of the day which corresponds to the date on which the period commenced to run.
      If there is no such corresponding date, the period shall expire at the end of the last
      day of the last month of the limitation period.
2.   The limitation period shall be calculated by reference to the date of the place
      where the legal proceedings are instituted.

Article 29

Where the last day of the limitation period falls on an official holiday or other dies non
juridicus precluding the appropriate legal action in the jurisdiction where the creditor
institutes legal proceedings or asserts a claim as envisaged in Article 13, 14, or 15, the
limitation period shall be extended so as not to expire until the end of the first day
following that official holiday or dies non juridicus on which such proceedings could be
instituted or on which such a claim could be asserted in that jurisdiction.

International effect

Article 30

The acts and circumstances referred to in Articles 13 through 19 which have taken place in
one Contracting State shall have effect for the purposes of this Convention in another
Contracting State, provided that the creditor has taken all reasonable steps to ensure that
the debtor is informed of the relevant act or circumstances as soon as possible.

PART II

Articles 31–33 [Omitted].

PART III

Articles 34–40 [Omitted].

PART IV

Articles 41–46 [Omitted].

MONTREAL ADDITIONAL PROTOCOL NO 1, 1975
ADDITIONAL PROTOCOL NO 1 TO AMEND THE CONVENTION FOR THE UNIFICATION
OF CERTAIN RULES RELATING TO INTERNATIONAL CARRIAGE BY AIR SIGNED AT
WARSAW ON 12TH OCTOBER 1929

CHAPTER I
AMENDMENTS TO THE CONVENTION

Article I

The Convention which the provisions of the present Chapter modify is the Warsaw
Convention, 1929.

Article II

Article 22 of the Convention shall be deleted and replaced by the following—
'Article 22
1. In the carriage of passengers the liability of the carrier for each passenger is limited to the sum of 8,300 Special Drawing Rights. Where, in accordance with the law of the court seised of the case, damages may be awarded in the form of periodic payments, the equivalent capital value of the said payments shall not exceed this limit. Nevertheless, by special contract, the carrier and the passenger may agree to a higher limit of liability.
2. In the carriage of registered baggage and of cargo, the liability of the carrier is limited to a sum of 17 Special Drawing Rights per kilogramme unless the consignor has made, at the time when the package as handed over to the carrier, a special declaration of interest in delivery at destination and has paid a supplementary sum if the case so requires. In that case the carrier will be liable to pay a sum not exceeding the declared sum, unless he proves that that sum is greater than the consignor's actual interest in delivery at destination.
3. As regards objects of which the passenger takes charge himself the liability of the carrier is limited to 32 Special Drawing Rights per passenger.
4. The sums mentioned in terms of the Special Drawing Right in this Article shall be deemed to refer to the Special Drawing Right as defined by the International Monetary Fund. Conversion of the sums into national currencies shall, in case of judicial proceedings, be made according to the value of such currencies in terms of the Special Drawing Right at the date of the judgment. The value of a national currency, in terms of the Special Drawing Right, of a High Contracting Party which is a Member of the International Monetary Fund, shall be calculated in accordance with the method of valuation applied by the International Monetary Fund, in effect at the date of the judgment, for its operations and transactions. The value of a national currency, in terms of the Special Drawing Right, of a High Contracting Party which is not a Member of the International Monetary Fund, shall be calculated in a manner determined by that High Contracting Party.
    Nevertheless those States which are not Members of the International Monetary Fund and whose law does not permit the application of the provisions of paragraphs 1, 2 and 3 of Article 22 may at the time of ratification or accession or at any time thereafter declare that the limit of liability of the carrier in judicial proceedings in their territories is fixed at a sum of 125,000 monetary units per passenger with respect to paragraph 1 of Article 22; 250 monetary units per kilogramme with respect to paragraph 2 of Article 22; and 5,000 monetary units per passenger with respect to paragraph 3 of Article 22. This monetary unit corresponds to sixty-five and a half milligrammes of gold of millesimal fineness nine hundred These sums may be converted into the national currency concerned in round figures. The conversion of these sums into national currency shall be made according to the law of the State concerned.'

CHAPTER II
SCOPE OF APPLICATION OF CONVENTION AS AMENDED

Article III

The Warsaw Convention as amended by this Protocol shall apply to international carriage as detailed in Article I of the Convention provided that the place of departure and destination referred to in that Article are situated either in the territories of two Parties to this Protocol or within the territory of a single Party to this Protocol with an agreed stopping place in the territory of another State.

CHAPTER III
FINAL CLAUSES

Articles IV–XII [Omitted].

MONTREAL ADDITIONAL PROTOCOL NO 2, 1975
ADDITIONAL PROTOCOL NO 2 TO AMEND THE CONVENTION FOR THE UNIFICATION OF CERTAIN RULES RELATING TO INTERNATIONAL CARRIAGE BY AIR SIGNED AT WARSAW ON 12TH OCTOBER 1929 AS AMENDED BY THE PROTOCOL DONE AT THE HAGUE ON 28TH SEPTEMBER 1955

CHAPTER I
AMENDMENTS TO THE CONVENTION

Article I

The Convention which the provisions of the present Chapter modify is the Warsaw Convention as amended at The Hague in 1955.

Article II

Article 22 of the Convention shall be deleted and replaced by the following—
'Article 22

1.   In the carriage of persons the liability of the carrier for each passenger is limited to the sum of 16,600 Special Drawing Rights. Where, in accordance with the law of the court seised of the case, damages may be awarded in the form of periodic payments, the equivalent capital value of the said payments shall not exceed this limit. Nevertheless, by special contract, the carrier and the passenger may agree to a higher limit of liability.

2.   (a) In the carriage of registered baggage and of cargo, the liability of the carrier is limited to a sum of 17 Special Drawing Rights per kilogramme, unless the passenger or consignor has made, at the time when the package was handed over to the carrier, a special declaration of interest in delivery at destination and has paid a supplementary sum if the case so requires. In that case the carrier will be liable to pay a sum not exceeding the declared sum, unless he proves that that sum is greater than the passenger's or consignor's actual interest in delivery at destination.

      (b) In the case of loss, damage or delay of part of registered baggage or cargo, or of any object contained therein, the weight to be taken into consideration in determining the amount to which the carrier's liability is limited shall be only the total weight of the package or packages concerned. Nevertheless, when the loss, damage or delay of a part of the registered baggage or cargo, or of an object contained therein, affects the value of other packages covered by the same baggage check or the same air waybill, the total weight of such package or packages shall also be taken into consideration in determining the limit of liability.

3.   As regards objects of which the passenger takes charge himself the liability of the carrier is limited to 332 Special Drawing Rights per passenger.

4. The limits prescribed in this Article shall not prevent the court from awarding, in accordance with its own law, in addition, the whole or part of the court costs and of the other expenses of the litigation incurred by the plaintiff. The foregoing provision shall not apply if the amount of the damages awarded, excluding court costs and other expenses of the litigation, does not exceed the sum which the carrier has offered in writing to the plaintiff within a period of six months from the date of the occurrence causing the damage, or before the commencement of the action, if that is later.

5. The sums mentioned in terms of the Special Drawing Right in this Article shall be deemed to refer to the Special Drawing Right as defined by the International Monetary Fund. Conversion of the sums into national currencies shall, in case of judicial proceedings, be made according to the value of such currencies in terms of the Special Drawing Right at the date of the judgment. The value of a national currency, in terms of the Special Drawing Right, of a High Contracting Party which is a Member of the International Monetary Fund, shall be calculated in accordance with the method of valuation applied by the International Monetary Fund, in effect at the date of the judgment, for its operations and transactions. The value of a national currency, in terms of the Special Drawing Right, of a High Contracting Party which is not a Member of the International Monetary Fund, shall be calculated in a manner determined by that High Contracting Party.

Nevertheless, those States which are not Members of the International Monetary Fund and whose law does not permit the application of the provisions of paragraphs 1, 2(a) and 3 of Article 22 may at the time of ratification or accession or at any time thereafter, declare that the limit of liability of the carrier in judicial proceedings in their territories is fixed at a sum of 250,000 monetary units per passenger with respect to paragraph 1 of Article 22; 250 monetary units per kilogramme with respect to paragraph 2(a) of Article 22; and 5,000 monetary units per passenger with respect to paragraph 3 of Article 22. This monetary unit corresponds to sixty-five and a half milligrammes of gold of millesimal fineness nine hundred. These sums may be converted into the national currency concerned in round figures. The conversion of these sums into national currency shall be made according to the law of the State concerned.'

CHAPTER II
SCOPE OF APPLICATION OF THE CONVENTION AS AMENDED

Article III

The Warsaw Convention as amended at The Hague in 1955 and by this Protocol shall apply to international carriage as defined in Article I of the Convention, provided that the places of departure and destination referred to in that Article are situated either in the territories of two Parties to this Protocol or within the territory of a single Party to this Protocol with an agreed stopping place in the territory of another State.

CHAPTER III
FINAL CLAUSES

Articles IV–XIII [Omitted].

MONTREAL ADDITIONAL PROTOCOL NO 3, 1975
ADDITIONAL PROTOCOL NO 3 TO AMEND THE CONVENTION FOR THE UNIFICATION OF CERTAIN RULES RELATING TO INTERNATIONAL CARRIAGE BY AIR SIGNED AT WARSAW ON 12TH OCTOBER 1929 AS AMENDED BY THE PROTOCOLS DONE AT THE HAGUE ON 28TH SEPTEMBER 1955 AND AT GUATEMALA CITY ON 8TH MARCH 1971

CHAPTER I
AMENDMENTS TO THE CONVENTION

Article I

The Convention which the provisions of the present Chapter modify is the Warsaw Convention as amended at The Hague in 1955 and at Guatemala City in 1971.

Article II

Article 22 of the Convention shall be deleted and replaced by the following—
'Article 22

1. (a) In the carriage of persons the liability of the carrier is limited to the sum of 100,000 Special Drawing Rights for the aggregate of the claims, however founded, in respect of damage suffered as a result of the death or personal injury of each passenger. Where, in accordance with the law of the court seised of the case, damages may be awarded in the form of periodic payments, the equivalent capital value of the said payments shall not exceed 100,000 Special Drawing Rights.

   (b) In the case of delay in the carriage of persons the liability of the carrier for each passenger is limited to 4,150 Special Drawing Rights.

   (c) In the carriage of baggage the liability of the carrier in the case of destruction, loss, damage or delay is limited to 1,000 Special Drawing Rights for each passenger.

2. (a) In the carriage of cargo, the liability of the carrier is limited to a sum of 17 Special Drawing Rights per kilogramme, unless the consignor has made, at the time when the package was handed over to the carrier, a special declaration of interest in delivery at destination and has paid a supplementary sum if the case so requires. In that case the carrier will be liable to pay a sum not exceeding the declared sum, unless he proves that that sum is greater than the consignor's actual interest in delivery at destination.

   (b) In the case of loss, damage or delay of part of the cargo, or of any object contained therein, the weight to be taken into consideration in determining the amount to which the carrier's liability is limited shall be only the total weight of the package or packages concerned. Nevertheless, when the loss, damage or delay of a part of the cargo, or of an object contained therein, affects the value of other packages covered by the same air waybill, the total weight of such package or packages shall also be taken into consideration in determining the limit of liability.

3. (a) The courts of the High Contracting Parties which are not authorised under their law to award the costs of the action, including lawyers' fees, shall, in actions to which this Convention applies, have the power to award, in their discretion, to the claimant the whole or part of the cost of the action, including lawyers' fees which the court considers reasonable.

   (b) The costs of the action including lawyers' fees shall be awarded in accordance with subparagraph (a) only if the claimant gives a written notice to the carrier of the amount claimed including the particulars of the calculation of that amount and the carrier does not make, within a period of six months after his receipt of such notice a written offer of settlement in an amount at least equal to the compensation awarded within the applicable limit. This period will be extended until the time of commencement of the action if that is later.

(c) The costs of the action including lawyers' fees will not be taken into account in applying the limits under this Article.

4. The sums mentioned in terms of Special Drawing Right in this Article shall be deemed to refer to the Special Drawing Right as defined by the International Monetary Fund. Conversion of the sums into national currencies shall, in case of judicial proceedings, be made according to the value of such currencies in terms of the Special Drawing Right at the date of the judgment. The value of a national currency, in terms of the Special Drawing Right, of a High Contracting Party which is a Member of the International Monetary Fund, shall be calculated in accordance with the method of valuation applied by the International Monetary Fund, in effect at the date of the judgment, for its operations and transactions. The value of a national currency, in terms of the Special Drawing Right, of a High Contracting Party which is not a Member of the International Monetary Fund, shall be calculated in a manner determined by that High Contracting Party.

Nevertheless, those States which are not Members of the International Monetary Fund and whose law does not permit the application of the provisions of paragraphs 1 and 2(a) of Article 22 may, at the time of ratification or accession or at any time thereafter declare that the limit of liability of the carrier in judicial proceedings in their territories is fixed at a sum of l,50,000 monetary units per passenger with respect to paragraph 1(a) of Article 22; 62,500 monetary units per passenger with respect to paragraph 1(b) of Article 22; 15,000 monetary units per passenger with respect to paragraph 1(c) of Article 22; and 250 monetary units per kilogramme with respect to paragraph 2(a) of Article 22. A State applying the provisions of this paragraph may also declare that the sum referred to in paragraphs 2 and 3 of Article 42 shall be the sum of 187,500 monetary units. This monetary unit corresponds to sixty-five and a half milligrammes of gold of millesimal fineness nine hundred. These sums may be converted into the national currency concerned in round figures. The conversion of these sums into national currency shall be made according to the law of the State concerned.'

Article III

In Article 42 of the Convention—
paragraphs 2 and 3 shall be deleted and replaced by the following:

'2. At each of the Conferences mentioned in paragraph 1 of this Article the limit of liability in Article 22, paragraph 1(a) in force at the respective date of these Conferences shall not be increased by an amount exceeding 12,500 Special Drawing Rights.

3. Subject to paragraph 2 of this article, unless before the thirty-first December of the fifth and tenth year after the date of entry into force of the Protocol referred to in paragraph 1 of this Article the aforesaid Conferences decide otherwise by a two-thirds majority vote of the Parties present and voting, the limit of liability in Article 22 paragraph 1(a) in force at the respective dates of these Conferences shall on those dates be increased by 12,500 Special Drawing Rights.'

CHAPTER II
SCOPE OF APPLICATION OF THE CONVENTION AS AMENDED

Article IV

The Warsaw Convention as amended at The Hague in 1955 and at Guatemala City in 1971 and by this Protocol shall apply to international carriage as defined in Article I of the Convention, provided that the place of departure and destination referred to in that Article are situated either in the territories of two Parties to this Protocol or within the territory of a single Party to this Protocol with an agreed stopping place in the territory of another State.

CHAPTER III
FINAL CLAUSES

Articles V–XIV [Omitted].

MONTREAL ADDITIONAL PROTOCOL NO 4, 1975
ADDITIONAL PROTOCOL NO 4 TO AMEND THE CONVENTION FOR THE UNIFICATION OF CERTAIN RULES RELATING TO INTERNATIONAL CARRIAGE BY AIR SIGNED AT WARSAW ON 12TH OCTOBER 1929 AS AMENDED BY THE PROTOCOL DONE AT THE HAGUE ON 28TH SEPTEMBER 1955

CHAPTER I
AMENDMENTS TO THE CONVENTION

Article I

The Convention which the provisions of the present Chapter modify is the Warsaw Convention as amended at The Hague in 1955.

Article II

In Article 2 of the Convention—
    paragraph 2 shall be deleted and replaced by the following:
    '2.   In the carriage of postal items the carrier shall be liable only to the relevant postal administration in accordance with the rules applicable to the relationship between the carriers and the postal administrations.
    3.   Except as provided in paragraph 2 of this Article, the provisions of this Convention shall not apply to the carriage of postal items.'

Article III

In Chapter II of the Convention—
    Section III (Articles 5 to 16) shall be deleted and replaced by the following:
    'Section III—Documentation relating to cargo
    Article 5
    1.   In respect of the carriage or cargo an air waybill shall be delivered.

2. Any other means which would preserve a record of the carriage to be performed may, with the consent of the consignor, be substituted for the delivery of an air waybill. If such other means are used, the carrier shall if so requested by the consignor deliver to the consignor a receipt for the cargo permitting identification of the consignment and access to the information contained in the record preserved by such other means.

3. The impossibility of using, at points of transit and destination, the other means which would preserve the record of the carriage referred to in paragraph 2 of this Article does not entitle the carrier to refuse to accept the cargo for carriage.

Article 6

1. The air waybill shall be made out by the consignor in three original parts.

2. The first part shall be marked 'for the carrier'; it shall be signed by the consignor. The second part shall be marked 'for the consignee'; it shall be signed by the consignor and by the carrier. The third part shall be signed by the carrier and handed by him to the consignor after the cargo has been accepted.

3. The signature of the carrier and that of the consignor may be printed or stamped.

4. If, at the request of the consignor, the carrier makes out the air waybill, he shall be deemed, subject to proof to the contrary, to have done so on behalf of the consignor.

Article 7

When there is more than one package —

(a) the carrier of cargo has the right to require the consignor to make out separate air waybills;

(b) the consignor has the right to require the carrier to deliver separate receipts when the other means referred to in paragraph 2 of Article 5 are used.

Article 8

The air waybill and receipt for the cargo shall contain —

(a) an indication of the places of departure and destination;

(b) if the places of departure and destination are within the territory of a single High Contracting Party, one or more agreed stopping places being within the territory of another State, an indication of at least one such stopping place; and

(c) an indication of the weight of the consignment.

Article 9

Non-compliance with the provisions of Articles 5 to 8 shall not affect the existence or the validity of the contract of carriage, which shall, none the less, be subject to the rules of this Convention including those relating to limitation of liability.

Article 10

1. The consignor is responsible for the correctness of the particulars and statements relating to the cargo inserted by him or on his behalf in the air waybill or furnished by him or on his behalf to the carrier for insertion in the receipt for the cargo or for insertion in the record preserved by the other means referred to in paragraph 2 of Article 5.

2. The consignor shall indemnify the carrier against all damage suffered by him, or by any other person to whom the carrier is liable, by reason of the irregularity, incorrectness or incompleteness of the particulars and statements furnished by the consignor or on his behalf.

3. Subject to the provisions of paragraphs 1 and 2 of this Article, the carrier shall indemnify the consignor against all damage suffered by him, or by any other person to whom the consignor is liable, by reason of the irregularity, incorrectness or incompleteness of the particulars and statements inserted

by the carrier or on his behalf in the receipt for the cargo or in the record preserved by the other means referred to in paragraph 2 of Article 5.

Article 11

1. The air waybill or the receipt for the cargo is *prima facie* evidence of the conclusion of the contract, of the acceptance of the cargo and of the conditions of carriage mentioned therein.

2. Any statements in the air waybill or the receipt for the cargo relating to the weight, dimensions and packing of the cargo, as well as those relating to the number of packages, are *prima facie* evidence of the facts stated; those relating to the quantity, volume and condition of the cargo do not constitute evidence against the carrier except so far as they both have been, and are stated in the air waybill to have been, checked by him in the presence of the consignor or relate to the apparent condition of the cargo.

Article 12

1. Subject to his liability to carry out all his obligations under the contract of carriage, the consignor has the right to dispose of the cargo by withdrawing it at the airport of departure or destination, or by stopping it in the course of the journey on any landing, or by calling for it to be delivered at the place of destination or in the course of the journey to a person other than the consignee originally designated, or by requiring it to be returned to the airport of departure. He must not exercise this right of disposition in such a way as to prejudice the carrier or other consignor and he must repay any expenses occasioned by the exercise of this right.

2. If it is impossible to carry out the orders of the consignor, the carrier has to inform him forthwith.

3. If the carrier obeys the orders of the consignor for the disposition of the cargo without requiring the production of the part of the air waybill or the receipt for the cargo delivered to the latter, he will be liable, without prejudice to his right of recovery from the consignor, for any damage which may be caused thereby to any person who is lawfully in possession of that part of the air waybill or the receipt for the cargo.

4. The right conferred on the consignor ceases at the moment when that of the consignee begins in accordance with Article 13. Nevertheless, if the consignee declines to accept the cargo, or if he cannot be communicated with, the consignor resumes his right of disposition.

Article 13

1. Except when the consignor has exercised his right under Article 12, the consignee is entitled, on arrival of the cargo at the place of destination, to require the carrier to deliver the cargo to him, on payment of the charges due and on complying with the conditions of carriage.

2. Unless it is otherwise agreed, it is the duty of the carrier to give notice to the consignee as soon as the cargo arrives.

3. If the carrier admits the loss of the cargo or if the cargo has not arrived at the expiration of seven days after the date on which it ought to have arrived, the consignee is entitled to enforce against the carrier the rights which flow from the contract of carriage.

Article 14

The consignor and the consignee can respectively enforce all the rights given them by Articles 12 and 13, each in his own name, whether he is acting in his own interest or in the interest of another, provided that he carries out the obligations imposed by the contract of carriage.

Article 15

1. Articles 12, 13 and 14 do not affect the relations of the consignor and the consignee with each other or the mutual relations of third parties whose rights are derived either from the consignor or from the consignee.

2. The provisions of Articles 12, 13 and 14 can only be varied by express provision in the air waybill or the receipt for the cargo.

Article 16

1. The consignor must furnish such information and such documents as are necessary to meet the formalities of customs, octroi or police before the cargo can be delivered to the consignee. The consignor is liable to the carrier for any damage occasioned by the absence, insufficiency or irregularity of any such information or documents unless the damage is due to the fault of the carrier, his servants or agents.

2. The carrier is under no obligation to enquire into the correctness or sufficiency of the information or documents.'

Article IV

Article 18 of the Convention shall be deleted and replaced by the following—

'Article 18

1. The carrier is liable for damage sustained in the event of the destruction or loss of, or damage to any registered baggage, if the occurrence which caused the damage so sustained took place during the carriage by air.

2. The carrier is liable for damage sustained in the event of the destruction or loss of, or damage to, cargo upon condition only that the occurrence which caused the damage so sustained took place during the carriage by air.

3. However, the carrier is not liable if he proves that the destruction, loss of, or damage to, the cargo resulted from one or more of the following—
   (a) inherent defect, quality or vice of that cargo;
   (b) defective packing of that cargo performed by a person other than the carrier or his servants or agents;
   (c) an act of war or an armed conflict;
   (d) an act of public authority carried out in connexion with the entry, exit or transit of the cargo.

4. The carriage by air within the meaning of the preceding paragraphs of this Article comprises the period during which the baggage or cargo is in the charge of the carrier, whether in an airport or on board an aircraft, or, in the case of a landing outside an airport, in any place whatsoever.

5. The period of the carriage by air does not extend to any carriage by land, by sea or by river performed outside an airport. If, however, such carriage takes place in the performance of a contract for carriage by air, for the purpose of loading, delivery or transhipment, any damage is presumed, subject to proof to the contrary, to have been the result of an event which took place during the carriage by air.'

Article V

Article 20 of the Convention shall be deleted and replaced by the following:

'Article 20

In the case of passengers and baggage, and in the case of damage occasioned by delay in the carriage of cargo, the carrier shall not be liable if he proves that he and his servants and agents have taken all necessary measures to avoid the damage or that it was impossible for them to take such measures.'

Article VI

Article 21 of the Convention shall be deleted and replaced by the following:

'Article 21

1. In the carriage of passengers and baggage, if the carrier proves that the damage was caused by or contributed to by the negligence of the person

suffering the damage the Court may, in accordance with the provisions of its own law, exonerate the carrier wholly or partly from his liability.

2.   In the carriage of cargo, if the carrier proves that the damage was caused by or contributed to by the negligence or other wrongful act or omission of the person claiming compensation, or the person from whom he derives his rights, the carrier shall be wholly or partly exonerated from his liability to the claimant to the extent that such negligence or wrongful act or omission caused or contributed to the damage.'

Article VII

In Article 22 of the Convention—

(a)   in paragraph 2 (a) the words 'and of cargo' shall be deleted.

(b)   after paragraph 2 (a) the following paragraph shall be inserted:

'(b) In the carriage of cargo, the liability of the carrier is limited to a sum of 17 Special Drawing Rights per kilogramme, unless the consignor has made, at the time when the package was handed over to the carrier, a special declaration of interest in delivery at destination and has paid a supplementary sum if the case so requires. In that case the carrier will be liable to pay a sum not exceeding the declared sum, unless he proves that the sum is greater than the consignor's actual interest in delivery at destination.'

(c)   paragraph 2 (b) shall be designated as paragraph 2(c).

(d)   after paragraph 5 the following paragraph shall be inserted

'6. The sums mentioned in terms of the Special Drawing Right in this Article shall be deemed to refer to the Special Drawing Right as defined by the International Monetary Fund. Conversion of the sums into national currencies shall, in case of judicial proceedings, be made according to the value of such currencies in terms of the Special Drawing Right at the date of the judgment. The value of a national currency, in terms of the Special Drawing Right, of a High Contracting Party which is a Member of the International Monetary Fund, shall be calculated in accordance with the method of valuation applied by the International Monetary Fund, in effect at the date of the judgment for its operations and transactions. The value of a national currency, in terms of the Special Drawing Right, of a High Contracting Party which is not a Member of the International Monetary Fund, shall be calculated in a manner determined, by that High Contracting Party.

Nevertheless, those States which are not Members of the International Monetary Fund and whose law does not permit the application of the provisions of paragraph 2 (b) of Article 22 may, at the time of ratification or accession or at any time thereafter, declare that the limit of liability of the carrier in judicial proceedings in their territories is fixed at a sum of two hundred and fifty monetary units per kilogramme This monetary unit corresponds to sixty-five and a half milligrammes of gold of millesimal fineness nine hundred. This sum may be converted into the national currency concerned in round figures. The conversion of this sum into the national currency shall be made according to the laws of the State concerned.'

Article VIII

Article 24 of the Convention shall be deleted and replaced by the following—

'Article 24

1.   In the carriage of passengers and baggage, any action for damages, however founded, can only be brought subject to the conditions and limits set out in

this Convention, without prejudice to the question as to who are the persons who have the right to bring suit and what are their respective rights.

2. In the carriage of cargo, any action for damages, however founded, whether under this Convention or in contract or in tort or otherwise, can only be brought subject to the conditions and limits of liability set out in this Convention, without prejudice to the question as to who are the persons who have the right to bring suit and what are their respective rights. Such limit of liability constitute maximum limits and may not be exceeded whatever the circumstances which gave rise to the liability.'

Article IX

Article 25 of the Convention shall be deleted and replaced by the following —
'Article 25

In the carriage of passengers and baggage, the limits of liability specified in Article 22 shall not apply if it is proved that the damage resulted from an act or omission of the carrier, his servants or agents, done with intent to cause damage or recklessly and with knowledge that damage would probably result; provided that, in the case of such act or omission of a servant or agent, it is also proved that he was acting within the scope of his employment.'

Article X

In Article 25A of the Convention —
paragraph 3 shall be deleted and replaced by the following:
'3. In the carriage of passengers and baggage, the provisions of paragraphs 1 and 2 of this Article shall not apply if it is proved that the damage resulted from an act or omission of the servant or agent done with intent to cause damage or recklessly and with knowledge that damage would probably result.'

Article XI

After Article 30 of the Convention, the following Article shall be inserted —
'Article 30A

Nothing in this Convention shall prejudice the question whether a person liable for damage in accordance with its provisions has a right of recourse against any other person.'

Article XII

Article 33 of the Convention shall be deleted and replaced by the following —
'Article 33

Except as provided in paragraph 3 of Article 5 nothing in this Convention shall prevent the carrier either from refusing to enter into any contract of carriage or from making regulations which do not conflict with the provisions of this Convention.'

Article XIII

Article 34 of the Convention shall be deleted and replaced by the following —
'Article 34

The provisions of Articles 3 to 8 inclusive relating to documents of carriage shall not apply in the case of carriage performed in extraordinary circumstances outside the normal scope of an air carrier's business.'

CHAPTER II
SCOPE OF APPLICATION OF THE CONVENTION AS AMENDED

Article XIV

The Warsaw Convention as amended at The Hague in 1955 and by this Protocol shall apply to international carriage as defined in Article I of the Convention, provided that the places of departure and destination referred to in that Article are situated either in the territories of two Parties to this Protocol or within the territory of a single Party to this Protocol with an agreed stopping place in the territory of another State.

CHAPTER III
FINAL CLAUSES

Articles XV–XXV [Omitted].

CONVENTION ON LIMITATION OF LIABILITY FOR MARITIME CLAIMS, 1976

See the Schedule to the Merchant Shipping Act 1979 for text of the Convention.

UNITED NATIONS CONVENTION ON THE CARRIAGE OF GOODS BY SEA, HAMBURG, 1978 (HAMBURG RULES)

PART I
GENERAL PROVISIONS

Article 1
Definitions

In this Convention—

1. 'Carrier' means any person by whom or in whose name a contract of carriage of goods by sea has been concluded with a shipper.
2. 'Actual carrier' means any person to whom the performance of the carriage of the goods, or of part of the carriage, has been entrusted by the carrier, and includes any other person to whom such performance has been entrusted.
3. 'Shipper' means any person by whom or in whose name or on whose behalf a contract of carriage of goods by sea has been concluded with a carrier, or any person by whom or in whose name or on whose behalf the goods are actually delivered to the carrier in relation to the contract of carriage by sea.
4. 'Consignee' means the person entitled to take delivery of the goods.
5. 'Goods' includes live animals; where the goods are consolidated in a container, pallet or similar article of transport or where they are packed, 'goods' includes such article of transport or packaging if supplied by the shipper.
6. 'Contract of carriage by sea' means any contract whereby the carrier undertakes against payment of freight to carry goods by sea from one port to another; however, a contract which involves carriage by sea and also carriage by some other means is deemed to be a contract of carriage by sea for the purposes of this Convention only in so far as it relates to the carriage by sea.
7. 'Bill of lading' means a document which evidences a contract of carriage by sea and the taking over or loading of the goods by the carrier, and by which the carrier

undertakes to deliver the goods against surrender of the document. A provision in the document that the goods are to be delivered to the order of a named person, or to order, or to bearer, constitutes such an undertaking.

8.   'Writing' includes, *inter alia*, telegram and telex.

Article 2
Scope of application

1.   The provisions of this Convention are applicable to all contracts of carriage by sea between two different States, if —
   (a)   the port of loading as provided for in the contract of carriage by sea is located in a Contracting State; or
   (b)   the port of discharge as provided for in the contract of carriage by sea is located in a Contracting State; or
   (c)   one of the optional ports of discharge provided for in the contract of carriage by sea is the actual port of discharge and such port is located in a Contracting State; or
   (d)   the bill of lading or other document evidencing the contract of carriage by sea is issued in a Contracting State; or
   (e)   the bill of lading or other document evidencing the contract of carriage by sea provides that the provisions of this Convention or the legislation of any State giving effect to them are to govern the contract.

2.   The provisions of this Convention are applicable without regard to the nationality of the ship, the carrier, the actual carrier, the shipper, the consignee or any other interested person.

3.   The provisions of this Convention are not applicable to charter-parties. However, where a bill of lading is issued pursuant to a charter-party, the provisions of the Convention apply to such a bill of lading if it governs the relation between the carrier and the holder of the bill of lading, not being the charterer.

4.   If a contract provides for future carriage of goods in a series of shipments during an agreed period, the provisions of this Convention apply to each shipment. However, where a shipment is made under a charter-party, the provisions of paragraph 3 of this Article apply.

Article 3
Interpretation of the Convention

In the interpretation and application of the provisions of this Convention regard shall be had to its international character and to the need to promote uniformity.

PART II
LIABILITY OF THE CARRIER

Article 4
Period of responsibility

1.   The responsibility of the carrier for the goods under this Convention covers the period during which the carrier is in charge of the goods at the port of loading, during the carriage and at the port of discharge.

2.   For the purpose of paragraph 1 of this Article, the carrier is deemed to be in charge of the goods —
   (a)   from the time he has taken over the goods from;
      (i)   the shipper, or a person acting on his behalf; or

       (ii) an authority or other third party to whom, pursuant to law or regulations applicable at the port of loading, the goods must be handed over for shipment;

    (b) until the time he has delivered the goods:

       (i) by handing over the goods to the consignee; or

       (ii) in cases where the consignee does not receive the goods from the carrier, by placing them at the disposal of the consignee in accordance with the contract or with the law or with the usage of the particular trade, applicable at the port of discharge; or

       (iii) by handing over the goods to an authority or other third party to whom, pursuant to law or regulations applicable at the port of discharge, the goods must be handed over.

3.   In paragraphs 1 and 2 of this Article, reference to the carrier or to the consignee means, in addition to the carrier or the consignee, the servants or agents, respectively of the carrier or the consignee.

Article 5
Basis of liability

1.   The carrier is liable for loss resulting from loss of or damage to the goods, as well as from delay in delivery, if the occurrence which caused the loss, damage or delay took place while the goods were in his charge as defined in Article 4, unless the carrier proves that he, his servants or agents took all measures that could reasonably be required to avoid the occurrence and its consequences.

2.   Delay in delivery occurs when the goods have not been delivered at the port of discharge provided for in the contract of carriage by sea within the time expressly agreed upon or, in the absence of such agreement, within the time which it would be reasonable to require of a diligent carrier, having regard to the circumstances of the case.

3.   The person entitled to make a claim for the loss of goods may treat the goods as lost if they have not been delivered as required by Article 4 within 60 consecutive days following the expiry of the time for delivery according to paragraph 2 of this Article.

4.   —

    (a) The carrier is liable:

       (i) for loss of or damage to the goods or delay in delivery caused by fire, if the claimant proves that the fire arose from fault or neglect on the part of the carrier, his servants or agents;

       (ii) for such loss, damage or delay in delivery which is proved by the claimant to have resulted from the fault or neglect of the carrier, his servants or agents, in taking all measures that could reasonably be required to put out the fire and avoid or mitigate its consequences.

    (b) In case of fire on board the ship affecting the goods, if the claimant or the carrier so desires, a survey in accordance with shipping practices must be held into the cause and circumstances of the fire, and a copy of the surveyor's report shall be made available on demand to the carrier and the claimant.

5.   With respect to live animals, the carrier is not liable for loss, damage or delay in delivery resulting from any special risks inherent in that kind of carriage. If the carrier proves that he has complied with any special instructions given to him by the shipper respecting the animals and that, in the circumstances of the case, the loss, damage or delay in delivery could be attributed to such risks, it is presumed that the loss, damage or delay in delivery was so caused, unless there is proof that all or a part of the loss, damage or delay in delivery resulted from fault or neglect on the part of the carrier, his servants or agents.

6.   The carrier is not liable, except in general average, where loss, damage or delay in delivery resulted from measures to save life or from reasonable measures to save property at sea.

7.   Where fault or neglect on the part of the carrier, his servants or agents combines with another cause to produce loss, damage or delay in delivery the carrier is liable only to the extent that the loss, damage or delay in delivery is attributable to such fault or neglect, provided that the carrier proves the amount of the loss, damage or delay in delivery not attributable thereto.

Article 6
Limits of liability

1.   —
   (a)   The liability of the carrier for loss resulting from loss of or damage to goods according to the provisions of Article 5 is limited to an amount equivalent to 835 units of account per package or other shipping unit or 2.5 units of account per kilogram of gross weight of the goods lost or damaged, whichever is the higher.
   (b)   The liability of the carrier for delay in delivery according to the provisions of Article 5 is limited to an amount equivalent to two and a half times the freight payable for the goods delayed, but not exceeding the total freight payable under the contract of carriage of goods by sea.
   (c)   In no case shall the aggregate liability of the carrier, under both subparagraphs (a) and (b) of this paragraph, exceed the limitation which would be established under subparagraph (a) of this paragraph for total loss of the goods with respect to which such liability was incurred.

2.   For the purpose of calculating which amount is the higher in accordance with paragraph 1(a) of this Article, the following rules apply—
   (a)   where a container, pallet or similar article of transport is used to consolidate goods, the package or other shipping units enumerated in the bill of lading, if issued, or otherwise in any other document evidencing the contract of carriage by sea, as packed in such article of transport are deemed packages or shipping units. Except as aforesaid the goods in such article of transport are deemed one shipping unit;
   (b)   in cases where the article of transport itself has been lost or damaged, that article of transport, if not owned or otherwise supplied by the carrier, is considered one separate shipping unit.

3.   Unit of account means the unit of account mentioned in Article 26.

4.   By agreement between the carrier and the shipper, limits of liability exceeding those provided for in paragraph 1 may be fixed.

Article 7
Application to non-contractual claims

1.   The defences and limits of liability provided for in this Convention apply in any action against the carrier in respect of loss or damage to the goods covered by the contract of carriage by sea, as well as of delay in delivery whether the action is founded in contract, in tort or otherwise.

2.   If such an action is brought against a servant or agent of the carrier, such servant or agent, if he proves that he acted within the scope of his employment, is entitled to avail himself of the defences and limits of liability which the carrier is entitled to invoke under this Convention.

3.   Except as provided in Article 8, the aggregate of the amounts recoverable from the carrier and from any persons referred to in paragraph 2 of this Article shall not exceed the limits of liability provided for in this convention.

Article 8
Loss of right to limit responsibility

1. The carrier is not entitled to the benefit of the limitation of liability provided for in Article 6 if it is proved that the loss, damage or delay in delivery resulted from an act or omission of the carrier done with the intent to cause such loss, damage or delay, or recklessly and with knowledge that such loss, damage or delay would probably result.

2. Notwithstanding the provisions of paragraph 2 of Article 7, a servant or agent of the carrier is not entitled to the benefit of the limitation of liability provided for in Article 6 if it is proved that the loss, damage or delay in delivery resulted from an act or omission of such servant or agent, done with the intent to cause such loss, damage or delay, or recklessly and with knowledge that such loss, damage or delay would probably result.

Article 9
Deck cargo

1. The carrier is entitled to carry the goods on deck only is such carriage is in accordance with an agreement with the shipper or with the usage of the particular trade or is required by statutory rules or regulations.

2. If the carrier and the shipper have agreed that the goods shall or may be carried on deck, the carrier must insert in the bill of lading or other document evidencing the contract of carriage by sea a statement to that effect. In the absence of such a statement the carrier has the burden of proving that an agreement for carriage on deck has been entered into; however, the carrier is not entitled to invoke such an agreement against a third party, including a consignee, who has acquired the bill of lading in good faith.

3. Where the goods have been carried on deck contrary to the provisions of paragraph 1 of this Article or where the carrier may not under paragraph 2 of this Article invoke an agreement for carriage on deck, the carrier, notwithstanding the provisions of paragraph 1 of Article 5, is liable for loss of or damage to the goods, as well as for delay in delivery, resulting solely from the carriage on deck, and the extent of his liability is to be determined in accordance with the provisions of Article 6 or Article 8 of this Convention, as the case may be.

4. Carriage of goods on deck contrary to express agreement for carriage under deck is deemed to be an act or omission of the carrier within the meaning of Article 8.

Article 10
Liability of the carrier and actual carrier

1. Where the performance of the carriage or part thereof has been entrusted to an actual carrier, whether or not in pursuance of a liberty under the contract of carriage by sea to do so, the carrier nevertheless remains responsible for the entire carriage according to the provisions of this Convention. The carrier is responsible, in relation to the carriage performed by the actual carrier, for the acts and omissions of the actual carrier and of his servants and agents acting within the scope of their employment.

2. All the provisions of this Convention governing the responsibility of the carrier also apply to the responsibility of the actual carrier for the carriage performed by him. The provisions of paragraphs 2 and 3 of Article 7 and of paragraph 2 of Article 8 apply if an action is brought against a servant or agent of the actual carrier.

3. Any special agreement under which the carrier assumes obligations not imposed by this Convention or waives rights conferred by this Convention affects the actual carrier only if agreed to by him expressly and in writing. Whether or not the actual

carrier has so agreed, the carrier nevertheless remains bound by the obligations or waivers resulting from such special agreement.

4. Where and to the extent that both the carrier and the actual carrier are liable, their liability is joint and several.

5. The aggregate of the amounts recoverable from the carrier; the actual carrier and their servants and agents shall not exceed the limits of liability provided for in this Convention.

6. Nothing in this Article shall prejudice any right of recourse as between the carrier and the actual carrier.

Article 11
Through carriage

1. Notwithstanding the provisions of paragraph 1 of Article 10, where a contract of carriage by sea provides explicitly that a specified part of the carriage covered by the said contract is to be performed by a named person other than the carrier, the contract may also provide that the carrier is not liable for loss, damage or delay in delivery caused by an occurrence which takes place while the goods are in the charge of the actual carrier during such part of the carriage. Nevertheless, any stipulation limiting or excluding such liability is without effect if no judicial proceedings can be instituted against the actual carrier in a court competent under paragraph 1 or 2 of Article 21. The burden of proving that any loss, damage or delay in delivery has been caused by such an occurrence rests upon the carrier.

2. The actual carrier is responsible in accordance with the provisions of paragraph 2 of Article 10 for loss, damage or delay in delivery caused by an occurrence which takes place while the goods are in his charge.

PART III
LIABILITY OF THE SHIPPER

Article 12
General rule

The shipper is not liable for loss sustained by the carrier or the actual carrier, or for damage sustained by the ship, unless such loss or damage was caused by the fault or neglect of the shipper, his servants or agents, Nor is any servant or agent of the shipper liable for such loss or damage unless the loss or damage was caused by fault or neglect on his part.

Article 13
Special rules on dangerous goods

1. The shipper must mark or label in a suitable manner dangerous goods as dangerous.

2. Where the shipper hands over dangerous goods to the carrier or an actual carrier, as the case may be, the shipper must inform him of the dangerous character of the goods and, if necessary, of the precautions to be taken. If the shipper fails to do so and such carrier or actual carrier does not otherwise have knowledge of their dangerous character—

    (a) the shipper is liable to the carrier and any actual carrier for the loss resulting from the shipment of such goods; and

    (b) the goods may at any time be unloaded, destroyed or rendered innocuous, as the circumstances may require, without payment of compensation.

3. The provisions of paragraph 2 of this Article may not be invoked by any person if during the carriage he has taken the goods in his charge with knowledge of their dangerous character.

4. If, in cases where the provisions of paragraph 2, subparagraph b, of this Article do not apply or may not be invoked, dangerous goods become an actual danger to life or property, they may unloaded, destroyed or rendered innocuous, as the circumstances may require, without payment of compensation except where there is an obligation to contribute in general average or where the carrier is liable in accordance with the provisions of Article 5.

PART IV
TRANSPORT DOCUMENTS

Article 14
Issue of bill of lading

1. When the carrier or the actual carrier takes the goods in his charge, the carrier must, on demand of the shipper, issue to the shipper a bill of lading.

2. The bill of lading may be signed by a person having authority from the carrier. A bill of lading signed by the master of the ship carrying the goods is deemed to have been signed on behalf of the carrier.

3. The signature on the bill of lading may be in handwriting, printed in facsimile, perforated, stamped, in symbols, or made by any other mechanical or electronic means, if not inconsistent with the law of the country where the bill of lading is issued.

Article 15
Contents of bill of lading

1. The bill of lading must include, *inter alia*, the following particulars—
   (a) the general nature of the goods, the leading marks necessary for identification of the goods, an express statement, if applicable, as to the dangerous character of the goods, the number of packages or pieces, and the weight of the goods or their quantity otherwise expressed, all such particulars as furnished by the shipper;
   (b) the apparent condition of the goods;
   (c) the name and principal place of business of the carrier;
   (d) the name of the shipper;
   (e) the consignee if named by the shipper;
   (f) the port of loading under the contract of carriage by sea and the date on which the goods were taken over by the carrier at the port of loading;
   (g) the port of discharge under the contract of carriage by sea;
   (h) the number of originals of the bill of lading, if more than one;
   (i) the place of issuance of the bill of lading;
   (j) the signature of the carrier or a person acting on his behalf;
   (k) the freight to the extent payable by the consignee or other indication that freight is payable by him;
   (l) the statement referred to in paragraph 3 of Article 23;
   (m) the statement, if applicable, that the goods shall or may be carried on deck;
   (n) the date or the period of delivery of the goods at the port of discharge if expressly agreed upon between the parties; and
   (o) any increased limit or limits of liability where agreed in accordance with paragraph 4 of Article 6.

2. After the goods have been loaded on board, if the shipper so demands, the carrier must issue to the shipper a 'shipped' bill of lading which, in addition to the

particulars required under paragraph 1 of this Article, must state that the goods are on board a named ship or ships, and the date or dates of loading. If the carrier has previously issued to the shipper a bill of lading or other document of title with respect to any of such goods, on request of the carrier, the shipper must surrender such document in exchange for a 'shipped' bill of lading. The carrier may amend any previously issued document in order to meet the shipper/s demand for a 'shipped' bill of lading if, as amended, such document includes all the information required to be contained in a 'shipped' bill of lading.

3. The absence in the bill of lading of one or more particulars referred to in this Article does not affect the legal character of the document as a bill of lading provided that it nevertheless meets the requirements set out in paragraph 7 of Article 1.

Article 16
Bills of lading: reservations and evidentiary effect

1. If the bill of lading contains particulars concerning the general nature, leading marks, number of packages or pieces, weight or quantity of the goods which the carrier or other person issuing the bill of lading on his behalf knows or has reasonable grounds to suspect do not accurately represent the goods actually taken over or, where a 'shipped' bill of lading is issued, loaded, or if he had no reasonable means of checking such particulars, the carrier or such other person must insert in the bill of lading a reservation specifying these inaccuracies, grounds of suspicion or the absence of reasonable means of checking.

2. If the carrier or other person issuing the bill of lading on his behalf fails to note on the bill of lading the apparent condition of the goods, he is deemed to have noted on the bill of lading that the goods were in apparent good condition.

3. Except for particulars in respect of which and to the extent to which a reservation permitted under paragraph 1 of this Article has been entered—

    (a) the bill of lading is *prima facie* evidence of the taking over or, where a 'shipped' bill of lading is issued, loading, by the carrier of the goods as described in the bill of lading; and

    (b) proof to the contrary by the carrier is not admissible if the bill of lading has been transferred to a third party, including a consignee, who in good faith has acted in reliance on the description of the goods therein.

4. A bill of lading which does not, as provided in paragraph 1 subparagraph h of Article 15, set forth the freight or otherwise indicate that freight is payable by the consignee or does not set forth demurrage incurred at the port of loading payable by the consignee, is *prima facie* evidence that no freight or such demurrage is payable by him. However, proof to the contrary by the carrier is not admissible when the bill of lading has been transferred to a third party, including a consignee, who in good faith has acted in reliance on the absence in the bill of lading of any such indication.

Article 17
Guarantees by the shipper

1. The shipper is deemed to have guaranteed to the carrier the accuracy of particulars relating to the general nature of the goods, their marks, number, weight and quantity as furnished by him for insertion in the bill of lading. The shipper must indemnify the carrier against the loss resulting from inaccuracies in such particulars. The shipper remains liable even if the bill of lading has been transferred by him. The right of the carrier to such indemnity in no way limits his liability under the contract of carriage by sea to any person other than the shipper.

2. Any letter of guarantee or agreement by which the shipper undertakes to indemnify the carrier against loss resulting from the issuance of the bill of lading by

the carrier, or by a person acting on his behalf, without entering a reservation relating to particulars furnished by the shipper for insertion in the bill of lading, or to the apparent condition of the goods, is void and of no effect as against any third party, including a consignee, to whom the bill of lading has been transferred.

3.   Such letter of guarantee or agreement is valid as against the shipper unless the carrier or the person acting on his behalf, by omitting the reservation referred to in paragraph 2 of this Article, intends to defraud a third party, including a consignee, who acts in reliance on the description of the goods in the bill of lading. In the latter case, if the reservation omitted relates to particulars furnished by the shipper for insertion in the bill of lading the carrier has no right of indemnity from the shipper pursuant to paragraph 1 of this Article.

4.   In the case of intended fraud referred to in paragraph 3 of this Article the carrier is liable, without the benefit of the limitation of liability provided for in this Convention, for the loss incurred by a third party, including a consignee, because he has acted in reliance on the description of the goods in the bill of lading.

Article 18
Documents other than bills of lading

Where a carrier issues a document other than a bill of lading to evidence the receipt of the goods to be carried, such a document is *prima facie* evidence of the conclusion of the contract of carriage by sea and the taking over by the carrier of the goods as therein described.

PART V
CLAIMS AND ACTIONS

Article 19
Notice of loss, damage or delay

1.   Unless notice of loss or damage, specifying the general nature of such loss or damage, is given in writing by the consignee to the carrier not later than the working day after the day when the goods were handed over to the consignee, such handing over is *prima facie* evidence of the delivery by the carrier of the goods as described in the document of transport or, if no such document has been issued, in good condition.

2.   Where the loss or damage is not apparent, the provisions of paragraph 1 of this Article apply correspondingly if notice in writing is not given within 15 consecutive days after the day when the goods were handed over to the consignee.

3.   If the state of the goods at the time they were handed over to the consignee has been the subject of a joint survey or inspection by the parties, notice in writing need not be given of loss or damage ascertained during such survey or inspection.

4.   In the case of any actual or apprehended loss or damage the carrier and the consignee must give all reasonable facilities to each other for inspecting and tallying the goods.

5.   No compensation shall be payable for loss resulting from delay in delivery unless a notice has been given in writing to the carrier within 60 consecutive days after the day when the goods were handed over to the consignee.

6.   If the goods have been delivered by an actual carrier, any notice given under this Article to him shall have the same effect as if it had been given to the carrier and any notice given to the carrier shall have effect as if given to such actual carrier.

7.   Unless notice of loss or damage, specifying the general nature of the loss or damage, is given in writing by the carrier or actual carrier to the shipper not later than 90 consecutive days after the occurrence of such loss or damage or after the delivery of the goods in accordance with paragraph 2 of Article 4, whichever is later,

the failure to give such notice is *prima facie* evidence that the carrier or the actual carrier has sustained no loss or damage due to the fault or neglect of the shipper, his servants or agents.

8. For the purpose of this Article, notice given to a person acting on the carrier's or the actual carrier's behalf, including the master or the officer in charge of the ship, or to a person acting on the shipper's behalf is deemed to have been given to the carrier, to the actual carrier or to the shipper, respectively.

Article 20
Limitation of actions

1. Any action relating to carriage of goods under this convention is time-barred if judicial or arbitral proceedings have not been instituted within a period of two years.
2. The limitation period commences on the day on which the carrier has delivered the goods or part thereof or, in cases where no goods have been delivered, on the last day on which the goods should have been delivered.
3. The day on which the limitation period commences is not included in the period.
4. The person against whom a claim is made may at any time during the running of the limitation period extend that period by a declaration in writing to the claimant. This period may be further extended by another declaration or declarations.
5. An action for indemnity by a person held liable may be instituted even after the expiration of the limitation period provided for in the preceding paragraphs if instituted within the time allowed by the law of the state where proceedings are instituted. However, the time allowed shall not be less than 90 days commencing from the day when the person instituting such action for indemnity has settled the claim or has been served with process in the action against himself.

Article 21
Jurisdiction

1. In judicial proceedings relating to carriage of goods under this convention the plaintiff, at his option, may institute an action in a court which, according to the law of the State where the court is situated, is competent and within the jurisdiction of which is situated one of the following places—
   (a) the principal place of business or, in the absence thereof, the habitual residence of the defendant; or
   (b) the place where the contract was made provided that the defendant has there a place of business, branch of agency through which the contract was made; or
   (c) the port of loading or the port of discharge; or
   (d) any additional place designated for that purpose in the contract of carriage by sea.
2. —
   (a) Notwithstanding the preceding provisions of this Article, an action may be instituted in the courts of any port or place in a Contracting State at which the carrying vessel or any other vessel of the same ownership may have been arrested in accordance with applicable rules of the law of that State and of international law. However, in such a case, at the petition of the defendant, the claimant must remove the action, at his choice, to one of the jurisdictions referred to in paragraph 1 of this Article for the determination of the claim, but before such removal the defendant must furnish security sufficient to ensure payment of any judgment that may subsequently be awarded to the claimant in the action.
   (b) All questions relating to the sufficiency or otherwise of the security shall be determined by the court of the port or place of the arrest.

3.   No judicial proceedings relating to carriage of goods under this convention may be instituted in a place not specified in paragraph 1 or 2 of this Article. The provisions of this paragraph do not constitute an obstacle to the jurisdiction of the Contracting States for provisional or protective measures.

4.   —

    (a)   Where an action has been instituted in a court competent under paragraph 1 or 2 of this Article or where judgment has been delivered by such a court, no new action may be started between the same parties on the same grounds unless the judgment of the court before which the first action was instituted is not enforceable in the country in which the new proceedings are instituted.

    (b)   For the purpose of this Article the institution of measures with a view to obtaining enforcement of a judgment is not to be considered as the starting of a new action.

    (c)   For the purpose of this Article, the removal of an action to a different court within the same country, or to a court in another country, in accordance with paragraph 2(a) of this Article, is not to be considered as the starting of a new action.

5.   Notwithstanding the provisions of the preceding paragraphs, an agreement made by the parties, after a claim under the contract of carriage by sea has arisen, which designates the place where the claimant may institute an action, is effective.

Article 22
Arbitration

1.   Subject to the provisions of this Article, parties may provide by agreement evidenced in writing that any dispute that may arise relating to carriage of goods under this Convention shall be referred to arbitration.

2.   Where a charter-party contains a provision that disputes arising thereunder shall be referred to arbitration and a bill of lading issued pursuant to the charter-party does not contain a special annotation providing that such provision shall be binding upon the holder of the bill of lading, the carrier may not invoke such provision as against a holder having acquired the bill of lading in good faith.

3.   The arbitration proceedings shall, at the option of the claimant, be instituted at one of the following places—

    (a)   a place in a state within whose territory is situated:

        (i)   the principal place of business of the defendant or, in the absence thereof, the habitual residence of the defendant; or

        (ii)   the place where the contract was made, provided that the defendant has there a place of business, branch or agency through which the contract was made; or

        (iii)   the port of loading or the port of discharge; or

    (b)   any place designated for that purpose in the arbitration clause or agreement.

4.   The arbitrator or arbitration tribunal shall apply the rules of this Convention.

5.   The provisions of paragraphs 3 and 4 of this Article are deemed to be part of every arbitration clause or agreement, and any term, of such clause or agreement which is inconsistent therewith is null and void.

6.   Nothing in this Article affects the validity of an agreement relating to arbitration made by the parties after the claim under the contract of carriage by sea has arisen.

PART VI
SUPPLEMENT PROVISION

Article 23
Contractual stipulations

1. Any stipulation in a contract of carriage by sea, in a bill of lading, or in any other document evidencing the contract of carriage by sea is null and void to the extent that it derogates, directly or indirectly, from the provisions of this Convention. The nullity of such a stipulation does not affect the validity of the other provisions of the contract or document of which it forms a part. A clause assigning benefit of insurance of the goods in favour of the carrier, or any similar clause, is null and void.
2. Notwithstanding the provisions of paragraph 1 of this Article, a carrier may increase his responsibilities and obligations under this Convention.
3. Where a bill of lading or any other document evidencing the contract of carriage by sea is issued, it must contain a statement that the carriage is subject to the provisions of this Convention which nullify any stipulation derogating therefrom to the detriment of the shipper or the consignee.
4. Where the claimant in respect of the goods has incurred loss as a result of a stipulation which is null and void by virtue of the present Article, or as a result of the omission of the statement referred to in paragraph 3 of this Article, the carrier must pay compensation to the extent required in order to give the claimant compensation in accordance with the provisions of this Convention for any loss of or damage to the goods as well as for delay in delivery. The carrier must, in addition, pay compensation for costs incurred by the claimant for the purpose of exercising his right, provided that costs incurred in the action where the foregoing provision is invoked are to be determined in accordance with the law of the State where proceedings are instituted.

Article 24
General average

1. Nothing in this Convention shall prevent the application of provisions in the contract of carriage by sea or national law regarding the adjustment of general average.
2. With the exception of Article 20, the provisions of this Convention relating to the liability of the carrier for loss of or damage to the goods also determine whether the consignee may refuse contribution in general average and the liability of the carrier to indemnify the consignee in respect of any such contribution made or any salvage paid.

Article 25
Other conventions

1. This Convention does not modify the rights or duties of the carrier, the actual carrier and their servants and agents, provided for in international conventions or national law relating to the limitation of liability of owners of seagoing ships.
[2.–4. Omitted].
5. Nothing contained in this Convention prevents a Contracting State from applying any other international convention which is already in force at the date of this Convention and which applies mandatorily to contracts of carriage of goods primarily by a mode of transport other than transport by sea. This provision also applies to any subsequent revision or amendment of such international convention.

Article 26
Unit of account

1. The unit of account referred to in Article 6 of this Convention is the Special Drawing Right as defined by the International Monetary Fund. The amounts mentioned in Article 6 are to be converted into the national currency of a State according to the value of such currency at the date of judgment or the date agreed upon by the parties. The value of a national currency, in terms of the Special Drawing Right, of a Contracting State which is a member of the International Monetary Fund is to be calculated in accordance with the method of valuation applied by the International Monetary Fund in effect at the date in question for its operations and transactions. The value of a national currency in terms of the Special Drawing Right of a Contracting State which is not a member of the International Monetary Fund is to be calculated in a manner determined by that State.

2. Nevertheless, those States which are not members of the International Monetary Fund and whose law does not permit the application of the provisions of paragraph 1 of this Article may, at the time of signature, or at the time of ratification, acceptance, approval or accession or at any time thereafter, declare that the limits of liability provided for in this Convention to be applied in their territories shall be fixed as —
    12,500 monetary units per package or other shipping unit or 37.5 monetary units per kilogram of gross weight of the goods.

3. The monetary unit referred to in paragraph 2 of this Article corresponds to sixty-five and a half milligrams of gold of millesimal fineness nine hundred. the conversion of the amounts referred to in paragraph 2 into the national currency is to be made according to the law of the state concerned.

4. The calculation mentioned in the last sentence of paragraph 1 and the conversion mentioned in paragraph 3 of this Article is to be made in such a manner as to express in the national currency of the Contracting State as far as possible the same real value for the amounts in Article 6 as is expressed there in units of account. Contracting States must communicate to the depository the manner of calculation pursuant to paragraph 1 of this Article, or the result of the conversion mentioned in paragraph 3 of this Article, as the case may be, at the time of signature or when depositing their instruments of ratification, acceptance, approval or accession, or when availing themselves of the option provided for in paragraph 2 of this Article and whenever there is a change in the manner of such calculation or in the result of such conversion.

PART VII

Articles 27–34 [Omitted].

EEC CONVENTION ON LAW APPLICABLE TO CONTRACTUAL OBLIGATIONS, ROME, 1980

See Schedule I to the Contracts (Applicable Law) Act 1990 for text of the Convention.

PROTOCOL AMENDING THE CONVENTION ON THE LIMITATION PERIOD IN THE INTERNATIONAL SALE OF GOODS, VIENNA, 1980

Article I

1.   Paragraph 1 of Article 3 is replaced by the following provisions—
     '1.   This Convention shall apply only—
        (a)   if, at the time of the conclusion of the contract, the places of business of the parties to a contract of international sale of goods are in Contracting States; or
        (b)   if the rules of private international law make the law of a Contracting State applicable to the contract of sale.'
2.   paragraph 2 of Article 3 is deleted.
3.   paragraph 3 of Article 3 is renumbered as paragraph 2.

Article II

1.   Subparagraph (a) of Article 4 is deleted and replaced by the following provision—
     '(a)   of goods bought for personal, family or household use, unless the seller, at any time before or at the conclusion of the contract, neither knew nor ought to have known that the goods were bought for any such use;'
2.   Subparagraph (e) of Article 4 is deleted and is replaced by the following provision:
     '(e)   of ships, vessels, hovercraft or aircraft;'

Articles III–XIV [Omitted].

UNIFORM RULES CONCERNING THE CONTRACT FOR INTERNATIONAL CARRIAGE OF GOODS BY RAIL (CIM), 1980

TITLE 1
GENERAL PROVISIONS

Article 1
Scope

1.   Subject to the exceptions provided for in Article 2, the Uniform rules shall apply to all consignments of goods for carriage under a through consignment note made out for a route over the territories of at least two States and exclusively over lines or services included in the list provided for in Articles 3 and 10 of the convention.
2.   In the Uniform rules the expression 'station' covers: railway stations, ports used by shipping services and all other establishments of transport undertakings, open to the public for the execution of the contract of carriage.

Article 2
Exceptions from scope

1.   Consignments between sending and destination stations situated in the territory of the same State, which pass through the territory of another State only in transit, shall not be subject to the Uniform Rules—

(a)   if the lines or services over which the transit occurs are exclusively operated by a railway of the State of departure; or

(b)   if the States or the railways concerned have agreed not to regard such consignments as international.

2.   Consignments between stations in two adjacent States and between stations in two States in transit through the territory of a third State shall, if the lines over which the consignments are carried are exclusively operated by a railway of one of those three States, be subject to the internal traffic regulations applicable to that railway if the sender, by using the appropriate consignment note, so elects and where there is nothing to the contrary in the laws and regulation of any of the States concerned.

Article 3
Obligation to carry

1.   The railway shall be bound to undertake all carriage of any goods in complete wagon-loads, subject to the terms of the Uniform rules, provided that—

(a)   the sender complies with the Uniform rules, the supplementary provisions and the tariffs;

(b)   carriage can be undertaken by the normal staff and transport resources which suffice to meet usual traffic requirements;

(c)   carriage is not prevented by circumstances which the railway cannot avoid and which it is not in a position to remedy.

2.   The railway shall not be obliged to accept goods of which the loading, trans-shipment or unloading requires the use of special facilities unless the stations concerned have such facilities at their disposal.

3.   The railway shall only be obliged to accept goods the carriage of which can take place without delay; the provisions in force at the forwarding station shall determine the circumstances in which goods not complying with that condition must be temporarily stored.

4.   When the competent authority decides that—

(a)   a service shall be discontinued or suspended totally or partially;

(b)   certain consignments shall be refused or accepted only subject to conditions, these measures shall, without delay, be brought to the notice of the public and the railways; the latter shall inform the railways of the other States with a view to their publication.

5.   The railways may, by joint agreement, concentrate goods traffic between certain places on specified frontier points and transit countries. These measures shall be notified to the Central Office. They shall be entered by the railways in special lists, published in the manner laid down for international tariffs, and shall come into force one month after the date of notification to the Central Office.

6.   Any contravention of this Article by the railway may constitute a cause of action for compensation for loss or damage caused.

Article 4
Articles not acceptable for carriage

The following shall not be accepted for carriage—

(a)   articles the carriage of which is prohibited in any one of the territories in which the articles would be carried;

(b)   articles the carriage of which is a monopoly of the postal authorities in any one of the territories in which the articles would be carried;

(c)   articles which, by reason of their dimensions, their mass, or their packaging, are not suitable for the carriage proposed, having regard to the installations or rolling stock of any one of the railways which would be used;

(d)   substances and articles which are not acceptable for carriage under the Regulations
concerning the international carriage of dangerous goods by rail (RID), Annex 1 to
the Uniform rules, subject to the exceptions provided for in Articles 5, §2.

Article 5
Articles acceptable for carriage subject to conditions

1.   The following shall be acceptable for carriage subject to conditions—
    (a)   substances and articles acceptable for carriage subject to the conditions laid
down in the RID or in the agreements and tariff clauses provided for in §2;
    (b)   funeral consignments, railway rolling stock running on its own wheels, live
animals and consignments the carriage of which presents special difficulties
by reason of their dimensions, their mass or their packaging: subject to the
conditions laid down in the supplementary provision; these may derogate
from the Uniform rules.
    Live animals must be accompanied by an attendant provided by the consignor.
Nevertheless an attendant shall not be required when the international tariffs
permit or when the railways participating in the carriage so permit at the
consignor's request; in such cases, unless there is an agreement to the contrary, the
railway shall not be liable for any loss or damage resulting from any risk which the
attendant was intended to avert.
2.   Two or more States, by agreement, or two or more railways, by tariff clauses, may
jointly determine the conditions with which certain substances or articles not
acceptable for carriage under the RID must comply if they are nevertheless to be
accepted. States or railways may, in the same manner, make the conditions for
acceptance laid down in the RID less rigorous. Such agreements and tariff clauses
must be published and notified to the Central Office which will bring them to the
notice of the States.

Article 6
Tariffs, private agreements [Omitted]

Article 7
Unit of account. Rate of exchange or of acceptance of foreign currency

1.   The unit of account referred to in the Uniform rules shall be the Special Drawing
Right as defined by the International Monetary Fund.
    The value in Special Drawing Right of the national currency of a State which is a
Member of the International Monetary fund shall be calculated in accordance with
the method of valuation applied by the International Monetary Fund for its own
operations and transactions.
2.   The value in Special Drawing Right of the national currency of a State which is not a
member of the International Monetary Fund shall be calculated by the method
determined by that State.
    The calculation must express in the national currency a real value approximating
as closely to that which would result from the application of §1.
3.   In the case of a state which is not a member of the International Monetary Fund
and whose legislation does not permit the application of §1 or §2 above, the unit of
account referred to in the Uniform Rules shall be deemed to be equal to three gold
francs.
    The gold franc is defined as 10/31 of a gram of gold of millesimal fineness 900.
    The conversion of the gold franc must express in the national currency a real
value approximating as closely to that which would result from the application of
§1.
4.   Within three months after the entry into force of the Convention and each time
that a change occurs in their method of calculation or in the value of their national

currency in relation to the unit of account, States shall notify the Central Office of their method of calculation in accordance with §2, or the results of the conversion in accordance with §3.

The Central Office shall notify the States of this information.

5.   The railway shall publish the rates at which—
   (a)   it converts sums expressed in foreign currencies but payable in domestic currency (rates of conversion);
   (b)   It accepts payment in foreign currencies (rates of acceptance).

Article 8
Special provisions for certain types of transport

1.   In the case of the haulage of privately owned wagons, special provisions are laid down in the Regulations concerning the international haulage of private owners' wagons by rail (RIP), Annex II to the Uniform Rules.
2.   In the case of the carriage of containers, special provisions are laid down in the Regulations concerning the international carriage of containers by rail (RICo), Annex III to the Uniform Rules.
3.   In the case of express parcels traffic, railways may, by tariff clauses, agree on special provisions in accordance with the Regulations concerning the international carriage of express parcels by rail (RIEx), Annex IV to the Uniform Rules.
4.   Two or more States, by special agreement, or two or more railways by supplementary provisions or by tariff clauses, may agree on terms derogating from the Uniform Rules for the following types of consignments—
   (a)   consignments under cover of a negotiable document;
   (b)   consignments to be delivered only against return of the duplicate of the consignment note;
   (c)   consignments of newspapers;
   (d)   consignment intended for fairs or exhibitions;
   (e)   consignment of loading tackle and of equipment for protection of goods in transit against heat or cold;
   (f)   consignments over all or part of the route under cover of consignment notes which are not used for charging and billing;
   (g)   consignments sent under cover of an instrument suitable for automatic data transmission.

Article 9
Supplementary provision

1.   Two or more States or two or more railways may make supplementary provisions for the execution of the Uniform Rules. They may not derogate from the Uniform Rules unless the latter expressly so provide.
2.   The supplementary provisions shall be put into force and published in the manner required by the laws and regulations of each State. The Central Office shall be notified of the supplementary provisions and of their coming into force.

Article 10
National law

1.   In the absence of provisions in the Uniform rules, supplementary provisions or international tariffs, national law shall apply.
2.   'National law' means the law of the State in which the person entitled asserts his rights, including the rules relating to conflict of laws.

TITLE II
MAKING AND EXECUTION OF THE CONTRACT OF CARRIAGE

Article 11
Making of the contract of carriage

1. The contract of carriage shall come into existence as soon as the forwarding railway has accepted the goods for carriage together with the consignment note. Acceptance is established by the application to the consignment note and, where appropriate, to each additional sheet, of the stamp of the forwarding station, or accounting machine entry, showing the date of acceptance.

2. The procedure laid done in §1 must be carried out immediately after all the goods to which the consignment note relates have been handed over for carriage and—where the provisions in force at the forwarding station so require—such charges as the consignor has undertaken to pay have been paid or a security deposited in accordance with Article 15, §7. The procedure shall be carried out in the presence of the consignor if he so requests.

3. When the stamp has been affixed or the accounting machine entry has been made, the consignment note shall be evidence of the making and content of the contract.

4. Nevertheless, when the loading of the goods is the duty of the consignor in accordance with tariffs or agreements existing between him and the railway, and provided that such agreements are authorised at the forwarding station, the particulars in the consignment note relating to the mass of the goods or to the number of packages shall only be evidence against the railway when that weight or number of packages has been verified by the railway and certified in the consignment note. If necessary these particulars may be proved by other means.

    If it is obvious that there is no actual deficiency corresponding to the discrepancy between the mass or number of packages and the particulars in the consignment note, the latter shall not be evidence against the railway. This shall apply in particular when the wagon is handed over to the consignee with the original seals intact.

5. The railway shall certify receipt of the goods and the date of acceptance for carriage by affixing the date stamp to or making the accounting machine entry on the duplicate of the consignment note before returning the duplicate to the consignor. The duplicate shall not have effect as the consignment note accompanying the goods, nor as a bill of lading.

Article 12
Consignment note

1. The consignor shall present a consignment note duly completed. A separate consignment note shall be made out for each consignment. One and the same consignment note may not relate to more than a single wagon load. The supplementary provisions may derogate from these rules.

2. The railways shall prescribe, for both *petite vitesse* and *grande vitesse* traffic, a standard form of consignment note, which must include a duplicate for the consignor. The choice of consignment note by the consignor shall indicate whether the goods are to be carried by *petite vitesse* or by *grande vitesse*. A request for *grande vitesse* over one part of the route and *petite vitesse* over the remainder will not be allowed except by agreement between all the railways concerned.

    In the case of certain traffic, notably between adjacent countries, the railways may prescribe, in the tariffs, the use of a simplified form of consignment note.

3.   The consignment note must be printed in two or where necessary in three languages, at least one of which shall be one of the working languages of the Organisation.

        International tariffs may determine the language in which the particulars to be filled in by the consignor in the consignment note shall be entered. In the absence of such provisions, they must be entered in one of the official languages of the State of departure and a translation in one of the working languages of the Organisation must be added unless the particulars have been entered in one of those languages. The particulars entered by the consignor in the consignment note shall be in Roman lettering, save where the supplementary provisions or international tariffs otherwise provide.

Article 13
Wording of the consignment note

1.   The consignment note must contain —
      (a)   the name of the destination station;
      (b)   the name and address of the consignee; only one individual or legal person shall be shown as consignee;
      (c)   the description of the goods;
      (d)   the mass, or failing that, comparable information in accordance with the provisions in force at the forwarding station;
      (e)   the number of packages and a description of the packing in the case of consignments in less than wagon loads, and in the case of complete wagon loads comprising one or more packages, forwarded by rail-sea and requiring to be trans-shipped;
      (f)   the number of the wagon and also, for privately-owned wagons, the tare, in the case of goods where the loading is the duty of the consignor;
      (g)   a detailed list of the documents which are required by Customs or other administrative authorities and are attached to the consignment note or shown as held at the disposal of the railway at a named station or at an office of the Customs or of any other authority;
      (h)   the name and address of the consignor; only one individual or legal person shall be shown as the consignor; if the provisions in force at the forwarding station so require, the consignor shall add to his name and address his written, printed or stamped signature.
        The provisions in force at the forwarding station shall determine the meanings of the terms 'wagon load' and 'less than wagon load' for the whole of the route.
2.   The consignment note must, where appropriate, contain all the other particulars provided for in the Uniform Rules. It shall not contain other particulars unless they are required or allowed by the laws and regulations of a State, the supplementary provisions or the tariffs, and are not contrary to the Uniform Rules.
3.   Nevertheless, the consignor may insert in the consignment note in the space set apart for the purpose, but as information for the consignee, remarks relating to the consignment, without involving the railway in any obligation or liability.
4.   The consignment note shall not be replaced by other documents or supplemented by documents other than those prescribed or allowed by the Uniform Rules, the supplementary provisions or the tariffs.

Article 14
Route and tariffs applicable

1.   The consignor may stipulate in the consignment note the route to be followed, indicating it by reference to frontier points or frontier stations and where appropriate, to transit stations between railways. He may only stipulate frontier

points and frontier stations which are open to traffic between the forwarding and destination places concerned.

2. The following shall be regarded as routing instructions—

(a) designation of stations where formalities required by customs or other administrative authorities are to be carried out, and of stations where special care is to be given to the goods (attention to animals, re-icing, etc);

(b) designation of the tariffs to be applied, if this is sufficient to determine the stations between which the tariffs requested are to be applied;

(c) instructions as to the payment of the whole or a part of the charges up to X (X indicating by name the point at which the tariffs of adjacent countries are applied).

3. Except in the cases specified in Article 3 §§4 and 5, and Article 33 §1, the railway may not carry the goods by a route other than that stipulated by the consignor unless both—

(a) the formalities required by customs or other administrative authorities, as well as the special care to be given to the goods, will in any event be carried out at the stations indicated by the consignor; and

(b) the charges and the transit periods will not be greater than the charges and transit periods calculated according to the route stipulated by the consignor.

Sub-paragraph (a) shall not apply to consignments in less than wagon loads if one of the participating railways is unable to adhere to the route chosen by the consignor by virtue of the routing instructions arising from its arrangements for the international carriage of consignments in less than wagon loads.

4. Subject to the provisions of §3, the charges and transit periods shall be calculated according to the route stipulated by the consignor or, in the absence of any such indication, according to the route chosen by the railway.

5. The consignor may stipulate in the consignment note which tariffs are to be applied. The railway must apply such tariffs if the conditions laid down for their application have been fulfilled.

6. If the instructions given by the consignor are not sufficient to indicate the route or tariffs to be applied, or if any of those instructions are inconsistent with one another, the railway shall choose the route or tariffs which appear to it to be the most advantageous to the consignor.

7. The railway shall not be liable for any loss or damage suffered as a result of the choice made in accordance with §6, except in the case of wilful misconduct or gross negligence.

8. If an international tariff exists from the forwarding to the destination station and if, in the absence of adequate instructions from the consignor, the railway has applied that tariff, the railway shall, at the request of the person entitled, refund him the difference between the carriage charges thus applied and those which the application of other tariffs would have produced over the same route, when such difference exceeds four units of account per consignment note.

The same shall apply if, in the absence of adequate instructions from the consignor, the railway has applied consecutive tariffs, even though there is an international tariff offering a more advantageous charge, all other conditions being the same.

Article 15
Payment of charges

1. The charges (carriage charges, supplementary charges, Customs duties and other charges incurred from the time of acceptance for carriage to the time of delivery) shall be paid by the consignor or the consignee in accordance with the following provisions.

In applying these provisions, charges which, according to the applicable tariff, must be added to the standard rates or special rates when calculating the carriage charges, shall be deemed to be carriage charges.

2.   A consignor who undertakes to pay a part or all of the charges shall indicate this on the consignment note by using one of the following phrases—

       (a)   —

            (i)   'carriage charges paid', if he undertakes to pay carriage charges only;

            (ii)   'carriage charges paid including...', if he undertakes to pay charges additional to those for carriage; he shall give an exact description of those charges; additional indications, which may relate only to the supplementary charges or other charges incurred from the time of acceptance for carriage until the time of delivery as well as to sums collected either by customs or other administrative authorities shall not result in any division of the total amount of any one category of charges (for example, the total amount of Customs duties and of other amounts payable to Customs, value added tax being regarded as a separate category);

            (iii)   'carriage charges paid to X' (X indicating by name the point at which the tariffs of adjacent countries are applied), if he undertakes to pay carriage charges to X;

            (iv)   'carriage chargers paid to X including...' (X indicating by name the point at which the tariffs of adjacent countries are applied), if he undertakes to pay charges additional to those for carriage to X, but excluding all charges relating to the subsequent country or railway; the provisions of (ii) shall apply analogously;

       (b)   'all charges paid', if he undertakes to pay all charges (carriage charges, supplementary charges, customs duties and other charges);

       (c)   'charges paid not exceeding...', if he undertakes to pay a fixed sum; save where the tariffs otherwise provide, this sum shall be expressed in the currency of the country of departure.

Supplementary and other charges which, according to the provisions in force at the forwarding station, are to be calculated for the whole of the route concerned, and the charge for interest in delivery laid down in Article 16, §2, shall always be paid in full by the consignor in the case of payment of the charges in accordance with (a)(iv).

3.   The international tariffs may, as regards payment of charges, prescribe the exclusive use of certain phrases set out in §2 of this Article or the use of other phrases.

4.   The charges which the consignor has not undertaken to pay shall be deemed to be payable by the consignee. Nevertheless, such charges shall be payable by the consignor if the consignee has not taken possession of the consignment note nor asserted his rights under Article 28, §4, nor modified the contract of carriage in accordance with Article 31.

5.   Supplementary charges, such as charges for demurrage and standage, warehousing and weighing, which arise from an act attributable to the consignee or from a request which he has made, shall always be paid by him.

6.   The forwarding railway may require the consignor to prepay the charges in the case of goods which in its opinion are liable to undergo rapid deterioration or which, by reason of their low value or their nature, do not provide sufficient cover for such charges.

7.   If the amount of the charges which the consignor undertakes to pay cannot be ascertained exactly at the time the goods are handed over for carriage, such charges shall be entered in a charges note and a settlement of accounts shall be made with the consignor not later than thirty days after the expiry of the transit period. The railway may require as security a deposit approximating to the amount of such charges, for which a receipt shall be given. A detailed account of charges

drawn up from the particulars in the charges note shall be delivered to the consignor in return for the receipt.

8. The forwarding station shall specify, in the consignment note and in the duplicate, the charges which have been prepaid, unless the provisions in force at the forwarding station provide that those charges are only to be specified in the duplicate. In the case provided for in §7 of this Article these charges are not to be specified either in the consignment note or in the duplicate.

Article 16
Interest in delivery

1. Any consignment may be the subject of a declaration of interest in delivery. The amount declared shall be shown in figures in the consignment note in the currency of the country of departure, in another currency determined by the tariffs or in units of account.

2. The charge for interest in delivery shall be calculated for the whole of the route concerned, in accordance with the tariffs of the forwarding railway.

Article 17
Cash on delivery and disbursements

1. The consignor may make the goods subject to a cash on delivery payment not exceeding their value at the time of acceptance at the forwarding station. The amount of such cash on delivery payment shall be expressed in the currency of the country of departure; the tariffs may provide for exceptions.

2. The railway shall not be obliged to pay over any amount representing a cash on delivery payment unless the amount in question has been paid by the consignee. That amount shall be placed at the consignor's disposal within thirty days of payment by the consignee; interest at five per cent per annum shall be payable from the date of the expiry of that period.

3. If the goods have been delivered, wholly or in part, to the consignee without prior collection of the amount of the cash on delivery payment, the railway shall pay the consignor the amount of any loss or damage sustained up to the total amount of the cash on delivery payment without prejudice to any right of recovery from the consignee.

4. Cash on delivery consignment shall be subject to a collection fee laid down in the tariffs; such fee shall be payable notwithstanding cancellation or reduction of the amount of the cash on delivery payment by modification of the contract of carriage in accordance with Article 30, §1.

5. Disbursements shall only be allowed if made in accordance with the provisions in force in force at the forwarding station.

6. The amounts of the cash on delivery payment and of disbursements shall be entered in figures on the consignment note.

Article 18
Responsibility for particulars furnished in the consignment note

The consignor shall be responsible for the correctness of the particulars inserted by, or for, him, in the consignment note. He shall bear all the consequences in the event of those particulars being irregular, incorrect, incomplete, or not entered in the allotted space. If that space is insufficient, the consignor shall indicate therein the place in the consignment note where the rest of the particulars are to be found.

Article 19
Condition, packing and marking of goods

1.   When the railway accepts for carriage goods showing obvious signs of damage, it may require the condition of such goods to be indicated in the consignment note.
2.   When the nature of the goods is such as to require packing, the consignor shall pack them in such a way as to protect them from total or partial loss and from damage in transit and to avoid risk of injury or damage to persons, equipment or other goods.
     Moreover the packing shall comply with the provisions in force at the forwarding station.
3.   If the consignor has not complied with the provisions of §2, the railway may either refuse the goods or require the sender to acknowledge in the consignment note the absence of packing or the defective condition of the packing, with an exact description thereof.
4.   The consignor shall be liable for all the consequences of the absence of packing or defective condition of packing and shall in particular make good any loss or damage suffered by the railway from this cause. In the absence of any particulars in the consignment note, the burden of proof of such absence of packing or defective condition of the packing shall rest upon the railway.
5.   Save where the tariffs otherwise provide, the consignor of a consignment amounting to less than a wagon load shall indicate on each package or on a label approved by the railway in a clear and indelible manner which will avoid confusion and correspond exactly with the particulars in the consignment note —
     (a)   the name and address of the consignee;
     (b)   the destination station.
     The details required under a and b above shall also be shown on each article or package comprised in a wagon load forwarded by rail/sea and requiring to be trans-shipped.
     Old markings or labels shall be obliterated or removed by the consignor.
6.   Save where the supplementary provisions or the tariffs otherwise provide, goods which are fragile or may become scattered in wagons and goods which may taint or damage other goods shall be carried only in complete wagon loads, unless packed or fastened together in such a manner that they cannot become broken or lost, or taint or damage other goods.

Article 20
Handing over of goods for carriage and loading of goods

1.   The handing over of goods for carriage shall be governed by the provisions in force at the forwarding station.
2.   Loading shall be the duty of the railway or the consignor according to the provisions in force at the forwarding station, unless otherwise provided in the Uniform Rules or unless the consignment note includes a reference to a special agreement between the consignor and the railway.
     When the loading is the responsibility of the consignor, he shall comply with the load limit. If different load limits are in force on the lines traversed, the lowest load limit shall be applicable to the whole route. The provisions laying down load limit shall be applicable to the whole route. The provisions laying down load limits shall be published in the same manner as tariffs. If the consignor so requests, the railway shall inform him of the permitted load limit.
3.   The consignor shall be liable for all the consequences of defective loading carried out by him and shall, in particular, make good any loss or damage suffered by the railway through this cause. Nevertheless Article 15 shall apply to the payment of costs arising from the reloading of goods in the event of defective loading. The burden of proof of defective loading shall rest upon the railway.

4.   Unless otherwise provided in the Uniform Rules, goods shall be carried in covered wagons, open wagons, sheeted open wagons or specially equipped wagons according to the international tariffs. If there are no international tariffs, or if they do not contain any provisions on the subject, the provisions in force at the forwarding station shall apply throughout the whole of the route.

5   he affixing of seals to wagons shall be governed by the provisions in force at the forwarding station.

The consignor shall indicate in the consignment note the number and description of the seals affixed to the wagons by him.

Article 21
Verification

1.   The railway shall always have the right to verify that the consignment corresponds with the particulars furnished in the consignment note by the consignor and that the provisions relating to the carriage of goods accepted subject to conditions have been complied with.

2.   If the contents of the consignment are examined for this purpose, the consignor or the consignee, according to whether the verification takes place at the forwarding station or the destination station, shall be invited to be present. Should the interested party not attend, or should the verification take place in transit, it shall be carried out in the presence of two witnesses not connected with the railway, unless the laws or regulations of the State where the verification takes place provide otherwise. The railway may not, however, carry out the verification in transit unless compelled to do so by operational necessities or by the requirements of the Customs or of other administrative authorities.

3.   The result of the verification of the particulars in the consignment note shall be entered therein. If verification takes place at the forwarding station, the result shall also be recorded in the duplicate of the consignment note if it is held by the railway.

If the consignment does not correspond with the particulars in the consignment note or if the provisions relating to the carriage of goods accepted subject to conditions have not been complied with, the costs of the verification shall be charged against the goods, unless paid at the time.

Article 22
Ascertainment of weight and number of packages

1.   The provisions in force in each State shall determine the circumstances in which the railway must ascertain the mass of the goods or the number of packages and the actual tare of the wagons.

The railway shall enter in the consignment note the results ascertained.

2.   If weighing by the railway, after the contract of carriage has been made, reveals a difference, the mass ascertained by the forwarding station or, failing that, the mass declared by the consignor, shall still be the basis for calculating the carriage charges—

(a)   if the difference is manifestly due to the nature of the goods or to atmospheric conditions; or

(b)   the weighing takes place on a weighbridge and does not reveal a difference exceeding two per cent of the mass ascertained by the forwarding station or, failing that, of that declared by the consignor.

Article 23
Overloading

1. When overloading of a wagon is established by the forwarding station or by an intermediate station, the excess load may be removed from the wagon even if no surcharge is payable. Where necessary the consignor or, if the contract of carriage has been modified in accordance with Article 31, the consignee shall be asked without delay to give instructions concerning the excess load.

2. Without prejudice to the payment of surcharges under Article 24, the excess load shall be charged for the distance covered in accordance with the carriage charges applicable to the main load. If the excess load is unloaded, the charge for unloading shall be determined by the tariffs of the railway which carries out the unloading.

    If the person entitled directs that the excess load be forwarded to the same destination station as the main load or to another destination station, or directs that it be returned to the forwarding station, the excess load shall be treated as a separate consignment.

Article 24
Surcharges

1. Without prejudice to the railway's entitlement to the difference in carriage charges and to compensation for any possible loss or damage, the railway may impose—
    (a) a surcharge equal to one unit of account per kilogram of gross mass of the whole package;
        (i)   in the case of irregular, incorrect or incomplete description of substances and articles not acceptable for carriage under the RID;
        (ii) in the case of irregular, incorrect or incomplete description of substances and articles which under the RID are acceptable for carriage subject to conditions, or in the case of failure to observe such conditions;
    (b) a surcharge equal to five units of account per 100 kilograms of mass in excess of the load limit, where the wagon has been loaded by the consignor;
    (c) a surcharge equal to twice the difference:
        (i)   between the carriage charge which should have been payable from the forwarding station to the destination station and that which had been charged, in the case of irregular, incorrect or incomplete description of goods other than those referred to in a, or in general where the description of the consignment would enable it to be carried at a lower tariff than the one that is actually applicable;
        (ii) between the carriage charge for the mass declared and that for the ascertained mass, where the mass declared is less than the real mass.

    When a consignment is composed of goods charged at different rates and their mass can be separately determined without difficulty, the surcharge shall be calculated on the basis of the rates respectively applicable to such goods if this method of calculation results in a lower surcharge.

2. Should there be both an under-declaration of mass and overloading in respect of one and the same wagon, the surcharges payable in respect thereof shall be cumulative.

3. The surcharges shall be charged against the goods irrespective of the place where the facts giving rise to the surcharges were established.

4. The amount of the surcharges and the reason for imposing them must be entered in the consignment note.

5. No surcharge shall be due in the case of:
    (a) an incorrect declaration of mass, if the railway is bound to weigh the goods under the provisions in force at the forwarding station;

(b) an incorrect declaration of mass, or overloading, if the consignor has requested in the consignment note that the railway should weigh the goods;

(c) overloading arising in the course of carriage from atmospheric conditions if it is proved that the load on the wagon did not exceed the load limit when it was consigned;

(d) an increase in mass during carriage, without overloading, if it is proved that the increase was due to atmospheric conditions;

(e) an incorrect declaration of mass, without overloading, if the difference between the mass indicated in the consignment note and the ascertained mass does not exceed three per cent of the declared mass;

(f) overloading of a wagon when the railway has neither published nor informed the consignor of the load limit in a way which would enable him to observe it.

Article 25
Documents for completion of administrative formalities, custom seals

1. The consignor must attach to the consignment note the documents necessary for the completion of formalities required by customs or other administrative authorities before delivery of the goods. Such documents shall relate only to goods which are the subject of one and the same consignment note, unless otherwise provided by the requirements of Customs or of other administrative authorities or by the tariffs.

    However, when these documents are not attached to the consignment note or if they are to be provided by the consignee, the consignor shall indicate in the consignment note the station, the Customs office or the office of any other authority where the respective documents will be made available to the railway and where the formalities must be completed. If the consignor will himself be present or be represented by an agent when the formalities required by Customs or other administrative authorities are carried out, it will suffice for the documents to be produced at the time when those formalities are carried out.

2. The railway shall not be obliged to check whether the documents furnished are sufficient and correct.

3. The consignor shall be liable to the railway for any loss or damage resulting from the absence or insufficiency of or any irregularity in such documents, save in the case of fault by the railway. The railway shall, where it is at fault, be liable for any consequences arising from the loss, non-use or misuse of the documents referred to in the consignment note and accompanying it or deposited with the railway; nevertheless any compensation shall not exceed that payable in the event of loss of the goods.

4. The consignor must comply with the requirements of Customs or of other administrative authorities with respect to the packing and sheeting of the goods. If the consignor has not packed or sheeted the goods in accordance with those requirements the railway shall be entitled to do so; the resulting costs shall be charged against the goods.

5. The railway may refuse consignments when the seals affixed by Customs or other administrative authorities are damaged or defective.

Article 26
Completion of administrative formalities

1. In transit, the formalities required by customs or other administrative authorities shall be completed by the railway. The railway may, however, delegate that duty to an agent.

2. In completing such formalities, the railway shall be liable for any fault committed by itself or by its agent; nevertheless, any compensation shall not exceed that payable in the event of loss of the goods.

3.   The consignor, by so indicating in the consignment note, or the consignee by giving orders as provided for in Article 31, may ask—

     (a)   to be present himself or to be represented by an agent when such formalities are carried out, for the purpose of furnishing any information or explanations required;

     (b)   to complete such formalities himself or to have them completed by an agent, in so far as the laws and regulations of the State in which they are to be carried out so permit;

     (c)   to pay Customs duties and other charges, when he or his agent is present at or completes such formalities, in so far as the laws and regulations of the State in which they carried out permit such payment.

     Neither the consignor, nor the consignee who has the right of disposal, nor the agent of either may take possession of the goods.

4.   If, for the completion of the formalities, the consignor designated a station where the provision in force do not permit of their completion, or if he has stipulated for the purpose any other procedure which cannot be followed, the railway shall act in the manner which appears to it to be the most favourable to the interests of the person entitled and shall inform the consignor of the measures taken.

     If the consignor, by an entry in the consignment note, has undertaken to pay charges including Customs duty, the railway shall have the choice of completing Customs formalities either in transit or at the destination station.

5.   Subject to the exception provided for in the second subparagraph §4, the consignee may complete Customs formalities at the destination station if that station has a Customs office and the consignment note requests Customs clearance on arrival, or, in the absence of such request, if the goods arrive under customs control. The consignee may also complete these formalities at a destination station that has no Customs officer if the national laws and regulations so permit or it the prior authority of the railway and the Customs authorities has been obtained. If the consignee exercises any of these rights, he shall pay in advance the amounts chargeable against the goods.

     Nevertheless, the railway may proceed in accordance with §4 if the consignee has not taken possession of the consignment note within the period fixed by the provisions in force at the destination station.

Article 27
Transit periods

1.   The transit periods shall be specified either by agreement between the railways participating in the carriage, or by the international tariffs applicable from the forwarding station to the destination station. For certain special types of traffic and on certain routes these periods may also be established on the basis of transport plans applicable between the railways concerned; in that case they must be included in international tariffs or special agreements which, where appropriate, may provide for derogations from §§3 to 9 below.

     Such periods shall not in any case exceed those which would result from the application of the following paragraphs.

2.   In the absence of any indication in regard to the transit periods as provided for in §1, and subject to the following paras, the transit periods shall be as follows—

     (a)   for wagon-load consignments:

        (i)   by *grande vitesse*:

            period for despatch   12 hours

            period for carriage, for each 400 km or fraction thereof   24 hours

        (ii)   by *petite vitesse*:

            period for despatch   24 hours

            period for carriage, for each 300 km or fraction thereof   24 hours

(b) for less than wagon-load consignments:
  (i) by *grande vitesse*:
     period for despatch 12 hours
     period for carriage, for each 300 km
     or fraction thereof   24 hours
  (ii) by *petite vitesse*:
     period for despatch 24 hours
     period for carriage, for each 200 km
     or fraction thereof   24 hours
All these distances shall relate to the kilometric distances contained in the tariffs.

3. The period for carriage shall be calculated on the total distance between the forwarding station and the destination station. the period for despatch shall be counted only one, irrespective of the number of systems traversed.

4. The railway may fix additional transit periods of specified duration in the following cases —
  (a) consignments handed in for carriage, or to be delivered, at places other than stations;
  (b) consignments to be carried:
     (i) by a line or system not equipped to deal rapidly with consignments;
     (ii) by a junction line connecting two lines of the same system or of different systems;
     (iii) by a second line;
     (iv) by lines of different gauge;
     (v) by sea or inland navigable waterway;
     (vi) by road if there is no rail link;
  (c) consignments charged at reduced rates in accordance with special or exceptional internal tariffs;
  (d) exceptional circumstances causing an exceptional increase in traffic or exceptional operating difficulties.

5. The additional transit period provided for in §4 (a) to (c) shall be shown in the tariffs or in the provisions duly published in each State.
  Those provided for in §4 (d) must be published and may not come into force before their publication.

6. The transit period shall run from midnight next following acceptance of the goods for carriage. In the case, however, of traffic consigned *grande vitesse* the period shall start twenty-four hours later if the day which follows the day of acceptance for carriage is a Sunday or a statutory holiday and if the forwarding station is not open for *grande vitesse* traffic on that Sunday or statutory holiday.

7. Except in the case of any fault by the railway, the transit period shall be extended by the duration of the period necessitated by —
  (a) verification or ascertainment in accordance with Article 21 and Article 22, §1, which reveals differences from the particulars shown in the consignment note;
  (b) completion of the formalities required by Customs or other administrative authorities;
  (c) modification of the contract of carriage under Article 30 or 31;
  (d) special care to be given to the goods;
  (e) the trans-shipment or reloading of any goods loaded defectively by the consignor;
  (f) any interruption of traffic temporarily preventing the commencement or continuation of carriage.
The reason for and the duration of such extensions shall be entered in the consignment note. If necessary proof may be furnished by other means.

8. The transit period shall be suspended for —
  (a) *petite vitesse*, on Sundays and statutory holidays;

(b)   *grande vitesse*, on Sundays and certain statutory holidays when the provisions in force in any State provide for the suspension of domestic railway transit periods on those days;

(c)   *grande vitesse* and *petite vitesse*, on Saturdays when the provisions in force in any State provide for the suspension of domestic railway transit periods on those days.

9.   When the transit period ends after the time at which the destination station closes, the period shall be extended until two hours after the time at which the station next opens.

In addition, in the case of *grande vitesse* consignments, if the transit period ends on a Sunday or a holiday as defined in 8(b) the period shall be extended until the same time on the next working day.

10.   The transit period is observed if, before its expiry—

(a)   in cases where consignments are to be delivered at a station and notice of arrival must be given, such notice is given and the goods are held at the disposal of the consignee;

(b)   in cases where consignments are to be delivered at a station and notice of arrival need not be given, the goods are held at the disposal of the consignee;

(c)   in the case of consignments which are to be delivered at places other than stations, the goods are placed at the disposal of the consignee.

Article 28
Delivery

1.   The railway shall hand over the consignment note and deliver the goods to the consignee at the destination station against a receipt and payment of the amounts chargeable to the consignee by the railway.

Acceptance of the consignment note obliges the consignee to pay to the railway the amounts chargeable to him.

2.   It shall be equivalent to delivery to the consignee if, in accordance with the provisions in force at the destination station—

(a)   the goods have been handed over to Customs or Octroi authorities at their premises or warehouses, when these are not subject to railway supervision;

(b)   the goods have been deposited for storage with the railway, with a forwarding agent or in a public warehouse.

3.   The provisions in force at the destination station or the terms of any agreements with the consignee shall determine whether the railway is entitled or obliged to hand over the goods to the consignee elsewhere than at the destination station, whether in a private siding, at his domicile or in a railway depot. If the railway hands over the goods, or arranges for them to be handed over in a private siding, at his domicile or in a depot, delivery shall be deemed to have been effected at the time when they are so handed over. Save where the railway and the user of a private siding have agreed otherwise, operations carried out by the railway on behalf of and under the instructions of that user shall not be covered by the contract of carriage.

4.   After the arrival of the goods at the destination station, the consignee may require the railway to hand over the consignment note and deliver the goods to him.

If the loss of the goods is established or if the goods have not arrived on the expiry of the period provided for in Article 39, §1, the consignee may assert, in his own name, any rights against the railway which he may have acquired by reason of the contract of carriage.

5.   The person entitled may refuse to accept the goods, even when he has received the consignment note and paid the charges, so long as an examination for which he has asked in order to establish alleged loss or damage has not been made.

6.   In all other respects, delivery of goods shall be carried out in accordance with the provisions in force at the destination station.

Article 29
Correction of charges

1. In case of incorrect application of a tariff or of error in the calculation or collection of charges, overcharges shall be repaid by the railway and undercharges paid to the railway only if they exceed four units of account per consignment note. The repayment shall be made as a matter of course.
2. If the consignee has not taken possession of the consignment note the consignor shall be obliged to pay to the railway any amounts undercharged. When the consignment note has been accepted by the consignee or the contract of carriage modified in accordance with Article 31, the consignor shall be obliged to pay any undercharge only to the extent that it relates to the costs which he has undertaken to pay by an entry in the consignment note. Any balance of the undercharge shall be paid by the consignee.
3. Sums due under this Article shall bear interest at five per cent per annum from the day of receipt of the demand for payment or from the day of the claim referred to in Article 53 or, if there has been no such demand or claim, from the day on which legal proceedings are instituted.

    If, within a reasonable period allotted to him, the person entitled does not submit to the railway the supporting documents required for the amount of the claim to be finally settled, no interest shall accrue between the expiry of the period laid down and the actual submission of such documents.

TITLE III

MODIFICATION OF THE CONTRACT OF CARRIAGE

Article 30
Modification by the consignor

1. The consignor may modify the contract of carriage by giving subsequent orders—
    (a) for the goods to be withdrawn at the forwarding station;
    (b) for the goods to be stopped in transit;
    (c) for delivery of the goods to be delayed;
    (d) for the goods to be delivered to a person other than the consignee shown in the consignment note;
    (e) for the goods to be delivered at a station other than the destination station shown in the consignment note;
    (f) for the goods to be returned to the forwarding station;
    (g) for the consignment to be made subject to a cash on delivery payment;
    (h) for a cash on delivery payment to be increased, reduced or cancelled;
    (i) for charges relating to a consignment which has not been prepaid to be debited to him, or for charges which he has undertaken to pay in accordance with Article 15, §2 to be increased.
    The tariffs of the forwarding railway may provide that orders specified in (g) to (i) are not acceptable.

    The supplementary provisions or the international tariffs in force between the railways participating in the carriage may provide for the acceptance of orders other than those listed above.

    Orders must not in any event have the effect of splitting the consignment.
2. Such orders shall be given to the forwarding station by means of a written declaration in the form laid down and published by the railway. The declaration shall be reproduced and signed by the consignor in the duplicate of the consignment note which shall be presented to the railway at the same time. The forwarding station shall certify that the order has been received by affixing its date

stamp on the duplicate note below the declaration made by the consignor and the duplicate shall then be returned to him.

If the consignor asks for a cash on delivery payment to be increased, reduced or cancelled, he shall produce the document which was delivered to him. Where the cash on delivery payment is to be increased or reduced, such document shall be returned to the consignor after correction; in the event of cancellation it shall not be returned. Any order given in a form other than that prescribed shall be null and void.

3.   If the railway complies with the consignor's orders without requiring the production of the duplicate, where this has been sent to the consignee, the railway shall be liable to the consignee for any loss or damage caused thereby. Nevertheless, any compensation shall not exceed that payable in the event of loss of the goods.

4.   The consignor's right to modify the contract of carriage shall, notwithstanding that he is in possession of the duplicate of the consignment note, be extinguished in cases where the consignee—

    (a)   has taken possession of the consignment note;

    (b)   has accepted the goods;

    (c)   has asserted his rights in accordance with Article 28, §4;

    (d)   is entitled, in accordance with Article 31, to give orders as soon as the consignment had entered the Customs territory of the country of destination.

From that time onwards, the railway shall comply with the orders and instructions of the consignee.

Article 31
Modification by the consignee

1.   When the consignor has not undertaken to pay the charges relating to carriage in the country of destination, and has not inserted in the consignment note the words 'Consignee not authorised to give subsequent orders', the consignee may modify the contact of carriage by giving subsequent orders—

    (a)   for the goods to be stopped in transit;

    (b)   for delivery of the goods to be delayed;

    (c)   for the goods to be delivered in the country of destination to a person other than the consignee shown in the consignment note;

    (d)   for the goods to be delivered in the country of destination at a station other than the destination station shown in the consignment note, subject to contrary provisions in international tariffs;

    (e)   for formalities required by customs or other administrative authorities to be carried out in accordance with Article 26, §3.

The supplementary provisions or the international tariffs in force between the railways participating in the carriage may provide for the acceptance of orders other than those listed above.

Orders must not in any case have the effect of splitting the consignment. the consignee's orders shall only be effective after the consignment has entered the Customs territory of the country of destination.

2.   Such orders shall be given either to the destination station or to the station of entry into the country of destination, by means of a written declaration in the form laid down and published by the railway.

Any order given in a form other than that prescribed shall be null and void.

3.   The consignee's right to modify the contract of carriage shall be extinguished in cases where he has—

    (a)   taken possession of the consignment note;

    (b)   accepted the goods;

    (c)   asserted his rights in accordance with Article 28, §4;

(d)   designated a person in accordance with §1 (c) and that person has taken possession of the consignment note or asserted his rights in accordance with Article 28, §4.

4.   If the consignee has given instructions for delivery of the goods to another person, that person shall not be entitled to modify the contract of carriage.

Article 32
Execution of subsequent orders

1.   The railway may not refuse to execute orders given under Articles 30 or 31 or delay doing so save where—
    (a)   it is no longer possible to execute the orders by the time they reach the station responsible for doing so;
    (b)   compliance with the orders would interfere with normal railway operations;
    (c)   a change of destination station would contravene the laws and regulations of a State, and in particular the requirements of the Customs or of other administrative authorities;
    (d)   in the case of a change of destination station, the value of the goods will not, in the railway's view, cover all the charges which would be payable on the goods on arrival at the new destination, unless the amount of such charges is paid or guaranteed immediately.

The person who has given the orders shall be informed as soon as possible of any circumstances which prevent their execution.

    If the railway is not in a position to foresee such circumstances, the person who has given the orders shall be liable for all the consequences of starting to execute them.

2.   The charges arising from the execution of an order, except those arising from any fault by the railway, shall be paid in accordance with Article 15.

3.   Subject to §1, the railway shall, in the case of any fault on its part, be liable for the consequences of failure to execute an order or failure to execute it properly. Nevertheless, any compensation shall not exceed that payable in the event of loss of the goods.

Article 33
Circumstances preventing carriage

1.   When circumstances prevent the carriage of goods, the railway shall decide whether it is preferable to carry the goods as a matter of course by modifying the route or whether it is advisable in the consignor's interest to ask him for instructions and at the same time give him any relevant information available to the railway.

    Save fault on its part, the railway may recover the carriage charges applicable to the route followed and shall be allowed the transit periods applicable to such route.

2.   If it is impossible to continue carrying the goods, the railway shall ask the consignor for instructions. It shall not be obliged to do so in the event of carriage being temporarily prevented as a result of measures taken in accordance with Article 3, §4.

3.   The consignor may enter in the consignment note instructions to cover the event of circumstances preventing carriage. If the railway considers that such instructions cannot be executed, it shall ask for fresh instructions.

4.   The consignor, on being notified of circumstances preventing carriage, may give his instructions either to the forwarding station or to the station where the goods are being held. If those instructions change the consignee or the destination station or are given to the station where the goods are being held, the consignor must enter them in the duplicate of the consignment note and present this to the railway.

5.   If the railway complies with the consignor's instructions without requiring the production of the duplicate, when this has been sent to the consignee, the railway shall be liable to the consignee for any loss or damage caused thereby. Nevertheless, any compensation shall not exceed that payable in the event of loss of the goods.

6.   If the consignor, on being notified of a circumstance preventing carriage, fails to give within a reasonable time instructions which can be executed, the railway shall take action in accordance with the provisions relating to circumstances preventing delivery, in force at the place where the goods have been held up. If the goods have been sold, the proceeds of sale, less any amounts chargeable against the goods, shall be held at the disposal of the consignor. If the proceeds are less than those costs, the consignor shall pay the difference.

7.   When the circumstances preventing carriage cease to obtain before the arrival of instructions from the consignor, the goods shall be forwarded to their destination without waiting for such instructions; the consignor shall be notified to that effect as soon as possible.

8.   When the circumstances preventing carriage arise after the consignee has modified the contract of carriage in accordance with Article 31, the railway shall notify the consignee. §§ 2, 6, 7 and 9 shall apply analogously.

9.   Save fault on its part, the railway may raise demurrage or standage charges if circumstances prevent carriage.

10. Article 32 shall apply to carriage undertaken in accordance with Article 33.

Article 34
Circumstances preventing delivery

1.   When circumstances prevent delivery of the goods, the destination station shall without delay notify the consignor through the forwarding station, and ask for his instructions. The consignor shall be notified direct, either in writing, by telegram or by teleprinter, if he has so requested in the consignment note; the costs of such notification shall be charged against the goods.

2.   If the circumstances preventing delivery cease to obtain before the arrival at the destination station of instructions from the consignor the goods shall be delivered to the consignee. The consignor shall be notified without delay be registered letter; the costs of such notification shall be charged against the goods.

3.   If the consignee refuses the goods, the consignor shall be entitled to give instructions even if he is unable to produce the duplicate of the consignment note.

4.   The consignor may also request, by an entry in the consignment note, that the goods be returned to him as a matter of course in the event of circumstances preventing delivery. Unless such request is made, his express consent is required.

5.   Unless the tariffs otherwise provide, the consignor's instructions shall be given through the forwarding station.

6.   Except as otherwise provided for above, the railway responsible for delivery shall proceed in accordance with the provisions in force at the place of delivery. If the goods have been sold, the proceeds of sale, less any costs chargeable against the goods, shall be held at the disposal of the consignor. If such proceeds are less than those costs, the consignor shall pay the difference.

7.   When the circumstances preventing delivery arise after the consignee has modified the contract of carriage in accordance with Article 31, the railway shall notify the consignee. §§ 1, 2 and 6 shall apply analogously.

8.   Article 32 shall apply to carriage undertaken in accordance with Article 34.

TITLE IV
LIABILITY

Article 35
Collective responsibility of railways

1.   The railway which has accepted goods for carriage with the consignment note shall be responsible for the carriage over the entire route up to delivery.
2.   Each succeeding railway, by the very act of taking over the goods with the consignment note, shall become a party to the contract of carriage in accordance with the terms of that document and shall assume the obligations arising therefrom, without prejudice to the provisions of Article 55, §3, relating to the railway of destination.

Article 36
Extent of liability

1.   The railway shall be liable for loss or damage resulting from the total or partial loss of, or damage to, the goods between the time of acceptance for carriage and the time of delivery and for the loss or damage resulting from the transit period being exceeded.
2.   The railway shall be relieved of such liability if the loss or damage or the exceeding of the transit period was caused by a fault on the part of the person entitled, by an order given by the person entitled other than as a result of a fault on the part of the railway, by inherent vice of the goods (decay, wastage, etc) or by circumstances which the railway could not avoid and the consequences of which it was unable to prevent.
3.   The railways shall be relieved of such liability when the loss or damage arises from the special risks inherent in one or more of the following circumstances—
      (a)   carriage in open wagons under the conditions applicable thereto or under an agreement made between the consignor and the railway and referred to in the consignment note;
      (b)   absence or inadequacy of packing in the case of goods which by their nature are liable to loss or damage when not packed or when not properly packed;
      (c)   loading operations carried out by the consignor or unloading operations carried out by the consignee under the provisions applicable thereto or under an agreement made between the consignor and the railway and referred to in the consignment note, or under an agreement between the consignee and the railway;
      (d)   defective loading, when loading has been carried out by the consignor under the provisions applicable thereto or under an agreement made between the consignor and the railway and referred to in the consignment note;
      (e)   completion by the consignor, the consignee or an agent of either, of the formalities required by Customs or other administrative authorities;
      (f)   the nature of certain goods which renders them inherently liable to total or partial loss or damage, especially through breakage, rust, interior and spontaneous decay, desiccation or wastage;
      (g)   irregular, incorrect or incomplete description of articles not acceptable for carriage or acceptable subject to conditions, or failure on the part of the consignor to observe the prescribed precautions in respect of articles acceptable subject to conditions;
      (h)   carriage of live animals;
      (i)   carriage which, under the provisions applicable or under an agreement made between the consignor and the railway and referred to in the consignment

note, must be accompanied by an attendant, if the loss or damage results from any risk which the attendant was intended to avert.

Article 37
Burden of proof

1. The burden of proving that the loss, the damage or the exceeding of the transit period was due to one of the causes specified in Article 36, §2 shall rest upon the railway.
2. When the railway establishes that, having regard to the circumstances of a particular case, the loss or damage could have arisen from one or more of the special risks referred to in Article 36, §3, it shall be presumed that it did so arise. The person entitled shall, however, have the right to prove that the loss or damage was not attributable either wholly or partly to one of those risks.

   This presumption shall not apply in the case referred to in Article 36, §3 (a) if an abnormally large quantity has been lost or if a package has been lost.

Article 38
Presumption in case of reconsignment

1. When a consignment despatched in accordance with the Uniform rules has been reconsigned subject to the same rules and partial loss or damage has been ascertained after the reconsignment, it shall be presumed that it occurred during the latest contract of carriage if the consignment remained in the care of the railway and was reconsigned in the same condition as it arrived at the station from which it was reconsigned.
2. This presumption shall also apply when the contract of carriage prior to the reconsignment was not subject to the Uniform Rules, if the rules would have applied in the case of a through consignment from the original forwarding station to the final destination station.

Article 39
Presumption of loss of goods

1. The person entitled may, without being required to furnish further proof, consider the goods lost when they have not been delivered to the consignee or are not being held at his disposal within thirty days after the expiry of the transit periods.
2. The person entitled may, on compensation for the lost goods, make a written request to be notified without delay should the goods be recovered within one year after the payment of compensation. The railway shall give a written acknowledgement of such request.
3. Within thirty days after receipt of such notification, the person entitled may require the goods to be delivered to him at any station on the route. In that case he shall pay the charges in respect of carriage from the forwarding station to the station where delivery is effected and shall refund the compensation received, less any costs which may have been included therein. Nevertheless he shall retain his rights to claim compensation for exceeding the transit period provided for in Articles 43 and 46.
4. In the absence of the request mentioned in §2 or of any instructions given within the period specified in §3, or if the goods are recovered more than one year after the payment of compensation, the railway shall dispose of them in accordance with the laws and regulations of the State having jurisdiction over the railway.

Article 40
Compensation for loss

1. In the event of total or partial loss of the goods the railway must pay, to the exclusion of all other damages, compensation calculated according to the commodity exchange quotation or, if there is no such quotation, according to the current market price, or if there is neither such quotation nor such price, according to the normal value of goods of the same kind and quality at the time and place at which the goods were accepted for carriage.

2. Compensation shall not exceed 17 units of account per kilogram of gross mass short, subject to the limit provided for in Article 45.

3. The railway shall in addition refund carriage charges, Customs duties and other amounts incurred in connection with carriage of the lost goods.

4. When the calculation of compensation requires the conversion of amounts expressed in foreign currencies, conversion shall be at the rate of exchange applicable at the time and place of payment of compensation.

Article 41
Liability for wastage in transit

1. In respect of goods which, by reason of their nature, are generally subject to wastage in transit by the sole fact of carriage, the railway shall only be liable to the extent that the wastage exceeds the following allowances, whatever the length of the route—
   (a) two per cent of the mass for liquid goods or goods consigned in a moist condition, and also for the following goods:

Bark	Leather
Bones, whole or ground	Liquorice root
Coal and coke	Mushrooms, fresh
Dye-woods, grated or ground	Peat and turf
Fats	Putty or mastic, fresh
Fish, dried	Roots
Fruit, fresh, dried or cooked	Salt
Furs	Sinews, animal
Hide cuttings	Soap and solidified oils
Hides	Tobacco, cut
Hog bristles	Tobacco leaves, fresh
Hops	Vegetables, fresh
Horns and hooves	Wool
Horsehair	

   (b) one per cent of the weight for all other dry goods.

2. The limitation of liability provided for in §1 may not be invoked if, having regard to the circumstances of a particular case, it is proved that the loss was not due to cause which would justify an allowance.

3. Where several packages are carried under a single consignment note, the wastage in transit shall be calculated separately for each package if its mass on despatch is shown separately in the consignment note or can otherwise be ascertained.

4. In the event of total loss of the goods, no deduction for wastage in transit shall be made in calculating the compensation payable.

5. This Article shall not derogate from Articles 36 and 37.

Article 42
Compensation for damage

1. In case of damage to goods, the railway must pay compensation equivalent to the loss in value of the goods, to the exclusion of all other damages. The amount shall

be calculated by applying to the value of the goods as defined in Article 40 the percentage of loss in value noted at the place of destination.

2.   The compensation may not exceed—
       (a)   if the whole consignment has lost value through damage, the amount which would have been payable in case of total loss;
       (b)   if only part of the consignment has lost value through damage, the amount which would have been payable had that part been lost.

3.   The railway shall in addition refund the amounts provided for in Article 40, §3, in the proportion set out in §1.

Article 43
Compensation for exceeding the transit period

1.   If loss or damage has resulted from the transit period being exceeded, the railway shall pay compensation not exceeding three times the carriage charger.

2.   In case of total loss of the goods, the compensation provided for in §1 shall not be payable in addition to that provided for in Article 40.

3.   In case of partial loss of the goods, the compensation provided for in §1 shall not exceed three times the carriage charges in respect of that part of the consignment which has not been lost.

4.   In case of damage to the goods, not resulting from the transit period being exceeded, the compensation provided for in §1 shall, where appropriate, be payable in addition to that provided for in Article 42.

5.   In no case shall the total of compensation payable under §1 together with that payable under Articles 40 and 42 exceed the compensation which would be payable in the event of total loss of the goods.

6.   The railway may provide, in international tariffs or in special agreements for other forms of compensation than those provided for in §1 when, in accordance with Article 27, §1, the transit period has been established on the basis of transport plans.

       If, in this case, the transit periods provided for in Article 27, §2 are exceeded, the person entitled may demand either the compensation provided for in §1 above or that determined by the international tariff or the special agreement applied.

Article 44
Compensation in case of wilful misconduct or gross negligence

When the loss, damage or exceeding of the transit period, or the failure to perform or failure to perform properly the railway's additional services provided for in the Uniform Rules, has been caused by wilful misconduct or gross negligence on the part of the railway, full compensation for the loss or damage proved shall be paid to the person entitled by the railway.

In case of gross negligence, liability shall, however, be limited to twice the maxima specified in Articles 25, 26, 30, 32, 33, 40, 42, 43, 45 and 46.

Article 45
Limitation of compensation under certain tariffs

When the railway agrees to special conditions of carriage through special or exceptional tariffs, involving a reduction in the carriage charge calculated on the basis of the general tariffs, it may limit the amount of compensation payable to the person entitled in the event of loss, damage or exceeding of the transit period, provided that such limit is indicated in the tariff.

When the special conditions of carriage apply only to part of the route, the limit may only be invoked if the event giving rise to the compensation occurred on that part of the route.

Article 46
Compensation in case of interest in delivery

In case of a declaration of interest in delivery, further compensation for loss or damage proved may be claimed, in addition to the compensation provided for in Articles 40, 42, 43 and 45, up to the amount declared.

Article 47
Interest on compensation

1. The person entitled may claim interest on compensation payable, calculated at five per cent per annum, from the date of the claim referred to in Article 53 or, if no such claim has been made, from the day on which legal proceedings are instituted.
2. Interest shall only be payable if the compensation exceeds four units of account per consignment note.
3. If, within a reasonable period allotted to him, the person entitled does not submit to the railway the supporting documents required for the amount of the claim to be finally settled, no interest shall accrue between the expiry of the period laid down and the actual submission of such documents.

Article 48
Liability in respect of rail-sea traffic

1. In rail-sea transport by the services referred to in Article 2, §2 of the Convention each State may, by requesting that a suitable note be included in the list of lines or services to which the Uniform Rules apply, indicate that the following grounds for exemption from liability will apply in their entirety in addition to those provided for in Article 36.

    The carrier may only avail himself to these grounds for exemption if he proves that the loss, damage or exceeding of the transit period occurred in the course of the sea journey between the time when the goods were loaded on board the ship and the time when they were discharged from the ship.

    The grounds for exemption are as follows—
    (a) act, neglect or default on the part of the master, a mariner, pilot or the carrier's servants in the navigation or management of the ship;
    (b) unseaworthiness of the ship, if the carrier proves that the unseaworthiness is not attributable to lack of due diligence on his part to make the ship seaworthy, to ensure that it is properly manned, equipped and supplied or to make all parts of the ship in which the goods are loaded fit and safe for their reception, carriage and protection;
    (c) fire, if the carrier proves that it was not caused by his act or fault, or that of the master, a mariner, pilot or the carrier's servants;
    (d) perils, dangers and accidents of the sea or the navigable waters;
    (e) saving or attempting to save life or property at sea;
    (f) the loading of goods on the deck of the ship, if they are so loaded with the consent of the consignor given in the consignment note and are not in wagons.

    The above grounds for exemption in no way affect the general obligations of the carrier and, in particular, his obligation to exercise due diligence to make the ship seaworthy, to ensure that it is properly manned, equipped and supplied and to make all parts of the ship in which the goods are loaded fit and safe for their reception, carriage and protection.

    Even when the carrier can rely on the foregoing grounds for exemption, he shall nevertheless remain liable if the person entitled proves that the loss, damage or exceeding of the transit period is due to a fault of the carrier, the master, a mariner, pilot or the carrier's servants, fault other than provided for under (a).

2.   Where one and the same sea route is served by several undertakings included in the list referred to in Articles 3 and 10 of the Convention, the regime of liability applicable to that route shall be the same for all those undertakings.

In addition, where such undertakings have been included in the list at the request of several States, the adoption of this regime shall be the subject of prior agreement between those states.

3.   The measures taken under this Article shall be notified to the Central Office. They shall come into force at the earliest at the expiry of a period of thirty days from the date of the letter by which the Central Office notifies them to the other states.

Consignments already in transit shall not be affected by such measures.

Article 49
Liability in case of nuclear incidents

The railway shall be relieved of liability under the Uniform Rules for less or damage caused by a nuclear incident when the operator of a nuclear installation or another person who is substituted for him is liable for the loss or damage pursuant to a State's laws and regulations governing liability in the field of nuclear energy.

Article 50
Liability of the railway for its servants

The railway shall be liable for its servants and for any other persons whom it employs to perform the carriage. If, however, such servants and other persons, at the request of an interested party, make out consignment notes, make translations or render other services which the railway itself is under no obligation to render, they shall be deemed to be acting on behalf of the person to whom the services are rendered.

Article 51
Other actions

In all cases to which the Uniform Rules apply, any action in respect of liability on any grounds whatsoever may be brought against the railway only subject to the conditions and limitations laid down in the Rules. The same shall apply to any action brought against those servants and other persons for whom the railway is liable under Article 50.

TITLE V

ASSERTION OF RIGHTS

Article 52
Ascertainment of partial loss or damage

1.   When partial loss of, or damage to, goods is discovered or presumed by the railway or alleged by the person entitled, the railway must without delay, and if possible in the presence of the person entitled, draw up a report stating, according to the nature of the loss or damage, the condition of the goods, their mass and, as far as possible, the extent of the loss or damage, its cause and the time of its occurrence.

A copy of the report must be supplied free of charge to the person entitled.

2.   Should the person entitled not accept the findings in the report, he may request that the condition and mass of the goods and the cause and amount of the loss or damage be ascertained by an expert appointed either by the parties or by a court. The procedure to be followed shall be governed by the laws and regulations in the State in which such ascertainment takes place.

Article 53
Claims

1.   Claims relating to the contract of carriage shall be made in writing to the railway
     specified in Article 55.
2.   A claim may be made by persons who have the right to bring an action against the
     railway under Article 54.
3.   To make the claim, the consignor must produce the duplicate of the consignment
     note. Failing this, he must produce an authorisation from the consignee or furnish
     proof that the consignee has refused to accept the consignment. To make the
     claim, the consignee must produce the consignment note if it has been handed
     over to him.
4.   The consignment note, the duplicate and any other documents which the person
     entitled thinks fit to submit with the claim shall be produced either in the original
     or as copies, the copies to be duly authenticated if the railway so requires. On
     settlement of the claim, the railway may require the production, in the original
     form, of the consignment note, the duplicate or the cash on delivery voucher so
     that they may be endorsed to the effect that settlement has been made.

Article 54
Persons who may bring an action against the railway

1.   An action for the recovery of a sum paid under the contract of carriage may only be
     brought by the person who made the payment.
2.   An action in respect of the cash on delivery payments provided for in Article 17 may
     only be brought by the consignor.
3.   Other actions arising from the contract of carriage may be brought—
     (a)   by the consignor, until such time as the consignee has:
           (i)   taken possession of the consignment note;
           (ii)   accepted the goods; or
           (iii) asserted his rights under Article 28, §4 or Article 31;
     (b)   by the consignee, from the time when he has:
           (i)   taken possession of the consignment note;
           (ii)   accepted the goods;
           (iii) asserted his rights under Article 28, §4; or
           (iv)   asserted his rights under Article 31 provided that the right of action shall
                  be extinguished from the time when the person designated by the
                  consignee in accordance with Article 31, §1 (c) has taken possession of
                  the consignment note, accepted the goods, or asserted his rights under
                  Article 28, §4.
4.   In order to bring an action, the consignor must produce the duplicate of the
     consignment note. Failing this, in order to bring an action under §3 (a) he must
     produce an authorisation from the consignee or furnish proof that the consignee
     has refused to accept the consignment. In order to bring an action, the consignee
     shall produce the consignment note if it has been handed over to him.

Article 55
Railways against which an action may be brought

1.   An action for the recovery of a sum paid under the contract of carriage may be
     brought against the railway which has collected that sum or against the railway on
     whose behalf it was collected.
2.   An action in respect of the cash on delivery payments provided for in Article 17 may
     only be brought against the forwarding railway.
3.   Other actions arising from the contact of carriage may be brought against the
     forwarding railway, the railway of destination or the railway on which the event

giving rise to the proceedings occurred. Such actions may be brought against the railway of destination even if it has received neither the goods nor the consignment note.

4.   If the plaintiff can choose between several railways, his right to choose shall be extinguished as soon as he brings an action against any one of them.

5.   An action may be brought against a railway other than those specified in §§1, 2 and 3 when instituted by way of counterclaim or by way of exception to the principal claim based on the same contract of carriage.

Article 56
Competence

Actions brought under the Uniform Rules may only be instituted in the competent court of the State having jurisdiction over the defendant railway, unless otherwise provided in agreements between States or in acts of concession. When a railway operates independent railway systems in different States, each system shall be regarded as a separate railway for the purposes of this Article.

Article 57
Extinction of right of action against the railway

1.   Acceptance of the goods by the person entitled shall extinguish all rights of action against the railway arising from the contract in case of partial loss, damage or exceeding of the transit period.

2.   Nevertheless, the right of action shall not be extinguished—
      (a)   in the case of partial loss or of damage, if:
            (i)   the loss or damage was ascertained before the acceptance of the goods in accordance with Article 52 by the person entitled;
            (ii)   the ascertainment which should have been carried out under Article 52 was omitted solely through the fault of the railway;
      (b)   in the case of loss or damage which is not apparent and is not ascertained until after acceptance of the goods by the person entitled, provided that he:
            (i)   asks for ascertainment in accordance with Article 52 immediately after discovery of the loss or damage and not later than seven days after the acceptance of the goods;
            (ii)   and, in addition, proves that the loss or damage occurred between the time of acceptance for carriage and the time of delivery;
      (c)   in cases where the transit period has been exceeded, if the person entitled has, within sixty days, asserted his rights against one of the railways referred to in Article 55, §3;
      (d)   if the person entitled furnishes proof that the loss or damage was caused by wilful misconduct or gross negligence on the part of the railway.

3.   If the goods have been reconsigned in accordance with Article 38, §1 rights of action in case of partial loss or of damage, arising from one of the previous contracts of carriage, shall be extinguished as if there had been only one contract of carriage.

Article 58
Limitation of action

1.   The period of limitation for an action arising from the contract of carriage shall be one year. Nevertheless, the period of limitation shall be two years in the case of an action—
      (a)   to recover a cash on delivery payment collected by the railway from the consignee;
      (b)   to recover the proceeds of a sale affected by the railway;

    (c)   for loss or damage caused by wilful misconduct;

    (d)   for fraud;

    (e)   arising from one of the contracts of carriage prior to the reconsignment in the case provided for in Article 38, §1.

2.   The period of limitation shall run—

    (a)   in actions for compensation for total loss, from the thirtieth day after the expiry of the transit period;

    (b)   in actions for compensation for partial loss, for damage or for exceeding the transit period, from the day when delivery took place;

    (c)   in actions for payment or refund of carriage charges, supplementary charges, other charges or surcharges, or for correction of charges in case of a tariff being wrongly applied or of an error in calculation or collection:

        (i)   if payment has been made, from the day of payment;

        (ii)   if payment has not been made, from the day when the goods were accepted for carriage if payment is due from the consignor, or from the day when the consignee took possession of the consignment note if payment is due from him;

        (iii)   in the case of sums to be paid under a charge note, from the day on which the railway submits to the consignor the account of charges provided for in Article 15, §7; if no such account has been submitted, the period in respect of sums due to the railway shall run from the thirtieth day following the expiry of the transit period;

    (d)   in an action by the railway for recovery of a sum which has been paid by the consignee instead of by the consignor or vice versa and which the railway is required to refund to the person entitled, from the day of the claim for a refund;

    (e)   in actions relating to cash on delivery as provided for in Article 17, from the thirtieth day following the expiry of the transit period;

    (f)   in actions to recover the proceeds of a sale, from the day of the sale;

    (g)   in actions to recover additional duty demanded by Customs or other administrative authorities, from the day of the demand made by such authorities;

    (h)   in all other cases, from the day when the right of action arises.

The day indicated for the commencement of the period of limitation shall not be included in the period.

3.   When a claim is presented to a railway in accordance with Article 53 together with the necessary supporting documents, the period of limitation shall be suspended until the day that the railway rejects the claim by notification in writing and returns the documents. If part of the claim is admitted, the period of limitation shall recommence in respect of that part of the claim still in dispute. The burden of proof of receipt of the claim or of the reply and of the return of the documents shall rest on the party who relies on those facts.

The period of limitation shall not be suspended by further claims having the same object.

4.   A right of action which has become time-barred may not be exercised by way of counter claim or relied upon by way of exception.

5.   Subject to the foregoing provisions, the suspension and interruption of periods of limitation shall be governed by national law.

TITLE VI
RELATIONS BETWEEN RAILWAYS

Article 59
Settlement of accounts between railways

1. Any railway which has collected, either at the time of forwarding or on arrival, charges or other sums due under the contract of carriage must pay to the railways concerned their respective shares.

   The methods of payment shall be settled by agreements between railways.

2. Subject to its rights of recovery against the consignor, the forwarding railway shall be liable for carriage and other charges which it has failed to collect when the consignor has undertaken to pay them in accordance with Article 15.

3. Should the railway of destination deliver the goods without collecting charges or other sums due under the contract of carriage, it shall be liable for them to the railways which have taken part in the carriage and to the other parties concerned.

4. Should one railway default in payment and such default be confirmed by the Central Office at the request of one of the creditor railways, the consequences thereof shall be borne by all the other railways which have taken part in the carriage in proportion to their shares of the carriage charges.

   The right of recovery against the defaulting railway shall not be affected.

Article 60
Recourse in case of loss or damage

1. A railway which has paid compensation in accordance with the Uniform Rules, for total or partial loss or for damage, has a right of recourse against the other railways which have taken part in the carriage in accordance with the following provision—
   (a) the railway which has caused the loss or damage shall be solely liable for it;
   (b) when the loss or damage has been caused by more than one railway, each shall be liable for the loss or damage it has caused; if such distinction cannot be made, the compensation shall be apportioned between those railways in accordance with (c);
   (c) if it cannot be proved that the loss or damage has been caused by one or more railways in particular, the compensation shall be apportioned between all the railways which have taken part in the carriage, except those which can prove that the loss or damage was not caused on their lines; such apportionment shall be in proportion to the kilometric distances contained in the tariffs.

2. In the case of the insolvency of any one of the railways, the unpaid share due from it shall be apportioned among all the other railways which have taken part in the carriage, in proportion to the kilometric distances contained in the tariffs.

Article 61
Recourse in case of exceeding the transit period

1. Article 60 shall apply where compensation is paid for exceeding the transit period. If this has been caused by more than one railway, the compensation shall be apportioned between such railways in proportion to the length of the delay occurring on their respective lines.

2. The transit periods specified in Article 27 shall be apportioned in the following manner—
   (a) where two railways have taken part in the carriage;
       (i) the period for despatch shall be divided equally;

(ii) the period for transport shall be divided in proportion to the kilometric distances contained in the tariffs;

(b) where three or more railways have taken part in the carriage:

(i) the period for despatch shall be divided equally between the forwarding railway and the railway of destination;

(ii) the period for transport shall be divided between all the railways:
— one third in equal shares,
— the remaining two thirds in proportion to the kilometric distances contained in the tariffs.

3. Any additional periods to which a railway may be entitled shall be allocated to that railway.

4. The interval between the time when the goods are handed over to the railway and commencement of the period for despatch shall be allocated exclusively to the forwarding railway.

5. Such apportionment shall only apply if the total transit period has been exceeded.

Article 62
Procedure for recourse

1. The validity of the payment made by the railway exercising one of the rights of recourse under Articles 60 and 61 may not be disputed by the railway against which the right of recourse is exercised, when compensation has been determined by a court and when the latter railway duly served with notice, has been afforded an opportunity to intervene in the proceedings. The court seised of the main proceedings shall determine what time shall be allowed for such notification and for intervention in the proceedings.

2. A railway exercising its right of recourse must take proceedings by one and the same action against all the railways concerned with which it has not reached a settlement, failing which it shall lose its right of recourse in the case of those against which it has not taken proceedings.

3. The court shall give its decision in one and the same judgment on all recourse claims brought before it.

4. The railways against which such action has been brought shall have no further right of recourse.

5. Recourse proceedings may not be joined with proceedings for compensation taken by the person entitled on the basis of the contract of carriage.

Article 63
Competence for recourse

1. The courts of the country in which the railway against which the recourse claim has been made, has its headquarters shall have exclusive competence for all recourse claims.

2. When the action is to be brought against several railways, the plaintiff railway shall be entitled to choose the court in which it will bring the proceedings from among those having competence under §1.

Article 64
Agreements concerning recourse

By agreement, railways may derogate from the provisions concerning reciprocal rights of recourse set out in Title VI, apart from that contained in Article 62, §5.

Articles 65–66 [Omitted].

UNITED NATIONS CONVENTION ON CONTRACTS FOR THE INTERNATIONAL SALE OF GOODS, VIENNA, 1980

PART I
SPHERE OF APPLICATION AND GENERAL PROVISIONS

CHAPTER I
SPHERE OF APPLICATION

Article 1

1. This Convention applies to contracts of sale of goods between parties whose places of business are in different States—
   - (a)   when the States are Contracting States; or
   - (b)   when the rules of private international law lead to the application of the law of a Contracting State.
2. The fact that the parties have their places of business in different States is to be disregarded whenever this fact does not appear either from the contract or from any dealings between, or from information disclosed by, the parties at any time before or at the conclusion of the contract.
3. Neither the nationality of the parties nor the civil or commercial character of the parties or of the contract is to be taken into consideration in determining the application of this Convention.

Article 2

This Convention does not apply to sales—
- (a)   of goods bought for personal, family or household use, unless the seller, at any time before or at the conclusion of the contract, neither knew nor ought to have known that the goods were bought for any such use;
- (b)   by auction;
- (c)   on execution or otherwise by authority of law;
- (d)   of stocks, shares, investment securities, negotiable instruments or money;
- (e)   of ships, vessels, hovercraft or aircraft;
- (f)   of electricity.

Article 3

1. Contracts for the supply of goods to be manufactured or produced are to be considered sales unless the party who orders the goods undertakes to supply a substantial part of the materials necessary for such manufacture or production.
2. This convention does not apply to contracts in which the preponderant part of the obligation of the party who furnishes the goods consists in the supply of labour or other services.

Article 4

This Convention governs only the formation of the contract of sale and the rights and obligations of the seller and the buyer arising from such a contract. In particular, except as otherwise expressly provided in this Convention, it is not concerned with—
- (a)   the validity of the contract or of any of its provisions or of any usage;
- (b)   the effect which the contract may have on the property in the goods sold.

Article 5

This convention does not apply to the liability of the seller for death or personal injury caused by the goods to any person.

Article 6

The parties may exclude the application of this Convention or, subject to Article 12, derogate from or vary the effect of any of its provisions.

CHAPTER II
GENERAL PROVISIONS

Article 7

1. In the interpretation of this Convention, regard is to be had to its international character and to the need to promote uniformity in its application and the observance of good faith in international trade.
2. Questions concerning matters governed by this Convention which are not expressly settled in it are to be settled in conformity with the general principles on which it is based or, in the absence of such principles, in conformity with the law applicable by virtue of the rules of private international law.

Article 8

1. For the purposes of this Convention statements made by and other conduct of a party are to be interpreted according to his intent where the other party knew or could not have been unaware what that intent was.
2. If the preceding paragraph is not applicable, statements made by and other conduct of a party are to be interpreted according to the understanding that a reasonable person of the same kind as the other party would have had in the same circumstances.
3. In determining the intent of a party or the understanding a reasonable person would have had, due consideration is to be given to all relevant circumstances of the case including the negotiations, any practices which the parties have established between themselves, usages and any subsequent conduct of the parties.

Article 9

1. The parties are bound by any usage to which they have agreed and by any practices which they have established between themselves.
2. The parties are considered, unless otherwise agreed, to have impliedly made applicable to their contract or its formation a usage of which the parties knew or ought to have known and which in international trade is widely known to, and regularly observed by, parties to contracts of the type involved in the particular trade concerned.

Article 10

For the purposes of this Convention—
(a) if a party has more than one place of business, the place of business is that which has the closest relationship to the contract and its performance, having regard to the circumstances known to or contemplated by the parties at any time before or at the conclusion of the contract;

(b)   if a party does not have a place of business, reference is to be made to his habitual residence.

Article 11

A contract of sale need not be concluded in or evidenced by writing and is not subject to any other requirement as to form. It may be proved by any means, including witnesses.

Article 12

Any provision of Article 11, Article 29 or Part II of this Convention that allows a contract of sale or its modification or termination by agreement or any offer, acceptance or other indication of intention to be made in any form other than in writing does not apply where any party has his place of business in a Contracting State which has made a declaration under Article 96 of this Convention. The parties may not derogate from or vary the effect of this Article.

Article 13

For the purposes of this Convention 'writing' includes telegram and telex.

PART II
FORMATION OF THE CONTRACT

Article 14

1.   A proposal for concluding a contract addressed to one or more specific persons constitutes an offer if it is sufficiently definite and indicates the intention of the offeror to be bound in case of acceptance. A proposal is sufficiently definite if it indicates the goods and expressly or implicitly fixes or makes provision for determining the quantity and the price.
2.   A proposal other than one addressed to one or more specific persons is to be considered merely as an invitation to make offers, unless the contrary is clearly indicated by the person making the proposal.

Article 15

1.   An offer becomes effective when it reaches the offeree.
2.   An offer, even if it is irrevocable, may be withdrawn if the withdrawal reaches the offeree before or at the same time as the offer.

Article 16

1.   Until a contract is concluded an offer may be revoked if the revocation reaches the offeree before he has dispatched an acceptance.
2.   However, an offer cannot be revoked—
      (a)   if it indicates, whether by stating a fixed time for acceptance or otherwise, that it is irrevocable; or
      (b)   if it was reasonable for the offeree to rely on the offer as being irrevocable and the offeree has acted in reliance on the offer.

Article 17

An offer, even if it is irrevocable, is terminated when a rejection reaches the offeror.

Article 18

1. A statement made by or other conduct of the offeree indicating assent to an offer is an acceptance. Silence or inactivity does not in itself amount to acceptance.

2. An acceptance of an offer becomes effective at the moment the indication of assent reaches the offeror. An acceptance is not effective if the indication of assent does not reach the offeror within the time he has fixed or, if no time is fixed, within a reasonable time, due account being taken of the circumstances of the transaction, including the rapidity of the means of communication employed by the offeror. An oral offer must be accepted immediately unless the circumstances indicate otherwise.

3. However, if, by virtue of the offer or as a result of practices which the parties have established between themselves or of usage, the offeree may indicate assent by performing an act, such as one relating to the dispatch of the goods or payment of the price, without notice to the offeror, the acceptance is effective at the moment the act is performed, provided that the act is performed within the period of time laid down in the preceding paragraph.

Article 19

1. A reply to an offer which purports to be an acceptance but contains additions, limitations or other modifications is a rejection of the offer and constitutes a counter-offer.

2. However, a reply to an offer which purports to be an acceptance but contains additional or different terms which do not materially alter the terms of the offer constitutes an acceptance, unless the offeror, without undue delay, objects orally to the discrepancy or dispatches a notice to that effect. If he does not so object, the terms of the contract are the terms of the offer with the modifications contained in the acceptance.

3. Additional or different terms relating, among other things, to the price, payment, quality and quantity of the goods, place and time of delivery, extent of one party's liability to the other or the settlement of disputes are considered to alter the terms of the offer materially.

Article 20

1. A period of time for acceptance fixed by the offeror in a telegram or a letter begins to run from the moment the telegram is handed in for dispatch or from the date shown on the letter or, if no such date is shown, from the date shown on the envelope. A period of time for acceptance fixed by the offeror by telephone, telex or other means of instantaneous communication, begins to run from the moment that the offer reaches the offeree.

2. Official holidays or non-business days occurring during the period for acceptance are included in calculating the period. However, if a notice of acceptance cannot be delivered at the address of the offeror on the last day of the period because that day falls on an official holiday or a non-business day at the place of business of the offeror, the period is extended until the first business day which follows.

Article 21

1. A late acceptance is nevertheless effective as an acceptance if without delay the offeror orally so informs the offeree or dispatches a notice to that effect.

2. If a letter or other writing containing a late acceptance shows that it has been sent in such circumstances that if its transmission had been normal it would have reached the offeror in due time, the late acceptance is effective as an acceptance

unless, without delay, the offeror orally informs the offeree that he considers his offer as having lapsed or dispatches a notice to that effect.

Article 22

An acceptance may be withdrawn if the withdrawal reaches the offeror before or at the same time as the acceptance would have become effective.

Article 23

A contract is concluded at the moment when an acceptance of an offer becomes effective in accordance with the provisions of this Convention.

Article 24

For the purposes of this Part of the Convention, an offer, declaration of acceptance or any other indication of intention 'reaches' the addressee when it is made orally to him or delivered by any other means to him personally, to his place of business or mailing address or, if he does not have a place of business or mailing address, to his habitual residence.

PART III
SALE OF GOODS

CHAPTER I
GENERAL PROVISIONS

Article 25

A breach of contract committed by one of the parties is fundamental if it results in such detriment to the other party as substantially to deprive him of what he is entitled to expect under the contract, unless the party in breach did not foresee and a reasonable person of the same kind in the same circumstances would not have foreseen such a result.

Article 26

A declaration of avoidance of the contract is effective only if made by notice to the other party.

Article 27

Unless otherwise expressly provided in this Part of the Convention, if any notice, request or other communication is given or made by a party in accordance with this Part and by means appropriate in the circumstances, a delay or error in the transmission of the communication or its failure to arrive does not deprive that party of the right to rely on the communication.

Article 28

If, in accordance with the provisions of this Convention, one party is entitled to require performance of any obligation by the other party, a court is not bound to enter a judgment for specific performance unless the court would do so under its own law in respect of similar contracts of sale not governed by this Convention.

Article 29

1.   A contract may be modified or terminated by the mere agreement of the parties.
2.   A contract in writing which contains a provision requiring any modification or
     termination by agreement to be in writing may not be otherwise modified or
     terminated by agreement. However, a party may be precluded by his conduct from
     asserting such a provision to the extent that the other party has relied on that
     conduct.

CHAPTER II
OBLIGATIONS OF THE SELLER

Article 30

The seller must deliver the goods, hand over any documents relating to them and transfer
the property in the goods, as required by the contract and this Convention.

SECTION I—DELIVERY OF THE GOODS AND HANDING OVER OF DOCUMENTS.

Article 31

If the seller is not bound to deliver the goods at any other particular place, his obligation
to deliver consists—
(a)   if the contract of sale involves carriage of the goods—in handing the goods over to
      the first carrier for transmission to the buyer;
(b)   if, in cases not within the preceding subpara, the contract relates to specific goods,
      or unidentified goods to be drawn from a specific stock or to be manufactured or
      produced, and at the time of the conclusion of the contract the parties knew that
      the goods were at, or were to be manufactured or produced at, a particular place—
      in placing the goods at the buyer's disposal at that place;
(c)   in other cases—in placing the goods at the buyer's disposal at the place where the
      seller had his place of business at the time of the conclusion of the contract.

Article 32

1.   If the seller, in accordance with the contract or this Convention, hands the goods
     over to a carrier and if the goods are not clearly identified to the contract by
     markings on the goods, by shipping documents or otherwise, the seller must give
     the buyer notice of the consignment specifying the goods.
2.   If the seller is bound to arrange for carriage of the goods, he must make such
     contracts as are necessary for carriage to the place fixed by means of transportation
     appropriate in the circumstances and according to the usual terms for such
     transportation.
3.   If the seller is not bound to effect insurance in respect of the carriage of the goods,
     he must, at the buyer's request, provide him with all available information
     necessary to enable him to effect such insurance.

Article 33

The seller must deliver the goods—
(a)   if a date is fixed by or determinable from the contract, on that date;
(b)   if a period of time is fixed by or determinable from the contract, at any time within
      that period unless circumstances indicate that the buyer is to choose a date; or
(c)   in any other case, within a reasonable time after the conclusion of the contract.

Article 34

If the seller is bound to hand over documents relating to the goods, he must hand them over at the time and place and in the form required by the contract. If the seller has handed over documents before that time, he may, up to that time, cure any lack of conformity in the documents, if the exercise of this right does not cause the buyer unreasonable inconvenience or unreasonable expense. However, the buyer retains any right to claim damages as provided for in this Convention.

SECTION II—CONFORMITY OF THE GOODS AND THIRD PARTY CLAIMS

Article 35

1.　The seller must deliver goods which are of the quantity, quality and description required by the contract and which are contained or packaged in the manner required by the contract.
2.　Except where the parties have agreed otherwise, the goods do not conform with the contract unless they—
　　(a)　are fit for the purposes for which goods of the same description would ordinarily be used;
　　(b)　are fit for any particular purpose expressly or impliedly made known to the seller at the time of the conclusion of the contract, except where the circumstances show that the buyer did not rely, or that it was unreasonable for him to rely, on the seller's skill and judgment;
　　(c)　possess the qualities of goods which the seller has held out to the buyer as a sample or model;
　　(d)　are contained or packaged in the manner usual for such goods or, where there is no such manner, in a manner adequate to preserve and protect the goods.
3.　The seller is not liable under subparagraphs a to d of the preceding paragraph for any lack of conformity of the goods if at the time of the conclusion of the contract the buyer knew or could not have been unaware of such lack of conformity.

Article 36

1.　The seller is liable in accordance with the contract and this Convention for any lack of conformity which exists at the time when the risk passes to the buyer, even though the lack of conformity becomes apparent only after that time.
2.　The seller is also liable for any lack of conformity which occurs after the time indicated in the preceding paragraph and which is due to a breach of any of his obligations, including a breach of any guarantee that for a period of time the goods will remain fit for their ordinary purpose or for some particular purpose or will retain specified qualities or characteristics.

Article 37

If the seller has delivered goods before the date for delivery, he may, up to that date, deliver any missing part or make up any deficiency in the quantity of the goods delivered, or deliver goods in replacement of any non-conforming goods delivered or remedy any lack of conformity in the goods delivered, provided that the exercise of this right does not cause the buyer unreasonable inconvenience or unreasonable expense. However, the buyer retains any right to claim damages as provided for in this Convention.

Article 38

1. The buyer must examine the goods, or cause them to be examined, within a short a period as is practicable in the circumstances.
2. If the contract involves carriage of the goods, examination may be deferred until after the goods have arrived at their destination.
3. If the goods are redirected in transit or redispatched by the buyer without a reasonable opportunity for examination by him and at the time of the conclusion of the contract the seller knew or ought to have known of the possibility of such redirection or redispatch, examination may be deferred until after the goods have arrived at the new destination.

Article 39

1. The buyer loses the right to rely on a lack of conformity of the goods if he does not give notice to the seller specifying the nature of the lack of conformity within a reasonable time after he has discovered it or ought to have discovered it.
2. In any event, the buyer loses the right to rely on a lack of conformity of the goods if he does not give the seller notice thereof at the latest within a period of two years from the date on which the goods were actually handed over to the buyer, unless this time-limit is inconsistent with a contractual period of guarantee.

Article 40

The seller is not entitled to rely on the provisions of Articles 38 and 39 if the lack of conformity relates to facts of which he knew or could not have been unaware and which he did not disclose to the buyer.

Article 41

The seller must deliver goods which are free from any right or claim of a third party, unless the buyer agreed to take the goods subject to that right or claim. However, if such right or claim is based on industrial property or other intellectual property, the seller's obligation is governed by Article 42.

Article 42

1. The seller must deliver goods which are free from any right or claim of a third party based on industrial property or other intellectual property, of which at the time of the conclusion of the contract the seller knew or could not have been unaware, provided that the right or claim is based on industrial property or other intellectual property—
   (a) under the law of the State where the goods will be resold or otherwise used, if it was contemplated by the parties at the time of the conclusion of the contract that the goods would be resold or otherwise used in that State; or
   (b) in any other case, under the law of the State where the buyer has his place of business.
2. The obligation of the seller under the preceding paragraph does not extend to cases where—
   (a) at the time of the conclusion of the contract the buyer knew or could not have been unaware of the right or claim; or
   (b) the right or claim results from the seller's compliance with technical drawings, designs, formulae or other such specifications furnished by the buyer.

Article 43

1.   The buyer loses the right to rely on the provisions of Article 41 or Article 42 if he does not give notice to the seller specifying the nature of the right or claim of the third party within a reasonable time after he has become aware or ought to have become aware of the right or claim.
2.   The seller is not entitled to rely on the provisions of the preceding paragraph if he knew of the right or claim of the third party and the nature of it.

Article 44

Notwithstanding the provisions of paragraph 1 of Article 39 and paragraph 1 of Article 43, the buyer may reduce the price in accordance with Article 50 or claim damages, except for loss of profit, if he has a reasonable excuse for his failure to give the required notice.

SECTION III—REMEDIES FOR BREACH OF CONTRACT BY THE SELLER

Article 45

1.   If the seller fails to perform any of his obligations under the contract or this Convention, the buyer may—
        (a)   exercise the rights provided in Articles 46 to 52;
        (b)   claim damages as provided in Articles 74 to 77.
2.   The buyer is not deprived of any right he may have to claim damages by exercising his right to other remedies.
3.   No period of grace may be granted to the seller by a court or arbitral tribunal when the buyer resorts to a remedy for breach of contract.

Article 46

1.   The buyer may require performance by the seller of his obligations unless the buyer has resorted to a remedy which is inconsistent with this requirement.
2.   If the goods do not conform with the contract, the buyer may require delivery of substitute goods only if the lack of conformity constitutes a fundamental breach of contract and a request for substitute goods is made either in conjunction with notice given under Article 39 or within a reasonable time thereafter.
3.   If the goods do not conform with the contract, the buyer may require the seller to remedy the lack of conformity by repair, unless this is unreasonable having regard to all the circumstances. A request for repair must be made either in conjunction with notice given under Article 39 or within a reasonable time thereafter.

Article 47

1.   The buyer may fix an additional period of time of reasonable length for performance by the seller of his obligations.
2.   Unless the buyer has received notice from the seller that he will not perform within the period so fixed, the buyer may not, during that period, resort to any remedy for breach of contract. However, the buyer is not deprived thereby of any right he may have to claim damages for delay in performance.

Article 48

1.   Subject to Article 49, the seller may, even after the date for delivery, remedy at his own expense any failure to perform his obligations, if he can do so without unreasonable delay and without causing the buyer unreasonable inconvenience or

uncertainty of reimbursement by the seller of expenses advanced by the buyer. However, the buyer retains any right to claim damages as provided for in this Convention.

2. If the seller requests the buyer to make known whether he will accept performance and the buyer does not comply with the request within a reasonable time, the seller may perform within the time indicated in his request. The buyer may not, during that period of time, resort to any remedy which is inconsistent with performance by the seller.

3. A notice by the seller that he will perform within a specified period of time is assumed to include a request, under the preceding paragraph, that the buyer make known his decision.

4. A request or notice by the seller under paragraph 2 or 3 of this Article is not effective unless received by the buyer.

Article 49

1. The buyer may declare the contract avoided —
    (a) if the failure by the seller to perform any of his obligations under the contract or this Convention amounts to a fundamental breach of contract; or
    (b) in case of non-delivery, if the seller does not deliver the goods within the additional period of time fixed by the buyer in accordance with paragraph 1 of Article 47 or declares that he will not deliver within the period so fixed.

2. However, in cases where the seller has delivered the goods, the buyer loses the right to declare the contract avoided unless he does so —
    (a) in respect of late delivery, within a reasonable time after he has become aware that delivery has been made;
    (b) in respect of any breach other than late delivery, within a reasonable time:
        (i)   after he knew or ought to have known of the breach;
        (ii) after the expiration of any additional period of time fixed by the buyer in accordance with paragraph 1 of Article 47, or after the seller has declared that he will not perform his obligations within such an additional period; or
        (iii) after the expiration of any additional period of time indicated by the seller in accordance with paragraph 2 of Article 48 or after the buyer has declared that he will not accept performance.

Article 50

If the goods do not conform with the contract and whether or not the price has already been paid, the buyer may reduce the price in the same proportion as the value that the goods actually delivered had at the time of the delivery bears to the value that conforming goods would have had at that time. However, if the seller remedies any failure to perform his obligations in accordance with Article 37 or Article 48 or if the buyer refuses to accept performance by the seller in accordance with those Articles, the buyer may not reduce the price.

Article 51

1. If the seller delivers only a part of the goods or if only a part of the goods delivered is in conformity with the contract, Articles 46 to 50 apply in respect of the part which is missing or which does not conform.

2. The buyer may declare the contract avoided in its entirety only if the failure to make delivery completely or in conformity with the contract amounts to a fundamental breach of the contract.

Article 52

1.   If the seller delivers the goods before the date fixed, the buyer may take delivery or refuse to take delivery.
2.   If the seller delivers a quantity of goods greater than that provided for in the contract, the buyer may take delivery or refuse to take delivery of the excess quantity. If the buyer takes delivery of all or part of the excess quantity, he must pay for it at the contract rate.

CHAPTER III
OBLIGATIONS OF THE BUYER

Article 53

The buyer must pay the price for the goods and take delivery of them as required by the contract and this Convention.

SECTION I—PAYMENT OF THE PRICE

Article 54

The buyer's obligation to pay the price includes taking such steps and complying with such formalities as may be required under the contract or any laws and regulations to enable payment to be made.

Article 55

Where a contract has been validly concluded but does not expressly or implicitly fix or make provision for determining the price, the parties are considered, in the absence of any indication to the contrary, to have impliedly made reference to the price generally charged at the time of the conclusion of the contract for such goods sold under comparable circumstances in the trade concerned.

Article 56

If the price is fixed according to the weight of the goods, in case of doubt it is to be determined by the net weight.

Article 57

1.   If the buyer is not bound to pay the price at any other particular place, he must pay it to the seller—
(a)   at the seller's place of business; or
(b)   if the payment is to be made against the handing over of the goods or of documents, at the place where the handing over takes place.
2.   The seller must bear any increase in the expenses incidental to payment which is caused by a change in his place of business subsequent to the conclusion of the contract.

Article 58

1.   If the buyer is not bound to pay the price at any other specific time, he must pay it when the seller places either the goods or documents controlling their disposition at the buyer's disposal in accordance with the contract and this Convention. The

seller may make such payment a condition for handing over the goods or documents.

2.   If the contract involves carriage of the goods, the seller may dispatch the goods on terms whereby the goods, or documents controlling their disposition, will not be handed over to the buyer except against payment of the price.

3.   The buyer is not bound to pay the price until he has had an opportunity to examine the goods, unless the procedures for delivery or payment agreed upon by the parties are inconsistent with his having such an opportunity.

Article 59

The buyer must pay the price on the date fixed by or determinable from the contract and this convention without the need for any request or compliance with any formality on the part of the seller.

SECTION II—TAKING DELIVERY

Article 60

The buyer's obligation to take delivery consists—

(a)   in doing all the acts which could reasonably be expected of him in order to enable the seller to make delivery; and

(b)   in taking over the goods.

SECTION III—REMEDIES FOR BREACH OF CONTRACT BY THE BUYER

Article 61

1.   If the buyer fails to perform any of his obligations under the contract or this Convention, the seller may—
      (a)   exercise the rights provided in Articles 62 to 65;
      (b)   claim damages as provided in Articles 74 to 77.

2.   The seller is not deprived of any right he may have to claim damages by exercising his right to other remedies.

3.   No period of grace may be granted to the buyer by a court or arbitral tribunal when the seller resorts to a remedy for breach of contract.

Article 62

The seller may require the buyer to pay the price, take delivery or perform his other obligations, unless the seller has resorted to a remedy which is inconsistent with this requirement.

Article 63

1.   The seller may fix an additional period of time of reasonable length for performance by the buyer of his obligations.

2.   Unless the seller has received notice from the buyer that he will not perform within the period so fixed, the seller may not, during that period, resort to any remedy for breach of contract. However, the seller is not deprived thereby of any right he may have to claim damages for delay in performance.

Article 64

1.   The seller may declare the contract avoided—
         (a)   if the failure by the buyer to perform any of his obligations under the contract
                or this Convention amounts to a fundamental breach of contract; or
         (b)   if the buyer does not, within the additional period of time fixed by the seller
                in accordance with paragraph 1 or Article 63, perform his obligation to pay
                the price or take delivery of the goods, or if he declares that he will not do so
                within the period so fixed.
2.   However, in cases where the buyer has paid the price, the seller loses the right to
         declare the contract avoided unless he does so—
         (a)   in respect of late performance by the buyer, before the seller has become
                aware that performance has been rendered; or
         (b)   in respect of any breach other than late performance by the buyer, within a
                reasonable time:
                (i)   after the seller knew or ought to have known of the breach; or
                (ii)   after the expiration of any additional period of time fixed by the seller in
                       accordance with paragraph 1 or Article 63, or after the buyer has declared
                       that he will not perform his obligations within such an additional period.

Article 65

1.   If under the contract the buyer is to specify the form, measurement or other
         features of the goods and he fails to make such specification either on the date
         agreed upon within a reasonable time after receipt of a request from the seller, the
         seller may, without prejudice to any other rights he may have, make the
         specification himself in accordance with the requirements of the buyer that may be
         known to him.
2.   If the seller makes the specification himself, he must inform the buyer of the details
         thereof and must fix a reasonable time within which the buyer may make a
         different specification. If, after receipt of such a communication, the buyer fails to
         do so within the time so fixed, the specification made by the seller is binding.

CHAPTER IV
PASSING OF RISK

Article 66

Loss of or damage to the goods after the risk has passed to the buyer does not discharge
him from his obligation to pay the price, unless the loss or damage is due to an act or
omission of the seller.

Article 67

1.   If the contract of sale involves carriage of the goods and the seller is not bound to
         hand them over at a particular place, the risk passes to the buyer when the goods
         are handed over to the first carrier for transmission to the buyer in accordance with
         the contract of sale. If the seller is bound to hand the goods over to a carrier at a
         particular place, the risk does not pass to the buyer until the goods are handed
         over to the carrier at that place. The fact that the seller is authorised to retain
         documents controlling the disposition of the goods does not affect the passage of
         the risk.
2.   Nevertheless, the risk does not pass to the buyer until the goods are clearly
         identified to the contract, whether by markings on the goods, by shipping
         documents, by notice given to the buyer or otherwise.

Article 68

The risk in respect of goods sold in transit passes to the buyer from the time of the conclusion of the contract. However, if the circumstances so indicate, the risk is assumed by the buyer from the time the goods were handed over to the carrier who issued the documents embodying the contract of carriage. Nevertheless, if at the time or the conclusion of the contract of sale the seller knew or ought to have known that the goods had been lost or damaged and did not disclose this to the buyer, the loss or damage is at the risk of the seller.

Article 69

1.   In cases not within Articles 67 and 68, the risk passes to the buyer when he takes over the goods or, if he does not do so in due time, from the time when the goods are placed at his disposal and he commits a breach of contract by failing to take delivery.
2.   However, if the buyer is bound to take over the goods at a place other than a place of business of the seller, the risk passes when delivery is due and the buyer is aware of the fact that the goods are placed at his disposal at that place.
3.   If the contract relates to goods not then identified, the goods are considered not to be placed at the disposal of the buyer until they are clearly identified to the contract.

Article 70

If the seller has committed a fundamental breach of contract, Articles 67, 68 and 69 do not impair the remedies available to the buyer on account of the breach.

CHAPTER V

PROVISIONS COMMON TO THE OBLIGATIONS OF THE
SELLER AND OF THE BUYER

SECTION I—ANTICIPATORY BREACH AND INSTALMENT CONTRACTS

Article 71

1.   A party may suspend the performance of his obligations if, after the conclusion of the contract, it becomes apparent that the other party will not perform a substantial part of his obligations as a result of—
      (a)   a serious deficiency in his ability to perform or in his credit worthiness; or
      (b)   his conduct in preparing to perform or in performing the contract.
2.   If the seller has already dispatched the goods before the grounds described in the preceding paragraph become evident, he may prevent the handing over of the goods to the buyer even though the buyer holds a document which entitles him to obtain them. The present paragraph relates only to the rights in the goods as between the buyer and the seller.
3.   A party suspending performance, whether before or after dispatch of the goods, must immediately give notice of the suspension to the other party and must continue with performance if the other party provides adequate assurance of his performance.

Article 72·

1. If prior to the date for performance of the contract it is clear that one of the parties will commit a fundamental breach of contract, the other party may declare the contract avoided.
2. If time allows, the party intending to declare the contract avoided must give reasonable notice to the other party in order to permit him to provide adequate assurance of his performance.
3. The requirements of the preceding paragraph do not apply if the other party has declared that he will not perform his obligations.

Article 73 ·

1. In the case of a contract for delivery of goods by instalments, if the failure of one party to perform any of his obligations in respect of any instalment constitutes a fundamental breach of contract with respect to that instalment, the other party may declare the contract avoided with respect to that instalment.
2. If one party's failure to perform any of his obligations in respect of any instalment gives the other party good grounds to conclude that a fundamental breach of contract will occur with respect to future instalments, he may declare the contract avoided for the future, provided that he does so within a reasonable time.
3. A buyer who declares the contract avoided in respect of any delivery may, at the same time, declare it avoided in respect of deliveries already made or of future deliveries if, by reason of their interdependence, those deliveries could not be used for the purpose contemplated by the parties at the time of the conclusion of the contract.

SECTION II—DAMAGES

Article 74

Damages for breach of contract by one party consist of a sum equal to the loss, including loss of profit, suffered by the other party as a consequence of the breach. Such damages may not exceed the loss which the party in breach foresaw or ought to have foreseen at the time of the conclusion of the contract, in the light of the facts and matters of which he then knew or ought to have known, as a possible consequence of the breach of contract.

Article 75

If the contract is avoided and if, in a reasonable manner and within a reasonable time after avoidance, the buyer has bought goods in replacement or the seller has resold the goods, the party claiming damages may recover the difference between the contract price and the price in the substitute transaction as well as any further damages recoverable under Article 74.

Article 76

1. If the contract is avoided and there is a current price for the goods, the party claiming damages may, if he has not made a purchase or resale under Article 75, recover the difference between the price fixed by the contract and the current price at the time of avoidance as well as any further damages recoverable under Article 74. If, however, the party claiming damages has avoided the contract after taking over the goods, the current price at the time of such taking over shall be applied instead of the current price at the time of avoidance.

2.   For the purposes of the preceding paragraph, the current price is the price prevailing at the place where delivery of the goods should have been made or, if there is no current price at that place, the price at such other place as serves as a reasonable substitute, making due allowance for differences in the cost of transporting the goods.

Article 77

A party who relies on a breach of contract must take such measures as are reasonable in the circumstances to mitigate the loss, including loss of profit, resulting from the breach. If he fails to take such measures, the party in breach may claim a reduction in the damages in the amount by which the loss should have been mitigated.

SECTION III—INTEREST

Article 78

If a party fails to pay the price or any other sum that is in arrears, the other party is entitled to interest on it, without prejudice to any claim for damages recoverable under Article 74.

SECTION IV—EXEMPTIONS

Article 79

1.   A party is not liable for a failure to perform any of his obligations if he proves that the failure was due to an impediment beyond his control and that he could not reasonably be expected to have taken the impediment into account at the time of the conclusion of the contract or to have avoided or overcome it or its consequences.
2.   If the party's failure is due to the failure by a third person whom he has engaged to perform the whole or a part of the contract, that party is exempt from liability only if—
      (a)   he is exempt under the preceding paragraph; and
      (b)   the person whom he has so engaged would be so exempt if the provisions of that paragraph were applied to him.
3.   The exemption provided by this Article has effect for the period during which the impediment exists.
4.   The party who fails to perform must give notice to the other party of the impediment and its effect on his ability to perform. If the notice is not received by the other party within a reasonable time after the party who fails to perform knew or ought to have known of the impediment, he is liable for damages resulting from such non-receipt.
5.   Nothing in this Article prevents either party from exercising any right other than to claim damages under this Convention.

Article 80

A party may not rely on a failure of the other party to perform, to the extent that such failure was caused by the first party's act or omission.

SECTION V—EFFECTS OF AVOIDANCE

Article 81

1. Avoidance of the contract releases both parties from their obligations under it, subject to any damages which may be due. Avoidance does not affect any provision of the contract for the settlement of disputes or any other provision of the contract governing the rights and obligations of the parties consequent upon the avoidance of the contract.

2. A party who has performed the contract either wholly or in part may claim restitution from the other party of whatever the first party has supplied or paid under the contract. If both parties are bound to make restitution, they must do so concurrently.

Article 82

1. The buyer loses the right to declare the contract avoided or to require the seller to deliver substitute goods if it is impossible for him to make restitution of the goods substantially in the condition in which he received them.

2. The preceding paragraph does not apply—
   (a) if the impossibility of making restitution of the goods or of making restitution of the goods substantially in the condition in which the buyer received them is not due to his act or omission;
   (b) if the goods or part of the goods have perished or deteriorated as a result of the examination provided for in Article 38; or
   (c) if the goods or part of the goods have been sold in the normal course of business or have been consumed or transformed by the buyer in the course of normal use before he discovered or ought to have discovered the lack of conformity.

Article 83

A buyer who has lost the right to declare the contract avoided or to require the seller to deliver substitute goods in accordance with Article 82 retains all other remedies under the contract and this Convention.

Article 84

1. If the seller is bound to refund the price, he must also pay interest on it, from the date on which the price was paid.

2. The buyer must account to the seller for all benefits which he has derived from the goods or part of them—
   (a) if he must make restitution of the goods or part of them; or
   (b) if it is impossible for him to make restitution of all or part of the goods or to make restitution of all or part of the goods substantially in the condition in which he received them, but he has nevertheless declared the contract avoided or required the seller to deliver substitute goods.

SECTION VI—PRESERVATION OF THE GOODS

Article 85

If the buyer is in delay in taking delivery of the goods or, where payment of the price and delivery of the goods are to be made concurrently, if he fails to pay the price, and the seller is either in possession of the goods or otherwise able to control their disposition, the seller must take such steps as are reasonable in the circumstances to preserve them. He is entitled to retain them until he has been reimbursed his reasonable expenses by the buyer.

Article 86

1. If the buyer has received the goods and intends to exercise any right under the contract or this Convention to reject them, he must take such steps to preserve them as are reasonable in the circumstances. He is entitled to retain them until he has been reimbursed his reasonable expenses by the seller.
2. If goods dispatched to the buyer have been placed at his disposal at their destination and he exercises the right to reject them, he must take possession of them on behalf of the seller, provided that this can be done without payment of the price and without unreasonable inconvenience or unreasonable expense. This provision does not apply if the seller or a person authorised to take charge of the goods on his behalf is present at the destination. If the buyer takes possession of the goods under this paragraph, his rights and obligations are governed by the preceding paragraph.

Article 87

A party who is bound to take steps to preserve the goods may deposit them in a warehouse of a third person at the expense of the other party provided that the expense incurred is not unreasonable.

Article 88

1. A party who is bound to preserve the goods in accordance with Article 85 or 86 may sell them by any appropriate means if there has been an unreasonable delay by the other party in taking possession of the goods or in taking them back or in paying the price or the cost of preservation, provided that reasonable notice of the intention to sell has been given to the other party.
2. If the goods are subject to rapid deterioration or their preservation would involve unreasonable expense, a party who is bound to preserve the goods in accordance with Article 85 or 86 must take reasonable measures to sell them. to the extent possible he must give notice to the other party of his intention to sell.
3. A party selling the goods has the right to retain out of the proceeds of sale an amount equal to the reasonable expenses of preserving the goods and of selling them. He must account to the other party for the balance.

PART IV

Articles 89–91 [Omitted].

Article 92

1. A Contracting State may declare at the time of the signature, ratification, acceptance, approval or accession that it will not be bound by Part II of this Convention or that it will not be bound by Part III of this Convention.
2. A Contracting State which makes a declaration in accordance with the preceding paragraph in respect of Part II or Part III of this Convention is not to be considered a contracting State within paragraph 1 or Article 1 of this Convention in respect of matters governed by the Part to which the declaration applies.

Article 93 [Omitted].

Article 94

1.   Two or more Contracting States which have the same or closely related legal rules on matters governed by this convention may at any time declare that the Convention is not to apply to contracts of sale or to their formation where the parties have their places of business in those States. Such declarations may be made jointly or by reciprocal unilateral declarations.
2.   A Contracting State which has the same or closely related legal rules on matters governed by this Convention as one or more non-Contracting States may at any time declare that the Convention is not to apply to contracts of sale or to their formation where the parties have their places of business in those States.
3.   [Omitted].

Article 95

Any State may declare at the time of the deposit of its instrument of ratification acceptance, approval or accession that it will not be bound by subparagraph 1 b of Article 1 of this Convention.

Article 96

A Contracting State whose legislation requires contracts of sale to be concluded in or evidenced by writing may at any time make a declaration in accordance with Article 12 that any provision of Article 11, Article 29, or Part II of this Convention, that allows a contract of sale or its modification or termination by agreement or any offer, acceptance, or other indication or intention to be made in any form other than in writing, does not apply where any party has his place of business in that State.

Articles 97–101 [Omitted].

UNITED NATIONS CONVENTION ON INTERNATIONAL MULTIMODAL TRANSPORT OF GOODS, GENEVA, 1980

PART I
GENERAL PROVISIONS

Article 1
Definitions

For the purposes of this Convention—
1.   'International multimodal transport' means the carriage of goods by at least two different modes of transport on the basis of a multimodal transport contract from a place in one country at which the goods are taken in charge by the multimodal transport operator to a place designated for delivery situated in a different country. The operation of pick-up and delivery of goods carried out in the performance of a unimodal transport contract, as defined in such contract, shall not be considered as international multimodal transport.
2.   'Multimodal transport operator' means any person who on his own behalf or through another person acting on his behalf concludes a multimodal transport contract and who acts as a principal, not as an agent or on behalf of the consignor

or of the carriers participating in the multimodal transport operations, and who assumes responsibility for the performance of the contract.

3. 'Multimodal transport contract' means a contract whereby a multimodal transport operator undertakes, against payment of freight, to perform or to procure the performance of international multimodal transport.

4. 'Multimodal transport document' means a document which evidences a multimodal transport contract, the taking in charge of the goods by the multimodal transport operator, and an undertaking by him to deliver the goods in accordance with the terms of that contract.

5. 'Consignor' means any person by whom or in whose name or on whose behalf a multimodal transport contract has been concluded with the multimodal transport operator, or any person by whom or in whose name or on whose behalf the goods are actually delivered to the multimodal transport operator in relation to the multimodal transport contract.

6. 'Consignee' means the person entitled to take delivery of the goods.

7. 'Goods' includes any container, pallet or similar article of transport or packaging, if supplied by the consignor.

8. 'International convention' means an international agreement concluded among States in written form and governed by international law.

9. 'Mandatory national law' means any statutory law concerning carriage of goods the provision of which cannot be departed from by contractual stipulation to the detriment of the consignor.

10. 'Writing' means, *inter alia*, telegram or telex.

Article 2
Scope of application

The provisions of this Convention shall apply to all contracts of multimodal transport between places in two States, if—

(a) The place for the taking in charge of the goods by the multimodal transport operator as provided for in the multimodal transport contract is located in a Contracting State; or

(b) The place for delivery of the goods by the multimodal transport operator as provided for in the multimodal transport contract is located in a Contracting State.

Article 3
Mandatory application

1. When a multimodal transport contract has been concluded which according to Article 2 shall be governed by this convention, the provisions of this convention shall be mandatorily applicable to such contract.

2. Nothing in this Convention shall affect the right of the consignor to choose between multimodal transport and segmented transport.

Article 4
Regulation and control of multimodal transport

1. This Convention shall not affect, or be incompatible with, the application of any international convention or national law relating to the regulation and control of transport operations.

2. This Convention shall not affect the right of each State to regulate and control at the national level multimodal transport operations and multimodal transport operators, including the right to take measures relating to consultations, especially before the introduction of new technologies and services, between multimodal transport operators, shippers, shippers' organisations and appropriate national authorities on terms and conditions of service; licensing of multimodal transport

operators; participation in transport; and all other steps in the national economic and commercial interest.

3.   The multimodal transport operator shall comply with the applicable law of the country in which he operates and with the provisions of this Convention.

PART II
DOCUMENTATION

Article 5
Issue of multimodal transport document

1.   When the goods are taken charge by the multimodal transport operator, he shall issue a multimodal transport document which, at the option of the consignor, shall be in either negotiable or non-negotiable form.

2.   The multimodal transport document shall be signed by the multimodal transport operator or by a person having authority from him.

3.   The signature on the multimodal transport document may be in hand-writing, printed in facsimile, perforated, stamped, in symbols, or made by any other mechanical or electronic means, if not inconsistent with the law of the country where the multimodal transport document is issued.

4.   If the consignor so agrees, a non-negotiable multimodal transport document may be issued by making use of any mechanical or other means preserving a record of the particulars stated in Article 8 to be contained in the multimodal transport document. In such a case the multimodal transport operator, after having taken the goods in charge, shall deliver to the consignor a readable document containing all the particulars so recorded, and such document shall for the purposes of the provisions of this Convention be deemed to be a multimodal transport document.

Article 6
Negotiable multimodal transport document

1.   Where a multimodal transport document is issued in negotiable form—
   (a)   It shall be made out to order or to bearer;
   (b)   If made out to order it shall be transferable by endorsement;
   (c)   If made out to bearer it shall be transferable without endorsement;
   (d)   If issued in a set of more than one original it shall indicate the number of originals in the set;
   (e)   If any copies are issued each copy shall be marked 'non-negotiable copy'.

2.   Delivery of the goods may be demanded from the multimodal transport operator or a person acting on his behalf only against surrender of the negotiable multimodal transport document duly endorsed where necessary.

3.   The multimodal transport operator shall be discharged from his obligation to deliver the goods if, where a negotiable multimodal transport document has been issued in a set of more than one original, he or a person acting on his behalf has in good faith delivered the goods against surrender of one of such originals.

Article 7
Non-negotiable multimodal transport

1.   Where a multimodal transport document is issued in non-negotiable form it shall indicate a named consignee.

2.   The multimodal transport operator shall be discharged from his obligation to deliver the goods if he makes delivery thereof to the consignee named in such non-negotiable multimodal transport document or to such other person as he may be duly instructed, as a rule, in writing.

Article 8
Contents of the multimodal transport document

1. The multimodal transport document shall contain the following particulars—
    (a) the general nature of the goods, the leading marks necessary for identification of the goods, an express statement, if applicable, as to the dangerous character of the goods, the number of packages or pieces, and the gross weight of the goods or their quantity otherwise expressed, all such particulars as furnished by the consignor;
    (b) the apparent condition of the goods;
    (c) the name and principal place of business of the multimodal transport operator;
    (d) the name of the consignor;
    (e) the consignee, if named by the consignor;
    (f) the place and date of taking in charge of the goods by the multimodal transport operator;
    (g) the place of delivery of the goods;
    (h) the date or the period of delivery of the goods at the place of delivery, if expressly agreed upon between the parties;
    (i) a statement indicating whether the multimodal transport document is negotiable or non-negotiable;
    (j) the place and date of issue of the multimodal transport document;
    (k) the signature of the multimodal transport operator or of a person having authority from him;
    (l) the freight for each mode of transport, if expressly agreed between the parties, or the freight including its currency, to the extent payable by the consignee or other indication that freight is payable by him;
    (m) the intended journey route, modes of transport and places of transhipment, if known at the time of issuance of the multimodal transport document;
    (n) the statement referred to in paragraph 3 of Article 28;
    (o) any other particulars which the parties may agree to insert in the multimodal transport document, if not inconsistent with the law of the country where the multimodal transport document is issued.
2. The absence from the multimodal transport document of one or more of the particulars referred to in paragraph 1 of this Article shall not affect the legal character of the document as a multimodal transport document provided that it nevertheless meets the requirements set out in paragraph 4 of Article 1.

Article 9
Reservations in the multimodal transport document

1. If the multimodal transport document contains particulars concerning the general nature, leading marks, number of packets or pieces, weight or quantity of the goods which the multimodal transport operator or a person acting on his behalf knows, or has reasonable grounds to suspect, do not accurately represent the goods actually taken in charge, or if he has no reasonable means of checking such particulars, the multimodal transport operator or a person acting on his behalf shall insert in the multimodal transport document a reservation specifying these inaccuracies, grounds of suspicion or the absence of reasonable means of checking.
2. If the multimodal transport operator or a person acting on his behalf fails to note on the multimodal transport document the apparent condition of the goods, he is deemed to have noted on the multimodal transport document that the goods were in apparent good condition.

Article 10
Evidentiary effect of the multimodal transport document

Except for particulars in respect of which and to the extent to which a reservation permitted under Article 9 has been entered —

(a)   the multimodal transport document shall be *prima facie* evidence of the taking in charge by the multimodal transport operator of the goods as described therein; and

(b)   proof to the contrary by the multimodal transport operator shall not be admissible if the multimodal transport document is issued in negotiable form and has been transferred to a third party, including a consignee, who has acted in good faith in reliance on the description of the goods therein.

Article 11
Liability for intentional misstatements or omissions

When the multimodal transport operator, with intent to defraud, gives in the multimodal transport document false information concerning the goods or omits any information required to be included under paragraph 1 a or b of Article 8 or under Article 9, he shall be liable, without the benefit of the limitation of liability provided for in this Convention, for any loss, damage or expenses incurred by a third party, including a consignee, who acted in reliance on the description of the goods in the multimodal transport document issued.

Article 12
Guarantee by the consignor

1.   The consignor shall be deemed to have guaranteed to the multimodal transport operator the accuracy, at the time the goods were taken in charge by the multimodal transport operator, of particulars relating to the general nature of the goods, their marks, number, weight and quantity and, if applicable, to the dangerous character of the goods, as furnished by him for insertion in the multimodal transport document.

2.   The consignor shall indemnify the multimodal transport operator against loss resulting from inaccuracies in or inadequacies of the particulars referred to in paragraph 1 of this Article. The consignor shall remain liable even if the multimodal transport document has been transferred to him. The right of the multimodal transport operator to such indemnity shall in no way limit his liability under the multimodal transport contract to any person other than the consignor.

Article 13
Other documents

The issue of the multimodal transport document does not preclude the issue, if necessary, of other documents relating to transport or other services involved in international multimodal transport, in accordance with applicable international conventions or national law. However, the issue of such other documents shall not affect the legal character of the multimodal transport document.

PART III
LIABILITY OF THE MULTIMODAL TRANSPORT OPERATOR

Article 14
Period of responsibility

1. The responsibility of the multimodal transport operator for the goods under this Convention covers the period from the time he takes the goods in his charge to the time of their delivery.
2. For the purpose of this Article, the multimodal transport operator is deemed to be in charge of the goods—
    (a) from the time he has taken over the goods from:
        (i)   the consignor or a person acting on his behalf; or
        (ii) an authority or other third party to whom, pursuant to law or regulations applicable at the place of taking in charge, the goods must be handed over for transport;
    (b) until the time he has delivered the goods:
        (i)   By handing over the goods to the consignee; or
        (ii) In cases where the consignee does not receive the goods from the multimodal transport operator, by placing them at the disposal of the consignee in accordance with the multimodal transport contract or with the law or with the usage of the particular trade applicable at the place of delivery; or
        (iii) By handing over the goods to an authority or other third party to whom, pursuant to law or regulations applicable at the place of delivery, the goods must be handed over.
3. In paragraphs 1 and 2 of this Article, reference to the multimodal transport operator shall include his servants or agents or any other person of whose services he makes use for the performance of the multimodal transport contract, and reference to the consignor or consignee shall include their servants or agents.

Article 15
The liability of the multimodal transport operator for his servants, agents and other persons

Subject to Article 21, the multimodal transport operator shall be liable for the acts and omissions of his servants or agents, when any such servant or agent is acting within the scope of his employment, or of any other person of whose services he makes use for the performance of the multimodal transport contract, when such person is acting in the performance of the contract, as if such acts and omissions were his own.

Article 16
Basis of liability

1. The multimodal transport operator shall be liable for loss resulting from loss or damage to the goods, as well as from delay in delivery, if the occurrence which caused the loss, damage or delay in delivery took place while the goods were in his charge as defined in Article 14, unless the multimodal transport operator proves that he, his servants or agents or any other person referred to in Article 15 took all measures that could reasonably be required to avoid the occurrence and its consequences.
2. Delay in delivery occurs when the goods have not been delivered within the time expressly agreed upon or, in the absence of such agreement, within the time which it would be reasonable to require of a diligent multimodal transport operator, having regard to the circumstances of the case.

3.   If the goods have not been delivered within 90 consecutive days following the date of delivery determined according to paragraph 2 of this Article, the claimant may treat the goods as lost.

Article 17
Concurrent causes

Where fault or neglect on the part of the multimodal transport operator, his servants or agents or any other person referred to in Article 15 combines with another cause to produce loss, damage or delay in delivery, the multimodal transport operator shall be liable only to the extent that the loss, damage or delay in delivery is attributable to such fault or neglect, provided that the multimodal transport operator proves the part of the loss, damage or delay in delivery not attributable thereto.

Article 18
Limitation of liability

1.   When the multimodal transport operator is liable for loss resulting from loss of or damage to the goods according to Article 16, his liability shall be limited to an amount not exceeding 920 units of account per package of other shipping unit or 2.75 units of account per kilogram of gross weight of the goods lost or damaged, whichever is the higher.
2.   For the purpose of calculating which amount is the higher in accordance with paragraph 1 of this Article, the following rules apply—
        (a)   where a container, pallet or similar article of transport is used to consolidate goods, the packages or other shipping units enumerated in the multimodal transport document as packed in such article of transport are deemed packages or shipping units. Except as aforesaid, the goods in such article of transport are deemed one shipping unit;
        (b)   in cases where the article of transport itself has been lost or damaged, that article of transport, if not owned or otherwise supplied by the multimodal transport operator, is considered one separate shipping unit.
3.   Notwithstanding the provisions of paragraphs 1 and 2 of this Article, if the international multimodal transport does not, according to the contract, include carriage of goods by sea or by inland waterways, the liability of the multimodal transport operator shall be limited to an amount not exceeding 8.33 units of account per kilogram of gross weight of the goods lost or damaged.
4.   The liability of the multimodal transport operator for loss resulting from delay in delivery according to the provisions of Article 16 shall be limited to an amount equivalent to two and a half times the freight payable for the goods delayed, but not exceeding the total freight payable under the multimodal transport contract.
5.   The aggregate liability of the multimodal transport operator, under paragraphs 1 and 4 or paragraphs 3 and 4 of this Article, shall not exceed the limit of liability for total loss of the goods as determined by paragraph 1 or 3 of this Article.
6.   By agreement between the multimodal transport operator and the consignor, limits of liability exceeding those provided for in paragraphs 1, 3 and 4 or this Article may be fixed in the multimodal transport document.
7.   'Unit of account' means the unit of account mentioned in Article 31.

Article 19
Localised damage

When the loss of or damage to the goods occurred during one particular of the multimodal transport, in respect of which an applicable international convention or mandatory national law provides a higher limit of liability than the limit that would follow from application of paragraphs 1 to 3 of Article 18, then the limit of the multimodal transport operator's liability for such loss or damage shall be determined by reference to the provisions of such convention or mandatory national law.

Article 20
Non-contractual liability

1.   The defences and limits of liability provided for in this Convention shall apply in any action against the multimodal transport operator in respect of loss resulting from loss of or damage to the goods, as well as from delay in delivery, whether the action be founded in contract, in tort or otherwise.
2.   If an action in respect of loss resulting from loss of or damage to the goods or from delay in delivery is brought against the servant or agent of the multimodal transport operator, if such servant or agent proves that he acted within the scope of his employment, or against any other person of whose services he makes use for the performance of the multimodal transport contract, if such other person proves that he acted within the performance of the contract, the servant or agent of such other person shall be entitled to avail himself of the defences and limits of liability which the multimodal transport operator is entitled to invoke under this Convention.
3.   Except as provided in Article 21, the aggregate of the amounts recoverable from the multimodal transport operator and from a servant or agent or any other person of whose services he makes use for the performance of the multimodal transport contract shall not exceed the limits of liability provided for in this Convention.

Article 21
Loss of the right to limit liability

1.   The multimodal transport operator is not entitled to the benefit of the limitation of liability provided for in this Convention if it is proved that the loss, damage or delay in delivery resulted from an act or omission of the multimodal transport operator done with the intent to cause such loss, damage or delay or recklessly and with knowledge that such loss, damage or delay would probably result.
2.   Notwithstanding paragraph 2 of Article 20, a servant or agent of the multimodal transport operator or other person of whose services he makes use for the performance of the multimodal transport contract is not entitled to the benefit of the limitation of liability provided for in this Convention if it is proved that the loss, damage or delay in delivery resulted from an act or omission of such servant, agent or other person, done with the intent to cause such loss, damage or delay or recklessly and with knowledge that such loss, damage or delay would probably result.

PART IV
LIABILITY OF THE CONSIGNOR

Article 22
General rule

The consignor shall be liable for loss sustained by the multimodal transport operator if such loss is caused by the fault or neglect of the consignor, or his servants or agents when such servants or agents are acting within the scope of their employment. Any servant or agent of the consignor shall be liable for such loss if the loss is caused by fault or neglect on his part.

Article 23
Special rules on dangerous goods

1. The consignor shall mark or label in a suitable manner dangerous goods as dangerous.
2. Where the consignor hands over dangerous goods to the multimodal transport operator or any person acting on his behalf, the consignor shall inform him of the dangerous character of the goods and, if necessary, the precautions to be taken. If the consignor fails to do so and the multimodal transport operator does not otherwise have knowledge of their dangerous character—
   (a) the consignor shall be liable to the multimodal transport operator for all loss resulting from the shipment of such goods; and
   (b) the goods may at any time be unloaded, destroyed or rendered innocuous, as the circumstances may require, without payment of compensation.
3. The provisions of paragraph 2 of this Article may not be invoked by any person if during the multimodal transport he has taken the goods in his charge with knowledge of their dangerous character.
4. If, in cases where the provisions of paragraph 2(b) of this Article do not apply or may not be invoked, dangerous goods become an actual danger to life or property, they may be unloaded, destroyed or rendered innocuous, as the circumstances may require, without payment of compensation except where there is an obligation to contribute in general average or where the multimodal transport operator is liable in accordance with the provisions of Article 16.

PART V
CLAIMS AND ACTIONS

Article 24
Notice of loss, damage or delay

1. Unless notice of loss or damage, specifying the general nature of such loss or damage, is given in writing by the consignee to the multimodal transport operator not later than the working day after the day when the goods were handed over to the consignee, such handing over is *prima facie* evidence of the delivery by the multimodal transport operator of the goods as described in the multimodal transport document.
2. Where the loss or damage is not apparent, the provisions of paragraph 1 of this Article apply correspondingly if notice in writing is not given within six consecutive days after the day when the goods were handed over to the consignee.
3. If the state of the goods at the time they were handed over to the consignee has been the subject of a joint survey or inspection by the parties or their authorised representatives at the place of delivery, notice in writing need not be given of loss or damage ascertained during such survey or inspection.
4. In the case of any actual or apprehended loss or damage the multimodal transport operator and the consignee shall give all reasonable facilities to each other for inspecting and tallying the goods.
5. No compensation shall be payable for loss resulting from delay in delivery unless notice has been given in writing to the multimodal transport operator within 60 consecutive days after the day when the goods were delivered by handing over to the consignee or when the consignee has been notified that the goods have been delivered in accordance with paragraph 2(b)(ii) or (iii) of Article 14.
6. Unless notice of loss or damage, specifying the general nature of the loss or damage, is given in writing by the multimodal transport operator to the consignor not later than 90 consecutive days after the occurrence of such loss of damage or after the delivery of the goods in accordance with paragraph 2(b) of Article 14,

whichever is later, the failure to give such notice is *prima facie* evidence that the multimodal transport operator has sustained no loss or damage due to the fault or neglect of the consignor, his servants or agents.

7. If any of the notice periods provided for in paragraphs 2, 5 and 6 of this Article terminates on a day which is not a working day at the place of delivery, such period shall be extended until the next working day.

8. For the purpose of this Article, notice given to a person acting on the multimodal transport operator's behalf, including any person of whose services he makes use at the place of delivery, or to a person acting on the consignor's behalf, shall be deemed to have been given to the multimodal transport operator, or to the consignor, respectively.

Article 25
Limitation of actions

1. Any action relating to international multimodal transport under this convention shall be time-barred if judicial or arbitral proceedings have not been instituted within a period of two years. However, if notification in writing, stating the nature and main particulars of the claim, has not been given within six months after the day when the goods were delivered or, where the goods have not been delivered, after the day on which they should have been delivered, the action shall be time-barred at the expiry of this period.

2. The limitation period commences on the day after the day on which the multimodal transport operator has delivered the goods or part thereof or, where the goods have not been delivered, on the day after the last day on which the goods should have been delivered.

3. The person against whom a claim is made may at any time during the running of the limitation period extend that period by a declaration in writing to the claimant. This period may be further extended by another declaration or declarations.

4. Provided that the provisions of another applicable international convention are not to the contrary, a recourse action for indemnity by a person held liable under this Convention may be instituted even after the expiration of the limitation period provided for in the preceding paragraphs if instituted within the time allowed by the law of the State where proceedings are instituted; however, the time allowed shall not be less than 90 days commencing from the day when the person instituting such action for indemnity has settled the claim or has been served with process in the action against himself.

Article 26
Jurisdiction

1. In judicial proceedings relating to international multimodal transport under this Convention, the plaintiff, at his option, may institute an action in a court which, according to the law of the State where the court is situated, is competent and within the jurisdiction of which is situated one of the following places—
   (a) the principal place of business or, in the absence thereof, the habitual residence of the defendant; or
   (b) the place where the multimodal transport contract was made, provided that the defendant has there a place of business, branch or agency through which the contract was made; or
   (c) the place of taking the goods in charge for international multimodal transport or the place of delivery; or
   (d) any other place designated for that purpose in the multimodal transport contract and evidenced in the multimodal transport document.

2. No judicial proceedings relating to international multimodal transport under this Convention may be instituted in a place not specified in paragraph 1 of this Article.

The provisions of this Article do not constitute an obstacle to the jurisdiction of the Contracting States for provisional or protective measures.

3.   Notwithstanding the preceding provisions of this Article, an agreement made by the parties after a claim has arisen, which designates the place where the plaintiff may institute an action, shall be effective.

4.   —

(a)   Where an action has been instituted in accordance with the provisions of this Article or where judgment in such an action has been delivered, no new action shall be instituted between the same parties on the same grounds unless the judgment in the first action is not enforceable in the country in which the new proceedings are instituted;

(b)   For the purposes of this Article neither the institution of measures to obtain enforcement of a judgment nor the removal of an action to a different court within the same country shall be considered as the starting of a new action.

Article 27
Arbitration

1.   Subject to the provisions of this Article, parties may provide by agreement evidenced in writing that any dispute that may arise relating to international multimodal transport under this Convention shall be referred to arbitration.

2.   The arbitration proceedings shall, at the option of the claimant, be instituted at one of the following places—

(a)   a place in a State within whose territory is situated:

(i)   the principal place of business of the defendant or, in the absence thereof, the habitual residence of the defendant; or

(ii)   the place where the multimodal transport contract was made, provided that the defendant has there a place of business, branch or agency through which the contract was made; or

(iii)   the place of taking the goods in charge for international multimodal transport or the place of delivery; or

(b)   any other place designated for that purpose in the arbitration clause or agreement.

3.   The arbitrator or arbitration tribunal shall apply the provisions of this Convention.

4.   The provisions of paragraphs 2 and 3 of this Article shall be deemed to be part of every arbitration clause or agreement and any term of such clause or agreement which is inconsistent therewith shall be null and void.

5.   Nothing in this Article shall affect the validity of an agreement on arbitration made by the parties after the claim relating to the international multimodal transport has arisen.

PART VI
SUPPLEMENTARY PROVISIONS

Article 28
Contractual stipulations

1.   Any stipulation in a multimodal transport contract or multimodal transport document shall be null and void to the extent that it derogates, directly or indirectly, from the provisions of this Convention. The nullity of such a stipulation shall not affect the validity of other provisions of the contract or document of which it forms a part. A clause assigning benefit of insurance of the goods in favour of the multimodal transport operator or any similar clause shall be null and void.

2. Notwithstanding the provisions of paragraph 1 of this Article, the multimodal transport operator may, with the agreement of the consignor, increase his responsibilities and obligations under this Convention.

3. The multimodal transport document shall contain a statement that the international multimodal transport is subject to the provisions of this Convention which nullify any stipulation derogating therefrom to the detriment of the consignor or the consignee.

4. Where the claimant in respect of the goods has incurred loss as a result of a stipulation which is null and void by virtue of the present Article, or as a result of the omission of the statement referred to in paragraph 3 of this Article, the multimodal transport operator must pay compensation to the extent required in order to give the claimant compensation in accordance with the provisions of this Convention for any loss of or damage to the goods as well as for delay in delivery. The multimodal transport operator must, in addition, pay compensation for costs incurred by the claimant for the purpose of exercising his right, provided that costs incurred in the action where the foregoing provision is invoked are to be determined in accordance with the law of the State where proceedings are instituted.

Article 29
General average

1. Nothing in this Convention shall prevent the application of provisions in the multimodal transport contract or national law regarding the adjustment of general average, if and to the extent applicable.

2. With the exception of Article 25, the provisions of this Convention relating to the liability of the multimodal transport operator for loss of or damage to the goods shall also determine whether the consignee may refuse contribution in general average and the liability of the multimodal transport operator to indemnify the consignee in respect of any such contribution made or any salvage paid.

Article 30
Other Conventions

1. This Convention does not modify the rights or duties provided for in the Brussels International Convention for the unification of certain rules relating to the limitation of the liability of owners of sea-going vessels of 25 August 1924; in the Brussels International Convention relating to the limitation of the liability of owners of sea-going ships of 10 October 1957; in the London convention on limitation of liability for maritime claims of 19 November 1976; and in the Geneva Convention relating to the limitation of the liability of owners of inland navigation vessels (CLN) of 1 March 1973, including amendments to these Conventions, or national law relating to the limitation of liability of owners of sea-going ships and inland navigation vessels.

2. The provisions of Articles 26 and 27 of this Convention do not prevent the application of the mandatory provisions of any other international convention relating to matters dealt with in the said Articles, provided that the dispute arises exclusively between parties having their principal place of business in States parties to such other Convention. However, this paragraph does not affect the application of paragraph 3 of Article 27 of this Convention.

3. [Omitted].

4. Carriage of goods such as carriage of goods in accordance with the Geneva Convention of 19 May 1956 on the Contract for the International Carriage of Goods by Road in Article 2, or the Berne Convention of 7 February 1970 concerning the Carriage of Goods by Rail, Article 2, shall not for States Parties to Conventions governing such carriage be considered as international multimodal transport

within the meaning of Article 1, paragraph 1, of this Convention, in so far as such States are bound to apply the provisions of such Conventions to such carriage of goods.

Article 31
Unit of account of monetary unit and conversion

1. The unit of account referred to in Article 18 of this Convention is the Special Drawing Right as defined by the International Monetary Fund. The amounts referred to in Article 18 shall be converted into the national currency of a State according to the value of such currency on the date of the judgment or award or the date agreed upon by the parties. The value of a national currency, in terms of Special Drawing Right, of a Contracting State which is a member of the International Monetary Fund, shall be calculated in accordance with the method of valuation applied by the International Monetary Fund, in effect on the date in question, for its operations and transactions. The value of a national currency in terms of the Special Drawing Right of a Contracting State which is not a member of the International Monetary Fund shall be calculated in a manner determined by that State.

2. Nevertheless, a State which is not a member of the International Monetary Fund and whose law does not permit the application of the provisions of paragraph 1 of this Article may, at the time of signature, ratification, acceptance, approval or accession, or at any time thereafter, declare that the limits of liability provided for in this Convention to be applied in its territory shall be fixed as follows: with regard to the limits provided for in paragraph 1 of Article 18, to 13,750 monetary units per package or other shipping unit or 41.25 monetary units per kilogram of gross weight of the goods, and with regard to the limit provided for in paragraph 3 of Article 18, to 124 monetary units.

3. The monetary unit referred to in paragraph 2 of this Article corresponds to sixty-five and a half milligrams of gold of millesimal fineness nine hundred. The conversion of the amount referred to in paragraph 2 of this Article into national currency shall be made according to the law of the State concerned.

4. The calculation mentioned in the last sentence of paragraph 1 of this Article and the conversion referred to in paragraph 3 of this Article shall be made in such a manner as to express in the national currency of the Contracting State as far as possible the same real value for the amounts in Article 18 as is expressed there in units of account.

5. Contracting States shall communicate to the depositary the manner of calculation pursuant to the last sentence of paragraph 1 of this Article, or the result of the conversion pursuant to paragraph 3 of this Article, as the case may be, at the time of signature or when depositing their instruments of ratification, acceptance, approval or accession, or when availing themselves of the option provided for in paragraph 2 of this Article and whenever there is a change in the manner of such calculation or in the result of such conversion.

PART VII

Article 32 [Omitted].

PART VIII

Article 33–40 [Omitted].

ANNEX: PROVISIONS ON CUSTOMS MATTERS RELATING TO INTERNATIONAL
MULTIMODAL TRANSPORT OF GOODS [OMITTED].

UNIDROIT CONVENTION ON AGENCY IN THE INTERNATIONAL SALE OF GOODS, GENEVA, 1983

CHAPTER 1
SPHERE OF APPLICATION AND GENERAL PROVISIONS

Article 1

1.   This Convention applies where one person, the agent, has authority or purports to have authority on behalf of another person, the principal, to conclude a contract of sale of goods with a third party.
2.   It governs not only the conclusion of such a contract by the agent but also any act undertaken by him for the purpose of concluding that contract or in relation to its performance.
3.   It is concerned only with relations between the principal or the agent on the one hand, and the third party on the other.
4.   It applies irrespective of whether the agent acts in his own name or in that of the principal.

Article 2

1.   This Convention applies only where the principal and the third party have their places of business in different States and—
   (a)   the agent has his place of business in a Contracting State; or
   (b)   the rules of private international law lead to the application of the law of a Contracting State.
2.   Where, at the time of contracting, the third party neither knew nor ought to have known that the agent was acting as an agent, the Convention only applies if the agent and the third party had their places of business in different States and if the requirements of paragraph 1 are satisfied.
3.   Neither the nationality of the parties nor the civil or commercial character of the parties or of the contract of sale is to be taken into consideration in determining the application of this Convention.

Article 3

1.   This Convention does not apply to—
   (a)   the agency of a dealer on a stock, commodity or other exchange;
   (b)   the agency of an auctioneer;
   (c)   agency by operation of law in family law, in the law of matrimonial property, or in the law of succession;
   (d)   agency arising from statutory or judicial authorisation to act for a person without capacity to act;
   (e)   agency by virtue of a decision of a judicial or quasi-judicial authority or subject to the direct control of such an authority.
2.   Nothing in this Convention affects any rule of law for the protection of consumers.

Article 4

For the purposes of this Convention —
(a)   an organ, officer, or partner of a corporation, association, partnership or other entity, whether or not possessing legal personality, shall not be regarded as the agent of that entity in so far as, in the exercise of his functions as such, he acts by virtue of an authority conferred by law or by the constitutive documents of that entity;
(b)   a trustee shall not be regarded as an agent of the trust, of the person who has created the trust, or of the beneficiaries.

Article 5

The principal, or an agent acting in accordance with the express or implied instructions of the principal, may agree with the third party to exclude the application of this Convention or, subject to Article 11, to derogate from or vary the effect of any of its provisions.

Article 6

1.   In the interpretation of this Convention, regard is to be had to its international character and to the need to promote uniformity in its application and the observance of good faith in international trade.
2.   Questions concerning matters governed by this Convention which are not expressly settled in it are to be settled in conformity with the general principles on which it is based or, in the absence of such principles, in conformity with the law applicable by virtue of the rules of private international law.

Article 7

1.   The principal or the agent on the one hand and the third party on the other are bound by any usage to which they have agreed and by any practices which they have established between themselves.
2.   They are considered, unless otherwise agreed, to have impliedly made applicable to their relations any usage of which they knew or ought to have known and which in international trade is widely known to, and regularly observed by, parties to agency relations of the type involved in the particular trade concerned.

Article 8

For the purposes of this Convention —
(a)   if a party has more than one place of business, the place of business is that which has the closest relationship to the contract of sale, having regard to the circumstances known to or contemplated by the parties at the time of contracting;
(b)   if a party does not have a place of business, reference is to be made to his habitual residence.

CHAPTER II
ESTABLISHMENT AND SCOPE OF THE AUTHORITY OF THE AGENT

Article 9

1.   The authorisation of the agent by the principal may be express or implied.
2.   The agent has authority to perform all acts necessary in the circumstances to achieve the purposes for which the authorisation was given.

Article 10

The authorisation need not be given in or evidenced by writing and is not subject to any other requirement as to form. It may be proved by any means, including witnesses.

Article 11

Any provision of Article 10, Article 15 or Chapter IV which allows an authorisation, a ratification or a termination of authority to be made in any form other than in writing does not apply where the principal or the agent has his place of business in a Contracting State which has made a declaration under Article 27. The parties may not derogate from or vary the effect of this paragraph.

CHAPTER III
LEGAL EFFECTS OF ACTS CARRIED OUT BY THE AGENT

Article 12

Where an agent acts on behalf of a principal within the scope of his authority and the third party knew or ought to have known that the agent was acting as an agent, the acts of the agent shall directly bind the principal and the third party to each other, unless it follows from the circumstances of the case, for example by a reference to a contract of commission, that the agent undertakes to bind himself only.

Article 13

1. Where the agent acts on behalf of a principal within the scope of this authority, his acts shall bind only the agent and the third party if—
   (a) the third party neither knew nor ought to have known that the agent was acting as an agent; or
   (b) it follows from the circumstances of the case, for example by a reference to a contract of commission, that the agent undertakes to bind himself only.
2. Nevertheless—
   (a) where the agent, whether by reason of the third party's failure of performance or for any other reason, fails to fulfil or is not in a position to fulfil his obligations to the principal, the principal may exercise against the third party the rights acquired on the principal's behalf by the agent, subject to any defences which the third party may set up against the agent;
   (b) where the agent fails to fulfil or is not in a position to fulfil his obligations to the third party, the third party may exercise against the principal the rights which the third party has against the agent, subject to any defences which the agent may set up against the third party and which the principal may set up against the agent.
3. The rights under paragraph 2 may be exercised only if notice of intention to exercise them is given to the agent and the third party or principal, as the case may be. As soon as the third party or principal has received such notice, he may no longer free himself from his obligations by dealing with the agent.
4. Where the agent fails to fulfil or is not in a position to fulfil his obligations to the third party because of the principal's failure of performance, the agent shall communicate the name of the principal to the third party.
5. Where the third party fails to fulfil his obligations under the contract to the agent, the agent shall communicate the name of the third party to the principal.
6. The principal may not exercise against the third party the rights acquired on his behalf by the agent if it appears from the circumstances of the case that the third

party, had he known the principal's identity, would not have entered into the contract.

7. An agent may, in accordance with the express or implied instructions of the principal, agree with the third party to derogate from or vary the effect of paragraph 2.

Article 14

1. Where an agent acts without authority or acts outside the scope of his authority, his acts do not bind the principal and the third party to each other.
2. Nevertheless, where the conduct of the principal causes the third party reasonably and in good faith to believe that the agent has authority to act on behalf of the principal and that the agent is acting within the scope of that authority, the principal may not invoke against the third party the lack of authority of the agent.

Article 15

1. An act by an agent who acts without authority or who acts outside the scope of his authority may be ratified by the principal. On ratification the act produces the same effects as if it had initially been carried out with authority.
2. Where, at the time of the agent's act, the third party neither knew nor ought to have known of the lack of authority, he shall not be liable to the principal, if, at any time before ratification, he gives notice of his refusal to become bound by a ratification. Where the principal ratifies but does not do so within a reasonable time, the third party may refuse to be bound by the ratification if he promptly notifies the principal.
3. Where, however, the third party knew or ought to have known of the lack of authority of the agent, the third party may not refuse to become bound by a ratification before the expiration of any time agreed for ratification, or failing agreement, such reasonable time as the third party may specify.
4. The third party may refuse to accept a partial ratification.
5. Ratification shall take effect when notice of it reaches the third party or the ratification otherwise comes to his attention. Once effective, it may not be revoked.
6. Ratification is effective notwithstanding that the act itself could not have been effectively carried out at the time of ratification.
7. Where the act has been carried out on behalf of a corporation or other legal person before its creation, ratification is effective only if allowed by the law of the State governing its creation.
8. Ratification is subject to no requirements as to form. It may be express or may be inferred from the conduct of the principal.

Article 16

1. An agent who acts without authority or who acts outside the scope of his authority shall, failing ratification, be liable to pay the third party such compensation as will place the third party in the same position as he would have been in if the agent had acted with authority and within the scope of his authority.
2. The agent shall not be liable, however, if the third party knew or ought to have known that the agent had no authority or was acting outside the scope of his authority.

CHAPTER IV
TERMINATION OF THE AUTHORITY OF THE AGENT

Article 17

The authority of the agent is terminated —
(a)   when this follows from any agreement between the principal and the agent;
(b)   on completion of the transaction or transactions for which the authority was created;
(c)   on revocation by the principal or renunciation by the agent, whether or not this is consistent with the terms of the agreement.

Article 18

The authority of the agent is also terminated when the applicable law so provides.

Article 19

The termination of the authority shall not affect the third party unless he knew or ought to have known of the termination or the facts which caused it.

Article 20

Notwithstanding the termination of his authority, the agent remains authorised to perform on behalf of the principal or his successors the acts which are necessary to prevent damage to their interests.

Articles 21–28 [Omitted].

Article 29

A Contracting State, the whole or specific parts of the foreign trade of which are carried on exclusively by specially authorised organisations, may at any time declare that, in cases where such organisations act either as buyers or sellers in foreign trade, all these organisations or the organisations specified in the declaration shall not be considered for the purposes of Article 13, paragraphs 2(b) and 4, as agents in their relations with other organisations having their place of business in the same State.

Article 30

1.   A Contracting State may at any time declare that it will apply the provisions of this Convention to specified cases falling outside its sphere of application.
2.   Such declaration may, for example, provide that the Convention shall apply to —
(a)   contracts other than contracts of sale of goods;
(b)   cases where the place of business mentioned in Article 2, paragraph 1, are not situated in Contracting States.

Articles 31–35 [Omitted].

CONVENTION ON THE LAW APPLICABLE TO CONTRACTS FOR THE INTERNATIONAL SALE OF GOODS, THE HAGUE, 1985

CHAPTER 1
SCOPE OF THE CONVENTION

Article 1

This Convention determines the law applicable to contracts of sale of goods—
(a)   between parties having their places of business in different States;
(b)   in all other cases involving a choice between the laws of different States, unless such a choice arises solely from a stipulation by the parties as to the applicable law, even if accompanied by a choice of court or arbitration.

Article 2

The Convention does not apply to—
(a)   sales by way of execution or otherwise by authority of law;
(b)   sales of stocks, shares, investment securities, negotiable instruments or money, it does, however, apply to the sale of goods based on documents;
(c)   sales of goods bought for personal, family or household use; it does, however, apply if the seller at the time of the conclusion of the contract neither knew nor ought to have known that the goods were bought for any such use.

Article 3

For the purposes of the Convention, 'goods' includes—
(a)   ships, vessels, boats, hovercraft and aircraft;
(b)   electricity.

Article 4

1.   Contracts for the supply of goods to be manufactured or produced are to be considered contracts of sale unless the party who orders the goods undertakes to supply a substantial part of the materials necessary for such manufacture or production.
2.   Contracts in which the preponderant part of the obligations of the party who furnishes goods consists of the supply of labour or other services are not to be considered contracts of sale.

Article 5

The Convention does not determine the law applicable to—
(a)   the capacity of the parties or the consequences of nullity or invalidity of the contract resulting from the incapacity of a party;
(b)   the question whether an agent is able to bind a principal, or an organ to bind a company or body corporate or unincorporate;
(c)   the transfer of ownership; nevertheless, the issues specifically mentioned in Article 12 are governed by the law applicable to the contract under the Convention;
(d)   the effect of the sale in respect of any person other than the parties;
(e)   agreements on arbitration or on choice of court, even if such an agreement is embodied in the contract of sale.

Article 6

The law determined under the Convention applies whether or not it is the law of a Contracting State.

CHAPTER II

APPLICABLE LAW

SECTION 1—DETERMINATION OF THE APPLICABLE LAW

Article 7

1. A contract of sale is governed by the law chosen by the parties. The parties' agreement on this choice must be express or be clearly demonstrated by the terms of the contract and the conduct of the parties, viewed in their entirety. Such a choice may be limited to a part of the contract.
2. The parties may at any time agree to subject the contract in whole or in part to a law other than that which previously governed it, whether or not the law previously governing the contract was chosen by the parties. Any change by the parties of the applicable law made after the conclusion of the contract does not prejudice its formal validity or the rights of third parties.

Article 8

1. To the extent that the law applicable to a contract of sale has not been chosen by the parties in accordance with Article 7, the contract is governed by the law of the State where the seller has his place of business at the time of conclusion of the contract.
2. However, the contract is governed by the law of the State where the buyer has his place of business at the time of conclusion of the contract, if—
   (a) negotiations were conducted, and the contract concluded by and in the presence of the parties, in that State; or
   (b) the contract provides expressly that the seller must perform his obligation to deliver the goods in that State; or
   (c) the contract was concluded on terms determined mainly by the buyer and in response to an invitation directed by the buyer to persons invited to bid (a call for tenders).
3. By way of exception, where, in the light of the circumstances as a whole, for instance any business relations between the parties, the contract is manifestly more closely connected with a law which is not the law which would otherwise be applicable to the contract under paragraphs 1 or 2 of this Article, the contract is governed by that other law.
4. Paragraph 3 does not apply if, at the time of the conclusion of the contract, the seller and the buyer have their places of business in States having made the reservation under Article 21 paragraph 1 sub-paragraph b.
5. Paragraph 3 does not apply in respect of issues regulated in the United Nations Convention on Contracts for the International Sale of Goods (Vienna, 11 April 1980) where, at the time for the conclusion of the contract, the seller and the buyer have their places of business in different States both of which are Parties to that Convention.

Article 9

A sale by auction or on a commodity or other exchange is governed by the law chosen by the parties in accordance with Article 7 to the extent to which the law of the State where the auction takes place or the exchange is located does not prohibit such choice. Failing a choice by the parties, or to the extent where the auction takes place or the exchange is located shall apply.

Article 10

1. Issues concerning the existence and material validity of the consent of the parties as to the choice of the applicable law are determined, where the choice of the applicable law are determined, where the choice satisfies the requirements of Article 7, by the law chosen. If under that law the choice is invalid, the law governing the contract is determined under Article 8.
2. The existence and material validity of a contract of sale, or of any term thereof, are determined by the law which under the Convention would govern the contract or term if it were valid.
3. Nevertheless, to establish that he did not consent to the choice of law, to the contract itself, or to any term thereof, a party may rely on the law of the State where he has his place of business, if in the circumstances it is not reasonable to determine that issue under the law specified in the preceding paragraphs.

Article 11

1. A contract of sale concluded between persons who are in the same State is formally valid if it satisfies the requirements either of the law which governs it under the Convention or of the law of the State where it is concluded.
2. A contract of sale concluded between persons who are in different States is formally valid if it satisfies the requirements either of the law which governs it under the Convention or of the law of one of those States.
3. Where the contract is concluded by an agent, the State in which the agent acts is the relevant State for the purposes of the preceding paragraphs.
4. An act intended to have legal effect relating to an existing or contemplated contract of sale is formally valid if it satisfies the requirements either of the law which under the Convention governs or would govern the contract, or to the law of the State where the act was done.
5. The Convention does not apply to the formal validity of a contract of sale where one of the parties to the contract has, at the time of its conclusion, his place of business in a State which has made the reservation provided for in Article 1 paragraph 1 sub-paragraph c.

SECTION 2—SCOPE OF THE APPLICABLE LAW

Article 12

The law applicable to a contract of sale by virtue of Articles 7, 8 or 9 governs in particular—
(a) interpretation of the contract;
(b) the rights and obligations of the parties and performance of the contract;
(c) the time at which the buyer becomes entitled to the products, fruits and income deriving from the goods;
(d) the time from which the buyer bears the risk with respect to the goods;
(e) the validity and effect as between the parties of clauses reserving title to the goods;
(f) the consequences of non performance of the contract, including the categories of loss for which compensation may be recovered, but without prejudice to the procedural law of the forum;
(g) the various ways of extinguishing obligations, as well as prescription and limitation of actions;
(h) the consequences of nullity or invalidity of the contract.

Article 13

In the absence of an express clause to the contrary, the law of the State where inspection of the goods takes place applies to the modalities and procedural requirements for such inspection.

CHAPTER III
GENERAL PROVISIONS

Article 14

1.   If a party has more than one place of business, the relevant place of business is that which has the closest relationship to the contract and its performance, having regard to the circumstance known to or contemplated by the parties at any time before or at the conclusion of the contract.
2.   If a party does not have a place of business, reference is to be made to his habitual residence.

Article 15

In the Convention 'law' means the law in force in a State other than its choice of law rules.

Article 16

In the interpretation of the Convention, regard is to be had to its international character and to the need to promote uniformity in its application.

Article 17

The Convention does not prevent the application of those provisions of the law of the forum that must be applied irrespective of the law that otherwise governs the contract.

Article 18

The application of a law determined by the Convention may be refused only where such application would be manifestly incompatible with public policy (*ordre public*).

Articles 19–20 [Omitted].

Article 21

1.   Any State may, at the time of signature, ratification, acceptance, approval or accession, make any of the following reservations—
     (a)   that it will not apply the Convention in cases covered by subparagraph (b) of Article 1;
     (b)   that it will not apply paragraph 3 of Article 8 except where neither party to the contract has his place of business in a State which has made a reservation provided for under this subparagraph;
     (c)   that for cases where its legislation requires contracts of sale to be concluded in or evidenced by writing, it will not apply the Convention to the formal validity of the contract, where any party has his place of business in its territory at the time of conclusion of the contract.
2.   [Omitted].
3.   [Omitted].

Articles 22–31 [Omitted].

UNIDROIT CONVENTION ON INTERNATIONAL FACTORING, OTTAWA, 1988

CHAPTER I
SPHERE OF APPLICATION AND GENERAL PROVISIONS

Article 1

1.   This Convention governs factoring contracts and assignments of receivables as described in this Chapter.
2.   For the purposes of this convention 'factoring contract' means a contract concluded between the party (the supplier) and another party (the factor) pursuant to which—
     (a)   the supplier may or will assign to the factor receivables arising from contracts of sale of goods made between the supplier and its customers (debtors) other than those for the sale of goods bought primarily for their personal, family or household use;
     (b)   the factor is to perform at least two of the following functions:
          —   finance for the supplier, including loans and advance payments;
          —   maintenance of accounts (ledgering) relating to the receivables;
          —   collection of receivables;
          —   protection against default in payment by debtors;
     (c)   notice of the assignment of the receivables is to be given to debtors.
3.   In this Convention references to 'goods' and 'sale of goods' shall include services and the supply of services.
4.   For the purposes of this Convention—
     (a)   a notice in writing need not be signed but must identify the person by whom or in whose name it is given;
     (b)   'notice in writing' includes, but is not limited to, telegrams, telex and any other telecommunication capable of being reproduced in tangible form;
     (c)   a notice in writing is given when it is received by the addressee.

Article 2

1.   This Convention applies whenever the receivables assigned pursuant to a factoring contract arise from a contract of sale of goods between a supplier and a debtor whose places of business are in different States and—
     (a)   those States and the State in which the factor has its place of business are Contracting States; or
     (b)   both the contract of sale of goods and the factoring contract are governed by the law of a Contracting State.
2.   A reference in this Convention to a party's place of business shall, if it has more than one place of business, mean the place of business which has the closest relationship to the relevant contract and its performance, having regard to the circumstances known to or contemplated by the parties at any time before or at the conclusion of that contract.

Article 3

1.   The application of this Convention may be excluded—
     (a)   by the parties to the factoring contract; or
     (b)   by the parties to the contract of sale of goods, as regards receivables arising at or after the time when the factor has been given notice in writing of such exclusion.

2.   Where the application of this Convention is excluded in accordance with the previous paragraph, such exclusion may be made only as regards the Convention as a whole.

Article 4

1.   In the interpretation of this Convention, regard is to be had to its object and purpose as set forth in the preamble, to its international character and to the need to promote uniformity in its application and the observance of good faith in international trade.
2.   Questions concerning matters governed by this convention which are not expressly settled in it are to be settled in conformity with the general principles on which it is based or, in the absence of such principles, in conformity with the law applicable by virtue of the rules of private international law.

CHAPTER II
RIGHTS AND DUTIES OF THE PARTIES

Article 5

As between the parties to the factoring contract—
(a)   a provision in the factoring contract for the assignment of existing or future receivables shall not be rendered invalid by the fact that contract does not specify them individually, if at the time of conclusion of the contract or when they come into existence they can be identified to the contract;
(b)   a provision in the factoring contract by which future receivables are assigned operates to transfer the receivables to the factor when they come into existence without the need for any new act of transfer.

Article 6

1.   The assignment of a receivable by the supplier to the factor shall be effective notwithstanding any agreement between the supplier and the debtor prohibiting such assignment.
2.   However, such assignment shall not be effective against the debtor when, at the time of conclusion of the contract of sale of goods, it has its place of business in a Contracting State which has made a declaration under Article 18 of this Convention.
3.   Nothing in paragraph 1 shall affect any obligation of good faith owed by the supplier to the debtor or any liability of the supplier to the debtor in respect of an assignment made in breach of the terms of the contract of sale of goods.

Article 7

A factoring contract may validly provide as between the parties thereto for the transfer, with or without a new act of transfer, of all or any of the supplier's rights deriving from the contract of sale of goods, including the benefit of any provision in the contract of sale of goods reserving to the supplier title to the goods or creating any security interest.

Article 8

1.   The debtor is under a duty to pay the factor if, and only if, the debtor does not have knowledge of any other person's superior right to payment and notice in writing of the assignment—
(a)   is given to the debtor by the supplier or by the factor with the supplier's authority;

    (b)   reasonably identifies the receivables which have been assigned and the factor to whom or for whose account the debtor is required to make payment; and

    (c)   relates to receivables arising under a contract of sale of goods made at or before the time the notice is given.

2.   Irrespective of any other ground on which payment by the debtor to the factor discharges the debtor from liability, payment shall be effective for this purpose if made in accordance with the previous paragraph.

Article 9

1.   In a claim by the factor against the debtor for payment of a receivable arising under a contract of sale of goods the debtor may set up against the factor all defences arising under that contract of which the debtor could have availed itself if such claim had been made by the supplier.

2.   The debtor may also assert against the factor any right of set-off in respect of claims existing against the supplier in whose favour the receivable arose and available to the debtor at the time a notice in writing of assignment conforming to Article 8(1) was given to the debtor.

Article 10

1.   Without prejudice to the debtor's rights under Article 9, non-performance or defective or late performance of the contract of sale of goods shall not by itself entitle the debtor to recover a sum paid by the debtor to the factor if the debtor has a right to recover that sum from the supplier.

2.   The debtor who has such a right to recover from the supplier a sum paid to the factor in respect of a receivable shall nevertheless be entitled to recover that sum from the factor to the extent that—

    (a)   the factor has not discharged an obligation to make payment to the supplier in respect of that receivable; or

    (b)   the factor made such payment at a time when it knew of the supplier's non-performance or defective or late performance as regards the goods to which the debtor's payment relates.

CHAPTER III
SUBSEQUENT ASSIGNMENTS

Article 11

1.   Where a receivable is assigned by a supplier to a factor pursuant to a factoring contract governed by this Convention—

    (a)   the rules set out in Articles 5 to 10 shall, subject to sub-paragraph b of this paragraph, apply to any subsequent assignment of the receivable by the factor or by a subsequent assignee;

    (b)   the provisions of Articles 8 to 10 shall apply as if the subsequent assignee were the factor.

2.   For the purposes of this Convention, notice to the debtor of the subsequent assignment also constitutes notice of the assignment to the factor.

Article 12

This Convention shall not apply to a subsequent assignment which is prohibited by the terms of the factoring contract.

CHAPTER IV

FINAL PROVISIONS

Articles 13–23 [Omitted].

**UNITED NATIONS CONVENTION ON INTERNATIONAL BILLS OF EXCHANGE
AND INTERNATIONAL PROMISSORY NOTES, 1988**

CHAPTER I
SPHERE OF APPLICATION AND FORM OF THE INSTRUMENT

Article 1

1.   This Convention applies to an international bill of exchange when it contains the heading 'International bill of exchange (UNCITRAL Convention)' and also contains in its text the words 'International bill of exchange (UNCITRAL Convention)'.
2.   This Convention applies to an international promissory note when it contains the heading 'International promissory note (UNCITRAL Convention)' and also contains in its text the words 'International promissory note (UNCITRAL Convention)'.
3.   This Convention does not apply to cheques.

Article 2

1.   An international bill of exchange is a bill of exchange which specifies at least two of the following places and indicates that any two so specified are situated in different States—
     (a)   the place where the bill is drawn;
     (b)   the place indicated next to the signature of the drawer;
     (c)   the place indicated next to the name of the drawee;
     (d)   the place indicated next to the name of the payee;
     (e)   the place of payment,
     provided that either the place where the bill is drawn or the place of payment is specified on the bill and that such place is situated in a Contracting State.
2.   An international promissory note is a promissory note which specifies at least two of the following places and indicates that any two so specified are situated in a different States—
     (a)   the place where the note is made;
     (b)   the place indicated next to the signature of the maker;
     (c)   the place indicated next to the name of the payee;
     (d)   the place of payment;
     provided that the place of payment is specified on the note and that such place is situated in a Contracting State.
3.   This Convention does not deal with the question of sanctions that may be imposed under national law in cases where an incorrect or false statement has been made on an instrument in respect of a place referred to in paragraph 1 or 2 of this Article. However, any such sanctions shall not affect the validity of the instrument or the application of this Convention.

Article 3

1.   A bill of exchange is a written instrument which—

     (a)   contains an unconditional order whereby the drawer directs the drawee to pay a definite sum of money to the payee or to his order;

     (b)   is payable on demand or at a definite time;

     (c)   is dated;

     (d)   is signed by the drawer.

2.   A promissory note is a written instrument which—

     (a)   contains an unconditional promise whereby the maker undertakes to pay a definite sum of money to the payee or to his order;

     (b)   is payable on demand or at a definite time;

     (c)   is dated;

     (d)   is signed by the maker.

CHAPTER II
INTERPRETATION

SECTION 1—GENERAL PROVISIONS

Article 4

In the interpretation of this Convention, regard is to be had to its international character and to the need to promote uniformity in its application and the observance of good faith in international transactions.

Article 5

In this Convention—

(a)   'Bill' means an international bill of exchange governed by this convention;

(b)   'Note' means an international promissory note governed by this Convention;

(c)   'Instrument' means a bill or a note;

(d)   'Drawee' means a person on whom a bill is drawn and who has not accepted it;

(e)   'Payee' means a person in whose favour the drawer directs payment to be made or to whom the maker promises to pay;

(f)   'Holder' means a person in possession of an instrument in accordance with Article 15;

(g)   'Protected Holder' means a holder who meets the requirements of Article 29;

(h)   'Guarantor' means any person any person who undertakes an obligation of guarantee under Article 46, whether governed by subparagraph b ('guaranteed') or subparagraph c ('*aval*') of paragraph 4 of Article 47;

(i)   'Party' means a person who has signed an instrument as drawer, maker, acceptor, endorser or guarantor;

(j)   'Maturity' means the time of payment referred to in paragraph 4, 5, 6 and 7 of Article 9;

(k)   'Signature' means a handwritten signature, its facsimile or an equivalent authentication effected by any other means; 'forged signature' includes a signature by the wrongful use of such means;

(l)   'Money' or 'currency' includes a monetary unit of account which is established by an intergovernmental institution or by agreement between two or more States, provided that this Convention shall apply without prejudice to the rules of the intergovernmental institution or to the stipulations of the agreement.

Article 6

For the purposes of this Convention, a person is considered to have knowledge of a fact if he has actual knowledge of that fact or could not have been unaware of its existence.

SECTION 2—INTERPRETATION OF FORMAL REQUIREMENTS

Article 7

The sum payable by an instrument is deemed to be a definite sum although the instrument states that it is to be paid—
(a)   with interest;
(b)   by instalments at successive dates;
(c)   by instalments at successive dates with a stipulation in the instrument that upon default in payment of any instalment the unpaid balance becomes due;
(d)   according to a rate of exchange indicated in the instrument or to be determined as directed by the instrument; or
(e)   in a currency other than the currency in which the sum is expressed in the instrument.

Article 8

1.   If there is a discrepancy between the sum expressed in words and the sum expressed in figures, the sum payable by the instrument is the sum expressed in words.
2.   If the sum is expressed more than once in words, and there is a discrepancy, the sum payable is the smaller sum. The same rule applies if the sum is expressed more than once in figures only, and there is a discrepancy.
3.   If the sum is expressed in a currency having the same description as that of at least one other State than the State where payment is to be made, as indicated in the instrument, and the specified currency is not identified as the currency of any particular State, the currency is to be considered as the currency of the State where payment is to be made.
4.   If an instrument states that the sum is to paid with interest, without specifying the date from which interest is to run, interest runs from the date of the instrument.
5.   A stipulation stating that the sum is to be paid with interest is deemed not to have been written on the instrument unless it indicates the rate at which interest is to be paid.
6.   A rate at which interest is to be paid may be expressed either as a definite rate or as a variable rate. For a variable rate to qualify for this purpose, it must vary in relation to one or more reference rates of interest in accordance with provisions stipulated in the instrument and each such reference rate must be published or otherwise available to the public and not be subject, directly or indirectly, to unilateral determination by a person who is named in the instrument at the time the bill is drawn or the note is made, unless the person is named only in the reference rate provisions.
7.   If the rate at which interest is to be paid is expressed as a variable rate, it may be stipulated expressly in the instrument that such rate shall not be less than or exceed a specified rate of interest, or that the variations are otherwise limited.
8.   If a variable rate does not qualify under paragraph 6 of this Article or for any reason it is not possible to determine the numerical value of the variable rate for any period, interest shall be payable for the relevant period at the rate calculated in accordance with paragraph 2 of Article 70.

Article 9

1.   An instrument is deemed to be payable on demand—
(a)   if it states that it is payable at sight or on demand or on presentment or if it contains words of similar import; or
(b)   if no time of payment is expressed.

2.   An instrument payable at a definite time which is accepted or endorsed or guaranteed after maturity is an instrument payable on demand as regards the acceptor, the endorser or the guarantor.

3.   An instrument is deemed to be payable at a definite time if it states that it is payable—
      (a)   on a stated date or at a fixed period after a stated date or at a fixed period after the date of the instrument; or
      (b)   at a fixed period after sight; or
      (c)   by instalments at successive dates; or
      (d)   by instalments at successive dates with the stipulation in the instrument that upon default in payment of any instalment the unpaid balance becomes due.

4.   The time of payment of an instrument payable at a fixed period after date is determined by reference to the date of the instrument.

5.   The time of payment of a bill payable at a fixed period after sight is determined by the date of acceptance or, if the bill is dishonoured by non-acceptance, by the date of protest or, if protest is dispensed with, by the date of dishonour.

6.   The time of payment of an instrument payable on demand is the date on which the instrument is presented for payment.

7.   The time of payment of a note payable at a fixed period after sight is determined by the date of the visa signed by the maker on the note or, if his visa is refused, by the date of presentment.

8.   If an instrument is drawn, or made, payable one or more months after a stated date or after a date of the instrument or after sight, the instrument is payable on the corresponding date of the month when payment must be made. If there is no corresponding date, the instrument is payable on the last day of that month.

Article 10

1.   A bill may be drawn—
      (a)   by two or more drawers;
      (b)   payable to two or more payees.

2.   A note may be made—
      (a)   by two or more makers;
      (b)   payable to two or more payees.

3.   If an instrument is payable to two or more payees in the alternative, it is payable to any one of them and any one of them in possession of the instrument may exercise the rights of a holder. In any other case the instrument is payable to all of them and the rights of a holder may be exercised only by all of them.

Article 11

A bill may be drawn by the drawer—
(a)   on himself;
(b)   payable to his order.

SECTION 3—COMPLETION OF AN INCOMPLETE INSTRUMENT

Article 12

1.   An incomplete instrument which satisfies the requirements set out in paragraph 1 of Article 1 and bears the signature of the drawer of the acceptance of the drawee, or which satisfies the requirements set out in paragraph 2 of Article 1 and subparagraph (d) of paragraph 2 of Article 3, but which lacks other elements pertaining to one or more of the requirements set out in Articles 2 and 3, may be completed, and the instrument so completed is effective as a bill or a note.

2.   If such an instrument is completed without authority or otherwise than in
accordance with the authority given—

(a)   a party who signed the instrument before the completion may invoke such
lack of authority as a defence against a holder who had knowledge of such
lack of authority when he became a holder;

(b)   a party who signed the instrument after the completion is liable according to
the terms of the instrument so completed.

CHAPTER III—TRANSFER

Article 13

An instrument is transferred—
(a)   by endorsement and delivery of the instrument by the endorser to the endorsee; or
(b)   by mere delivery of the instrument if the last endorsement is in blank.

Article 14

1.   An endorsement must be written on the instrument or on a slip affixed thereto
('*allonge*'). It must be signed.
2.   An endorsement may be—
(a)   in blank, that is, by a signature alone or by a signature accompanied by a
statement to the effect that the instrument is payable to a person in
possession of it;
(b)   special, that is, by a signature accompanied by an indication of the person to
whom the instrument is payable.
3.   A signature alone, other than that of the drawee, is an endorsement only if placed
on the back of the instrument.

Article 15

1.   A person is a holder if he is—
(a)   the payee in possession of the instrument; or
(b)   in possession of an instrument which has been endorsed to him, or on which
the last endorsement is in blank, and on which there appears an
uninterrupted series of endorsements, even if any endorsement was forged
or was signed by an agent without authority.
2.   If an endorsement in blank is followed by another endorsement, the person who
signed this last endorsement is deemed to be an endorsee by the endorsement in
blank.
3.   A person is not prevented from being a holder by the fact that the instrument was
obtained by him or any previous holder under circumstances, including incapacity
or fraud, duress or mistake of any kind, that would give rise to a claim to, or a
defence against liability on, the instrument.

Article 16

The holder of an instrument on which the last endorsement is in blank may—
(a)   further endorse it either by an endorsement in blank or by a special endorsement;
or
(b)   convert the blank endorsement into a special endorsement by indicating in the
endorsement that the instrument is payable to himself or to some other specified
person; or
(c)   transfer the instrument in accordance with subparagraph b of Article 13.

Article 17

1. If the drawer or the maker has inserted in the instrument such words as 'not acceptable', 'not transferable', 'not to order', 'pay (x) only', or words of similar import, the instrument may not be transferred except for purposes of collection, and any endorsement, even if it does not contain words authorising the endorsee to collect the instrument, is deemed to be an endorsement for collection.
2. If an endorsement contains the words 'not negotiable', 'not transferable', 'not to order', 'pay (x) only', or words of similar import, the instrument may not be transferred further except for purposes of collection, and any subsequent endorsement, even if it does not contain words authorising the endorsee to collect the instrument, is deemed to be an endorsement for collection.

Article 18

1. An endorsement must be unconditional.
2. A conditional endorsement transfers the instrument whether or not the condition is fulfilled. The condition is ineffective as to those parties and transferees who are subsequent to the endorsee.

Article 19

An endorsement in respect of a part of the sum due under the instrument is ineffective as an endorsement.

Article 20

If there are two or more endorsements, it is presumed, unless the contrary is proved, that each endorsement was made in the order in which it appears on the instrument.

Article 21

1. If an endorsement contains the words 'for collection', 'for deposit', 'value in collection', 'by procuration', 'pay any bank', or words of similar import authorising the endorsee to collect the instrument, the endorsee is a holder who—
    (a) may exercise all rights arising out of the instrument;
    (b) may endorse the instrument only for purposes of collection;
    (c) is subject only to the claims and defences which may be set up against the endorser.
2. The endorser for collection is not liable on the instrument to any subsequent holder.

Article 22

1. If an endorsement contains the words 'value in security', 'value in pledge', or any other words indicating a pledge, the endorsee is a holder who—
    (a) may exercise all rights arising out of the instrument;
    (b) may endorse the instrument only for purposes of collection;
    (c) is subject only to the claims and defences specified in Article 28 or 30.
2. If such an endorsee endorses for collection, he is not liable on the instrument to any subsequent holder.

Article 23

The holder of an instrument may transfer it to a prior party or to the drawee in accordance with Article 13; however, if the transferee has previously been a holder of the instrument, no endorsement is required, and any endorsement which would prevent him from qualifying as a holder may be struck out.

Article 24

An instrument may be transferred in accordance with Article 13 after maturity, except by the drawee, the acceptor or the maker.

Article 25

1. If an endorsement is forged, the person whose endorsement is forged, or a party who signed the instrument before the forgery, has the right to recover compensation for any damage that he may have suffered because of the forgery against—
    (a) the forger;
    (b) the person to whom the instrument was directly transferred by the forger;
    (c) a party or the drawee who paid the instrument to the forger directly or through one or more endorsees for collection.
2. However, an endorsee for collection is not liable under paragraph 1 of this Article if he is without knowledge of the forgery—
    (a) at the time he pays the principal or advises him of the receipt of payment; or
    (b) at the time he receives payment, if this is later,
    unless his lack of knowledge is due to his failure to act in good faith or to exercise reasonable care.
3. Furthermore, a party or the drawee who pays an instrument is not liable under paragraph 1 of this Article if, at the time he pays the instrument, he is without knowledge of the forgery, unless his lack of knowledge is due to his failure to act in good faith or to exercise reasonable care.
4. Except as against the forger, the damages recoverable under paragraph 1 of this Article may not exceed the amount referred to in Article 70 or 71.

Article 26

1. If an endorsement is made by an agent without authority or power to bind his principal in the matter, the principal, or a party who signed the instrument before such endorsement, has the right to recover compensation for any damage that he may have suffered because of such endorsement against—
    (a) the agent;
    (b) the person to whom the instrument was directly transferred by the agent;
    (c) a party or the drawee who paid the instrument to the agent directly or through one or more endorsees for collection.
2. However, an endorsee for collection is not liable under paragraph 1 of this Article if he is without knowledge that the endorsement does not bind the principal—
    (a) at the time he pays the principal or advises him of the receipt of payment; or
    (b) at the time he receives payment, if this is later,
    unless his lack of knowledge is due to his failure to act in good faith or to exercise reasonable care.
3. Furthermore, a party or the drawee who pays an instrument is not liable under paragraph 1 of this Article if, at the time he pays the instrument, he is without knowledge that the endorsement does not bind the principal, unless his lack of knowledge is due to his failure to act in good faith or to exercise reasonable care.
4. Except as against the agent, the damages recoverable under paragraph 1 of this Article may not exceed the amount referred to in Article 70 or 71.

CHAPTER IV
RIGHTS AND LIABILITIES

SECTION 1—THE RIGHTS OF A HOLDER AND A PROTECTED HOLDER

Article 27

1. The holder of an instrument has all the rights conferred on him by this Convention against the parties to the instrument.
2. The holder may transfer the instrument in accordance with Article 13.

Article 28

1. A party may set up against a holder who is not a protected holder—
   (a) any defence that may be set up against a protected holder in accordance with paragraph 1 of Article 30;
   (b) any defence based on the underlying transaction between himself and the drawer or between himself and his transferee, but only if the holder took the instrument with knowledge of such defence or if he obtained the instrument by fraud or theft or participated at any time in a fraud or theft concerning it;
   (c) any defence arising from the circumstances as a result of which he became a party, but only if the holder took the instrument with knowledge of such defence or if he obtained the instrument by fraud or theft or participated at any time in a fraud or theft concerning it;
   (d) any defence which may be raised against an action in contract between himself and the holder;
   (e) any other defence available under this Convention.
2. The rights to an instrument of a holder who is not a protected holder are subject to any valid claim to the instrument on the part of any person, but only if he took the instrument with knowledge of such claim or if he obtained the instrument by fraud or theft or participated at any time in a fraud or theft concerning it.
3. A holder who takes an instrument after the expiration of the time-limit for presentment for payment is subject to any claim to, or defence against liability on, the instrument to which his transferor is subject.
4. A party may not raise as a defence against a holder who is not a protected holder the fact that a third person has a claim to the instrument unless—
   (a) the third person asserted a valid claim to the instrument; or
   (b) the holder acquired the instrument by theft or forged the signature of the payee or an endorsee, or participated in the theft or the forgery.

Article 29

'Protected holder' means the holder of an instrument which was complete when he took it or which was incomplete within the meaning of paragraph 1 of Article 12 and was completed in accordance with authority given, provided that when he became a holder—
(a) he was without knowledge of a defence against liability on the instrument referred to in subparagraphs (a), (b), (c) and (e) of paragraph 1 of Article 28;
(b) he was without knowledge of a valid claim to the instrument of any person;
(c) he was without knowledge of the fact that it had been dishonoured by non-acceptance or by non-payment;
(d) the time-limit provided by Article 55 for presentment of that instrument for payment had not expired; and
(e) he did not obtain the instrument by fraud or theft or participate in a fraud or theft concerning it.

Article 30

1. A party may not set up against a protected holder any defence except—
    (a) defences under Articles 33 §1, 34, 35 §1, 36 §3, 53 §1, 57 §1, 63 §1 and 84 of this Convention;
    (b) defences based on the underlying transaction between himself and such holder or arising from any fraudulent act on the part of such holder in obtaining the signature on the instrument of that party;
    (c) defences based on his incapacity to incur liability on the instrument or on the fact that he signed without knowledge that his signature made him a party to the instrument, provided that his lack of knowledge was not due to his negligence and provided that he was fraudulently induced so to sign.
2. The rights to an instrument of a protected holder are not subject to any claim to the instrument on the part of any person, except a valid claim arising from the underlying transaction between himself and the person by whom the claim is raised.

Article 31

1. The transfer of an instrument by a protected holder vests in any subsequent holder the rights to and on the instrument which the protected holder had.
2. Those rights are not vested in a subsequent holder if—
    (a) he participated in a transaction which gives rise to a claim to, or a defence against liability on, the instrument;
    (b) he has previously been a holder, but not a protected holder.

Article 32

Every holder is presumed to be a protected holder unless the contrary is proved.

SECTION 2—LIABILITIES OF THE PARTIES

A GENERAL PROVISIONS

Article 33

1. Subject to the provisions of Articles 34 and 36, a person is not liable on an instrument unless he signs it.
2. A person who signs an instrument in a name which is not his own is liable as if he had signed it in his own name.

Article 34

A forged signature on an instrument does not impose any liability on the person whose signature was forged. However, if he consents to be bound by the forged signature or represents that it is his own, he is liable as if he had signed the instrument himself.

Article 35

1. If an instrument is materially altered—
    (a) a party who signs it after the material alteration is liable according to the terms of the altered text;
    (b) a party who signs it before the material alteration is liable according to the terms of the original text. However, if a party makes, authorises or assents to a material alteration, he is liable according to the terms of the altered text.

2.　　　A signature is presumed to have been placed on the instrument after the material alteration unless the contrary is proved.

3.　　　Any alteration is material which modifies the written undertaking on the instrument of any party in any respect.

Article 36

1.　　　An instrument may be signed by an agent.

2.　　　The signature of an agent placed by him on an instrument with the authority of his principal and showing on the instrument that he is signing in a representative capacity for that named principal, or the signature of a principal placed on the instrument by an agent with his authority, imposes liability on the principal and not on the agent.

3.　　　A signature placed on an instrument by a person as agent but who lacks authority to sign or exceeds his authority, or by an agent who has authority to sign but who does not show on the instrument that he is signing in a representative capacity for a named person, or who shows on the instrument that he is signing in a representative capacity but does not name the person whom he represents, imposes liability on the person signing and not on the person whom he purports to represent.

4.　　　The question whether a signature was placed on the instrument in a representative capacity may be determined only by reference to what appears on the instrument.

5.　　　A person who is liable pursuant to paragraph 3 of this Article and who pays the instrument has the same rights as the person for whom he purported to act would have had if that person had paid the instrument.

Article 37

The order to pay contained in a bill does not of itself operate as an assignment to the payee of funds made available for payment by the drawer with the drawee.

B   THE DRAWER

Article 38

1.　　　The drawee engages that upon dishonour of the bill by non-acceptance or by non-payment, and upon any necessary protest, he will pay the bill to the holder, or to any endorser or any endorser's guarantor who takes up and pays the bill.

2.　　　The drawer may exclude or limit his own liability for acceptance or for payment by an express stipulation in the bill. Such a stipulation is effective only with respect to the drawer. A stipulation excluding or limiting liability for payment is effective only if another party is or becomes liable on the bill.

C   THE MAKER

Article 39

1.　　　The maker engages that he will pay the note in accordance with its terms to the holder, or to any party who takes up and pays the note.

2.　　　The maker may not exclude or limit his own liability by a stipulation in the note. Any such stipulation is ineffective.

D   THE DRAWEE AND THE ACCEPTOR

Article 40

1.   The drawee is not liable on a bill until he accepts it.
2.   The acceptor engages that he will pay the bill in accordance with the terms of his acceptance to the holder, or to any party who takes up and pays the bill.

Article 41

1.   An acceptance must be written on the bill and may be affected—
     (a)   by the signature of the drawee accompanied by the word 'accepted' or by words of similar import; or
     (b)   by the signature alone of the drawee.
2.   An acceptance may be written on the front or on the back of the bill.

Article 42

1.   An incomplete bill which satisfies the requirements set out in paragraph 1 of Article 1 may be accepted by the drawee before it has been signed by the drawer, or while otherwise incomplete.
2.   A bill may be accepted before, at or after maturity, or after it has been dishonoured by non-acceptance or by non-payment.
3.   If a bill drawn payable at a fixed period after sight, or a bill which must be presented for acceptance before a specified date, is accepted, the acceptor must indicate the date of his acceptance; failing such indication by the acceptor, the drawer or the holder may insert the date of acceptance.
4.   If a bill drawn payable at a fixed period after sight is dishonoured by non-acceptance and the drawee subsequently accepts it, the holder is entitled to have the acceptance dated as of the date on which the bill was dishonoured.

Article 43

1.   An acceptance must be unqualified. An acceptance is qualified if it is conditional or varies the terms of the bill.
2.   If the drawee stipulates in the bill that his acceptance is subject to qualification—
     (a)   he is nevertheless bound according to the terms of his qualified acceptance;
     (b)   the bill is dishonoured by non-acceptance.
3.   An acceptance relating to only a part of the sum payable is a qualified acceptance. If the holder takes such an acceptance, the bill is dishonoured by non-acceptance only as to the remaining part.
4.   An acceptance indicating that payment will be made at a particular address or by a particular address or by a particular agent is not a qualified acceptance, provided that—
     (a)   the place in which payment is to be made is not changed;
     (b)   the bill is not drawn payable by another agent.

E   THE ENDORSER

Article 44

1.   The endorser engages that upon dishonour of the instrument by non- acceptance or by non-payment, and upon any necessary protest, he will pay the instrument to the holder, or to any subsequent endorser or any endorser's guarantor who takes up and pays the instrument.

2.   An endorser may exclude or limit his own liability by an express stipulation in the instrument. Such a stipulation is effective only with respect to that endorser.

F   THE TRANSFEROR BY ENDORSEMENT OR BY MERE DELIVERY

Article 45

1.   Unless otherwise agreed, a person who transfers an instrument, by endorsement and delivery or by mere delivery, represents to the holder to whom he transfers the instrument that—
   (a)   the instrument does not bear any forged or unauthorised signature;
   (b)   the instrument has not been materially altered;
   (c)   at the time of transfer, he has no knowledge of any fact which would impair the right of the transferee to payment of the instrument against the acceptor of a bill or, in the case of an unaccepted bill, the drawer, or against the maker of a note.

2.   Liability of the transferor under paragraph 1 of this Article is incurred only if the transferee took the instrument without knowledge of the matter giving rise to such liability.

3.   If the transferor is liable under paragraph 1 of this Article, the transferee may recover, even before maturity, the amount paid by him to the transferor, with interest calculated in accordance with Article 70 against return on the instrument.

G.   THE GUARANTOR

Article 46

1.   Payment of an instrument, whether or not it has been accepted, may be guaranteed, as to the whole or part of its amount, for the account of a party or the drawee. A guarantee may be given by any person, who may or may not already be a party.

2.   A guarantee must be written on the instrument or on a slip affixed thereto ('allonge').

3.   A guarantee is expressed by the words 'guaranteed', 'aval', 'good as aval' or words of similar import, accompanied by the signature of the guarantor. For the purposes of this Convention, the words 'prior endorsements guaranteed' or words of similar import do not constitute a guarantee.

4.   A guarantee may be effected by a signature alone on the front of the instrument. A signature alone on the front of the instrument, other than that of the maker, the drawer or the drawee, is a guarantee.

5.   A guarantor may specify the person for whom he has become guarantor. In the absence of such specification, the person for whom he has become guarantor is the acceptor or the drawee in the case of a bill, and the maker in the case of a note.

6.   A guarantor may not raise as a defence to his liability the fact that he signed the instrument before it was signed by the person for whom he is a guarantor, or while the instrument was incomplete.

Article 47

1.   The liability of a guarantor on the instrument is of the same nature as that of the party for whom he has become guarantor.

2.   If the person for whom he has become guarantor is the drawee, the guarantor engages—
   (a)   to pay the bill at maturity to the holder, or to any party who takes up and pays the bill;

    (b)   if the bill is payable at a definite time, upon dishonour by non-acceptance and upon any necessary protest, to pay it to the holder, or to any party who takes up and pays the bill.

3.   In respect of defences that are personal to himself, a guarantor may set up—
    (a)   against a holder who is not a protected holder only those defences which he may set up under paragraphs 1, 3 and 4 of Article 28;
    (b)   against a protected holder only those defences which he may set up under paragraph 1 of Article 30.

4.   In respect of defences that may be raised by the person for whom he has become a guarantor—
    (a)   a guarantor may set up against a holder who is not a protected holder only those defences which the person for whom he has become a guarantor may set up against such holder under paragraphs 1, 3 and 4 of Article 28;
    (b)   a guarantor who expresses his guarantee by the words 'guaranteed', 'payment guaranteed' or collection guaranteed', or words of similar import, may set up against a protected holder only those defences which the person for whom he has become a guarantor may set up against a protected holder under paragraph 1 of Article 30;
    (c)   a guarantor who expresses his guarantee by the words 'aval' or 'good as aval' may set up against a protected holder only:
        (i)   the defence, under subparagraph (b) of paragraph 1 of Article 30, that the protected holder obtained the signature on the instrument of the person for whom he has become a guarantor by a fraudulent act;
        (ii)   the defence, under Article 53 or 57, that the instrument was not presented for acceptance or for payment;
        (iii)   the defence, under Article 63, that the instrument was not duly protested for non-acceptance or for non-payment;
        (iv)   the defence, under Article 84, that a right of action may no longer be exercised against the person for whom he has become guarantor;
    (d)   a guarantor who is not a bank or other financial institution and who expresses his guarantee by a signature alone may set up against a protected holder only the defences referred to in subparagraph b of this paragraph;
    (e)   a guarantor which is a bank or other financial institution and which expresses its guarantee by a signature alone may set up against a protected holder only the defences referred to in subparagraph c of this paragraph.

Article 48

1.   Payment of an instrument by the guarantor in accordance with Article 72 discharges the party for whom he became guarantor of his liability on the instrument to the extent of the amount paid.

2.   The guarantor who pays the instrument may recover from the party for whom he has become guarantor and from the parties who are liable on it to that party the amount paid and any interest.

CHAPTER V
PRESENTMENT, DISHONOUR BY NON-ACCEPTANCE OR NON-PAYMENT, AND RECOURSE

SECTION 1—PRESENTMENT FOR ACCEPTANCE AND DISHONOUR BY NON-ACCEPTANCE

Article 49

1.   A bill may be presented for acceptance.

2.   A bill must be presented for acceptance—
      (a)   if the drawer has stipulated in the bill that it must be presented for acceptance;
      (b)   if the bill is payable at a fixed period after sight; or
      (c)   if the bill is payable elsewhere than at the residency or place of business of the drawee, unless it is payable on demand.

Article 50

1.   The drawer may stipulate in the bill that it must not be presented for acceptance before a specified date or before the occurrence of a specified event. Except where a bill must be presented for acceptance under subparagraph b or c of paragraph 2 of Article 49, the drawer may stipulate that it must not be presented for acceptance.
2.   If a bill is presented for acceptance notwithstanding a stipulation permitted under paragraph 1 of this Article and acceptance is refused, the bill is not thereby dishonoured.
3.   If the drawee accepts a bill notwithstanding a stipulation that it must not be presented for acceptance, the acceptance is effective.

Article 51

A bill is duly presented for acceptance if it is presented in accordance with the following rules—
(a)   the holder must present the bill to the drawee on a business day at a reasonable hour;
(b)   presentment for acceptance may be made to a person or authority other than the drawee if that person or authority is entitled under the applicable law to accept the bill;
(c)   if a bill is payable on a fixed date, presentment for acceptance must be made before or on that date;
(d)   a bill payable on demand or at a fixed period after sight must be presented for acceptance within one year of its date;
(e)   a bill in which the drawer has stated a date or time limit for presentment for acceptance must be presented on the stated date or within the stated time-limit.

Article 52

1.   A necessary or optional presentment for acceptance is dispensed with if—
      (a)   the drawee is dead, or no longer has the power freely to deal with his assets by reason of his insolvency, or is a fictitious person, or is a person not having capacity to incur liability on the instrument as an acceptor; or
      (b)   the drawee is a corporation, partnership, association or other legal entity which has ceased to exist.
2.   A necessary presentment for acceptance is dispensed with if—
      (a)   a bill is payable on a fixed date, and presentment for acceptance cannot be effected before or on that date due to circumstances which are beyond the control of the holder and which he could neither avoid nor overcome; or
      (b)   a bill is payable at a fixed period after sight, and presentment for acceptance cannot be effected within one year of its date due to circumstances which are beyond the control of the holder and which he could neither avoid nor overcome.
3.   Subject to paragraphs 1 and 2 of this Article, delay in a necessary presentment for acceptance is excused, but presentment for acceptance is not dispensed with, if the bill is drawn with a stipulation that it must be presented for acceptance within a stated time-limit, and the delay in presentment for acceptance is caused by circumstances which are beyond the control of the holder and which he could

neither avoid nor overcome. When the cause of the delay ceases to operate, presentment must be made with reasonable diligence.

Article 53

1. If a bill which must be presented for acceptance is not so presented, the drawer, the endorsers and their guarantors are not liable on the bill.
2. Failure to present a bill for acceptance does not discharge the guarantor of the drawee of liability on the bill.

Article 54

1. A bill is considered to be dishonoured by non-acceptance—
   (a) if the drawee, upon due presentment, expressly refuses to accept the bill or acceptance cannot be obtained with reasonable diligence or if the holder cannot obtain the acceptance to which he is entitled under this Convention;
   (b) if presentment for acceptance is dispensed with pursuant to Article 52, unless the bill is in fact accepted.
2. —
   (a) If a bill is dishonoured by non acceptance in accordance with subparagraph a of paragraph 1 of this Article, the holder may exercise an immediate right of recourse against the drawer, the endorsers and their guarantors, subject to the provisions of Article 59.
   (b) If a bill is dishonoured by non-acceptance in accordance with subparagraph (b) of paragraph 1 of this Article, the holder may exercise an immediate right of recourse against the drawer, the endorsers and their guarantors.
   (c) If a bill is dishonoured by non-acceptance in accordance with paragraph 1 of this Article, the holder may claim payment from the guarantor of the drawee upon any necessary protest.
3. If a bill payable on demand is presented for acceptance, but acceptance is refused, it is not considered to be dishonoured by non-acceptance.

SECTION 2—PRESENTMENT FOR PAYMENT AND DISHONOUR BY NON-PAYMENT

Article 55

An instrument is duly presented for payment if it is presented in accordance with the following rules—
(a) the holder must present the instrument to the drawee or to the acceptor or to the maker on a business day at a reasonable hour;
(b) a note signed by two or more makers may be presented to any one of them, unless the note clearly indicates otherwise;
(c) if the drawee or the acceptor or the maker is dead, presentment must be made to the persons who under the applicable law are his heirs or the persons entitled to administer his estate;
(d) presentment for payment may be made to a person or authority other than the drawee, the acceptor or the maker if that person or authority is entitled under the applicable law to pay the instrument;
(e) an instrument which is not payable on demand must be presented for payment on the date of maturity or on one of the two business days which follow;
(f) an instrument which is payable on demand must be presented for payment within one year of its date;
(g) an instrument must be presented for payment:
   (i) at the place of payment specified on the instrument; or

      (ii)   if no place of payment is specified, at the address of the drawee or the acceptor or the maker indicated in the instrument; or

      (iii)   if no place of payment is specified and the address of the drawee or the acceptor or the maker is not indicated, at the principal place of business or habitual residence of the drawee or the acceptor or the maker;

(h)   an instrument which is presented at a clearing-house is duly presented for payment if the law of the place where the clearing-house is located or the rules or customs of that clearing-house so provide.

Article 56

1.   Delay in making presentment for payment is excused if the delay is caused by circumstances which are beyond the control of the holder and which he could neither avoid nor overcome. When the cause of the delay ceases to operate, presentment must be made with reasonable diligence.

2.   Presentment for payment is dispensed with—

     (a)   if the drawer, an endorser or a guarantor has expressly waived presentment; such waiver:

        (i)   if made on the instrument by the drawer. binds any subsequent party and benefits any holder;

        (ii) if made on the instrument by a party other than the drawer, binds only that party but benefits any holder;

        (iii) if made outside the instrument, binds only the party making it and benefits only a holder in whose favour it was made;

     (b)   if an instrument is not payable on demand, and the cause of delay in making presentment referred to in paragraph 1 of this Article continues to operate beyond 30 days after maturity;

     (c)   if an instrument is payable on demand, and the cause of delay in making presentment referred to in paragraph 1 of this Article continues to operate beyond 30 days after the expiration of the time-limit for presentment for payment;

     (d)   if the drawee, the maker or the acceptor has no longer the power freely to deal with his assets by reason of his insolvency, or is a fictitious person or a person not having capacity to make payment, or if the drawee, the maker or the acceptor is a corporation, partnership, association or other legal entity which has ceased to exist;

     (e)   if there is no place at which the instrument must be presented in accordance with subparagraph (g) of Article 55.

3.   Presentment for payment is also dispensed with as regards a bill, if the bill has been protested for dishonour by non-acceptance.

Article 57

1.   If an instrument is not duly presented for payment, the drawer, the endorsers and their guarantors are not liable on it.

2.   Failure to present an instrument for payment does not discharge the acceptor, the maker and their guarantors or the guarantor of the drawee of liability on it.

Article 58

1.   An instrument is considered to be dishonoured by non-payment—

     (a)   if payment is refused upon due presentment or if the holder cannot obtain the payment to which he is entitled under this Convention;

     (b)   if presentment for payment is dispensed with pursuant to paragraph 2 of Article 56 and the instrument is unpaid at maturity.

2.   If a bill is dishonoured by non-payment, the holder may, subject to the provisions
      of Article 59, exercise a right of recourse against the drawer, the endorsers and their
      guarantors.
3.   If a note is dishonoured by non-payment, the holder may, subject to the provisions
      of Article 59, exercise a right of recourse against the endorsers and their
      guarantors.

SECTION 3—RECOURSE

Article 59

If an instrument is dishonoured by non-acceptance or by non-payment, the holder may
exercise a right of recourse only after the instrument has been duly protested for
dishonour in accordance with the provisions of Articles 60 to 62.

A   PROTEST

Article 60

1.   A protest is a statement of dishonour drawn up at the place where the instrument
      has been dishonoured and signed and dated by a person authorised in that respect
      by the law of that place. The statement must specify—
      (a)   the person at whose request the instrument is protested;
      (b)   the place of protest; and
      (c)   the demand made and the answer given, if any, or the fact that the drawee or
            the acceptor or the maker could not be found.
2.   A protest may be made—
      (a)   on the instrument or on a slip affixed thereto ('*allonge*'); or
      (b)   as a separate document, in which case it must clearly identify the instrument
            that has been dishonoured.
3.   Unless the instrument stipulates that protest must be made, a protest may be
      replaced by a declaration written on the instrument and signed and dated by the
      drawee or the acceptor or the maker, or, in the case of an instrument domiciled
      with a named person for payment, by that named person; the declaration must be
      to the effect that acceptance or payment is refused.
4.   A declaration made in accordance with paragraph 3 of this Article is a protest for
      the purpose of this Convention.

Article 61

Protest for dishonour of an instrument by non-acceptance or by non payment must be
made on the day on which the instrument is dishonoured or on one of the four business
days which follow.

Article 62

1.   Delay in protesting an instrument for dishonour is excused if the delay is caused by
      circumstances which are beyond the control of the holder and which he could
      neither avoid nor overcome. When the cause of the delay ceases to operate,
      protest must be made with reasonable diligence.
2.   Protest for dishonour by non-acceptance or by non-payment is dispensed with—
      (a)   if the drawer, an endorser or a guarantor has expressly waived protest; such
            waiver:
            (i)   if made on the instrument by the drawer, binds any subsequent party and
                  benefits any holder;

(ii) if made on the instrument by a party other than the drawer, binds only that party but benefits any holder;

(iii) if made outside the instrument, binds only the party making it an benefits only a holder in whose favour it was made;

(b) if the cause of the delay in making protest referred to in paragraph 1 of this Article continues to operate beyond 30 days after the date of dishonour;

(c) as regards the drawer of a bill, if the drawer and the drawee or the acceptor are the same person;

(d) if presentment for acceptance or for payment is dispensed with in accordance with Article 52 or paragraph 2 of Article 56.

Article 63

1. If an instrument which must be protested for non-acceptance or for non payment is not duly protested, the drawer, the endorsers and their guarantors are not liable on it.

2 Failure to protest an instrument does not discharge the acceptor, the maker and their guarantors or the guarantor of the drawee of liability on it.

B   NOTICE OF DISHONOUR

Article 64

1. The holder, upon dishonour of an instrument by non-acceptance or by non-payment, must give notice of such dishonour—
   (a) to the drawer and the last endorser; and
   (b) to all other endorsers and guarantors whose addresses the holder can ascertain on the basis of information contained in the instrument.

2. An endorser or a guarantor who receives notice must give notice of dishonour to the last party preceding him and liable on the instrument.

3. Notice of dishonour operates for the benefit of any party who has a right of recourse on the instrument against the party notified.

Article 65

1. Notice of dishonour may be given in any form whatever and in any terms which identify the instrument and State that it has been dishonoured. The return of the dishonoured instrument is sufficient notice, provided it is accompanied by a statement indicating that it has been dishonoured.

2. Notice of dishonour is duly given if it is communicated or sent to the party to be notified by means appropriate in the circumstances, whether or not it is received by that party.

3. The burden of proving that notice has been duly given rests upon the person who is required to give such notice.

Article 66

Notice of dishonour must be given within the two business days which follow—
(a) the day of protest or, if protest is dispensed with, the day of dishonour; or
(b) the day of receipt of notice of dishonour.

Article 67

1. Delay in giving notice of dishonour is excused if the delay is caused by circumstances which are beyond the control of the person required to give notice,

and which he could neither avoid nor overcome. When the cause of the delay
ceases to operate, notice must be given with reasonable diligence.

2.   Notice of dishonour is dispensed with—
      (a)   if, after the exercise of reasonable diligence, notice cannot be given;
      (b)   if the drawer, an endorser or a guarantor has expressly waived notice of
             dishonour; such waiver:
             (i)   if made on the instrument by the drawer, binds any subsequent party and
                    benefits any holder;
             (ii)   if made on the instrument by a party other than the drawer, binds only
                    that party but benefits any holder;
             (iii) if made outside the instrument, binds only the party making it and
                    benefits only a holder in whose favour it was made;
      (c)   as regards the drawer of the bill, if the drawer and the drawee or the acceptor
             are the same person.

Article 68

If a person who is required to give notice of dishonour fails to give it to a party who is
entitled to receive it, he is liable for any damages which that party may suffer from such
failure, provided that such damages do not exceed the amount referred to in Article 70 or 71.

SECTION 4—AMOUNT PAYABLE

Article 69

1.   The holder may exercise his rights on the instrument against any one party, or
      several or all parties, liable on it and is not obliged to observe the order in which
      the parties have become bound. Any party who takes up and pays the instrument
      may exercise his rights in the same manner against parties liable to him.
2.   Proceedings against a party do not preclude proceedings against any other party,
      whether or not subsequent to the party originally proceeded against.

Article 70

1.   The holder may recover from any party liable—
      (a)   at maturity: the amount of the instrument with interest, if interest has been
             stipulated for;
      (b)   after maturity:
             (i)   the amount of the instrument with interest, if interest has been
                    stipulated for, to the date of maturity;
             (ii)   if interest has been stipulated to be paid after maturity, interest at the rate
                    stipulated, or, in the absence of such stipulation, interest at the rate
                    specified in paragraph 2 of this Article, calculated from the date of
                    presentment on the sum specified in subparagraph (b)(i) of this
                    paragraph;
             (iii) any expenses of protest and of the notices given by him;
      (c)   before maturity:
             (i)   the amount of the instrument with interest, if interest has been
                    stipulated for, to the date of payment; or, if no interest has been
                    stipulated for, subject to a discount from the date of payment to the date
                    of maturity, calculated in accordance with paragraph 4 of this Article;
             (ii)   any expenses of protest and of the notices given by him.
2.   The rate of interest shall be the rate that would be recoverable in legal proceedings
      taken in the jurisdiction where the instrument is payable.

3.   Nothing in paragraph 2 of this Article prevents a court from awarding damages or compensation for additional loss caused to the holder by reason of delay in payment.

4.   The discount shall be at the official rate (discount rate) or other similar appropriate rate effective on the date when recourse is exercised at the place where the holder has his principal place of business, or, if he does not have a place of business his habitual residence, or, if there is no such rate, then at such rate as is reasonable in the circumstances.

Article 71

A party who pays an instrument and is thereby discharged in whole or in part of his liability on the instrument may recover from the parties liable to him—
(a)   the entire sum which he has paid;
(b)   interest on that sum at the rate specified in paragraph 2 of Article 70, from the date on which he made payment;
(c)   any expenses of the notices given by him.

CHAPTER VI
DISCHARGE

SECTION 1—DISCHARGE BY PAYMENT

Article 72

1.   A party is discharged of liability on the instrument when he pays the holder, or a party subsequent to himself who has paid the instrument and is in possession of it, the amount due pursuant to Article 70 or 71—
     (a)   at or after maturity; or
     (b)   before maturity, upon dishonour by non-acceptance.

2.   Payment before maturity other than under subparagraph (b) of paragraph 1 of this Article does not discharge the party making the payment of his liability on the instrument except in respect of the person to whom payment was made.

3.   A party is not discharged of liability if he pays a holder who is not a protected holder, or a party who has taken up and paid the instrument, and knows at the time of payment that the holder or that party acquired the instrument by theft or forged the signature of the payee or an endorsee, or participated in the theft or the forgery.

4.   —
     (a)   A person receiving payment of an instrument must, unless agreed otherwise, deliver:
         (i)   to the drawee making such payment, the instrument;
         (ii)   to any other person making such payment, the instrument, a receipted account, and any protest.
     (b)   In the case of an instrument payable by instalments at successive dates, the drawee or a party making a payment of the last instalment, may require that mention of such payment be made on the instrument or on a slip affixed thereto ('*allonge*') and that a receipt therefore be given to him.
     (c)   If an instrument payable by instalments at successive dates is dishonoured by non-acceptance or by non-payment as to any of its instalments and a party, upon dishonour, pays the instalment, the holder who receives such payment must give the party a certified copy of the instrument and any necessary authenticated protest in order to enable such party to exercise a right on the instrument.

(d)   The person from whom payment is demanded may withhold payment if the person demanding payment does not deliver the instrument to him. Withholding payment in these circumstances does not constitute dishonour by non-payment under Article 58.

(e)   If payment is made but the person paying, other than the drawee, fails to obtain the instrument, such person is discharged but the discharge cannot be set up as a defence against a protected holder to whom the instrument has been subsequently transferred.

Article 73

1.   The holder is not obliged to take partial payment.
2.   If the holder who is offered partial payment does not take it, the instrument is dishonoured by non-payment.
3.   If the holder takes partial payment from the drawee, the guarantor of the drawee, or the acceptor or the maker—
      (a)   the guarantor of the drawee, or the acceptor or the maker is discharged of his liability on the instrument to the extent of the amount paid; and
      (b)   the instrument is to be considered as dishonoured by non-payment as to the amount unpaid.
4.   If the holder takes partial payment from a party to the instrument other than the acceptor, the maker or the guarantor of the drawee—
      (a)   the party making payment is discharged of his liability on the instrument to the extent of the amount paid; and
      (b)   the holder must give such party a certified copy of the instrument and any necessary authenticated protest in order to enable such party to exercise a right on the instrument.
5.   The drawee or a party making partial payment may require that mention of such payment be made on the instrument and that a receipt therefor be given to him.
6.   If the balance is paid, the person who receives it and who is in possession of the instrument must deliver to the payor the receipted instrument and any authenticated protest.

Article 74

1.   The holder may refuse to take payment at a place other than the place where the instrument was presented for payment in accordance with Article 55.
2.   In such case if payment is not made at the place where the instrument was presented for payment in accordance with Article 55, the instrument is considered to be dishonoured by non-payment.

Article 75

1.   An instrument must be paid in the currency in which the sum payable is expressed.
2.   If the sum payable is expressed in a monetary unit of account within the meaning of subparagraph 1 of Article 5 and the monetary unit of account is transferable between the person making payment and the person receiving it, then, unless the instrument specifies a currency of payment, payment shall be made by transfer of monetary units of account. If the monetary unit of account is not transferable between those persons, payment shall be made in the currency specified in the instrument or, if no such currency is specified, in the currency of the place of payment.
3.   The drawer or the maker may indicate in the instrument that it must be paid in a specified currency other than the currency in which the sum payable is expressed. In that case—
      (a)   the instrument must be paid in the currency so specified;

    (b)   the amount payable is to be calculated according to the rate of exchange indicated in the instrument. Failing such indication, the amount payable is to be calculated according to the rate of exchange for sight drafts (or, if there is no such rate, according to the appropriate established rate of exchange) on the date of maturity:

        (i)   ruling at the place where the instrument must be presented for payment in accordance with subparagraph (g) of Article 55, if the specified currency is that of that place (local currency); or

        (ii) if the specified currency is not that of that place, according to the usages of the place where the instrument must be presented for payment in accordance with subparagraph (g) of Article 55;

    (c)   if such an instrument is dishonoured by non-acceptance, the amount payable is to be calculated:

        (i)   if the rate of exchange is indicated in the instrument, according to that rate;

        (ii) if no rate of exchange is indicated in the instrument, at the option of the holder, according to the rate of exchange ruling on the date of dishonour or on the date of actual payment;

    (d)   if such an instrument is dishonoured by non-payment, the amount payable is to be calculated according to that rate:

        (i)   if the rate of exchange is indicated in the instrument, according to that rate;

        (ii) if no rate of exchange is indicated in the instrument, at the option of the holder, according to the rate of exchange ruling on the date of maturity or on the date of actual payment.

4.   Nothing in this Article prevents a court from awarding damages for loss caused to the holder by reason of fluctuations in rates of exchange if such loss is caused by dishonour for non-acceptance or by non-payment.

5.   The rate of exchange ruling at a certain date is the rate of exchange ruling, at the option of the holder, at the place where the instrument must be presented for payment in accordance with subparagraph (g) of Article 55 or at the place of actual payment.

Article 76

1.   Nothing in this Convention prevents a Contracting State from enforcing exchange control regulations applicable in its territory and its provisions relating to the protection of its currency, including regulations which it is bound to apply virtue of international agreements to which it is a party.

2.   —

    (a)   If, by virtue of the application of paragraph 1 of this Article, an instrument drawn in a currency which is not that of the place of payment must be paid in local currency, the amount payable is to be calculated according to the rate of exchange for sight drafts (or, if there is no such rate, according to the appropriate established rate of exchange) on the date of presentment ruling at the place where the instrument must be presented for payment in accordance with subparagraph (g) of Article 55.

    (b)   —

        (i)   if such an instrument is dishonoured by non-acceptance, the amount payable is to be calculated, at the option of the holder, at the rate of exchange ruling on the date of dishonour or on the date of actual payment;

        (ii) if such an instrument is dishonest by non-payment, the amount is to be calculated, at the option of the holder, according to the rate of exchange ruling on the date of presentment or on the date of actual payment;

        (iii) paragraphs 4 and 5 of Article 75 are applicable where appropriate.

SECTION 2—DISCHARGE OF OTHER PARTIES

Article 77

1. If a party is discharged in whole or in part of his liability on the instrument, any party who has a right on the instrument against him is discharged to the same extent.
2. Payment by the drawee of the whole or a part of the amount of a bill to the holder, or to any party who takes up and pays the bill, discharges all parties of their liability to the same extent, except where the drawee pays a holder who is not a protected holder, or a party who has taken up and paid the bill, and knows at the time of payment that the holder or that party acquired the bill by theft or forged the signature of the payee or an endorsee, or participated in the theft or the forgery.

CHAPTER VII
LOST INSTRUMENTS

Article 78

1. If an instrument is lost, whether by destruction, theft or otherwise, the person who lost the instrument has, subject to the provisions of paragraph 2 of this Article, the same right to payment which he would have had if he had been in possession of the instrument. The party from whom payment is claimed cannot set up as a defence against liability on the instrument the fact that the person claiming payment is not in possession of the instrument.
2. —
    (a) The person claiming payment of a lost instrument must state in writing to the party from whom he claims payment:
         (i)   the elements of the lost instrument pertaining to the requirements set forth in paragraph 1 or 2 of Articles 1, 2 and 3; for this purpose the person claiming payment of the lost instrument may present to that party a copy of that instrument;
         (ii) the facts showing that, if he had been in possession of the instrument, he would have had a right to payment from the party from whom payment is claimed;
         (iii) the facts which prevent production of the instrument.
    (b) The party from whom payment of a lost instrument is claimed may require the person claiming payment to give security in order to indemnify him for any loss which he may suffer by reason of the subsequent payment of the lost instrument.
    (c) The nature of the security and its terms are to be determined by agreement between the person claiming payment and the party from whom payment is claimed. Failing such an agreement, the court may determine whether security is called for and, if so, the nature of the security and its terms.
    (d) If the security cannot be given, the court may order the party from whom payment is claimed to deposit the sum of the lost instrument, and any interest and expenses which may be claimed under Article 70 or 71, with the court or any other competent authority or institution, and may determine the duration of such deposit. Such deposit is to be considered as payment to the person claiming payment.

Article 79

1. A party who has paid a lost instrument and to whom the instrument is subsequently presented for payment by another person must give notice of such presentment to the person whom he paid.

2. Such notice must be given on the day the instrument is presented or on one of the two business days which follow and must state the name of the person presenting the instrument and the date and place of presentment.

3. Failure to give notice renders the party who has paid the lost instrument liable for any damages which the person whom he paid may suffer from such failure, provided that the damages do not exceed the amount referred to in Article 70 or 71.

4. Delay in giving notice is excused when the delay is caused by circumstances which are beyond the control of the person who has paid the lost instrument and which he could neither avoid nor overcome. When the cause of the delay ceases to operate, notice must be given with reasonable diligence.

5. Notice is dispensed with when the cause of delay in giving notice continues to operate beyond 30 days after the last day on which it should have been given.

Article 80

1. A party who has paid a lost instrument in accordance with the provisions of Article 78 and who is subsequently required to, and does, pay the instrument, or who, by reason of the loss of the instrument, then loses his right to recover from any party liable to him, has the right—
   (a) if security was given, to realise the security; or
   (b) if an amount was deposited with the court or other competent authority or institution, to reclaim the amount so deposited.

2. The person who has given security in accordance with the provisions of subparagraph (b) of paragraph 2 of Article 78 is entitled to obtain release of the security when the party for whose benefit the security was given is no longer at risk to suffer loss because of the fact that the instrument is lost.

Article 81

For the purpose of making protest for dishonour by non-payment, a person claiming payment of a lost instrument may use a written statement that satisfies the requirements of subparagraph (a) of paragraph 2 of Article 78.

Article 82

A person receiving payment of a lost instrument in accordance with Article 78 must deliver to the party paying the written statement required under subparagraph (a) of paragraph 2 of Article 78, receipted by him, and any protest and a receipted account.

Article 83

1. A party who pays a lost instrument in accordance with Article 78 has the same rights which he would have had if he had been in possession of the instrument.

2. Such party may exercise his rights only if he is in possession of the receipted written statement referred to in Article 82.

CHAPTER VIII
LIMITATION (PRESCRIPTION)

Article 84

1. A right of action arising on an instrument may no longer be exercised after four years have elapsed—
   (a) against the maker, or his guarantor, of a note payable on demand, from the date of the note;

    (b)   against the acceptor or the maker or their guarantor of an instrument payable at a definite time, from the date of maturity;

    (c)   against the guarantor of the drawee of a bill payable at a definite time, from the date of maturity or, if the bill is dishonoured by non-acceptance, from the date of protest for dishonour or, where protest is dispensed with, from the date of dishonour;

    (d)   against the acceptor of a bill payable on demand or his guarantor, from the date on which it was accepted or, if no such date is shown, from the date of the bill;

    (e)   against the guarantor of the drawee of a bill payable on demand, from the date on which he signed the bill or, if no such date is shown, from the date of the bill;

    (f)   against the drawer or an endorser or their guarantor, from the date of protest for dishonour by non-acceptance or by non-payment or, where protest is dispensed with, from the date of dishonour.

2.   A party who pays the instrument in accordance with Article 70 or 71 may exercise his right of action against a party liable to him within one year from the date on which he paid the instrument.

CHAPTER IX

Articles 85–90 [Omitted].

UNITED NATIONS CONVENTION ON THE LIABILITY OF OPERATORS OF TRANSPORT TERMINALS IN INTERNATIONAL TRADE, VIENNA, 1991

Article 1
Definitions

In this Convention:

    (a)   'Operator of a transport terminal' (hereinafter referred to as 'operator') means a person who, in the course of his business, undertakes to take in charge goods involved in international carriage in order to perform or to procure the performance of transport-related services with respect to the goods in an area under his control or in respect of which he has a right of access or use. However, a person is not considered an operator whenever he is a carrier under applicable rules of law governing carriage;

    (b)   Where goods are consolidated in a container, pallet or similar Article of transport or where they are packed, 'goods' includes such Article of transport or packaging if it was not supplied by the operator;

    (c)   'International carriage' means any carriage in which the place of departure and the place of destination are identified as being located in two different States when the goods are taken in charge by the operator;

    (d)   'Transport-related services' includes such services as storage, warehousing, loading, unloading, stowage, trimming, dunnaging and lashing;

    (e)   'Notice' means a notice given in a form which provides a record of the information contained therein;

    (f)   'Request' means a request made in a form which provides a record of the information contained therein.

Article 2
Scope of application

(1)   This Convention applies to transport-related services performed in relation to goods which are involved in international carriage:

    (a)   When the transport-related services are performed by an operator whose place of business is located in a State Party, or

    (b)   When the transport-related services are performed in a State Party, or

    (c)   When, according to the rules of private international law, the transport-related services are governed by the law of a State Party.

(2)   If the operator has more than one place of business, the place of business is that which has the closest relationship to the transport-related services as a whole.

(3)   If the operator does not have a place of business, reference is to be made to the operator's habitual residence.

Article 3
Period of responsibility

The operator is responsible for the goods from the time he has taken them in charge until the time he has handed them over to or has placed them at the disposal of the person entitled to take delivery of them.

Article 4
Issuance of document

(1)   The operator may, and at the customer's request shall, within a reasonable period of time, at the option of the operator, either:

    (a)   Acknowledge his receipt of the goods by signing and dating a document presented by the customer that identifies the goods, or

    (b)   Issue a signed document identifying the goods, acknowledging his receipt of the goods and the date thereof, and stating their condition and quantity in so far as they can be ascertained by reasonable means of checking.

(2)   If the operator does not act in accordance with either subparagraph (a) or (b) of paragraph (1), he is presumed to have received the goods in apparent good condition, unless he proves otherwise. No such presumption applies when the services performed by the operator are limited to the immediate transfer of the goods between means of transport.

(3)   A document referred to in paragraph (1) may be issued in any form which preserves a record of the information contained therein. When the customer and the operator have agreed to communicate electronically, a document referred to in paragraph (1) may be replaced by an equivalent electronic data interchange message.

(4)   The signature referred to in paragraph (1) means a handwritten signature, its facsimile or an equivalent authentication effected by any other means.

Article 5
Basis of liability

(1)   The operator is liable for loss resulting from loss of or damage to the goods, as well as from delay in handing over the goods, if the occurrence which caused the loss, damage or delay took place during the period of the operator's responsibility for the goods as defined in Article 3, unless he proves that he, his servants or agents or other persons of whose services the operator makes use for the performance of the transport-related services took all measures that could reasonably be required to avoid the occurrence and its consequences.

(2)   Where a failure on the part of the operator, his servants or agents or other persons of whose services the operator makes use for the performance of the transport-related services to take the measures referred to in paragraph (1) combines with another cause to produce loss, damage or delay, the operator is liable only to the extent that the loss resulting from such loss, damage or delay is attributable to that failure, provided that the operator proves the amount of the loss not attributable thereto.

(3)   Delay in handing over the goods occurs when the operator fails to hand them over to or place them at the disposal of a person entitled to take delivery of them within the time expressly agreed upon or, in the absence of such agreement, within a reasonable time after receiving a request for the goods by such person.

(4)   If the operator fails to hand over the goods to or place them at the disposal of a person entitled to take delivery of them within a period of 30 consecutive days after the date expressly agreed upon or, in the absence of such agreement, within a period of 30 consecutive days after receiving a request for the goods by such person, a person entitled to make a claim for the loss of the goods may treat them as lost.

Article 6
Limits of liability

(1)   (a)   The liability of the operator for loss resulting from loss of or damage to goods according to the provisions of Article 5 is limited to an amount not exceeding 8.33 units of account per kilogram of gross weight of the goods lost or damaged.

    (b)   However, if the goods are handed over to the operator immediately after carriage by sea or by inland waterways, or if the goods are handed over, or are to be handed over, by him for such carriage, the liability of the operator for loss resulting from loss of or damage to goods according to the provisions of Article 5 is limited to an amount not exceeding 2.75 units of account per kilogram of gross weight of the goods lost or damaged. For the purposes of this paragraph, carriage by sea or by inland waterways includes pick-up and delivery within a port.

    (c)   When the loss of or damage to a part of the goods affects the value of another part of the goods, the total weight of the lost or damaged goods and of the goods whose value is affected shall be taken into consideration in determining the limit of liability.

(2)   The liability of the operator for delay in handing over the goods according to the provisions of Article 5 is limited to an amount equivalent to two and a half times the charges payable to the operator for his services in respect of the goods delayed, but not exceeding the total of such charges in respect of the consignment of which the goods were a part.

(3)   In no case shall the aggregate liability of the operator under both paragraphs (1) and (2) exceed the limitation which would be established under paragraph (1) for total loss of the goods in respect of which such liability was incurred.

(4)   The operator may agree to limits of liability exceeding those provided for in paragraphs (1), (2) and (3).

Article 7
Application to non-contractual claims

(1)   The defences and limits of liability provided for in this Convention apply in any action against the operator in respect of loss of or damage to the goods, as well as delay in handing over the goods, whether the action is founded in contract, in tort or otherwise.

(2)   If such an action is brought against a servant or agent of the operator, or against another person of whose services the operator makes use for the performance of the transport-related services, such servant, agent or person, if he proves that he acted within the scope of his employment or engagement by the operator, is entitled to avail himself of the defences and limits of liability which the operator is entitled to invoke under this Convention.

(3)   Except as provided in Article 8, the aggregate of the amounts recoverable from the operator and from any servant, agent or person referred to in the preceding paragraph shall not exceed the limits of liability provided for in this Convention.

Article 8
Loss of right to limit liability

(1)   The operator is not entitled to the benefit of the limitation of liability provided for in Article 6 if it is proved that the loss, damage or delay resulted from an act or omission of the operator himself or his servants or agents done with the intent to cause such loss, damage or delay, or recklessly and with knowledge that such loss, damage or delay would probably result.

(2)   Notwithstanding the provision of paragraph (2) of Article 7, a servant or agent of the operator or another person of whose services the operator makes use for the performance of the transport-related services is not entitled to the benefit of the limitation of liability provided for in Article 6 if it is proved that the loss, damage or delay resulted from an act or omission of such servant, agent or person done with the intent to cause such loss, damage or delay, or recklessly and with knowledge that such loss, damage or delay would probably result.

Article 9
Special rules on dangerous goods

If dangerous goods are handed over to the operator without being marked, labelled, packaged or documented in accordance with any law or regulation relating to dangerous goods applicable in the country where the goods are handed over and if, at the time the goods are taken in charge by him, the operator does not otherwise know of their dangerous character, he is entitled:

(a)   To take all precautions the circumstances may require, including, when the goods pose an imminent danger to any person or property, destroying the goods, rendering them innocuous, or disposing of them by any other lawful means, without payment of compensation for damage to or destruction of the goods resulting from such precautions, and

(b)   To receive reimbursement for all costs incurred by him in taking the measures referred to in subparagraph (a) from the person who failed to meet any obligation under such applicable law or regulation to inform him of the dangerous character of the goods.

Article 10
Rights of security in goods

(1)   The operator has a right of retention over the goods for costs and claims which are due in connection with the transport-related services performed by him in respect of the goods both during the period of his responsibility for them and thereafter. However, nothing in this Convention affects the validity under the applicable law of any contractual arrangements extending the operator's security in the goods.

(2)   The operator is not entitled to retain the goods if a sufficient guarantee for the sum claimed is provided or if an equivalent sum is deposited with a mutually accepted third party or with an official institution in the State where the operator has his place of business.

(3)   In order to obtain the amount necessary to satisfy his claim, the operator is entitled, to the extent permitted by the law of the State where the goods are located, to sell all or part of the goods over which he has exercised the right of retention provided for in this Article. This right to sell does not apply to containers, pallets or similar Articles of transport or packaging which are owned by a party other than the carrier or the shipper and which are clearly marked as regards ownership except in respect of claims by the operator for the cost of repairs of or improvements to the containers, pallets or similar Articles of transport or packaging.

(4)   Before exercising any right to sell the goods, the operator shall make reasonable efforts to give notice of the intended sale to the owner of the goods, the person from whom the operator received them and the person entitled to take delivery of them from the operator. The operator shall account appropriately for the balance of the proceeds of the sale in excess of the sums due to the operator plus the reasonable costs of the sale. The right of sale shall in all other respects be exercised in accordance with the law of the State where the goods are located.

Article 11
Notice of loss, damage or delay

(1)   Unless notice of loss or damage, specifying the general nature of the loss or damage, is given to the operator not later than the third working day after the day when the goods were handed over by the operator to the person entitled to take delivery of them, the handing over is *prima facie* evidence of the handing over by the operator of the goods as described in the document issued by the operator pursuant to paragraph (1)(b) of Article 4 or, if no such document was issued, in good condition.

(2)   Where the loss or damage is not apparent, the provisions of paragraph (1) apply correspondingly if notice is not given to the operator within 15 consecutive days after the day when the goods reached the final recipient, but in no case later than 60 consecutive days after the day when the goods were handed over to the person entitled to take delivery of them.

(3)   If the operator participated in a survey or inspection of the goods at the time when they were handed over to the person entitled to take delivery of them, notice need not be given to the operator of loss or damage ascertained during that survey or inspection.

(4)   In the case of any actual or apprehended loss of or damage to the goods, the operator, the carrier and the person entitled to take delivery of the goods shall give all reasonable facilities to each other for inspecting and tallying the goods.

(5)   No compensation is payable for loss resulting from delay in handing over the goods unless notice has been given to the operator within 21 consecutive days after the day when the goods were handed over to the person entitled to take delivery of them.

Article 12
Limitation of actions

(1)   Any action under this Convention is time-barred if judicial or arbitral proceedings have not been instituted within a period of two years.

(2)   The limitation period commences:
   (a)   On the day the operator hands over the goods or part thereof to, or places them at the disposal of, a person entitled to take delivery of them, or
   (b)   In cases of total loss of the goods, on the day the person entitled to make a claim receives notice from the operator that the goods are lost, or on the day that person may treat the goods as lost in accordance with paragraph (4) of Article 5, whichever is earlier.

(3)   The day on which the limitation period commences is not included in the period.
(4)   The operator may at any time during the running of the limitation period extend
        the period by a notice to the claimant. The period may be further extended by
        another notice or notices.
(5)   A recourse action by a carrier or another person against the operator may be
        instituted even after the expiration of the limitation period provided for in the
        preceding paragraphs if it is instituted within 90 days after the carrier or other
        person has been held liable in an action against himself or has settled the claim
        upon which such action was based and if, within a reasonable period of time after
        the filing of a claim against a carrier or other person that may result in a recourse
        action against the operator, notice of the filing of such a claim has been given to the
        operator.

Article 13
Contractual stipulations

(1)   Unless otherwise provided in this Convention, any stipulation in a contract
        concluded by an operator or in any document signed or issued by the operator
        pursuant to Article 4 is null and void to the extent that it derogates, directly or
        indirectly, from the provisions of this Convention. The nullity of such a stipulation
        does not affect the validity of the other provisions of the contract or document of
        which it forms a part.
(2)   Notwithstanding the provisions of the preceding paragraph, the operator may
        agree to increase his responsibilities and obligations under this Convention.

Article 14
Interpretation of the Convention

In the interpretation of this Convention, regard is to be had to its international character
and to the need to promote uniformity in its application.

Article 15
International transport conventions

This Convention does not modify any rights or duties which may arise under an
international convention relating to the international carriage of goods which is binding
on a State which is a party to this Convention or under any law of such State giving effect
to a convention relating to the international carriage of goods.

Article 16
Unit of account

(1)   The unit of account referred to in Article 6 is the Special Drawing Right as defined
        by the International Monetary Fund. The amounts mentioned in Article 6 are to be
        expressed in the national currency of a State according to the value of such
        currency at the date of judgement or the date agreed upon by the parties. The
        equivalence between the national currency of a State Party which is a member of
        the International Monetary Fund and the Special Drawing Right is to be calculated
        in accordance with the method of valuation applied by the International Monetary
        Fund in effect at the date in question for its operations and transactions. The
        equivalence between the national currency of a State Party which is not a member
        of the International Monetary Fund and the Special Drawing Right is to be
        calculated in a manner determined by that State.
(2)   The calculation mentioned in the last sentence of the preceding paragraph is to be
        made in such a manner as to express in the national currency of the State Party as
        far as possible the same real value for amounts in Article 6 as is expressed there in

units of account. States Parties must communicate to the depositary the manner of calculation at the time of signature or when depositing their instrument of ratification, acceptance, approval or accession and whenever there is a change in the manner of such calculation.

FINAL CLAUSE

Articles 17–25 [Omitted].

UNITED NATIONS CONVENTION ON INDEPENDENT GUARANTEES AND STAND-BY LETTERS OF CREDIT, 1996

CHAPTER I
SCOPE OF APPLICATION

Article 1
Scope of application

(1)   This Convention applies to an international undertaking referred to in article 2—
    (a)   If the place of business of the guarantor/issuer at which the undertaking is issued is in a Contracting State; or
    (b)   If the rules of private international law lead to the application of the law of a Contracting State,
      unless the undertaking excludes the application of the Convention.
(2)   This Convention applies also to an international letter of credit not falling within article 2 if it expressly states that it is subject to this Convention.
(3)   The provisions of articles 21 and 22 apply to international undertakings referred to in article 2 independently of paragraph (1) of this article.

Article 2
Undertaking

(1)   For the purposes of this Convention, an undertaking is an independent commitment, known in international practice as an independent guarantee or as a stand-by letter of credit, given by a bank or other institution or person ('guarantor/issuer') to pay to the beneficiary a certain or determinable amount upon simple demand or upon demand accompanied by other documents, in conformity with the terms and any documentary conditions of the undertaking, indicating, or from which it is to be inferred, that payment is due because of a default in the performance of an obligation, or because of another contingency, or for money borrowed or advanced, or on account of any mature indebtedness undertaken by the principal/applicant or another person.
(2)   The undertaking may be given—
    (a)   at the request or on the instruction of the customer ('principal/applicant') of the guarantor/issuer;
    (b)   on the instruction of another bank, institution or person ('instructing party') that acts at the request of the customer ('principal/applicant') of that instructing party; or
    (c)   on behalf of the guarantor/issuer itself.
(3)   Payment may be stipulated in the undertaking to be made in any form, including—
    (a)   payment in a specified currency or unit of account;
    (b)   acceptance of a bill of exchange (draft);
    (c)   payment on a deferred basis;

(d)   supply of a specified item of value.

(4)   The undertaking may stipulate that the guarantor/issuer itself is the beneficiary when acting in favour of another person.

Article 3
Independence of undertaking

For the purposes of this Convention, an undertaking is independent where the guarantor/issuer's obligation to the beneficiary is not—

(a)   dependent upon the existence or validity of any underlying transaction, or upon any other undertaking (including stand-by letters of credit or independent guarantees to which confirmations or counter-guarantees relate); or

(b)   subject to any term or condition not appearing in the undertaking, or to any future, uncertain act or event except presentation of documents or another such act or event within a guarantor/issuer's sphere of operations.

Article 4
Internationality of undertaking

(1)   An undertaking is international if the places of business, as specified in the undertaking, of any two of the following persons are in different States: guarantor/issuer, beneficiary, principal/applicant, instructing party, confirmer.

(2)   For the purposes of the preceding paragraph—

(a)   if the undertaking lists more than one place of business for a given person, the relevant place of business is that which has the closest relationship to the undertaking;

(b)   if the undertaking does not specify a place of business for a given person but specifies its habitual residence, that residence is relevant for determining the international character of the undertaking.

CHAPTER II
INTERPRETATION

Article 5
Principles of interpretation

In the interpretation of this Convention, regard is to be had to its international character and to the need to promote uniformity in its application and the observance of good faith in the international practice of independent guarantees and stand-by letters of credit.

Article 6
Definitions

For the purposes of this Convention and unless otherwise indicated in a provision of this Convention or required by the context—

(a)   'Undertaking' includes 'counter-guarantee' and 'confirmation of an undertaking';

(b)   'Guarantor/issuer' includes 'counter-guarantor' and 'confirmer';

(c)   'Counter-guarantee' means an undertaking given to the guarantor/issuer of another undertaking by its instructing party and providing for payment upon simple demand or upon demand accompanied by other documents, in conformity with the terms and any documentary conditions of the undertaking, indicating, or from which it is to be inferred, that payment under that other undertaking has been demanded from, or made by, the person issuing that other undertaking;

(d)   'Counter-guarantor' means the person issuing a counter-guarantee;

(e)   'Confirmation' of an undertaking means an undertaking added to that of the guarantor/issuer, and authorized by the guarantor/issuer, providing the beneficiary with the option of demanding payment from the confirmer instead of from the guarantor/issuer, upon simple demand or upon demand accompanied by other documents, in conformity with the terms and any documentary conditions of the confirmed undertaking, without prejudice to the beneficiary's right to demand payment from the guarantor/issuer;

(f)   'Confirmer' means the person adding a confirmation to an undertaking;

(g)   'Document' means a communication made in a form that provides a complete record thereof.

CHAPTER III
FORM AND CONTENT OF UNDERTAKING

Article 7
Issuance, form and irrevocability of undertaking

(1)   Issuance of an undertaking occurs when and where the undertaking leaves the sphere of control of the guarantor/issuer concerned.

(2)   An undertaking may be issued in any form which preserves a complete record of the text of the undertaking and provides authentication of its source by generally accepted means or by a procedure agreed upon by the guarantor/issuer and the beneficiary.

(3)   From the time of issuance of an undertaking, a demand for payment may be made in accordance with the terms and conditions of the undertaking, unless the undertaking stipulates a different time.

(4)   An undertaking is irrevocable upon issuance, unless it stipulates that it is revocable.

Article 8
Amendment

(1)   An undertaking may not be amended except in the form stipulated in the undertaking or, failing such stipulation, in a form referred to in paragraph (2) of article 7.

(2)   Unless otherwise stipulated in the undertaking or elsewhere agreed by the guarantor/issuer and the beneficiary, an undertaking is amended upon issuance of the amendment if the amendment has previously been authorized by the beneficiary.

(3)   Unless otherwise stipulated in the undertaking or elsewhere agreed by the guarantor/issuer and the beneficiary, where any amendment has not previously been authorized by the beneficiary, the undertaking is amended only when the guarantor/issuer receives a notice of acceptance of the amendment by the beneficiary in a form referred to in paragraph (2) of article 7.

(4)   An amendment of an undertaking has no effect on the rights and obligations of the principal/applicant (or an instructing party) or of a confirmer of the undertaking unless such person consents to the amendment.

Article 9
Transfer of beneficiary's right to demand payment

(1)   The beneficiary's right to demand payment may be transferred only if authorized in the undertaking, and only to the extent and in the manner authorized in the undertaking.

(2)   If an undertaking is designated as transferable without specifying whether or not the consent of the guarantor/issuer or another authorized person is required for

the actual transfer, neither the guarantor/issuer nor any other authorized person is obliged to effect the transfer except to the extent and in the manner expressly consented to by it.

Article 10
Assignment of proceeds

(1)   Unless otherwise stipulated in the undertaking or elsewhere agreed by the guarantor/issuer and the beneficiary, the beneficiary may assign to another person any proceeds to which it may be, or may become, entitled under the undertaking.

(2)   If the guarantor/issuer or another person obliged to effect payment has received a notice originating from the beneficiary, in a form referred to in paragraph (2) of article 7, of the beneficiary's irrevocable assignment, payment to the assignee discharges the obligor, to the extent of its payment, from its liability under the undertaking.

Article 11
Cessation of right to demand payment

(1)   The right of the beneficiary to demand payment under the undertaking ceases when—
   (a)   the guarantor/issuer has received a statement by the beneficiary of release from liability in a form referred to in paragraph (2) of article 7;
   (b)   the beneficiary and the guarantor/issuer have agreed on the termination of the undertaking in the form stipulated in the undertaking or, failing such stipulation, in a form referred to in paragraph (2) of article 7;
   (c)   the amount available under the undertaking has been paid, unless the undertaking provides for the automatic renewal or for an automatic increase of the amount available or otherwise provides for continuation of the undertaking;
   (d)   the validity period of the undertaking expires in accordance with the provisions of article 12.

(2)   The undertaking may stipulate, or the guarantor/issuer and the beneficiary may agree elsewhere, that return of the document embodying the undertaking to the guarantor/issuer, or a procedure functionally equivalent to the return of the document in the case of the issuance of the undertaking in non-paper form, is required for the cessation of the right to demand payment, either alone or in conjunction with one of the events referred to in subparagraphs (a) and (b) of paragraph (1) of this article. However, in no case shall retention of any such document by the beneficiary after the right to demand payment ceases in accordance with subparagraph (c) or (d) of paragraph (1) of this article preserve any rights of the beneficiary under the undertaking.

Article 12
Expiry

The validity period of the undertaking expires—
(a)   at the expiry date, which may be a specified calendar date or the last day of a fixed period of time stipulated in the undertaking, provided that, if the expiry date is not a business day at the place of business of the guarantor/issuer at which the undertaking is issued, or of another person or at another place stipulated in the undertaking for presentation of the demand for payment, expiry occurs on the first business day which follows;
(b)   if expiry depends according to the undertaking on the occurrence of an act or event not within the guarantor/issuer's sphere of operations, when the guarantor/issuer is advised that the act or event has occurred by presentation of the

document specified for that purpose in the undertaking or, if no such document is specified, of a certification by the beneficiary of the occurrence of the act or event;
(c)   if the undertaking does not state an expiry date, or if the act or event on which expiry is stated to depend has not yet been established by presentation of the required document and an expiry date has not been stated in addition, when six years have elapsed from the date of issuance of the undertaking.

CHAPTER IV
RIGHTS, OBLIGATIONS AND DEFENCES

Article 13
Determination of rights and obligations

(1)   The rights and obligations of the guarantor/issuer and the beneficiary arising from the undertaking are determined by the terms and conditions set forth in the undertaking, including any rules, general conditions or usages specifically referred to therein, and by the provisions of this Convention.

(2)   In interpreting terms and conditions of the undertaking and in settling questions that are not addressed by the terms and conditions of the undertaking or by the provisions of this Convention, regard shall be had to generally accepted international rules and usages of independent guarantee or stand-by letter of credit practice.

Article 14
Standard of conduct and liability of guarantor/issuer

(1)   In discharging its obligations under the undertaking and this Convention, the guarantor/issuer shall act in good faith and exercise reasonable care having due regard to generally accepted standards of international practice of independent guarantees or stand-by letters of credit.

(2)   A guarantor/issuer may not be exempted from liability for its failure to act in good faith or for any grossly negligent conduct.

Article 15
Demand

(1)   Any demand for payment under the undertaking shall be made in a form referred to in paragraph (2) of article 7 and in conformity with the terms and conditions of the undertaking.

(2)   Unless otherwise stipulated in the undertaking, the demand and any certification or other document required by the undertaking shall be presented, within the time that a demand for payment may be made, to the guarantor/issuer at the place where the undertaking was issued.

(3)   The beneficiary, when demanding payment, is deemed to certify that the demand is not in bad faith and that none of the elements referred to in subparagraphs (a), (b) and (c) of paragraph (1) of article 19 are present.

Article 16
Examination of demand and accompanying documents

(1)   The guarantor/issuer shall examine the demand and any accompanying documents in accordance with the standard of conduct referred to in paragraph (1) of article 14. In determining whether documents are in facial conformity with the terms and conditions of the undertaking, and are consistent with one another, the guarantor/

issuer shall have due regard to the applicable international standard of independent guarantee or stand-by letter of credit practice.

(2)   Unless otherwise stipulated in the undertaking or elsewhere agreed by the guarantor/issuer and the beneficiary, the guarantor/issuer shall have reasonable time, but not more than seven business days following the day of receipt of the demand and any accompanying documents, in which to—

(a)   examine the demand and any accompanying documents;

(b)   decide whether or not to pay;

(c)   if the decision is not to pay, issue notice thereof to the beneficiary.

The notice referred to in subparagraph (c) above shall, unless otherwise stipulated in the undertaking or elsewhere agreed by the guarantor/issuer and the beneficiary, be made by teletransmission or, if that is not possible, by other expeditious means and indicate the reason for the decision not to pay.

Article 17
Payment

(1)   Subject to article 19, the guarantor/issuer shall pay against a demand made in accordance with the provisions of article 15. Following a determination that a demand for payment so conforms, payment shall be made promptly, unless the undertaking stipulates payment on a deferred basis, in which case payment shall be made at the stipulated time.

(2)   Any payment against a demand that is not in accordance with the provisions of article 15 does not prejudice the rights of the principal/applicant.

Article 18
Set-off

Unless otherwise stipulated in the undertaking or elsewhere agreed by the guarantor/ issuer and the beneficiary, the guarantor/issuer may discharge the payment obligation under the undertaking by availing itself of a right of set-off, except with any claim assigned to it by the principal/applicant or the instructing party.

Article 19
Exception to payment obligation

(1)   If it is manifest and clear that—

(a)   any document is not genuine or has been falsified;

(b)   no payment is due on the basis asserted in the demand and the supporting documents; or

(c)   judging by the type and purpose of the undertaking, the demand has no conceivable basis, the guarantor/issuer, acting in good faith, has a right, as against the beneficiary, to withhold payment.

(2)   For the purposes of subparagraph (c) of paragraph (1) of this article, the following are types of situations in which a demand has no conceivable basis—

(a)   the contingency or risk against which the undertaking was designed to secure the beneficiary has undoubtedly not materialized;

(b)   the underlying obligation of the principal/applicant has been declared invalid by a court or arbitral tribunal, unless the undertaking indicates that such contingency falls within the risk to be covered by the undertaking;

(c)   the underlying obligation has undoubtedly been fulfilled to the satisfaction of the beneficiary;

(d)   fulfilment of the underlying obligation has clearly been prevented by wilful misconduct of the beneficiary;

(e)   in the case of a demand under a counter-guarantee, the beneficiary of the counter-guarantee has made payment in bad faith as guarantor/issuer of the undertaking to which the counter- guarantee relates.

(3)   In the circumstances set out in subparagraphs (a), (b) and (c) of paragraph (1) of this article, the principal/applicant is entitled to provisional court measures in accordance with article 20.

CHAPTER V
PROVISIONAL COURT MEASURES

Article 20
Provisional court measures

(1)   Where, on an application by the principal/applicant or the instructing party, it is shown that there is a high probability that, with regard to a demand made, or expected to be made, by the beneficiary, one of the circumstances referred to in subparagraphs (a), (b) and (c) of paragraph (1) of article 19 is present, the court, on the basis of immediately available strong evidence, may—

(a)   issue a provisional order to the effect that the beneficiary does not receive payment, including an order that the guarantor/issuer hold the amount of the undertaking; or

(b)   issue a provisional order to the effect that the proceeds of the undertaking paid to the beneficiary are blocked, taking into account whether in the absence of such an order the principal/applicant would be likely to suffer serious harm.

(2)   The court, when issuing a provisional order referred to in paragraph (1) of this article, may require the person applying therefor to furnish such form of security as the court deems appropriate.

(3)   The court may not issue a provisional order of the kind referred to in paragraph (1) of this article based on any objection to payment other than those referred to in subparagraphs (a), (b) and (c) of paragraph (1) of article 19, or use of the undertaking for a criminal purpose.

CHAPTER VI
CONFLICT OF LAWS

Article 21
Choice of applicable law

The undertaking is governed by the law the choice of which is—

(a)   stipulated in the undertaking or demonstrated by the terms and conditions of the undertaking; or

(b)   agreed elsewhere by the guarantor/issuer and the beneficiary.

Article 22
Determination of applicable law

Failing a choice of law in accordance with article 21, the undertaking is governed by the law of the State where the guarantor/issuer has that place of business at which the undertaking was issued.

CHAPTER VII
FINAL CLAUSES

Articles 23–29 [Omitted].

CONVENTION FOR THE UNIFICATION OF CERTAIN RULES FOR INTERNATIONAL CARRIAGE BY AIR, MONTREAL, 1999

See Schedule 1B to the Carriage by Air Act 1961.

UNIFORM RULES CONCERNING THE CONTRACT OF INTERNATIONAL CARRIAGE OF GOODS BY RAIL (CIM) 1999

The editors and publisher thank OTIF (Intergovernmental Organisation for International Carriage by Rail) for their permission to reproduce CIM 1999.

TITLE I
GENERAL PROVISIONS

Article 1
Scope

§1   These Uniform Rules shall apply to every contract of carriage of goods by rail for reward when the place of taking over of the goods and the place designated for delivery are situated in two different Member States, irrespective of the place of business and the nationality of the parties to the contract of carriage.

§2   These Uniform Rules shall apply also to contracts of carriage of goods by rail for reward, when the place of taking over of the goods and the place designated for delivery are situated in two different States, of which at least one is a Member State and the parties to the contract agree that the contract is subject to these Uniform Rules.

§3   When international carriage being the subject of a single contract includes carriage by road or inland waterway in internal traffic of a Member State as a supplement to transfrontier carriage by rail, these Uniform Rules shall apply.

§4   When international carriage being the subject of a single contract of carriage includes carriage by sea or transfrontier carriage by inland waterway as a supplement to carriage by rail, these Uniform Rules shall apply if the carriage by sea or inland waterway is performed on services included in the list of services provided for in Article 24 §1 of the Convention.

§5   These Uniform Rules shall not apply to carriage performed between stations situated on the territory of neighbouring States, when the infrastructure of these stations is managed by one or more infrastructure managers subject to only one of those States.

§6   Any State which is a party to a convention concerning international through carriage of goods by rail comparable with these Uniform Rules may, when it makes an application for accession to the Convention, declare that it will apply these Uniform Rules only to carriage performed on part of the railway infrastructure situated on its territory. This part of the railway infrastructure must be precisely defined and connected to the railway infrastructure of a Member State. When a

State has made the above-mentioned declaration, these Uniform Rules shall apply
only on the condition —
- (a) that the place of taking over of the goods or the place designated for delivery,
  as well as the route designated in the contract of carriage, is situated on the
  specified infrastructure or
- (b) that the specified infrastructure connects the infrastructure of two Member
  States and that it has been designated in the contract of carriage as a route for
  transit carriage.

§7   A State which has made a reservation in accordance with § 6 may withdraw it at any
time by notification to the Depositary. This withdrawal shall take effect one month
after the day on which the Depositary notifies it to the Member States. The
declaration shall cease to have effect when the convention referred to in § 6, first
sentence, ceases to be in force for that State.

Article 2
Prescriptions of public law

Carriage to which these Uniform Rules apply shall remain subject to the prescriptions of
public law, in particular the prescriptions relating to the carriage of dangerous goods as
well as the prescriptions of customs law and those relating to the protection of animals.

Article 3
Definitions

For purposes of these Uniform Rules the term —
- (a) 'carrier' means the contractual carrier with whom the consignor has concluded the
  contract of carriage pursuant to these Uniform Rules, or a subsequent carrier who
  is liable on the basis of this contract;
- (b) 'substitute carrier' means a carrier, who has not concluded the contract of carriage
  with the consignor, but to whom the carrier referred to in letter (a) has entrusted, in
  whole or in part, the performance of the carriage by rail;
- (c) 'General Conditions of Carriage' means the conditions of the carrier in the form of
  general conditions or tariffs legally in force in each Member State and which have
  become, by the conclusion of the contract of carriage, an integral part of it;
- (d) 'intermodal transport unit' means a container, swap body, semi-trailer or other
  comparable loading unit used in intermodal transport.

Article 4
Derogations

§1   Member States may conclude agreements which provide for derogations from
these Uniform Rules for carriage performed exclusively between two stations on
either side of the frontier, when there is no other station between them.

§2   For carriage performed between two Member States, passing through a State which
is not a Member State, the States concerned may conclude agreements which
derogate from these Uniform Rules.

§3   Agreements referred to in §§ 1 and 2 as well as their coming into force shall be
notified to the Intergovernmental Organisation for International Carriage by Rail.
The Secretary General of the Organisation shall inform the Member States and
interested undertakings of these notifications.

Article 5
Mandatory law

Unless provided otherwise in these Uniform Rules, any stipulation which, directly or
indirectly, would derogate from these Uniform Rules shall be null and void. The nullity of

such a stipulation shall not involve the nullity of the other provisions of the contract of carriage. Nevertheless, a carrier may assume a liability greater and obligations more burdensome than those provided for in these Uniform Rules.

TITLE II
CONCLUSION AND PERFORMANCE OF THE CONTRACT OF CARRIAGE

Article 6
Contract of carriage

§1 By the contract of carriage, the carrier shall undertake to carry the goods for reward to the place of destination and to deliver them there to the consignee.

§2 The contract of carriage must be confirmed by a consignment note which accords with a uniform model. However, the absence, irregularity or loss of the consignment note shall not affect the existence or validity of the contract which shall remain subject to these Uniform Rules.

§3 The consignment note shall be signed by the consignor and the carrier. The signature can be replaced by a stamp, by an accounting machine entry or in any other appropriate manner.

§4 The carrier must certify the taking over of the goods on the duplicate of the consignment note in an appropriate manner and return the duplicate to the consignor.

§5 The consignment note shall not have effect as a bill of lading.

§6 A consignment note must be made out for each consignment. In the absence of a contrary agreement between the consignor and the carrier, a consignment note may not relate to more than one wagon load.

§7 In the case of carriage which enters the customs territory of the European Community or the territory on which the common transit procedure is applied, each consignment must be accompanied by a consignment note satisfying the requirements of Article 7.

§8 The international associations of carriers shall establish uniform model consignment notes in agreement with the customers' international associations and the bodies having competence for customs matters in the Member States as well as any intergovernmental regional economic integration organisation having competence to adopt its own customs legislation.

§9 The consignment note and its duplicate may be established in the form of electronic data registration which can be transformed into legible written symbols. The procedure used for the registration and treatment of data must be equivalent from the functional point of view, particularly so far as concerns the evidential value of the consignment note represented by those data.

Article 7
Wording of the consignment note

§1 The consignment note must contain the following particulars:
(a)   the place at which and the day on which it is made out;
(b)   the name and address of the consignor;
(c)   the name and address of the carrier who has concluded the contract of carriage;
(d)   the name and address of the person to whom the goods have effectively been handed over if he is not the carrier referred to in letter (c);
(e)   the place and the day of taking over of the goods;
(f)   the place of delivery;
(g)   the name and address of the consignee;

(h) the description of the nature of the goods and the method of packing, and, in case of dangerous goods, the description provided for in the Regulation concerning the International Carriage of Dangerous Goods by Rail (RID);

(i) the number of packages and the special marks and numbers necessary for the identification of consignments in less than full wagon loads;

(j) the number of the wagon in the case of carriage of full wagon loads;

(k) the number of the railway vehicle running on its own wheels, if it is handed over for carriage as goods;

(l) in addition, in the case of intermodal transport units, the category, the number or other characteristics necessary for their identification;

(m) the gross mass or the quantity of the goods expressed in other ways;

(n) a detailed list of the documents which are required by customs or other administrative authorities and are attached to the consignment note or held at the disposal of the carrier at the offices of a duly designated authority or a body designated in the contract;

(o) the costs relating to carriage (the carriage charge, incidental costs, customs duties and other costs incurred from the conclusion of the contract until delivery) in so far as they must be paid by the consignee or any other statement that the costs are payable by the consignee;

(p) a statement that the carriage is subject, notwithstanding any clause to the contrary, to these Uniform Rules.

§2 Where applicable the consignment note must also contain the following particulars:

(a) in the case of carriage by successive carriers, the carrier who must deliver the goods when he has consented to this entry in the consignment note;

(b) the costs which the consignor undertakes to pay;

(c) the amount of the cash on delivery charge;

(d) the declaration of the value of the goods and the amount representing the special interest in delivery;

(e) the agreed transit period;

(f) the agreed route;

(g) a list of the documents not mentioned in §1, letter (n) handed over to the carrier;

(h) the entries made by the consignor concerning the number and description of seals he has affixed to the wagon.

§3 The parties to the contract may enter on the consignment note any other particulars they consider useful.

Article 8
Responsibility for particulars entered on the consignment note

§1 The consignor shall be responsible for all costs, loss or damage sustained by the carrier by reason of—

(a) the entries made by the consignor in the consignment note being irregular, incorrect, incomplete or made elsewhere than in the allotted space, or

(b) the consignor omitting to make the entries prescribed by RID.

§2 If, at the request of the consignor, the carrier makes entries on the consignment note, he shall be deemed, unless the contrary is proved, to have done so on behalf of the consignor.

§3 If the consignment note does not contain the statement provided for in Article 7 §1, letter (p), the carrier shall be liable for all costs, loss or damage sustained through such omission by the person entitled.

Article 9
Dangerous goods

If the consignor has failed to make the entries prescribed by RID, the carrier may at any time unload or destroy the goods or render them innocuous, as the circumstances may require, without payment of compensation, save when he was aware of their dangerous nature on taking them over.

Article 10
Payment of costs

§1   Unless otherwise agreed between the consignor and the carrier, the costs (the carriage charge, incidental costs, customs duties and other costs incurred from the time of the conclusion of the contract to the time of delivery) shall be paid by the consignor.

§2   When by virtue of an agreement between the consignor and the carrier, the costs are payable by the consignee and the consignee has not taken possession of the consignment note nor asserted his rights in accordance with Article 17 §3, nor modified the contract of carriage in accordance with Article 18, the consignor shall remain liable to pay the costs.

Article 11
Examination

§1   The carrier shall have the right to examine at any time whether the conditions of carriage have been complied with and whether the consignment corresponds with the entries in the consignment note made by the consignor. If the examination concerns the contents of the consignment, this shall be carried out as far as possible in the presence of the person entitled; where this is not possible, the carrier shall require the presence of two independent witnesses, unless the laws and prescriptions of the State where the examination takes place provide otherwise.

§2   If the consignment does not correspond with the entries in the consignment note or if the provisions relating to the carriage of goods accepted subject to conditions have not been complied with, the result of the examination must be entered in the copy of the consignment note which accompanies the goods, and also in the duplicate of the consignment note, if it is still held by the carrier. In this case the costs of the examination shall be charged against the goods, if they have not been paid immediately.

§3   When the consignor loads the goods, he shall be entitled to require the carrier to examine the condition of the goods and their packaging as well as the accuracy of statements on the consignment note as to the number of packages, their marks and numbers as well as the gross mass of the goods or their quantity otherwise expressed. The carrier shall be obliged to proceed with the examination only if he has appropriate means of carrying it out. The carrier may demand the payment of the costs of the examination. The result of the examination shall be entered on the consignment note.

Article 12
Evidential value of the consignment note

§1   The consignment note shall be *prima facie* evidence of the conclusion and the conditions of the contract of carriage and the taking over of the goods by the carrier.

§2   If the carrier has loaded the goods, the consignment note shall be *prima facie* evidence of the condition of the goods and their packaging indicated on the consignment note or, in the absence of such indications, of their apparently good condition at the moment they were taken over by the carrier and of the accuracy of the statements in the consignment note concerning the number of packages, their marks and numbers as well as the gross mass of the goods or their quantity otherwise expressed.

§3 If the consignor has loaded the goods, the consignment note shall be *prima facie* evidence of the condition of the goods and of their packaging indicated in the consignment note or, in the absence of such indication, of their apparently good condition and of the accuracy of the statements referred to in § 2 solely in the case where the carrier has examined them and recorded on the consignment note a result of his examination which tallies.

§4 However, the consignment note will not be *prima facie* evidence in a case where it bears a reasoned reservation. A reason for a reservation could be that the carrier does not have the appropriate means to examine whether the consignment corresponds to the entries in the consignment note.

Article 13
Loading and unloading of the goods

§1 The consignor and the carrier shall agree who is responsible for the loading and unloading of the goods. In the absence of such an agreement, for packages the loading and unloading shall be the responsibility of the carrier whereas for full wagon loads loading shall be the responsibility of the consignor and unloading, after delivery, the responsibility of the consignee.

§2 The consignor shall be liable for all the consequences of defective loading carried out by him and must in particular compensate the carrier for the loss or damage sustained in consequence by him. The burden of proof of defective loading shall lie on the carrier.

Article 14
Packing

The consignor shall be liable to the carrier for any loss or damage and costs due to the absence of, or defects in, the packing of goods, unless the defectiveness was apparent or known to the carrier at the time when he took over the goods and he made no reservations concerning it.

Article 15
Completion of administrative formalities

§1 With a view to the completion of the formalities required by customs and other administrative authorities, to be completed before delivery of the goods, the consignor must attach the necessary documents to the consignment note or make them available to the carrier and furnish him with all the requisite information.

§2 The carrier shall not be obliged to check whether these documents and this information are correct and sufficient. The consignor shall be liable to the carrier for any loss or damage resulting from the absence or insufficiency of, or any irregularity in, such documents and information, save in the case of fault of the carrier.

§3 The carrier shall be liable for any consequences arising from the loss or misuse of the documents referred to in the consignment note and accompanying it or deposited with the carrier, unless the loss of the documents or the loss or damage caused by the misuse of the documents has been caused by circumstances which the carrier could not avoid and the consequences of which he was unable to prevent. Nevertheless any compensation payable shall not exceed that provided for in the event of loss of the goods.

§4   The consignor, by so indicating in the consignment note, or the consignee by giving orders as provided for in Article 18 § 3 may ask—
      (a)   to be present himself or to be represented by an agent when the customs or other administrative formalities are carried out, for the purpose of furnishing any information or explanation required;
      (b)   to complete the customs or other administrative formalities himself or to have them completed by an agent, in so far as the laws and prescriptions of the State in which they are to be carried out so permit;
      (c)   to pay customs duties and other charges, when he or his agent is present at or completes the customs or other administrative formalities, in so far as the laws and prescriptions of the State in which they are carried out permit such payment.
      In such circumstances neither the consignor, nor the consignee who has the right of disposal, nor the agent of either may take possession of the goods.
§5   If, for the completion of the customs or other administrative formalities, the consignor has designated a place where the prescriptions in force do not permit their completion, or if he has stipulated for the purpose any other procedure which cannot be followed, the carrier shall act in the manner which appears to him to be the most favourable to the interests of the person entitled and shall inform the consignor of the measures taken.
§6   If the consignor has undertaken to pay customs duties, the carrier shall have the choice of completing customs formalities either in transit or at the destination place.
§7   However, the carrier may proceed in accordance with §5 if the consignee has not taken possession of the consignment note within the period fixed by the prescriptions in force at the destination place.
§8   The consignor must comply with the prescriptions of customs or other administrative authorities with respect to the packing and sheeting of the goods. If the consignor has not packed or sheeted the goods in accordance with those prescriptions the carrier shall be entitled to do so; the resulting cost shall be charged against the goods.

Article 16
Transit periods

§1   The consignor and the carrier shall agree the transit period. In the absence of an agreement, the transit period must not exceed that which would result from the application of §§2 to 4.
§2   Subject to §§3 and 4, the maximum transit periods shall be as follows:
      (a)   for wagon-load consignments
            —   period for consignment   12 hours,
            —   period for carriage, for each 400 km or fraction thereof   24 hours;
      (b)   for less than wagon-load consignment
            —   period for consignments   24 hours,
            —   period for carriage, for each 200 km or fraction thereof   24 hours.
      The distances shall relate to the agreed route or, in the absence thereof, to the shortest possible route.
§3   The carrier may fix additional transit periods of specified duration in the following cases:
      (a)   consignments to be carried
            —   by lines of a different gauge,
            —   by sea or inland waterway,
            —   by road if there is no rail link;
      (b)   exceptional circumstances causing an exceptional increase in traffic or exceptional operating difficulties.

The duration of the additional transit periods must appear in the General Conditions of Carriage.

§4 The transit period shall start to run after the taking over of the goods; it shall be extended by the duration of a stay caused without any fault of the carrier. The transit period shall be suspended on Sundays and statutory holidays.

Article 17
Delivery

§1 The carrier must hand over the consignment note and deliver the goods to the consignee at the place designated for delivery against receipt and payment of the amounts due according to the contract of carriage.

§2 It shall be equivalent to delivery to the consignee if, in accordance with the prescriptions in force at the place of destination,

(a) the goods have been handed over to customs or octroi authorities at their premises or warehouses, when these are not subject to the carrier's supervision;

(b) the goods have been deposited for storage with the carrier, with a forwarding agent or in a public warehouse.

§3 After the arrival of the goods at the place of destination, the consignee may ask the carrier to hand over the consignment note and deliver the goods to him. If the loss of the goods is established or if the goods have not arrived on the expiry of the period provided for in Article 29 §1, the consignee may assert, in his own name, his rights against the carrier under the contract of carriage.

§4 The person entitled may refuse to accept the goods, even when he has received the consignment note and paid the charges resulting from the contract of carriage, so long as an examination which he has demanded in order to establish alleged loss or damage has not been carried out.

§5 In other respects, delivery of the goods shall be carried out in accordance with the prescriptions in force at the place of destination.

§6 If the goods have been delivered without prior collection of a cash on delivery charge, the carrier shall be obliged to compensate the consignor up to the amount of the cash on delivery charge without prejudice to his right of recourse against the consignee.

Article 18
Right to dispose of the goods

§1 The consignor shall be entitled to dispose of the goods and to modify the contract of carriage by giving subsequent orders. He may in particular ask the carrier—

(a) to discontinue the carriage of the goods;

(b) to delay the delivery of the goods;

(c) to deliver the goods to a consignee different from the one entered on the consignment note;

(d) to deliver the goods at a place other than the place of destination entered on the consignment note.

§2 The consignor's right to modify the contract of carriage shall, notwithstanding that he is in possession of the duplicate of the consignment note, be extinguished in cases where the consignee—

(a) has taken possession of the consignment note;

(b) has accepted the goods;

(c) has asserted his rights in accordance with Article 17 §3;

(d) is entitled, in accordance with §3, to give orders; from that time onwards, the carrier shall comply with the orders and instructions of the consignee.

§3   The consignee shall have the right to modify the contract of carriage from the time when the consignment note is drawn up, unless the consignor indicates to the contrary on the consignment note.

§4   The consignee's right to modify the contract of carriage shall be extinguished in cases where he has—

(a)   taken possession of the consignment note;

(b)   accepted the goods;

(c)   asserted his rights in accordance with Article 17 §3;

(d)   given instructions for delivery of the goods to another person in accordance with §5 and when that person has asserted his rights in accordance with Article 17 §3.

§5   If the consignee has given instructions for delivery of the goods to another person, that person shall not be entitled to modify the contract of carriage.

Article 19
Exercise of the right to dispose of the goods

§1   If the consignor or, in the case referred to in Article 18 § 3, the consignee wishes to modify the contract of carriage by giving subsequent orders, he must produce to the carrier the duplicate of the consignment note on which the modifications have to be entered.

§2   The consignor or, in the case referred to in Article 18 § 3, the consignee must compensate the carrier for the costs and the prejudice arising from the carrying out of subsequent modifications.

§3   The carrying out of the subsequent modifications must be possible, lawful and reasonable to require at the time when the orders reach the person who is to carry them out, and must in particular neither interfere with the normal working of the carrier's undertaking nor prejudice the consignors or consignees of other consignments.

§4   The subsequent modifications must not have the effect of splitting the consignment.

§5   When, by reason of the conditions provided for in § 3, the carrier cannot carry out the orders which he receives he shall immediately notify the person from whom the orders emanate.

§6   In the case of fault of the carrier he shall be liable for the consequences of failure to carry out an order or failure to carry it out properly. Nevertheless, any compensation payable shall not exceed that provided for in case of loss of the goods.

§7   If the carrier implements the consignor's subsequent modifications without requiring the production of the duplicate of the consignment note, the carrier shall be liable to the consignee for any loss or damage sustained by him if the duplicate has been passed on to the consignee. Nevertheless, any compensation payable shall not exceed that provided for in case of loss of the goods.

Article 20
Circumstances preventing carriage

§1   When circumstances prevent the carriage of goods, the carrier shall decide whether it is preferable to carry the goods as a matter of course by modifying the route or whether it is advisable, in the interest of the person entitled, to ask him for instructions while giving him any relevant information available to the carrier.

§2   If it is impossible to continue carrying the goods, the carrier shall ask for instructions from the person who has the right to dispose of the goods. If the carrier is unable to obtain instructions within a reasonable time he must take such steps as seem to him to be in the best interests of the person entitled to dispose of the goods.

Article 21
Circumstances preventing delivery

§1   When circumstances prevent delivery, the carrier must without delay inform the consignor and ask him for instructions, save where the consignor has requested, by an entry in the consignment note, that the goods be returned to him as a matter of course in the event of circumstances preventing delivery.

§2   When the circumstances preventing delivery cease to exist before arrival of instructions from the consignor to the carrier the goods shall be delivered to the consignee. The consignor must be notified without delay.

§3   If the consignee refuses the goods, the consignor shall be entitled to give instructions even if he is unable to produce the duplicate of the consignment note.

§4   When the circumstances preventing delivery arise after the consignee has modified the contract of carriage in accordance with Article 18 §§3 to 5 the carrier must notify the consignee.

Article 22
Consequences of circumstances preventing carriage and delivery

§1   The carrier shall be entitled to recover the costs occasioned by—
      (a)   his request for instructions,
      (b)   the carrying out of instructions received,
      (c)   the fact that instructions requested do not reach him or do not reach him in time,
      (d)   the fact that he has taken a decision in accordance with Article 20 §1, without having asked for instructions,
      unless such costs were caused by his fault. The carrier may in particular recover the carriage charge applicable to the route followed and shall be allowed the transit periods applicable to such route.

§2   In the cases referred to in Article 20 §2 and Article 21 §1 the carrier may immediately unload the goods at the cost of the person entitled. Thereupon the carriage shall be deemed to be at an end. The carrier shall then be in charge of the goods on behalf of the person entitled. He may, however, entrust them to a third party, and shall then be responsible only for the exercise of reasonable care in the choice of such third party. The charges due under the contract of carriage and all other costs shall remain chargeable against the goods.

§3   The carrier may proceed to the sale of the goods, without awaiting instructions from the person entitled, if this is justified by the perishable nature or the condition of the goods or if the costs of storage would be out of proportion to the value of the goods. In other cases he may also proceed to the sale of the goods if within a reasonable time he has not received from the person entitled instructions to the contrary which he may reasonably be required to carry out.

§4   If the goods have been sold, the proceeds of sale, after deduction of the costs chargeable against the goods, must be placed at the disposal of the person entitled. If the proceeds of sale are less than those costs, the consignor must pay the difference.

§5   The procedure in the case of sale shall be determined by the laws and prescriptions in force at, or by the custom of, the place where the goods are situated.

§6   If the consignor, in the case of circumstances preventing carriage or delivery, fails to give instructions within a reasonable time and if the circumstances preventing carriage or delivery cannot be eliminated in accordance with §§2 and 3, the carrier may return the goods to the consignor or, if it is justified, destroy them, at the cost of the consignor.

TITLE III
LIABILITY

Article 23
Basis of liability

§1 The carrier shall be liable for loss or damage resulting from the total or partial loss of, or damage to, the goods between the time of taking over of the goods and the time of delivery and for the loss or damage resulting from the transit period being exceeded, whatever the railway infrastructure used.

§2 The carrier shall be relieved of this liability to the extent that the loss or damage or the exceeding of the transit period was caused by the fault of the person entitled, by an order given by the person entitled other than as a result of the fault of the carrier, by an inherent defect in the goods (decay, wastage etc.) or by circumstances which the carrier could not avoid and the consequences of which he was unable to prevent.

§3 The carrier shall be relieved of this liability to the extent that the loss or damage arises from the special risks inherent in one or more of the following circumstances:

(a) carriage in open wagons pursuant to the General Conditions of Carriage or when it has been expressly agreed and entered in the consignment note; subject to damage sustained by the goods because of atmospheric influences, goods carried in intermodal transport units and in closed road vehicles carried on wagons shall not be considered as being carried in open wagons; if for the carriage of goods in open wagons, the consignor uses sheets, the carrier shall assume the same liability as falls to him for carriage in open wagons without sheeting, even in respect of goods which, according to the General Conditions of Carriage, are not carried in open wagons;

(b) absence or inadequacy of packaging in the case of goods which by their nature are liable to loss or damage when not packed or when not packed properly;

(c) loading of the goods by the consignor or unloading by the consignee;

(d) the nature of certain goods which particularly exposes them to total or partial loss or damage, especially through breakage, rust, interior and spontaneous decay, desiccation or wastage;

(e) irregular, incorrect or incomplete description or numbering of packages;

(f) carriage of live animals;

(g) carriage which, pursuant to applicable provisions or agreements made between the consignor and the carrier and entered on the consignment note, must be accompanied by an attendant, if the loss or damage results from a risk which the attendant was intended to avert.

Article 24
Liability in case of carriage of railway vehicles as goods

§1 In case of carriage of railway vehicles running on their own wheels and consigned as goods, the carrier shall be liable for the loss or damage resulting from the loss of, or damage to, the vehicle or to its removable parts arising between the time of taking over for carriage and the time of delivery and for loss or damage resulting from exceeding the transit period, unless he proves that the loss or damage was not caused by his fault.

§2 The carrier shall not be liable for loss or damage resulting from the loss of accessories which are not mentioned on both sides of the vehicle or in the inventory which accompanies it.

Article 25
Burden of proof

§1 The burden of proving that the loss, damage or exceeding of the transit period was due to one of the causes specified in Article 23 §2 shall lie on the carrier.

§2 When the carrier establishes that, having regard to the circumstances of a particular case, the loss or damage could have arisen from one or more of the special risks referred to in Article 23 § 3, it shall be presumed that it did so arise. The person entitled shall, however, have the right to prove that the loss or damage was not attributable either wholly or in part to one of those risks.

§3 The presumption according to § 2 shall not apply in the case provided for in Article 23 §3, letter (a) if an abnormally large quantity has been lost or if a package has been lost.

Article 26
Successive carriers

If carriage governed by a single contract is performed by several successive carriers, each carrier, by the very act of taking over the goods with the consignment note, shall become a party to the contract of carriage in accordance with the terms of that document and shall assume the obligations arising therefrom. In such a case each carrier shall be responsible in respect of carriage over the entire route up to delivery.

Article 27
Substitute carrier

§1 Where the carrier has entrusted the performance of the carriage, in whole or in part, to a substitute carrier, whether or not in pursuance of a right under the contract of carriage to do so, the carrier shall nevertheless remain liable in respect of the entire carriage.

§2 All the provisions of these Uniform Rules governing the liability of the carrier shall also apply to the liability of the substitute carrier for the carriage performed by him. Articles 36 and 41 shall apply if an action is brought against the servants and any other persons whose services the substitute carrier makes use of for the performance of the carriage.

§3 Any special agreement under which the carrier assumes obligations not imposed by these Uniform Rules or waives rights conferred by these Uniform Rules shall be of no effect in respect of the substitute carrier who has not accepted it expressly and in writing. Whether or not the substitute carrier has accepted it, the carrier shall nevertheless remain bound by the obligations or waivers resulting from such special agreement.

§4 Where and to the extent that both the carrier and the substitute carrier are liable, their liability shall be joint and several.

§5 The aggregate amount of compensation payable by the carrier, the substitute carrier and their servants and other persons whose services they make use of for the performance of the carriage shall not exceed the limits provided for in these Uniform Rules.

§6 This article shall not prejudice rights of recourse which may exist between the carrier and the substitute carrier.

Article 28
Presumption of loss or damage in case of reconsignment

§1 When a consignment consigned in accordance with these Uniform Rules has been reconsigned subject to these same Rules and partial loss or damage has been ascertained after that reconsignment, it shall be presumed that it occurred under the latest contract of carriage if the consignment remained in the charge of the carrier and was reconsigned in the same condition as when it arrived at the place from which it was reconsigned.

§2   This presumption shall also apply when the contract of carriage prior to the reconsignment was not subject to these Uniform Rules, if these Rules would have applied in the case of a through consignment from the first place of consignment to the final place of destination.

§3   This presumption shall also apply when the contract of carriage prior to the reconsignment was subject to a convention concerning international through carriage of goods by rail comparable with these Uniform Rules, and when this convention contains the same presumption of law in favour of consignments consigned in accordance with these Uniform Rules.

Article 29
Presumption of loss of the goods

§1   The person entitled may, without being required to furnish further proof, consider the goods as lost when they have not been delivered to the consignee or placed at his disposal within thirty days after the expiry of the transit periods.

§2   The person entitled may, on receipt of the payment of compensation for the goods lost, make a written request to be notified without delay should the goods be recovered within one year after the payment of compensation. The carrier shall acknowledge such request in writing.

§3   Within thirty days after receipt of a notification referred to in §2, the person entitled may require the goods to be delivered to him against payment of the costs resulting from the contract of carriage and against refund of the compensation received, less, where appropriate, costs which may have been included therein. Nevertheless he shall retain his rights to claim compensation for exceeding the transit period provided for in Articles 33 and 35.

§4   In the absence of the request referred to in § 2 or of instructions given within the period specified in §3, or if the goods are recovered more than one year after the payment of compensation, the carrier shall dispose of them in accordance with the laws and prescriptions in force at the place where the goods are situated.

Article 30
Compensation for loss

§1   In case of total or partial loss of the goods, the carrier must pay, to the exclusion of all other damages, compensation calculated according to the commodity exchange quotation or, if there is no such quotation, according to the current market price, or if there is neither such quotation nor such price, according to the usual value of goods of the same kind and quality on the day and at the place where the goods were taken over.

§2   Compensation shall not exceed 17 units of account per kilogramme of gross mass short.

§3   In case of loss of a railway vehicle running on its own wheels and consigned as goods, or of an intermodal transport unit, or of their removable parts, the compensation shall be limited, to the exclusion of all other damages, to the usual value of the vehicle or the intermodal transport unit, or their removable parts, on the day and at the place of loss. If it is impossible to ascertain the day or the place of the loss, the compensation shall be limited to the usual value on the day and at the place where the vehicle has been taken over by the carrier.

§4   The carrier must, in addition, refund the carriage charge, customs duties already paid and other sums paid in relation to the carriage of the goods lost except excise duties for goods carried under a procedure suspending those duties.

Article 31
Liability for wastage in transit

§1   In respect of goods which, by reason of their nature, are generally subject to wastage in transit by the sole fact of carriage, the carrier shall only be liable to the extent that the wastage exceeds the following allowances, whatever the length of the route:

(a)   two per cent of the mass for liquid goods or goods consigned in a moist condition;

(b)   one per cent of the mass for dry goods.

§2   The limitation of liability provided for in § 1 may not be invoked if, having regard to the circumstances of a particular case, it is proved that the loss was not due to causes which would justify the allowance.

§3   Where several packages are carried under a single consignment note, the wastage in transit shall be calculated separately for each package if its mass on consignment is shown separately on the consignment note or can be ascertained otherwise.

§4   In case of total loss of goods or in case of loss of a package, no deduction for wastage in transit shall be made in calculating the compensation.

§5   This Article shall not derogate from Articles 23 and 25.

Article 32
Compensation for damage

§1   In case of damage to goods, the carrier must pay compensation equivalent to the loss in value of the goods, to the exclusion of all other damages. The amount shall be calculated by applying to the value of the goods defined in accordance with Article 30 the percentage of loss in value noted at the place of destination.

§2   The compensation shall not exceed:

(a)   if the whole consignment has lost value through damage, the amount which would have been payable in case of total loss;

(b)   if only part of the consignment has lost value through damage, the amount which would have been payable had that part been lost.

§3   In case of damage to a railway vehicle running on its own wheels and consigned as goods, or of an intermodal transport unit, or of their removable parts, the compensation shall be limited, to the exclusion of all other damages, to the cost of repair. The compensation shall not exceed the amount payable in case of loss.

§4   The carrier must also refund the costs provided for in Article 30 §4, in the proportion set out in §1.

Article 33
Compensation for exceeding the transit period

§1   If loss or damage results from the transit period being exceeded, the carrier must pay compensation not exceeding four times the carriage charge.

§2   In case of total loss of the goods, the compensation provided for in §1 shall not be payable in addition to that provided for in Article 30.

§3   In case of partial loss of the goods, the compensation provided for in §1 shall not exceed four times the carriage charge in respect of that part of the consignment which has not been lost.

§4   In case of damage to the goods, not resulting from the transit period being exceeded, the compensation provided for in §1 shall, where appropriate, be payable in addition to that provided for in Article 32.

§5   In no case shall the total of compensation provided for in §1 together with that provided for in Articles 30 and 32 exceed the compensation which would be payable in case of total loss of the goods.

§6   If, in accordance with Article 16 §1, the transit period has been established by agreement, other forms of compensation than those provided for in §1 may be so agreed. If, in this case, the transit periods provided for in Article 16 §§2 to 4 are exceeded, the person entitled may claim either the compensation provided for in the agreement mentioned above or that provided for in §§1 to 5.

Article 34
Compensation in case of declaration of value

The consignor and the carrier may agree that the consignor shall declare in the consignment note a value for the goods exceeding the limit provided for in Article 30 §2. In such a case the amount declared shall be substituted for that limit.

Article 35
Compensation in case of interest in delivery

The consignor and the carrier may agree that the consignor may declare, by entering an amount in figures in the consignment note, a special interest in delivery, in case of loss, damage or exceeding of the transit period. In case of a declaration of interest in delivery further compensation for loss or damage proved may be claimed, in addition to the compensation provided for in Articles 30, 32 and 33, up to the amount declared.

Article 36
Loss of right to invoke the limits of liability

The limits of liability provided for in Article 15 §3, Article 19 §§6 and 7, Article 30 and Articles 32 to 35 shall not apply if it is proved that the loss or damage results from an act or omission, which the carrier has committed either with intent to cause such loss or damage, or recklessly and with knowledge that such loss or damage would probably result.

Article 37
Conversion and interest

§1   Where the calculation of the compensation requires the conversion of sums expressed in foreign currency, conversion shall be at the exchange rate applicable on the day and at the place of payment of compensation.

§2   The person entitled may claim interest on compensation, calculated at five per cent per annum, from the day of the claim provided for in Article 43 or, if no such claim has been made, from the day on which legal proceedings were instituted.

§3   If the person entitled does not submit to the carrier, within a reasonable time allotted to him, the supporting documents required for the amount of the claim to be finally settled, no interest shall accrue between the expiry of the time allotted and the actual submission of such documents.

Article 38
Liability in respect of rail-sea traffic

§1   In rail-sea carriage by the services referred to in Article 24 §1 of the Convention any Member State may, by requesting that a suitable note be included in the list of services to which these Uniform Rules apply, add the following grounds for exemption from liability in their entirety to those provided for in Article 23:
      (a)   fire, if the carrier proves that it was not caused by his act or default, or that of the master, a mariner, the pilot or the carrier's servants;
      (b)   saving or attempting to save life or property at sea;

(c)   loading of goods on the deck of the ship, if they are so loaded with the consent of the consignor given on the consignment note and are not in wagons;

(d)   perils, dangers and accidents of the sea or other navigable waters.

§2   The carrier may only avail himself of the grounds for exemption referred to in §1 if he proves that the loss, damage or exceeding the transit period occurred in the course of the journey by sea between the time when the goods were loaded on board the ship and the time when they were unloaded from the ship.

§3   When the carrier relies on the grounds for exemption referred to in §1, he shall nevertheless remain liable if the person entitled proves that the loss, damage or exceeding the transit period is due to the fault of the carrier, the master, a mariner, the pilot or the carrier's servants.

§4   Where a sea route is served by several undertakings included in the list of services in accordance with Article 24 §1 of the Convention, the liability regime applicable to that route must be the same for all those undertakings. In addition, where those undertakings have been included in the list at the request of several Member States, the adoption of this regime must be the subject of prior agreement between those States.

§5   The measures taken in accordance with §§1 and 4 shall be notified to the Secretary General. They shall come into force at the earliest at the expiry of a period of thirty days from the day on which the Secretary General notifies them to the other Member States. Consignments already in transit shall not be affected by such measures.

Article 39
Liability in case of nuclear incidents

The carrier shall be relieved of liability pursuant to these Uniform Rules for loss or damage caused by a nuclear incident when the operator of a nuclear installation or another person who is substituted for him is liable for the loss or damage pursuant to the laws and prescriptions of a State governing liability in the field of nuclear energy.

Article 40
Persons for whom the carrier is liable

The carrier shall be liable for his servants and other persons whose services he makes use of for the performance of the carriage, when these servants and other persons are acting within the scope of their functions. The managers of the railway infrastructure on which the carriage is performed shall be considered as persons whose services the carrier makes use of for the performance of the carriage.

Article 41
Other actions

§1   In all cases where these Uniform Rules shall apply, any action in respect of liability, on whatever grounds, may be brought against the carrier only subject to the conditions and limitations laid down in these Uniform Rules.

§2   The same shall apply to any action brought against the servants or other persons for whom the carrier is liable pursuant to Article 40.

TITLE IV
ASSERTION OF RIGHTS

Article 42
Ascertainment of partial loss or damage

§1   When partial loss or damage is discovered or presumed by the carrier or alleged by the person entitled, the carrier must without delay, and if possible in the presence of the person entitled, draw up a report stating, according to the nature of the loss or damage, the condition of the goods, their mass and, as far as possible, the extent of the loss or damage, its cause and the time of its occurrence.

§2   A copy of the report must be supplied free of charge to the person entitled.

§3   Should the person entitled not accept the findings in the report, he may request that the condition and mass of the goods and the cause and amount of the loss or damage be ascertained by an expert appointed either by the parties to the contract of carriage or by a court or tribunal. The procedure to be followed shall be governed by the laws and prescriptions of the State in which such ascertainment takes place.

Article 43
Claims

§1   Claims relating to the contract of carriage must be addressed in writing to the carrier against whom an action may be brought.

§2   A claim may be made by persons who have the right to bring an action against the carrier.

§3   To make the claim the consignor must produce the duplicate of the consignment note. Failing this he must produce an authorisation from the consignee or furnish proof that the consignee has refused to accept the goods.

§4   To make the claim the consignee must produce the consignment note if it has been handed over to him.

§5   The consignment note, the duplicate and any other documents which the person entitled thinks fit to submit with the claim must be produced either in the original or as copies, the copies, where appropriate, duly certified if the carrier so requests.

§6   On settlement of the claim the carrier may require the production, in the original form, of the consignment note, the duplicate or the cash on delivery voucher so that they may be endorsed to the effect that settlement has been made.

Article 44
Persons who may bring an action against the carrier

§1   Subject to §§3 and 4 actions based on the contract of carriage may be brought:
     (a)   by the consignor, until such time as the consignee has—
         1.   taken possession of the consignment note,
         2.   accepted the goods, or
         3.   asserted his rights pursuant to Article 17 §3 or Article 18 §3;
     (b)   by the consignee, from the time when he has—
         1.   taken possession of the consignment note,
         2.   accepted the goods, or
         3.   asserted his rights pursuant to Article 17 §3 or Article 18 §3.

§2   The right of the consignee to bring an action shall be extinguished from the time when the person designated by the consignee in accordance with Article 18 §5 has taken possession of the consignment note, accepted the goods or asserted his rights pursuant to Article 17 §3.

§3   An action for the recovery of a sum paid pursuant to the contract of carriage may only be brought by the person who made the payment.

§4   An action in respect of cash on delivery payments may only be brought by the consignor.

§5   In order to bring an action the consignor must produce the duplicate of the consignment note. Failing this he must produce an authorisation from the consignee or furnish proof that the consignee has refused to accept the goods. If necessary, the consignor must prove the absence or the loss of the consignment note.

§6   In order to bring an action the consignee must produce the consignment note if it has been handed over to him.

Article 45
Carriers against whom an action may be brought

§1   Subject to §§3 and 4 actions based on the contract of carriage may be brought only against the first carrier, the last carrier or the carrier having performed the part of the carriage on which the event giving rise to the proceedings occurred.

§2   When, in the case of carriage performed by successive carriers, the carrier who must deliver the goods is entered with his consent on the consignment note, an action may be brought against him in accordance with §1 even if he has received neither the goods nor the consignment note.

§3   An action for the recovery of a sum paid pursuant to the contract of carriage may be brought against the carrier who has collected that sum or against the carrier on whose behalf it was collected.

§4   An action in respect of cash on delivery payments may be brought only against the carrier who has taken over the goods at the place of consignment.

§5   An action may be brought against a carrier other than those specified in §§1 to 4 when instituted by way of counter-claim or by way of exception in proceedings relating to a principal claim based on the same contract of carriage.

§6   To the extent that these Uniform Rules apply to the substitute carrier, an action may also be brought against him.

§7   If the plaintiff has a choice between several carriers, his right to choose shall be extinguished as soon as he brings an action against any one of them; this shall also apply if the plaintiff has a choice between one or more carriers and a substitute carrier.

Article 46
Forum

§1   Actions based on these Uniform Rules may be brought before the courts or tribunals of Member States designated by agreement between the parties or before the courts or tribunals of a State on whose territory—

    (a)   the defendant has his domicile or habitual residence, his principal place of business or the branch or agency which concluded the contract of carriage, or

    (b)   the place where the goods were taken over by the carrier or the place designated for delivery is situated.

    Other courts or tribunals may not be seised.

§2   Where an action based on these Uniform Rules is pending before a court or tribunal competent pursuant to §1, or where in such litigation a judgment has been delivered by such a court or tribunal, no new action may be brought between the same parties on the same grounds unless the judgment of the court or tribunal before which the first action was brought is not enforceable in the State in which the new action is brought.

Article 47
Extinction of right of action

§1   Acceptance of the goods by the person entitled shall extinguish all rights of action against the carrier arising from the contract of carriage in case of partial loss, damage or exceeding of the transit period.

§2   Nevertheless, the right of action shall not be extinguished:
   (a)   in case of partial loss or damage, if—
          1.   the loss or damage was ascertained in accordance with Article 42 before the acceptance of the goods by the person entitled;
          2.   the ascertainment which should have been carried out in accordance with Article 42 was omitted solely through the fault of the carrier;
   (b)   in case of loss or damage which is not apparent whose existence is ascertained after acceptance of the goods by the person entitled, if he—
          1.   asks for ascertainment in accordance with Article 42 immediately after discovery of the loss or damage and not later than seven days after the acceptance of the goods, and
          2.   in addition, proves that the loss or damage occurred between the time of taking over and the time of delivery;
   (c)   in cases where the transit period has been exceeded, if the person entitled has, within sixty days, asserted his rights against one of the carriers referred to in Article 45 §1;
   (d)   if the person entitled proves that the loss or damage results from an act or omission, done with intent to cause such loss or damage, or recklessly and with knowledge that such loss or damage would probably result.

§3   If the goods have been reconsigned in accordance with Article 28 rights of action in case of partial loss or in case of damage, arising from one of the previous contracts of carriage, shall be extinguished as if there had been only a single contract of carriage.

Article 48
Limitation of actions

§1   The period of limitation for an action arising from the contract of carriage shall be one year. Nevertheless, the period of limitation shall be two years in the case of an action—
   (a)   to recover a cash on delivery payment collected by the carrier from the consignee;
   (b)   to recover the proceeds of a sale effected by the carrier;
   (c)   for loss or damage resulting from an act or omission done with intent to cause such loss or damage, or recklessly and with knowledge that such loss or damage would probably result;
   (d)   based on one of the contracts of carriage prior to the reconsignment in the case provided for in Article 28.

§2   The period of limitation shall run for actions—
   (a)   for compensation for total loss, from the thirtieth day after expiry of the transit period;
   (b)   for compensation for partial loss, damage or exceeding of the transit period, from the day when delivery took place;
   (c)   in all other cases, from the day when the right of action may be exercised.
        The day indicated for the commencement of the period of limitation shall not be included in the period.

§3   The period of limitation shall be suspended by a claim in writing in accordance with Article 43 until the day that the carrier rejects the claim by notification in writing and returns the documents submitted with it. If part of the claim is admitted, the period of limitation shall start to run again in respect of the part of the claim still in dispute. The burden of proof of receipt of the claim or of the reply and of the return of the documents shall lie on the party who relies on those facts. The period of limitation shall not be suspended by further claims having the same object.

§4 A right of action which has become time-barred may not be exercised further, even by way of counter-claim or relied upon by way of exception.

§5 Otherwise, the suspension and interruption of periods of limitation shall be governed by national law.

TITLE V
RELATIONS BETWEEN CARRIERS

Article 49
Settlement of accounts

§1 Any carrier who has collected or ought to have collected, either at departure or on arrival, charges or other costs arising out of the contract of carriage must pay to the carriers concerned their respective shares. The methods of payment shall be fixed by agreement between the carriers.

§2 Article 12 shall also apply to the relations between successive carriers.

Article 50
Right of recourse

§1 A carrier who has paid compensation pursuant to these Uniform Rules shall have a right of recourse against the carriers who have taken part in the carriage in accordance with the following provisions:
(a) the carrier who has caused the loss or damage shall be solely liable for it;
(b) when the loss or damage has been caused by several carriers, each shall be liable for the loss or damage he has caused; if such distinction is impossible, the compensation shall be apportioned between them in accordance with letter (c);
(c) if it cannot be proved which of the carriers has caused the loss or damage, the compensation shall be apportioned between all the carriers who have taken part in the carriage, except those who prove that the loss or damage was not caused by them; such apportionment shall be in proportion to their respective shares of the carriage charge.

§2 In the case of insolvency of any one of these carriers, the unpaid share due from him shall be apportioned among all the other carriers who have taken part in the carriage, in proportion to their respective shares of the carriage charge.

Article 51
Procedure for recourse

§1 The validity of the payment made by the carrier exercising a right of recourse pursuant to Article 50 may not be disputed by the carrier against whom the right of recourse is exercised, when compensation has been determined by a court or tribunal and when the latter carrier, duly served with notice of the proceedings, has been afforded an opportunity to intervene in the proceedings. The court or tribunal seised of the principal action shall determine what time shall be allowed for such notification of the proceedings and for intervention in the proceedings.

§2 A carrier exercising his right of recourse must make his claim in one and the same proceedings against all the carriers with whom he has not reached a settlement, failing which he shall lose his right of recourse in the case of those against whom he has not taken proceedings.

§3   The court or tribunal must give its decision in one and the same judgment on all recourse claims brought before it.

§4   The carrier wishing to enforce his right of recourse may bring his action in the courts or tribunals of the State on the territory of which one of the carriers participating in the carriage has his principal place of business, or the branch or agency which concluded the contract of carriage.

§5   When the action must be brought against several carriers, the plaintiff carrier shall be entitled to choose the court or tribunal in which he will bring the proceedings from among those having competence pursuant to §4.

§6   Recourse proceedings may not be joined with proceedings for compensation taken by the person entitled under the contract of carriage.

Article 52
Agreements concerning recourse

The carriers may conclude agreements which derogate from Articles 49 and 50.

COUNCIL OF EUROPE CONVENTION ON CYBERCRIME, BUDAPEST, 2001

CHAPTER I
USE OF TERMS

Article 1
Definitions

For the purposes of this Convention:

(a)   'computer system' means any device or a group of inter-connected or related devices, one or more of which, pursuant to a program, performs automatic processing of data;

(b)   'computer data' means any representation of facts, information or concepts in a form suitable for processing in a computer system, including a program suitable to cause a computer system to perform a function;

(c)   'service provider' means:

(i)   any public or private entity that provides to users of its service the ability to communicate by means of a computer system, and

(ii)   any other entity that processes or stores computer data on behalf of such communication service or users of such service.

(d)   'traffic data' means any computer data relating to a communication by means of a computer system, generated by a computer system that formed a part in the chain of communication, indicating the communication's origin, destination, route, time, date, size, duration, or type of underlying service.

CHAPTER II
MEASURES TO BE TAKEN AT THE NATIONAL LEVEL

SECTION 1—SUBSTANTIVE CRIMINAL LAW

TITLE 1
OFFENCES AGAINST THE CONFIDENTIALITY, INTEGRITY AND AVAILABILITY OF COMPUTER DATA AND SYSTEMS

Article 2
Illegal access

Each Party shall adopt such legislative and other measures as may be necessary to establish as criminal offences under its domestic law, when committed intentionally, the access to the whole or any part of a computer system without right. A Party may require that the offence be committed by infringing security measures, with the intent of obtaining computer data or other dishonest intent, or in relation to a computer system that is connected to another computer system.

Article 3
Illegal interception

Each Party shall adopt such legislative and other measures as may be necessary to establish as criminal offences under its domestic law, when committed intentionally, the interception without right, made by technical means, of non-public transmissions of computer data to, from or within a computer system, including electromagnetic emissions from a computer system carrying such computer data. A Party may require that the offence be committed with dishonest intent, or in relation to a computer system that is connected to another computer system.

Article 4
Data interference

1.   Each Party shall adopt such legislative and other measures as may be necessary to establish as criminal offences under its domestic law, when committed intentionally, the damaging, deletion, deterioration, alteration or suppression of computer data without right.
2.   A Party may reserve the right to require that the conduct described in paragraph 1 result in serious harm.

Article 5
System interference

Each Party shall adopt such legislative and other measures as may be necessary to establish as criminal offences under its domestic law, when committed intentionally, the serious hindering without right of the functioning of a computer system by inputting, transmitting, damaging, deleting, deteriorating, altering or suppressing computer data.

Article 6
Misuse of devices

1.   Each Party shall adopt such legislative and other measures as may be necessary to establish as criminal offences under its domestic law, when committed intentionally and without right:

(a)   the production, sale, procurement for use, import, distribution or otherwise making available of:

    (i)   a device, including a computer program, designed or adapted primarily for the purpose of committing any of the offences established in accordance with Article 2 through 5;

    (ii)   a computer password, access code, or similar data by which the whole or any part of a computer system is capable of being accessed,

    with intent that it be used for the purpose of committing any of the offences established in Articles 2 through 5; and

(b)   the possession of an item referred to in paragraphs (a)(1) or (2) above, with intent that it be used for the purpose of committing any of the offences established in Articles 2 through 5. A Party may require by law that a number of such items be possessed before criminal liability attaches.

2.   This article shall not be interpreted as imposing criminal liability where the production, sale, procurement for use, import, distribution or otherwise making available or possession referred to in paragraph 1 of this Article is not for the purpose of committing an offence established in accordance with articles 2 through 5 of this Convention, such as for the authorised testing or protection of a computer system.

3.   Each Party may reserve the right not to apply paragraph 1 of this Article, provided that the reservation does not concern the sale, distribution or otherwise making available of the items referred to in paragraph 1(a)(ii) of this Article.

TITLE 2
COMPUTER-RELATED OFFENCES

Article 7
Computer-related forgery

Each Party shall adopt such legislative and other measures as may be necessary to establish as criminal offences under its domestic law, when committed intentionally and without right, the input, alteration, deletion, or suppression of computer data, resulting in inauthentic data with the intent that it be considered or acted upon for legal purposes as if it were authentic, regardless whether or not the data is directly readable and intelligible. A Party may require an intent to defraud, or similar dishonest intent, before criminal liability attaches.

Article 8
Computer-related fraud

Each Party shall adopt such legislative and other measures as may be necessary to establish as criminal offences under its domestic law, when committed intentionally and without right, the causing of a loss of property to another by:

(a)   any input, alteration, deletion or suppression of computer data,

(b)   any interference with the functioning of a computer system,

with fraudulent or dishonest intent of procuring, without right, an economic benefit for oneself or for another.

TITLE 3
CONTENT-RELATED OFFENCES

Article 9
Offences related to child pornography
[Omitted].

TITLE 4
OFFENCES RELATED TO INFRINGEMENTS OF COPYRIGHT AND RELATED RIGHTS

Article 10
Offences related to infringements of copyright and related rights

1. Each Party shall adopt such legislative and other measures as may be necessary to establish as criminal offences under its domestic law the infringement of copyright, as defined under the law of that Party pursuant to the obligations it has undertaken under the Paris Act of 24 July 1971 revising the Bern Convention for the Protection of Literary and Artistic Works, the Agreement on Trade-Related Aspects of Intellectual Property Rights and the WIPO Copyright Treaty, with the exception of any moral rights conferred by such Conventions, where such acts are committed wilfully, on a commercial scale and by means of a computer system.

2. Each Party shall adopt such legislative and other measures as may be necessary to establish as criminal offences under its domestic law the infringement of related rights, as defined under the law of that Party, pursuant to the obligations it has undertaken under the International Convention for the Protection of Performers, Producers of Phonograms and Broadcasting Organisations (Rome Convention), the Agreement on Trade-Related Aspects of Intellectual Property Rights and the WIPO Performances and Phonograms Treaty, with the exception of any moral rights conferred by such Conventions, where such acts are committed wilfully, on a commercial scale and by means of a computer system.

3. A Party may reserve the right not to impose criminal liability under paragraphs 1 and 2 of this article in limited circumstances, provided that other effective remedies are available and that such reservation does not derogate from the Party's international obligations set forth in the international instruments referred to in paragraphs 1 and 2 of this article.

TITLE 5
ANCILLARY LIABILITY AND SANCTIONS

Article 11
Attempt and aiding or abetting

1. Each Party shall adopt such legislative and other measures as may be necessary to establish as criminal offences under its domestic law, when committed intentionally, aiding or abetting the commission of any of the offences established in accordance with Articles 2 through 10 of the present Convention with intent that such offence be committed.

2. Each Party shall adopt such legislative and other measures as may be necessary to establish as criminal offences under its domestic law, when committed intentionally, an attempt to commit any of the offences established in accordance with Articles 3 through 5, 7, 8, 9(1)a and 9(1)c of this Convention.

3. Each Party may reserve the right not to apply, in whole or in part, paragraph 2 of this article.

Article 12
Corporate liability

1. Each Party shall adopt such legislative and other measures as may be necessary to ensure that a legal person can be held liable for a criminal offence established in accordance with this Convention, committed for its benefit by any natural person,

acting either individually or as part of an organ of the legal person, who has a leading position within the legal person, based on:

(a)   a power of representation of the legal person;
(b)   an authority to take decisions on behalf of the legal person;
(c)   an authority to exercise control within the legal person.

2.   Apart from the cases already provided for in paragraph 1, each Party shall take the measures necessary to ensure that a legal person can be held liable where the lack of supervision or control by a natural person referred to in paragraph 1 has made possible the commission of a criminal offence established in accordance with this Convention for the benefit of that legal person by a natural person acting under its authority.

3.   Subject to the legal principles of the Party, the liability of a legal person may be criminal, civil or administrative.

4.   Such liability shall be without prejudice to the criminal liability of the natural persons who have committed the offence.

Article 13
Sanctions and measures

1.   Each Party shall adopt such legislative and other measures as may be necessary to ensure that the criminal offences established in accordance with Articles 2 through 11 are punishable by effective, proportionate and dissuasive sanctions, which include deprivation of liberty.

2.   Each Party shall ensure that legal persons held liable in accordance with Article 12 shall be subject to effective, proportionate and dissuasive criminal or non-criminal sanctions or measures, including monetary sanctions.

SECTION 2—PROCEDURAL LAW

TITLE 1
COMMON PROVISIONS

Article 14
Scope of procedural provisions

1.   Each Party shall adopt such legislative and other measures as may be necessary to establish the powers and procedures provided for in this Section for the purpose of specific criminal investigations or proceedings.

2.   Except as specifically otherwise provided in Article 21, each Party shall apply the powers and procedures referred to in paragraph 1 to:

(a)   the criminal offences established in accordance with Articles 2 through 11 of this Convention;
(b)   other criminal offences committed by means of a computer system; and
(c)   the collection of evidence in electronic form of a criminal offence.

3.   (a)   Each Party may reserve the right to apply the measures referred to in Article 20 only to offences or categories of offences specified in the reservation, provided that the range of such offences or categories of offences is not more restricted than the range of offences to which it applies the measures referred to in Article 21. Each Party shall consider restricting such a reservation to enable the broadest application of the measure referred to in Article 20.

(b)   Where a Party, due to limitations in its legislation in force at the time of the adoption of the present Convention, is not able to apply the measures referred to in Articles 20 and 21 to communications being transmitted within a computer system of a service provider, which system:

(i)   is being operated for the benefit of a closed group of users, and

(ii)   does not employ public communications networks and is not connected with another computer system, whether public or private,

that Party may reserve the right not to apply these measures to such communications. Each Party shall consider restricting such a reservation to enable the broadest application of the measures referred to in Articles 20 and 21.

Article 15
Conditions and safeguards

1.   Each Party shall ensure that the establishment, implementation and application of the powers and procedures provided for in this Section are subject to conditions and safeguards provided for under its domestic law, which shall provide for the adequate protection of human rights and liberties, including rights arising pursuant to obligations it has undertaken under the 1950 Council of Europe Convention for the Protection of Human Rights and Fundamental Freedoms, the 1966 United Nations International Covenant on Civil and Political Rights, and other applicable international human rights instruments, and which shall incorporate the principle of proportionality.

2.   Such conditions and safeguards shall, as appropriate in view of the nature of the power or procedure concerned, *inter alia*, include judicial or other independent supervision, grounds justifying application, and limitation on the scope and the duration of such power or procedure.

3.   To the extent that it is consistent with the public interest, in particular the sound administration of justice, a Party shall consider the impact of the powers and procedures in this Section upon the rights, responsibilities and legitimate interests of third parties.

TITLE 2
EXPEDITED PRESERVATION OF STORED COMPUTER DATA

Article 16
Expedited preservation of stored computer data

1.   Each Party shall adopt such legislative and other measures as may be necessary to enable its competent authorities to order or similarly obtain the expeditious preservation of specified computer data, including traffic data, that has been stored by means of a computer system, in particular where there are grounds to believe that the computer data is particularly vulnerable to loss or modification.

2.   Where a Party gives effect to paragraph 1 above by means of an order to a person to preserve specified stored computer data in the person's possession or control, the Party shall adopt such legislative and other measures as may be necessary to oblige that person to preserve and maintain the integrity of that computer data for a period of time as long as necessary, up to a maximum of 90 days, to enable the competent authorities to seek its disclosure. A Party may provide for such an order to be subsequently renewed.

3.   Each Party shall adopt such legislative or other measures as may be necessary to oblige the custodian or other person who is to preserve the computer data to keep confidential the undertaking of such procedures for the period of time provided for by its domestic law.

4.   The powers and procedures referred to in this article shall be subject to Articles 14 and 15.

Article 17
Expedited preservation and partial disclosure of traffic data

1. Each Party shall adopt, in respect of traffic data that is to be preserved under Article 16, such legislative and other measures as may be necessary to:
    (a) ensure that such expeditious preservation of traffic data is available regardless of whether one or more service providers were involved in the transmission of that communication; and
    (b) ensure the expeditious disclosure to the Party's competent authority, or a person designated by that authority, of a sufficient amount of traffic data to enable the Party to identify the service providers and the path through which the communication was transmitted.
2. The powers and procedures referred to in this article shall be subject to Articles 14 and 15.

TITLE 3
PRODUCTION ORDER

Article 18
Production order

1. Each Party shall adopt such legislative and other measures as may be necessary to empower its competent authorities to order:
    (a) a person in its territory to submit specified computer data in that person's possession or control, which is stored in a computer system or a computer-data storage medium; and
    (b) a service provider offering its services in the territory of the Party to submit subscriber information relating to such services in that service provider's possession or control;
2. The powers and procedures referred to in this article shall be subject to Articles 14 and 15.
3. For the purpose of this article, 'subscriber information' means any information, contained in the form of computer data or any other form, that is held by a service provider, relating to subscribers of its services, other than traffic or content data, by which can be established:
    (a) the type of the communication service used, the technical provisions taken thereto and the period of service;
    (b) the subscriber's identity, postal or geographic address, telephone and other access number, billing and payment information, available on the basis of the service agreement or arrangement;
    (c) any other information on the site of the installation of communication equipment available on the basis of the service agreement or arrangement.

TITLE 4
SEARCH AND SEIZURE OF STORED COMPUTER DATA

Article 19
Search and seizure of stored computer data

1. Each Party shall adopt such legislative and other measures as may be necessary to empower its competent authorities to search or similarly access:
    (a) a computer system or part of it and computer data stored therein; and
    (b) a computer-data storage medium in which computer data may be stored in its territory.

2.   Each Party shall adopt such legislative and other measures as may be necessary to ensure that where its authorities search or similarly access a specific computer system or part of it, pursuant to paragraph 1(a), and have grounds to believe that the data sought is stored in another computer system or part of it in its territory, and such data is lawfully accessible from or available to the initial system, such authorities shall be able to expeditiously extend the search or similar accessing to the other system.

3.   Each Party shall adopt such legislative and other measures as may be necessary to empower its competent authorities to seize or similarly secure computer data accessed according to paragraphs 1 or 2. These measures shall include the power to:
        (a)   seize or similarly secure a computer system or part of it or a computer-data storage medium;
        (b)   make and retain a copy of those computer data;
        (c)   maintain the integrity of the relevant stored computer data; and
        (d)   render inaccessible or remove those computer data in the accessed computer system.

4.   Each Party shall adopt such legislative and other measures as may be necessary to empower its competent authorities to order any person who has knowledge about the functioning of the computer system or measures applied to protect the computer data therein to provide, as is reasonable, the necessary information, to enable the undertaking of the measures referred to in paragraphs 1 and 2.

5.   The powers and procedures referred to in this article shall be subject to Articles 14 and 15.

TITLE 5
REAL-TIME COLLECTION OF COMPUTER DATA

Article 20
Real-time collection of traffic data

1.   Each Party shall adopt such legislative and other measures as may be necessary to empower its competent authorities to:
        (a)   collect or record through application of technical means on the territory of that Party, and
        (b)   compel a service provider, within its existing technical capability:
                (i)   to collect or record through application of technical means on the territory of that Party, or
                (ii)   to co-operate and assist the competent authorities in the collection or recording of,
                traffic data, in real-time, associated with specified communications in its territory transmitted by means of a computer system.

2.   Where a Party, due to the established principles of its domestic legal system, cannot adopt the measures referred to in paragraph 1(a), it may instead adopt legislative and other measures as may be necessary to ensure the real-time collection or recording of traffic data associated with specified communications in its territory through the application of technical means on that territory.

3.   Each Party shall adopt such legislative and other measures as may be necessary to oblige a service provider to keep confidential the fact of the execution of any power provided for in this Article and any information relating to it.

4.   The powers and procedures referred to in this article shall be subject to Articles 14 and 15.

Article 21
Interception of content data

1.   Each Party shall adopt such legislative and other measures as may be necessary, in relation to a range of serious offences to be determined by domestic law, to empower its competent authorities to:
       (a)   collect or record through application of technical means on the territory of that Party, and
       (b)   compel a service provider, within its existing technical capability,
              (i)   to collect or record through application of technical means on the territory of that Party, or
              (ii)   to co-operate and assist the competent authorities in the collection or recording of,
              content data, in real-time, of specified communications in its territory transmitted by means of a computer system.
2.   Where a Party, due to the established principles of its domestic legal system, cannot adopt the measures referred to in paragraph 1(a), it may instead adopt legislative and other measures as may be necessary to ensure the real-time collection or recording of content data of specified communications in its territory through application of technical means on that territory.
3.   Each Party shall adopt such legislative and other measures as may be necessary to oblige a service provider to keep confidential the fact of and any information about the execution of any power provided for in this Article.
4.   The powers and procedures referred to in this article shall be subject to Articles 14 and 15.

SECTION 3—JURISDICTION

Article 22
Jurisdiction

1.   Each Party shall adopt such legislative and other measures as may be necessary to establish jurisdiction over any offence established in accordance with Articles 2 through 11 of this Convention, when the offence is committed:
       (a)   in its territory; or
       (b)   on board a ship flying the flag of that Party; or
       (c)   on board an aircraft registered under the laws of that Party; or
       (d)   by one of its nationals, if the offence is punishable under criminal law where it was committed or if the offence is committed outside the territorial jurisdiction of any State.
2.   Each Party may reserve the right not to apply or to apply only in specific cases or conditions the jurisdiction rules laid down in paragraphs (1)b through (1)d of this article or any part thereof.
3.   Each Party shall adopt such measures as may be necessary to establish jurisdiction over the offences referred to in Article 24, paragraph (1) of this Convention, in cases where an alleged offender is present in its territory and it does not extradite him or her to another Party, solely on the basis of his or her nationality, after a request for extradition.
4.   This Convention does not exclude any criminal jurisdiction exercised in accordance with domestic law.
5.   When more than one Party claims jurisdiction over an alleged offence established in accordance with this Convention, the Parties involved shall, where appropriate, consult with a view to determining the most appropriate jurisdiction for prosecution.

CHAPTER III
INTERNATIONAL CO-OPERATION

SECTION 1—GENERAL PRINCIPLES

TITLE 1
GENERAL PRINCIPLES RELATING TO INTERNATIONAL CO-OPERATION

Article 23
General principles relating to international co-operation

The Parties shall co-operate with each other, in accordance with the provisions of this chapter, and through application of relevant international instruments on international co-operation in criminal matters, arrangements agreed on the basis of uniform or reciprocal legislation, and domestic laws, to the widest extent possible for the purposes of investigations or proceedings concerning criminal offences related to computer systems and data, or for the collection of evidence in electronic form of a criminal offence.

TITLE 2
PRINCIPLES RELATING TO EXTRADITION

Article 24
Extradition

1. (a)   This article applies to extradition between Parties for the criminal offences established in accordance with Articles 2 through 11 of this Convention, provided that they are punishable under the laws of both Parties concerned by deprivation of liberty for a maximum period of at least one year, or by a more severe penalty.

    (b)   Where a different minimum penalty is to be applied under an arrangement agreed on the basis of uniform or reciprocal legislation or an extradition treaty, including the European Convention on Extradition (ETS No. 24), applicable between two or more parties, the minimum penalty provided for under such arrangement or treaty shall apply.

2. The criminal offences described in paragraph 1 of this Article shall be deemed to be included as extraditable offences in any extradition treaty existing between or among the Parties. The Parties undertake to include such offences as extraditable offences in any extradition treaty to be concluded between or among them.

3. If a Party that makes extradition conditional on the existence of a treaty receives a request for extradition from another Party with which it does not have an extradition treaty, it may consider this Convention as the legal basis for extradition with respect to any criminal offence referred to in paragraph 1 of this article.

4. Parties that do not make extradition conditional on the existence of a treaty shall recognise the criminal offences referred to in paragraph 1 of this article as extraditable offences between themselves.

5. Extradition shall be subject to the conditions provided for by the law of the requested Party or by applicable extradition treaties, including the grounds on which the requested Party may refuse extradition.

6. If extradition for a criminal offence referred to in paragraph 1 of this article is refused solely on the basis of the nationality of the person sought, or because the requested Party deems that it has jurisdiction over the offence, the requested Party shall submit the case at the request of the requesting Party to its competent authorities for the purpose of prosecution and shall report the final outcome to the

requesting Party in due course. Those authorities shall take their decision and conduct their investigations and proceedings in the same manner as in the case of any other offence of a comparable nature under the law of that Party.

7. (a) Each Party shall, at the time of signature or when depositing its instrument of ratification, acceptance, approval or accession, communicate to the Secretary General of the Council of Europe the name and address of each authority responsible for making or receiving requests for extradition or provisional arrest in the absence of a treaty.

    (b) The Secretary General of the Council of Europe shall set up and keep updated a register of authorities so designated by the Parties. Each Party shall ensure that the details held on the register are correct at all times.

TITLE 3
GENERAL PRINCIPLES RELATING TO MUTUAL ASSISTANCE

Article 25
General principles relating to mutual assistance

1. The Parties shall afford one another mutual assistance to the widest extent possible for the purpose of investigations or proceedings concerning criminal offences related to computer systems and data, or for the collection of evidence in electronic form of a criminal offence.

2. Each Party shall also adopt such legislative and other measures as may be necessary to carry out the obligations set forth in Articles 27 through 35.

3. Each Party may, in urgent circumstances, make requests for mutual assistance or communications related thereto by expedited means of communication, including fax or e-mail, to the extent that such means provide appropriate levels of security and authentication (including the use of encryption, where necessary), with formal confirmation to follow, where required by the requested Party. The requested Party shall accept and respond to the request by any such expedited means of communication.

4. Except as otherwise specifically provided in articles in this chapter, mutual assistance shall be subject to the conditions provided for by the law of the requested Party or by applicable mutual assistance treaties, including the grounds on which the requested Party may refuse co-operation. The requested Party shall not exercise the right to refuse mutual assistance in relation to the offences referred to in Articles 2 to 11 solely on the ground that the request concerns an offence which it considers a fiscal offence.

5. Where, in accordance with the provisions of this chapter, the requested Party is permitted to make mutual assistance conditional upon the existence of dual criminality, that condition shall be deemed fulfilled, irrespective of whether its laws place the offence within the same category of offence or denominate the offence by the same terminology as the requesting Party, if the conduct underlying the offence for which assistance is sought is a criminal offence under its laws.

Article 26
Spontaneous information

1. A Party may, within the limits of its domestic law and without prior request, forward to another Party information obtained within the framework of its own investigations when it considers that the disclosure of such information might assist the receiving Party in initiating or carrying out investigations or proceedings concerning criminal offences established in accordance with this Convention or might lead to a request for co-operation by that Party under this chapter.

2. Prior to providing such information, the providing Party may request that it be kept confidential or used subject to conditions. If the receiving Party cannot comply with such request, it shall notify the providing Party, which shall then determine whether the information should nevertheless be provided. If the receiving Party accepts the information subject to the conditions, it shall be bound by them.

TITLE 4
PROCEDURES PERTAINING TO MUTUAL ASSISTANCE REQUESTS IN THE ABSENCE OF APPLICABLE INTERNATIONAL AGREEMENTS

Article 27
Procedures pertaining to mutual assistance requests in the absence of applicable international agreements

1. Where there is no mutual assistance treaty or arrangement on the basis of uniform or reciprocal legislation in force between the requesting and requested Parties, the provisions of paragraphs 2 through 9 of this article shall apply. The provisions of this article shall not apply where such treaty, arrangement or legislation is available, unless the Parties concerned agree to apply any or all of the remainder of this article in lieu thereof.

2. (a) Each Party shall designate a central authority or authorities that shall be responsible for sending and answering requests for mutual assistance, the execution of such requests, or the transmission of them to the authorities competent for their execution.

    (b) The central authorities shall communicate directly with each other.

    (c) Each Party shall, at the time of signature or when depositing its instrument of ratification, acceptance, approval or accession, communicate to the Secretary General of the Council of Europe the names and addresses of the authorities designated in pursuance of this paragraph.

    (d) The Secretary General of the Council of Europe shall set up and keep updated a register of central authorities so designated by the Parties. Each Party shall ensure that the details held on the register are correct at all times.

3. Mutual assistance requests under this Article shall be executed in accordance with the procedures specified by the requesting Party except where incompatible with the law of the requested Party.

4. The requested Party may, in addition to the grounds for refusal available under Article 25, paragraph (4), refuse assistance if:

    (a) the request concerns an offence which the requested Party considers a political offence or an offence connected with a political offence; or

    (b) it considers that execution of the request is likely to prejudice its sovereignty, security, *ordre public* or other essential interests.

5. The requested Party may postpone action on a request if such action would prejudice criminal investigations or proceedings conducted by its authorities.

6. Before refusing or postponing assistance, the requested Party shall, where appropriate after having consulted with the requesting Party, consider whether the request may be granted partially or subject to such conditions as it deems necessary.

7. The requested Party shall promptly inform the requesting Party of the outcome of the execution of a request for assistance. Reasons shall be given for refusal or postponement of the request. The requested Party shall also inform the requesting Party of any reasons that render impossible the execution of the request or are likely to delay it significantly.

8. The requesting Party may request that the requested Party keep confidential the fact of any request made under this chapter as well as its subject, except to the extent necessary for its execution. If the requested Party cannot comply with the

request for confidentiality, it shall promptly inform the requesting Party, which shall then determine whether the request should nevertheless be executed.

9.   (a)   In the event of urgency, requests for mutual assistance or communications related thereto may be sent directly by judicial authorities of the requesting Party to such authorities of the requested Party. In any such cases a copy shall be sent at the same time to the central authority of the requested Party through the central authority of the requesting Party.

      (b)   Any request or communication under this paragraph may be made through the International Criminal Police Organisation (Interpol).

      (c)   Where a request is made pursuant to subparagraph (a) and the authority is not competent to deal with the request, it shall refer the request to the competent national authority and inform directly the requesting Party that it has done so.

      (d)   Requests or communications made under this paragraph that do not involve coercive action may be directly transmitted by the competent authorities of the requesting Party to the competent authorities of the requested Party.

      (e)   Each Party may, at the time of signature or when depositing its instrument of ratification, acceptance, approval or accession inform the Secretary General of the Council of Europe that, for reasons of efficiency, requests made under this paragraph are to be addressed to its central authority.

Article 28
Confidentiality and limitation on use

1.   When there is no mutual assistance treaty or arrangement on the basis of uniform or reciprocal legislation in force between the requesting and the requested Parties, the provisions of this article shall apply. The provisions of this article shall not apply where such treaty, arrangement or legislation exists, unless the Parties concerned agree to apply any or all of the remainder of this article in lieu thereof.

2.   The requested Party may make the furnishing of information or material in response to a request dependent on the condition that it is:

      (a)   kept confidential where the request for mutual legal assistance could not be complied with in the absence of such condition, or

      (b)   not used for investigations or proceedings other than those stated in the request.

3.   If the requesting Party cannot comply with a condition referred to in paragraph 2, it shall promptly inform the other Party, which shall then determine whether the information is nevertheless provided. When the requesting Party accepts the condition, it shall be bound by it.

4.   Any Party that furnishes information or material subject to a condition referred to in paragraph 2 may require the other Party to explain, in relation to that condition, the use made of such information or material.

SECTION 2—SPECIFIC PROVISIONS

TITLE 1
MUTUAL ASSISTANCE REGARDING PROVISIONAL MEASURES

Article 29
Expedited preservation of stored computer data

1.   A Party may request another Party to order or otherwise obtain the expeditious preservation of data stored by means of a computer system, which is located within the territory of that other Party and in respect of which the requesting Party intends

to submit a request for mutual assistance for the search or similar access, seizure or similar securing, or disclosure of the data.

2. A request for preservation made under paragraph 1 shall specify:
   (a) the authority that is seeking the preservation;
   (b) the offence that is the subject of a criminal investigation or proceeding and a brief summary of related facts;
   (c) the stored computer data to be preserved and its relationship to the offence;
   (d) any available information to identify the custodian of the stored computer data or the location of the computer system;
   (e) the necessity of the preservation; and
   (f) that the Party intends to submit a request for mutual assistance for the search or similar access, seizure or similar securing, or disclosure of the stored computer data.

3. Upon receiving the request from another Party, the requested Party shall take all appropriate measures to preserve expeditiously the specified data in accordance with its domestic law. For the purposes of responding to a request, dual criminality shall not be required as a condition to providing such preservation.

4. A Party that requires dual criminality as a condition for responding to a request for mutual assistance for the search or similar access, seizure or similar securing, or disclosure of stored data may, in respect of offences other than those established in accordance with Articles 2 through 11 of this Convention, reserve the right to refuse the request for preservation under this article in cases where it has reason to believe that at the time of disclosure the condition of dual criminality cannot be fulfilled.

5. In addition, a request for preservation may only be refused if:
   (a) the request concerns an offence which the requested Party considers a political offence or an offence connected with a political offence; or
   (b) the requested Party considers that execution of the request is likely to prejudice its sovereignty, security, *ordre public* or other essential interests.

6. Where the requested Party believes that preservation will not ensure the future availability of the data or will threaten the confidentiality of or otherwise prejudice the requesting Party's investigation, it shall promptly so inform the requesting Party, which shall then determine whether the request should nevertheless be executed.

7. Any preservation effected in response to the request referred to in paragraph 1 shall be for a period not less than 60 days in order to enable the requesting Party to submit a request for the search or similar access, seizure or similar securing, or disclosure of the data. Following the receipt of such a request, the data shall continue to be preserved pending a decision on that request.

Article 30
Expedited disclosure of preserved traffic data

1. Where, in the course of the execution of a request made under Article 29 to preserve traffic data concerning a specific communication, the requested Party discovers that a service provider in another State was involved in the transmission of the communication, the requested Party shall expeditiously disclose to the requesting Party a sufficient amount of traffic data in order to identify that service provider and the path through which the communication was transmitted.

2. Disclosure of traffic data under paragraph 1 may only be withheld if:
   (a) the request concerns an offence which the requested Party considers a political offence or an offence connected with a political offence; or
   (b) the requested Party considers that execution of the request is likely to prejudice its sovereignty, security, *ordre public* or other essential interests.

TITLE 2
MUTUAL ASSISTANCE REGARDING INVESTIGATIVE POWERS

Article 31
Mutual assistance regarding accessing of stored computer data

1. A Party may request another Party to search or similarly access, seize or similarly secure, and disclose data stored by means of a computer system located within the territory of the requested Party, including data that has been preserved pursuant to Article 29.
2. The requested Party shall respond to the request through application of international instruments, arrangements and laws referred to in Article 23, and in accordance with other relevant provisions of this Chapter.
3. The request shall be responded to on an expedited basis where:
    (a) there are grounds to believe that relevant data is particularly vulnerable to loss or modification; or
    (b) the instruments, arrangements and laws referred to in paragraph 2 otherwise provide for expedited co-operation.

Article 32
Trans-border access to stored computer data with consent or where publicly available

A Party may, without obtaining the authorisation of another Party:
(a) access publicly available (open source) stored computer data, regardless of where the data is located geographically; or
(b) access or receive, through a computer system in its territory, stored computer data located in another Party, if the Party obtains the lawful and voluntary consent of the person who has the lawful authority to disclose the data to the Party through that computer system.

Article 33
Mutual assistance regarding the real-time collection of traffic data

1. The Parties shall provide mutual assistance to each other in the real-time collection of traffic data associated with specified communications in their territory transmitted by means of a computer system. Subject to the provisions of paragraph 2, assistance shall be governed by the conditions and procedures provided for under domestic law.
2. Each Party shall provide such assistance at least with respect to criminal offences for which real-time collection of traffic data would be available in a similar domestic case.

Article 34
Mutual assistance regarding the interception of content data

The Parties shall provide mutual assistance to each other in the real-time collection or recording of content data of specified communications transmitted by means of a computer system to the extent permitted under their applicable treaties and domestic laws.

TITLE 3
24/7 NETWORK

Article 35
24/7 Network

1. Each Party shall designate a point of contact available on a 24 hour, 7 day per week basis in order to ensure the provision of immediate assistance for the purpose of investigations or proceedings concerning criminal offences related to computer systems and data, or for the collection of evidence in electronic form of a criminal offence. Such assistance shall include facilitating, or, if permitted by its domestic law and practice, directly carrying out the following measures:
    (a)   the provision of technical advice;
    (b)   the preservation of data pursuant to Articles 29 and 30; and
    (c)   the collection of evidence, the provision of legal information, and locating of suspects.
2. (a)   A Party's point of contact shall have the capacity to carry out communications with the point of contact of another Party on an expedited basis.
    (b)   If the point of contact designated by a Party is not part of that Party's authority or authorities responsible for international mutual assistance or extradition, the point of contact shall ensure that it is able to co-ordinate with such authority or authorities on an expedited basis.
3. Each Party shall ensure that trained and equipped personnel are available in order to facilitate the operation of the network.

CHAPTER IV
FINAL PROVISIONS

Articles 36–48 [Omitted].

SECTION V
RULES AND MODEL LAWS

1.   Scope of application
These rules shall apply whenever the parties so agree.

2.   Definitions
(a)   'Contract of Carriage', means any agreement to carry goods wholly or partly by sea.
(b)   'EDI', means Electronic Data Interchange, that is, the interchange of trade data effected by teletransmission.
(c)   'UN/EDIFACT' means the United Nations Rules for Electronic Data Interchange for Administration, Commerce and Transport.
(d)   'Transmission' means one or more messages electronically sent together as one unit of dispatch which includes heading and terminating data.
(e)   'Confirmation' means a Transmission which advises that the content of a Transmission appears to be complete and correct, without prejudice to any subsequent consideration or action that the content may warrant.
(f)   'Private Key' means any technically appropriate form, such as a combination of numbers and/or letters, which the parties may agree for securing the authenticity and integrity of a Transmission.
(g)   'Holder' means the party who is entitled to the rights described in Article 7(a) by virtue of its possession of a valid Private Key.
(h)   'Electronic Monitoring System' means the device by which a computer system can be examined for the transactions that it recorded, such as a Trade Data Log or an Audit Trail.
(i)   'Electronic Storage' means any temporary, intermediate or permanent storage of electronic data including the primary and the back-up storage of such data.

3.   Rules of procedure
(a)   When not in conflict with these Rules, the Uniform Rules of Conduct for Interchange of Trade Data by Teletransmission, 1987 (UNCID) shall govern the conduct between the parties.
(b)   The EDI under these Rules should conform with the relevant UN/EDIFACT standards. However, the parties may use any other method of trade data interchange acceptable to all of the users.
(c)   Unless otherwise agreed, the document format for the Contract of Carriage shall conform to the UN Layout Key or compatible national standard for bills of lading.
(d)   Unless otherwise agreed, a recipient of a Transmission is not authorised to act on a Transmission unless he has sent a Confirmation.
(e)   In the event of a dispute arising between the parties as to the data actually transmitted, an Electronic Monitoring System may be used to verify the data received. Data concerning other transactions not related to the data in dispute are to be considered as trade secrets and thus not available for examination. If such data are unavoidably revealed as part of the examination of the Electronic Monitoring System, they must be treated as confidential and not released to any outside party or used for any other purpose.
(f)   Any transfer of rights to the goods shall be considered to be private information, and shall not be released to any outside party not connected to the transport or clearance of the goods.

4.   **Form and content of the receipt message**
  (a)   The carrier, upon receiving the goods from the shipper, shall give notice of the receipt of the goods to the shipper by a message at the electronic address specified by the shipper.
  (b)   This receipt message shall include—
    (i)   the name of the shipper;
    (ii)   the description of the goods, with any representations and reservations, in the same tenor as would be required if a paper bill of lading were issued;
    (iii)   the date and place of the receipt of the goods;
    (iv)   a reference to the carrier's terms and conditions of carriage; and
    (v)   the Private Key to be used in subsequent Transmissions.
    The shipper must confirm this receipt message to the carrier, upon which Confirmation the shipper shall be the Holder.
  (c)   Upon demand of the Holder, the receipt message shall be updated with the date and place of shipment as soon as the goods have been loaded on board.
  (d)   The information contained in (ii), (iii) and (iv) of paragraph (b) above including the date and place of shipment if updated in accordance with paragraph (c) of this Rule, shall have the same force and effect as if the receipt message were contained in a paper bill of lading.

5.   **Terms and conditions of the Contract of Carriage**
  (a)   It is agreed and understood that whenever the carrier makes a reference to its terms and conditions of carriage, these terms and conditions shall form part of the Contract of Carriage.
  (b)   Such terms and conditions must be readily available to the parties to the Contract of Carriage.
  (c)   In the event of any conflict or inconsistency between such terms and conditions and these Rules, these Rules shall prevail.

6.   **Applicable law**
  The Contract of Carriage shall be subject to any international convention or national law which would have been compulsorily applicable if a paper bill of lading had been issued.

7.   **Right of Control and Transfer**
  (a)   The Holder is the only party who may, as against the carrier—
    (1)   claim delivery of the goods;
    (2)   nominate the consignee or substitute a nominated consignee for any other party, including itself;
    (3)   transfer the Right of Control and Transfer to another party;
    (4)   instruct the carrier on any other subject concerning the goods, in accordance with the terms and conditions of the Contract of Carriage, as if he were the holder of a paper bill of lading.
  (b)   A transfer of the Right of Control and Transfer shall be effected: (i) by notification of the current Holder to the carrier of its intention to transfer its Right of Control and Transfer to a proposed new Holder, and (ii) confirmation by the carrier of such notification message, whereupon (iii) the carrier shall transmit the information as referred to in article 4 (except for the Private Key) to the proposed new Holder, whereafter (iv) the proposed new Holder shall advise the carrier of its acceptance of the Right of Control and Transfer, whereupon (v) the carrier shall cancel the current Private Key and issue a new Private Key to the new Holder.
  (c)   If the proposed new Holder advises the carrier that it does not accept the Right of Control and Transfer or fails to advise the carrier of such acceptance within a reasonable time, the proposed transfer of the Right of Control and

Transfer shall not take place. The carrier shall notify the current Holder accordingly and the current Private Key shall retain its validity.

(d)   The transfer of the Right of Control and Transfer in the manner described above shall have the same effects as the transfer of such rights under a paper bill of lading.

8.   The Private Key

(a)   The Private Key is unique to each successive Holder. It is not transferable by the Holder. The carrier and the Holder shall each maintain the security of the Private Key.

(b)   The carrier shall only be obliged to send a Confirmation of an electronic message to the last Holder to whom it issued a Private Key, when such Holder secures the Transmission containing such electronic message by the use of the Private Key.

(c)   The Private Key must be separate and distinct from any means used to identify the Contract of Carriage, and any security password or identification used to access the computer network.

9.   Delivery

(a)   The carrier shall notify the Holder of the place and date of intended delivery of the goods. Upon such notification the Holder has a duty to nominate a consignee and to give adequate delivery instructions to the carrier with verification by the Private Key. In the absence of such nomination, the Holder will be deemed to be the consignee.

(b)   The carrier shall deliver the goods to the consignee upon production of proper identification in accordance with the delivery instructions specified in paragraph (a) above; such delivery shall automatically cancel the Private Key.

(c)   The carrier shall be under no liability for misdelivery if it can prove that it exercised reasonable care to ascertain that the party who claimed to be the consignee was in fact that party.

10.   Option to receive a paper document

(a)   The Holder has the option at any time prior to delivery of the goods to demand from the carrier a paper bill of lading. Such document shall be made available at a location to be determined by the Holder, provided that no carrier shall be obliged to make such document available at a place where it has no facilities and in such instance the carrier shall only be obliged to make the document available at the facility nearest to the location determined by the Holder. The carrier shall not be responsible for delays in delivering the goods resulting from the Holder exercising the above option.

(b)   The carrier has the option at any time prior to delivery of the goods to issue to the Holder a paper bill of lading unless the exercise of such option could result in undue delay or disrupts the delivery of the goods.

(c)   A bill of lading issued under Rules 10(a) or (b) shall include: the information set out in the receipt message referred to in Rule 4 (except for the Private Key); and (ii) a statement to the effect that the bill of lading has been issued upon termination of the procedures for EDI under the CMI Rules for Electronic Bills of Lading. The aforementioned bill of lading shall be issued at the option of the Holder either to the order of the Holder whose name for this purpose shall then be inserted in the bill of lading or 'to bearer'.

(d)   The issuance of a paper bill of lading under Rule 10(a) or (b) shall cancel the Private Key and terminate the procedures for EDI under these Rules. Termination of these procedures by the Holder or the carrier will not relieve any of the parties to the Contract of Carriage of their rights, obligations or liabilities while performing under the present Rules nor of their rights, obligations or liabilities under the Contract of Carriage.

(e)   The Holder may demand at any time the issuance of a print-out of the receipt message referred to in Rule 4 (except for the Private Key) marked as 'non-negotiable copy'. The issuance of such a print-out shall not cancel the Private Key nor terminate the procedures for EDI.

11. Electronic data is equivalent to writing

The carrier and the shipper and all subsequent parties utilizing these procedures agree that any national or local law, custom or practice requiring the Contract of Carriage to be evidenced in writing and signed, is satisfied by the transmitted and confirmed electronic data residing on computer data storage media displayable in human language on a video screen or as printed out by a computer. In agreeing to adopt these Rules, the parties shall be taken to have agreed not to raise the defence that this contract is not in writing.

CMI UNIFORM RULES FOR SEA WAYBILLS 1990

---

1. Scope of application

(i)   These Rules shall be called the 'CMI Uniforms Rules for Sea Waybills'.

(ii)   They shall apply when adopted by a contract of carriage which is not covered by a bill of lading or similar document of title, whether the contract be in writing or not.

2. Definitions

In these Rules—

'Contract of carriage' shall mean any contract of carriage subject to these Rules which is to be performed wholly or partly by sea.

'Goods' shall mean any goods carried or received for carriage under a contract of carriage.

'Carrier' and 'Shipper' shall mean the parties named in or identifiable as such from the contract of carriage.

'Consignee' shall mean the party named in or identifiable as such from the contract of carriage, or any person substituted as consignee in accordance with rule 6(i).

'Right of Control' shall mean the rights and obligations referred to in rule 6.

3. Agency

(i)   The shipper on entering into the contract of carriage does so not only on his own behalf but also as agent for and on behalf of the consignee, and warrants to the carrier that he has authority so to do.

(ii)   This rule shall apply if, and only if, it be necessary by the law applicable to the contract of carriage so as to enable the consignee to sue and be sued thereon. The consignee shall be under no greater liability than he would have been had the contract of carriage been covered by a bill of lading or similar document of title.

4. Rights and responsibilities

(i)   The contract of carriage shall be subject to any International Convention or National Law which is, or if the contract of carriage had been covered by a bill of lading or similar document of title would have been, compulsorily applicable thereto. Such convention or law shall apply notwithstanding anything inconsistent therewith in the contract of carriage.

(ii)   Subject always to subrule (i), the contract of carriage is governed by:

(a) these Rules;

(b) unless otherwise agreed by the parties, the carrier's standard terms and conditions for the trade, if any, including any terms and conditions relating to the non-sea part of the carriage;

(c) any other terms and conditions agreed by the parties.

(iii) In the event of any inconsistency between the terms and conditions mentioned under subrule (ii)(b) or (c) and these Rules, these Rules shall prevail.

5. Description of the goods

(i) The shipper warrants the accuracy of the particulars furnished by him relating to the goods, and shall indemnify the carrier against any loss, damage or expense resulting from any inaccuracy.

(ii) In the absence of reservation by the carrier, any statement in a sea waybill or similar document as to the quantity or condition of the goods shall:

(a) as between the carrier and the shipper be *prima facie* evidence of receipt of the goods as so stated;

(b) as between the carrier and the consignee be conclusive evidence of receipt of the goods as so stated, and proof to the contrary shall not be permitted, provided always that the consignee has acted in good faith.

6. Right of control

(i) Unless the shipper has exercised his option under subrule (ii) below, he shall be the only party entitled to give the carrier instructions in relation to the contract of carriage. Unless prohibited by the applicable law, he shall be entitled to change the name of the consignee at any time up to the consignee claiming delivery of the goods after their arrival at destination, provided he gives the carrier reasonable notice in writing, or by some other means acceptable to the carrier, thereby undertaking to indemnify the carrier against any additional expense caused thereby.

(ii) The shipper shall have the option, to be exercised not later than the receipt of the goods by the carrier, to transfer the right of control to the consignee. The exercise of this option must be noted on the sea waybill or similar document, if any. Where the option has been exercised the consignee shall have such rights as are referred to in subrule (i) above and the shipper shall cease to have such rights.

7. Delivery

(i) The carrier shall deliver the goods to the consignee upon production of proper identification.

(ii) The carrier shall be under no liability for wrong delivery if he can prove that he has exercised reasonable care to ascertain that the party claiming to be the consignee is in fact that party.

8. Validity

In the event of anything contained in these Rules or any such provisions as are incorporated into the contract of carriage by virtue of rule 4, being inconsistent with the provisions of any International Convention or National Law compulsorily applicable to the contract of carriage, such Rules and provisions shall to that extent but no further be null and void.

UNCITRAL ARBITRATION RULES 1976

SECTION I—INTRODUCTORY RULES

SCOPE OF APPLICATION

Article 1

1. Where the parties to a contract have agreed in writing* that disputes in relation to that contract shall be referred to arbitration under the UNCITRAL Arbitration Rules, then such disputes shall be settled in accordance with these Rules subject to such modification as the parties may agree in writing.
2. These Rules shall govern the arbitration except that where any of these Rules is in conflict with a provision of the law applicable to the arbitration from which the parties cannot derogate, that provision shall prevail.

NOTICE, CALCULATION OF PERIODS OF TIME

Article 2

1. For the purposes of these Rules, any notice, including a notification, communication or proposal, is deemed to have been received if it is physically delivered to the addressee or if it is delivered at his habitual residence, place of business or mailing address, or, if none of these can he found after making reasonable inquiry, then at the addressee's last known residence or place of business. Notice shall be deemed to have been received on the day it is so delivered.
2. For the purposes of calculating a period of time under these Rules, such period shall begin to run on the day following the day when a notice, notification, communication or proposal is received. If the last day of such period is an official holiday or a non-business day at the residence or place of business of the addressee, the period is extended until the first business day which follows. Official holidays or non-business days occurring during the running of the period of time are included in calculating the period.

* MODEL ARBITRATION CLAUSE
Any dispute, controversy or claim arising out of or relating to this contract, or the breach, termination or invalidity thereof, shall be settled by arbitration in accordance with the UNCITRAL Arbitration Rules as at present in force.
    Note — Parties may wish to consider adding—
(a)   the appointing authority shall be ... (name of institution or person);
(b)   the number of arbitrators shall be ... (one or three);
(c)   the place of arbitration shall be ... (town or country);
(d)   the language(s) to be used in the arbitral proceedings shall be ...

NOTICE OF ARBITRATION

Article 3

1. The party initiating recourse to arbitration (hereinafter called the 'claimant') shall give to the other party (hereinafter called the 'respondent') a notice of arbitration.
2. Arbitral proceedings shall be deemed to commence on the date on which the notice of arbitration is received by the respondent.

3.   The notice of arbitration shall include the following—
   (a)   a demand that the dispute be referred to arbitration;
   (b)   the names and addresses of the parties;
   (c)   a reference to the arbitration clause or the separate arbitration agreement that is invoked;
   (d)   a reference to the contract out of or in relation to which the dispute arises;
   (e)   the general nature of the claim and an indication of the amount involved, if any;
   (f)   the relief or remedy sought;
   (g)   a proposal as to the number of arbitrators (ie one or three), if the parties have not previously agreed thereon.
4.   The notice of arbitration may also include—
   (a)   the proposals for the appointments of a sole arbitrator and an appointing authority referred to in article 6, paragraph 1;
   (b)   the notification of the appointment of an arbitrator referred to in article 7;
   (c)   the statement of claim referred to in article 18.

REPRESENTATION AND ASSISTANCE

Article 4

The parties may be represented or assisted by persons of their choice. The names and addresses of such persons must be communicated in writing to the other party; such communication must specify whether the appointment is being made for purposes of representation or assistance.

SECTION II—COMPOSITION OF THE ARBITRAL TRIBUNAL

NUMBER OF ARBITRATORS

Article 5

If the parties have not previously agreed on the number of arbitrators (ie, one or three), and if within 15 days after the receipt by the respondent of the notice of arbitration the parties have not agreed that there shall be only one arbitrator, three arbitrators shall be appointed.

APPOINTMENT OF ARBITRATORS (ARTICLES 6 TO 8)

Article 6

1.   If a sole arbitrator is to be appointed, either party may propose to the other—
   (a)   the names of one or more persons, one of whom would serve as the sole arbitrator; and
   (b)   if no appointing authority has been agreed upon by the parties, the name or names of one or more institutions or persons, one of whom would serve as appointing authority.
2.   If within 30 days after receipt by a party of a proposal made in accordance with paragraph 1 the parties have not reached agreement on the choice of a sole arbitrator, the sole arbitrator shall be appointed by the appointing authority agreed upon by the parties. If no appointing authority has been agreed upon by the parties, or if the appointing authority agreed upon refuses to act or fails to appoint the arbitrator within 60 days of the receipt of a party's request therefor, either party may request the Secretary-General of the Permanent Court of Arbitration at The Hague to designate an appointing authority.

3.   The appointing authority shall, at the request of one of the parties, appoint the sole arbitrator as promptly as possible. In making the appointment the appointing authority shall use the following list-procedure, unless both parties agree that the list-procedure should not be used or unless the appointing authority determines in its discretion that the use of the list-procedure is not appropriate for the case—

   (a)   at the request of one of the parties the appointing authority shall communicate to both parties an identical list containing at least three names;

   (b)   within 15 days after the receipt of his list, each party may return the list to the appointing authority after having deleted the name or names to which he objects and numbered the remaining names on the list in the order of his preference;

   (c)   after the expiration of the above period of time the appointing authority shall appoint the sole arbitrator from among the names approved on the lists returned to it and in accordance with the order of preference indicated by the parties;

   (d)   if for any reason the appointment cannot be made according to this procedure, the appointing authority may exercise its discretion in appointing the sole arbitrator.

4.   In making the appointment, the appointing authority shall have regard to such considerations as are likely to secure the appointment of an independent and impartial arbitrator and shall take into account as well the advisability of appointing an arbitrator of a nationality other than the nationalities of the parties.

Article 7

1.   If three arbitrators are to be appointed, each party shall appoint one arbitrator. The two arbitrators thus appointed shall choose the third arbitrator who will act as the presiding arbitrator of the tribunal.

2.   If within 30 days after the receipt of a party's notification of the appointment of an arbitrator the other party has not notified the first party of the arbitrator he has appointed—

   (a)   the first party may request the appointing authority previously designated by the parties to appoint the second arbitrator; or

   (b)   if no such authority has been previously designated by the parties, or if the appointing authority previously designated refuses to act or fails to appoint the arbitrator within 30 days after receipt of a party's request therefor, the first party may request the Secretary-General of the Permanent Court of Arbitration at The Hague to designate the appointing authority. The first party may then request the appointing authority so designated to appoint the second arbitrator. In either case, the appointing authority may exercise its discretion in appointing the arbitrator.

3.   If within 30 days after the appointment of the second arbitrator the two arbitrators have not agreed on the choice of the presiding arbitrator, the presiding arbitrator shall be appointed by an appointing authority in the same way as a sole arbitrator would be appointed under article 6.

Article 8

1.   When an appointing authority is requested to appoint an arbitrator pursuant to article 6 or article 7, the party which makes the request shall send to the appointing authority a copy of the notice of arbitration, a copy of the contract out of or in relation to which the dispute has arisen and a copy of the arbitration agreement if it is not contained in the contract. The appointing authority may require from either party such information as it deems necessary to fulfil its function.

2.   Where the names of one or more persons are proposed for appointment as arbitrators, their full names, addresses and nationalities shall be indicated, together with a description of their qualifications.

CHALLENGE OF ARBITRATORS (ARTICLES 9 TO 12)

Article 9

A prospective arbitrator shall disclose to those who approach him in connexion with his possible appointment any circumstances likely to give rise to justifiable doubts as to his impartiality or independence. An arbitrator, once appointed or chosen, shall disclose such circumstances to the parties unless they have already been informed by him of these circumstances.

Article 10

1.   Any arbitrator may be challenged if circumstances exist that give rise to justifiable doubts as to the arbitrators impartiality or independence.
2.   A party may challenge the arbitrator appointed by him only for reasons of which he becomes aware after the appointment has been made.

Article 11

1.   A party who intends to challenge an arbitrator shall send notice of his challenge within 15 days after the appointment of the challenged arbitrator has been notified to the challenging party or within 15 days after the circumstances mentioned in articles 9 and 10 became known to that party.
2.   The challenge shall be notified to the other party, to the arbitrator who is challenged and to the other members of the arbitral tribunal. The notification shall be in writing and shall state the reasons for the challenge.
3.   When an arbitrator has been challenged by one party, the other party may agree to the challenge. The arbitrator may also, after the challenge, withdraw from his office. In neither case does this imply acceptance of the validity of the grounds for the challenge. In both cases the procedure provided in article 6 or 7 shall be used in full for the appointment of the substitute arbitrator, even if during the process of appointing the challenged arbitrator a party had failed to exercise his right to appoint or to participate in the appointment.

Article 12

1.   If the other party does not agree to the challenge and the challenged arbitrator does not withdraw, the decision on the challenge will be made—
        (a)   when the initial appointment was made by an appointing authority, by that authority;
        (b)   when the initial appointment was not made by an appointing authority, but an appointing authority has been previously designated, by that authority;
        (c)   in all other cases, by the appointing authority to be designated in accordance with the procedure for designating an appointing authority as provided for in article 6.
2.   If the appointing authority sustains the challenge, a substitute arbitrator shall be appointed or chosen pursuant to the procedure applicable to the appointment or choice of an arbitrator as provided in articles 6 to 9 except that, when this procedure would call for the designation of an appointing authority, the appointment of the arbitrator shall be made by the appointing authority which decided on the challenge.

REPLACEMENT OF AN ARBITRATOR

Article 13

1. In the event of the death or resignation of an arbitrator during the course of the arbitral proceedings a substitute arbitrator shall be appointed or chosen pursuant to the procedure provided for in articles 6 to 9 that was applicable to the appointment or choice of the arbitrator being replaced.
2. In the event that an arbitrator fails to act or in the event of the de jure or de facto impossibility of his performing his functions, the procedure in respect of the challenge and replacement of an arbitrator as provided in the preceding articles shall apply.

REPETITION OF HEARINGS IN THE EVENT OF THE REPLACEMENT OF AN ARBITRATOR

Article 14

If under articles 11 to 13 the sole or presiding arbitrator is replaced, any hearings held previously shall be repeated; if any other arbitrator is replaced, such prior hearings may be repeated at the discretion of the arbitral tribunal.

SECTION III—ARBITRAL PROCEEDINGS

GENERAL PROVISIONS

Article 15

1. Subject to these Rules, the arbitral tribunal may conduct the arbitration in such manner as it considers appropriate, provided that the parties are treated with equality and that at any stage of the proceedings each party is given a full opportunity of presenting his case.
2. If either party so requests at any stage of the proceedings, the arbitral tribunal shall hold hearings for the presentation of evidence by witnesses, including expert witnesses, or for oral argument. In the absence of such a request, the arbitral tribunal shall decide whether to hold such hearings or whether the proceedings shall be conducted on the basis of documents and other materials.
3. All documents or information supplied to the arbitral tribunal by one party shall at the same time be communicated by that party to the other party.

PLACE OF ARBITRATION

Article 16

1. Unless the parties have agreed upon the place where the arbitration is to be held, such place shall be determined by the arbitral tribunal, having regard to the circumstances of the arbitration.
2. The arbitral tribunal may determine the locale of the arbitration within the country agreed upon by the parties. It may hear witnesses and hold meetings for consultation among its members at any place it deems appropriate, having regard to the circumstances of the arbitration.
3. The arbitral tribunal may meet at any place it deems appropriate for the inspection of goods, other property or documents. The parties shall be given sufficient notice to enable them to be present at such inspection.
4. The award shall be made at the place of arbitration.

LANGUAGE

Article 17

1. Subject to an agreement by the parties, the arbitral tribunal shall, promptly after its appointment, determine the language or languages to be used in the proceedings. This determination shall apply to the statement of claim, the statement of defence, and any further written statements and, if oral hearings take place, to the language or languages to be used in such hearings.
2. The arbitral tribunal may order that any documents annexed to the statement of claim or statement of defence, and any supplementary documents or exhibits submitted in the course of the proceedings, delivered in their original language, shall be accompanied by a translation into the language or languages agreed upon by the parties or determined by the arbitral tribunal.

STATEMENT OF CLAIM

Article 18

1. Unless the statement of claim was contained in the notice of arbitration, within a period of time to be determined by the arbitral tribunal, the claimant shall communicate his statement of claim in writing to the respondent and to each of the arbitrators. A copy of the contract, and of the arbitration agreement if not contained in the contract, shall be annexed thereto. The statement of claim shall include the following particulars—
    (a)   the names and addresses of the parties;
    (b)   a statement of the facts supporting the claim;
    (c)   the points at issue;
    (d)   the relief or remedy sought.
    The claimant may annex to his statement of claim all documents he deems relevant or may add a reference to the documents or other evidence he will submit.

STATEMENT OF DEFENCE

Article 19

1. Within a period of time to be determined by the arbitral tribunal, the respondent shall communicate his statement of defence in writing to the claimant and to each of the arbitrators.
2. The statement of defence shall reply to the particulars (b), (c) and (d) of the statement of claim (article 18, para 2). The respondent may annex to his statement the documents on which he relies for his defence or may add a reference to the documents or other evidence he will submit.
3. In his statement of defence, or at a later stage in the arbitral proceedings if the arbitral tribunal decides that the delay was justified under the circumstances the respondent may make a counter-claim arising out of the same contract or rely on a claim arising out of the same contract for the purpose of a set-off.
4. The provisions of article 18, paragraph 2, shall apply to a counter-claim and a claim relied on for the purpose of a set-off.

AMENDMENTS TO THE CLAIM OR DEFENCE

Article 20

During the course of the arbitral proceedings either party may amend or supplement his claim or defence unless the arbitral tribunal considers it inappropriate to allow such amendment having regard to the delay in making it or prejudice to the other party or any other circumstances. However, a claim may not be amended in such a manner that the amended claim falls outside the scope of the arbitration clause or separate arbitration agreement.

PLEAS AS TO THE JURISDICTION OF THE ARBITRAL TRIBUNAL

Article 21

1.   The arbitral tribunal shall have the power to rule on objections that it has no jurisdiction, including any objections with respect to the existence or validity of the arbitration clause or of the separate arbitration agreement.
2.   The arbitral tribunal shall have the power to determine the existence or the validity of the contract of which an arbitration clause forms a part. For the purposes of article 21, an arbitration clause which forms part of a contract and which provides for arbitration under these Rules shall be treated as an agreement independent of the other terms of the contract. A decision by the arbitral tribunal that the contract is null and void shall not entail *ipso jure* the invalidity of the arbitration clause.
3.   A plea that the arbitral tribunal does not have jurisdiction shall be raised not later than in the statement of defence or, with respect to a counter-claim, in the reply to the counter-claim.
4.   In general, the arbitral tribunal should rule on a plea concerning its jurisdiction as a preliminary question. However, the arbitral tribunal may proceed with the arbitration and rule on such a plea in their final award.

FURTHER WRITTEN STATEMENTS

Article 22

The arbitral tribunal shall decide which further written statements, in addition to the statement of claim and the statement of defence, shall be required from the parties or may be presented by them and shall fix the periods of time for communicating such statements.

PERIODS OF TIME

Article 23

The periods of time fixed by the arbitral tribunal for the communication of written statements (including the statement of claim and statement of defence) should not exceed 45 days. However, the arbitral tribunal may extend the time-limits if it concludes that an extension is justified.

EVIDENCE AND HEARINGS (ARTICLES 24 AND 25)

Article 24

1.   Each party shall have the burden of proving the facts relied on to support his claim or defence.

2.   The arbitral tribunal may, if it considers it appropriate, require a party to deliver to the tribunal and to the other party, within such a period of time as the arbitral tribunal shall decide, a summary of the documents and other evidence which that party intends to present in support of the facts in issue set out in his statement of claim or statement of defence.

3.   At any time during the arbitral proceedings the arbitral tribunal may require the parties to produce documents, exhibits or other evidence within such a period of time as the tribunal shall determine.

Article 25

1.   In the event of an oral hearing, the arbitral tribunal shall give the parties adequate advance notice of the date, time and place thereof.

2.   If witnesses are to be heard, at least 15 days before the hearing each party shall communicate to the arbitral tribunal and to the other party the names and addresses of the witnesses he intends to present, the subject upon and the languages in which such witnesses will give their testimony.

3.   The arbitral tribunal shall make arrangements for the translation of oral statements made at a hearing and for a record of the hearing if either is deemed necessary by the tribunal under the circumstances of the case, or if the parties have agreed thereto and have communicated such agreement to the tribunal at least 15 days before the hearing.

4.   Hearings shall be held in camera unless the parties agree otherwise. The arbitral tribunal may require the retirement of any witness or witnesses during the testimony of other witnesses. The arbitral tribunal is free to determine the manner in which witnesses are examined.

5.   Evidence of witnesses may also be presented in the form of written statements signed by them.

6.   The arbitral tribunal shall determine the admissibility, relevance, materiality and weight of the evidence offered.

INTERIM MEASURES OF PROTECTION

Article 26

1.   At the request of either party, the arbitral tribunal may take any interim measures it deems necessary in respect of the subject-matter of the dispute, including measures for the conservation of the goods forming the subject-matter in dispute, such as ordering their deposit with a third person or the sale of perishable goods.

2.   Such interim measures may be established in the form of an interim award. The arbitral tribunal shall be entitled to require security for the costs of such measures.

3.   A request for interim measures addressed by any party to a judicial authority shall not be deemed incompatible with the agreement to arbitrate, or as a waiver of that agreement.

EXPERTS

Article 27

1.   The arbitral tribunal may appoint one or more experts to report to it, in writing, on specific issues to be determined by the tribunal. A copy of the expert's terms of reference, established by the arbitral tribunal, shall be communicated to the parties.

2.   The parties shall give the expert any relevant information or produce for his inspection any relevant documents or goods that he may require of them. Any

dispute between a party and such expert as to the relevance of the required information or production shall be referred to the arbitral tribunal for decision.

3. Upon receipt of the expert's report, the arbitral tribunal shall communicate a copy of the report to the parties who shall be given the opportunity to express, in writing, their opinion on the report. A party shall be entitled to examine any document on which the expert has relied in his report.

4. At the request of either party the expert, after delivery of the report, may be heard at a hearing where the parties shall have the opportunity to be present and to interrogate the expert. At this hearing either party may present expert witnesses in order to testify on the points at issue. The provisions of article 25 shall be applicable to such proceedings.

DEFAULT

Article 28

1. If, within the period of time fixed by the arbitral tribunal, the claimant has failed to communicate his claim without showing sufficient cause for such failure, the arbitral tribunal shall issue an order for the termination of the arbitral proceedings. If, within the period of time fixed by the arbitral tribunal, the respondent has failed to communicate his statement of defence without showing sufficient cause for such failure, the arbitral tribunal shall order that the proceedings continue.

2. If one of the parties, duly notified under these Rules, fails to appear at a hearing, without showing sufficient cause for such failure, the arbitral tribunal may proceed with the arbitration.

3. If one of the parties, duly invited to produce documentary evidence, fails to do so within the established period of time, without showing sufficient cause for such failure, the arbitral tribunal may make the award on the evidence before it.

CLOSURE OF HEARINGS

Article 29

1. The arbitral tribunal may inquire of the parties if they have any further proof to offer or witnesses to be heard or submissions to make and, if there are none, it may declare the hearings closed.

2. The arbitral tribunal may, if it considers it necessary owing to exceptional circumstances, decide on its own motion or upon application of a party, to reopen the hearings at any time before the award is made.

WAIVER OF RULES

Article 30

A party who knows that any provision of, or requirement under, these Rules has not been complied with and yet proceeds with the arbitration without promptly stating his objection to such non-compliance, shall be deemed to have waived his right to object.

SECTION IV—THE AWARD

DECISIONS

Article 31

1. When there are three arbitrators, any award or other decision of the arbitral tribunal shall be made by a majority of the arbitrators.

2. In the case of questions of procedure, when there is no majority or when the arbitral tribunal so authorizes, the presiding arbitrator may decide on his own, subject to revision, if any, by the arbitral tribunal.

FORM AND EFFECT OF THE AWARD

Article 32

1. In addition to making a final award, the arbitral tribunal shall be entitled to make interim, interlocutory, or partial awards.
2. The award shall be made in writing and shall be final and binding on the parties. The parties undertake to carry out the award without delay.
3. The arbitral tribunal shall state the reasons upon which the award is based, unless the parties have agreed that no reasons are to be given.
4. An award shall be signed by the arbitrators and it shall contain the date on which and the place where the award was made. Where there are three arbitrators and one of them fails to sign, the award shall state the reason for the absence of the signature.
5. The award may be made public only with the consent of both parties.
6. Copies of the award signed by the arbitrators shall be communicated to the parties by the arbitral tribunal.
7. If the arbitration law of the country where the award is made requires that the award be filed or registered by the arbitral tribunal, the tribunal shall comply with this requirement within the period of time required by law.

APPLICABLE LAW, AMIABLE COMPOSITEUR

Article 33

1. The arbitral tribunal shall apply the law designated by the parties as applicable to the substance of the dispute. Failing such designation by the parties, the arbitral tribunal shall apply the law determined by the conflict of laws rules which it considers applicable.
2. The arbitral tribunal shall decide as *amiable compositeur* or *ex aequo et bono* only if the parties have expressly authorized the arbitral tribunal to do so and if the law applicable to the arbitral procedure permits such arbitration.
3. In all cases, the arbitral tribunal shall decide in accordance with the terms of the contract and shall take into account the usages of the trade applicable to the transaction.

SETTLEMENT OR OTHER GROUNDS FOR TERMINATION

Article 34

1. If before the award is made, the parties agree on a settlement of the dispute, the arbitral tribunal shall either issue an order for the termination of the arbitral proceedings or, if requested by both parties and accepted by the tribunal, record the settlement in the form of an arbitral award on agreed terms. The arbitral tribunal is not obliged to give reasons for such an award.
2. If, before the award is made, the continuation of the arbitral proceedings becomes unnecessary or impossible for any reason not mentioned in paragraph 1, the arbitral tribunal shall inform the parties of its intention to issue an order for the termination of the proceedings. The arbitral tribunal shall have the power to issue such an order unless a party raises justifiable grounds for objection.

3.   Copies of the order for termination of the arbitral proceedings or of the arbitral award on agreed terms, signed by the arbitrators, shall be communicated by the arbitral tribunal to the parties. Where an arbitral award on agreed terms is made, the provisions of article 32, paragraphs 2 and 4 to 7, shall apply.

INTERPRETATION OF THE AWARD

Article 35

1.   Within 30 days after the receipt of the award, either party, with notice to the other party, may request that the arbitral tribunal give an interpretation of the award.
2.   The interpretation shall be given in writing within 45 days after the receipt of the request. The interpretation shall form part of the award and the provisions of article 32, paragraphs 2 to 7, shall apply.

CORRECTION OF THE AWARD

Article 36

1.   Within 30 days after the receipt of the award, either party, with notice to the other party, may request the arbitral tribunal to correct in the award any errors in computation, any clerical or typographical errors, or any errors of similar nature. The arbitral tribunal may within 30 days after the communication of the award make such corrections on its own initiative.
2.   Such corrections shall be in writing, and the provisions of article 32, paragraphs 2 to 7, shall apply.

ADDITIONAL AWARD

Article 37

1.   Within 30 days after the receipt of the award, either party, with notice to the other party, may request the arbitral tribunal to make an additional award as to claims presented in the arbitral proceedings but omitted from the award.
2.   If the arbitral tribunal considers the request for an additional award to be justified and considers that the omission can be rectified without any further hearings or evidence, it shall complete its award within 60 days after the receipt of the request.
3.   When an additional award is made, the provisions of article 32, paragraphs 2 to 7, shall apply.

COSTS (ARTICLES 38 TO 40)

Article 38

The arbitral tribunal shall fix the costs of arbitration in its award. The term 'costs' includes only—
(a)   the fees of the arbitral tribunal to be stated separately as to each arbitrator and to be fixed by the tribunal itself in accordance with article 39;
(b)   the travel and other expenses incurred by the arbitrators;
(c)   the costs of expert advice and of other assistance required by the arbitral tribunal;
(d)   the travel and other expenses of witnesses to the extent such expenses are approved by the arbitral tribunal;
(e)   the costs for legal representation and assistance of the successful party if such costs were claimed during the arbitral proceedings, and only to the extent that the arbitral tribunal determines that the amount of such costs is reasonable;

(f)   any fees and expenses of the appointing authority as well as the expenses of the Secretary General of the Permanent Court of Arbitration at The Hague.

Article 39

1.   The fees of the arbitral tribunal shall be reasonable in amount, taking into account the amount in dispute, the complexity of the subject-matter, the time spent by the arbitrators and any other relevant circumstances of the case.
2.   If an appointing authority has been agreed upon by the parties or designated by the Secretary-General of the Permanent Court of Arbitration at The Hague, and if that authority has issued a schedule of fees for arbitrators in international cases which it administers, the arbitral tribunal in fixing its fees shall take that schedule of fees into account to the extent that it considers appropriate in the circumstances of the case.
3.   If such appointing authority has not issued a schedule of fees for arbitrators in international cases, any party may at any time request the appointing authority to furnish a statement setting forth the basis for establishing fees which is customarily followed in international cases in which the authority appoints arbitrators. If the appointing authority consents to provide such a statement, the arbitral tribunal in fixing its fees shall take such information into account to the extent that it considers appropriate in the circumstances of the case.
4.   In cases referred to in paragraphs 2 and 3, when a party so requests and the appointing authority consents to perform the function, the arbitral tribunal shall fix its fees only after consultation with the appointing authority which may make any comment it deems appropriate to the arbitral tribunal concerning the fees.

Article 40

1.   Except as provided in paragraph 2, the costs of arbitration shall in principle be borne by the unsuccessful party. However, the arbitral tribunal may apportion each of such costs between the parties if it determines that apportionment is reasonable, taking into account the circumstances of the case.
2.   With respect to the costs of legal representation and assistance referred to in article 38, paragraph (e), the arbitral tribunal, taking into account the circumstances of the case, shall be free to determine which party shall bear such costs or may apportion such costs between the parties if it determines that apportionment is reasonable.
3.   When the arbitral tribunal issues an order for the termination of the arbitral proceedings or makes an award on agreed terms, it shall fix the costs of arbitration referred to in article 38 and article 39, paragraph 1, in the text of that order or award.
4.   No additional fees may be charged by an arbitral tribunal for interpretation or correction or completion of its award under articles 35 to 37.

DEPOSIT OF COSTS

Article 41

1.   The arbitral tribunal, on its establishment, may request each party to deposit an equal amount as an advance for the costs referred to in article 38, paragraphs (a), (b) and (c).
2.   During the course of the arbitral proceedings the arbitral tribunal may request supplementary deposits from the parties.
3.   If an appointing authority has been agreed upon by the parties or designated by the Secretary-General of the Permanent Court of Arbitration at The Hague, and when a party so requests and the appointing authority consents to perform the

function, the arbitral tribunal shall fix the amounts of any deposits or supplementary deposits only after consultation with the appointing authority which may make any comments to the arbitral tribunal which it deems appropriate concerning the amount of such deposits and supplementary deposits.

4.   If the required deposits are not paid in full within 30 days after the receipt of the request, the arbitral tribunal shall so inform the parties in order that one or another of them may make the required payment. If such payment is not made, the arbitral tribunal may order the suspension or termination of the arbitral proceedings.

5.   After the award has been made, the arbitral tribunal shall render an accounting to the parties of the deposits received and return any unexpended balance to the parties.

UNCITRAL CONCILIATION RULES 1980

APPLICATION OF THE RULES

Article 1

(1)   These Rules apply to conciliation of disputes arising out of or relating to a contractual or other legal relationship where the parties seeking an amicable settlement of their dispute have agreed that the UNCITRAL Conciliation Rules apply.

(2)   The parties may agree to exclude or vary any of these Rules at any time.

(3)   Where any of these Rules is in conflict with a provision of law from which the parties cannot derogate, that provision prevails.

COMMENCEMENT OF CONCILIATION PROCEEDINGS

Article 2

(1)   The party initiating conciliation sends to the other party a written invitation to conciliate under these Rules, briefly identifying the subject of the dispute.

(2)   Conciliation proceedings commence when the other party accepts the invitation to conciliate. If the acceptance is made orally, it is advisable that it be confirmed in writing.

(3)   If the other party rejects the invitation, there will be no conciliation proceedings.

(4)   If the party initiating conciliation does not receive a reply within thirty days from the date on which he sends the invitation, or within such other period of time as specified in the invitation, he may elect to treat this as a rejection of the invitation to conciliate. If he so elects, he informs the other party accordingly.

NUMBER OF CONCILIATORS

Article 3

There shall be one conciliator unless the parties agree that there shall be two or three conciliators. Where there is more than one conciliator, they ought, as a general rule, to act jointly.

APPOINTMENT OF CONCILIATORS

Article 4

(1)　(a)　In conciliation proceedings with one conciliator, the parties shall endeavour to reach agreement on the name of a sole conciliator;

　　(b)　In conciliation proceedings with two conciliators, each party appoints one conciliator;

　　(c)　In conciliation proceedings with three conciliators, each party appoints one conciliator. The parties shall endeavour to reach agreement on the name of the third conciliator.

(2)　Parties may enlist the assistance of an appropriate institution or person in connexion with the appointment of conciliators. In particular—

　　(a)　a party may request such an institution or person to recommend the names of suitable individuals to act as conciliator; or

　　(b)　the parties may agree that the appointment of one or more conciliators be made directly by such an institution or person.

In recommending or appointing individuals to act as conciliator, the institution or person shall have regard to such considerations as are likely to secure the appointment of an independent and impartial conciliator and, with respect to a sole or third conciliator, shall take into account the advisability of appointing a conciliator of a nationality other than the nationalities of the parties.

SUBMISSION OF STATEMENTS TO CONCILIATOR

Article 5

(1)　The conciliator,* upon his appointment, requests each party to submit to him a brief written statement describing the general nature of the dispute and the points at issue. Each party sends a copy of his statement to the other party.

(2)　The conciliator may request each party to submit to him a further written statement of his position and the facts and grounds in support thereof, supplemented by any documents and other evidence that such party deems appropriate. The party sends a copy of his statement to the other party.

(3)　At any stage of the conciliation proceedings the conciliator may request a party to submit to him such additional information as he deems appropriate.

* In this and all following articles, the term 'conciliator' applies to a sole conciliator, two or three conciliators, as the case may be.

REPRESENTATION AND ASSISTANCE

Article 6

The parties may be represented or assisted by persons of their choice. The names and addresses of such persons are to be communicated in writing to the other party and to the conciliator; such communication is to specify whether the appointment is made for purposes of representation or of assistance.

ROLE OF CONCILIATOR

Article 7

(1)　The conciliator assists the parties in an independent and impartial manner in their attempt to reach an amicable settlement of their dispute.

(2)   The conciliator will be guided by principles of objectivity, fairness and justice, giving consideration to, among other things, the rights and obligations of the parties, the usages of the trade concerned and the circumstances surrounding the dispute, including any previous business practices between the parties.

(3)   The conciliator may conduct the conciliation proceedings in such a manner as he considers appropriate taking into account the circumstances of the case, the wishes the parties may express, including any request by a party that the conciliator hear oral statements, and the need for a speedy settlement of the dispute.

(4)   The conciliator may, at any stage of the conciliation proceedings, make proposals for a settlement of the dispute. Such proposals need not be in writing and need not be accompanied by a statement of the reasons therefor.

ADMINISTRATIVE ASSISTANCE

Article 8

In order to facilitate the conduct of the conciliation proceedings, the parties, or the conciliator with the consent of the parties, may arrange for administrative assistance by a suitable institution or person.

COMMUNICATION BETWEEN CONCILIATOR AND PARTIES

Article 9

(1)   The conciliator may invite the parties to meet with him or may communicate with them orally or in writing. He may meet or communicate with the parties together or with each of them separately.

(2)   Unless the parties have agreed upon the place where meetings with the conciliator are to be held, such place will be determined by the conciliator, after consultation with the parties, having regard to the circumstances of the conciliation proceedings.

DISCLOSURE OF INFORMATION

Article 10

When the conciliator receives factual information concerning the dispute from a party, he discloses the substance of that information to the other party in order that the other party may have the opportunity to present any explanation which he considers appropriate. However, when a party gives any information to the conciliator subject to a specific condition that it be kept confidential, the conciliator does not disclose that information to the other party.

CO-OPERATION OF PARTIES WITH CONCILIATOR

Article 11

The parties will in good faith co-operate with the conciliator and, in particular, will endeavour to comply with requests by the conciliator to submit written materials, provide evidence and attend meetings.

SUGGESTIONS BY PARTIES FOR SETTLEMENT OF DISPUTE

Article 12

Each party may, on his own initiative or at the invitation of the conciliator, submit to the conciliator suggestions for the settlement of the dispute.

SETTLEMENT AGREEMENT

Article 13

(1)   When it appears to the conciliator that there exist elements of a settlement which would be acceptable to the parties, he formulates the terms of a possible settlement and submits them to the parties for their observations. After receiving the observations of the parties, the conciliator may reformulate the terms of a possible settlement in the light of such observations.

(2)   If the parties reach agreement on a settlement of the dispute, they draw up and sign a written settlement agreement.** If requested by the parties, the conciliator draws up, or assists the parties in drawing up, the settlement agreement.

(3)   The parties by signing the settlement agreement put an end to the dispute and are bound by the agreement.

** The parties may wish to consider including in the settlement agreement a clause that any dispute arising out of or relating to the settlement agreement shall be submitted to arbitration.

CONFIDENTIALITY

Article 14

The Conciliator and the parties must keep confidential all matters relating to the conciliation proceedings. Confidentiality extends also to the settlement agreement, except where its disclosure is necessary for purposes of implementation and enforcement.

TERMINATION OF CONCILIATION PROCEEDINGS

Article 15

The conciliation proceedings are terminated—
(a)   by the signing of the settlement agreement by the parties, on the date of the agreement; or
(b)   by a written declaration of the conciliator, after consultation with the parties, to the effect that further efforts at conciliation are no longer justified, on the date of the declaration; or
(c)   by a written declaration of the parties addressed to the conciliator to the effect that the conciliation proceedings are terminated, on the date of the declaration; or
(d)   by a written declaration of a party to the other party and the conciliator, if appointed, to the effect that the conciliation proceedings are terminated, on the date of the declaration.

RESORT TO ARBITRAL OR JUDICIAL PROCEEDINGS

Article 16

The parties undertake not to initiate, during the conciliation proceedings, any arbitral or judicial proceedings in respect of a dispute that is the subject of the conciliation proceedings, except that a party may initiate arbitral or judicial proceedings where, in his opinion, such proceedings are necessary for preserving his rights.

COSTS

Article 17

(1)   Upon termination of the conciliation proceedings, the conciliator fixes the costs of
       the conciliation and gives written notice thereof to the parties. The term 'costs'
       includes only—
       (a)   the fee of the conciliator which shall be reasonable in amount;
       (b)   the travel and other expenses of the conciliator;
       (c)   the travel and other expenses of witnesses requested by the conciliator with
              the consent of the parties;
       (d)   The cost of any expert advice requested by the conciliator with the consent of
              the parties;
       (e)   The cost of any assistance provided pursuant to articles 4, paragraph (2)(b),
              and 8 of these Rules.
(2)   The costs, as defined above, are borne equally by the parties unless the settlement
       agreement provides for a different apportionment. All other expenses incurred by
       a party are borne by that party.

DEPOSITS

Article 18

(1)   The conciliator, upon his appointment, may request each party to deposit an equal
       amount as an advance for the costs referred to in article 17, paragraph (1) which he
       expects will be incurred.
(2)   During the course of the conciliation proceedings the conciliator may request
       supplementary deposits in an equal amount from each party.
(3)   If the required deposits under paragraphs (1) and (2) of this article are not paid in
       full by both parties within thirty days, the conciliator may suspend the proceedings
       or may make a written declaration of termination to the parties, effective on the
       date of that declaration.
(4)   Upon termination of the conciliation proceedings, the conciliator renders an
       accounting to the parties of the deposits received and returns any unexpended
       balance to the parties.

ROLE OF CONCILIATOR IN OTHER PROCEEDINGS

Article 19

The parties and the conciliator undertake that the conciliator will not act as an arbitrator
or as a representative or counsel of a party in any arbitral or judicial proceedings in
respect of a dispute that is the subject of the conciliation proceedings. The parties also
undertake that they will not present the conciliator as a witness in any such proceedings.

ADMISSIBILITY OF EVIDENCE IN OTHER PROCEEDINGS

Article 20

The parties undertake not to rely on or introduce as evidence in arbitral or judicial
proceedings, whether or not such proceedings relate to the dispute that is the subject of
the conciliation proceedings—
(a)   views expressed or suggestions made by the other party in respect of a possible
       settlement of the dispute;
(b)   admissions made by the other party in the course of the conciliation proceedings;

(c)   proposals made by the conciliator;
(d)   the fact that the other party had indicated his willingness to accept a proposal for settlement made by the conciliator.

MODEL CONCILIATION CLAUSE

Where, in the event of a dispute arising out of or relating to this contract, the parties wish to seek an amicable settlement of that dispute by conciliation, the conciliation shall take place in accordance with the UNCITRAL Conciliation Rules as at present in force.
   (The parties may agree on other conciliation clauses.)

UNCITRAL MODEL LAW ON ELECTRONIC COMMERCE 1996, AS AMENDED 1998

PART ONE
ELECTRONIC COMMERCE IN GENERAL

CHAPTER I
GENERAL PROVISIONS

Article 1
*Sphere of application**

This Law** applies to any kind of information in the form of a data message used in the context*** of commercial**** activities.

* The Commission suggests the following text for States that might wish to limit the applicability of this Law to international data messages:
   'This Law applies to a data message as defined in paragraph (1) of article 2 where the data message relates to international commerce.'

** This Law does not override any rule of law intended for the protection of consumers.

*** The Commission suggests the following text for States that might wish to extend the applicability of this Law: 'This Law applies to any kind of information in the form of a data message, except in the following situations: [...].'

**** The term 'commercial' should be given a wide interpretation so as to cover matters arising from all relationships of a commercial nature, whether contractual or not. Relationships of a commercial nature include, but are not limited to, the following transactions: any trade transaction for the supply or exchange of goods or services; distribution agreement, commercial representation or agency; factoring; leasing; construction of works; consulting; engineering, licensing; investment; financing; banking; insurance; exploitation agreement or concession; joint venture and other forms of industrial or business cooperation; carriage of goods or passengers by air, sea, rail or road.

Article 2
Definitions

For the purposes of this Law—
(a)   'Data message' means information generated, sent, received or stored by electronic, optical or similar means including, but not limited to, electronic data interchange (EDI), electronic mail, telegram, telex or telecopy.
(b)   'Electronic data interchange (EDI)' means the electronic transfer from computer to computer of information using an agreed standard to structure the information.
(c)   'Originator' of a data message means a person by whom, or on whose behalf, the data message purports to have been sent or generated prior to storage, if any, but it does not include a person acting as an intermediary with respect to that data message.

(d)   'Addressee' of a data message means a person who is intended by the originator to receive the data message, but does not include a person acting as an intermediary with respect to that data message.

(e)   'Intermediary', with respect to a particular data message, means a person who, on behalf of another person, sends, receives or stores that data message or provides other services with respect to that data message.

(f)   'Information system' means a system for generating, sending, receiving, storing or otherwise processing data messages.

Article 3
Interpretation

(1)   In the interpretation of this Law, regard is to be had to its international origin and to the need to promote uniformity in its application and the observance of good faith.

(2)   Questions concerning matters governed by this Law which are not expressly settled in it are to be settled in conformity with the general principles on which this Law is based.

Article 4
Variation by agreement

(1)   As between parties involved in generating, sending, receiving, storing or otherwise processing data messages, and except as otherwise provided, the provisions of chapter III may be varied by agreement.

(2)   Paragraph (1) does not affect any right that may exist to modify by agreement any rule of law referred to in chapter II.

CHAPTER II
APPLICATION OF LEGAL REQUIREMENTS TO DATA MESSAGES

Article 5
Legal recognition of data messages

Information shall not be denied legal effect, validity or enforceability solely on the grounds that it is in the form of a data message.

Article 5 bis
Incorporation by reference

Information shall not be denied legal effect, validity or enforceability solely on the grounds that it is not contained in the data message purporting to give rise to such legal effect, but is merely referred to in that data message.

Article 6
Writing

(1)   Where the law requires information to be in writing, that requirement is met by a data message if the information contained therein is accessible so as to be usable for subsequent reference.

(2)   Paragraph (1) applies whether the requirement therein is in the form of an obligation or whether the law simply provides consequences for the information not being in writing.

(3)   The provisions of this article do not apply to the following: [...].

Article 7
Signature

(1)   Where the law requires a signature of a person, that requirement is met in relation to a data message if—
    (a)   a method is used to identify that person and to indicate that person's approval of the information contained in the data message; and
    (b)   that method is as reliable as was appropriate for the purpose for which the data message was generated or communicated, in the light of all the circumstances, including any relevant agreement.

(2)   Paragraph (1) applies whether the requirement therein is in the form of an obligation or whether the law simply provides consequences for the absence of a signature.

(3)   The provisions of this article do not apply to the following: [...].

Article 8
Original

(1)   Where the law requires information to be presented or retained in its original form, that requirement is met by a data message if:
    (a)   there exists a reliable assurance as to the integrity of the information from the time when it was first generated in its final form, as a data message or otherwise; and
    (b)   where it is required that information be presented, that information is capable of being displayed to the person to whom it is to be presented.

(2)   Paragraph (1) applies whether the requirement therein is in the form of an obligation or whether the law simply provides consequences for the information not being presented or retained in its original form.

(3)   For the purposes of subparagraph (a) of paragraph (1)—
    (a)   the criteria for assessing integrity shall be whether the information has remained complete and unaltered, apart from the addition of any endorsement and any change which arises in the normal course of communication, storage and display; and
    (b)   the standard of reliability required shall be assessed in the light of the purpose for which the information was generated and in the light of all the relevant circumstances.

(4)   The provisions of this article do not apply to the following: [...].

Article 9
Admissibility and evidential weight of data messages

(1)   In any legal proceedings, nothing in the application of the rules of evidence shall apply so as to deny the admissibility of a data message in evidence—
    (a)   on the sole ground that it is a data message; or
    (b)   if it is the best evidence that the person adducing it could reasonably be expected to obtain, on the grounds that it is not in its original form.

(2)   Information in the form of a data message shall be given due evidential weight. In assessing the evidential weight of a data message, regard shall be had to the reliability of the manner in which the data message was generated, stored or communicated, to the reliability of the manner in which the integrity of the information was maintained, to the manner in which its originator was identified, and to any other relevant factor.

Article 10
Retention of data messages

(1)   Where the law requires that certain documents, records or information be retained, that requirement is met by retaining data messages, provided that the following conditions are satisfied—

    (a)   the information contained therein is accessible so as to be usable for subsequent reference; and

    (b)   the data message is retained in the format in which it was generated, sent or received, or in a format which can be demonstrated to represent accurately the information generated, sent or received; and

    (c)   such information, if any, is retained as enables the identification of the origin and destination of a data message and the date and time when it was sent or received.

(2)   An obligation to retain documents, records or information in accordance with paragraph (1) does not extend to any information the sole purpose of which is to enable the message to be sent or received.

(3)   A person may satisfy the requirement referred to in paragraph (1) by using the services of any other person, provided that the conditions set forth in subparagraphs (a), (b) and (c) of paragraph (1) are met.

CHAPTER III
COMMUNICATION OF DATA MESSAGES

Article 11
Formation and validity of contracts

(1)   In the context of contract formation, unless otherwise agreed by the parties, an offer and the acceptance of an offer may be expressed by means of data messages. Where a data message is used in the formation of a contract, that contract shall not be denied validity or enforceability on the sole ground that a data message was used for that purpose.

(2)   The provisions of this article do not apply to the following: [...].

Article 12
Recognition by parties of data messages

(1)   As between the originator and the addressee of a data message, a declaration of will or other statement shall not be denied legal effect, validity or enforceability solely on the grounds that it is in the form of a data message.

(2)   The provisions of this article do not apply to the following: [...].

Article 13
Attribution of data messages

(1)   A data message is that of the originator if it was sent by the originator itself.

(2)   As between the originator and the addressee, a data message is deemed to be that of the originator if it was sent—

    (a)   by a person who had the authority to act on behalf of the originator in respect of that data message; or

    (b)   by an information system programmed by, or on behalf of, the originator to operate automatically.

(3)   As between the originator and the addressee, an addressee is entitled to regard a data message as being that of the originator, and to act on that assumption, if—

       (a)   in order to ascertain whether the data message was that of the originator, the addressee properly applied a procedure previously agreed to by the originator for that purpose; or

       (b)   the data message as received by the addressee resulted from the actions of a person whose relationship with the originator or with any agent of the originator enabled that person to gain access to a method used by the originator to identify data messages as its own.

(4)   Paragraph (3) does not apply:

       (a)   as of the time when the addressee has both received notice from the originator that the data message is not that of the originator, and had reasonable time to act accordingly; or

       (b)   in a case within paragraph (3)(b), at any time when the addressee knew or should have known, had it exercised reasonable care or used any agreed procedure, that the data message was not that of the originator.

(5)   Where a data message is that of the originator or is deemed to be that of the originator, or the addressee is entitled to act on that assumption, then, as between the originator and the addressee, the addressee is entitled to regard the data message as received as being what the originator intended to send, and to act on that assumption. The addressee is not so entitled when it knew or should have known, had it exercised reasonable care or used any agreed procedure, that the transmission resulted in any error in the data message as received.

(6)   The addressee is entitled to regard each data message received as a separate data message and to act on that assumption, except to the extent that it duplicates another data message and the addressee knew or should have known, had it exercised reasonable care or used any agreed procedure, that the data message was a duplicate.

Article 14
Acknowledgement of receipt

(1)   Paragraphs (2) to (4) of this article apply where, on or before sending a data message, or by means of that data message, the originator has requested or has agreed with the addressee that receipt of the data message be acknowledged.

(2)   Where the originator has not agreed with the addressee that the acknowledgement be given in a particular form or by a particular method, an acknowledgement may be given by—

       (a)   any communication by the addressee, automated or otherwise; or

       (b)   any conduct of the addressee,

sufficient to indicate to the originator that the data message has been received.

(3)   Where the originator has stated that the data message is conditional on receipt of the acknowledgement, the data message is treated as though it has never been sent, until the acknowledgement is received.

(4)   Where the originator has not stated that the data message is conditional on receipt of the acknowledgement, and the acknowledgement has not been received by the originator within the time specified or agreed or, if no time has been specified or agreed, within a reasonable time, the originator—

       (a)   may give notice to the addressee stating that no acknowledgement has been received and specifying a reasonable time by which the acknowledgement must be received; and

       (b)   if the acknowledgement is not received within the time specified in subparagraph (a), may, upon notice to the addressee, treat the data message as though it had never been sent, or exercise any other rights it may have.

(5)   Where the originator receives the addressee's acknowledgement of receipt, it is presumed that the related data message was received by the addressee. That presumption does not imply that the data message corresponds to the message received.

(6)   Where the received acknowledgement states that the related data message met technical requirements, either agreed upon or set forth in applicable standards, it is presumed that those requirements have been met.

(7)   Except in so far as it relates to the sending or receipt of the data message, this article is not intended to deal with the legal consequences that may flow either from that data message or from the acknowledgement of its receipt.

Article 15
Time and place of dispatch and receipt of data messages

(1)   Unless otherwise agreed between the originator and the addressee, the dispatch of a data message occurs when it enters an information system outside the control of the originator or of the person who sent the data message on behalf of the originator.

(2)   Unless otherwise agreed between the originator and the addressee, the time of receipt of a data message is determined as follows—

(a)   if the addressee has designated an information system for the purpose of receiving data messages, receipt occurs:

(i)   at the time when the data message enters the designated information system; or

(ii) if the data message is sent to an information system of the addressee that is not the designated information system, at the time when the data message is retrieved by the addressee;

(b)   if the addressee has not designated an information system, receipt occurs when the data message enters an information system of the addressee.

(3)   Paragraph (2) applies notwithstanding that the place where the information system is located may be different from the place where the data message is deemed to be received under paragraph (4).

(4)   Unless otherwise agreed between the originator and the addressee, a data message is deemed to be dispatched at the place where the originator has its place of business, and is deemed to be received at the place where the addressee has its place of business. For the purposes of this paragraph—

(a)   if the originator or the addressee has more than one place of business, the place of business is that which has the closest relationship to the underlying transaction or, where there is no underlying transaction, the principal place of business;

(b)   if the originator or the addressee does not have a place of business, reference is to be made to its habitual residence.

(5)   The provisions of this article do not apply to the following: [...].

PART TWO
ELECTRONIC COMMERCE TO SPECIFIC AREAS

CHAPTER I
CARRIAGE OF GOODS

Article 16
Actions related to contracts of carriage of goods

Without derogating from the provisions of part one of this Law, this chapter applies to any action in connection with, or in pursuance of, a contract of carriage of goods, including but not limited to—

(a)   (i)   furnishing the marks, number, quantity or weight of goods;

(ii) stating or declaring the nature or value of goods;

(iii) issuing a receipt for goods;

        (iv)   confirming that goods have been loaded;

(b)   (i)   notifying a person of terms and conditions of the contract;

        (ii)   giving instructions to a carrier;

(c)   (i)   claiming delivery of goods;

        (ii)   authorizing release of goods;

        (iii)   giving notice of loss of, or damage to, goods;

(d)   giving any other notice or statement in connection with the performance of the contract;

(e)   undertaking to deliver goods to a named person or a person authorized to claim delivery;

(f)   granting, acquiring, renouncing, surrendering, transferring or negotiating rights in goods;

(g)   acquiring or transferring rights and obligations under the contract.

Article 17
Transport documents

(1)   Subject to paragraph (3), where the law requires that any action referred to in article 16 be carried out in writing or by using a paper document, that requirement is met if the action is carried out by using one or more data messages.

(2)   Paragraph (1) applies whether the requirement therein is in the form of an obligation or whether the law simply provides consequences for failing either to carry out the action in writing or to use a paper document.

(3)   If a right is to be granted to, or an obligation is to be acquired by, one person and no other person, and if the law requires that, in order to effect this, the right or obligation must be conveyed to that person by the transfer, or use of, a paper document, that requirement is met if the right or obligation is conveyed by using one or more data messages, provided that a reliable method is used to render such data message or messages unique.

(4)   For the purposes of paragraph (3), the standard of reliability required shall be assessed in the light of the purpose for which the right or obligation was conveyed and in the light of all the circumstances, including any relevant agreement.

(5)   Where one or more data messages are used to effect any action in subparagraphs (f) and (g) of article 16, no paper document used to effect any such action is valid unless the use of data messages has been terminated and replaced by the use of paper documents. A paper document issued in these circumstances shall contain a statement of such termination. The replacement of data messages by paper documents shall not affect the rights or obligations of the parties involved.

(6)   If a rule of law is compulsorily applicable to a contract of carriage of goods which is in, or is evidenced by, a paper document, that rule shall not be inapplicable to such a contract of carriage of goods which is evidenced by one or more data messages by reason of the fact that the contract is evidenced by such data message or messages instead of by a paper document.

(7)   The provisions of this article do not apply to the following: [...].

UNCITRAL MODEL LAW ON ELECTRONIC SIGNATURES, 2001

Article 1
Sphere of application

This Law applies where electronic signatures are used in the context* of commercial** activities. It does not override any rule of law intended for the protection of consumers.

* The Commission suggests the following text for States that might wish to extend the applicability of this Law:
'This Law applies where electronic signatures are used, except in the following situations: [...].'

** The term 'commercial' should be given a wide interpretation so as to cover matters arising from all relationships of a commercial nature, whether contractual or not. Relationships of a commercial nature include, but are not limited to, the following transactions: any trade transaction for the supply or exchange of goods or services; distribution agreement; commercial representation or agency; factoring; leasing; construction of works; consulting; engineering; licensing; investment; financing; banking; insurance; exploitation agreement or concession; joint venture and other forms of industrial or business cooperation; carriage of goods or passengers by air, sea, rail or road.

Article 2
Definitions

For the purposes of this Law:
(a)   'Electronic signature' means data in electronic form in, affixed to or logically associated with, a data message, which may be used to identify the signatory in relation to the data message and to indicate the signatory's approval of the information contained in the data message;
(b)   'Certificate' means a data message or other record confirming the link between a signatory and signature creation data;
(c)   'Data message' means information generated, sent, received or stored by electronic, optical or similar means including, but not limited to, electronic data interchange (EDI), electronic mail, telegram, telex or telecopy; and acts either on its own behalf or on behalf of the person it represents;
(d)   'Signatory' means a person that holds signature creation data and acts either on its own behalf or on behalf of the person it represents;
(e)   'Certification service provider' means a person that issues certificates and may provide other services related to electronic signatures;
(f)   'Relying party' means a person that may act on the basis of a certificate or an electronic signature.

Article 3
Equal treatment of signature technologies

Nothing in this Law, except article 5, shall be applied so as to exclude, restrict or deprive of legal effect any method of creating an electronic signature that satisfies the requirements referred to in article 6, paragraph 1, or otherwise meets the requirements of applicable law.

Article 4
Interpretation

1.   In the interpretation of this Law, regard is to be had to its international origin and to the need to promote uniformity in its application and the observance of good faith.
2.   Questions concerning matters governed by this Law which are not expressly settled in it are to be settled in conformity with the general principles on which this Law is based.

Article 5
Variation by agreement

The provisions of this Law may be derogated from or their effect may be varied by agreement, unless that agreement would not be valid or effective under applicable law.

Article 6
Compliance with a requirement for a signature

1.   Where the law requires a signature of a person, that requirement is met in relation to a data message if an electronic signature is used that is as reliable as was appropriate for the purpose for which the data message was generated or communicated, in the light of all the circumstances, including any relevant agreement.

2.   Paragraph 1 applies whether the requirement referred to therein is in the form of an obligation or whether the law simply provides consequences for the absence of a signature.

3.   An electronic signature is considered to be reliable for the purpose of satisfying the requirement referred to in paragraph 1 if:

   (a)   The signature creation data are, within the context in which they are used, linked to the signatory and to no other person;

   (b)   The signature creation data were, at the time of signing, under the control of the signatory and of no other person;

   (c)   Any alteration to the electronic signature, made after the time of signing, is detectable; and

   (d)   Where a purpose of the legal requirement for a signature is to provide assurance as to the integrity of the information to which it relates, any alteration made to that information after the time of signing is detectable.

4.   Paragraph 3 does not limit the ability of any person:

   (a)   To establish in any other way, for the purpose of satisfying the requirement referred to in paragraph 1, the reliability of an electronic signature; or

   (b)   To adduce evidence of the non-reliability of an electronic signature.

5.   The provisions of this article do not apply to the following: [...].

Article 7
Satisfaction of article 6

1.   *[Any person, organ or authority, whether public or private, specified by the enacting State as competent]* may determine which electronic signatures satisfy the provisions of article 6 of this Law.

2.   Any determination made under paragraph 1 shall be consistent with recognized international standards.

3.   Nothing in this article affects the operation of the rules of private international law.

Article 8
Conduct of the signatory

1.   Where signature creation data can be used to create a signature that has legal effect, each signatory shall:

   (a)   Exercise reasonable care to avoid unauthorized use of its signature creation data;

   (b)   Without undue delay, utilize means made available by the certification service provider pursuant to article 9 of this Law, or otherwise use reasonable efforts, to notify any person that may reasonably be expected by the signatory to rely on or to provide services in support of the electronic signature if:

      (i)   The signatory knows that the signature creation data have been compromised; or

      (ii)   The circumstances known to the signatory give rise to a substantial risk that the signature creation data may have been compromised;

   (c)   Where a certificate is used to support the electronic signature, exercise reasonable care to ensure the accuracy and completeness of all material representations made by the signatory that are relevant to the certificate throughout its life cycle or that are to be included in the certificate.

2. A signatory shall bear the legal consequences of its failure to satisfy the requirements of paragraph 1.

Article 9
Conduct of the certification service provider

1. Where a certification service provider provides services to support an electronic signature that may be used for legal effect as a signature, that certification service provider shall:
   - (a) Act in accordance with representations made by it with respect to its policies and practices;
   - (b) Exercise reasonable care to ensure the accuracy and completeness of all material representations made by it that are relevant to the certificate throughout its life cycle or that are included in the certificate;
   - (c) Provide reasonably accessible means that enable a relying party to ascertain from the certificate:
     - (i) The identity of the certification service provider;
     - (ii) That the signatory that is identified in the certificate had control of the signature creation data at the time when the certificate was issued;
     - (iii) That signature creation data were valid at or before the time when the certificate was issued;
   - (d) Provide reasonably accessible means that enable a relying party to ascertain, where relevant, from the certificate or otherwise:
     - (i) The method used to identify the signatory;
     - (ii) Any limitation on the purpose or value for which the signature creation data or the certificate may be used;
     - (iii) That the signature creation data are valid and have not been compromised;
     - (iv) Any limitation on the scope or extent of liability stipulated by the certification service provider;
     - (v) Whether means exist for the signatory to give notice pursuant to article 8, paragraph 1(b), of this Law;
     - (vi) Whether a timely revocation service is offered;
   - (e) Where services under subparagraph (d)(v) are offered, provide a means for a signatory to give notice pursuant to article 8, paragraph 1(b), of this Law and, where services under subparagraph (d)(vi) are offered, ensure the availability of a timely revocation service;
   - (f) Utilize trustworthy systems, procedures and human resources in performing its services.

2. A certification service provider shall bear the legal consequences of its failure to satisfy the requirements of paragraph 1.

Article 10
Trustworthiness

For the purposes of article 9, paragraph 1(f), of this Law in determining whether, or to what extent, any systems, procedures and human resources utilized by a certification service provider are trustworthy, regard may be had to the following factors:

(a) Financial and human resources, including existence of assets;

(b) Quality of hardware and software systems;

(c) Procedures for processing of certificates and applications for certificates and retention of records;

(d) Availability of information to signatories identified in certificates and to potential relying parties;

(e)   Regularity and extent of audit by an independent body;
(f)   The existence of a declaration by the State, an accreditation body or the certification service provider regarding compliance with or existence of the foregoing; or
(g)   Any other relevant factor.

Article 11
Conduct of the relying party

A relying party shall bear the legal consequences of its failure:
(a)   To take reasonable steps to verify the reliability of an electronic signature; or
(b)   Where an electronic signature is supported by a certificate, to take reasonable steps:
       (i)   To verify the validity, suspension or revocation of the certificate; and
       (ii)   To observe any limitation with respect to the certificate.

Article 12
Recognition of foreign certificates and electronic signatures

1.   In determining whether, or to what extent, a certificate or an electronic signature is legally effective, no regard shall be had:
       (a)   To the geographic location where the certificate is issued or the electronic signature created or used; or
       (b)   To the geographic location of the place of business of the issuer or signatory.
2.   A certificate issued outside [the enacting State] shall have the same legal effect in [the enacting State] as a certificate issued in [the enacting State] if it offers a substantially equivalent level of reliability.
3.   An electronic signature created or used outside [the enacting State] shall have the same legal effect in [the enacting State] as an electronic signature created or used in [the enacting State] if it offers a substantially equivalent level of reliability.
4.   In determining whether a certificate or an electronic signature offers a substantially equivalent level of reliability for the purposes of paragraph 2 or 3, regard shall be had to recognized international standards and to any other relevant factors.
5.   Where, notwithstanding paragraphs 2, 3 and 4, parties agree, as between themselves, to the use of certain types of electronic signatures or certificates, that agreement shall be recognized as sufficient for the purposes of cross-border recognition, unless that agreement would not be valid or effective under applicable law.

UNCITRAL MODEL LAW ON INTERNATIONAL COMMERCIAL ARBITRATION 1985

CHAPTER I
GENERAL PROVISIONS

Article 1
Scope of application*

(1)   This Law applies to international commercial** arbitration, subject to any agreement in force between this State and any other State or States.
(2)   The provisions of this Law, except articles 8, 9, 35 and 36, apply only if the place of arbitration is in the territory of this State.
(3)   An arbitration is international if—

- (a)   the parties to an arbitration agreement have, at the time of the conclusion of that agreement, their places of business in different States; or
- (b)   one of the following places is situated outside the State in which the parties have their places of business:
    - (i)   the place of arbitration if determined in, or pursuant to, the arbitration agreement;
    - (ii)   any place where a substantial part of the obligations of the commercial relationship is to be performed or the place with which the subject-matter of the dispute is most closely connected; or
- (c)   the parties have expressly agreed that the subject-matter of the arbitration agreement relates to more than one country.
- (4)   For the purposes of paragraph (3) of this article—
    - (a)   if a party has more than one place of business, the place of business is that which has the closest relationship to the arbitration agreement;
    - (b)   if a party does not have a place of business, reference is to be made to his habitual residence.
- (5)   This Law shall not affect any other law of this State by virtue of which certain disputes may not be submitted to arbitration or may be submitted to arbitration only according to provisions other than those of this Law.

* Article headings are for reference purposes only and are not to be used for purposes of interpretation.

** The term 'commercial' should be given a wide interpretation so as to cover matters arising from all relationships of a commercial nature, whether contractual or not. Relationships of a commercial nature include, but are not limited to, the following transactions: any trade transaction for the supply or exchange of goods or services; distribution agreement; commercial representation or agency; factoring; leasing; construction of works; consulting; engineering; licensing; investment; financing; banking; insurance; exploitation agreement or concession; joint venture and other forms of industrial or business co-operation; carriage of goods or passengers by air, sea, rail or road.

Article 2
Definitions and rules of interpretation

For the purposes of this Law—
- (a)   'Arbitration' means any arbitration whether or not administered by a permanent arbitral institution.
- (b)   'Arbitral tribunal' means a sole arbitrator or a panel of arbitrators.
- (c)   'Court' means a body or organ of the judicial system of a State.
- (d)   Where a provision of this Law, except article 28, leaves the parties free to determine a certain issue, such freedom includes the right of the parties to authorize a third party, including an institution, to make that determination.
- (e)   Where a provision of this Law refers to the fact that the parties have agreed or that they may agree or in any other way refers to an agreement of the parties, such agreement includes any arbitration rules referred to in that agreement.
- (f)   Where a provision of this Law, other than in articles 25(a) and 32(2)(a), refers to a claim, it also applies to a counter-claim, and where it refers to a defence, it also applies to a defence to such counter-claim.

Article 3
Receipt of written communications

- (1)   Unless otherwise agreed by the parties—
    - (a)   any written communication is deemed to have been received if it is delivered to the addressee personally or if it is delivered at his place of business, habitual residence or mailing address; if none of these can be found after making a reasonable inquiry, a written communication is deemed to have been received if it is sent to the addressee's last-known place of business,

habitual residence or mailing address by registered letter or any other means which provides a record of the attempt to deliver it;

(b)   the communication is deemed to have been received on the day it is so delivered.

(2)   The provisions of this article do not apply to communications in court proceedings.

Article 4
Waiver of right to object

A party who knows that any provision of this Law from which the parties may derogate or any requirement under the arbitration agreement has not been complied with and yet proceeds with the arbitration without stating his objection to such non-compliance without undue delay or, if a time-limit is provided therefor, within such period of time, shall be deemed to have waived his right to object.

Article 5
Extent of court intervention

In matters governed by this Law, no court shall intervene except where so provided in this Law.

Article 6
Court or other authority for certain functions of arbitration assistance and supervision

The functions referred to in articles 11(3), 11(4), 13(3), 14, 16(3) and 34(2) shall be performed by … [Each State enacting this model law specifies the court, courts or, where referred to therein, other authority competent to perform these functions.]

CHAPTER II
ARBITRATION AGREEMENT

Article 7
Definition and form of arbitration agreement

(1)   'Arbitration agreement' is an agreement by the parties to submit to arbitration all or certain disputes which have arisen or which may arise between them in respect of a defined legal relationship, whether contractual or not. An arbitration agreement may be in the form of an arbitration clause in a contract or in the form of a separate agreement.

(2)   The arbitration agreement shall be in writing. An agreement is in writing if it is contained in a document signed by the parties or in an exchange of letters, telex, telegrams or other means of telecommunication which provide a record of the agreement, or in an exchange of statements of claim and defence in which the existence of an agreement is alleged by one party and not denied by another. The reference in a contract to a document containing an arbitration clause constitutes an arbitration agreement provided that the contract is in writing and the reference is such as to make that clause part of the contract.

Article 8
Arbitration agreement and substantive claim before court

(1)   A court before which an action is brought in a matter which is the subject of an arbitration agreement shall, if a party so requests not later than when submitting his first statement on the substance of the dispute, refer the parties to arbitration

unless it finds that the agreement is null and void, inoperative or incapable of being performed.

(2)   Where an action referred to in paragraph (1) of this article has been brought, arbitral proceedings may nevertheless be commenced or continued, and an award may be made, while the issue is pending before the court.

Article 9
Arbitration agreement and interim measures by court

It is not incompatible with an arbitration agreement for a party to request, before or during arbitral proceedings, from a court an interim measure of protection and for a court to grant such measure.

CHAPTER III
COMPOSITION OF ARBITRAL TRIBUNAL

Article 10
Number of arbitrators

(1)   The parties are free to determine the number of arbitrators.
(2)   Failing such determination, the number of arbitrators shall be three.

Article 11
Appointment of arbitrators

(1)   No person shall be precluded by reason of his nationality from acting as an arbitrator, unless otherwise agreed by the parties.
(2)   The parties are free to agree on a procedure of appointing the arbitrator or arbitrators, subject to the provisions of paragraphs (4) and (5) of this article.
(3)   Failing such agreement—
    (a)   in an arbitration with three arbitrators, each party shall appoint one arbitrator, and the two arbitrators thus appointed shall appoint the third arbitrator; if a party fails to appoint the arbitrator within thirty days of receipt of a request to do so from the other party, or if the two arbitrators fail to agree on the third arbitrator within thirty days of their appointment, the appointment shall be made, upon request of a party, by the court or other authority specified in article 6;
    (b)   in an arbitration with a sole arbitrator, if the parties are unable to agree on the arbitrator, he shall be appointed, upon request of a party, by the court or other authority specified in article 6.
(4)   Where, under an appointment procedure agreed upon by the parties—
    (a)   a party fails to act as required under such procedure; or
    (b)   the parties, or two arbitrators, are unable to reach an agreement expected of them under such procedure; or
    (c)   a third party, including an institution, fails to perform any function entrusted to it under such procedure,
any party may request the court or other authority specified in article 6 to take the necessary measure, unless the agreement on the appointment procedure provides other means for securing the appointment.
(5)   A decision on a matter entrusted by paragraph (3) or (4) of this article to the court or other authority specified in article 6 shall be subject to no appeal. The court or other authority, in appointing an arbitrator, shall have due regard to any qualifications required of the arbitrator by the agreement of the parties and to such considerations as are likely to secure the appointment of an independent and impartial arbitrator and, in the case of a sole or third arbitrator, shall take into

account as well the advisability of appointing an arbitrator of a nationality other than those of the parties.

Article 12
Grounds for challenge

(1)   When a person is approached in connection with his possible appointment as an arbitrator, he shall disclose any circumstances likely to give rise to justifiable doubts as to his impartiality or independence. An arbitrator, from the time of his appointment and throughout the arbitral proceedings, shall without delay disclose any such circumstances to the parties unless they have already been informed of them by him.

(2)   An arbitrator may be challenged only if circumstances exist that give rise to justifiable doubts as to his impartiality or independence, or if he does not possess qualifications agreed to by the parties. A party may challenge an arbitrator appointed by him, or in whose appointment he has participated, only for reasons of which he becomes aware after the appointment has been made.

Article 13
Challenge procedure

(1)   The parties are free to agree on a procedure for challenging an arbitrator, subject to the provisions of paragraph (3) of this article.

(2)   Failing such agreement, a party who intends to challenge an arbitrator shall, within fifteen days after becoming aware of the constitution of the arbitral tribunal or after becoming aware of any circumstance referred to in article 12(2), send a written statement of the reasons for the challenge to the arbitral tribunal. Unless the challenged arbitrator withdraws from his office or the other party agrees to the challenge, the arbitral tribunal shall decide on the challenge.

(3)   If a challenge under any procedure agreed upon by the parties or under the procedure of paragraph (2) of this article is not successful, the challenging party may request, within thirty days after having received notice of the decision rejecting the challenge, the court or other authority specified in article 6 to decide on the challenge, which decision shall be subject to no appeal; while such a request is pending, the arbitral tribunal, including the challenged arbitrator, may continue the arbitral proceedings and make an award.

Article 14
Failure or impossibility to act

(1)   If an arbitrator becomes de jure or de facto unable to perform his functions or for other reasons fails to act without undue delay, his mandate terminates if he withdraws from his office or if the parties agree on the termination. Otherwise, if a controversy remains concerning any of these grounds, any party may request the court or other authority specified in article 6 to decide on the termination of the mandate, which decision shall be subject to no appeal.

(2)   If, under this article or article 13(2), an arbitrator withdraws from his office or a party agrees to the termination of the mandate of an arbitrator, this does not imply acceptance of the validity of any ground referred to in this article or article 12(2).

Article 15
Appointment of substitute arbitrator

Where the mandate of an arbitrator terminates under article 13 or 14 or because of his withdrawal from office for any other reason or because of the revocation of his mandate by agreement of the parties or in any other case of termination of his mandate, a substitute arbitrator shall be appointed according to the rules that were applicable to the appointment of the arbitrator being replaced.

CHAPTER IV
JURISDICTION OF ARBITRAL TRIBUNAL

Article 16
Competence of arbitral tribunal to rule on its jurisdiction

(1)   The arbitral tribunal may rule on its own jurisdiction, including any objections with respect to the existence or validity of the arbitration agreement. For that purpose, an arbitration clause which forms part of a contract shall be treated as an agreement independent of the other terms of the contract. A decision by the arbitral tribunal that the contract is null and void shall not entail ipso jure the invalidity of the arbitration clause.

(2)   A plea that the arbitral tribunal does not have jurisdiction shall be raised not later than the submission of the statement of defence. A party is not precluded from raising such a plea by the fact that he has appointed, or participated in the appointment of, an arbitrator. A plea that the arbitral tribunal is exceeding the scope of its authority shall be raised as soon as the matter alleged to be beyond the scope of its authority is raised during the arbitral proceedings. The arbitral tribunal may, in either case, admit a later plea if it considers the delay justified.

(3)   The arbitral tribunal may rule on a plea referred to in paragraph (2) of this article either as a preliminary question or in an award on the merits. If the arbitral tribunal rules as a preliminary question that it has jurisdiction, any party may request, within thirty days after having received notice of that ruling, the court specified in article 6 to decide the matter, which decision shall be subject to no appeal, while such a request is pending, the arbitral tribunal may continue the arbitral proceedings and make an award.

Article 17
Power of arbitral tribunal to order interim measures

Unless otherwise agreed by the parties, the arbitral tribunal may, at the request of a party, order any party to take such interim measure of protection as the arbitral tribunal may consider necessary in respect of the subject-matter of the dispute. The arbitral tribunal may require any party to provide appropriate security in connection with such measure.

CHAPTER V
CONDUCT OF ARBITRAL PROCEEDINGS

Article 18
Equal treatment of parties

The parties shall be treated with equality and each party shall be given a full opportunity of presenting his case.

Article 19
Determination of rules of procedure

(1)   Subject to the provisions of this Law, the parties are free to agree on the procedure to be followed by the arbitral tribunal in conducting the proceedings.

(2)   Failing such agreement, the arbitral tribunal may, subject to the provisions of this Law, conduct the arbitration in such manner as it considers appropriate. The power

conferred upon the arbitral tribunal includes the power to determine the admissibility, relevance, materiality and weight of any evidence.

Article 20
Place of arbitration

(1)   The parties are free to agree on the place of arbitration. Failing such agreement, the place of arbitration shall be determined by the arbitral tribunal having regard to the circumstances of the case, including the convenience of the parties.

(2)   Notwithstanding the provisions of paragraph (1) of this article, the arbitral tribunal may, unless otherwise agreed by the parties, meet at any place it considers appropriate for consultation among its members, for hearing witnesses, experts or the parties, or for inspection of goods, other property or documents.

Article 21
Commencement of arbitral proceedings

Unless otherwise agreed by the parties, the arbitral proceedings in respect of a particular dispute commence on the date on which a request for that dispute to be referred to arbitration is received by the respondent.

Article 22
Language

(1)   The parties are free to agree on the language or languages to be used in the arbitral proceedings. Failing such agreement, the arbitral tribunal shall determine the language or languages to be used in the proceedings. This agreement or determination, unless otherwise specified therein, shall apply to any written statement by a party, any hearing and any award, decision or other communication by the arbitral tribunal.

(2)   The arbitral tribunal may order that any documentary evidence shall be accompanied by a translation into the language or languages agreed upon by the parties or determined by the arbitral tribunal.

Article 23
Statements of claim and defence

(1)   Within the period of time agreed by the parties or determined by the arbitral tribunal, the claimant shall state the facts supporting his claim, the points at issue and the relief or remedy sought, and the respondent shall state his defence in respect of these particulars, unless the parties have otherwise agreed as to the required elements of such statements. The parties may submit with their statements all documents they consider to be relevant or may add a reference to the documents or other evidence they will submit.

(2)   Unless otherwise agreed by the parties, either party may amend or supplement his claim or defence during the course of the arbitral proceedings, unless the arbitral tribunal considers it inappropriate to allow such amendment having regard to the delay in making it.

Article 24
Hearings and written proceedings

(1)   Subject to any contrary agreement by the parties, the arbitral tribunal shall decide whether to hold oral hearings for the presentation of evidence or for oral argument, or whether the proceedings shall be conducted on the basis of documents and other materials. However, unless the parties have agreed that no

hearings shall be held, the arbitral tribunal shall hold such hearings at an appropriate stage of the proceedings, if so requested by a party.

(2)   The parties shall be given sufficient advance notice of any hearing and of any meeting of the arbitral tribunal for the purposes of inspection of goods, other property or documents.

(3)   All statements, documents or other information supplied to the arbitral tribunal by one party shall be communicated to the other party. Also any expert report or evidentiary document on which the arbitral tribunal may rely in making its decision shall be communicated to the parties.

Article 25
Default of a party

Unless otherwise agreed by the parties, if, without showing sufficient cause —

(a)   the claimant fails to communicate his statement of claim in accordance with article 23(1), the arbitral tribunal shall terminate the proceedings;

(b)   the respondent fails to communicate his statement of defence in accordance with article 23(1), the arbitral tribunal shall continue the proceedings without treating such failure in itself as an admission of the claimant's allegations;

(c)   any party fails to appear at a hearing or to produce documentary evidence, the arbitral tribunal may continue the proceedings and make the award on the evidence before it.

Article 26
Expert appointed by arbitral tribunal

(1)   Unless otherwise agreed by the parties, the arbitral tribunal —

(a)   may appoint one or more experts to report to it on specific issues to be determined by the arbitral tribunal;

(b)   may require a party to give the expert any relevant information or to produce, or to provide access to, any relevant documents, goods or other property for his inspection.

(2)   Unless otherwise agreed by the parties, if a party so requests or if the arbitral tribunal considers it necessary, the expert shall, after delivery of his written or oral report, participate in a hearing where the parties have the opportunity to put questions to him and to present expert witnesses in order to testify on the points at issue.

Article 27
Court assistance in taking evidence

The arbitral tribunal or a party with the approval of the arbitral tribunal may request from a competent court of this State assistance in taking evidence. The court may execute the request within its competence and according to its rules on taking evidence.

CHAPTER VI
MAKING OF AWARD AND TERMINATION OF PROCEEDINGS

Article 28
Rules applicable to substance of dispute

(1)   The arbitral tribunal shall decide the dispute in accordance with such rules of law as are chosen by the parties as applicable to the substance of the dispute. Any designation of the law or legal system of a given State shall be construed, unless

otherwise expressed, as directly referring to the substantive law of that State and not to its conflict of laws rules.

(2)   Failing any designation by the parties, the arbitral tribunal shall apply the law determined by the conflict of laws rules which it considers applicable.

(3)   The arbitral tribunal shall decide *ex aequo et bono* or as amiable compositeur only if the parties have expressly authorized it to do so.

(4)   In all cases, the arbitral tribunal shall decide in accordance with the terms of the contract and shall take into account the usages of the trade applicable to the transaction.

Article 29
Decision making by panel of arbitrators

In arbitral proceedings with more than one arbitrator, any decision of the arbitral tribunal shall be made, unless otherwise agreed by the parties, by a majority of all its members. However, questions of procedure may be decided by a presiding arbitrator, if so authorized by the parties or all members of the arbitral tribunal.

Article 30
Settlement

(1)   If, during arbitral proceedings, the parties settle the dispute, the arbitral tribunal shall terminate the proceedings and, if requested by the parties and not objected to by the arbitral tribunal, record the settlement in the form of an arbitral award on agreed terms.

(2)   An award on agreed terms shall be made in accordance with the provisions of article 31 and shall state that it is an award. Such an award has the same status and effect as any other award on the merits of the case.

Article 31
Form and contents of award

(1)   The award shall be made in writing and shall be signed by the arbitrator or arbitrators. In arbitral proceedings with more than one arbitrator, the signatures of the majority of all members of the arbitral tribunal shall suffice, provided that the reason for any omitted signature is stated.

(2)   The award shall state the reasons upon which it is based, unless the parties have agreed that no reasons are to be given or the award is an award on agreed terms under article 30.

(3)   The award shall state its date and the place of arbitration as determined in accordance with article 20(1). The award shall be deemed to have been made at that place.

(4)   After the award is made, a copy signed by the arbitrators in accordance with paragraph (1) of this article shall be delivered to each party.

Article 32
Termination of proceedings

(1)   The arbitral proceedings are terminated by the final award or by an order of the arbitral tribunal in accordance with paragraph (2) of this article.

(2)   The arbitral tribunal shall issue an order for the termination of the arbitral proceedings when—

   (a)   the claimant withdraws his claim, unless the respondent objects thereto and the arbitral tribunal recognizes a legitimate interest on his part in obtaining a final settlement of the dispute;

   (b)   the parties agree on the termination of the proceedings;

(c)   the arbitral tribunal finds that the continuation of the proceedings has for any other reason become unnecessary or impossible.

(3)   The mandate of the arbitral tribunal terminates with the termination of the arbitral proceedings, subject to the provisions of articles 33 and 34(4).

Article 33
Correction and interpretation of award; additional award

(1)   Within thirty days of receipt of the award, unless another period of time has been agreed upon by the parties—

(a)   a party, with notice to the other party, may request the arbitral tribunal to correct in the award any errors in computation, any clerical or typographical errors or any errors of similar nature;

(b)   if so agreed by the parties, a party, with notice to the other party, may request the arbitral tribunal to give an interpretation of a specific point or part of the award.

If the arbitral tribunal considers the request to be justified, it shall make the correction or give the interpretation within thirty days of receipt of the request. The interpretation shall form part of the award.

(2)   The arbitral tribunal may correct any error of the type referred to in paragraph (1)(a) of this article on its own initiative within thirty days of the date of the award.

(3)   Unless otherwise agreed by the parties, a party, with notice to the other party, may request, within thirty days of receipt of the award, the arbitral tribunal to make an additional award as to claims presented in the arbitral proceedings but omitted from the award. If the arbitral tribunal considers the request to be justified, it shall make the additional award within sixty days.

(4)   The arbitral tribunal may extend, if necessary, the period of time within which it shall make a correction, interpretation or an additional award under paragraph (1) or (3) of this article.

(5)   The provisions of article 31 shall apply to a correction or interpretation of the award or to an additional award.

CHAPTER VII
RECOURSE AGAINST AWARD

Article 34
Application for setting aside as exclusive recourse against arbitral award

(1)   Recourse to a court against an arbitral award may be made only by an application for setting aside in accordance with paragraphs (2) and (3) of this article.

(2)   An arbitral award may be set aside by the court specified in article 6 only if—

(a)   the party making the application furnishes proof that:

(i)   a party to the arbitration agreement referred to in article 7 was under some incapacity; or the said agreement is not valid under the law to which the parties have subjected it or, failing any indication thereon, under the law of this State; or

(ii)   the party making the application was not given proper notice of the appointment of an arbitrator or of the arbitral proceedings or was otherwise unable to present his case; or

(iii)   the award deals with a dispute not contemplated by or not falling within the terms of the submission to arbitration, or contains decisions on matters beyond the scope of the submission to arbitration, provided that, if the decisions on matters submitted to arbitration can be separated from those not so submitted, only that part of the award which contains decisions on matters not submitted to arbitration may be set aside; or

(iv) the composition of the arbitral tribunal or the arbitral procedure was not in accordance with the agreement of the parties, unless such agreement was in conflict with a provision of this Law from which the parties cannot derogate, or, failing such agreement, was not in accordance with this Law; or

(b) the court finds that:

    (i) the subject-matter of the dispute is not capable of settlement by arbitration under the law of this State; or

    (ii) the award is in conflict with the public policy of this State.

(3) An application for setting aside may not be made after three months have elapsed from the date on which the party making that application had received the award or, if a request had been made under article 33, from the date on which that request had been disposed of by the arbitral tribunal.

(4) The court, when asked to set aside an award, may, where appropriate and so requested by a party, suspend the setting aside proceedings for a period of time determined by it in order to give the arbitral tribunal an opportunity to resume the arbitral proceedings or to take such other action as in the arbitral tribunal's opinion will eliminate the grounds for setting aside.

CHAPTER VIII
RECOGNITION AND ENFORCEMENT OF AWARDS

Article 35
Recognition and enforcement

(1) An arbitral award, irrespective of the country in which it was made, shall be recognized as binding and, upon application in writing to the competent court, shall be enforced subject to the provisions of this article and of article 36.

(2) The party relying on an award or applying for its enforcement shall supply the duly authenticated original award or a duly certified copy thereof, and the original arbitration agreement referred to in article 7 or a duly certified copy thereof. If the award or agreement is not made in an official language of this State, the party shall supply a duly certified translation thereof into such language.***

*** The conditions set forth in this paragraph are intended to set maximum standards. It would, thus, not be contrary to the harmonization to be achieved by the model law if a State retained even less onerous conditions.

Article 36
Grounds for refusing recognition or enforcement

(1) Recognition or enforcement of an arbitral award, irrespective of the country in which it was made, may be refused only:

(a) at the request of the party against whom it is invoked, if that party furnishes to the competent court where recognition or enforcement is sought proof that:

    (i) a party to the arbitration agreement referred to in article 7 was under some incapacity; or the said agreement is not valid under the law to which the parties have subjected it or, failing any indication thereon, under the law of the country where the award was made; or

    (ii) the party against whom the award is invoked was not given proper notice of the appointment of an arbitrator or of the arbitral proceedings or was otherwise unable to present his case; or

    (iii) the award deals with a dispute not contemplated by or not falling within the terms of the submission to arbitration, or it contains decisions on matters beyond the scope of the submission to arbitration, provided that, if the decisions on matters submitted to arbitration can be separated from those not so submitted, that part of the award which contains decisions on matters submitted to arbitration may be recognized and enforced; or

(iv) the composition of the arbitral tribunal or the arbitral procedure was not in accordance with the agreement of the parties or, failing such agreement, was not in accordance with the law of the country where the arbitration took place; or

(v) the award has not yet become binding on the parties or has been set aside or suspended by a court of the country in which, or under the law of which, that award was made; or

(b) if the court finds that:

(i) the subject-matter of the dispute is not capable of settlement by arbitration under the law of this State; or

(ii) the recognition or enforcement of the award would be contrary to the public policy of this State.

(2) If an application for setting aside or suspension of an award has been made to a court referred to in paragraph (1)(a)(v) of this article, the court where recognition or enforcement is sought may, if it considers it proper, adjourn its decision and may also, on the application of the party claiming recognition or enforcement of the award, order the other party to provide appropriate security.

UNCITRAL MODEL LAW ON INTERNATIONAL COMMERCIAL CONCILIATION, 2003

Article 1
Scope of application and definitions

(1) This Law applies to international* commercial** conciliation.

(2) For the purposes of this Law, 'conciliator' means a sole conciliator or two or more conciliators, as the case may be.

(3) For the purposes of this Law, 'conciliation' means a process, whether referred to by the expression conciliation, mediation or an expression of similar import, whereby parties request a third person or persons ('the conciliator') to assist them in their attempt to reach an amicable settlement of their dispute arising out of or relating to a contractual or other legal relationship. The conciliator does not have the authority to impose upon the parties a solution to the dispute.

(4) A conciliation is international if:

(a) The parties to an agreement to conciliate have, at the time of the conclusion of that agreement, their places of business in different States; or

(b) The State in which the parties have their places of business is different from either:

(i) The State in which a substantial part of the obligations of the commercial relationship is to be performed; or

(ii) The State with which the subject matter of the dispute is most closely connected.

(5) For the purposes of this article:

(a) If a party has more than one place of business, the place of business is that which has the closest relationship to the agreement to conciliate;

(b) If a party does not have a place of business, reference is to be made to the party's habitual residence.

(6) This Law also applies to a commercial conciliation when the parties agree that the conciliation is international or agree to the applicability of this Law.

(7) The parties are free to agree to exclude the applicability of this Law.

(8)   Subject to the provisions of paragraph (9) of this article, this Law applies irrespective of the basis upon which the conciliation is carried out, including agreement between the parties whether reached before or after a dispute has arisen, an obligation established by law, or a direction or suggestion of a court, arbitral tribunal or competent governmental entity.

(9)   This Law does not apply to:

    (a)   Cases where a judge or an arbitrator, in the course of judicial or arbitral proceedings, attempts to facilitate a settlement; and

    (b)   [...].

* States wishing to enact this Model Law to apply to domestic as well as international conciliation may wish to consider the following changes to the text:

    —   Delete the word 'international' in paragraph (1) of article 1; and
    —   Delete paragraphs (4), (5) and (6) of article 1.

** The term 'commercial' should be given a wide interpretation so as to cover matters arising from all relationships of a commercial nature, whether contractual or not. Relationships of a commercial nature include, but are not limited to, the following transactions: any trade transaction for the supply or exchange of goods or services; distribution agreement; commercial representation or agency; factoring; leasing; construction of works; consulting; engineering; licensing; investment; financing; banking; insurance; exploitation agreement or concession; joint venture and other forms of industrial or business cooperation; carriage of goods or passengers by air, sea, rail or road.

Article 2
Interpretation

(1)   In the interpretation of this Law, regard is to be had to its international origin and to the need to promote uniformity in its application and the observance of good faith.

(2)   Questions concerning matters governed by this Law which are not expressly settled in it are to be settled in conformity with the general principles on which this Law is based.

Article 3
Variation by agreement

Except for the provisions of article 2 and article 6, paragraph (3), the parties may agree to exclude or vary any of the provisions of this Law.

Article 4
Commencement of conciliation proceedings***

(1)   Conciliation proceedings in respect of a dispute that has arisen commence on the day on which the parties to that dispute agree to engage in conciliation proceedings.

(2)   If a party that invited another party to conciliate does not receive an acceptance of the invitation within thirty days from the day on which the invitation was sent, or within such other period of time as specified in the invitation, the party may elect to treat this as a rejection of the invitation to conciliate.

Article 5
Number and appointment of conciliators

(1)   There shall be one conciliator, unless the parties agree that there shall be two or more conciliators.

(2)   The parties shall endeavour to reach agreement on a conciliator or conciliators, unless a different procedure for their appointment has been agreed upon.

(3)   Parties may seek the assistance of an institution or person in connection with the appointment of conciliators. In particular:

(a)   A party may request such an institution or person to recommend suitable persons to act as conciliator; or

(b)   The parties may agree that the appointment of one or more conciliators be made directly by such an institution or person.

(4)   In recommending or appointing individuals to act as conciliator, the institution or person shall have regard to such considerations as are likely to secure the appointment of an independent and impartial conciliator and, where appropriate, shall take into account the advisability of appointing a conciliator of a nationality other than the nationalities of the parties.

(5)   When a person is approached in connection with his or her possible appointment as conciliator, he or she shall disclose any circumstances likely to give rise to justifiable doubts as to his or her impartiality or independence. A conciliator, from the time of his or her appointment and throughout the conciliation proceedings, shall without delay disclose any such circumstances to the parties unless they have already been informed of them by him or her.

*** The following text is suggested for States that might wish to adopt a provision on the suspension of the limitation period:

Article X
Suspension of limitation period

(1)   When the conciliation proceedings commence, the running of the limitation period regarding the claim that is the subject matter of the conciliation is suspended.

(2)   Where the conciliation proceedings have terminated without a settlement agreement, the limitation period resumes running from the time the conciliation ended without a settlement agreement.

Article 6
Conduct of conciliation

(1)   The parties are free to agree, by reference to a set of rules or otherwise, on the manner in which the conciliation is to be conducted.

(2)   Failing agreement on the manner in which the conciliation is to be conducted, the conciliator may conduct the conciliation proceedings in such a manner as the conciliator considers appropriate, taking into account the circumstances of the case, any wishes that the parties may express and the need for a speedy settlement of the dispute.

(3)   In any case, in conducting the proceedings, the conciliator shall seek to maintain fair treatment of the parties and, in so doing, shall take into account the circumstances of the case.

(4)   The conciliator may, at any stage of the conciliation proceedings, make proposals for a settlement of the dispute.

Article 7
Communication between conciliator and parties

The conciliator may meet or communicate with the parties together or with each of them separately.

Article 8
Disclosure of information

When the conciliator receives information concerning the dispute from a party, the conciliator may disclose the substance of that information to any other party to the conciliation. However, when a party gives any information to the conciliator, subject to a specific condition that it be kept confidential, that information shall not be disclosed to any other party to the conciliation.

Article 9
Confidentiality

Unless otherwise agreed by the parties, all information relating to the conciliation proceedings shall be kept confidential, except where disclosure is required under the law or for the purposes of implementation or enforcement of a settlement agreement.

Article 10
Admissibility of evidence in other proceedings

(1)   A party to the conciliation proceedings, the conciliator and any third person, including those involved in the administration of the conciliation proceedings, shall not in arbitral, judicial or similar proceedings rely on, introduce as evidence or give testimony or evidence regarding any of the following:

   (a)   An invitation by a party to engage in conciliation proceedings or the fact that a party was willing to participate in conciliation proceedings;

   (b)   Views expressed or suggestions made by a party in the conciliation in respect of a possible settlement of the dispute;

   (c)   Statements or admissions made by a party in the course of the conciliation proceedings;

   (d)   Proposals made by the conciliator;

   (e)   The fact that a party had indicated its willingness to accept a proposal for settlement made by the conciliator;

   (f)   A document prepared solely for purposes of the conciliation proceedings.

(2)   Paragraph (1) of this article applies irrespective of the form of the information or evidence referred to therein.

(3)   The disclosure of the information referred to in paragraph (1) of this article shall not be ordered by an arbitral tribunal, court or other competent governmental authority and, if such information is offered as evidence in contravention of paragraph (1) of this article, that evidence shall be treated as inadmissible. Nevertheless, such information may be disclosed or admitted in evidence to the extent required under the law or for the purposes of implementation or enforcement of a settlement agreement.

(4)   The provisions of paragraphs (1), (2) and (3) of this article apply whether or not the arbitral, judicial or similar proceedings relate to the dispute that is or was the subject matter of the conciliation proceedings.

(5)   Subject to the limitations of paragraph (1) of this article, evidence that is otherwise admissible in arbitral or judicial or similar proceedings does not become inadmissible as a consequence of having been used in a conciliation.

Article 11
Termination of conciliation proceedings

The conciliation proceedings are terminated:

(a)   By the conclusion of a settlement agreement by the parties, on the date of the agreement;

(b)   By a declaration of the conciliator, after consultation with the parties, to the effect that further efforts at conciliation are no longer justified, on the date of the declaration;

(c)   By a declaration of the parties addressed to the conciliator to the effect that the conciliation proceedings are terminated, on the date of the declaration; or

(d)   By a declaration of a party to the other party or parties and the conciliator, if appointed, to the effect that the conciliation proceedings are terminated, on the date of the declaration.

Article 12
Conciliator acting as arbitrator

Unless otherwise agreed by the parties, the conciliator shall not act as an arbitrator in respect of a dispute that was or is the subject of the conciliation proceedings or in respect of another dispute that has arisen from the same contract or legal relationship or any related contract or legal relationship.

Article 13
Resort to arbitral or judicial proceedings

Where the parties have agreed to conciliate and have expressly undertaken not to initiate during a specified period of time or until a specified event has occurred arbitral or judicial proceedings with respect to an existing or future dispute, such an undertaking shall be given effect by the arbitral tribunal or the court until the terms of the undertaking have been complied with, except to the extent necessary for a party, in its opinion, to preserve its rights. Initiation of such proceedings is not of itself to be regarded as a waiver of the agreement to conciliate or as a termination of the conciliation proceedings.

Article 14
Enforceability of settlement agreement****

If the parties conclude an agreement settling a dispute, that settlement agreement is binding and enforceable ... [the enacting State may insert a description of the method of enforcing settlement agreements or refer to provisions governing such enforcement].

**** When implementing the procedure for enforcement of settlement agreements, an enacting State may consider the possibility of such a procedure being mandatory.

UNIDROIT PRINCIPLES OF INTERNATIONAL COMMERCIAL CONTRACTS, 1994*

PREAMBLE—PURPOSE OF THE PRINCIPLES

These Principles set forth general rules for international commercial contracts.
    They shall be applied when the parties have agreed that their contract be governed by.
    They may be applied when the parties have agreed that their contracts be governed by general principles of law, the *lex mercatoria* or the like.
    They may provide a solution to an issue raised when it proves impossible to establish the relevant rule of applicable law.
    They may be used to interpret or supplement international uniform law instruments.
    They may serve as a model for national and international legislators.

CHAPTER 1
GENERAL PROVISIONS

Article 1.1
Freedom of contract

The parties are free to enter into a contract and determine its content.

Article 1.2
No form required

Nothing in these Principles requires a contract to be concluded in or evidenced by writing. It may be proved by any means, including witnesses.

Article 1.3
Binding character of contract

A contract validly entered into is binding upon the parties. It can only be modified or terminated in accordance with its terms or by agreement or as otherwise provided in these Principles.

Article 1.4
Mandatory rules

Nothing in these Principles shall restrict the application of mandatory rules, whether of national, international or supranational origin, which are applicable in accordance with the relevant rules of private international law.

Article 1.5
Exclusion or modification by the parties

The parties may exclude the application of these Principles or derogate from or vary the effect of any of their provisions, except as otherwise provided in the Principles.

Article 1.6
Interpretation and supplementation of the principles

(1)   In the interpretation of these Principles, regard is to be had to their international character and to their purposes including the need to promote uniformity in their application.
(2)   Issues within the scope of these Principles but not expressly settled by them are as far as possible to be settled in accordance with their underlying general principles.

Article 1.7
Good faith and fair dealing

(1)   Each party must act in accordance with good faith and fair dealing in international trade.
(2)   The parties may not exclude or limit this duty.

Article 1.8
Usages and practices

(1)   The parties are bound by any usage to which they have agreed and by any practices which they have established between themselves.
(2)   The parties are bound by a usage that is widely known to and regularly observed in international trade by parties in the particular trade concerned except where the application of such usage would be unreasonable.

Article 1.9
Notice

(1)   Where notice is required it may be given by any means appropriate to the circumstances.

(2)   A notice is effective when it reaches the person to whom it is given.
(3)   For the purpose of paragraph (2) a notice 'reaches' a person when given to that person orally or delivered at that person's place of business or mailing address.
(4)   For the purpose of this article 'notice' includes a declaration, demand, request or any other communication of intention.

Article 1.10
Definitions

In these Principles—
—   court' includes an arbitral tribunal;
—   where a party has more than one place of business the relevant 'place of business' is that which has the closest relationship to the contract and its performance, having regard to the circumstances known to or contemplated by the parties at any time before or at the conclusion of the contract;
—   'obligor' refers to the party who is to perform an obligation and 'obligee' refers to the party who is entitled to performance of that obligation;
—   'writing' means any mode of communication that preserves a record of the information contained therein and is capable of being reproduced in tangible form.

CHAPTER 2
FORMATION

Article 2.1
Manner of formation

A contract may be concluded either by the acceptance of an offer or by conduct of the parties that is sufficient to show agreement.

Article 2.2
Definition of offer

A proposal for concluding a contract constitutes an offer if it is sufficiently definite and indicates the intention of the offeror to be bound in case of acceptance.

Article 2.3
Withdrawal of offer

(1)   An offer becomes effective when it reaches the offeree.
(2)   An offer, even if it is irrevocable, may be withdrawn if the withdrawal reaches the offeree before or at the same time as the offer.

Article 2.4
Revocation of offer

(1)   Until a contract is concluded an offer may be revoked if the revocation reaches the offeree before it has dispatched an acceptance.
(2)   However, an offer cannot be revoked—
       (a)   if it indicates, whether by stating a fixed time for acceptance or otherwise, that it is irrevocable; or
       (b)   if it was reasonable for the offeree to rely on the offer as being irrevocable and the offeree has acted in reliance of the offer.

Article 2.5
Rejection of offer

An offer is terminated when a rejection reaches the offeror.

Article 2.6
Mode of acceptance

(1)   A statement made by or other conduct of the offeree indicating assent to an offer is an acceptance. Silence or inactivity does not in itself amount to acceptance.
(2)   An acceptance of an offer becomes effective when the indication of assent reaches the offeror.
(3)   However, if, by virtue of the offer or as a result of practices which the parties have established between themselves or of usage, the offeree may indicate assent by performing an act without notice to the offeror, the acceptance is effective when the act is performed.

Article 2.7
Time of acceptance

An offer must be accepted within the time the offeror has fixed or, if no time is fixed, within a reasonable time having regard to the circumstances, including the rapidity of the means of communication employed by the offeror. An oral offer must be accepted immediately unless the circumstances indicate otherwise.

Article 2.8
Acceptance within a fixed period of time

(1)   A period of time for acceptance fixed by the offeror in a telegram or a letter begins to run from the moment the telegram is handed in for dispatch or from the date shown on the letter or, if no such date is shown, from the date shown on the envelope. A period of time for acceptance fixed by the offeror by means of instantaneous communication begins to run from the moment that offer reaches the offeree.
(2)   Official holidays or non-business days occurring during the period for acceptance are included in calculating the period. However, if a notice of acceptance cannot be delivered at the address of the offeror on the last day of the period because that day falls on an official holiday or a non-business day at the place of business of the offeror, the period is extended until the first business day which follows.

Article 2.9
Late acceptance; delay in transmission

(1)   A late acceptance is nevertheless effective as an acceptance if without undue delay the offeror so informs the offeree or gives notice to that effect.
(2)   If a letter or other writing containing a late acceptance shows that it has been sent in such circumstances that if its transmission had been normal it would have reached the offeror in due time, the late acceptance is effective as an acceptance, unless without undue delay, the offeror informs the offeree that it considers the offer as having lapsed.

Article 2.10
Withdrawal of acceptance

An acceptance may be withdrawn if the withdrawal reaches the offeror before or at the same time as the acceptance would have become effective.

Article 2.11
Modified acceptance

(1)   A reply to an offer which purports to be an acceptance but contains additions, limitations or other modifications is a rejection of the offer and constitutes a counter-offer.

(2)   However, a reply to an offer which purports to be an acceptance but contains additional or different terms which do not materially alter the terms of the offer constitutes an acceptance, unless the offeror without undue delay, objects to the discrepancy. If the offeror does not object, the terms of the contract are the terms of the offer with the modifications contained in the acceptance.

Article 2.12
Writings in confirmation

If a writing which is sent within a reasonable time after the conclusion of the contract and which purports to be a confirmation of the contract contains additional or different terms, such terms become part of the contract, unless they materially alter the contract or the recipient, without undue delay, objects to the discrepancy.

Article 2.13
Conclusion of contract dependent on agreement on specific matters or in a specific form

Where in the course of negotiations one of the parties insists that the contract is not concluded until there is agreement on specific matters or in a specific form, no contract is concluded before agreement is reached on those matters or in that form.

Article 2.14
Contract with terms deliberately left open

(1)   If the parties intend to conclude a contract, the fact that they intentionally leave a term to be agreed upon in further negotiations or to be determined by a third person does not prevent a contract from coming into existence.

(2)   The existence of the contract is not affected by the fact that subsequently—
      (a)   the parties reach no agreement on the terms; or
      (b)   the third person does not determine the term, provided that there is an alternative means of rendering the term definite that is reasonable in the circumstances, having regard to the intention of the parties.

Article 2.15
Negotiations in bad faith

(1)   A party is free to negotiate and is not liable for failure to reach an agreement.

(2)   However, a party who negotiates or breaks off negotiations in bad faith is liable for the losses caused to the other party.

(3)   It is bad faith, in particular, for a party to enter into or continue negotiations when intending not to reach an agreement with the other party.

Article 2.16
Duty of confidentiality

Where information is given as confidential by one party in the course of negotiations, the other party is under a duty not to disclose that information or to use it improperly for its own purposes, whether or not a contract is subsequently concluded. Where appropriate, the remedy for breach of that duty may include compensation based on the benefit received by the other party.

Article 2.17
Merger clause

A contract in writing which contains a clause indicating that the writing completely embodies the terms on which the parties have agreed cannot be contradicted or supplemented by evidence of prior statements or agreements. However, such statements or agreements may be used to interpret the writing.

Article 2.18
Written modification clause

A contract in writing which contains a clause requiring any modification or termination by agreement to be in writing may not be otherwise modified or terminated. However, a party may be precluded by its conduct from asserting such a clause to the extent that the other party has acted in reliance on that conduct.

Article 2.19
Contracting under standard terms

(1)   Where one party or both parties use standard terms in concluding a contract, the general rules of formation apply, subject to Articles 2.20–2.22.
(2)   Standard terms are provisions which are prepared in advance for general and repeated use by one party and which are actually used without negotiation with the other party.

Article 2.20
Surprising terms

(1)   No term contained in standard terms which is of such a character that the other party could not reasonably have expected it, is effective unless it has been expressly accepted by that party.
(2)   In determining whether a term is of such a character regard is to be had to its content, language and presentation.

Article 2.21
Conflict between standard terms and non-standard terms

In case of conflict between a standard term and a term which is not a standard term the latter prevails.

Article 2.22
Battle of forms

Where both parties use standard terms and reach agreement except on those terms, a contract is concluded on the basis of the agreed terms and of any standard terms which are common in substance unless one party clearly indicates in advance, or later and without undue delay informs the other party, that it does not intend to be bound by such a contract.

CHAPTER 3
VALIDITY

Article 3.1
Matters not covered

These Principles do not deal with invalidity arising from—
(a)   lack of capacity;
(b)   lack of authority;
(c)   immorality or illegality.

Article 3.2
Validity of mere agreement

A contract is concluded, modified or terminated by the mere agreement of the parties, without any further requirements.

Article 3.3
Initial impossibility

(1)   The mere fact that at the time of the conclusion of the contract the performance of the obligation assumed was impossible does not affect the validity of the contract.
(2)   The mere fact that at the time of the conclusion of the contract a party was not entitled to dispose of the assets to which the contract relates does not affect the validity of the contract.

Article 3.4
Definition of mistake

Mistake is an erroneous assumption relating to facts or to law existing when the contract was concluded.

Article 3.5
Relevant mistake

(1)   A party may only avoid the contract for mistake if, when the contract was concluded, the mistake was of such importance that a reasonable person in the same situation as the party in error would only have concluded the contract on materially different terms or would not have concluded it at all if the true state of affairs had been known, and—
(a)   the other party made the same mistake, or caused the mistake, or knew or ought to have known of the mistake and it was contrary to reasonable commercial standards of fair dealing to leave the mistaken party in error; or
(b)   the other party had not at the time of avoidance acted in reliance on the contract.
(2)   However, a party may not avoid the contract if—
(a)   it was grossly negligent in committing the mistake; or
(b)   the mistake relates to a matter in regard to which the risk of mistake was assumed or, having regard to the circumstances, should be borne by the mistaken party.

Article 3.6
Error in expression or transmission

An error occurring in the expression or transmission of a declaration is considered to be a mistake of the person from whom the declaration emanated.

Article 3.7
Remedies for non-performance

A party is not entitled to avoid the contract on the ground of mistake if the circumstances on which that party relies afford, or could have afforded, a remedy for non-performance.

Article 3.8
Fraud

A party may avoid the contract when it has been led to conclude the contract by the other party's fraudulent representation, including language or practices, or fraudulent non-disclosure of circumstances which, according to reasonable commercial standards of fair dealing, the latter party should have disclosed.

Article 3.9
Threat

A party may avoid the contract when it has been led to conclude the contract by the other party's unjustified threat which, having regard to the circumstances, is so imminent and serious as to leave the first party no reasonable alternative. In particular, a threat is unjustified if the act or omission with which a party has been threatened is wrongful in itself, or is wrong to use it as a means to obtain the conclusion of the contract.

Article 3.10
Gross disparity

(1)   A party may avoid the contract or an individual term of it if, at the time of the conclusion of the contract, the contract term unjustifiably gave the other party an excessive advantage. Regard is to be had, among other factors, to—
   (a)   the fact that the other party has taken unfair advantage of the first party's dependence, economic distress or urgent needs, or of its improvidence, ignorance, inexperience or lack of bargaining skill; and
   (b)   the nature and purpose of the contract.
(2)   Upon the request of the party entitled to avoidance, a court may adapt the contract or term in order to make it accord with reasonable commercial standards of fair dealing.
(3)   A court may also adapt the contract or term upon the request of the party receiving notice of avoidance, provided that that party informs the other party of its request promptly after receiving such notice and before the other party has acted in reliance on it. The provisions of Article 3.13(2) apply accordingly.

Article 3.11
Third persons

(1)   Where fraud, threat, gross disparity or a party's mistake is imputable to, or is known or ought to be known by, a third person for whose acts the other party is responsible, the contract may be avoided under the same conditions as if the behaviour or knowledge had been that of the party itself.
(2)   Where fraud, threat or gross disparity is imputable to a third person for whose acts the other party is not responsible, the contract may be avoided if that party knew or ought to have known of the fraud, threat or disparity, or has not at the time of avoidance acted in reliance on the contract.

Article 3.12
Confirmation

If the party entitled to avoid the contract expressly or impliedly confirms the contract after the period of time for giving notice of avoidance has begun to run, avoidance of contract is excluded.

Article 3.13
Loss of right to avoid

(1)   If a party is entitled to avoid the contract for mistake but the other party declares itself willing to perform or performs the contract as it was understood by the party entitled to avoidance, the contract is considered to have been concluded as the latter party understood it. The other party must make such a declaration or render such performance promptly after having been informed of the manner in which the party entitled to avoidance had understood the contract and before that party has acted in reliance on a notice of avoidance.

(2)   After such a declaration or performance the right to avoidance is lost and any earlier notice of avoidance is ineffective.

Article 3.14
Notice of avoidance

The right of a party to avoid the contract is exercised by notice to the other party.

Article 3.15
Time limits

(1)   Notice of avoidance shall be given within a reasonable time, having regard to the circumstances, after the avoiding party knew or could not have been unaware of the relevant facts or became capable of acting freely.

(2)   Where an individual term of the contract may be avoided by a party under Article 3.10, the period of time for giving notice of avoidance begins to run when that term is asserted by the other party.

Article 3.16
Partial avoidance

Where a ground of avoidance affects only individual terms of the contract, the effect of avoidance is limited to those terms unless, having regard to the circumstances, it is unreasonable to uphold the remaining contract.

Article 3.17
Retroactive effect of avoidance

(1)   Avoidance takes effect retroactively.

(2)   On avoidance either party may claim restitution of whatever is supplied under the contract or the part of it avoided, provided that it concurrently makes restitution of whatever it has received under the contract or the part of it avoided or, if it cannot make restitution in kind, it makes an allowance for what it has received.

Article 3.18
Damages

Irrespective of whether or not the contract has been avoided, the party who knew or ought to have known of the ground for avoidance is liable for damages so as to put the other party in the same position in which it would have been if it had not concluded the contract.

Article 3.19
Mandatory character of the provision

The provisions of this Chapter are mandatory, except insofar as they relate to the binding force of mere agreement, initial impossibility or mistake.

Article 3.20
Unilateral Declarations

The provisions of this Chapter apply with appropriate adaptations to any communication of intention addressed by one party to the other.

CHAPTER 4
INTERPRETATION

Article 4.1
Intention of the parties

(1)   A contract shall be interpreted according to the common intention of the parties.
(2)   If such an intention cannot be established, the contract shall be interpreted according to the meaning that reasonable persons of the same kind as the parties would give to it in the same circumstances.

Article 4.2
Interpretation of statements and other conduct

(1)   The statements and other conduct of a party shall be interpreted according to that party's intention if the other party knew or could not have been unaware of that intention.
(2)   If the preceding paragraph is not applicable, such statements and other conduct shall be interpreted according to the meaning that a reasonable person of the same kind as the other party would give to it in the same circumstances.

Article 4.3
Relevant circumstances

In applying Articles 4.1 and 4.2, regard shall be had to all the circumstances, including—
(a)   preliminary negotiations between the parties;
(b)   practices which the parties have established between themselves;
(c)   the conduct of the parties subsequent to the conclusion of the contract;
(d)   the nature and purpose of the contract;
(e)   the meaning commonly given to terms and expressions in the trade concerned;
(f)   usages.

Article 4.4
Reference to contract or statement as a whole

Terms and expressions shall be interpreted in the light of the whole contract or statement in which they appear.

Article 4.5
All terms to be given effect

Contract terms shall be interpreted so as to give effect to all the terms rather than to deprive some of them of effect.

Article 4.6
Contra proferentem rule

If contract terms supplied by one party are unclear, an interpretation against that party is preferred.

Article 4.7
Linguistic discrepancies

Where a contract is drawn up in two or more language versions which are equally authoritative there is, in case of discrepancy between the versions, a preference for the interpretation according to a version in which the contract was originally drawn up.

Article 4.8
Supplying an omitted term

(1)   Where the parties to a contract have not agreed with respect to a term which is important for a determination of their rights and duties, a term which is appropriate in the circumstances shall be supplied.

(2)   In determining what is an appropriate term regard shall be had, among other factors to—
   (a)   the intention of the parties;
   (b)   the nature and purpose of the contract;
   (c)   good faith and fair dealing;
   (d)   reasonableness.

CHAPTER 5
CONTENT

Article 5.1
Express and implied obligations

The contractual obligations of the parties may be express or implied.

Article 5.2
Implied obligations

Implied obligations stem from—
(a)   the nature and purpose of the contract;
(b)   practices established between the parties and usages;
(c)   good faith and fair dealing;
(d)   reasonableness.

Article 5.3
Co-operation between the parties

Each party shall co-operate with the other party when such co-operation may reasonably be expected for the performance of that party's obligations.

Article 5.4
Duty to achieve a specific result; duty of best efforts

(1)   To the extent that an obligation of a party involves a duty to achieve a specific result, that party is bound to achieve that result.
(2)   To the extent that an obligation of a party involves a duty of best efforts in the performance of an activity, that party is bound to make such efforts as would be made by a reasonable person of the same kind in the same circumstances.

Article 5.5
Determination of kind of duty involved

In determining the extent to which an obligation of a party involves a duty of best efforts in the performance of an activity or duty to achieve a specific result, regard shall be had, among other factors, to—
(a)   the way in which the obligation is expressed in the contract;
(b)   the contractual price and other terms of the contract;
(c)   the degree of risk normally involved in achieving the expected result;
(d)   the ability of the other party to influence the performance of the obligation.

Article 5.6
Determination of quality of performance

Where the quality of performance is neither fixed by, nor determinable from, the contract a party is bound to render a performance of a quality that is reasonable and not less than average in the circumstances.

Article 5.7
Price determination

(1)   Where a contract does not fix or make provision for determining the price, the parties are considered, in the absence of any indication to the contrary, to have made reference to the price generally charged at the time of the conclusion of the contract for such performance in comparable circumstances in the trade concerned or, if no such price is available, to a reasonable price.
(2)   Where the price is to be determined by one party and that determination is manifestly unreasonable, a reasonable price shall be substituted notwithstanding any contract term to the contrary.
(3)   Where the price is to be fixed by a third person, and that person cannot or will not do so, the price shall be a reasonable price.
(4)   Where the price is to be fixed by reference to factors which do not exist or have ceased to exist or to be accessible, the nearest equivalent factor shall be treated as a substitute.

Article 5.8
Contract for an indefinite period

A contract for an indefinite period may be ended by either party by giving notice a reasonable time in advance.

CHAPTER 6
PERFORMANCE

SECTION 1—PERFORMANCE IN GENERAL

Article 6.1.1
Time of performance

A party must perform its obligations—
(a)   if a time is fixed by or determinable from the contract, at that time;
(b)   if a period of time is fixed by or determinable from the contract, at any time within
       that period unless circumstances indicate that the other party is to choose a time;
(c)   in any other case, within a reasonable time after the conclusion of the contract.

Article 6.1.2
Performance at one time or in instalments

In cases under Article 6.1 (b) or (c), a party must perform its obligations at one time if that
performance can be rendered at one time and the circumstances do not indicate
otherwise.

Article 6.1.3
Partial performance

(1)   The obligee may reject an offer to perform in part at the time performance is due,
       whether or not such offer is coupled with an assurance as to the balance of the
       performance, unless the obligee has no legitimate interest in so doing.
(2)   Additional expenses caused to the obligee by partial performance are to be borne
       by the obligor without prejudice to any other remedy.

Article 6.1.4
Order of performance

(1)   To the extent that the performances of the parties can be rendered simultaneously,
       the parties are bound to render them simultaneously unless the circumstances
       indicate otherwise.
(2)   To the extent that the performance of only one party requires a period of time, that
       party is bound to render its performance first, unless the circumstances indicate
       otherwise.

Article 6.1.5
Earlier performance

(1)   The obligee may reject an earlier performance unless it has no legitimate interest in
       so doing.
(2)   Acceptability by a party of an earlier performance does not affect the time for the
       performance of its own obligations if that time has been fixed irrespective of the
       performance of the other party's obligations.
(3)   Additional expenses caused to the obligee by earlier performance are to be borne
       by the obligor, without prejudice to any other remedy.

Article 6.1.6
Place of performance

(1)   If the place of performance is neither fixed by, nor determinable from the contract, a party is to perform—
    (a)   a monetary obligation, at the obligee's place of business;
    (b)   any other obligation, at its own place of business.
(2)   A party must bear any increase in the expenses incidental to performance which is caused by a change in its place of business subsequent to the conclusion of the contract.

Article 6.1.7
Payment by cheque or other instrument

(1)   Payment may be made in any form used in the ordinary course of business at the place for payment.
(2)   However, an obligee who accepts, either by virtue of paragraph (1) or voluntarily, a cheque, any other order to pay or a promise to pay, is presumed to do so only on condition that it will be honoured.

Article 6.1.8
Payment by funds transfer

(1)   Unless the obligee has indicated a particular account, payment may be made by a transfer to any of the financial institutions in which the obligee has made it known that it has an account.
(2)   In case of payment by a transfer of the obligation of the obligor is discharged when the transfer to the obligee's financial institution becomes effective.

Article 6.1.9
Currency of payment

(1)   If a monetary obligation is expressed in a currency other than that of the place of payment, it may be paid by the obligor in the currency of the place for payment unless—
    (a)   the currency is freely convertible; or
    (b)   the parties have agreed that payment should be made only in the currency in which the monetary obligation is expressed.
(2)   If it is impossible for the obligor to make payment in the currency in which the monetary obligation is expressed, the obligee may require payment in the currency of the place for payment, even in the case referred to in paragraph (1)(b).
(3)   Payment in the currency of the place for payment is to be made according to the applicable rate of exchange prevailing there when payment is due.
(4)   However, if the obligor has not paid at the time when payment is due, the obligee may require payment according to the applicable rate of exchange prevailing either when payment is due or at the time of actual payment.

Article 6.1.10
Currency not expressed

Where a monetary obligation is not expressed in a particular currency, payment must be made in the currency of the place where payment is to be made.

Article 6.1.11
Costs of performance

Each party shall bear the costs of performance of its obligations.

Article 6.1.12
Imputation of payments

(1)   An obligor owing several monetary obligations to the same obligee may specify at the time of payment the debt to which it intends the payment to be applied. However, the payment discharges first any expenses, then interest due and finally the principal.
(2)   If the obligor makes no such specification, the obligee may, within a reasonable time after payment, declare to the obligor the obligation to which it imputes the payment, provided that the obligation is due and undisputed.
(3)   In the absence of imputation under paragraphs (1) or (2), payment is imputed to that obligation which satisfies one of the following criteria and in the order indicated—
       (a)   an obligation which is due or which is the first to fall due;
       (b)   the obligation for which the obligee has least security;
       (c)   the obligation which is the most burdensome for the obligor;
       (d)   the obligation which has arisen first.
       If none of the preceding criteria applies, payment is imputed to all the obligations proportionally.

Article 6.1.13
Imputation of non-monetary obligations

Article 6.1.12 applies with appropriate adaptations to the imputation of performance of non- monetary obligations.

Article 6.1.14
Application for public permission

Where the law of a State requires a public permission affecting the validity of the contract or its performance and neither that law nor the circumstances indicate otherwise—
(a)   if only one party has its place of business in that State, that party shall take the measures necessary to obtain the permission;
(b)   in any other case the party whose performance requires permission shall take the necessary measures.

Article 6.1.15
Procedure in applying for permission

(1)   The party required to take the measures necessary to obtain the permission shall do so without undue delay and shall bear any expenses incurred.
(2)   That party shall whenever appropriate give the other party notice of the grant or refusal of such permission without undue delay.

Article 6.1.16
Permission neither granted nor refused

(1)   If, notwithstanding the fact that the party responsible has taken all measures required, permission is neither granted nor refused within an agreed period or, where no period has been agreed, within a reasonable time from the conclusion of the contract, either party is entitled to terminate the contract.

(2)   Where the permission affects some terms only, paragraph (1) does not apply if, having regard to the circumstances, it is reasonable to uphold the remaining contract even if the permission is refused.

Article 6.1.17
Permission Refused

(1)   The refusal of a permission affecting the validity of the contract renders the contract void. If the refusal affects the validity of some terms only, only such terms are void if, having regard to the circumstances, it is reasonable to uphold the remaining contract.

(2)   Where the refusal of a permission renders the performance of the contract impossible in whole or in part, the rules on non-performance apply.

SECTION 2—HARDSHIP

Article 6.2.1
Contract to be observed

Where the performance of a contract becomes more onerous for one of the parties, that party is nevertheless bound to perform its obligations subject to the following provisions on hardship.

Article 6.2.2
Definition of hardship

There is hardship where the occurrence of events fundamentally alters the equilibrium of the contract either because the cost of a party's performance has increased or because the value of the performance a party receives has diminished, and—

(a)   the events occur or become known to the disadvantaged party after the conclusion of the contract;

(b)   the events could not reasonably have been taken into account by the disadvantaged party at the time of the conclusion of the contract;

(c)   the events are beyond the control of the disadvantaged party; and

(d)   the risk of the events was not assumed by the disadvantaged party.

Article 6.2.3
Effects of hardship

(1)   In case of hardship the disadvantaged party is entitled to request renegotiations. The request shall be made without undue delay and shall indicate the grounds on which it is based.

(2)   The request for renegotiation does not itself entitle the disadvantaged party to withhold performance.

(3)   Upon failure to reach agreement within a reasonable time either party may resort to the court.

(4)   If the court finds hardship it may, if reasonable—

(a)   terminate the contract at a date and on terms to be fixed; or

(b)   adapt the contract with a view to restoring its equilibrium.

CHAPTER 7
NON-PERFORMANCE

SECTION 1—NON-PERFORMANCE IN GENERAL

Article 7.1.1
Non-performance defined

Non-performance is failure by a party to perform any of its obligations under the contract, including defective performance or late performance.

Article 7.1.2
Interference by the other party

A party may not rely on the non-performance of the other party to the extent that such non- performance was caused by the first party's act or omission or by another event as to which the first party bears the risk.

Article 7.1.3
Withholding performance

(1)   Where the parties are to perform simultaneously, either party may withhold performance until the other party tenders performance.
(2)   Where the parties are to perform consecutively, the party that is to perform later may withhold its performance until the first party has performed.

Article 7.1.4
Cure by non-performing party

(1)   The non-performing party may, at its own expense, cure any non-performance, provided that—
       (a)   without undue delay, it gives notice indicating the proposed manner and timing of the cure;
       (b)   cure is appropriate in the circumstances;
       (c)   the aggrieved party has no legitimate interest in refusing cure; and
       (d)   cure is effected promptly.
(2)   The right to cure is not precluded by notice of termination.
(3)   Upon effective notice of cure, rights of the aggrieved party that are inconsistent with the non-performing party's performances are suspended until the time for cure has expired.
(4)   The aggrieved party may withhold performance pending cure.
(5)   Notwithstanding cure, the aggrieved party retains the right to claim damages for delay as well as for any harm caused or not prevented by the cure.

Article 7.1.5
Additional period for performance

(1)   In a case of non-performance the aggrieved party may by notice to the other party allow an additional period of time for performance.
(2)   During the additional period the aggrieved party may withhold performance of its own reciprocal obligations and may claim damages but may not resort to any other remedy. If it receives notice from the other party that the latter will not perform within that period, or if upon expiry of that period due performance has not been made, the aggrieved party may resort to any of the remedies that may be available under this Chapter.

(3) Where in a case of delay in performance which is not fundamental the aggrieved party has given notice allowing an additional period of time of reasonable length, it may terminate the contract at the end of that period. If the additional period allowed is not of reasonable length it shall be extended to a reasonable length. The aggrieved party may in its notice provide that if the other party fails to perform within the period allowed by the notice the contract shall automatically terminate.

(4) Paragraph (3) does not apply where the obligation which has not been performed is only a minor part of the contractual obligation of the non-performing party.

Article 7.1.6
Exemption clauses

A clause which limits or excludes one party's liability for non-performance or which permits one party to tender performance substantially different from what the other party reasonably expected may not be invoked if it would be grossly unfair to do so, having regard to the purpose of the contract.

Article 7.1.7
Force majeure

(1) Non-performance by a party is excused if that party proves that the non-performance was due to an impediment beyond its control and that it could not reasonably be expected to have taken the impediment into account at the time of the conclusion of the contract or to have avoided or overcome it or its consequences.

(2) When the impediment is only temporary, the excuse shall have effect for such period as is reasonable having regard to the effect of the impediment on performance of the contract.

(3) The party who fails to perform must give notice to the other party of the impediment and its effect on its ability to perform. If the notice is not received by the other party within a reasonable time after the party who fails to perform knew or ought to have known of the impediment, it is liable for damages resulting from such non-receipt.

(4) Nothing in this article prevents a party from exercising a right to terminate the contract or to withhold performance or request interest on money due.

SECTION 2—RIGHT TO PERFORMANCE

Article 7.2.1
Performance of monetary obligation

Where a party who is obliged to pay money does not do so, the other may require payment.

Article 7.2.2
Performance of non-monetary obligation

Where a party who owes an obligation other than one to pay money does not perform, the other party may require performance, unless—

(a) performance is impossible in law or fact;

(b) performance or, where relevant, enforcement is unreasonably burdensome or expensive;

(c) the party entitled to performance may reasonably obtain performance from another source;

(d) performance is of an exclusively personal character; or

(e)   the party entitled to performance does not require performance within a reasonable time after it has, or ought to have, become aware of the non-performance.

Article 7.2.3
Repair and replacement of defective performance

The right to performance includes in appropriate cases the right to require repair, replacement, or other cure of defective performance. The provisions of Articles 7.2.1 and 7.2.2 apply accordingly.

Article 7.2.4
Judicial penalty

(1)   Where the court orders a party to perform, it may also direct that this party pay a penalty if it does not comply with the order.
(2)   The penalty shall be paid to the aggrieved party unless mandatory provisions of the law of the forum provide otherwise. Payment of the penalty to the aggrieved party does not exclude any claim for damages.

Article 7.2.5
Change of remedy

(1)   An aggrieved party who has required performance of a non-monetary obligation and who has not received performance within a period fixed or otherwise within a reasonable period of time may invoke any other remedy.
(2)   Where the decision of a court for performance of a non-monetary obligation cannot be enforced, the aggrieved party may invoke any other remedy.

SECTION 3—TERMINATION

Article 7.3.1
Right to terminate the contract

(1)   A party may terminate the contract where the failure of the other party to perform an obligation under the contract amounts to a fundamental non-performance.
(2)   In determining whether a failure to perform an obligation amounts to a fundamental non-performance regard shall be had, in particular, to whether—
    (a)   the non-performance substantially deprives the aggrieved party of what it was entitled to expect under the contract unless the other party did not foresee and could not reasonably have foreseen such result;
    (b)   strict compliance with the obligation which has not been performed is of essence under the contract;
    (c)   the non-performance is intentional or reckless;
    (d)   the non-performance gives the aggrieved party reason to believe that it cannot rely on the other party's future performance;
    (e)   the non-performing party will suffer disproportionate loss as a result of the preparation or performance if the contract is terminated.
(3)   In the case of delay the aggrieved party may also terminate the contract if the other party fails to perform before the time allowed under Article 7.1.5 has expired.

Article 7.3.2
Notice of termination

(1)   The right of a party to terminate the contract is exercised by notice to the other party.
(2)   If performance has been offered late or otherwise does not conform to the contract the aggrieved party will lose its right to terminate the contract unless it gives notice to the other party within a reasonable time after it has or ought to have become aware of the non-conforming performance.

Article 7.3.3
Anticipatory non-performance

Where prior to the date for performance by one of the parties it is clear that there will be a fundamental non-performance by that party, the other party may terminate the contract.

Article 7.3.4
Adequate assurance of due performance

A party who reasonably believes that there will be a fundamental non-performance by the other party may demand adequate assurance of due performance and may meanwhile withhold its own performance. Where this assurance is not provided within a reasonable time the party demanding it may terminate the contract.

Article 7.3.5
Effects of termination in general

(1)   Termination of the contract releases both parties from their obligation to effect and to receive future performance.
(2)   Termination does not preclude a claim for damages for non-performance.
(3)   Termination does not affect any provision in the contract for the settlement of disputes or any other term of the contract which is to operate even after termination.

Article 7.3.6
Restitution

(1)   On termination of contract either party may claim restitution of whatever it has supplied, provided that such party concurrently makes restitution of whatever it has received. If restitution in kind is not possible or appropriate allowance should be made in money whenever reasonable.
(2)   However, if performance of the contract has extended over a period of time and the contract is divisible, such restitution can only be claimed for the period after termination has taken effect.

SECTION 4—DAMAGES

Article 7.4.1
Right to damages

Any non-performance gives the aggrieved party a right to damages either exclusively or in conjunction with any other remedies except where the non-performance is excused under these Principles.

Article 7.4.2
Full compensation

(1)   The aggrieved party is entitled to full compensation for harm sustained as a result of the non-performance. Such harm includes both any loss which it suffered and any gain of which it was deprived, taking into account any gain to the aggrieved party resulting from its avoidance of cost or harm.
(2)   Such harm may be non-pecuniary and includes, for instance, physical suffering or emotional distress.

Article 7.4.3
Certainty of harm

(1)   Compensation is due only for harm, including future harm, that is established with a reasonable degree of certainty.
(2)   Compensation may be due for the loss of a chance in proportion to the stability of its occurrence.
(3)   Where the amount of damages cannot be established with a sufficient degree of certainty, the assessment is at the discretion of the court.

Article 7.4.4
Foreseeability of harm

The non-performing party is liable only for harm which it foresaw or could reasonably have foreseen at the time of the conclusion of the contract as being likely to result from its non-performance.

Article 7.4.5
Proof of harm in case of replacement transaction

Where the aggrieved party has terminated the contract and has made a replacement transaction within a reasonable time and in a reasonable manner it may recover the difference between the contract price and the price of the replacement transaction as well as damages for any further harm.

Article 7.4.6
Proof of harm by current price

(1)   Where the aggrieved party has terminated the contract and has not made a replacement transaction but there is a current price for the performance contracted for, it may recover the difference between the contract price and the price current at the time the contract is terminated as well as damages for any further harm.
(2)   Current price is the price generally charged for goods delivered or services rendered in comparable circumstances at the place where the contract should have been performed or, if there is no current price at that place, the current price at such other place that appears reasonable to take as a reference.

Article 7.4.7
Harm due in part to aggrieved party

Where the harm is due in part to an act or omission of the aggrieved party or to another event as to which that party bears the risk, the amount of damages shall be reduced to the extent that these factors have contributed to the harm, having regard to the conduct of the parties.

Article 7.4.8
Mitigation of harm

(1)   The non-performing party is not liable for harm suffered by the aggrieved party to the extent that the harm could have been reduced by the latter party's taking reasonable steps.

(2)   The aggrieved party is entitled to recover any expenses reasonably incurred in attempting to reduce the harm.

Article 7.4.9
Interest for failure to pay money

(1)   If a party does not pay a sum of money when it falls due the aggrieved party is entitled to interest upon that sum from the time when payment is due to the time of payment whether or not the nonpayment is excused.

(2)   The rate of interest shall be the average bank short-term lending rate to prime borrowers prevailing for the currency of payment at the place for payment, or where no such rate exists at that place, then the same rate in the State of the currency of payment. In the absence of such a rate at either place the rate of interest shall be the appropriate rate fixed by the law of the State of the currency of payment.

(3)   The aggrieved party is entitled to additional damages if the non-payment caused it a greater harm.

Article 7.4.10
Interest on damages

Unless otherwise agreed, interest on damages for non-performance of non-monetary obligations accrues as from the time of non-performance.

Article 7.4.11
Manner of monetary redress

(1)   Damages are to be paid in a lump sum. However, they may be payable in instalments where the nature of the harm makes this appropriate.

(2)   Damages to be paid in instalments may be indexed.

Article 7.4.12
Currency in which to assess damages

Damages are to be assessed either in the currency in which the monetary obligation was expressed or in the currency in which the harm was suffered, whichever is more appropriate.

Article 7.4.13
Agreed payment for non-performance

(1)   Where the contract provides that a party who does not perform is to pay a specified sum to the aggrieved party for such non-performance, the aggrieved party is entitled to that sum irrespective of its actual harm.

(2)   However, notwithstanding any agreement to the contrary the specified sum may be reduced to a reasonable amount where it is grossly excessive in relation to the harm resulting from the non-performance and to the other circumstances.

THE YORK-ANTWERP RULES 1994

RULE OF INTERPRETATION

In the adjustment of general average the following Rules shall apply to the exclusion of any Law and Practice inconsistent therewith.

Except as provided by the Rule Paramount and the numbered Rules, general average shall be adjusted according to the lettered Rules.

RULE PARAMOUNT

In no case shall there be any allowance for sacrifice or expenditure unless reasonably made or incurred.

RULE A

There is a general average act when, and only when, any extraordinary sacrifice or expenditure is intentionally and reasonably made or incurred for the common safety for the purpose of preserving from peril the property involved in a common maritime adventure.

General average sacrifices and expenditures shall be borne by the different contributing interests on the basis hereinafter provided.

RULE B

There is a common maritime adventure when one or more vessels are towing or pushing another vessel or vessels, provided that they are all involved in commercial activities and not in a salvage operation.

When measures are taken to preserve the vessels and their cargoes, if any, from a common peril, these Rules shall apply.

A vessel is not in common peril with another vessel or vessels if by simply disconnecting from the other vessel or vessels she is in safety; but if the disconnection is itself a general average act the common maritime adventure continues.

RULE C

Only such losses, damages or expenses which are the direct consequence of the general average act shall be allowed as general average.

In no case shall there be any allowance in general average for losses, damages or expenses incurred in respect of damage to the environment or in consequence of the escape or release of pollutant substances from the property involved in the common maritime adventure.

Demurrage, loss of market, and any loss or damage sustained or expense incurred by reason of delay, whether on the voyage or subsequently, and any indirect loss whatsoever, shall not be admitted as general average.

RULE D

Rights to contribution in general average shall not be affected, though the event which gave rise to the sacrifice or expenditure may have been due to the fault of one of the parties to the adventure; but this shall not prejudice any remedies or defences which may be open against or to that party in respect of such fault.

RULE E

The onus of proof is upon the party claiming in general average to show that the loss or expense claimed is properly allowable as general average.

All parties claiming in general average shall give notice in writing to the average adjuster of the loss or expense in respect of which they claim contribution within 12 months of the date of the termination of the common maritime adventure.

Failing such notification, or if within 12 months of a request for the same any of the parties shall fail to supply evidence in support of a notified claim, or particulars of value in respect of a contributory interest, the average adjuster shall be at liberty to estimate the extent of the allowance or the contributory value on the basis of the information available to him, which estimate may be challenged only on the ground that it is manifestly incorrect.

RULE F

Any additional expense incurred in place of another expense which would have been allowable as general average shall be deemed to be general average and so allowed without regard to the saving, if any, to other interests, but only up to the amount of the general average expense avoided.

RULE G

General average shall be adjusted as regards both loss and contribution upon the basis of values at the time and place when and where the adventure ends.

This rule shall not affect the determination of the place at which the average statement is to be made up.

When a ship is at any port or place in circumstances which would give rise to an allowance in general average under the provisions of Rules X and XI, and the cargo or part thereof is forwarded to destination by other means, rights and liabilities in general average shall, subject to cargo interests being notified if practicable, remain as nearly as possible the same as they would have been in the absence of such forwarding, as if the adventure had continued in the original ship for so long as justifiable under the contract of affreightment and the applicable law.

The proportion attaching to cargo of the allowances made in general average by reason of applying the third paragraph of this Rule shall not exceed the cost which would have been borne by the owners of cargo if the cargo had been forwarded at their expense.

Rule I
Jettison of cargo

No jettison of cargo shall be made good as general average, unless such cargo is carried in accordance with the recognised custom of the trade.

Rule II
Loss or damage by sacrifices for the common safety

Loss of or damage to the property involved in the common maritime adventure by or in consequence of a sacrifice made for the common safety, and by water which goes down a ship's hatches opened or other opening made for the purpose of making a jettison for the common safety, shall be made good as general average.

Rule III
Extinguishing fire on shipboard

Damage done to a ship and cargo, or either of them, by water or otherwise, including damage by beaching or scuttling a burning ship, in extinguishing a fire on board the ship, shall be made good as general average, except that no compensation shall be made for damage by smoke however caused or by heat of the fire.

Rule IV
Cutting away wreck

Loss or damage sustained by cutting away wreck or parts of the ship which have previously been carried away or are effectively lost by accident shall not be made good as general average.

Rule V
Voluntary stranding

When a ship is intentionally run on shore for the common safety, whether or not she might have been driven on shore, the consequent loss or damage to the property involved in the common maritime adventure shall be allowed in general average.

Rule VI
Salvage remuneration

(a)   Expenditure incurred by the parties to the adventure in the nature of salvage, whether under contract or otherwise, shall be allowed in general average provided that the salvage operations were carried out for the purpose of preserving from peril the property involved in the common maritime adventure.
Expenditure allowed in general average shall include any salvage remuneration in which the skill and efforts of the salvors in preventing or minimising damage to the environment such as is referred to in Article 13 paragraph 1(b) of the International Convention on Salvage, 1989 have been taken into account.

(b)   Special compensation payable to a salvor by the shipowner under Article 14 of the said Convention to the extent specified in paragraph 4 of that Article or under any other provision similar in substance shall not be allowed in general average.

Rule VII
Damage to machinery and boilers

Damage caused to any machinery and boilers of a ship which is ashore and in a position of peril, in endeavouring to refloat, shall be allowed in general average when shown to have arisen from an actual intention to float the ship for the common safety at the risk of such damage; but where a ship is afloat no loss or damage caused by working propelling machinery and boilers shall in any circumstances be made good as general average.

Rule VIII
Expenses lightening a ship when ashore, and consequent damage

When a ship is ashore and cargo and ship's fuel and stores or any of them are discharged as a general average act, the extra cost of lightening, lighter hire and reshipping (if incurred), and any loss or damage to the property involved in the common maritime adventure in consequence thereof, shall be admitted as general average.

Rule IX
Cargo, ship's materials and stores used for fuel

Cargo, ship's materials and stores, or any of them, necessarily used for fuel for the common safety at a time of peril shall be admitted as general average, but when such an allowance is made for the cost of ship's materials and stores the general average shall be credited with the estimated cost of the fuel which would otherwise have been consumed in prosecuting the intended voyage.

Rule X
Expenses of port of refuge, etc

(a)   When a ship shall have entered a port or place of refuge or shall have returned to her port or place of loading in consequence of accident, sacrifice or other extraordinary circumstances which render that necessary for the common safety, the expenses of entering such port or place shall be admitted as general average; and when she shall have sailed thence with her original cargo, or a part of it, the corresponding expenses of leaving such port or place of refuge consequent upon such entry or return shall likewise be admitted as general average.

When a ship is at any port or place of refuge and is necessarily removed to another port or place because repairs cannot be carried out in the first port or place, the provisions of this Rule shall be applied to the second port or place as if it were a port or place of refuge and the cost of such removal including temporary repairs and towage shall be admitted as general average. The provisions of Rule XI shall be applied to the prolongation of the voyage occasioned by such removal.

(b)   The cost of handling on board or discharging cargo, fuel or stores whether at a port or place of loading, call or refuge, shall be admitted as general average, when the handling or discharge was necessary for the common safety or to enable damage to the ship caused by sacrifice or accident to be repaired, if the repairs were necessary for the safe prosecution of the voyage, except in cases where the damage to the ship is discovered at a port or place of loading or call without any accident or other extraordinary circumstances connected with such damage having taken place during the voyage.

The cost of handling on board or discharging cargo, fuel or stores shall not be admissible as general average when incurred solely for the purpose of restowage due to shifting during the voyage, unless such restowage is necessary for the common safety.

(c)   Whenever the cost of handling or discharging cargo, fuel or stores is admissible as general average, the costs of storage, including insurance if reasonably incurred, reloading and stowing of such cargo, fuel or stores shall likewise be admitted as general average. The provisions of Rule XI shall be applied to the extra period of detention occasioned by such reloading or restowing.

But when the ship is condemned or does not proceed on her original voyage, storage expenses shall be admitted as general average only up to the date of the ship's condemnation or of the abandonment of the voyage or up to the date of completion of discharge of cargo if the condemnation or abandonment takes place before that date.

Rule XI
Wages and maintenance of crew and other expenses bearing up for and
in a port of refuge, etc

(a)   Wages and maintenance of master, officers and crew reasonably incurred and fuel and stores consumed during the prolongation of the voyage occasioned by a ship entering a port or place of refuge or returning to her port or place of loading shall be admitted as general average when the expenses of entering such port or place are allowable in general average in accordance with Rule X(a).

(b)   When a ship shall have entered or been detained in any port or place in consequence of accident, sacrifice or other extraordinary circumstances which render that necessary for the common safety, or to enable damage to the ship caused by sacrifice or accident to be repaired, if the repairs were necessary for the safe prosecution of the voyage, the wages and maintenance of the master, officers and crew reasonably incurred during the extra period of detention in such port or place until the ship shall or should have been ready to proceed upon her voyage, shall be admitted in general average.

Fuel and stores consumed during the extra period of detention shall be admitted as general average, except such fuel and stores as are consumed in effecting repairs not allowable in general average.

Port charges incurred during the extra period of detention shall likewise be admitted as general average except such charges as are incurred solely by reason of repairs not allowable in general average.

Provided that when damage to the ship is discovered at a port or place of loading or call without any accident or other extraordinary circumstance connected with such damage having taken place during the voyage, then the wages and maintenance of master, officers and crew and fuel and stores consumed and port charges incurred during the extra detention for repairs to damages so discovered shall not be admissible as general average, even if the repairs are necessary for the safe prosecution of the voyage.

When the ship is condemned or does not proceed on her original voyage, the wages and maintenance of the master, officers and crew and fuel and stores consumed and port charges shall be admitted as general average only up to the date of the ship's condemnation or of the abandonment of the voyage or up to the date of completion of discharge of cargo if the condemnation or abandonment takes place before that date.

(c)   For the purpose of this and the other Rules wages shall include all payments made to or for the benefit of the master, officers and crew whether such payments be imposed by law upon the shipowners or be made under the terms of articles of employment.

(d)   The cost of measures undertaken to prevent or minimise damage to the environment shall be allowed in general average when incurred in any or all of the following circumstances:

(i)   as part of an operation performed for the common safety which, had it been undertaken by a party outside the common maritime adventure, would have entitled such party to a salvage reward;

(ii)   as a condition of entry into or departure from any port or place in the circumstances prescribed in Rule X(a);

(iii)   as a condition of remaining at any port or place in the circumstances prescribed in Rule X(a), provided that when there is an actual escape or release of pollutant substances the cost of any additional measures required on that account to prevent or minimise pollution or environmental damage shall not be allowed as general average;

(iv)   necessarily in connection with the discharging, storing or reloading of cargo whenever the cost of those operations is admissible as general average.

Rule XII
Damage to cargo in discharging, etc

Damage to or loss of cargo, fuel or stores sustained in consequence of their handling, discharging, storing, reloading and stowing shall be made good as general average, when and only when the cost of those measures respectively is admitted as general average.

Rule XIII
Deduction from cost of repairs

Repairs to be allowed in general average shall not be subject to deductions in respect of 'new or old' where old material or parts are replaced by new unless the ship is over fifteen years old in which case there shall be a deduction of one third. The deductions shall be regulated by the age of the ship from the 31st December of the year of completion of the construction to the date of the general average act, except for insulation, life and similar boats, communications and navigational apparatus and equipment, machinery and boilers for which the deductions shall be regulated by the age of the particular parts to which they apply.

The deductions shall be made only from the cost of the new material or parts when finished and ready to be installed in the ship.

No deductions shall be made in respect of provisions, stores, anchors and chain cables.

Drydock and slipway dues and costs of shifting the ship shall be allowed in full.

The costs of cleaning, painting or coating of bottom shall not be allowed in general average unless the bottom has been painted or coated within the twelve months preceding the date of the general average act in which case one half of such costs shall be allowed.

Rule XIV
Temporary repairs

Where temporary repairs are effected to a ship at a port of loading, call or refuge, for the common safety, or of damage caused by general average sacrifice, the cost of such repairs shall be admitted as general average.

Where temporary repairs of accidental damage are effected in order to enable the adventure to be completed, the cost of such repairs shall be admitted as general average without regard to the saving, if any, to other interests, but only up to the saving in expense which would have been incurred and allowed in general average if such repairs had not been effected there.

No deductions 'new for old' shall be made from the cost of temporary repairs allowable as general average.

Rule XV
Loss of freight

Loss of freight arising from damage to or loss of cargo shall be made good as general average, either when caused by a general average act, or when the damage to or loss of cargo is so made good.

Deduction shall be made from the amount of gross freight lost, of the charges which the owner thereof would have incurred to earn such freight, but has, in consequence of the sacrifice, not incurred.

Rule XVI
Amount to be made good for cargo lost or damaged by sacrifice

The amount to be made good as general average for damage to or loss of cargo sacrificed shall be the loss which has been sustained thereby based on the value at the time of discharge, ascertained from the commercial invoice rendered to the receiver or if there is no such invoice from the shipped value. The value at the time of discharge shall include the cost of insurance and freight except insofar as such fright is at the risk of interests other than the cargo.

When cargo so damaged is sold and the amount of the damage has not been otherwise agreed, the loss to be made good in general average shall be the difference between the net proceeds of sale and the net sound value as computed in the first paragraph of this Rule.

Rule XVII
Contributory values

The contribution to a general average shall be made upon the actual net values of the property at the termination of the adventure except that the value of cargo shall be the value at the time of discharge, ascertained from the commercial invoice rendered to the receiver or if there is no such invoice from the shipped value. The value of the cargo shall include the cost of insurance and freight unless and insofar as such freight is at the risk of interests other than the cargo, deducting therefrom any loss or damage suffered by the cargo prior to or at the time of discharge. The value of the ship shall be assessed without taking into account the beneficial or detrimental effect of any demise or time charterparty to which the ship may be committed.

To these values shall be added the amount made good as general average for property sacrificed, if not already included, deduction being made from the freight and passage money at risk of such charges and crew's wages as would not have been incurred in earning the freight had the ship and cargo been totally lost at the date of the general average act and have not been allowed as general average, deduction being also made from the value of the property of all extra charges incurred in respect thereof subsequently to the general average act, except such charges as are allowed in general average or fall upon the ship by virtue of an award for special compensation under Article 14 of the International Convention on Salvage, 1989 or under any other provision similar in substance.

In the circumstances envisaged in the third paragraph of Rule G, the cargo and other property shall contribute on the basis of its value upon delivery at original destination unless sold or otherwise disposed of short of that destination, and the ship shall contribute upon its actual net value at the time of completion of discharge of cargo.

Where cargo is sold short of destination, however, it shall contribute upon the actual net proceeds of sale, with the addition of any amount made good as general average.

Mails, passenger's luggage, personal effects and accompanied private motor vehicles shall not contribute in general average.

Rule XVIII
Damage to ship

The amount to be allowed as general average for damage or loss to the ship, her machinery and/ or gear caused by a general average act shall be as follows —
(a)   When repaired or replaced:
        The actual reasonable cost of repairing or replacing such damage or loss, subject to deductions in accordance with Rule XIII;
(b)   When not repaired or replaced:
        The reasonable depreciation arising from such damage or loss, but not exceeding the estimated cost of repairs. But where the ship is an actual total loss or when the cost of repairs of the damage would exceed the value of the ship when repaired, the amount to be allowed as general average shall be the difference between the estimated sound value of the ship after deducting therefrom the estimated cost of repairing damage which is not general average and the value of the ship in her damaged state which may be measured by the net proceeds of sale, if any.

Rule XIX
Undeclared or wrongfully declared cargo

Damage or loss caused to goods loaded without the knowledge of the shipowner or his agent or to goods wilfully misdescribed at time of shipment shall not be allowed as general average, but such goods shall remain liable to contribute, if saved.

Damage or loss caused to goods which have been wrongfully declared on shipment at a value which is lower than their real value shall be contributed for at the declared value, but such goods shall contribute upon their actual value.

Rule XX
Provision of funds

A commission of 2 per cent. on general average disbursements, other than the wages and maintenance of masters, officers and crew and fuel and stores not replaced during the voyage, shall be allowed in general average.

The capital loss sustained by the owners of goods sold for the purpose of raising funds to defray general average disbursements shall be allowed in general average.

The cost of insuring general average disbursements shall also be admitted in general average.

Rule XXI
Interest on losses made good in general average

Interest shall be allowed on expenditure, sacrifices and allowances in general average at the rate of 7 per cent per annum, until three months after the date of issue of the general average adjustment, due allowance being made for any payment on account by the contributory interests or from the general average deposit fund.

Rule XXII
Treatment of cash deposits

Where cash deposits have been collected in respect of cargo's liability for general average, salvage or special charges, such deposits shall be paid without any delay into a special account in the joint names of a representative nominated on behalf of the shipowner and a representative nominated on behalf of the depositors in a bank to be approved by both. The sum so deposited, together with accrued interest, if any, shall be held as security for payment to the parties entitled thereto of the general average, salvage or special charges payable by cargo in respect to which the deposits have been collected. Payments on account or refunds of deposits may be made if certified to in writing by the average adjuster. Such deposits and payments or refunds shall be without prejudice to the ultimate liability of the parties.

SECTION VI
STANDARD FORMS

INSTITUTE CARGO CLAUSES (A)

1/1/82   (FOR USE ONLY WITH THE NEW MARINE POLICY FORM)

INSTITUTE CARGO CLAUSES (A)

RISKS COVERED

1   This insurance covers all risks of loss of or damage to the subject-matter insured except as provided in Clauses 4, 5, 6 and 7 below.   *Risks Clause*

2   This insurance covers general average and salvage charges, adjusted or determined according to the contract of affreightment and/or the governing law and practice, incurred to avoid or in connection with the avoidance of loss from any cause except those excluded in Clauses 4, 5, 6 or 7 or elsewhere in this insurance.   *General Average Clause*

3   This insurance is extended to indemnify the Assured against such proportion of liability under the contract of affreightment "Both to Blame Collision" Clause as is in respect of a loss recoverable hereunder. In the event of any claim by shipowners under the said Clause the Assured agree to notify the Underwriters who shall have the right, at their own cost and expense, to defend the Assured against such claim.   *"Both to Blame Collision" Clause*

EXCLUSIONS

4   In no case shall this insurance cover   *General Exclusions Clause*

    4.1   loss damage or expense attributable to wilful misconduct of the Assured

    4.2   ordinary leakage, ordinary loss in weight or volume, or ordinary wear and tear of the subject-matter insured

    4.3   loss damage or expense caused by insufficiency or unsuitability of packing or preparation of the subject-matter insured (for the purpose of this Clause 4.3 "packing" shall be deemed to include stowage in a container or liftvan but only when such stowage is carried out prior to attachment of this insurance or by the Assured or their servants)

    4.4   loss damage or expense caused by inherent vice or nature of the subject-matter insured

    4.5   loss damage or expense proximately caused by delay, even though the delay be caused by a risk insured against (except expenses payable under Clause 2 above)

    4.6   loss damage or expense arising from insolvency or financial default of the owners managers charterers or operators of the vessel

    4.7   loss damage or expense arising from the use of any weapon of war employing atomic or nuclear fission and/or fusion or other like reaction or radioactive force or matter.

5   5.1   In no case shall this insurance cover loss damage or expense arising from   *Unseaworthiness and Unfitness Exclusion Clause*

        unseaworthiness of vessel or craft,

        unfitness of vessel craft conveyance container or liftvan for the safe carriage of the subject-matter insured,

      where the Assured or their servants are privy to such unseaworthiness or unfitness, at the time the subject-matter insured is loaded therein.

    5.2   The Underwriters waive any breach of the implied warranties of seaworthiness of the ship and fitness of the ship to carry the subject-matter insured to destination, unless the Assured or their servants are privy to such unseaworthiness or unfitness.

6   In no case shall this insurance cover loss damage or expense caused by   *War Exclusion Clause*

    6.1   war civil war revolution rebellion insurrection, or civil strife arising therefrom, or any hostile act by or against a belligerent power

    6.2   capture seizure arrest restraint or detainment (piracy excepted), and the consequences thereof or any attempt thereat

    6.3   derelict mines torpedoes bombs or other derelict weapons of war.

7   In no case shall this insurance cover loss damage or expense   *Strikes Exclusion Clause*

    7.1   caused by strikers, locked-out workmen, or persons taking part in labour disturbances, riots or civil commotions

    7.2   resulting from strikes, lock-outs, labour disturbances, riots or civil commotions

    7.3   caused by any terrorist or any person acting from a political motive.

DURATION

8   8.1   This insurance attaches from the time the goods leave the warehouse or place of storage at the place named herein for the commencement of the transit, continues during the ordinary course of transit and terminates either   *Transit Clause*

    8.1.1   on delivery to the Consignees' or other final warehouse or place of storage at the destination named herein,

    8.1.2   on delivery to any other warehouse or place of storage, whether prior to or at the destination named herein, which the Assured elect to use either

    8.1.2.1   for storage other than in the ordinary course of transit or

    8.1.2.2   for allocation or distribution,

        or

    8.1.3   on the expiry of 60 days after completion of discharge overside of the goods hereby insured from the oversea vessel at the final port of discharge,

    whichever shall first occur.

    8.2   If, after discharge overside from the oversea vessel at the final port of discharge, but prior to termination of this insurance, the goods are to be forwarded to a destination other than that to which they are insured hereunder, this insurance, whilst remaining subject to termination as provided for above, shall not extend beyond the commencement of transit to such other destination.

    8.3   This insurance shall remain in force (subject to termination as provided for above and to the provisions of Clause 9 below) during delay beyond the control of the Assured, any deviation, forced discharge, reshipment or transhipment and during any variation of the adventure arising from the exercise of a liberty granted to shipowners or charterers under the contract of affreightment.

(Continued)

9   If owing to circumstances beyond the control of the Assured either the contract of carriage is terminated at a port or place other than the destination named therein or the transit is otherwise terminated before delivery of the goods as provided for in Clause 8 above, then this insurance shall also terminate *unless prompt notice is given to the Underwriters and continuation of cover is requested when the insurance shall remain in force, subject to an additional premium if required by the Underwriters,* either

     9.1   until the goods are sold and delivered at such port or place, or, unless otherwise specially agreed, until the expiry of 60 days after arrival of the goods hereby insured at such port or place, whichever shall first occur,

         or

     9.2   if the goods are forwarded within the said period of 60 days (or any agreed extension thereof) to the destination named herein or to any other destination, until terminated in accordance with the provisions of Clause 8 above.

10   Where, after attachment of this insurance, the destination is changed by the Assured, *held covered at a premium and on conditions to be arranged subject to prompt notice being given to the Underwriters.*

CLAIMS

11   11.1   In order to recover under this insurance the Assured must have an insurable interest in the subject-matter insured at the time of the loss.

     11.2   Subject to 11.1 above, the Assured shall be entitled to recover for insured loss occurring during the period covered by this insurance, notwithstanding that the loss occurred before the contract of insurance was concluded, unless the Assured were aware of the loss and the Underwriters were not.

12   Where, as a result of the operation of a risk covered by this insurance, the insured transit is terminated at a port or place other than that to which the subject-matter is covered under this insurance, the Underwriters will reimburse the Assured for any extra charges properly and reasonably incurred in unloading storing and forwarding the subject-matter to the destination to which it is insured hereunder.

This Clause 12, which does not apply to general average or salvage charges, shall be subject to the exclusions contained in Clauses 4, 5, 6 and 7 above, and shall not include charges arising from the fault negligence insolvency or financial default of the Assured or their servants.

13   No claim for Constructive Total Loss shall be recoverable hereunder unless the subject-matter insured is reasonably abandoned either on account of its actual total loss appearing to be unavoidable or because the cost of recovering, reconditioning and forwarding the subject-matter to the destination to which it is insured would exceed its value on arrival.

14   14.1   If any Increased Value insurance is effected by the Assured on the cargo insured herein the agreed value of the cargo shall be deemed to be increased to the total amount insured under this insurance and all Increased Value insurances covering the loss, and liability under this insurance shall be in such proportion as the sum insured herein bears to such total amount insured.

In the event of claim the Assured shall provide the Underwriters with evidence of the amounts insured under all other insurances.

     14.2   **Where this insurance is on Increased Value the following clause shall apply:**
The agreed value of the cargo shall be deemed to be equal to the total amount insured under the primary insurance and all Increased Value insurances covering the loss and effected on the cargo by the Assured, and liability under this insurance shall be in such proportion as the sum insured herein bears to such total amount insured.

In the event of claim the Assured shall provide the Underwriters with evidence of the amounts insured under all other insurances.

BENEFIT OF INSURANCE

15   This insurance shall not inure to the benefit of the carrier or other bailee.

MINIMISING LOSSES

16   It is the duty of the Assured and their servants and agents in respect of loss recoverable hereunder

     16.1   to take such measures as may be reasonable for the purpose of averting or minimising such loss, and

     16.2   to ensure that all rights against carriers, bailees or other third parties are properly preserved and exercised

and the Underwriters will, in addition to any loss recoverable hereunder, reimburse the Assured for any charges properly and reasonably incurred in pursuance of these duties.

17   Measures taken by the Assured or the Underwriters with the object of saving, protecting or recovering the subject-matter insured shall not be considered as a waiver or acceptance of abandonment or otherwise prejudice the rights of either party.

AVOIDANCE OF DELAY

18   It is a condition of this insurance that the Assured shall act with reasonable despatch in all circumstances within their control.

LAW AND PRACTICE

19   This insurance is subject to English law and practice.

NOTE:— *It is necessary for the Assured when they become aware of an event which is "held covered" under this insurance to give prompt notice to the Underwriters and the right to such cover is dependent upon compliance with this obligation.*

(Margin notes, top to bottom): Termination of Contract of Carriage Clause — Change of Voyage Clause — Insurable Interest Clause — Forwarding Charges Clause — Constructive Total Loss Clause — Increased Value Clause — Not to Inure Clause — Duty of Assured Clause — Waiver Clause — Reasonable Despatch Clause — English Law and Practice Clause

INSTITUTE CARGO CLAUSES (B)

1/1/82   **(FOR USE ONLY WITH THE NEW MARINE POLICY FORM)**

INSTITUTE CARGO CLAUSES (B)

RISKS COVERED

1   This insurance covers, except as provided in Clauses 4, 5, 6 and 7 below,   *Risks Clause*

    1.1   loss of or damage to the subject-matter insured reasonably attributable to

    1.1.1   fire or explosion

    1.1.2   vessel or craft being stranded grounded sunk or capsized

    1.1.3   overturning or derailment of land conveyance

    1.1.4   collision or contact of vessel craft or conveyance with any external object other than water

    1.1.5   discharge of cargo at a port of distress

    1.1.6   earthquake volcanic eruption or lightning,

    1.2   loss of or damage to the subject-matter insured caused by

    1.2.1   general average sacrifice

    1.2.2   jettison or washing overboard

    1.2.3   entry of sea lake or river water into vessel craft hold conveyance container liftvan or place of storage,

    1.3   total loss of any package lost overboard or dropped whilst loading on to, or unloading from, vessel or craft.

2   This insurance covers general average and salvage charges, adjusted or determined according to the contract of affreightment and/or the governing law and practice, incurred to avoid or in connection with the avoidance of loss from any cause except those excluded in Clauses 4, 5, 6 and 7 or elsewhere in this insurance.   *General Average Clause*

3   This insurance is extended to indemnify the Assured against such proportion of liability under the contract of affreightment "Both to Blame Collision" Clause as is in respect of a loss recoverable hereunder. In the event of any claim by shipowners under the said Clause the Assured agree to notify the Underwriters who shall have the right, at their own cost and expense, to defend the Assured against such claim.   *"Both to Blame Collision" Clause*

EXCLUSIONS

4   In no case shall this insurance cover   *General Exclusions Clause*

    4.1   loss damage or expense attributable to wilful misconduct of the Assured

    4.2   ordinary leakage, ordinary loss in weight or volume, or ordinary wear and tear of the subject-matter insured

    4.3   loss damage or expense caused by insufficiency or unsuitability of packing or preparation of the subject-matter insured (for the purpose of this Clause 4.3 "packing" shall be deemed to include stowage in a container or liftvan but only when such stowage is carried out prior to attachment of this insurance or by the Assured or their servants)

    4.4   loss damage or expense caused by inherent vice or nature of the subject-matter insured

    4.5   loss damage or expense proximately caused by delay, even though the delay be caused by a risk insured against (except expenses payable under Clause 2 above)

    4.6   loss damage or expense arising from insolvency or financial default of the owners managers charterers or operators of the vessel

    4.7   deliberate damage to or deliberate destruction of the subject-matter insured or any part thereof by the wrongful act of any person or persons

    4.8   loss damage or expense arising from the use of any weapon of war employing atomic or nuclear fission and/or fusion or other like reaction or radioactive force or matter.

5   5.1   In no case shall this insurance cover loss damage or expense arising from   *Unseaworthiness and Unfitness Exclusion Clause*

        unseaworthiness of vessel or craft,

        unfitness of vessel craft conveyance container or liftvan for the safe carriage of the subject-matter insured,

    where the Assured or their servants are privy to such unseaworthiness or unfitness, at the time the subject-matter insured is loaded therein.

    5.2   The Underwriters waive any breach of the implied warranties of seaworthiness of the ship and fitness of the ship to carry the subject-matter insured to destination, unless the Assured or their servants are privy to such unseaworthiness or unfitness.

6   In no case shall this insurance cover loss damage or expense caused by   *War Exclusion Clause*

    6.1   war civil war revolution rebellion insurrection, or civil strife arising therefrom, or any hostile act by or against a belligerent power

    6.2   capture seizure arrest restraint or detainment, and the consequences thereof or any attempt thereat

    6.3   derelict mines torpedoes bombs or other derelict weapons of war.

7   In no case shall this insurance cover loss damage or expense   *Strikes Exclusion Clause*

    7.1   caused by strikers, locked-out workmen, or persons taking part in labour disturbances, riots or civil commotions

    7.2   resulting from strikes, lock-outs, labour disturbances, riots or civil commotions

    7.3   caused by any terrorist or any person acting from a political motive.

DURATION

8   8.1   This insurance attaches from the time the goods leave the warehouse or place of storage at the place named herein for the commencement of the transit, continues during the ordinary course of transit and terminates either   *Transit Clause*

    8.1.1   on delivery to the Consignees' or other final warehouse or place of storage at the destination named herein,

    8.1.2   on delivery to any other warehouse or place of storage, whether prior to or at the destination named herein, which the Assured elect to use either

    8.1.2.1   for storage other than in the ordinary course of transit or

    8.1.2.2   for allocation or distribution,

        or

    8.1.3   on the expiry of 60 days after completion of discharge overside of the goods hereby insured from the oversea vessel at the final port of discharge,

    whichever shall first occur.

8.2   If, after discharge overside from the oversea vessel at the final port of discharge, but prior to termination of this insurance, the goods are to be forwarded to a destination other than that to which they are insured hereunder, this insurance, whilst remaining subject to termination as provided for above, shall not extend beyond the commencement of transit to such other destination.

8.3   This insurance shall remain in force (subject to termination as provided for above and to the provisions of Clause 9 below) during delay beyond the control of the Assured, any deviation, forced discharge, reshipment or transhipment and during any variation of the adventure arising from the exercise of a liberty granted to shipowners or charterers under the contract of affreightment.

9   If owing to circumstances beyond the control of the Assured either the contract of carriage is terminated at a port or place other than the destination named therein or the transit is otherwise terminated before delivery of the goods as provided for in Clause 8 above, then this insurance shall also terminate *unless prompt notice is given to the Underwriters and continuation of cover is requested when the insurance shall remain in force, subject to an additional premium if required by the Underwriters,* either   Termination of Contract of Carriage Clause

9.1   until the goods are sold and delivered at such port or place, or, unless otherwise specially agreed, until the expiry of 60 days after arrival of the goods hereby insured at such port or place, whichever shall first occur,

or

9.2   if the goods are forwarded within the said period of 60 days (or any agreed extension thereof) to the destination named herein or to any other destination, until terminated in accordance with the provisions of Clause 8 above.

10   Where, after attachment of this insurance, the destination is changed by the Assured, *held covered at a premium and on conditions to be arranged subject to prompt notice being given to the Underwriters.*   Change of Voyage Clause

CLAIMS

11   11.1   In order to recover under this insurance the Assured must have an insurable interest in the subject-matter insured at the time of the loss.   Insurable Interest Clause

11.2   Subject to 11.1 above, the Assured shall be entitled to recover for insured loss occurring during the period covered by this insurance, notwithstanding that the loss occurred before the contract of insurance was concluded, unless the Assured were aware of the loss and the Underwriters were not.

12   Where, as a result of the operation of a risk covered by this insurance, the insured transit is terminated at a port or place other than that to which the subject-matter is covered under this insurance, the Underwriters will reimburse the Assured for any extra charges properly and reasonably incurred in unloading storing and forwarding the subject-matter to the destination to which it is insured hereunder.   Forwarding Charges Clause

This Clause 12, which does not apply to general average or salvage charges, shall be subject to the exclusions contained in Clauses 4, 5, 6 and 7 above, and shall not include charges arising from the fault negligence insolvency or financial default of the Assured or their servants.

13   No claim for Constructive Total Loss shall be recoverable hereunder unless the subject-matter insured is reasonably abandoned either on account of its actual total loss appearing to be unavoidable or because the cost of recovering, reconditioning and forwarding the subject-matter to the destination to which it is insured would exceed its value on arrival.   Constructive Total Loss Clause

14   14.1   If any Increased Value insurance is effected by the Assured on the cargo insured herein the agreed value of the cargo shall be deemed to be increased to the total amount insured under this insurance and all Increased Value insurances covering the loss, and liability under this insurance shall be in such proportion as the sum insured herein bears to such total amount insured.   Increased Value Clause

In the event of claim the Assured shall provide the Underwriters with evidence of the amounts insured under all other insurances.

14.2   **Where this insurance is on Increased Value the following clause shall apply:**
The agreed value of the cargo shall be deemed to be equal to the total amount insured under the primary insurance and all Increased Value insurances covering the loss and effected on the cargo by the Assured, and liability under this insurance shall be in such proportion as the sum insured herein bears to such total amount insured.

In the event of claim the Assured shall provide the Underwriters with evidence of the amounts insured under all other insurances.

BENEFIT OF INSURANCE

15   This insurance shall not inure to the benefit of the carrier or other bailee.   Not to Inure Clause

MINIMISING LOSSES

16   It is the duty of the Assured and their servants and agents in respect of loss recoverable hereunder   Duty of Assured Clause

16.1   to take such measures as may be reasonable for the purpose of averting or minimising such loss, and

16.2   to ensure that all rights against carriers, bailees or other third parties are properly preserved and exercised

and the Underwriters will, in addition to any loss recoverable hereunder, reimburse the Assured for any charges properly and reasonably incurred in pursuance of these duties.

17   Measures taken by the Assured or the Underwriters with the object of saving, protecting or recovering the subject-matter insured shall not be considered as a waiver or acceptance of abandonment or otherwise prejudice the rights of either party.   Waiver Clause

AVOIDANCE OF DELAY

18   It is a condition of this insurance that the Assured shall act with reasonable despatch in all circumstances within their control.   Reasonable Despatch Clause

LAW AND PRACTICE

19   This insurance is subject to English law and practice.   English Law and Practice Clause

---

NOTE:— It is necessary for the Assured when they become aware of an event which is "held covered" under this insurance to give prompt notice to the Underwriters and the right to such cover is dependent upon compliance with this obligation.

CL. 253.

INSTITUTE CARGO CLAUSES (C)

1/1/82   (FOR USE ONLY WITH THE NEW MARINE POLICY FORM)

INSTITUTE CARGO CLAUSES (C)

RISKS COVERED

1   This insurance covers, except as provided in Clauses 4, 5, 6 and 7 below,   Risks Clause

    1.1   loss of or damage to the subject-matter insured reasonably attributable to

    1.1.1   fire or explosion

    1.1.2   vessel or craft being stranded grounded sunk or capsized

    1.1.3   overturning or derailment of land conveyance

    1.1.4   collision or contact of vessel craft or conveyance with any external object other than water

    1.1.5   discharge of cargo at a port of distress,

    1.2   loss of or damage to the subject-matter insured caused by

    1.2.1   general average sacrifice

    1.2.2   jettison.

2   This insurance covers general average and salvage charges, adjusted or determined according to the contract of affreightment and/or the governing law and practice, incurred to avoid or in connection with the avoidance of loss from any cause except those excluded in Clauses 4, 5, 6 and 7 or elsewhere in this insurance.   General Average Clause

3   This insurance is extended to indemnify the Assured against such proportion of liability under the contract of affreightment "Both to Blame Collision" Clause as is in respect of a loss recoverable hereunder. In the event of any claim by shipowners under the said Clause the Assured agree to notify the Underwriters who shall have the right, at their own cost and expense, to defend the Assured against such claim.   "Both to Blame Collision" Clause

EXCLUSIONS

4   In no case shall this insurance cover   General Exclusions Clause

    4.1   loss damage or expense attributable to wilful misconduct of the Assured

    4.2   ordinary leakage, ordinary loss in weight or volume, or ordinary wear and tear of the subject-matter insured

    4.3   loss damage or expense caused by insufficiency or unsuitability of packing or preparation of the subject-matter insured (for the purpose of this Clause 4.3 "packing" shall be deemed to include stowage in a container or liftvan but only when such stowage is carried out prior to attachment of this insurance or by the Assured or their servants)

    4.4   loss damage or expense caused by inherent vice or nature of the subject-matter insured

    4.5   loss damage or expense proximately caused by delay, even though the delay be caused by a risk insured against (except expenses payable under Clause 2 above)

    4.6   loss damage or expense arising from insolvency or financial default of the owners managers charterers or operators of the vessel

    4.7   deliberate damage to or deliberate destruction of the subject-matter insured or any part thereof by the wrongful act of any person or persons

    4.8   loss damage or expense arising from the use of any weapon of war employing atomic or nuclear fission and/or fusion or other like reaction or radioactive force or matter.

5   5.1   In no case shall this insurance cover loss damage or expense arising from   Unseaworthiness and Unfitness Exclusion Clause

        unseaworthiness of vessel or craft,

        unfitness of vessel craft conveyance container or liftvan for the safe carriage of the subject-matter insured,

        where the Assured or their servants are privy to such unseaworthiness or unfitness, at the time the subject-matter insured is loaded therein.

    5.2   The Underwriters waive any breach of the implied warranties of seaworthiness of the ship and fitness of the ship to carry the subject-matter insured to destination, unless the Assured or their servants are privy to such unseaworthiness or unfitness.

6   In no case shall this insurance cover loss damage or expense caused by   War Exclusion Clause

    6.1   war civil war revolution rebellion insurrection, or civil strife arising therefrom, or any hostile act by or against a belligerent power

    6.2   capture seizure arrest restraint or detainment, and the consequences thereof or any attempt thereat

    6.3   derelict mines torpedoes bombs or other derelict weapons of war.

7   In no case shall this insurance cover loss damage or expense   Strikes Exclusion Clause

    7.1   caused by strikers, locked-out workmen, or persons taking part in labour disturbances, riots or civil commotions

    7.2   resulting from strikes, lock-outs, labour disturbances, riots or civil commotions

    7.3   caused by any terrorist or any person acting from a political motive.

DURATION

8   8.1   This insurance attaches from the time the goods leave the warehouse or place of storage at the place named herein for the commencement of the transit, continues during the ordinary course of transit and terminates either   Transit Clause

    8.1.1   on delivery to the Consignees' or other final warehouse or place of storage at the destination named herein,

    8.1.2   on delivery to any other warehouse or place of storage, whether prior to or at the destination named herein, which the Assured elect to use either

    8.1.2.1   for storage other than in the ordinary course of transit or

    8.1.2.2   for allocation or distribution,

        or

    8.1.3   on the expiry of 60 days after completion of discharge overside of the goods hereby insured from the oversea vessel at the final port of discharge,

        whichever shall first occur.

Continued   **9**

8.2   If, after discharge overside from the oversea vessel at the final port of discharge, but prior to termination of this insurance, the goods are to be forwarded to a destination other than that to which they are insured hereunder, this insurance, whilst remaining subject to termination as provided for above, shall not extend beyond the commencement of transit to such other destination.

8.3   This insurance shall remain in force (subject to termination as provided for above and to the provisions of Clause 9 below) during delay beyond the control of the Assured, any deviation, forced discharge, reshipment or transhipment and during any variation of the adventure arising from the exercise of a liberty granted to shipowners or charterers under the contract of affreightment.

9   If owing to circumstances beyond the control of the Assured either the contract of carriage is terminated at a port or place other than the destination named therein or the transit is otherwise terminated before delivery of the goods as provided for in Clause 8 above, then this insurance shall also terminate *unless prompt notice is given to the Underwriters and continuation of cover is requested when the insurance shall remain in force, subject to an additional premium if required by the Underwriters*, either   *Termination of Contract of Carriage Clause*

9.1   until the goods are sold and delivered at such port or place, or, unless otherwise specially agreed, until the expiry of 60 days after arrival of the goods hereby insured at such port or place, whichever shall first occur,

or

9.2   if the goods are forwarded within the said period of 60 days (or any agreed extension thereof) to the destination named herein or to any other destination, until terminated in accordance with the provisions of Clause 8 above.

10   Where, after attachment of this insurance, the destination is changed by the Assured, *held covered at a premium and on conditions to be arranged subject to prompt notice being given to the Underwriters.*   *Change of Voyage Clause*

CLAIMS

11   11.1   In order to recover under this insurance the Assured must have an insurable interest in the subject-matter insured at the time of the loss.   *Insurable Interest Clause*

11.2   Subject to 11.1 above, the Assured shall be entitled to recover for insured loss occurring during the period covered by this insurance, notwithstanding that the loss occurred before the contract of insurance was concluded, unless the Assured were aware of the loss and the Underwriters were not.

12   Where, as a result of the operation of a risk covered by this insurance, the insured transit is terminated at a port or place other than that to which the subject-matter is covered under this insurance, the Underwriters will reimburse the Assured for any extra charges properly and reasonably incurred in unloading storing and forwarding the subject-matter to the destination to which it is insured hereunder.   *Forwarding Charges Clause*

This Clause 12, which does not apply to general average or salvage charges, shall be subject to the exclusions contained in Clauses 4, 5, 6 and 7 above, and shall not include charges arising from the fault negligence insolvency or financial default of the Assured or their servants.

13   No claim for Constructive Total Loss shall be recoverable hereunder unless the subject-matter insured is reasonably abandoned either on account of its actual total loss appearing to be unavoidable or because the cost of recovering, reconditioning and forwarding the subject-matter to the destination to which it is insured would exceed its value on arrival.   *Constructive Total Loss Clause*

14   14.1   If any Increased Value insurance is effected by the Assured on the cargo insured herein the agreed value of the cargo shall be deemed to be increased to the total amount insured under this insurance and all Increased Value insurances covering the loss, and liability under this insurance shall be in such proportion as the sum insured herein bears to such total amount insured.   *Increased Value Clause*
In the event of claim the Assured shall provide the Underwriters with evidence of the amounts insured under all other insurances.

14.2   **Where this insurance is on Increased Value the following clause shall apply:**
The agreed value of the cargo shall be deemed to be equal to the total amount insured under the primary insurance and all Increased Value insurances covering the loss and effected on the cargo by the Assured, and liability under this insurance shall be in such proportion as the sum insured herein bears to such total amount insured.
In the event of claim the Assured shall provide the Underwriters with evidence of the amounts insured under all other insurances.

BENEFIT OF INSURANCE

15   This insurance shall not inure to the benefit of the carrier or other bailee.   *Not to Inure Clause*

MINIMISING LOSSES

16   It is the duty of the Assured and their servants and agents in respect of loss recoverable hereunder   *Duty of Assured Clause*

16.1   to take such measures as may be reasonable for the purpose of averting or minimising such loss, and

16.2   to ensure that all rights against carriers, bailees or other third parties are properly preserved and exercised

and the Underwriters will, in addition to any loss recoverable hereunder, reimburse the Assured for any charges properly and reasonably incurred in pursuance of these duties.

17   Measures taken by the Assured or the Underwriters with the object of saving, protecting or recovering the subject-matter insured shall not be considered as a waiver or acceptance of abandonment or otherwise prejudice the rights of either party.   *Waiver Clause*

AVOIDANCE OF DELAY

18   It is a condition of this insurance that the Assured shall act with reasonable despatch in all circumstances within their control.   *Reasonable Despatch Clause*

LAW AND PRACTICE

19   This insurance is subject to English law and practice.   *English Law and Practice Clause*

NOTE:— *It is necessary for the Assured when they become aware of an event which is "held covered" under this insurance to give prompt notice to the Underwriters and the right to such cover is dependent upon compliance with this obligation.*

INSTITUTE STRIKES CLAUSES (CARGO)

1/1/82   (FOR USE ONLY WITH THE NEW MARINE POLICY FORM)

INSTITUTE STRIKES CLAUSES (CARGO)

RISKS COVERED

1   This insurance covers, except as provided in Clauses 3 and 4 below, loss of or damage to the subject-matter insured caused by   *Risks Clause*

   1.1   strikers, locked-out workmen, or persons taking part in labour disturbances, riots or civil commotions

   1.2   any terrorist or any person acting from a political motive.

2   This insurance covers general average and salvage charges, adjusted or determined according to the contract of affreightment and/or the governing law and practice, incurred to avoid or in connection with the avoidance of loss from a risk covered under these clauses.   *General Average Clause*

EXCLUSIONS

3   In no case shall this insurance cover   *General Exclusions Clause*

   3.1   loss damage or expense attributable to wilful misconduct of the Assured

   3.2   ordinary leakage, ordinary loss in weight or volume, or ordinary wear and tear of the subject-matter insured

   3.3   loss damage or expense caused by insufficiency or unsuitability of packing or preparation of the subject-matter insured (for the purpose of this Clause 3.3 "packing" shall be deemed to include stowage in a container or liftvan but only when such stowage is carried out prior to attachment of this insurance or by the Assured or their servants)

   3.4   loss damage or expense caused by inherent vice or nature of the subject-matter insured

   3.5   loss damage or expense proximately caused by delay, even though the delay be caused by a risk insured against (except expenses payable under Clause 2 above)

   3.6   loss damage or expense arising from insolvency or financial default of the owners managers charterers or operators of the vessel

   3.7   loss damage or expense arising from the absence shortage or withholding of labour of any description whatsoever resulting from any strike, lockout, labour disturbance, riot or civil commotion

   3.8   any claim based upon loss of or frustration of the voyage or adventure

   3.9   loss damage or expense arising from the use of any weapon of war employing atomic or nuclear fission and/or fusion or other like reaction or radioactive force or matter.

   3.10   loss damage or expense caused by war civil war revolution rebellion insurrection, or civil strife arising therefrom, or any hostile act by or against a belligerent power.

4   4.1   In no case shall this insurance cover loss damage or expense arising from   *Unseaworthiness and Unfitness Exclusion Clause*

      unseaworthiness of vessel or craft,

      unfitness of vessel craft conveyance container or liftvan for the safe carriage of the subject-matter insured,

   where the Assured or their servants are privy to such unseaworthiness or unfitness, at the time the subject-matter insured is loaded therein.

   4.2   The Underwriters waive any breach of the implied warranties of seaworthiness of the ship and fitness of the ship to carry the subject-matter insured to destination, unless the Assured or their servants are privy to such unseaworthiness or unfitness.

DURATION

5   5.1   This insurance attaches from the time the goods leave the warehouse or place of storage at the place named herein for the commencement of the transit, continues during the ordinary course of transit and terminates either   *Transit Clause*

   5.1.1   on delivery to the Consignees' or other final warehouse or place of storage at the destination named herein,

   5.1.2   on delivery to any other warehouse or place of storage, whether prior to or at the destination named herein, which the Assured elect to use either

   5.1.2.1   for storage other than in the ordinary course of transit or

   5.1.2.2   for allocation or distribution,

   or

   5.1.3   on the expiry of 60 days after completion of discharge overside of the goods hereby insured from the oversea vessel at the final port of discharge,

   whichever shall first occur.

   5.2   If, after discharge overside from the oversea vessel at the final port of discharge, but prior to termination of this insurance, the goods are to be forwarded to a destination other than that to which they are insured hereunder, this insurance, whilst remaining subject to termination as provided for above, shall not extend beyond the commencement of transit to such other destination.

   5.3   This insurance shall remain in force (subject to termination as provided for above and to the provisions of Clause 6 below) during delay beyond the control of the Assured, any deviation, forced discharge, reshipment or transhipment and during any variation of the adventure arising from the exercise of a liberty granted to shipowners or charterers under the contract of affreightment.

Continued

13

6 If owing to circumstances beyond the control of the Assured either the contract of carriage is terminated at a port or place other than the destination named therein or the transit is otherwise terminated before delivery of the goods as provided for in Clause 5 above, then this insurance shall also terminate *unless prompt notice is given to the Underwriters and continuation of cover is requested when the insurance shall remain in force, subject to an additional premium if required by the Underwriters,* either

 6.1 until the goods are sold and delivered at such port or place, or, unless otherwise specially agreed, until the expiry of 60 days after arrival of the goods hereby insured at such port or place, whichever shall first occur,

  or

 6.2 if the goods are forwarded within the said period of 60 days (or any agreed extension thereof) to the destination named herein or to any other destination, until terminated in accordance with the provisions of Clause 5 above.

7 Where, after attachment of this insurance, the destination is changed by the Assured, *held covered at a premium and on conditions to be arranged subject to prompt notice being given to the Underwriters.*

CLAIMS

8 **8.1** In order to recover under this insurance the Assured must have an insurable interest in the subject-matter insured at the time of the loss.

 8.2 Subject to 8.1 above, the Assured shall be entitled to recover for insured loss occurring during the period covered by this insurance, notwithstanding that the loss occurred before the contract of insurance was concluded, unless the Assured were aware of the loss and the Underwriters were not.

9 **9.1** If any Increased Value insurance is effected by the Assured on the cargo insured herein the agreed value of the cargo shall be deemed to be increased to the total amount insured under this insurance and all Increased Value insurances covering the loss, and liability under this insurance shall be in such proportion as the sum insured herein bears to such total amount insured.

  In the event of claim the Assured shall provide the Underwriters with evidence of the amounts insured under all other insurances.

 9.2 **Where this insurance is on an Increased Value the following clause shall apply:**
  The agreed value of the cargo shall be deemed to be equal to the total amount insured under the primary insurance and all Increased Value insurances covering the loss and effected on the cargo by the Assured, and liability under this insurance shall be in such proportion as the sum insured herein bears to such total amount insured.

  In the event of claim the Assured shall provide the Underwriters with evidence of the amounts insured under all other insurances.

BENEFIT OF INSURANCE

10 This insurance shall not inure to the benefit of the carrier or other bailee.

MINIMISING LOSSES

11 It is the duty of the Assured and their servants and agents in respect of loss recoverable hereunder

 11.1 to take such measures as may be reasonable for the purpose of averting or minimising such loss, and

 11.2 to ensure that all rights against carriers, bailees or other third parties are properly preserved and exercised

 and the Underwriters will, in addition to any loss recoverable hereunder, reimburse the Assured for any charges properly and reasonably incurred in pursuance of these duties.

12 Measures taken by the Assured or the Underwriters with the object of saving, protecting or recovering the subject-matter insured shall not be considered as a waiver or acceptance of abandonment or otherwise prejudice the rights of either party.

AVOIDANCE OF DELAY

13 It is a condition of this insurance that the Assured shall act with reasonable despatch in all circumstances within their control.

LAW AND PRACTICE

14 This insurance is subject to English law and practice.

Marginal notes: Termination of Contract of Carriage Clause · Change of Voyage Clause · Insurable Interest Clause · Increased Value Clause · Not to Inure Clause · Duty of Assured Clause · Waiver Clause · Reasonable Despatch Clause · English Law and Practice Clause

---

NOTE:— It is necessary for the Assured when they become aware of an event which is "held covered" under this insurance to give prompt notice to the Underwriters and the right to such cover is dependent upon compliance with this obligation.

INSTITUTE WAR CLAUSES (CARGO)

1/1/82 (FOR USE ONLY WITH THE NEW MARINE POLICY FORM)

INSTITUTE WAR CLAUSES (CARGO)

RISKS COVERED

1 This insurance covers, except as provided in Clauses 3 and 4 below, loss of or damage to the subject-matter insured caused by
    1.1   war civil war revolution rebellion insurrection, or civil strife arising therefrom, or any hostile act by or against a belligerent power
    1.2   capture seizure arrest restraint or detainment, arising from risks covered under 1.1 above, and the consequences thereof or any attempt threat
    1.3   derelict mines torpedoes bombs or other derelict weapons of war.

Risks Clause

2 This insurance covers general average and salvage charges, adjusted or determined according to the contract of affreightment and/or the governing law and practice, incurred to avoid or in connection with the avoidance of loss from a risk covered under these clauses.

General Average Clause

EXCLUSIONS

3 In no case shall this insurance cover
    3.1   loss damage or expense attributable to wilful misconduct of the Assured
    3.2   ordinary leakage, ordinary loss in weight or volume, or ordinary wear and tear of the subject-matter insured
    3.3   loss damage or expense caused by insufficiency or unsuitability of packing or preparation of the subject-matter insured (for the purpose of this Clause 3.3 "packing" shall be deemed to include stowage in a container or liftvan but only when such stowage is carried out prior to attachment of this insurance or by the Assured or their servants)
    3.4   loss damage or expense caused by inherent vice or nature of the subject-matter insured
    3.5   loss damage or expense proximately caused by delay, even though the delay be caused by a risk insured against (except expenses payable under Clause 2 above)
    3.6   loss damage or expense arising from insolvency or financial default of the owners managers charterers or operators of the vessel
    3.7   any claim based upon loss of or frustration of the voyage or adventure
    3.8   loss damage or expense arising from any hostile use of any weapon of war employing atomic or nuclear fission and/or fusion or other like reaction or radioactive force or matter.

General Exclusions Clause

4   4.1   In no case shall this insurance cover loss damage or expense arising from
        unseaworthiness of vessel or craft,
        unfitness of vessel craft conveyance container or liftvan for the safe carriage of the subject-matter insured,
        where the Assured or their servants are privy to such unseaworthiness or unfitness, at the time the subject-matter insured is loaded therein.
    4.2   The Underwriters waive any breach of the implied warranties of seaworthiness of the ship and fitness of the ship to carry the subject-matter insured to destination, unless the Assured or their servants are privy to such unseaworthiness or unfitness.

Unseaworthiness and Unfitness Exclusion Clause

DURATION

5   5.1   This insurance
    5.1.1   attaches only as the subject-matter insured and as to any part as that part is loaded on an oversea vessel
        and
    5.1.2   terminates, subject to 5.2 and 5.3 below, either as the subject-matter insured and as to any part as that part is discharged from an oversea vessel at the final port or place of discharge,
        or
        on expiry of 15 days counting from midnight of the day of arrival of the vessel at the final port or place of discharge,
        whichever shall first occur;
        nevertheless,
        subject to prompt notice to the Underwriters and to an additional premium, such insurance
    5.1.3   reattaches when, without having discharged the subject-matter insured at the final port or place of discharge, the vessel sails therefrom,
        and
    5.1.4   terminates, subject to 5.2 and 5.3 below, either as the subject-matter insured and as to any part as that part is thereafter discharged from the vessel at the final (or substituted) port or place of discharge,
        or
        on expiry of 15 days counting from midnight of the day of re-arrival of the vessel at the final port or place of discharge or arrival of the vessel at a substituted port or place of discharge,
        whichever shall first occur.
    5.2   If during the insured voyage the oversea vessel arrives at an intermediate port or place to discharge the subject-matter insured for on-carriage by oversea vessel or by aircraft, or the goods are discharged from the vessel at a port or place of refuge, then, subject to 5.3 below and to an additional premium if required, this insurance continues until the expiry of 15 days counting from midnight of the day of arrival of the vessel at such port or place, but thereafter reattaches as the subject-matter insured and as to any part as that part is loaded on an on-carrying oversea vessel or aircraft. During the period of 15 days the insurance remains in force after discharge only whilst the subject-matter insured and as to any part as that part is at such port or place. If the goods are on-carried within the said period of 15 days or if the insurance reattaches as provided in this Clause 5.2
    5.2.1   where the on-carriage is by oversea vessel this insurance continues subject to the terms of these clauses,
        or
    5.2.2   where the on-carriage is by aircraft, the current Institute War Clauses (Air Cargo) (excluding sendings by Post) shall be deemed to form part of this insurance and shall apply to the on-carriage by air.

Transit Clause

Continued

11

5.3   If the voyage in the contract of carriage is terminated at a port or place other than the destination agreed therein, such port or place shall be deemed the final port of discharge and such insurance terminates in accordance with 5.1.2. If the subject-matter insured is subsequently reshipped to the original or any other destination, then *provided notice is given to the Underwriters before the commencement of such further transit and subject to an additional premium*, such insurance reattaches

5.3.1   in the case of the subject-matter insured having been discharged, as the subject-matter insured and as to any part as that part is loaded on the on-carrying vessel for the voyage;

5.3.2   in the case of the subject-matter not having been discharged, when the vessel sails from such deemed final port of discharge;

thereafter such insurance terminates in accordance with 5.1.4.

5.4   The insurance against the risks of mines and derelict torpedoes, floating or submerged, is extended whilst the subject-matter insured or any part thereof is on craft whilst in transit to or from the oversea vessel, but in no case beyond the expiry of 60 days after discharge from the oversea vessel unless otherwise specially agreed by the Underwriters.

5.5   *Subject to prompt notice to Underwriters, and to an additional premium if required,* this insurance shall remain in force within the provisions of these Clauses during any deviation, or any variation of the adventure arising from the exercise of a liberty granted to shipowners or charterers under the contract of affreightment.

(For the purpose of Clause 5

''arrival'' shall be deemed to mean that the vessel is anchored, moored or otherwise secured at a berth or place within the Harbour Authority area. If such a berth or place is not available, arrival is deemed to have occurred when the vessel first anchors, moors or otherwise secures either at or off the intended port or place of discharge

''oversea vessel'' shall be deemed to mean a vessel carrying the subject-matter from one port or place to another where such voyage involves a sea passage by that vessel)

6   Where, after attachment of this insurance, the destination is changed by the Assured, *held covered at a premium and on conditions to be arranged subject to prompt notice being given to the Underwriters.*   Change of Voyage Clause

7   **Anything contained in this contract which is inconsistent with Clauses 3.7, 3.8 or 5 shall, to the extent of such inconsistency, be null and void.**

CLAIMS

8   8.1   In order to recover under this insurance the Assured must have an insurable interest in the subject-matter insured at the time of the loss.   Insurable Interest Clause

      8.2   Subject to 8.1 above, the Assured shall be entitled to recover for insured loss occurring during the period covered by this insurance, notwithstanding that the loss occurred before the contract of insurance was concluded, unless the Assured were aware of the loss and the Underwriters were not.

9   9.1   If any Increased Value insurance is effected by the Assured on the cargo insured herein the agreed value of the cargo shall be deemed to be increased to the total amount insured under this insurance and all Increased Value insurances covering the loss, and liability under this insurance shall be in such proportion as the sum insured herein bears to such total amount insured.   Increased Value Clause
            In the event of claim the Assured shall provide the Underwriters with evidence. of the amounts insured under all other insurances.

      9.2   **Where this insurance is on Increased Value the following clause shall apply:**
            The agreed value of the cargo shall be deemed to be equal to the total amount insured under the primary insurance and all Increased Value insurances covering the loss and effected on the cargo by the Assured, and liability under this insurance shall be in such proportion as the sum insured herein bears to such total amount insured.
            In the event of claim the Assured shall provide the Underwriters with evidence of the amounts insured under all other insurances.

BENEFIT OF INSURANCE

10   This insurance shall not inure to the benefit of the carrier or other bailee.   Not to Inure Clause

MINIMISING LOSSES

11   It is the duty of the Assured and their servants and agents in respect of loss recoverable hereunder   Duty of Assured Clause

      11.1   to take such measures as may be reasonable for the purpose of averting or minimising such loss, and

      11.2   to ensure that all rights against carriers, bailees or other third parties are properly preserved and exercised

      and the Underwriters will, in addition to any loss recoverable hereunder, reimburse the Assured for any charges properly and reasonably incurred in pursuance of these duties.

12   Measures taken by the Assured or the Underwriters with the object of saving, protecting or recovering the subject-matter insured shall not be considered as a waiver or acceptance of abandonment or otherwise prejudice the rights of either party.   Waiver Clause

AVOIDANCE OF DELAY

13   It is a condition of this insurance that the Assured shall act with reasonable despatch in all circumstances within their control.   Reasonable Despatch Clause

LAW AND PRACTICE

14   This insurance is subject to English law and practice.   English Law and Practice Clause

NOTE:— *It is necessary for the Assured when they become aware of an event which is ''held covered'' under this insurance to give prompt notice to the Underwriters and the right to such cover is dependent upon compliance with this obligation.*

MARINE POLICY FORM

The Institute of London Underwriters

Companies Marine Policy

WE, THE COMPANIES, hereby agree, in consideration of the payment to us by or on behalf of the Assured of the premium specified in the Schedule, to insure against loss damage liability or expense in the proportions and manner hereinafter provided. Each Company shall be liable only for its own respective proportion.

This insurance shall be subject to the exclusive jurisdiction of the English Courts, except as may be expressly provided herein to the contrary.

IN WITNESS whereof the General Manager and Secretary of The Institute of London Underwriters has subscribed his name on behalf of each Company.

....
General Manager and Secretary
The Institute of London Underwriters

This Policy is not valid unless it bears the embossment of the Policy Department of The Institute of London Underwriters.

MAR 91

SCHEDULE

POLICY NUMBER

NAME OF ASSURED

VESSEL

VOYAGE OR PERIOD OF INSURANCE

SUBJECT-MATTER INSURED

AGREED VALUE
   (if any)

AMOUNT INSURED HEREUNDER

PREMIUM

CLAUSES, ENDORSEMENTS, SPECIAL CONDITIONS AND WARRANTIES

COMPANIES' PROPORTIONS

For use by the Policy Department

of

The Institute of London Underwriters

In all communications please quote the following reference	

The Institute of London Underwriters

Companies Marine Policy

This Policy is subscribed by Insurance Companies
Members of The Institute of London Underwriters
49, Leadenhall Street,
London, EC3A 2BE

SECTION VII
STANDARD TRADING CONDITIONS

Acknowledgment: The editors and publisher thank BIFA (British International Freight Association) for their permission to reproduce BIFA Terms and Conditions 2000(b).

The Customer's attention is drawn to the Clauses hereof which exclude or limit the Company's liability and those which require the Customer to indemnify the Company in certain circumstances.

DEFINITIONS AND APPLICATION

1. In these Conditions:
   'Company' is the BIFA Member trading under these Conditions.
   'Person' includes persons or any Body or Bodies Corporate.
   'The Owner' means the Owner of the goods (including any packaging, containers or equipment) to which any business concluded under these Conditions relates and any other person who is or may become interested in them.
   'Customer' means any person at whose request or on whose behalf the Company undertakes any business or provides advice, information or services.

2. (A) Subject to Sub-Paragraph (B) below, all and any activities of the Company in the course of business whether gratuitous or not are undertaken subject to these Conditions.

   (B) If any legislation is compulsorily applicable to any business undertaken, these Conditions shall, as regards such business, be read as subject to such legislation and nothing in these Conditions shall be construed as a surrender by the Company of any of its rights or immunities or as an increase of any of its responsibilities or liabilities under such legislation and if any part of these Conditions be repugnant to such legislation to any extent such part shall as regards such business be overridden to that extent and no further.

3. The Customer warrants that he is either the Owner or the authorised Agent of the Owner and also that he is accepting these Conditions not only for himself but also as Agent for and on behalf of the Owner.

THE COMPANY

4. (A) Subject to Clauses 11 and 12 below, the Company shall be entitled to procure any or all of its services as an Agent or to provide those services as a Principal.

   (B) The Company shall on demand by the Customer provide evidence of any Contract entered into as Agent for the Customer. Insofar as the Company may be in default of this obligation, it shall be deemed to have contracted with the Customer as a Principal for the performance of the Customer's instructions.

5. When the Company contracts as a Principal for any services, it shall have full liberty a) to perform such services itself, or b) to subcontract the whole or any part of such services to third parties (including the Company's own parent, subsidiary, or associated companies).

6. When the Company acts as an Agent on behalf of the Customer, the Company shall be entitled (and the Customer hereby expressly authorises the Company) to enter into all such Contracts on behalf of the Customer as may be necessary or desirable to fulfil the Customer's instructions and subject to the trading conditions of the parties with whom such contracts are made.

7. The Company reserves to itself a reasonable liberty as to the means, route and procedure to be followed in the handling, storage and transportation of goods.

8. (A) Subject to Sub-Clause (B) hereof, the Company shall have a general lien on all goods and documents relating to goods in its possession, custody or control for all sums due at any time from the Customer or Owner, and shall be

entitled to sell or dispose of such goods or documents as Agent for and at the expense of the Customer and apply the proceeds in or towards the payment of such sums on 28 days notice in writing to the Customer. Upon accounting to the Customer for any balance remaining after payment of any sum due to the Company and the costs of sale or disposal the Company shall be discharged of any liability whatsoever in respect of the goods or documents.

(B)   When the goods are liable to perish or deteriorate, the Company's right to sell or dispose of the goods shall arise immediately upon any sum becoming due to the Company subject only to the Company taking reasonable steps to bring to the Customer's attention its intention of selling or disposing of the goods before doing so.

9.   The Company shall be entitled to retain and be paid all brokerages, commissions, allowances and other remunerations customarily retained by or paid to Freight Forwarders.

10.   (A)   If delivery of the goods or any part thereof is not taken by the Customer, Consignee or Owner, at the time and place when and where the Company is entitled to call upon such person to take delivery thereof, the Company shall be entitled to store the goods or any part thereof at the sole risk of the Customer, whereupon the liability of the Company in respect of the goods or that part thereof stored as aforesaid shall wholly cease and the cost of such storage if paid for or payable by the Company or any Agent or Sub-Contractor of the Company shall forthwith upon demand be paid by the Customer to the Company.

(B)   The Company shall be entitled at the expense of the Customer to dispose of (by sale or otherwise as may be reasonable in all the circumstances):

(i)   on 28 days notice in writing to the Customer, or (where the Customer cannot be traced and reasonable efforts have been made to contact any parties who may reasonably be supposed by the Company to have any interest in the goods) without notice, any goods which have been held by the Company for 90 days and which cannot be delivered as instructed; and

(ii)   without prior notice, goods which have perished, deteriorated or altered or are in immediate prospect of doing so in a manner which has caused or may reasonably be expected to cause loss or damage to the Company or Third Parties or to contravene any applicable laws or regulations.

11.   (A)   No Insurance will be effected except upon express instructions given in writing by the Customer and all Insurances effected by the Company are subject to the usual exceptions and conditions of the Policies of the Insurance Company or Underwriters taking the risk. Unless otherwise agreed in writing the Company shall not be under any obligation to effect a separate Insurance on each consignment but may declare it on any open or general Policy held by the Company.

(B)   Insofar as the Company agrees to effect Insurance, the Company acts solely as Agent for the Customer. The limits of liability under Clause 27(A)(ii) of these Conditions shall not apply to the Company's obligations under Clauses 11(A) and (B).

12.   (A)   Except under special arrangements previously made in writing or under the terms of a printed document signed by the Company, any instructions relating to the delivery or release of goods in specified circumstances only, such as (but without prejudice to the generality of this Clause) against payment or against surrender of a particular document, are accepted by the Company where the Company has to engage third parties to effect compliance with the instructions, only as Agents for the Customer.

(B)   The Company shall not be under any liability in respect of such arrangements as are referred to under Sub-Clause (A) hereof save where such arrangements are made in writing.

(C)   In any event, the Company's liability in respect of the performance or arranging the performance of such instructions shall not exceed the limits set out in Clause 27(A)(ii) of these Conditions.

13.   Advice and information, in whatever form it may be given, is provided by the Company for the Customer only and the Customer shall not pass such advice or information to any Third Party without the Company's written agreement. The Customer shall indemnify the Company against all loss and damage suffered as a consequence of any breach of this Condition by the Customer.

14.   (A)   Except under special arrangement previously made in writing the Company will not accept or deal with bullion, coin, precious stones, jewellery, valuables, antiques, pictures, human remains, livestock, pets or plants. Should any Customer nevertheless deliver any such goods to the Company or cause the Company to handle or deal with any such goods otherwise than under special arrangements previously made in writing the Company shall be under no liability whatsoever for or in connection with such goods howsoever arising.

      (B)   The Company may at any time waive its rights and exemptions from liability under Sub-Clause (A) above in respect of any one or more of the categories of goods mentioned herein or of any part of any category. If such waiver is not in writing, the onus of proving such waiver shall be on the Customer.

15.   Except following instructions previously received in writing and accepted by the Company, the Company will not accept or deal with goods of a dangerous or damaging nature, nor with goods likely to harbour or encourage vermin or other pests, nor with goods liable to taint or affect other goods. If such goods are accepted pursuant to a special arrangement and then in the opinion of the Company they constitute a risk to other goods, property, life or health, the Company shall where reasonably practicable contact the Customer, but reserves the right at the expense of the Customer to remove or otherwise deal with the goods.

16.   Where there is a choice of rates according to the extent or degree of the liability assumed by carriers, warehousemen or others, no declaration of value where optional will be made except under special arrangements previously made in writing.

THE CUSTOMER

17.   The Customer warrants:

      (A)   that the description and particulars of any goods furnished by or on behalf of the Customer are full and accurate.

      (B)   that all goods have been properly and sufficiently prepared, packed, stowed, labelled and/or marked, and that the preparation, packing, stowage, labelling and marking are appropriate to any operations or transactions affecting the goods and the characteristics of the goods.

      (C)   that where the Company receives the goods from the Customer already stowed in or on a container, trailer, tanker, or any other device specifically constructed for the carriage of goods by land, sea or air (each hereafter individually referred to as 'the transport unit'), the transport unit is in good condition, and is suitable for the carriage to the intended destination of the goods loaded therein or thereon.

18.   Should the Customer otherwise than under special arrangements previously made in writing as set out in Clause 15 above deliver to the Company or cause the Company to deal with or handle goods of a dangerous or damaging nature, or goods likely to harbour or encourage vermin or other pests, or goods liable to taint or affect other goods, he shall be liable for all loss or damage arising in connection with such goods and shall indemnify the Company against all penalties, claims, damages, costs and expenses whatsoever arising in connection therewith, and the

goods may be dealt with in such manner as the Company or any other person in whose custody they may be at any relevant time shall think fit.

19. The Customer undertakes that no claim shall be made against any Director, Servant, or Employee of the Company which imposes or attempts to impose upon them any liability in connection with any services which are the subject of these Conditions and if any such claim should nevertheless be made, to indemnify the Company against all consequences thereof.

20. The Customer shall save harmless and keep the Company indemnified from and against:

    (A)   All liability, loss, damage, costs and expenses whatsoever (including without prejudice to the generality of the foregoing, all duties, taxes, imposts, levies, deposits and outlays of whatsoever nature levied by any authority in relation to the goods) arising out of the Company acting in accordance with the Customer's instructions or arising from any breach by the Customer of any Warranty contained in these Conditions or from the negligence of the Customer, and

    (B)   Without derogation from Sub-Clause (A) above, any liability assumed or incurred by the Company when by reason of carrying out the Customer's instructions the Company has reasonably become liable or may become liable to any other party, and

    (C)   All claims, costs and demands whatsoever and by whomsoever made or preferred in excess of the liability of the Company under the terms of these Conditions regardless whether such claims, costs and demands arise from or in connection with the negligence or breach of duty of the Company, its Servants, Sub-Contractors or Agents, and

    (D)   Any claims of a General Average nature which may be made on the Company.

21. (A)   The Customer shall pay to the Company in cash or as otherwise agreed all sums immediately when due without reduction or deferment on account of any claim, counterclaim or set-off.

    (B)   In respect of all sums, which are overdue, the Customer shall be liable to pay to the Company interest calculated at 8% above the prevailing Base Rate of the London clearing banks.

22. Despite the acceptance by the Company of instructions to collect freight, duties, charges or other expenses from the Consignee or any other person the Customer shall remain responsible for such freight, duties, charges or expenses on receipt of evidence of proper demand and in the absence of evidence of payment (for whatever reason) by such Consignee or other person when due.

23. Where liability for General Average arises in connection with the goods, the Customer shall promptly provide security to the Company or to any other party designated by the Company in a form acceptable to the Company.

LIABILITY AND LIMITATION

24. The Company shall perform its duties with a reasonable degree of care, diligence, skill and judgement.

25. The Company shall be relieved of liability for any loss or damage if and to the extent that such loss or damage is caused by:

    (A)   strike, lock-out, stoppage or restraint of labour, the consequences of which the Company is unable to avoid by the exercise of reasonable diligence;

    (B)   any cause or event which the Company is unable to avoid and the consequences whereof the Company is unable to prevent by the exercise of reasonable diligence.

26. Except under special arrangements previously made in writing the Company accepts no responsibility for departure or arrival dates of goods.

27. (A) Subject to clause 2(B) and 11(B) above and sub-clause (D) below the Company's liability howsoever arising and notwithstanding that the cause of loss or damage be unexplained shall not exceed:

(i) in the case of claims for loss or damage to goods: (a) the value of any goods lost or damaged, or (b) a sum at the rate of two Special Drawing Rights as defined by the International Monetary Fund (hereinafter referred to as SDRs), per kilo of the gross weight of any goods lost or damaged whichever shall be the least.

(ii) in the case of all other claims:

(a) the value of the goods the subject of the relevant transaction between the Company and its Customer, or

(b) a sum at the rate of two SDRs per kilo of the gross weight of the goods the subject of the said transaction, or

(c) 75,000 SDRs in respect of any one transaction whichever shall be the least.

For the purposes of Clause 27(A) the value of the goods shall be their value when they were or should have been shipped. The value of SDRs shall be calculated as at the date when the claim is received by the Company in writing.

(B) Subject to Clause 2(B) above, and Sub-Clause (D) below, the Company's liability for loss or damage as a result of failure to deliver or arrange delivery of goods in a reasonable time or (where there is a special arrangement under Clause 26) to adhere to agreed departure or arrival dates shall not in any circumstances whatever exceed a sum equal to twice the amount of the Company's charges in respect of the relevant transaction.

(C) Save in respect of such loss or damage as is referred to at Sub-Clause (B) and subject to Clause 2(B) above and Sub-Clause (D) below, the Company shall not in any circumstances whatsoever be liable for indirect or consequential loss such as (but not limited to) loss of profit, loss of market or the consequences of delay or deviation however caused.

(D) By special arrangement agreed in writing, the Company may accept liability in excess of the limits set out in Sub-Clauses (A) to (C) above upon the Customer agreeing to pay the Company's additional charges for accepting such increased liability. Details of the Company's additional charges will be provided upon request.

28. (A) Any claim by the Customer against the Company arising in respect of any service provided for the Customer or which the Company has undertaken to provide shall be made in writing and notified to the Company within 14 days of the date upon which the Customer became or should have become aware of any event or occurrence alleged to give rise to such claim and any claim not made and notified as aforesaid shall be deemed to be waived and absolutely barred except where the Customer can show that it was impossible for him to comply with this Time Limit and that he has made the claim as soon as it was reasonably possible for him to do so.

(B) Notwithstanding the provisions of Sub-Paragraph (A) above the Company shall in any event be discharged of all liability whatsoever howsoever arising in respect of any service provided for the Customer or which the Company has undertaken to provide unless suit be brought and written notice thereof given to the Company within nine months from the date of the event or occurrence alleged to give rise to a cause of action against the Company.

JURISDICTION AND LAW

29. These Conditions and any act or contract to which they apply shall be governed by English Law and any dispute arising out of any act or contract to which these Conditions apply shall be subject to the exclusive jurisdiction of the English Courts.

INDEX

Uniform Rules Concerning the
Contract for International Carriage
of Goods by Rail (CIM), 1980 382–413

Uniform Rules Concerning the
Contract of International Carriage
of Goods by Rail (CIM), 1999. 494–514